ANIMAL LAW: WELFARE, INTERESTS, AND RIGHTS

ASPEN ELECTIVE SERIES

ANIMAL LAW: WELFARE, INTERESTS, AND RIGHTS

SECOND EDITION

DAVID S. FAVRE
PROFESSOR OF LAW
MICHIGAN STATE UNIVERSITY COLLEGE OF LAW

Wolters Kluwer
Law & Business

Printed in the United States of America.

1 2 3 4 5 6 7 8 9 0

ISBN 978-1-4548-0266-2

Library of Congress Cataloging-in-Publication Data
Favre, David S.
  Animal law : welfare, interests, and rights / David Favre. — 2nd ed.
  p. cm. — (Aspen elective series)
  Includes index.
  ISBN 978-1-4548-0266-2
1. Domestic animals — Law and legislation — United States. 2. Animal welfare — Law and legislation — United States. I. Title.

KF390.5.A5F38 2011
344.7304'9 — dc22

2011017526

Cover photograph by John Devins, of Eloise Reavis.

About Wolters Kluwer Law & Business

Wolters Kluwer Law & Business is a leading global provider of intelligent information and digital solutions for legal and business professionals in key specialty areas, and respected educational resources for professors and law students. Wolters Kluwer Law & Business connects legal and business professionals as well as those in the education market with timely, specialized authoritative content and information-enabled solutions to support success through productivity, accuracy and mobility.

Serving customers worldwide, Wolters Kluwer Law & Business products include those under the Aspen Publishers, CCH, Kluwer Law International, Loislaw, Best Case, ftwilliam.com and MediRegs family of products.

CCH products have been a trusted resource since 1913, and are highly regarded resources for legal, securities, antitrust and trade regulation, government contracting, banking, pension, payroll, employment and labor, and healthcare reimbursement and compliance professionals.

Aspen Publishers products provide essential information to attorneys, business professionals and law students. Written by preeminent authorities, the product line offers analytical and practical information in a range of specialty practice areas from securities law and intellectual property to mergers and acquisitions and pension/benefits. Aspen's trusted legal education resources provide professors and students with high-quality, up-to-date and effective resources for successful instruction and study in all areas of the law.

Kluwer Law International products provide the global business community with reliable international legal information in English. Legal practitioners, corporate counsel and business executives around the world rely on Kluwer Law journals, looseleafs, books, and electronic products for comprehensive information in many areas of international legal practice.

Loislaw is a comprehensive online legal research product providing legal content to law firm practitioners of various specializations. Loislaw provides attorneys with the ability to quickly and efficiently find the necessary legal information they need, when and where they need it, by facilitating access to primary law as well as state-specific law, records, forms and treatises.

Best Case Solutions is the leading bankruptcy software product to the bankruptcy industry. It provides software and workflow tools to flawlessly streamline petition preparation and the electronic filing process, while timely incorporating ever-changing court requirements.

ftwilliam.com offers employee benefits professionals the highest quality plan documents (retirement, welfare and non-qualified) and government forms (5500/PBGC, 1099 and IRS) software at highly competitive prices.

MediRegs products provide integrated health care compliance content and software solutions for professionals in healthcare, higher education and life sciences, including professionals in accounting, law and consulting.

Wolters Kluwer Law & Business, a division of Wolters Kluwer, is headquartered in New York. Wolters Kluwer is a market-leading global information services company focused on professionals.

SUMMARY OF CONTENTS

TABLE OF CONTENTS

PREFACE

This is a picture of Moppet. Moppet is a being, a being who lives with me. She is alive. Look into her eyes; she is aware, aware of me but perhaps not self-aware. She is quiet, quick, and potentially dead-ly to other small beings who come into our place. To touch her is to feel like you are touching a cloud. She is soft and flowing, with sharp points hidden in her paws. Her spirit is pos-itive and engaging.

Moppet generally makes good decisions, but they are not always the same decisions that I would make (for a time her nickname was "Deathwish Moppet"). She likes human companionship and the warmth of the sun and seeks out both. To us she is the essence of innocence, of cute-ness, of goodness. To her, she simply is. Moppet has become an occa-sional companion to Rocky, the 100-pound Great Pyrenees, and they spend quality time together until he gets too playful. She wanders about in our part of the world, answering to a drummer that I can-not hear. She knows where home is, and who the members are of our multiple-species family. Moppet lives her life as best she can, as do I.

The world of philosophy and law does not normally intrude into this world. But we need to explore just what Moppet's status is in my world of moral and legal obligations. We need to reflect upon who she is and how we humans ought to deal with her and the millions of animals that she might represent.

This book will allow the reader to explore the present and poten-tial dynamics of the relationships between human beings and other beings. Given the long-standing interactions between our species and so many others, there is a rich matrix of context through which to view the relationships among all these beings: law, cultural, ecologi-cal, neurological, philological, economic, and psychological. Although the primary focus of this book is for the student of law, the non-law student will also be provided a thread of discovery. For the student focused on the law, be aware that this book contains more than just "the law." As the issue of the status of animals within the legal system is presently in considerable flux, there is a necessity to present considerable nonlegal material to allow readers to make their own judgments about the "oughts" of the legal system. I am of strong opinion that the present state of the legal system is inadequate in its treatment of animals, but there is much room for debate about what possibilities exist for its future growth. This requires us to examine where we are now, what problems exist with the present state of affairs, and where we might want to go.

Animal Law: Welfare, Interests, and Rights is a part of a more extensive set of materials available on the Animal Law and History Center Website, which is hosted by the Michigan State University College of Law.

Additional material on many of the topics covered in this book can be found within the website, www.animallaw.info.

David S. Favre
April 2011

ACKNOWLEDGMENTS

I also would like to acknowledge the following organizations and individuals for the use of their materials:

Stephen Burr, *Toward Legal Rights for Animals*, 4 Env't. Aff. 205 (1975) (Boston College Law School).

Chai (Animal welfare organization based in Israel), *Dog and Cat Fur Products*, *available at* www.chai-online.org/en/compassion/clothes_fur.htm#cats_dogs (Dec. 2007).

Larry Cunningham, *The Case Against Dog Breed Discrimination by Homeowners' Insurance Companies*, 11 Conn. Ins. L.J. 1 (2004) (Connecticut Insurance Law Journal).

David Favre, *Equitable Self-Ownership for Animals*, 50 Duke L.J. 473 (2000).

David Favre and Vivien Tsang, *The Development of Anti-Cruelty Laws During the 1800's*, 1993 Detroit Coll. of Law Review 1 (1993).

Hanna Gibson, *Introduction: What is Dog Fighting?* Animal Legal and Historical Center (2005), *available at* http://www.animallaw.info.

Iredell Jenkins, *The Concept of Rights and the Competence of Courts*, Am. J. of Jurisprudence (Notre Dame Law School).

Thomas Kelch, *The Role of the Rational and the Emotive in a Theory of Animal Rights*, 27 Bost. Col. Env't. Aff. L. Rev. 1 (1999) (Boston College School of Law).

Mary Midgley, *Persons and Non-Persons*, from Peter Singer (ed.), In Defense of Animals, 52–62 (1985 Blackwell).

Richard Posner and Peter Singer, *A Dialogue on Animal Rights*, Slate Magazine, June 2001, *available at* http://www.slate.com/id/110101/entry/110109/.

Roscoe Pound, Vol. 3 Jurisprudence (1959 West Publishing Co.).

RSPCA (Royal Society for the Prevention of Cruelty to Animals – U.K.) *Chicken Standards & Freedom Foods*, *available at* http://www.rspca.org.uk/.

Paige M. Tomaselli, *International Comparative Animal Cruelty Laws*, Animal Legal and Historical Center (2003), *available at* http://www. animallaw.info/articles/ddusicacl.htm.

Voiceless (An animal focused organization in Australia) From Paddocks to Prisons: Pigs in New South Wales, Current Practices, Future Directions (Dec. 2005), *available at* http://www.voiceless.org.au.

Steve Wise, *How Nonhuman Animals Were Trapped in a Nonexistent Universe*, 1 Animal Law 15 (1995).

ANIMAL LAW: WELFARE, INTERESTS, AND RIGHTS

CHAPTER 1

Introduction

Although the focus of the materials in this book is on the United States, the reader must be aware that animal issues are global in reach. Therefore, occasionally international materials will be included for general discussion or comparison with approaches in the United States.

Section 1

A Few Issues of Public Policy

Dog- and Cat-Fur Products

Cats and Dogs

In spite of a deep aversion to the exploitation of companion animals in the West, the market for cat and dog fur is a burgeoning international industry, said to amount to more than 2 million lives a year. Bans exist in the United States and in many European Union (EU) countries, such as Italy, yet these laws set limitations based only on the sales value of an individual item. This means that any inexpensive item is considered completely legal, and this category covers the widest use of cat and dog fur, namely as trim or small items with a value under $150. Animal-hair tests reveal that cat and dog fur is commonly used in jackets, linings in garments, boots, gloves, handbags, hats, collars, scarves, lap rugs (sought after in Germany and Switzerland to treat arthritis and rheumatism), dolls, and even toys for cats and dogs themselves. (In addition to clothing, the skin has a broad range of other uses.) And that's just the legal trade.

The main originating sources are China, South Korea, Thailand, and the Philippines, where cats and dogs are collected and, more recently, commercially bred and farmed. To support this flourishing trade, family pets are commonly stolen and sold. Rows of crates, tightly stuffed with live cats and dogs, are openly displayed in outdoor stalls across Southeast Asia. The cats are usually snared in a wire loop (garrote) and strangled by hanging. The dogs are muzzled, tethered with their legs often over their backs, and then bled to death by slashing their thighs or paws. They all will be skinned and their fur processed for shipment.

This is an international market of trade, export, import, and re-export designed to blur the origin and exact nature of the pelt. Most typically, the fur is collected in one country, processed in another, and assembled in a third to circumvent import restrictions. Creative labeling and fraudulent mislabeling helps manufacturers and retailers thwart bans and oversight and deceive consumers. Investigators have discovered whole garments for sale in the United States and across Europe, in contravention of current bans. At least one reporter revealed active fur trafficking in stolen pet cats from England, whose hides were offered for sale in Belgium.

www.chai-online.org/en/compassion/clothes_fur.htm#cats_dogs (July 2006)

McCartney to Boycott China over Animal Cruelty

Paul Lewis, Nov. 29, 2005
The Guardian online

Sir Paul McCartney says he will never perform in China after watching a secretly taped film of animals being abused and killed for their fur. In one scene, shot in a fur market in Guangzhou, southern China, and due to be broadcast on the BBC's Six O'Clock News last night, workers throw cats into boiling water. The film was watched by Sir Paul and his wife, Heather, at a preview screening.

Anonymous photograph from the Web: Dogs off to slaughter in China.

Sir Paul said yesterday: "I wouldn't dream of going over there to play, in the same way I wouldn't go to a country that supported apartheid. This is just disgusting. It's against every rule of humanity."

Questions & Notes

1. What is your reaction to the information in the story and to the picture? Is the picture, or are the sentences, more emotionally compelling? Why?

2. Do you think the boycott of China by McCartney is a good approach for dealing with the problem?

3. Do you think the use of dogs and cats as food and fur is morally acceptable? Is the method of death morally acceptable? Would you eat dog? Why or why not? If it is acceptable in the Chinese culture, do we have the right to question it? Is there the risk of cultural imperialism? As of 2011 there is no national criminal anticruelty law in China. Do you think they will adopt one in the next ten years?

4. As of the summer of 2006, the State Forestry Administration has responsibility for animal welfare issues. On being shown pictures of the live skinning of dogs and cats at an animal market outside Beijing, officials from the agency expressed horror and shock, claiming that such actions are illegal; but in fact, it is not clear that there is any law on point. For a detailed discussion of the Chinese trying to figure out how to respond to these new Western concerns about animal welfare, see the editorial "Progress against dog and cat fur in China," *Animal People*, June 2006, p. 3.

5. The United States banned the use of or importation of dog- or cat-fur products in 2000. See 10 USC 1308. On November 20, 2006, the European Union adopted a ban on the importation, export, and sale of dog and cat fur. In 2010 Congress adopted the Truth in Fur Labeling Act (H.R. 2480) to eliminate some of the loop holes in the original law.

Section 2

Pain and Suffering

While the sensation of pain is a universal experience, hard wired in the brain long ago in the evolutionary process, suffering is a more difficult concept. Pain (and suffering) is a word with an inherent negative context, yet the experience of pain may be useful and necessary. When you pick up a hot object, pain is the signal from the fingers relayed to the brain and, without internal discussion, the signal "you dummy drop that thing" results in fingers letting go, helping save the flesh of the fingers. The often used statement is that we should seek to avoid the infliction of "unnecessary pain and suffering" on others. Can you give an example of unnecessary pain? What is the context for judging unnecessary?

Suffering is a more diffuse idea; the following will help provide some context.

http://en.wikipedia.org/wiki/Suffering:

> The word suffering is sometimes used in the narrow sense of physical pain, but more often it refers to mental or emotional pain, or more often yet to pain in the broad sense, i.e. to any unpleasant feeling, emotion or sensation. The word pain usually refers to physical pain, but it is also a common synonym of suffering. The words pain and suffering are often used both together in different ways. For instance, they may be used as interchangeable synonyms. Or they may be used in 'contradistinction' to one another, as in "pain is physical, suffering is mental", or "pain is inevitable, suffering is optional". Or they may be used to define each other, as in "pain is physical suffering", or "suffering is severe physical or mental pain".

> Qualifiers, such as mental, emotional, psychological, and spiritual, are often used for referring to certain types of pain or suffering. In particular, mental pain (or suffering) may be used in relationship with physical pain (or suffering) for distinguishing between two wide categories of pain or suf-

fering. A first caveat concerning such a distinction is that it uses physical pain in a sense that normally includes not only the "typical sensory experience of physical pain" but also other unpleasant bodily experiences such as itching or nausea. A second caveat is that the terms physical or mental should not be taken too literally: physical pain or suffering, as a matter of fact, happens through conscious minds and involves emotional aspects, while mental pain or suffering happens through physical brains and, being an emotion, involves important physiological aspects.

http://www.newworldencyclopedia.org/entry/Suffering:

Suffering is usually described as a negative basic feeling or emotion that involves a subjective character of unpleasantness, aversion, harm, or threat of harm.

Suffering may be said to be physical or mental, depending whether it refers to a feeling or emotion that is linked primarily to the body or to the mind. Examples of physical suffering are pain, illness, disability, hunger, poverty, and death. Examples of mental suffering are grief, hatred, frustration, heartbreak, guilt, humiliation, anxiety, loneliness, and self-pity. Attitudes towards suffering may vary hugely according to how much one deems it to be light or severe, avoidable or unavoidable, useful or useless, of little or of great consequence, deserved or undeserved, chosen or unwanted, acceptable or unacceptable.

Physical suffering can often be ameliorated by medical, political, and economic measures that can alleviate disease and poverty and put an end to conflicts and wars. Mental suffering persists, however, even in the most ideal physical circumstances. Even as regards to physical suffering, science offers no cure for the ultimate physical suffering—death.

Questions & Notes

1. Have you ever seen an animal experience human-created pain? What happened? Was it justified?

2. What can we say about human suffering? Is there ever a good outcome from suffering? Example? Can an animal suffer?

3. Is a chimpanzee in a 10′ x 20′ cement room with bars on one side in a physical place that will necessarily induce suffering? How? would we know if a chimpanzee is suffering? What might cause

suffering for a house cat? For a mouse? What justifies animal suffering: human food needs or entertainment perhaps? Do we have an ethical guideline for deciding when human inflicted suffering might or might not be unnecessary?

4. Is death suffering?

Section 3

Horses as Food

In 2003 a *Washington Post* article noted that,

> Of an estimated 7-million-plus horses in the United States, about 50,000 end up each year in the Texas slaughterhouses, where they are stunned by a four-inch retractable bolt shot into the brain, then hung up by a hind leg to have their throats slit so they can be bled out. The method, required by the federal Humane Methods of Slaughter Act, is the same used for beef cattle. (Tamara Jones, *Washington Post*, Sunday, January 19, 2003, p. A01.)

At the time this article was written, a number of individuals in Texas were trying to shut down the plant, one of only three in existence in the United States at the time—two of these plants happened to be in Texas. Some of the horse meat was destined to be used as feed for zoo animals, but much of the meat was intended for human consumption overseas. A large group of organizations took up the issue and sought to shut down any commercial horse slaughter in the United States.

At the federal level a number of attempts have been made over the past few years to outlaw the slaughter of horses for human consumption, but thus far nothing has been signed into law. At the state level, a combination of state law and cases have, as of the beginning of 2008, shut down the three old plants. See 225 ILCS 635/1.5 – "Slaughter for human consumption unlawful." However, it should be noted that the Illinois law does not make it illegal to slaughter horses for consumption by dogs or tigers, only as food for humans.

A lingering question now that the slaughterhouses have been shut down: What is happening to the approximately 70,000 horses that were being killed annually at those slaughter plants?

Apparently there is no law prohibiting the shipment of live horses to Mexico.

> "It's super, super sad," said Hillary Bogley, who bought the underweight appaloosa in Front Royal from her Middleburg Humane Foundation. "Now they'll all go to Mexico, where we have no regulation and the animals will suffer even more. Horse slaughter is not going to go away unless people regulate the breeding industry to stop overpopula-

tion." (Tamara Jones, *Washington Post*, Sunday, January 19, 2003, p. A01)

It is much more expensive to deal with horse overpopulation than with dog overpopulation. Is the slaughter of horses a moral issue or a management approach to overpopulation?

Questions & Notes

1. Why are horses viewed any differently than cows? Do you think sending horses to Mexico increased their suffering? Is it necessary suffering?

2. Is this a personal decision or a matter of public policy debate? Do all of the people who wrote Congress opposing horse slaughter now have an obligation to provide for the care of unwanted horses?

3. Is it illegal for an owner to take a horse out into open space and shoot him or her?

4. As of the end of 2010 no federal legislation has been passed to outlaw the slaughter of horses for human consumption, even though a bill to that purpose has been introduced several times. However, several western states are considering the adoption of laws that would specifically allow the slaughter of horses if the meat is for export.

Section 4

An Innocent Inquiry into a Very Difficult Topic

Proposed Farm Animal Protection Ad #45

Scene Set-Up

The camera is looking down one of the long aisles in a large food store. A mother and child are standing in front of the meat counter and the mother takes up a package. Camera zooms up close enough to have half-body shots of the two and pick up their voices:

Scene

Daughter (about five years old, nicely dressed, look of intelligence): Mommy, what is that?

Mother: It's a package of chicken for dinner tomorrow.

Daughter (slight pause while thinking): But chickens have pretty feathers and walk around on two feet, crowing out the welcome song.

Mother: Well, yes but this one was killed so we could have the meat to eat.

Daughter: Did it hurt to be killed? What happened to the feathers?

Mother: I hope it did not hurt the chicken, and I don't know what happened to the feathers.

Daughter: Where did the chicken live? How old was it when it was killed? (pause) How did they kill it?

Mother: Ok, enough of the questions. Let's go find the eggs…

Daughter: Are the chickens that lay the eggs the same ones we eat? Where do they live?

Mother: I have no idea, now stop all the questions. I have to find the donuts.

Scene dissolves. Phase in a picture of five chickens in a small cage. Voiceover with male voice: "Do you know where your eggs or chickens come from? Do you know how they lived and died? Shouldn't you?"

◇◇

A Few Chicken Facts

How many chickens are we talking about? At the end of 2010 the US Dept. of Agriculture reported that in year 2009, 8,658,860,000 chickens were slaughtered in the U.S. Also, as of December 1, 2010 there were 283,000,000 commercial chickens laying eggs at the rate of 75 eggs per day per 100 birds, or 212,200,000 eggs per day. Where are all these chickens? Meat chickens are mostly in large buildings and walk around on the floor. The chickens that lay eggs are kept in rows of cages stacked four or five high, also in windowless buildings.

In August 2005 there was a large fire in one of about eight major buildings on a ten-acre site west of Lansing, Michigan. The buildings, 150 x 600 feet, are windowless, and anyone driving by would have no idea that millions of chickens are contained in them. This is truly an animal industrial site. The fire destroyed the one building and killed approximately 250,000 chickens. Considerable effort by rural firefighters saved the chickens in the other buildings. The comment of the owner was that he was thankful that no one had been injured.

Fire Kills 250,000 Chickens at One of Michigan's Largest Poultry Farms, August 10, 2005. www.freep.com/news/statewire/sw119654_20050810.htm.

Questions & Notes

1. Clearly the owner of the facility where the fire occurred did not consider chickens of moral concern. They were not "persons." Should chickens be in our moral universe?

2. Note that between 1970 and 1990 there was a 13% reduction in the number of hens, but the same number of eggs were produced. How is that possible? Is this good, or more suffering?

3. Who do you think are the major purchasers of eggs? Do you think individuals would pay more for chicken meat and eggs for a better quality of life for the animals? What about corporations?

4. Why is it acceptable to eat chickens but not dogs or horses?

5. The conditions of industrial chicken production will be considered in Chapter 9 in more detail. For the moment it should be noted that no federal law covers the raising or slaughter of chickens. Why might this be?

6. In 2005 it was announced that seafood producers in both Norway and Japan are turning to new ways of peddling whale-based products in the hopes of boosting sagging markets for whale meat. They are promoting the consumption of "whale burgers" to compete with hamburgers: *www.aftenposten.no/english/local/article1087535.ece?service=print*. As of 2011 this effort does not seem to have succeeded.

   Do you think there are any differences between developing a market for whale meat from that of a market for chicken meat?

7. What about the consumption of primates?

   Jane Goodall, a world primate expert, said the population of apes in the continent, particularly the Congo basin, had been strained by a thriving bush meat market and a rapid destruction of forests that provide habitat.

   "The bush-meat crisis is very, very serious. Animals are being eaten into extinction and the problem is all over in Asia, South America and Africa," Goodall told reporters on the sidelines of the 21st congress of the International Primatological Society, taking place at a hotel on the shores of Lake Victoria. Sapa-AFP, Published on the Web by IOL on 2006-06-30 07:17:28.

   Unlike the whale issue, the sale of primates as bush meat is illegal almost everywhere. Primates are protected under international law. This illegal meat has been found in Europe's major cities. How might this be different from eating the meat of chickens?

Section 5

Big Thinkers: It All Started with the Greeks

How Nonhuman Animals Were Trapped in a Nonexistent Universe[1]

by Steven Wise, 1 *Animal Law* 15 (1995) [This is an edited version of portions of the article.]

I. Introduction

In a famous lecture, Oliver Wendell Holmes, Jr., emphasized the importance of the knowledge of history to an ability rationally to analyze the present value of legal principles. In Holmes' view, an understanding of history "is the first step toward an enlightened skepticism, that is toward a *deliberate reconsideration* of the worth of those rules"; the alternative is mere "blind imitation of the past." As [l]aw is a scavenger ... [that] grows by feeding on ideas from outside, not by inventing new ones of its own," its history and evolution intimately weave among the histories and evolutions of other disciplines.

II. Aristotle, the "Great Chain of Being," and the Early Denial of Justice to Nonhuman Animals

Thales, Anaximander, and Anaximenes were the trio of sixth-century, B.C., Milesian philosophers who, it is said, invented Western philosophy and physical science. In their work first glimmered a universe that operated by the cause and effect of physical laws and not through divine caprice or myth; theirs was a cosmography, not a theogony. Ever so lightly, they uncoupled humanity from sacred nature. Humans, for the first time, viewed the world without seeing their own reflections. This idea, which occurred just once, and then in a form so primitive that even scientific experiment lay beyond the horizon, was to take a very long time to mature. A century later, Xenophon, the Greek soldier and historian, claimed that Socrates, whom he had known as a youth in late fifth-century, B.C., Athens, believed that animals existed for humans.

In the fourth century, B.C., Aristotle attributed the idea of a nature resulting from intelligent design to Anaxagoras, who lived in the fifth century, B.C. Empedocles, a contemporary of Anaxagoras, was, in Aristotle's view, the source of the competing claim that nature, including animals, had originated not from an intelligent design, but by chance. But Aristotle ranged far wider in his discussions of cosmology.

First, Aristotle explicitly rejected the theory of Empedocles that nature operated by chance and not design. In the *Physics*, he conceived that everything in nature had been created for a purpose; everything had a "final cause" for which it existed. Everything acted for the sake of something else. To understand a part of nature, one had to know its purpose.

In the *Politics*, Aristotle identified the purposes of plants and animals, along with various kinds of human beings. One could infer that plants existed for animals, and that the other animals exist for the sake of man, the tame for use and food, the wild, if not all, at least the greater part of them, for food and for the provisions of clothing and various instruments. Now if nature makes nothing incomplete, and nothing in vain, the inference must be that she has made all animals for the sake of man.

In short, Aristotelian nature was teleological, in that nature and all her processes were directed towards some goal.

Second, Aristotle postulated a world populated by species that had once been created and never changed. The natural world of Classical and Hellenistic Greece was identical to the world as it had been created and as it would forever remain.

Third, from Aristotle emerged the partially inconsistent but influential ideas of continuity, which included the continuity of biological organisms, and of a natural hierarchy of beings. Two things were "continuous when the limits of each, with which they touch and are kept together, become one and the same." There was a seamless continuity, for example, between the inanimate and the animate, and from plant to animal. Aristotle discussed several ways in which organisms could be classified within a linear hierarchy. One conception accorded each type of organism its natural degree of perfection. Heat was his measure. The greater the heat an animal generated, the more it developed. Women, colder than men, were less perfect. Equally, if not more powerful, was his classification according to the characteristics possessed by the soul of each kind of organism. Plants, animals and humans were imbued with souls of increasing and ascending complexity, as their heat increased.

"[S]ome kinds of living things … possess all, some less than all, others one only. Those [souls] we have mentioned are the nutritive, the appetitive, the sensory, the locomotive, and the power of thinking. Plants have none but the first, the nutritive, while another order of living things has this *plus* the sensory. If an order of living things has the sensory, it must also have the appetitive; … now all animals have one sense at least. … Certain kinds of animals possess in addition the power of locomotion, and still others, i.e., man and possibly another order like man or superior to him, the power of thinking, and thought."

This classification of souls suggested both continuity, in that the lower souls are subsumed within the higher souls, and a hierarchal discontinuity, in that portions of the higher souls had no antecedents in the lower.

Plato had believed that every conceivable kind of living being that could exist, did. The historian of ideas, Arthur O. Lovejoy, called this Plato's "principle of plenitude." It was, as usually understood, inconsistent with any belief in progress, or, indeed, in any sort of significant change in the universe as a whole. Aristotle's idea of linear hierarchy fused with Plato's principle of plenitude to form the "Great Chain of Being." It became, in Lovejoy's words, "one of the half-dozen most potent and persistent presuppositions in Western thought. It was, in fact, until not much more than a century ago, probably the most widely familiar conception of the general *scheme* of things," it was "explicitly and vehemently antievolutionary."

As plants, animals, and humans were assigned their permanent places in this natural and designed hierarchy, so were there different natural and permanent levels within orders of beings. Akin to fractals, each segment of the Great Chain of Being appeared to recapitulate the whole. All humans were not equally imbued with a rational soul. Aristotle differentiated that portion of the rational soul that could reason from that which could merely listen to and appreciate the reasoning of another. Some humans, males, free men, and adults, for example, occupied superior positions with respect to others, such as females, slaves, and children. Women, believed deficient in reason and, in a sense, in justice, occupied a place between men and nonhuman animals. That species of "thinking property," the natural human slave, was endowed with just that portion of the rational soul that permitted the appreciation of reason. Two thousand years later, Chief Justice Taney alluded to the Great Chain in *Dred Scott*, when he claimed that blacks "had been looked upon as so far below [whites] in the scale of created beings." Children could not fully reason. Their ability to "deliberate" was a higher form of reason than mere appreciation, though it was inferior to mature reason. Whatever place each organism, human, nonhuman animal, or plant, occupied was its appropriate, necessary, and permanent place in the natural hierarchy ordained by a designed and ordered universe.

Aristotle lodged such powers of the inner mental world as intellect, reason, thought, and belief exclusively in human beings. Nonhuman animals could merely use their senses to perceive. These sense perceptions gave them the capacity for memory and therefore experience, for experiences consisted of a chain of memories. Nonhuman animals could also feel pleasure and pain; they could even learn. But because they lacked reason, they lacked true emotion. They could, however, *act* as if they had emotion, but remained in the end oblivious to justice and injustice, to good and bad, even to their own harm and benefit.

It was important for Aristotle to separate those who could reason, to any degree, from those who could not. For those who could reason would neither share friendship nor agreements nor systems of law with those who could not. Justice, which complete reasoners owed only one to the other, was no more owed to slaves or nonhuman animals than it was owed to lifeless tools.

◇◇

Endnotes

1. Steven M. Wise has been a practicing animal protection lawyer for 30 years and is president of the Center for the Expansion of Fundamental Rights, Inc. He is the author of *Rattling the Cage – Toward Legal Rights for Animals* (2000); *Drawing the Line – Science and the Case for Animal*

Rights (2003); and *Though the Heavens May Fall – The Landmark Trial That Led to the End of Human Slavery* (2005). He has taught Animal Rights Law at the Harvard, Vermont, John Marshall, St. Thomas, and Lewis and Clark Law Schools.

Questions & Notes

1. In summary, how did the Greeks set the stage for the Western view of animals? To what degree do you believe that the view still exists?

Section 6

Big Thinkers: Rene Descartes

Letter of November 23, 1646, to Marquess of Newcastle

I cannot share the opinion of Montaigne and others who attribute understanding or thought to animals. I am not worried that people say that men have an absolute empire over all the other animals; because I agree that some of them are stronger than us, and believe that there may also be some who have an instinctive cunning capable of deceiving the shrewdest human beings. But I observe that they only imitate or surpass us in those of our actions which are not guided by our thoughts. It often happens that we walk or eat without thinking at all about what we are doing; and similarly, without using our reason, we reject things which are harmful for us, and parry the blows aimed at us. Indeed, even if we expressly willed not to put our hands in front of our head when we fall, we could not prevent ourselves. I think also that if we had no thought we would eat, as the animals do, without having to learn to; and it is said that those who walk in their sleep sometimes swim across streams in which they would drown if they were awake. As for the movements of our passions, even though in us they are accompanied with thought because we have the faculty of thinking, it is none the less very clear that they do not depend on thought, because they often occur in spite of us. Consequently they can also occur in animals, even more violently than they do in human beings, without our being able to conclude from that that they have thoughts.

In fact, none of our external actions can show anyone who examines them that our body is not just a self-moving machine but contains a soul with thoughts, with the exception of words, or other signs that are relevant to particular topics without expressing any passion. I say words or other signs, because deaf-mutes use signs as we use spoken words; and I say that these signs must be relevant, to exclude the speech of parrots, without excluding the speech of madmen, which is relevant to particular topics even though it does not follow reason. I add also that these words or signs must not express any passion, to rule out not only cries of joy or sadness and the like, but also whatever can be taught by training to animals. If you teach a magpie to say good-day to its mistress, when it sees her approach, this can only be by making the utterance of this word the expressing of one of its passions. For instance it will be an expression of the hope of eating, if it has always been given a tidbit when it says it. Similarly, all the things which dogs, horses, and monkeys are taught to perform are only expressions of their fear, their hope, or their joy; and consequently they can be performed without any thought. Now it seems to me very striking that the use of words, so defined, is something peculiar to human beings. Montaigne and Charron may have said that there is more difference between one human being and another than between a human being and an animal; but there has never been known an animal so perfect as to use a sign to make other animals understand something which expressed no passion; and there is no human being so imperfect as not to do so, since even deaf-mutes invent special signs to express their thoughts. This seems to me a very strong argument to prove that the reason why animals do not speak as we do is not that they lack the organs but that they have no thoughts. It cannot be said that they speak to each other and that we cannot understand them; because since dogs and some other animals express their passions to us, they would express their thoughts also if they had any.

Section 7

Big Thinkers: Voltaire, *Animals* in Philosophical Dictionary

A Response to Descartes

What a pitiful, what a sorry thing to have said that animals are machines bereft of understanding and feeling, which perform their operations always in the same way, which learn nothing, perfect nothing, etc.!

What! that bird which makes its nest in a semi-circle when it is attaching it to a wall, which builds it in a quarter circle when it is in an angle, in a circle upon a tree; that bird acts always in the same way? That hunting-dog which you have disciplined for three months, does it not know more at the end of this time than it knew before your lessons? Does the canary to which you teach a tune repeat it at once? Do you not spend a considerable time in teaching it? Have you not seen that it has made a mistake and that it corrects itself?

Is it because I speak to you, that you judge that I have feeling, memory, ideas? Well, I do not speak to you; you see me going home looking disconsolate, seeking a paper anxiously, opening the desk where I remember having shut it, finding it, reading it joyfully. You judge that I have experienced the feeling of distress and that of pleasure, that I have memory and understanding.

Bring the same judgment to bear on this dog which has lost its master, which has sought him on every road with sorrowful cries, which enters the house agitated, uneasy, which goes down the stairs, up the stairs, from room to room, which at last finds in his study the master it loves, and which shows him its joy by its cries of delight, by its leaps, by its caresses.

Barbarians seize this dog, which in friendship surpasses man so prodigiously; they nail it on a table, and they dissect it alive in order to show the mesenteric veins. You discover in it all the same organs of feeling that are in yourself. Answer me, machinist, has nature arranged all the means of feeling in this animal, so that it may not feel? Has it nerves in order to be impassible? Do not suppose this impertinent contradiction in nature.

Questions & Notes

1. Why are Descartes and Voltaire debating the point?

2. Do you know any nonhuman animals? Do they ever think? Do they have emotions? Do they have thoughts?

3. Are animals morally relevant to humans? To Descartes or Voltaire?

Section 8

AMA Surveys Public About Attitudes Toward Animals

In September 1989 the American Medical Association (AMA) issued a paper entitled, "Public Attitudes About the Use of Animals in Biomedical Research." The AMA paper was compiled from surveys done by LaScola Qualitative Research and Meilman & Lazarus, Inc. Both surveys were done in 1989.

The findings listed in the AMA report were:

Views Toward Using Animals	% In Favor	% Opposed
Fur Coats	17	81
Testing Cosmetics on Animals	21	75
Leather Shoes	37	57
Testing Household Products on Animals	32	63
Finding Cures for Alcohol or Drug Abuse	49	46
Scientific Experiments	55	38
Food	70	25

Questions & Notes

1. Do you think the relative judgments reflected above have changed now that 20 years have passed?

Section 9

Use of Chimpanzees in Research and Entertainment

A national survey of 1,217 adults was performed by Zogby International on behalf of the Doris Day Animal League (© 2001 — margin of error is given as +/- 3%). Among the many questions asked, 85% of the individuals agreed that "like humans, chimpanzees have complex social, intellectual and emotional lives." When asked if it was acceptable to use chimpanzees for research that causes them to suffer distress for human benefit, 40% found it acceptable while 54% said it was not. However, when asked about specific research, the numbers changed. Sixty-four percent found it acceptable to use chimpanzees for cancer research, 32% not acceptable. On the issue of product testing, only 28% thought it was acceptable; 69% thought it unacceptable.

Section 10

Speech of Senator Byrd

Here is the speech made by Senator Robert Byrd (D-WV), on July 9, 2001, preceding an action that would help strengthen the Humane Slaughter Act. While ten years have passed, and Senator Byrd has passed away, it is still very reflective of the middle American view of animals

Mr. President, a few months ago a lady by the name of Sara McBurnett accidentally tapped a sports utility vehicle from behind on a busy highway in California. The angry owner of the bumped vehicle, Mr. Andrew Burnett, stormed back to Ms. McBurnett's car and began yelling at her; and then reached through her open car window with both hands, grabbed her little white dog and hurled it onto the busy roadway. The lady sat helplessly watching in horror as her frightened little pet ran for its life, dodging speeding traffic to no avail. The traffic was too heavy and the traffic was too swift.

Imagine her utter horror. Recently, Mr. Burnett was found guilty of animal cruelty by a jury in a California court, so my faith in the wisdom of juries was restored. Ever since I first heard about this monstrous, brutal, barbaric act, I have wondered what would drive any sane person to do such a thing. There are some people who have blamed this senseless and brutal incident on road rage. But it was not just road rage, it was bestial cruelty. It was and is an outrage. It was an act of sheer depravity to seize a fluffy, furry, innocent little dog, and toss it onto a roadway, and most certainly to be crushed under tons of onrushing steel, iron, glass, and rubber, while its terrified owner, and perhaps other people in other vehicles, watched.

There is no minimizing such cruelty and resorting to the lame excuse that, "after all, it was just a dog." The dog owner, Ms. McBurnett, puts the incident in perspective. Here is what she said: It wasn't just a dog to me. For me, it was my child. A majority of pet owners do believe their pets to be family members. That is the way I look at my little dog, my little dog Billy—Billy Byrd. I look at him as a family member. When he passes away, I will shed tears. I know that. He is a little white Maltese Terrier. As a pet owner and dog lover, I know exactly what that lady means, and so did millions of other dog lovers who could never even fathom such an act.

For my wife and me, Billy Byrd is a key part of our lives at the Byrd House in McLean. He brings us great joy and wonderful companionship. As I said on this floor just a few months ago, if I ever saw in this world anything that was made by the Creator's hand that is more dedicated, more true, more faithful, more trusting, more undeviant than this little dog, I am at a loss to state what it is. Such are the feelings of many dog owners.

Dogs have stolen our hearts and made a place in our homes for thousands of years. Dogs fill an emotional need in man and they have endured as our close companions. They serve as guards and sentries and watchdogs; they are hunting companions. Some, like Lassie and Rin Tin Tin, have become famous actors. But mostly, these sociable little creatures are valued especially as loyal comforters to their human masters. Petting a dog can make our blood pressure drop. Try it. Our heart rate slows down. Try it. Our sense of anxiety diminishes, just goes away. Researchers in Australia have found that dog owners have a lower risk of heart disease, lower blood pressure, and lower cholesterol levels than those people who do not own dogs. Researchers in England have demonstrated that dog owners have far fewer minor health complaints than those people without a dog. Our dogs are about the most devoted, steadfast companions that the Creator could have designed. They are said to be man's best friend and, indeed, who can dispute it?

The affection that a dog provides is not only unlimited, it is unqualified, unconditional. A faithful dog does not judge its owner, it does not criticize him or her, it simply accepts him or her; it accepts us as we are, for who we are, no matter how we dress, no matter how much money we have or don't have, and no matter what our social standing might be or might not be. No matter what happens, one's dog is still one's friend.

A long, frustrating day at work melts into insignificance—gone—with the healing salve of warm, excited greetings from one's ever faithful, eternally loyal dog.

President Truman was supposed to have remarked: If you want a friend in Washington, buy a dog. I often think about Mr. Truman's words. No wonder so many political leaders have chosen the dog as a faithful companion and canine confidante. Former Senate Republican leader, Robert Dole, was constantly bringing his dog, "Leader"—every day—to work with him.

President Bush has "Barney" and "Spot." President Truman had an Irish setter named "Mike." President Ford had a golden retriever named "Lucky." The first President Bush had "Millie".

...

So, just a little pat, a little treat, a little attention for the dog is all that a pet asks. How many members of the human species can love so completely? How does man return that kind of affection?

I remember a recent news program that told of a man who was going around killing dogs and selling the meat from them. A couple of years ago, NBC News reported that American companies were importing and selling toys made in China that were decorated with the fur from dogs that were raised and then slaughtered just for that purpose.

And now we have this monster—I do not hesitate to overrate him—who, because of cruelty and rage, decided that he had the right to grab a harmless little dog and hurl it to its certain death. It makes one ponder the question, doesn't it, Which was the animal? Burnett, or Leo, the little dog? Of course we know the answer.

The point is this: We have a responsibility to roundly condemn such abject cruelty. Apathy regarding incidents such as this will only lead to more deviant behavior. And respect for life, all life, and for humane treatment of all creatures is something that must never be lost.

The Scriptures say in the Book of Proverbs, "A righteous man regardeth the life of his beast, but the tender mercies of the wicked are cruel."

Mr. President, I am concerned that cruelty toward our faithful friend, the dog, may be reflective of an overall trend toward animal cruelty. Recent news accounts have been saturated with accounts of such brutal behavior. A year or two ago, it was revealed that macabre videos showing small animals, including hamsters, kittens, and monkeys, being crushed to death were selling for as much as $300 each. And just a few days ago, there were local news accounts of incidents in Maryland involving decapitated geese being left on the doorsteps of several homes in a Montgomery County community.

Our inhumane treatment of livestock is becoming widespread and more and more barbaric. Six-hundred-pound hogs—they were pigs at one time—raised in two-foot-wide metal cages called gestation crates, in which the poor beasts are unable to turn around or lie down in natural positions, and this way they live for months at a time.

On profit-driven factory farms, veal calves are confined to dark wooden crates so small that they are prevented from lying down or scratching themselves. These creatures feel; they know pain. They suffer pain just as we humans suffer pain. Egg-laying hens are confined to battery cages. Unable to spread their wings, they are reduced to nothing more than an egg-laying machine.

Last April, the Washington Post detailed the inhumane treatment of livestock in our Nation's slaughterhouses. A 23-year-old Federal law requires that cattle and hogs to be slaughtered must first be stunned, thereby rendered insensitive to pain, but mounting evidence indicates that this is not always being done, that these animals are sometimes cut, skinned, and scalded while still able to feel pain.

A Texas beef company, with 22 citations for cruelty to animals, was found chopping the hooves off live cattle. In another Texas plant with about two dozen violations, Federal officials found nine live cattle dangling from an overhead chain. Secret videos from an Iowa pork plant show hogs squealing and kicking as they are being lowered into the boiling water that will soften their hides, soften the bristles on the hogs and make them easier to skin.

I used to kill hogs. I used to help lower them into the barrels of scalding water, so that the bristles could be removed easily. But those hogs were dead when we lowered them into the barrels.

The law clearly requires that these poor creatures be stunned and rendered insensitive to pain before this process begins. Federal law is being ignored. Animal cruelty abounds. It is sickening. It is infuriating. Barbaric treatment of helpless, defenseless creatures must not be tolerated even if these animals are being raised for food—and even more so, more so. Such insensitivity is insidious and can spread and is dangerous. Life must be respected and dealt with humanely in a civilized society.

So for this reason I have added language in the supplemental appropriations bill that directs the Secretary of Agriculture to report on cases of inhumane animal treatment in regard to livestock production, and to document the response of USDA regulatory agencies.

The U.S. Department of Agriculture agencies have the authority and the capability to take action to reduce the disgusting cruelty about which I have spoken.

Oh, these are animals, yes. But they, too, feel pain. These agencies can do a better job, and with this provision they will know that the U.S. Congress expects them to do better in their inspections, to do better in their enforcement of the law, and in their research for new, humane technologies. Additionally, those who perpetuate such barbaric practices will be put on notice that they are being watched.

I realize that this provision will not stop all the animal life in the United States from being mistreated. It will not even stop all beef, cattle, hogs and other livestock from being tortured. But it can serve as an important step toward alleviating cruelty and unnecessary suffering by these creatures.

Let me read from the Book of Genesis. First chapter, verses 24–26 reads:

And God said—

Who said? God said.

And God said, Let the Earth bring forth the living creature after his kind, cattle, and creeping thing, and beast of the Earth after his kind: and it was so.

And God made—

Who made?

And God made the beasts of the earth after his kind, and cattle after their kind, and every thing that creepeth upon the earth after his kind: and God saw that it was good.

And God said—

Who said? God said. Who said?

And God said, Let us make man in our image, after our likeness: and let them have dominion over the fish of the sea, and over the fowl of the air, and over the cattle, and over all the earth, and over every creeping thing that creepeth upon the Earth.

Thus, Mr. President, God gave man dominion over the Earth. We are only the stewards of this planet. We are only the stewards of His planet. Let us not fail in our Divine mission. Let us strive to be good stewards and not defile God's creatures or ourselves by tolerating unnecessary, abhorrent, and repulsive cruelty.

Mr. President, I yield the floor and suggest the absence of a quorum.

Senator Byrd's speech was distributed over the Web by DawnWatch, an animal rights media watch group that looks at animal issues in the media and facilitates one-click responses to the relevant media outlets.

Section 11

An Old Case
People v. Tinsdale

10 Abbott's Prac. Rept. (New) 374 (N.Y. 1868)

New York General Sessions, February, 1868.

Before Hon. John K. Hackett, *Recorder.*

Indictment for a misdemeanor in violating the provisions of 1 *Laws of 1867*, ch. 375, being an "Act for the more effectual prevention of Cruelty to Animals."

The indictment was as follows:

"City and County of New York, ss.

"The jurors of the people of the State of New York, in and for the body of the city and county of New York, upon their oath present: That George W. Tinsdale, late of the first ward of the city of New York in the county of New York aforesaid, he then and there being a conductor of a passenger car, on the Bleecker-street and Fulton Ferry Railroad of the city of New York, and Arthur Taggart, late of the same place, he then and there being the driver of said passenger car of said railroad, on the second day of January, in the year of our Lord one thousand eight hundred and sixty-eight, at the ward, city and county aforesaid, with force and arms did unnecessarily overload and procure said passenger car to be overloaded, then and there being attached to said passenger car two living creatures, to wit, two horses: by means whereof on a certain portion of the route of the said railroad the horses so attached to said passenger car were unable to draw said passenger car, but were, by reason of the premises aforesaid, overloaded, overdriven, tortured, and tormented; against the form of the statute in such case made and provided, and against the peace of the people of the State of New York, and their dignity.

"Oakley Hall,

District-Attorney."

The prisoners were arraigned, pleaded not guilty, and were tried jointly before Hon. John K. Hackett, Recorder, and a jury, February 7, 1868. Gunning S. Bedford, Jr., Assistant District-Attorney, for the people Charles S. Spencer, for the prisoners.

The facts upon the trial of the case appear in the charge to the jury. Hackett, recorder, charged the jury as follows:

Gentlemen of the Jury: The statute, for an alleged violation of which the accused are at the bar, was intended and enacted for a wise and beneficial purpose; and that it should only recently have been the subject of legislative action, is a matter of reproach.

No statute determines the limit or number of passengers that may be carried in cars propelled by steam or horse power; and that no such provision of law exists is with many a subject of regret, and it must be within your experience, that not an hour or moment of the day passes, but that human beings are packed in cars, and, as alleged, simply for the gain and cupidity of railroad directors and stockholders. If true, they are as much obnoxious to the charge of cruelty to human beings, as the accused now stand charged with inhumanity to dumb animals.

As matter of law, I charge you that no exemption from liability accrues to the accused from the fact developed in this case, that they were then in the employ of a railroad company. The law (1 *Laws of 1867*, ch. 375, § 1, p. 834) plainly recites that "If any person shall overdrive, overload, torture, torment, deprive of necessary sustenance, or unnecessarily or cruelly beat, or needlessly mutilate or kill, or cause or procure to be overdriven, overloaded, torture, tormented or deprived of necessary sustenance, or to be unnecessarily or cruelly beaten or needlessly mutilated or killed, as aforesaid, any living creature, every such offender shall, for every such offense, be guilty of a misdemeanor." The conductor who has charge of the car, and the driver who drives the horses, whilst in the performance of the several duties allotted to them, are equally responsible for a violation of the law referred to. The law does not make president, directors, or other officers of the company responsible for the acts of their employees, but only those who have charge of the car; which charge is especially given to the conductor on the one hand, and the driver, on the other, each having separate and distinct duties. If they, or either, are guilty of a violation of this law, their offense is not extenuated by the fact that they are each acting under orders from superiors. Were I to direct either of you to commit assault and battery on another, and should this direction be followed, you would be responsible. No company can compel their conductor or other employee to do an act which is against the law.

It follows that there is nothing in the argument of the counsel for the accused, that no crime exists, except there be an intention to transgress. If one commits a murder, it would be absurd to interpose the defense that he did not so intend. If a man overloads a car, beyond the ability of the horses attached to it to draw, he is within the act in question, and guilty of cruelty, and, therefore, responsible. The intention is assumed directly from the act itself.

In the case at bar, although it appears that Mr. Tinsdale was simply the conductor of the car, I charge you that if you find him guilty at all upon the evidence, he (Tinsdale) is just as much responsible and just as much guilty as the driver; in fact, perhaps, more so, for the reason that a driver is usually held in subjection to the orders of the conductor.

I will briefly call your attention to portions of the testimony in this case, which I regard as most material. The police officer who appears to be perfectly disinterested, and who has been complimented for his fairness by the counsel for the accused, testifies that the car was unusually crowded, that one of the horses slipped twice, and that some of the passengers were compelled to aid the horses in putting the car in motion. If the testimony did not expressly establish the fact, the right belongs to you to infer the fact that without the aid of the passengers and also of the conductor, the car could not have been set in motion. You are to regard all the testimony in determining the question, whether or not the car was overloaded upon the occasion referred to. Mr. Bergh testifies that the car was crowded and was ascending the steepest grade in the city; that the horses attached were light in weight and strength; that they slipped, and one of them fell twice, whilst straining propel the overloaded car, and were evidently unsuited for such labor. Mr. Bergh further states, that, in his opinion, the car could not have been placed in motion without the aid of the passengers and conductor. Mr. Hill, a witness for the defense (a driver by occupation, and on the occasion a passenger upon the car), testifies that the stoppage was occasioned by the passage of a truck in front, and when the horses started, one slipped; but corroborates the statement that the passengers had to aid the horses in their endeavor to start the car. Mr. Morris, a witness for the accused, testified that the record of the passengers disclosed *thirty-two* upon the down trip. His statement is at variance with the testimony of the officer and that of Mr. Bergh. Mr. Hill also testifies that there were no more than thirty-two passengers, and further, that conductors and drivers were not limited as to the number of passengers to be carried. It is to be regretted that such a salutary law does not exist; but the fact that none such existed should not prejudice the accused in your estimation. They should not be held responsive for the wrongs committed by their superiors.

I leave this matter with you. If you believe from the testimony in this case, that, upon the occasion of the arrest of the accused, the one was acting as conductor of the car, and the other as driver; and that such car was overloaded, or laden with passengers in connection with the grade to such an extent as to be beyond the ordinary and proper capacity of the horses attached to it to draw it, then you will find the accused guilty.

A statement has been made by the counsel for the accused, who has so ably defended them, which may have improperly operated upon your minds, to the effect that the penalty upon conviction is a very serious one. With that you have nothing to do. It is within the power of the court, in administering the law, to impose fines, from one cent up to an amount of two hundred and fifty dollars, or imprisonment from one day to one year. In the event of conviction, I shall be guided by my sense of duty; but neither the extent nor character of the punishment prescribed by law, should affect your minds in considering upon your verdict. The jury rendered a verdict of "Guilty," against both defendants, and the court thereupon imposed a fine of two hundred and fifty dollars upon each of them.

Section 12

A New Case

In the spring of 2006 on Lake Lansing in Michigan, a pair of mute swans successfully hatched out three baby birds. It was a joy for the many people who lived on the lake. Their progress was watched by many human shore

residences. On June 12, 2006, one resident observed a powerboat doing a partial circle around the swans and then turn toward them and run over the group apparently killing two of the babies. This was reported on page one of the *Lansing State Journal* on Friday, June 16, 2006. The next day in the editorial column there was a call to find the persons who had done the act and with the hope that the doers of the act would be "dealt with." LSJ page 6A, June 17, 2006. A week later a 22-year-old man was identified as the possible doer of the act. No charges have ever been filed.

Questions & Notes

1. Why would someone commit such an act? Is it an immoral act? Do you think the act was illegal? If not, would you make it illegal? Define the crime. What is the appropriate punishment?

2. Why was it reported on page one of the newspaper? That same day many animals died because of the intentional acts of humans—food animals were slaughtered, unwanted pets were killed, and rats were trapped or poisoned. Is it the death of an animal that is news?

Section 13

Being a Lawyer: Harm to Humans
Fact Pattern #1

Note: This fact pattern and the following fact pattern are from e-mails sent unsolicited from the general public to the editor of the Animal Legal and Historical Web Center (2005). The identification of the parties has been changed.

My name is Mary and I live in Maryland. On May 31, 2004, my twelve-year-old son Scott was attacked and severely injured by an unleashed Rottweiller in the park across the street from our house. The dog bit him over ten times on his left arm and he actually ate a large part of my son's tricep muscle. Adam had to undergo surgery and therapy to regain the strength in his left arm, and he still has permanent scars and tremors. My dilemma is that the people who owned the dog are renting their home. They have not paid any of his hospital or therapy expenses. I have contacted the landlord and he has assumed no responsibility either. The owners of the dog refused to have the dog put to sleep after he attacked our son. My husband and I then requested a hearing to ask that the dog be put to sleep. While we were waiting to hear from the county regarding the status of our request, we found out that the same dog who bit Adam actually bit the owner's little boy. The police were called and the dog was so violent that he had to be immediately put to sleep. As a mother, I am extremely frustrated. I cannot understand why no one is assuming the responsibility of my child being hurt. My husband and I are still paying hospital bills. My son is still terrified of dogs. He won't go back to the park, which is right across the street from our home. The family that owned the dog still lives in the neighborhood. The landlord insists that he did not know that they owned a dog. He never checks his property. He says that their lease did not allow for animals. If that's the case, they were in violation of their lease, but he still allowed them to stay. We live in a quiet neighborhood of homeowners. Until recently, we didn't have renters in our neighborhood. It is ironic that the renters that have moved in have brought dogs that no one holds them responsible for. It is even more ironic that the county put leash-law signs in the park after Adam was bitten. Could you please contact me and give me some insight about how to proceed. My son has been damaged both physically and emotionally by this incident. Sometimes, I am still overwhelmed when I think that I almost lost my only child. Thank you so much for your help.

Questions & Notes

1. Is this fair? Are the actions of the dog's owner moral?

2. Is there a legal cause of action, against the owner, landlord, or city? Are there recoverable damages?

3. Should the dog have had a due process hearing?

4. Can justice be done?

5. Setting aside the concerns of the individual in this case, what broader issues of public policy exist? How about banning the breed? Should the state punish the owners or the dog? Can the state help prevent this kind of harm?

Fact Pattern #2

I'll try to give you the *Reader's Digest* version of this story...

I was the private chef/house manager for a couple on Cape Cod. I lived at the house for two years with my cat when the house was sold to a new owner. I had my own wing at the home.

The new owner's fiancée's parents brought their two Jack Russells out to the house in January of this year, and somehow (and I'll never know how exactly, but I think it was the parents) the dogs got into my wing and attacked my 13-year-old cat, Virginia, while I was upstairs working. I heard barking, but the dogs barked all the time, and what kills me is that I was trying not to be a control freak, against my better judgment, and I assumed because there was a note on my door that they would respect that and not enter my part of the house. So my cat died in my arms—she was like my baby and slept on my bed every night. I had nightmares for months and I still have flashbacks—I try not to think about it, and I literally have to turn it around when she pops into my head.

Obviously there is no bringing her back, and it was impossible to continue to work at the house with all of the scratch marks in the floor where she was dragged. I ended up resigning four months later (I would have quit sooner but the salary was very high—120K/year—and those positions are hard to come by); we ended on a very bad note and now they refuse to give me a favorable reference, and they actually accused me of attempting to steal their property in an attempt to discredit my reputation. I have all of the emails that we exchanged in the disagreement that ensued.

I have been looking for almost three months now for a full-time position in this area—there's nothing.

Is there anything I can do, legally, or can I sue them for lack of employment, or mental trauma? I did see a counselor a couple of times when my cat first died, but it didn't really help.

Thank you

Questions & Notes

1. Has a wrong occurred (moral/legal)?
2. Can justice be done?
3. What can you say to the house manager who lost her cat?

Section 14

Summary Questions & Notes

1. How many different types of attitudes about animals might exist among humans? Make up a chart going from intentional inflictors of pain to animal-rights advocates.

2. How many different categories of animal/human relationships might exist and what are the different rules of the relationship?

3. Consider the following:
   - Pets
   - Traditional Farm Animals
   - Industrial Farm Animals
   - Wildlife
   - Genetically Created Animals

   Would you add additional categories?

CHAPTER 2

Animal Ownership

Section 1

What Is Ownership?

Equitable Self-Ownership for Animals
by David Favre, 50 Duke L.J. 473 (2000)

A. An Overview of Ownership

The concept of property is one of the fundamental organizing points for any legal system. Anything of physical substance is subject to its conceptual organization. The right to control, direct, or consume things—living or nonliving—is allocated or decided within our society under the legal concept of title to property. The rules of each sovereign country control the property within its jurisdictional boundaries.

Before proceeding to animal-specific issues, consideration must be given to the concept of title. To have title is to have a cluster of legally enforceable rights relative to a given object. Concepts of title are entirely abstract and dependent upon the legal system in which the object is located. Legal rights, or the relationship between the title holder and the object, may well change as the object moves from one jurisdiction to another. For example, historically, in some states within the United States, humans were the property of other humans, and the slave laws of those states established the property rights of the owners. If an owner took a slave into another jurisdiction, then different laws would apply. At one point, England adopted the proposition that any slave brought into its jurisdiction was freed immediately, thus entirely destroying the property interest of the slave owner. There is therefore an inherent flexibility in the property world.

There are no characteristics within physical objects that demand a particular set of rules or definitions of the concept of title. However, because of the nature of human beings, rules of title are a prerequisite to order and efficiency within human society. Humans seek to possess, use, and consume objects. The rules of title create a predictable matrix that sets out who may use which type of objects and what kinds of uses may be made of the object [and how to transfer ownership between individuals]. Rules of property interrelate closely to help direct the economic structure of a country. As these rules are an ordering point for human society, they have a profound impact on how the members of that society view the world around them. The property rules also reflect the ethical and moral positions within a society. As those positions change or evolve so can the laws of property. What is seen today as the rules of property do not have to remain so into the future.

In the United States, the governments of the individual states control ownership under property law concepts. As the concept of title predates the creation of our state governments, it is a common law topic. As such, either the state courts or the state legislatures are fully empowered to deal with the issue of ownership of animals. One other preliminary point is that our common law system allows for a distinction between title and possession. As we will see, while human possession may be critical to create initial "title" in an animal, once title to an object is obtained, then possession by the title holder need not be retained in order to prove title. Title to your cat or dog is not transferred when you let a friend borrow him or her for a week; instead, a bailment is created.

Questions & Notes

1. Is it good or bad that animals are property? Has there ever been a time in recorded human history that some animals were not property of humans?

2. As will be revealed in the following materials, the economic value of most individual animals is modest at best, and therefore, there is only modest pressure on the legal system to develop the rules for determining ownership of animals. Animal legal issues do not get first-level attention of judges, and cases seldom rise to a state supreme court level. Laws that deal with property generally, for example the Uniform Commercial Code, divorce laws, lost property laws, and trust and will laws, often do not take into account the living nature of this category of property. For this reason many of the case studies in this topic arise not out of filed cases but from e-mail inquires from the general public to the Animal Legal and Historical Center from individuals without lawyers looking for answers to their problems. Unfortunately, it is often the case that there is no clear answer in the legal system, or for the high transaction costs that make legal action impractical.

3. Sometimes people want to claim ownership, usually to enjoy a benefit. Sometimes, to avoid an obligation or liability, they seek to disclaim any ownership. Sometimes the law will impose liability regardless of the wishes of the individual. And sometimes the law, particularly when dealing with dogs, allows the summary destruction of dogs in circumstances not allowed when dealing with other types of property.

4. The threads of property law wander throughout this book. Chapter 6 considers the criminal abuse of an animal by individuals. In Chapter 5 the efforts of the state and local jurisdictions to restrict and control ownership and possession of animal property are set out in detail. Chapter 8 considers the lack of standards that govern the most abundant category of do-

> **Think About It**
>
> There are now three categories of property: real property, personal property, and intellectual property,
>
> Perhaps it is time to add a fourth: living property.

mestic animals: animals within industrial agriculture. This chapter has a focus on pets, as that group of animals is presently challenging the traditional nature of the property laws that govern ownership and transfer of ownership between private individuals.

5. The category of living property is easily distinguished from the other property categories as physical, movable living objects—not human—that have an inherent self-interest in their continued well-being and existence. To what degree does the law treat this category of property different from the others?

Dogs as Property—A Special Case

Animal Law and Dog Behavior

Dogs

Dogs have always had a special status in the legal system, clearly being the most regulated of all the nonhuman animals. Because of their unique character, they were historically considered separate from the domestic v. wildlife classification. Because, historically, "domestic animals" have a context of economic value, dogs (and other pets) lacking economic value were not initially given the status of property. In an 1897 case, the Supreme Court, while discussing a Louisiana statute, gives an extensive historical overview of the human attitude toward dogs:

> The very fact that they are without the protection of the criminal laws shows that property in dogs is of an imperfect or qualified nature, and that they stand, as it were, between animals ferae naturae in which until killed or subdued, there is no property, and domestic animals, in which the right of property is perfect and complete. They are not considered as being upon the same plane with horses, cattle, sheep and other domesticated animals, but rather in the category of cats, monkeys, parrots, singing birds and similar animals kept for pleasure, curiosity or caprice. They have no intrinsic value, by which we understand a value common to all dogs as such, and independent of the particular breed or individual. Unlike other domestic animals, they are useful neither as beasts of burden, for draught (except to a limited extent), nor for food. They are peculiar in the fact that they differ among themselves more widely than any other class of animals, and can hardly be said to have a characteristic common to the entire race. While the higher breeds rank among the noblest representatives of the animal kingdom and are justly esteemed for their intelligence, sagacity, fidel-

ity, watchfulness, affection, and above all, for their natural companionship with man, others are afflicted with such serious infirmities of temper as to be little better than a public nuisance. All are more or less subject to attacks of hydrophobic madness.

Sentell v. New Orleans & Carrolton R.R. Co., 166 U.S. 698, 701 (1897).

It is perhaps the wide array of dog behavior, including their potential for causing serious harm to humans and their property, that has led to this special status. It is generally recognized that attacks on humans by dogs, when they do occur, can be most serious in consequence. The trend of the court decisions since the 1930s has been to eliminate the special status of dogs and treat them as any other domestic animal.

This trend has not been without its reversals and holdouts. A 1933 Pennsylvania case found a dog to be a domestic animal for purposes of a larceny statute, but in 1966 the statute was amended to remove dogs from the scope of the statute. A number of states have clarified the dog's legal status by statute, declaring them to be personal property. In 1977 a cruelty conviction was overturned because the Florida court did not believe the general cruelty statute was intended to protect dogs. **Daniels v. State**, 351 So.2d 749. Because cases that turn on the status of dogs do not arise in each jurisdiction on a regular basis, many of the old cases represent an outmoded position that ought to change as new cases arise. In the context of more recent issues, the status of the dog, as personal property, is important when deciding whether the constitutional requirements of due process must be satisfied when the government seeks to take or remove a dog from the possession of its owner, because if the dog is not property, then constitutional protections for the owner do not attach.

> **News Bits**
>
> **Science News**, "Three Dog Eves: Canine Diaspora from East Asia to Americas," by Susan Milius (Nov. 23, 2002)
>
> Two genetic studies have just rewritten the history of humanity's best friend. The new version has moved the origins of the domestic dog from the Middle East to East Asia and argues that the first people to venture into the Americas brought their dogs with them. Analysis of 654 dogs from around the world suggests that their earliest female ancestors originated from several lineages of wolves primarily in one region. The patterns of genetic diversity point to East Asia as the likeliest place for the canine, about 15,000 years ago.

◇◇◇

Unintended Ownership

Case Study 2A

Hello,

I am trying to find information or get an opinion regarding ownership of cats in West Virginia. I currently own a cat who I provide very well for. Recently a stray cat started coming through the cat door I have for my cat and eating his food. I saw the cat a couple of times and it ran off. About a week ago, my dog cornered the cat and I was able to get close enough to it to see that it had an injury and infection in its face and around it's mouth. It was obviously a very sick animal. I called my local Humane Society and explained the situation to them and asked them to come and get the animal. I could not get close enough to the cat to catch it and was not sure what was wrong with it. The animal control office told me that since I had seen the cat before and it had eaten the food I was providing for my cat I was now the owner of the cat and it was my responsibility to capture it and provide it with medical attention. With some help I was able to catch the poor cat and took it myself to the humane society. I was told I would have to fill out a paper saying I was surrendering the animal. I was told they keep these on file and use them when considering an application for future adoption of a pet. I am a little put off by this since my only intention was to help a sick animal.

I have done some research and what I have found has not been specific. If you have any insight it would be appreciated. Is or was this cat truly mine based on the fact that it had taken my cats food? Was this considered providing for an animal and thereby assuming ownership?

Received December 2005 by editor, Animal Legal & Historical Web Center.

This relatively simple fact pattern raises a number of property and public policy issues.

1. What was the legal status of the cat before she saw it? Before she touched it?

2. When she caught the cat (taking dominion and control) did it change the legal status of the cat?

3. What was her intention and does it matter? Did she have the authority to turn over the cat for treatment or death to the humane society?

4. Are there any public policy issues that push us toward wanting to hold her responsible or not hold her responsible for the cat?

5. Is it fair that her humane society "record" reflect a negative for turning in a sick wild cat? Should the law do anything about that?

It should be recognized that when the cat is turned over to the humane society the humane society has the ownership of the cat and the authority to decide to treat the cat, perhaps adopt it out or to kill* the cat.

> * Note: Other terms such as "put down" are often used in such sentences to shield those who have to do such acts from the harshness of what they are doing. Out of respect for the animals who are killed, I shall not hide the reality behind soft phrases.

As you ponder those questions, consider the following statutory language from West Virginia:

> **§ 19-9-1. Definitions** (for the Chapter Dealing with Diseases Among Domestic Animals)
>
> > (b) "Animal," any domestic equine or bovine animal, sheep, goat, swine, dog, cat or poultry;
> >
> > (c) "Owner," any person who owns, leases or hires any domestic animal from another, **or who allows a domestic animal habitually to remain about the premises** inhabited by such person;
>
> § 19-20-9a. Dogs, cats, etc.; rabies observation
>
> > (a) Any person who owns or **harbors** any dog, cat or other domesticated animal, whether licensed or unlicensed, which bites any person, shall forthwith confine and quarantine the animal for a period of ten days for rabies observation.
>
> § 19-20A-2. Vaccination of dogs and cats.
>
> Whoever owns, keeps or **harbors** a dog or cat within the boundaries of any county in the state of West Virginia shall, on or before the first day of June, one thousand nine hundred eighty-seven …

Questions & Notes

1. Sort out the difference between the key scoping words "owner," "keeper," and "harbors." How does the word "feral" work into this?

2. What is the public policy goal of the West Virginia law? Is this a good and useful approach? Will it work? Do you think some individuals seek to avoid responsi-

> **Think About It**
>
> Is it in the best interest of the cat to become the property of the humans who live in the house that the cat chooses to use as a food source? To get medical treatment, will the cat have to become property?

bility by saying that the cat or dog they feed is not theirs but instead a neighborhood stray?

3. For a detailed consideration of the the terms "keep" and "harbor, see **Pawlowski v. American Family Mutual Ins. Co.,** 777 N.W.2d 67 (Wis. S. Ct., 2009). "Harboring means to afford lodging, to shelter or to give refuge to a dog."

4. Might we be able to say that a nonhuman-owned cat or dog is self-owned? At common law there were only two categories: a domestic animal was either owned with full rights and responsibilities, or it was not owned, with no ownership and no responsibilities. Perhaps a new category is needed of partial ownership and partial responsibility?

Section 2

Obtaining, Transferring, and Losing Ownership Status

Obtaining Title

Domestic Animals—Title by Birth

The Latin maxim *partus sequitur ventrem* (the offspring follows the mother) summarizes the legal concept of title by birth. Ownership of a newborn animal will lie with the owner of the mother regardless of the title to the land upon which the mother is maintained or the ownership of the father. Such ownership will continue, unless divested by some contract, into the indefinite future. The newborn was historically referred to as the "increase." A daughter may subsequently have increase or offspring of its own, and ownership will continue to be traced through the mother's side. Two policy reasons are generally suggested to support this point of law. First, the sire (father) of the offspring may be difficult to ascertain. While DNA may make this easier today, it is still too expensive to be used for most animals. Second, the mother (dam) is often of little economic value during pregnancy, yet must be maintained at the owner's expense. Therefore, certainty and fairness mandates that the title to the offspring go to the owner of the mother.

Obtaining Private Ownership of Wildlife

There are two major hurdles confronting anyone wishing to obtain title to wildlife. The first is the laws and regulations of the state where the wildlife is located. The second is the property law requirement of possession. An uncluttered statement of property law is that any individual who obtains lawful possession of any wild animal shall be the owner of the animal and have all property rights accorded ownership in wild animals, which may not be the same set of rights given to owners of domesticated animals. Originally, wild animals were considered to be without owners so that title simply went to the first person to properly reduce the animal to possession. This concept has been modified by the state ownership doctrine in the United States. The result is that even where possession would be considered sufficient under property law, it may be unlawful.

The classic case is that of **Pierson v. Post**, 3 Caines (NY) 175, 2 Am. Dec. 264 (1805). Post was in full pursuit of a particular fox with horses and hounds. Pierson, with full knowledge of Post's pursuit, shot and killed the fox, taking physical possession of the fox. Post claimed his pursuit sufficiently diligent and active to give him a superior interest in the fox. The court disagreed, saying that pursuit, without mortal wounding, circumventing, or ensnaring, so as to deprive an animal of natural liberty and gain control over it, was insufficient to give rise to any property interest in the fox.

Finding a Domestic Animal—Common Law

When a person finds a domestic animal, the status of the title will be determined primarily by the intentions of the prior owner. If the prior owner has abandoned the animal, then the finder obtains full title immediately. On the other hand, if the animal strayed away and the owner had no intention of giving up title, then the finder, while having a duty to try and find the original owner, will be considered to have full title against all the world except the original owner. The practical difficulty with the law is that when an animal is simply wandering about, it is most difficult to determine the intentions of the prior owner. Thus, the rights and duties of the finder are often cloudy. Additionally, there can be state statutory duties that may require giving notice which a finder must satisfy before he can obtain good title. Statutory duties and the rights of individuals, animal shelters, and government pounds often frustrate and confuse the common law rules just set out.

Most statutory "finder" laws do not seem appropriate to the many varied situations that can arise with animals. If a cat wanders into your backyard and settles down for a nap under a shrub, are you a finder of the cat? No, to be a finder one must:

a. have knowledge of the animal,

b. have intention both to reduce it to possession and assert title, and

c. in fact exert an appropriate degree of dominion and control over the animal.

Therefore, to be a finder of the cat just suggested one would first have to be aware of the cat's presence in the yard; second, intend to take possession of the cat; and finally, take possession—not an easy thing to do. Feeding the cat off the back step is insufficient action at common law because the human is exerting no real dominion and control over the cat. If the cat consents to spend the night in the house, there is a stronger argument. The best proof obviously would be to cage the cat, but there may be certain practical difficulties with this option. The elements of "finding" must be considered on a case-by-case basis, with some allowance for the nature of the animal at issue. However, remember the discussion of "harboring" a cat in West Virginia, *supra*.

Once the status of "finder" can be properly applied, there still remains the issue of what type of title the finder will get. Because the issue will arise only in case of a conflict between the finder and another person, it will be helpful to divide conflicts into two groups. First, as between finder and prior owner, normal property concepts will apply. Ordinarily, the prior owner will retain title and have the right to regain possession, unless it can be shown that the previous owner abandoned the animal. One interesting twist to this conflict is the effect of humane statutes that prohibit the abandonment of animals. Such a provision does not preclude the reality of the abandonment and the subsequent transfer of title. Rather, the provision makes the abandonment of an animal a criminal offense without changing the property law outcome.

Unless from the surrounding circumstances it is apparent the animal has been abandoned, the finder is under a duty to make an appropriate effort to discover the true owner. The degree of effort may vary with the apparent value of the animal, the locations involved (backyard, airport, country road, etc.), and various state statutes. Until the finder has made the appropriate effort to find the true owner, he is in the position of a bailee. Only after the effort has failed may the finder begin to assert the full rights of ownership.

The second group of conflicts is between third parties and the finder. Notwithstanding the various statutes, it would be appropriate in these situations to presume the finder/possessor to be the owner of the animal after six months or one year has lapsed without any evidence of a true owner coming forward. Because a possessor can be charged with the liability of an owner, it seems appropriate that the possessor have full ownership rights unless another party can show better title in the animal.

Think About It

Can you prove who owns the nonhuman animal in your household?

CASE BY CASE

Morgan v. Kroupa

167 Vt. 99, 702 A. 2d 630 (1997)

MORSE, JUSTICE.

Defendant Zane Kroupa appeals from a judgment awarding possession of a dog named Boy (a/k/a Max) to plaintiff Mary Morgan. We affirm.

Defendant adopted a mixed-breed puppy when it was six to eight weeks old and trained it to be a hunting dog. In July 1994, when the dog was five years old, it broke free of its collar, ran away and became lost. Defendant immediately informed his friends and local businesses, and notified the Addison County Humane Society of the dog's escape.

About two weeks later, plaintiff found the dog walking down Route 17 in the Town of Addison and brought it home. She called the Addison County Humane Society and gave a description of the dog; the Humane Society told her to keep the dog until she, or they, could find the owner. She apparently never heard back from them. Plaintiff also posted notices in three State Parks and four general stores in the area, and arranged to have a local radio station broadcast at least two announcements concerning the dog. Although defendant resided in Addison, a rural town of approximately 1,000 residents, he allegedly did not locate the dog for more than one year after it became lost.

Plaintiff took care of the dog and fed and sheltered it. She considered it the household pet. In September 1995, a friend of defendant's told him that he had seen the dog at a house only two miles down the road. Defendant drove to the house, which belonged to plaintiff's boyfriend, and sought unsuccessfully to have the dog returned. As defendant prepared to leave, however, the dog jumped in his truck and defendant left with the animal. Shortly thereafter, plaintiff brought this action in replevin to recover the dog.

The trial court, sitting without a jury, ruled in favor of plaintiff and returned Max to her. In so holding, the court noted that the case could be analyzed under several different theories. The first was to treat the matter as a simple property case, applying the Vermont "lost property" statute, 27 V.S.A. §§ 1101-1110. The second was to analogize it to a child custody case, inquiring into what was in the "best interests" of the dog. The third was to base the judgment on the emotional "attachment" of the contending parties. The trial court essentially chose the first approach, ruling that plaintiff had "substantially compl[ied]" with the statute and was therefore entitled to possession.

Vermont's lost property statute provides that a person who

> finds money or goods, to the value of $3.00 or more, or takes
> up a stray beast, the owner of which is not known, shall,
> within six days thereafter, make two notices, describing

such money, goods or beast, with the natural or artificial marks, with the time and place of finding or taking up the same, and post them in two public places in town in which such property was found.

27 V.S.A. § 1101. If the value of the property exceeds $10.00, the finder must additionally "immediately cause a copy of the notice to be published three weeks successively in some newspaper circulating in such town." 27 V.S.A. § 1103. If the owner does not appear and claim the property within twenty days of the notice, the finder must additionally "cause a copy of the notice to be recorded in the office of the clerk of such town." 27 V.S.A. § 1104. Should the owner not claim the property within ninety days, other provisions of the statute allow the finder to "sell it at public auction" and retain a portion of the proceeds to defray the "expenses of keeping the property," the balance to be "paid to the town treasurer," 27 V.S.A. § 1105, and to further "put such beast to reasonable labor ... allow[ing] the owner a reasonable compensation therefor." 27 V.S.A. § 1109.

From its plain terms and judicial application over time it is evident that the statute—which dates from the late-eighteenth and early-nineteenth centuries—was designed for agricultural animals of substantial monetary value, not lost pets. Although no direct legislative history is extant, the legislature undoubtedly intended the phrase "stray beasts" to include, as the trial court here observed, "animals that had very significant value" such as cows, oxen, horses, sheep, swine, and other farm animals that formed the basis of a largely agricultural economy. The specific and exacting notice requirements, provision for public *auction*, and the allowance for "put[ting] such beast[s] to reasonable *labor*" all presume, and seek to protect the owner's and finder's interest in, an animal of significant financial value. 27 V.S.A. § 1109.

Thus, modern courts have recognized that pets generally do not fit neatly within traditional property law principles. "[A] pet is not just a thing but occupies a special place somewhere in between a person and a piece of personal property." *Corso v. Crawford Dog & Cat Hosp., Inc.,* 97 Misc.2d 530, 415 N.Y.S.2d 182, 183 (City Civ. Ct. 1979). Ordinary common law or statutory rules governing lost personal property therefore do not provide a useful framework for resolving disputes over lost pets. Instead, courts must fashion and apply rules that recognize their unique status, and protect the interests of both owner and finder, as well as the public. In this regard, the trial court was correct that family law provides an imperfect analogue. However strong the emotional attachments between pets and humans, courts simply cannot evaluate the "best interests" of an animal. Recognizing, however, the substantial value that society places on domestic animals, it is proper that the law encourage finders to take in and care for lost pets. A stray dog obviously requires care and shelter, and left unattended could pose hazards to traffic, spread rabies, or exacerbate an animal overpopulation problem if unneutered. A rule of decision that made it difficult or impossible for the finder to keep the animal after many months or years of care and companionship might deter these salutary efforts, and would not be in the public interest.

The value of a pet to its human companions has already been noted. Accordingly, apart from providing care and shelter, finders of stray pets should also be encouraged to make every reasonable effort to find the animal's owner. Although circumstances will vary, this might include contacting the local humane society, veterinarians, or the police department, posting notices near where the animal was found, and placing newspaper or radio advertisements. Additionally, owners of lost pets should be enjoined to undertake reasonable efforts to locate their animals by contacting local humane societies and other appropriate agencies, printing and placing notices, or taking out appropriate advertisements. Together these requirements provide an incentive to finders to care for stray pets and attempt to locate their owners, and place the onus on owners to conscientiously search for their pet.

When confronted with a case of this nature, therefore, courts should factor these practical and policy considerations into any decision. Indeed, this was essentially the approach taken by the trial court here. Although couched in terms of "substantial compliance" with the lost-property statute, the [lower] court basically held that where the finder of a lost pet makes a reasonable effort to locate its owner, and responsibly cares for the animal over a reasonably extensive period of time, the finder may acquire possession of the animal.

Having found that plaintiff diligently attempted to locate the dog's owner and responsibly sheltered and cared for the animal for over a year, the trial court was clearly within its discretion in awarding possession to plaintiff.

GIBSON, JUSTICE, dissenting.

Because I believe that Vermont's lost-property statute, 27 V.S.A. §§ 1101-1110, rejected by the Court herein, outlines the rights and responsibilities of both true owners and finders of stray domesticated animals, including dogs, and that, under the provisions of that statute, Boy (a/k/a Max) should be returned to defendant, I respectfully dissent.

… In this case, the Court follows neither the lost-property statute nor the generally accepted common-law rule. Instead, without benefit of citation to any supporting authority, the Court fashions its own solution in a manner that will be difficult, if not impossible, to apply in a consistent manner in future cases. The Court asserts that the statute applies only to animals having "significant value."

Although the Court believes its holding will encourage finders of lost animals to take them in and give them a home, I am concerned about the consequences of removing pets from the animal-theft protections of the lost-property statute. The lost-property statute was designed in part to remove incentives for animal theft and make it difficult for the finder to profit from selling a stray animal. See 27 V.S.A. § 1105 (if finder sells unwanted stray animal, proceeds of sale go to town after reimbursing finder for expenses). The Court, however, holds that any person who "finds" a dog and makes a "reasonable" effort to locate the owner may claim title to the animal superior to that of the true owner after an undefined "reasonable" amount of time.

Despite the Court's professions to the contrary, I cannot agree that plaintiff made a "reasonable effort" or "diligently attempted" to locate the dog's owner. Although she posted notices, they simply read "lost dog" and listed a phone number, without describing the dog's breed, sex, approximate age (puppy or adult), color, markings or distinctive features, or whether the dog had a collar. While plaintiff also requested community-service radio ads, these ran for two days only, and there is no indication they were any more detailed than her posted notices. Thus, plaintiff failed to provide even the minimal notice necessary to qualify as "reasonable," much less comply with the lost-property statute.

Questions & Notes

1. Why does the Court assume the dog was lost? Is the dog lost, or is the problem that the owner does not know where the dog is? Define "lost" in an animal context.

2. Consider the inadequacy of the state law for finders of lost property. The Vermont law is representative of the older laws found in most states. More recent are the state laws that authorize humane societies or government pounds to dispose of lost animals after only a short holding period. See next case.

3. The court rejects the "best interest" of the animal as an approach to deciding the case. Why was that? What might be made of the fact that the dog chose to go home with the defendant after nearly a year's absence? If you were trying to decide the case on the best interest of the dog, what factors would you use to decide the case?

4. What is the new rule that comes out of this case? What public policy supports the rule? Do you agree with the outcome? In light of the information in the dissenting opinion about the efforts of the plaintiff in trying to find the defendant, do you agree the plaintiff's efforts were adequate? Do you share the dissenting judge's concerns that the new rule will make it easier for individuals to steal dogs and sell them to research facilities? Should private parties be required to turn over found animals to public or private animal shelters?

5. There does not seem to be any concern about how the plaintiff had been treating the dog. What if the plaintiff chained the dog to a tree ten hours a day, and in the time they had the dog had never taken it to a veterinarian for care?

Case Study 2B

hi, my name is jimmy and i was hoping you could possibly answer a few questions i have about dog theft. my fiancé was recently charged with theft of a dog, and faces a possible 10 years in prison and a $5,000 fine. the dog had broken its runner cable and went to her mothers house. this happened on the day we were moving, so she had went to her mothers house to borrow her truck so we could move. well, the dog was there and had no tags to tell whom the dog belonged to. her mother had removed the remaining cable. when she left, the dog followed her a short distance down the road. she was afraid the dog was going to get hurt, or worse, killed. she stopped the truck, let down the tail gate, and the dog jumped in. we started moving our stuff, and while we were at the place we were moving to, the dog got out. we gave it some dog food and water, and had to leave to get more of our stuff. her intentions were to keep the dog until someone claimed it, in which case someone did claim it a day or two later, but the dog had ran away and we could not find it, and we have been unable to find it. now the owner of the dog is trying to charge her with theft, a class 5 felony. i was wondering if you had any advice on what to do, or could tell me someone who would. she has never committed a crime or anything of the sort, so this is her first offense. when she let the dog into the bed of the truck, she didnt think she was doing anything wrong … she was only trying to help keep the dog from getting hurt until the owner claimed it. i hope to get a response soon.

Received December 2005 by the Animal Legal & Historical Web Center.

Statutory Termination of Title

CASE BY CASE

Lamare v. North Country Animal League
170 Vt. 115, 743 A. 2d 598 (1999)

MORSE, J. [This is same judge that wrote the majority opinion for the prior lost dog case.]

The following facts are undisputed. Plaintiffs were the co-owners of a five and one-half year old female German Sheppard named Billy. They acquired the dog as a puppy and registered it with the American Kennel Club. On June 3, 1997, Billy and her five-month-old puppy broke free from their tether at plaintiffs' residence in Wolcott. Although licensed with the Town of Wolcott, Billy was not wearing her license tags at the time of her escape. The puppy returned several hours later. When Billy failed to return, plaintiffs contacted their neighbors, friends, and family with the hope that she had gone to someone's home. During the next month, plaintiffs continued to search for Billy when they had time, but her continued absence caused them to speculate that she had been injured, killed, or stolen.

In fact, Billy was found several hours after her escape, running on the road, by a couple who brought her to Lamoille Kennel. An employee of Lamoille Kennel notified Gilbert Goff, the Wolcott animal control officer. Goff assumed control and custody of the dog under the Wolcott dog control ordinance.

As required by the ordinance, Goff placed notices describing the dog in the village store, post office, and town clerk's office. After holding Billy for nine days from the date of impoundment without any response to the notices, Goff transferred Billy into the care and custody of defendant North Country Animal League, where Billy remained for approximately three weeks.

On Sunday, July 6, plaintiff Arnold's mother contacted Goff, who told her that he had placed a dog in the League's custody. Plaintiffs called the League that day and left a message on the answering machine concerning their lost dog. On Monday, July 7, plaintiffs again contacted the League and were told that it still had the dog in its possession. Plaintiffs arrived at the League shortly thereafter and identified the dog. They asked that the dog be returned, provided American Kennel Club papers to prove ownership, and offered to pay all boarding costs. A League employee, defendant Darcy Fitzgerald, told them that the dog belonged to the League and that the only way to gain possession was to fill out an adoption application. Plaintiffs immediately completed the application, but were told that their personal references had to be contacted. Two days later, plaintiffs called the League to inquire about the status of their adoption application. A League employee informed plaintiffs that their application had been denied. When plaintiffs questioned the reason for the denial, they were told that it was not in the dog's best interests to be returned to them. Plaintiffs later learned that, in fact, the League had approved "Jane and John Doe's" adoption of Billy on July 5, prior to plaintiffs' application. Billy was spayed on July 8 and adopted by the Doe family that same day. None of the references listed in plaintiffs' application was ever contacted.

Plaintiffs then filed this action to recover their dog from the Does and for damages from the League for violation of their due process rights guaranteed by the United States Constitution.

I.

In *Morgan*, [*supra*] we held that when the finder of a lost dog makes a reasonable effort to locate the owner and responsibly cares for the animal over a reasonably extensive period of time, the finder may be awarded possession of the dog. *Morgan* involved a dispute between private parties and was governed by common law principles. This case, in contrast, concerns the rights and responsibilities of a public entity vis a vis the owners of a lost dog and is controlled by state statutes and local ordinances. Thus, the trial court's task here was confined to interpreting and applying the pertinent legislative enactments and determining their validity. The trial court's application of *Morgan* was therefore inapposite, but as we reach the same result on different grounds we need not reverse the judgment.

The Wolcott dog control ordinance provides:

> If the owner of the dog is unknown, the officer shall, within forty-eight (48) hours of impoundment, post an advertisement in the Town Clerk's Office and at least one public place in the Town. Said notice shall describe the dog, state when and where the dog was impounded and declare that unless the owner or person entitled to possession of the dog shall claim the same and pay all charges set forth below within seven (7) days after posting of such notice, the dog office shall sell the dog, give the dog away or dispose of it in a humane way.

Town of Wolcott Dog Control Ordinance, § 7(C).

The record evidence supports the trial court's conclusion that the local animal control officer complied with the notice requirements of the ordinance, and properly transferred ownership of the dog to the League under its provisions. Indeed, plaintiffs do not challenge these findings, but instead contend that the ordinance was invalid because it was not authorized by state statute and violated their constitutional right to due process.

II.

There is no dispute that the statute authorizing towns to regulate the running at large of domestic pets empowered the town to take possession of Billy when she was found running on the road unattended and without license tags. Yet, plaintiffs argue that once having taken possession, the town lacked the corollary authority to transfer possession of the dog and responsibility for its upkeep to the League after the requisite seven-day redemption period had passed. The argument is unpersuasive. The town must have the ability to make some humane disposition of the animal after a certain period of impoundment has expired. Plaintiffs' narrow construction of the statute would effectively compel the town to care for impounded domestic animals in perpetuity if the rightful owner never came forward, a result plainly at odds with reason and sound policy. We conclude, therefore, that the provision of the ordinance authorizing the town to sell or otherwise dispose of the animal in a humane fashion constituted a necessary and essential power under the enabling statute, and therefore did not exceed the town's authority.

III.

Plaintiffs next assert that the ordinance violated their due process rights by depriving them of property without adequate notice and an opportunity to be heard.

We have recently reaffirmed the principle that " 'property' in domestic pets is of a highly qualified nature, possession of which may be subject to limitation and control." *Morgan,* 167 Vt. at 104, 702 A.2d at 634. As we noted in *Morgan,* state law provides that an animal shall be deemed abandoned if placed in the custody of a veterinarian, kennel or other establishment for treatment, board, or care for a specified period of time. See *id.* (citing 20 V.S.A. § 3511). Domestic pets suspected of having been exposed to rabies may be confined or impounded, see 20 V.S.A. § 3806, or even killed if reasonably necessary, see *id.* § 3807(a), and "vicious" domestic pets may be removed from the owner and "disposed of in a humane way." *Id.* § 3546(c).

The qualified right to possession of dogs and other animals, and the strong public interest in assuring their permanent placement in a suitable environment, amply supports the town's decision to provide for the sale or transfer of impounded dogs if unclaimed after seven days.

These common sense requirements, together with the town's additional ordinances requiring that owners provide their dogs with license tags, and that the dog control officer directly contact the owner of an impounded dog if the identity is known, establish that the risks of an erroneous deprivation under the ordinance are small. Only in the limited circumstances where the owner of a lost dog has not complied with the license requirements, and has failed to take the reasonable steps of inquiring with the local pound or checking notices in the town office and other public places, is it possible that an owner will fail to receive notice within the seven-day notice period. The fact that plaintiffs in this case did not take these reasonable steps does not render the ordinance unconstitutional.

We conclude, in sum, that the town's posting of descriptive notices in the town clerk's office, post office, and village store — in conformity with the ordinance — did not deprive plaintiffs of their constitutional right to due process.

V.

Any case involving possession of a domestic pet predictably arouses broad public interest and concern. The actions of the League in this case certainly warrant such concern; it was, to say the least, insensitive in its dealings with plaintiffs. Although plaintiffs' action for repossession of the dog and for damages based upon alleged constitutional violations lacks merit, this is not to say that a future case seeking recovery for the emotional distress or other damages resulting from the negligent handling of an impounded animal — a claim not alleged here — would be unsuccessful.

Questions & Notes

1. Did the humane society have a legal duty to return the dog to its original owner? Whether or not there is a duty, can they decide to not return the dog to its owner because they think the owners are not fit for pet responsibility (e.g., the son wants the dog back but the father in the family abuses/beats the dog on a regular basis)?

2. If a law requires five days of holding an animal, how is that calculated? Twenty-four-hour clocks? What about weekends when no one answers the phone? There have been a number of cases where hours make the difference between life and death for animals.

3. The Humane Society of the U.S. filed an amicus brief in support of the defendant. Why did they do that? What would be the consequence to future actions of humane societies if the court had found a duty to hold and return the lost dog? Why is the time period so short?

4. If this was private party owner versus private party finder, did the owner make a reasonable effort to locate the lost animal? Note the lack of an identification collar and what flowed from that. Would this give support for the law requiring the obtaining and displaying of a dog license or other identification?

5. Because the court found that the owner had lost title by the time that the dog was delivered to the humane society, the court did not really address the actions of the humane society. Would you allow a cause of action against the humane society for how they handled the events? What damages might be appropriate?

6. Part of the difficulty of the legal structure in which this case arises is that general finder laws are poorly integrated with shelter holding rules, and the average citizen may not be aware of the quick time limitations which exist in shelter holding laws. Normally one criterion for a good law is that it is aligned with the expectations of an average citizen who is subject to the law. Do you think this is the case for this area of the law?

7. See also **Johnson v. Atlanta Humane Society**, 326 S.E.2d 585 (Ga. Ct. App. 1985); **Lamare v. N. Country Animal League**, 743 A.2d 598 (1999). In both cases, the courts found that as long as the humane society complied with statutory mandates, its transfer of title to a third person (or killing the animal) was upheld against the owner's original title because the owner was found to have forfeited title by losing the animal. In **Richardson v. Fairbanks N. Star Borough**, 705 P.2d 454 (Al. 1985), the owner was successful in a suit against an animal shelter

that killed his dog before the minimum holding period had expired. The owner was able to recover market value damages.

Transferring Title

Sales

As animals are personal property, a common method for the transfer of title is by sale. It is clear that animals are "goods" as defined under the Uniform Commercial Code, and therefore the sale of most animals would be subject to those provisions. We will leave a full consideration of all the possible sales issues to the course on contract law and discuss only a few that relate directly to the uniqueness of pet animals.

While a wide variety of dogs and cats are available at shelters for the minor cost of adoption, the price for "purebred" animals can easily run $500 to $1,500. If a mother dog has six puppies, then the value of a litter can be $3,000 to $9,000. This level of sales is a sufficient incentive for many humans to get into the dog breeding business (and many do who should not). While the federal Animal Welfare Act controls the physical conditions of commercial breeders, it does not control "home" or hobby breeders. There is no law that sorts individuals for commercial breeding based on resources available, knowledge, or skills.

A key problem in the area of dog sales is the reality that many consumers buy dogs on impulse and quickly become emotionally attached to the animals. Additionally, when a puppy or kitten is offered for sale, only a veterinarian or a well-trained eye can see the genetic difficulties or diseases that an animal might have. It is a reality that many of the dogs offered to the public should not have been bred in the first place, as they had to endure poor living conditions and may carry fatal diseases. Their mothers may be treated as breeding machines (money machines) with two or more litters per year for a number of years—until they die of exhaustion. The social concerns are not only with the human buyer to which the rule of "buyer beware" certainly applies, but to a market place where the property being sold faces a life of pain and suffering because of unscrupulous breeders trying to make money without regards to the quality of the animals being produced. All of these risks are amplified in a world where individuals are willing to buy dogs over the Internet, sight unseen, and move them across the country.

So how do the laws handle consumers who get the new dog home and two days later find they don't really want to deal with a puppy or notice that one eye is weeping or the back leg is not working? Even more difficult is when a year or more after the purchase of a dog, when the dog is well ingrained into the hearts of all the family members, a congenital disease comes to the forefront causing much anguish, cost of treatment, and suffering to the dog.

Added to these difficulties is the reality that the legal system's cost of engagement is so high that justice is difficult to obtain. Even at $1,000 purchase price and $500 in veterinarian bills, the hiring of an attorney for proceeding to court is difficult to justify. (Human pain and suffering and animal pain and suffering are not available as damages because the claim is based on contract and a buyer is usually limited to actual and incidental damages.) See Chapter 4 for full discussion of damages.

Besides the health and well-being of the animals, the other major issue that surrounds dogs in particular is the ability to register the purchased dog in the AKC system (American Kennel Club). Does the dog have his or her "papers"? Sellers have to have their breeding dogs registered and have to provide additional paperwork for sold animals. This does not always happen, and sometimes there is intentional misrepresentation by the seller. The AKC registration is about genetic purity and says nothing about the health and well-being of a particular dog. AKC registration is usually a prerequisite to showing a dog or to do breed-specific breeding, which can get the higher prices.

Given the complexities of the situations and the limitations of the Uniform Commercial Code, over a dozen states have adopted laws specifically focused on the sale of pets.

Questions & Notes

1. Pennsylvania has a statute that is five pages long with many complexities (full text available at *www.animallaw.info*). The heart of the provisions provide:

    § **201-9.3. Dog purchaser protection** (b) If, within ten days after the date of purchase, a dog purchased from a seller is determined, through physical examination, diagnostic tests or necropsy by a veterinarian, to be clinically ill or dies from any contagious or infectious illness or any parasitic illness which renders it unfit for purchase or results in its death, the purchaser may exercise one of the following options:

    (1) *Return the dog to the seller for a complete refund of the purchase price, not including the sales tax.*

    (2) *Return the dog to the seller for a replacement dog of equal value of the purchaser's choice, providing a replacement dog is available.*

    (3) *Retain the dog and be entitled to receive reimbursement from the seller for reasonable veterinary fees incurred in curing or attempting to cure the affected dog, subject to the limitation that the seller's liability for reimbursement shall not exceed the purchase price, not including sales tax, of the dog. This clause shall apply only if the purchaser's veterinarian determines the dog's illness*

can be treated and corrected by procedures that are appropriate and customary. The value of these services is considered reasonable if comparable to the value of similar services rendered by other licensed veterinarians in reasonable proximity to the treating veterinarian. Reimbursement shall not include the costs of the initial veterinary examination fee and diagnostic or treatment fees not directly related to the veterinarian's certification that the animal is unfit for purchase pursuant to this section. If, however, the purchaser's veterinarian determines the dog's illness is incurable, only the options in clauses (1) and (2) of this subsection shall apply.

(f)(3) If the seller fails to provide this documentation [for registration] within one hundred twenty days of the date of sale or fails to notify the purchaser of an extension under clause (2) of this subsection, the purchaser may elect one of the following remedies:

(i) *Return the dog and receive a full refund of the purchase price, not including sales tax.*

(ii) *Retain the dog and receive a refund from the seller in an amount equal to fifty per cent of the purchase price.*

The key phrase "unfit for purchase" is specifically defined:

(i) As used in this section: "Unfit for purchase" means any disease, deformity, injury, physical condition, illness or any defect which is congenital or hereditary and which severely affects the health of the animal or which was manifest, capable of diagnosis or likely to have been contracted on or before the sale and delivery of the animal to the consumer.

2. Do you think that the above provisions represent a fair balance between the interests of the sellers and buyers? Does this law reduce the incentives to create "puppy mills"? What practical difficulties might still exist?

Usually the individual consumer/purchaser has only the small claims court as a source of relief. Consider the following:

CASE BY CASE

Roberts v. Melendez

6 Misc. 3d 1015, 2005 WL 192353 (N.Y. City Civ. Ct.)

Unpublished Disposition.

1.

On October 27, 2003, plaintiff Courtney Roberts, purchased from defendant Le Petit Puppy, an eleven week old male dachshund puppy (Identification number D0107) for $1200. The parties entered into a sales agreement for this purchase. The written sales agreement was presented to the Court without objection. Ms. Roberts also received a dog information sheet along with a packet. Ms. Roberts presented without objection only the information sheet to the court. The information sheet revealed that Le Petit Puppy received the dog on October 15, 2003, and listed seven vaccinations administered to the dog as follows: Panacur de-worming on August 15, 2003, Progard CPV on September 17, 2003, Panacur de-worming on September 17, 2003, Vanguard DA2MP on September 24, 2003, Progard KC on October 1, 2003, Panacur de-worming on October 1, 2003, and Progard Puppy 7 DPV on October 5, 2003. Testimony revealed that Ms. Roberts had been to Le Petit Puppy on October 22, 2003, 5 days before the purchase of the dog, and made a separate purchase of a cat. She recalls getting a packet and paperwork in conjunction with that purchase as well.

Ms. Roberts took her newly purchased dog on an airplane to California. The animal was seen by her veterinarian in California on October 28, 2003, the day after she purchased the dog, as evidenced by medical records which were presented to the Court without objection. Plaintiff's veterinarian, Janet C. Lowery, DVM, administered a DHPP vaccine at that time. Dr. Lowery noted the dog to be "normal" in all of the following categories: attitude/appearance, oral cavity/teeth, mucous membranes, eyes, ears, cardiovascular, respiratory, gastrointestinal, musculoskeletal and nervous system. She noted that plaintiff reported that she had just gotten the dog the day before from a New York pet store and that the dog was sneezing a bit. Dr. Lowery's notes also report the doctor's inability to palpate one of the dog's testicles and her witnessing one flea. She directed the use of Advantage, an anti-flea medication.

The following day, on October 29, 2003, the dog presented with illness and was admitted to Dr. Lowery's care at her facility, Mid-Peninsula Animal Hospital. Over the course of the next days, the facility treated the puppy. At that point, the dog's white blood cell count was diminishing, and he appeared to show signs of Parvo. According to the medical records, a Parvo test was done "which was positive at that time, however, the fact that he was vaccinated the day prior potentially negates the test results."

2.

Ms. Roberts supplied to the Court without objection a letter from Dr. Lowery to Le Petit Puppy, dated December 1, 2003, which posits that the vaccination schedule may well have compromised the dog's immune system. Nevertheless, despite a fully disclosed vaccination schedule, Dr. Lowery also gave the dog a DHPP vaccine on October 28, 2003. While the animal could not be conclusively diagnosed as having Parvo because of that particular vaccination, the dog exhibited clinical symptoms consistent with Parvo. The Court notes that none of the vaccines received by the dog were administered by Le Petit Puppy. Doctor Lowery concludes in her letter that "[b]ecause Parvo typically has a prepatent period of 5–7 days this puppy was infected with the virus at the time of purchase. Certainly there may have been no clinical signs present at the time to signal this or there may have been just the beginnings of lethargy and diminished appetite."

> **Think About It**
>
> Never, never, ever buy an animal over the Internet.

Dr. Lowery concedes in her December 1, 2003 letter that, "[She] certainly understand[s] that this is the type of situation where you, as a pet store, cannot be held responsible for knowing what wasn't yet apparent, but the fact is that you sold a puppy that had been exposed to and was incubating Parvovirus."

Some time after the dog was euthanized, Ms. Roberts contacted Le Petit Puppy for the first time to alert them that the dog had been ill, treated and put down, and gave them a copy of her veterinarian's report. She sought reimbursement for $1687 in hospital costs, $1755 in emergency bills and $1400 for the cost of her taking the dog to California.

The sales agreement submitted to the Court, which bears Ms. Roberts' signature, provides in relevant part that:

> I. All pets sold are covered by a 14 (fourteen) day money-back warranty if a licensed veterinarian diagnoses the pet as unhealthy at the time of sale.
>
> II. Claims made under the above warranty must be accompanied by a statement from a veterinarian specifying, in detail, the medical conditions leading to his/her diagnosis. The seller, however, shave [sic] have the right to have the pet re-examined by another veterinarian …
>
> VI. Excepting appropriate provisions under the laws of the State of New York, the above 14 (fourteen) day money-back health warranty and one year serious congenital defects pet-replacement warranty shall constitute the only post-sale responsibility of Le Petit Puppy.

3.

Ms. Roberts seeks by this action reimbursement for the cost of the dog, the medical costs for the dog's treatment, and the cost of transporting the dog to California. Ms. Roberts provides without objection her credit card statement as proof of payment for the dog, but fails to provide any proof of payment of any medical bills submitted to the court.

[The court found that the defendant did not engage in any "deceptive practices" and therefore that attorney fees were unavailable to the plaintiff.]

The Court finds that the parties' contract clearly outlines the remedies available here. Those remedies mirror those provided by the General Business Law. Gen. Bus. § 753 et.seq., [Mckinneys 2005] Simply put, plaintiff could have contacted defendant and chosen one of a number of options involving the return of the dog, or keeping the dog while making the dog available for examination.

The question for this Court remains whether a purchaser may take advantage of a health warranty affording her reimbursement for the purchase price of the animal plus the cost of certification of the animal's unfitness for purchase, when that purchaser failed to afford the pet dealer the corresponding right to examine the animal?

Plaintiff, by her own admission, failed to notify defendant that the dog was ill, did not return the dog, and did not make the animal available so that the pet could be re-examined by another veterinarian (even one in California chosen by the dealer). While the law is sure to afford rights to the consumer, it also instills in them correlative duties, and provides a correlative right to the pet store.

Here defendant is at a disadvantage. Plaintiff used a New York City address when purchasing the animal, and promptly relocated to California. Many intervening variables could have affected the condition and health of the dog, such as a change in food, travel on an airplane, a disruption in environment, the new vaccine received in California, or administering Advantage to an 11 week old dog. Here, the pet store was not even notified of a problem until after the animal was euthanized, cremated and unavailable for examination.

4.

New York City Civil Court Act § 1804 authorizes this court to "conduct hearings upon small claims in such manner as to do substantial justice between the parties according to the rules of substantive law and shall not be bound by statutory provisions or rules of practice, procedure, pleading or evidence, except statutory provisions relating to privileged communications and personal transactions or communications with a decedent or mentally ill person." New York City Civil Court Rules §208.41(j) direct that the "court shall conduct the hearing in such manner as it deems best suited to discover the facts and to determine the justice of the case."

It is undisputed that the consumer never afforded the pet dealer the right to contest a demand for reimbursement, and failed to produce the animal for examination by a licensed veterinarian designated by such dealer. The Court notes that as a result, the pet dealer is also without recourse as against the breeder. Nevertheless, Ms. Roberts' sought care for her dog and such action should be encouraged. Thus, this Court finds that substantial justice would be attained by the parties sharing in the cost of the dog, namely the $1303.50 ($1200 plus tax of $103.50).

The clerk of the Court is directed to enter judgment in favor of claimant and against Narciso Melendez d/b/a Le Petit Puppy in the amount of $651.75 plus interest from the date of filing, June 17, 2004.

Questions & Notes

1. Was "substantial justice" done? What would have been the outcome in other than a small claims court? It should be noted that in many states, plaintiffs are specifically not allowed to use an attorney in small claims court.

2. What is parvo? If the plaintiff had read the papers do you think the average person would understood the nature of the risk — suppressed immunity?

3. What about the fact that the seller had not personally done anything wrong? Will the seller get reimbursement from the breeder?

Case Study 2C

I recently bought a puppy online from a breeder in texas well lets just say I didn't get the puppy I wanted so he sent me a second one and said I could keep both due to the fact of my inconvenience or I could ship the first puppy back well I could not send the first puppy back I spent 1,400.00 on vet bills that he would not help cover, bothe puppys were sick the first puppy ended up dieing but he told me not to waste my money on the puppy he instructed me to starve the puppy to death instead, and said not to spend more money on the second puppy that she would be okay, well the second puppy was also ill, so my vet told me to report him I need to know what to do I am in california he is in texas but he told me to kill the puppy because my vet refused to put it to sleep at first only because we thought she was hypoglimic and we then ran blood work to find out the puppy was in kidney failure and liver failure along with carona virus and other things so can you help me … if so please email me at xxx@verizon.net and tell me what I can do to get this breeder to stop breeding sick animals and to start to cover the medical bills from the sick animals he ships to people
thank you
Received November 2005, Animal Law Web Center
What advice do you give?

4. In July of 2010 an advisory committee within San Francisco considered the adoption of a law that would have outlawed the sale of all pets except fish. What are the pros and cons of such a proposal?

More materials available: See Robyn F. Katz, Commercial Breeders and Puppy Mills, Animal Legal and Historical Center (2008). http://www.animal-law.info/articles/dduscommercialbreeders.htm.

◇◇

Adoption

Today when an individual visits an animal shelter in hopes of taking home a dog or cat, they will find that it is a more complex process than that which occurs at the pet store in the mall. The shelters talk in terms of placement and adoption rather than sale, and just because you are willing to take a pet does not mean that you meet their qualifications for adoption or placement of a particular animal. The term "adoption" clearly denotes something different from the mere sale of an animal. This is the intention of most groups that adopt out or place animals. It is clearly meant to mimic the process by which children are placed in new families. It is out of respect for the animal—recognition that a dog or cat is fundamentally different from a car.

But the question that must be asked is whether the legal system allows for this new method of transfer of title, for no state has changed the status of animals from that of personal property. Regardless of the heading at the top of a paper, the legal concepts of gifts, contracts, and sales constitute the legal context for the consideration of the provisions of an adoption agreement. While a few states' laws do make reference to adoption by humane societies; no state has fully considered how to deal with the process that is occurring every day across the country.

Shelters have three primary concerns when placing animals in new homes. First, they want the right outcome to occur for the animal in their care. As part of this, they often seek to control ownership and possession of the animal after the placement of the animal in a new home. Second, there is a concern of tort liability if the animal causes harm when placed in a home. This is a liability beyond the contract remedy for return of defective goods. Third, there are limited resources available with which to deal with the unending flow of animals arriving at their front door.

Normal Process

The shelters sort animals by being aware of species traits and needs, taking the history of an animal if available, performing veterinary check-ups, and engaging in behavior observation of each animal. The first decision is whether the animal is adoptable at all; and if he or she is not adoptable, then death may be the only option, unless the shelter is committed to keeping animals indefinitely. (No-kill shelters raise issues of their own.)

Questions & Notes

1. Is a life in a cage in a shelter for unadoptable animals necessarily in the best interests of the animal? Is this suffering?

2. When is the adopting group just meddling in a family's personal decisions about how to deal with a pet? On the other hand, most humane groups are involved with enforcement of anti-cruelty laws, so perhaps some level of meddling is acceptable. Should this be by state law or private contract?

∞

Title Revocation by Statute

The statutory direction about adoption that exists in some states arises from a separate public policy concern, that of pet overpopulation. The number of dogs and cats born every year in the United States is more than our capacity to care for them.

One approach to reducing the number of dogs and cats is to require the mandatory spaying and neutering of all animals adopted out by humane societies. Over half of the states have adopted legislation to promote this goal. The legislature usually pays little attention to broader property law issues; rather, the focus is on getting the animals "fixed." The issue of the nature and legal consequences of the adoption process is not touched upon.

The seriousness of this issue to the legislatures can be judged by the rather summary transfers of title back to the placement/adoption agency. Consider:

1. **Arkansas** §20-19-103(B) – It is unlawful for shelter to release unsterilized animal; if an extension is granted, not exceeding 30 days, and owner does not comply, **animal shall be returned to releasing agency and title reverts to releasing agency**.

2. **Texas**: § 828.009. Reclamation

(a) A releasing agency that does not receive a letter under Section 828.005, 828.006, or 828.007 after the expiration of the seventh day after the sterilization completion date agreed to under Section 828.002 **may promptly reclaim the animal from the new owner**.

3. **Utah**: § 10-17-105. Failure to comply with sterilization agreement

If a recipient fails to comply with the sterilization agreement under Subsection 10-17-103(2):

> (1) the failure is ground for seizure and impoundment of the animal by the animal shelter from whom the recipient obtained the animal;

> (2) **the recipient relinquishes all ownership rights regarding** the animal and any claim to expenses incurred in maintenance and care of the animal; and

> (3) the recipient forfeits the sterilization deposit.

It appears that in the zeal to assure sterilization, the legislatures have not thought through the property law aspects of conditional ownership. Additionally, in many states there is no law to support humane shelters or pounds that engage in the adoption approach. In these cases, contract law is really the primary tool available for legal analysis. It is the common practice of many shelters and pounds to impose conditions and oversight on the transfer of title to the new owners. While contract law is available as a context of analysis, there are some terms found in these contracts that cause difficulty in a property law context:

1. Restraints on alienation—can the new owner sell or gift the adopted animal to a third party without permission of adopting agency? And if the adopting owner did so, can the adopting group get the animal back? (void vs. voidable title)

2. Would the conditions (covenants), such as the duty to spay or neuter the animal, run to a purchaser of the adopting individual? Can title be burdened beyond the person signing the contract?

3. Can the adopting group continue to enforce a duty of good care provision against subsequent purchasers? If they can, are they limited to damages or can they get a return of the animal?

The difficulty of these issues is increased when there is no oversight by the state in either the contract terms or the decisions of adoption engaged in by various organizations, and the likelihood of court involvement is low.

Case Study 2D

I have a rather urgent question for you. To try to summarize, I have an acquaintance who adopted a dog through a rescue organization but due to some miscommunications between myself and within the organization itself, the group is now saying that the dog shouldn't have been adopted because he needed to have a "recheck" on his temperament test. The dog is only 3–4 months old, has already passed a complete evaluation at the group, and has also been evaluated by 2 behaviorists outside the group who state that the dog is fine. However, the group is basically demanding that he bring the dog back for a recheck within the next couple weeks, even though they have already stated that the "recheck" is basically only a "courtesy" and that they pretty much intend to put the dog down based on what I feel are some off the cuff discussions and supposed "aggressive" behavior that some of the people at the group claim to have seen. The supposed "aggressive behavior" was seen by myself and two others as well and we do not agree that it was aggressive in any sort of possible interpretation. While I don't pretend to be an expert, I do put faith in the outside unbiased behaviorists who have evaluated the dog since this all started.

Based on this information, my question for you is 1.) Is it mandatory that the dog be returned for a "recheck" despite the fact that this person has already signed an adoption contract to adopt the dog, given the fact that it has already been pretty much decided that the dog will be put down no matter HOW great he does on his "recheck"? 2.) Is there any case law that you know of where a group tried to cancel an adoption contract after it had already been transacted? It seems crazy to me that a group would try to do this, especially on a dog that has already passed the groups own temperament test, and given the extreme length to which rescue groups go to ensure they are not held liable for any potential future behavior problems, but unfortunately this is the case. We are in a temporary holding pattern with the group right now, but are not sure what the next steps should be. And, given that the dog has displayed no aggressive behaviors, we are both fearful that he will be put down unfairly because no one within the group wants to dispute what someone else claims to have seen, whether true or not. Your advice would be greatly appreciated, if you know of any cases regarding such an issue, or where I might be able to do more research on the subject to determine our options that would be a big help as well.

Thank you so much in advance.

Submitted to Animal Legal and Historical Web Center May 2005

Questions & Notes

1. Draft a contract provision for waiver of tort liability for harm that might be done after the new owners take the pet home.

2. Draft a contract provision that allows the adopting agency to take the animal back if the animal is not properly cared for.

3. The adoption process seems acceptable when done by animal shelters, which in the vast majority of cases are large enough organizations for the public to have some level of confidence in their ability and judgments. After all, the shelters have had to build or buy a building and then obtain a license and fill it with animals; this requires a certain level of management skills and personnel sorting. However, breed-specific rescue groups also take it upon themselves to place animals. These groups can be one- or two-person operations by volunteers who may or may not have the education and experience to do this properly. An issue that the legal system does not really deal with: Who is qualified to be an adopter of animals? Do the rules of title transfer, which by statute apply to shelters, apply to rescue groups?

Think About It

In 2005 the disaster in the Gulf Coast created by Hurricane Katrina presented those dealing with pets a large number of legal questions:

- Is it appropriate to demand that people leave their pets when being taken out of disaster areas?

- If after the disaster pet rescuers believe a dog is in an abandoned home, can they break into the home to get the animal?

- What rules of foster care should govern animals rescued if the owners are not known? Many animals ended up 1,000 miles from their homes, just like their owners. Without the Internet listing of found animals, the reunion of animals with owners would have been almost impossible.

- What happens when an out-of-state foster parent refuses to return the dog?

See Megan McNabb, *Pets in the Eye of the Storm: Hurricane Katrina Floods the Courts with Pet Custody Disputes*, 14 Animal Law 71 (2007).

Disputes over Title and Control

Divorce of the Humans

When pet owners decide to go their separate ways, what to do with the pet can be as emotional as what to do with children, particularly if those in the relationship have pets but not children. In this context, treating the animal as property to be awarded along with the silverware and sofa seems very inappropriate. In this case it is not a private party making an adoption decision, but a court making a decision. In the past decade more and more courts have been asked to treat pets differently. Sometimes courts have treated pets like children, other times they have specifically refused to do so, saying that the law gives them no flexibility in this matter.

Professor Rebecca J. Huss, *Separation, Custody, and Estate Planning Issues Relating to Companion Animals*, 74 Univ. Colo. Law Review 181 (2003):

> Trial courts often approve settlement agreements that award custody and even support (sometimes referred to as "petimony") to one spouse in a divorce proceeding. One example is *Dickson v. Dickson*. [fn - No. 94-1072 (Ark. Garland County Ch. Ct. Oct. 14, 1994); see also Labrador Retrieval: Woman in Divorce Wins Custody and Dog Support, Dallas Morning News, Oct. 16, 1995, at 8D, available at 1995 WL 9066006 (discussing Dickson case). Note that the dog in this case had been given to the husband as a gift although the wife was given custody.] In Dickson, the divorcing parties agreed to have joint custody of their dog, with the wife as the primary custodian, subject to reasonable visitation rights by the husband. The husband was ordered to pay up to $150 per month for the dog's care and maintenance. The consent order was later modified due to a material change in circumstances that rendered the original order inequitable. In the modification, the wife was granted sole care and custody of the dog and the husband was ordered to pay half of the outstanding debts for the care and maintenance of the animal. Furthermore, the order stated that the husband had no further interest in the dog but would also have no further liability for the dog's care.
>
> There is judicial reluctance to award custody of animals using a "best interest of the animal" approach. An example is *Nuzzaci v. Nuzzaci*. [fn - 1995 WL 783006 (Del. Fam. Ct. Apr. 19, 1995).] There, the court declined to apply the best interests of the animal approach and refused to sign a Stipulation and Order for visitation rights relating to a golden retriever. The judge referenced the lack of statutory support for such orders and expressed concern as to the court's ability to make decisions on the custody or visitation of animals in the absence of the parties' agreement.

CASE BY CASE

Desanctis v. Pritchard

803 A. 2d 230 (Pa. Super. Ct. 2002)

In seeking "shared custody" and a "visitation" arrangement, Appellant appears to treat Barney, a dog, as a child. Despite the status owners bestow on their pets, Pennsylvania law considers dogs to be personal property. See 3 P.S. § 459-601(a); see also Price v. Brown, 545 Pa. 216, 680 A.2d 1149, 1153 n. 3 (1996). The Agreement in question explicitly awarded this property to Appellee. Appellant argues that 23 Pa. C.S.A. § 3105(a), which allows the court to enforce a supplementary agreement to a divorce decree whether or not it was merged or incorporated into the decree, controls this issue. Appellant, however, overlooks the fact that any terms set forth in the Agreement are void to the extent that they attempt to award custodial visitation with or shared custody of personal property. See Pa. C.S.A. § 3502 (setting forth guidelines for distribution of property as opposed to custody or visitation). As the trial court aptly noted, Appellant is seeking an arrangement analogous, in law, to a visitation schedule for a table or a lamp. This result is clearly not contemplated by the statute. 23 Pa.C.S.A. §§ 3503-04. By the clear and unambiguous terms of the Agreement, Barney and his social schedule belong exclusively to Appellee. {FN2}

> FN2. It is interesting to note that Barney was purchased by Appellee two months prior to the parties' first separation, and from December, 1996 until October, 2000, Appellant never saw Barney.

This claim is meritless.

Questions & Notes

1. Do you think that the general public would accept the idea that when dealing with the issues of divorce, a court should be authorized to deal with pets as a special category, allowing cost and visitation rights to be discussed along with physical custody? Why or why not?

2. What standards do you think a court should adopt in deciding what to do with an animal?

3. What if a young man and woman are living together and the man buys a cat? Over the next few months the woman takes care of the pet and the cat ends up on the woman's lap most of the time. After a year, the humans decide to split up but have a dispute over who gets the cat. What should happen? Is there a role for the courts?

◇◇

CASE BY CASE

Houseman v. Dare

966 A. 2d 24 (N.J. Super. Ct. App. Div. 2009)

Plaintiff Doreen Houseman appeals from a judgment of the Family Part awarding her $1500 for a dog she and defendant Eric Dare jointly owned when they separated and ended their engagement to be married. Alleging that she and Dare had an oral agreement giving her possession of the dog that Dare breached by wrongfully retaining the dog after a post-separation visit, Houseman sought specific performance of the agreement and a judgment declaring her ownership of the animal. Prior to trial, the court determined that pets are personal property that lack the unique value essential to an award of specific performance. On appeal Houseman claims that the pretrial ruling was erroneous as a matter of law. We agree and remand for further proceedings. {FN2}

> FN2. By leave granted, the Animal Legal Defense Fund and Lawyers in Defense of Animals both filed a brief as amicus curiae. They urge us to adopt a rule that requires consideration of the best interests of the dog.

The following facts are not in dispute. Houseman and Dare had a relationship for thirteen years. In 1999 they purchased a residence, which they owned as joint tenants and made their home. In 2000 they engaged to marry, and in 2003 they purchased a pedigree dog for $1500, which they registered with the American Kennel Club reporting that they both owned the dog. In May 2006 Dare decided to end his relationship with Houseman. At that time, Dare wanted to stay in the house and purchase Houseman's interest in the property. In June 2006, Houseman signed a deed transferring her interest in the house to Dare. When she vacated the residence on July 4, 2006, Houseman took the dog and its paraphernalia with her. She left one of the dog's jerseys and some photographs behind as mementos for Dare.

The trial court limited presentation of evidence about the parties' dog in accordance with its pretrial ruling foreclosing Houseman's claim for specific performance and the parties' stipulation that $1500 was the intrinsic value of the dog.

Dare and Houseman did not have a written agreement about the dog, but after Houseman left the residence she allowed him to take the dog for visits after which he returned the pet to her. According to Houseman, when she asked Dare to memorialize their agreement about the dog in a writing, he told her she could trust him and he would not keep the dog from her. Although Dare admitted to making that promise in his answer to Houseman's complaint, he offered no testimony on that point at trial.

In late February 2007, Houseman left the dog with Dare when she went on vacation. On March 4, 2007, she asked Dare for the dog, but the pet was not returned. Houseman filed the complaint that initiated this litigation on March 16, 2007, and when trial commenced in December 2007 Dare still had the dog.

The court's conclusion that specific performance is not, as a matter of law, available to remedy a breach of an oral agreement about possession of a dog reached by its joint owners is not sustainable. The remedy of specific performance can be invoked to address a breach of an enforceable agreement when money damages are not adequate to protect the expectation interest of the injured party and an order requiring performance of the contract will not result in inequity to the offending party, reward the recipient for unfair dealing or conflict with public policy.

Specific performance is generally recognized as the appropriate remedy when an agreement concerns possession of property such as "heirlooms, family treasures and works of art that induce a strong sentimental attachment." Restatement (Second) of Contracts §§ 357, 358, 360, 364, 365 (1981). That is so because money damages cannot compensate the injured party for the special subjective benefits he or she derives from possession. And, consideration of special subjective value is equally appropriate when a court is called upon to exercise its equitable jurisdiction to resolve a dispute between joint owners of property that cannot be partitioned or sold without hardship or violation of public policy.

There is no reason for a court of equity to be more wary in resolving competing claims for possession of a pet based on one party's sincere affection for and attachment to it than in resolving competing claims based on one party's sincere sentiment for an inanimate object based upon a relationship with the donor. See Burr v. Bloomsburg, 101 N.J. Eq. 615, 621, 138 A. 876 (Ch. 1927). In both types of cases, a court of equity must consider the interests of the parties pressing competing claims for possession and public policies that may be implicated by an award of possession. Cf. Juelfs v. Gough, 41 P.3d 593, 597 (Alaska 2002) (approving modification of a property settlement agreement providing for shared possession of a dog because the arrangement assumed cooperation between the parties that did not exist).

In those fortunately rare cases when a separating couple is unable to agree about who will keep jointly held property with special subjective value (either because an agreement is in dispute or there is none) and the trial court deems division by forced sale an inappropriate or inadequate remedy given the nature of the property, our courts are equipped to determine whether the assertion of a special interest in possession is sincere and grounded in "facts and circumstances which endow the chattel with a special ... value" or based upon a sentiment assumed for the purpose of litigation out of greed, ill-will or other sentiment or motive similarly unworthy of protection in a court of equity. Burr, supra, 101 N.J. Eq. at 626, 138 A. 876. We are less confident that there are judicially discoverable and manageable standards for resolving questions of possession from the perspective of a pet, at least apart from cases involving abuse or neglect contrary to public policies expressed in laws designed to protect animals. see Morgan v. Kroupa, 167 Vt. 99, 702 A.2d 630, 633 (1997) (noting that "[h]owever strong the emotional attachments between pets and humans, courts simply cannot evaluate the 'best interests' of an animal" and resolving a dispute about possession in light of the interests asserted by the parties).

We conclude that the trial court erred by declining to consider the relevance of the oral agreement alleged on the ground that a pet is property. Agreements about property jointly held by cohabitants are material in actions concerning its division. They may be specifically enforced when that remedy is appropriate.

Houseman's evidence was adequate to require the trial court to consider the oral agreement and the remedy of specific performance. The special subjective value of the dog to Houseman can be inferred from her testimony about its importance to her and her prompt effort to enforce her right of possession when Dare took action adverse to her enjoyment of that right. Her stipulation to the dog's intrinsic monetary value cannot be viewed as a concession that the stipulated value was adequate to compensate her for loss of the special value given her efforts to pursue her claim for specific performance at trial.

Questions & Notes

1. Notice the openness and flexibility the court suggests for equitable consideration of this dispute. Should this be available in a divorce proceeding? Since it was not a formal dispute under the divorce laws of the state, the court had the historical non-legislative context of equitable distribution of joint owned property in which it could work.

2. Did the court adopt any form of "best interests of the animal" as a standard? How will the court decide on re-trial?

Pets in Trust and Wills

Under this heading there are two separate topics. First, at the death of the pet owner, what is to happen to the pet? How much power will the deceased have in the issue of pet disposition? What if the will directs that the pet be killed so that the animal may join the owner in heaven?

CASE BY CASE

In re Capers Estate

34 Pa. D. & C.2d 121 (1963)

RAHAUSER, J.

Ida M. Capers, the owner of two Irish setters named "Brickland" and "Sunny Birch", died January 27, 1963. Her will provided, among other things:

> "FIFTH: I direct that any dog which I may own at the time of my death be destroyed in a humane manner and I give and grant unto my Executors hereinafter named full and complete power and discretion necessary to carry out the same."

The executors of the estate filed a petition for declaratory judgment. The petition prays that the court determine the rights and duties of the executors by reason of the aforementioned clause in the will of the above decedent. There was uncertainty on the part of the executors, if they should take such drastic action without the authority of the court. The governor of the State ordered the Attorney General of Pennsylvania to intervene to prohibit the executors from carrying out the illegal purpose of the will.

It is apparent that testatrix was deeply interested in the humane care and treatment of animals. She left the greater part of her fortune for these purposes. The testimony at the hearing indicated that the chief objects of decedent's affection were the two Irish setters mentioned in her will. She was interested that they would be given the same care after her death that she gave them while she lived. She evidently feared that either they would grieve for her or that no one would afford them the same affection and kindness that they received during her life. She, accordingly, made the above provision in her will for their destruction. Testimony indicates that she was mistaken on both above points. [The animals had been temporarily placed with a family on a farm where the large dogs had considerable more ability to be outside and run free.]

This brings us to the third question. Is it against public policy to hold valid a clause in a will directing the summary destruction of certain of decedent's property after her death?

There is no question of the strength of the public sentiment in favor of preserving the lives of these animals. This is in accord with the upward development of the humane instinct in mankind for the preservation of life of all kinds, not only of human life but of the life of the lesser species. Man has come to realize that he has an ethical duty to preserve all life, human or not, unless the destruction of such other life is an absolute necessity. This ethic is epitomized in Albert Schweitzer's phrase "reverence for life" and is best expressed by that noble man in his book "Out of My Life and Thought." [The Court quotes extensively from the book.]

If affirmation of life and ethics are inseparably combined, it indeed would be unethical to carry out the literal provisions of paragraph five of decedent's will. Paragraph 5 of decedent's will would confiscate the life of the two setters for no purpose. It would be an act of cruelty that is not sanctioned by the traditions and purposes of this court, and would conflict with its established public policy.

[This is a 12-page opinion, with much more detailed consideration of the policy issues than is reproduced here.]

Decree

And now, to wit, November 12, 1964, the above case having been heard and briefs having been filed and the prayer for a declaratory judgment having been considered, it is ordered, adjudged and decreed that the fifth paragraph of decedent's will providing for the destruction of the two Irish setters, "Brickland" and "Sunny Birch," is void as not being within the purview of the Wills Act of the Commonwealth of Pennsylvania, and being against the public policy of the Commonwealth of Pennsylvania.

Questions & Notes

1. Do you agree with the court? Are there circumstances when you would agree with the directions of the decedent to kill the pets? This is not a highly litigated issue, but many pets have to be "dealt with" at the death of an owner. What if the children just don't want to deal with the old pet of their parents? Can they have it euthanized?

2. What happens with title to a pet at the moment of an owner's death?

3. For additional discussion, see Rachel Hirschfeld, *Ensure Your Pet's Future: Estate Planning for Owners and Their Animal Companions*, 9 Marq. Elder's Advisor 155 (2007), available at *http://www.animallaw.info/articles/arus9marqeldersadvisor155. htm*; Suzette Daniels, *An Introduction to Pet in Wills and Pet Euthanasia* (2004), Animal Legal and Historical Web Center. Available at *www.animallaw.info/articles/arusdanielssuzette2004. htm*.

◇◇

The second part of this topic is of a much more positive nature. How might an owner best take care of his or her pet after death? At common law there was/is a firm rule that animals could not be beneficiaries, as they are property, and property cannot be the owner of property. Then there is the common law Rule of Perpetuities, which would be violated if an animal received property or money for his or her life (trust me on this). Regardless of the position of the law, individuals have long sought to provide for their pets after death. The best they could do would be to create an honorary trust. This approach seeks to create a mechanism for the payment of money for care for the animal. However, nothing is enforceable as a matter of law, the owner will be dependent on the good will and ethical conduct of the particular individual in possession of the animal.

In 1990 things began to change. In the quiet little backwater of will drafting, animals have made significant progress in the world of jurisprudence. In 1990 the National Conference of Commissioners on Uniform State Laws revised the Uniform Probate Code to specifically allow for pet trusts. Section 2-907 was modified in 1993 and in part now states:

> (b) [Trust for Pets.] Subject to this subsection and subsection (c), a trust for the care of a designated domestic or pet animal is valid. The trust terminates when no living animal is covered by the trust. A governing instrument must be liberally construed to bring the transfer within this subsection, to presume against the merely precatory or honorary nature of the disposition, and to carry out the general intent of the transferor. Extrinsic evidence is admissible in determining the transferor's intent.

In 2000 the Uniform Trust act also added pet trust provisions. In this case the enforceability of the trust is made very clear with the adoption of the following language:

> 408 (b) A trust authorized by this section may be enforced by a person appointed in the terms of the trust or, if no person is so appointed, by a person appointed by the court. A person having an interest in the welfare of the animal may request the court to appoint a person to enforce the trust or to remove a person appointed.

Unlike the area of divorce, in the area of wills and trusts the United States is in the midst of a legislative transformation. The implementation of new probate and trust laws by over 40 state legislatures illustrates the flexibility of the state legal system. (The pet provisions were just one small part of a set of recommended changes. It is not known how many legislators actually understood the specifics of the pet provisions.)

Questions & Notes

1. Could a wealthy owner set aside $1,000,000 for the benefit of two cats? Could an owner direct that the home not be sold so long as the animals are alive and able to stay in the home? What about a pet obtained after the will was written but before death? Should the trust be able to cover the cost of the offspring of the pet (a pet fee tail)?

2. Draft a short list of questions for a client interview with someone who has animals and sufficient assets to provide for them.

3. Should the trustee and the caregiver be the same person?

4. Would it be acceptable for the caregiver to use trust money to buy a new car in which to transport the five cats to the vet office and visit friends? How about a new sound system for them to listen to music (assume it was provided for in the will)?

5. As of the beginning of 2011 no case had been reported that raised issues under the new pet trust provisions of any state. For additional discussion see: Gerry W. Beyer, *Pet Animals: What Happens When Their Humans Die?* 40 Santa Clara L. Rev. 617 (2000); Rebecca J. Huss, *Separation, Custody, and Estate Planning Issues Relating to Companion Animals*, 74 Colo. L. Rev. 181 (2003).

Section 3

Bailments

The Creation and Nature of Bailments

The broadest definition of a bailment is the lawful possession of an animal by someone other than the owner.

A few examples of bailment include: the million dollar stallion that spends a day on another's farm for a $10,000 stud fee; the family poodle who is at Fancy Dog's getting a cut and wash; and the weekend rider who rents a horse for four hours. In all of these situations, possession is in the hands of someone who is not the lawful owner of the animal. The laws of bailment will determine the rights and duties of the parties unless a legislature has changed the rules, as is the case with the Equine Liability Acts adopted in many states (see *http://www.animallaw.info/articles/dduseala.htm*). The primary legal rules that govern the relationship of a bailment are: first, that the bailee (possessor of the animal) is liable under common law tort rules for damages to the bailed animals during the bailment. Secondly, the bailee is absolutely liable for misdelivery of the animals to someone other than the bailor (title holder of the animal or other prior lawful possessor).

These rules arise only if it is first found that a bailment relationship exists. For the creation of a bailment, two elements are critical. First, there must be physical delivery of the property to the bailee. Second, there must be knowing acceptance of the property by the bailee.

The bailee may rent an animal for personal pleasure (horse stable), the bailor may loan an animal to a friend without charge, or the bailee may keep the animal as a favor or for the convenience of the bailor, without compensation. But most common animal bailments are of a commercial nature. By contract, a bailee may agree to take possession and responsibility for the feeding and raising of animals.

Duties of Bailor and Bailee

The easiest situation to deal with is the one least likely to occur. The bailee has a duty to redeliver the bailed item to the bailor. If the bailee delivers the animals to someone without authorization from the bailor, then the bailee is liable for their value at that point, without regard to the issue of negligence. The issue is not the reasonableness of the bailee's conduct; rather, the bailee is under an absolute duty to redeliver the bailed items, and lack of negligence will not constitute a defense. As might be imagined, misdelivery does not arise nearly as often as the problem of injury or death to the bailed animal while in the possession of the bailee.

The greatest number of problems arise over the question of the bailee's duty of care toward the animal in his or her possession. The term "care" in this context is not just the positive duty of providing adequate food, water, and shelter as set out in criminal anti-cruelty law, but also the broader general tort concept that includes an obligation to refrain from any action or nonaction that could forseeably result in injury to the bailed property.

The duty of the bailee is to provide the level of care appropriate to all the surrounding circumstances. This is a factual issue (that is, a jury question) that must be determined on a case-by-case basis. It is a "reasonable man" standard and presupposes familiarity with the animal's needs.

Case Study 2E

Cynthia Rock took two cats to Dr. Roy Carroll's veterinary clinic to be neutered. Rock phoned the clinic the next day and was told that one of the cats, Tigger, escaped and had been missing for several hours. When Rock arrived at the clinic, she was told by Carroll's staff that they had been looking for and would continue to search for Tigger, had called animal control, and would run an ad in the paper and post notices in an effort to locate the cat. A few weeks later, when Tigger had still not been found, Rock sued Dr. Carroll d/b/a The Animal Care Clinic for conversion or breach of bailment and emotional distress.

Carroll's veterinary technician testified that she watched as a kennel assistant tried to remove Tigger from a cage to administer an antibiotic. The cat scratched the assistant's neck and arms and she dropped him. The technician tried to catch Tigger by throwing a towel over him, but he escaped by tearing through a piece of plastic and some wire mesh that covered a space between the wall and an air conditioning unit. The technician immediately ran outside to catch the cat, but he jumped past her and ran away.

Does Cynthia have a cause of action? Will she win?

See **Carroll v. Rock**, 220 Ga.App. 260, 469 S.E.2d 391 (1996).

Case Study 2F

From an e-mail received Sept 10, 2008:

Hello, I am in a very difficult situation and am not quite sure how to handle it. I have 2 dogs, that I love more than anything else in the world. I got very very sick and so my mother volunteered to take them until I was well again. I was supposed to pick them up September 19th, before my mom goes away on vacation (I live in New York, she in Michigan) and I called her the other day to make arrangements. Unfortunately, she told me she turned them over to a rescue league, and one of them, Harry, has already been adopted. She made no mention of this to me, did not try to ask me to come for them sooner, or anything of the sort. On my last trip home, (about a month ago) we got into a huge fight, and have hardly spoken since. I never in a million years thought she would do this to me. When I spoke to the man from the rescue, he said that he would not help me get Harry back, even though he was just adopted on Friday. I have all of his papers in my name, and I never once gave my consent for my babies to be turned over. My heart is broken and all I want is to get BOTH of my dogs back. What is the best course of action to take? Please help me. I am devastated.

What is the legal category of each of the individuals? Can she get the dog back?

CASE BY CASE

A key aspect to the concept of bailment is the risk allocations between the owner and possessor of the bailed item/animal. As the next case demonstrates, the risk allocation is created through the burden-of-proof requirements.

Gebert v. Yank

172 Cal. App. 3d 544, 218 Cal. Rptr. 585 (1985)

HANSON, J.

By amended complaint, plaintiffs Rosemary Gebert and Florence M. Thuillier sought damages from defendant Albert Yank, Worldwide Bloodstock Agency, a California corporation. Five causes of action were stated concerning two thoroughbred horses the plaintiff-owners had entrusted to defendant Yank: (1) negligence; (2) breach of a bailment contract; (3) breach of an oral contract. [Four and five are omitted.]

Factual Background

Plaintiffs Gebert and Thuillier owned two thoroughbred yearling horses, a chestnut filly (sometimes referred to herein as Filly) and a gray colt (Colt). [FN4] Plaintiffs had extensive experience in ranching, and in raising thoroughbred horses for sale. Defendant is what is known as a bloodstock agent, selling thoroughbreds for a commission.

> FN4 Thoroughbred horses become yearlings on January 1 after their birth; yearlings are referred to customarily by their color and gender.

Plaintiff Gebert testified that she valued young Filly at $30,000 and was anxious to command the best price she could get. Acting upon the recommendation of an experienced ranch owner and fellow horse breeder, the plaintiffs decided to employ defendant Yank as their agent for the select sale. Yank was a widely known and respected bloodstock agent, with many years of experience. It was agreed that Filly would be transported to Yank's Swiss Ranch for preparation prior to the sale. On July 15, 1978, Filly was so transported. [FN5]

> FN5 The agreement of the parties and the delivery of Filly to the Swiss Ranch and into the care of bailee Yank were not controverted at trial—said facts were admitted by defendant.

On July 23, 1978, Filly was exercised by horse trainer Wally Dunne, an employee of defendant Yank, for about five minutes in a round pen. Dunne then turned over the horse to groom Diane Barnett, also an employee of defendant.

Filly was wearing a halter strapped on her head, with a ring under the chin. The groom held a leather shank, a strap approximately one inch wide and seven feet long; attached to the shank was a thirty-inch chain, which had been passed through the ring of the halter and reattached to itself, forming a loop. Filly had been observed by defendant and by Barnett to be a relatively docile young horse. Barnett led Filly to a patch of grass so that she could graze. Barnett, a former student at Cal Poly San Luis Obispo, had received instruction in handling horses and had recently been employed by defendant as a groom. She testified that she was watching Filly closely, standing on her left side which is the customary position, holding the shank tightly. She denied that the chain with the loop was dragging on the ground. Suddenly, however, Filly "struck out," i.e., raised her left hoof and leg; her hoof got entangled in the loop of the chain. As is typical of thoroughbreds, Filly resisted by pulling backwards, which increased the pressure on the halter on her head. She reared up, fell backward and injured herself. Barnett ran for help, and another employee came to the scene and cut the halter off of Filly's head. However, it was necessary to call a veterinarian and that same day Filly was euthanized, put to sleep.

At trial, the hotly disputed issue was whether the configuration of shank and looped chain around Filly's head and neck constituted thoroughbred horse handling of the negligent variety or met the requisite standard of care. There was sharp disagreement between the witnesses on this point. All seemed to agree that thoroughbred horses are high-strung, nervous, unpredictable animals, and that yearlings in particular, being very young horses, have even less capacity for withstanding ordinary distractions. Experienced horse breeder Ruth Betty Rutledge declared that the chain loop was very careless and should have been knotted to ensure the horse's safety. Trainer Leigh Howard, who had given instruction to groom Barnett, testified that Barnett had been properly instructed concerning shanks and chains and had never been told by her to graze an animal with a looped open 30-inch chain. On the other hand, expert Jimmy Mayer testified for the defense that it was customary in the breeding industry to use a 30-inch chain just as it had been utilized by groom Barnett. The last witness for the defense was Johnny Longden, a famous jockey and 77 years old at time of trial, who approved the use of a shank and a 30-inch chain in the manner utilized by Barnett; denied that knots were customarily tied in chains in the horsebreeding industry; he estimated that the odds of a horse putting its hoof through the chain shank were "one in three or four million," but declared that accidents happen to thoroughbreds frequently which cannot be prevented.

As indicated, the jury rejected plaintiffs' cause of action for negligence but found liability on the part of defendant for breach of the bailment contract regarding Filly.

Discussion

I.

"In a broad sense a bailment is the delivery of a thing to another for some special object or purpose, on a contract, express or implied, to conform to the objects or purposes of the delivery which may be as various as the transactions of men [citation]."

The jury in this case was told that "A bailee, the person who received the property, is not an insurer of the goods left in his possession. That is to say, he is not absolutely responsible if he does not redeliver the goods. He is only responsible if the failure to redeliver is caused by his negligence. When the goods are lost, destroyed or damaged by accident, without any fault on the part of the bailee, the loss must fall on the bailor." This is an accurate statement of California law.

However, the jury was also instructed that once plaintiffs had proved the existence of a bailment, the defendant/bailee had "the burden of establishing by a preponderance of the evidence all of the facts necessary to prove the following issue: that the loss of Filly occurred without negligence on the part of defendant." This rule is of relatively recent vintage in California.

The present rule, requiring the bailee to demonstrate lack of fault, was set forth in, where it was declared that if the burden remains with the bailor, "he will be faced in many cases with insuperable difficulties in securing and presenting evidence." It was concluded that "when a bailee who is under the duty of exercising ordinary care is unable to redeliver the subject of the bailment, it is not enough for him to show that the property was lost, stolen or destroyed, but that if he relies upon such fact to excuse his failure, he must go further and show that the loss occurred without negligence on his part. As heretofore stated, a contrary rule would place upon the plaintiff [bailor], in many cases, an impossible burden. It is just and fair that one who undertakes for reward to care for a chattel should have the burden of explaining its loss or destruction while in his custody and of negativing an inference of negligence on his part arising from such loss or destruction."

We decline to develop new rules for bailed animals and note that the issue as such was neither addressed nor litigated below. Civil Code section 1834 provides only that "A depositary of living animals must provide them with suitable food and shelter, and treat them kindly."

II.

Defendant claims that the jury verdict as to Filly was inconsistent as a matter of law, compelling reversal. Defendant specifically contends that since the jury rejected plaintiffs' cause of action for negligence, they were precluded from finding, as they did, for plaintiffs on the breach of bailment cause of action. As indicated previously, finding for plaintiffs on the breach of bailment cause of action did involve, of necessity, a determination that defendant was, to some degree, negligent in caring for Filly. Defendant, therefore, argues that the jury had to determine that defendant was either negligent or not, and could not make inconsistent determinations with respect to the two causes of action on the same set of facts.

Rarely does a case demonstrate, as this one does, the importance of burdens of proof in terms of the legal consequences. Plaintiffs pleaded two causes of action concerning the loss of Filly, one for negligence and one for breach of bailment. Pleading of alternative theories of relief on the same set of facts is, of course, quite proper and is often done where there is a legally recognized basis for recovery in both contract and tort. (4 Witkin, Cal. Procedure (3d ed. 1985) § 356, p. 411.) The jury was instructed that plaintiffs were proceeding with two alternative theories of recovery, and were instructed as to the elements of each cause of action. They were instructed, as to burdens of proof, that plaintiffs had the burden of proof as to the negligence cause of action but having established the bailment, plaintiffs did not have the burden of proof on negligence in the breach of bailment cause of action. Even aided by the instruction regarding res ipsa loquitur, the jury was not sufficiently persuaded of defendant's negligence to find for plaintiffs on the negligence theory, and thus the burden of proof operated to prevent recovery. The jury apparently did regard the evidence on the issue of negligence as very evenly divided, but the burden operated against the defendant on the breach of bailment cause of action because of his failure to completely refute fault on his part.

***

Disposition

The judgment is affirmed.

Questions & Notes

1. Do you agree that there was a bailment?

2. Was there negligence on the part the agent or the bailee?

3. Was there freedom from negligence on the part of the bailee?

4. If you were the attorney for the bailee, how would you satisfy your burden of proof?

5. Was the outcome fair in this case? As a general matter, is the allocation of risk as adopted by this case appropriate for animal bailments?

Section 4

Interfering with Owner's Rights and Expectations

A key attribute of the ownership of property is the ability of the owner to do as they wish with property, including the consumption or destruction of property. (Think doughnuts and cars.) This attribute of property acts as a presumption of freedom of action or inaction for the owner, but there are clearly circumstances when other private parties and the government itself will assert the power to interfere with that presumption. This will arise both when the use of the property interferes with other humans and their interests, and when it is necessary to intervene on behalf of the animal itself. The long existing anti-cruelty laws at the state level clearly limit what people may do to their living property, or that of another. This topic is so extensive as to require two chapters: Intentional Cruelty and Duty to Provide Care, Chapters 6 and 7. Additionally, the government asserts a general right of control over the types of animals that can be kept, as well as the living conditions that must be provided for the animals. This is covered in Chapter 5. A few federal laws, such as the Animal Welfare Act (Chapter 10), limit what owners can do with their animal property, but these laws are limited in their scope because property law is primarily a state law issue.

The brief materials that follow shall be considered a few other modes of interference.

Government Agents

The ultimate interference is when a third party kills another person's animal. When done by a private party the normal rules of torts apply, but the issue of damages provides some unique difficulties (see Chapter 4). What happens when the killing is done not by a private party, but by an agent of the government under the color of authority of the state? This can occur directly, on the street, and by taking the animal into possession and then killing the animal later.

These cases arise in the context of government action in violation of the Constitution's Fourth Amendment.

> The right of the people to be secure in their persons, houses, papers, and effects, against unreasonable seizures, shall not be violated ...

U.S. Const. Amend. 4

Police Shooting Pets — Detailed Discussion

by Pamela L. Roudebush, Animal Legal and Historical Center (www. animallaw.info) (2002)

The Supreme Court has stated unequivocally that a seizure of personal property occurs when "there is some meaningful interference with an individual's possessory interests in that property." **United States v. Jacobsen**, 466 U.S. 109, 113 (1984). The destruction of property is considered "meaningful interference" constituting a seizure under the Fourth Amendment because the destruction of property by state officials poses as much a threat, if not more, to people's right to be "secure ... in their effects" as does the physical taking of them.

Another question to be asked: Does the Fourth Amendment only cover seizures of personal property that occur during a criminal search? Again, the Supreme Court has clarified this issue and stated that the reason why an officer might enter onto a person's property or into a person's home does not vitiate the question of whether a seizure has occurred and whether the Fourth Amendment applies. The reason can be for searches and seizures relating to both criminal and civil issues. "In our view, the reason why an officer might enter a house or effectuate a seizure is *wholly irrelevant* to the threshold question whether the Amendment applies. *What matters is the intrusion on the people's security from governmental interference."* **Sobal v. Cook County**, 506 U.S. 56, 69 (1992) (emphasis added).

Generally speaking, destruction of property that is not necessary to a law official's duties is considered an unreasonable seizure of property under the Fourth Amendment. The courts, based on the individual facts of the case, will determine whether the destruction of the property was reasonable. Although the courts will decide the reasonableness of a seizure on a case by case basis, the person considering filing a lawsuit for a pet's death must have a general idea of whether the officer's conduct in their particular case was unreasonable.

Case Study 2G

The sad history of this section 1983 case began in 1988. Claire Bilida rescued an orphaned raccoon, which her family raised as a pet and kept in a cage attached to the back of the family's home in Warwick, Rhode Island. Raccoon Mia lived there for seven years until she was seized and destroyed in August 1995 by local officials. On August 8, 1995, a Warwick police officer named Kenneth Brierly entered Bilida's backyard in response to a security alarm signal. While investigating the alarm, which proved to be false, Brierly saw Mia in her cage. Uncertain whether possession of the raccoon was legal, he called Nora Legault, the city's animal control officer, and then left the premises. A half hour or so later, Brierly and Nora returned to find Bilida at home. They asked for her permit from the department, which is required under Rhode Island law for possession of raccoons and certain other animal species. Bilida told Legault that she had a permit but then was unable to produce one. The department then sent two of its officers to Bilida's home where the officers—who had no warrant—entered Bilida's gated backyard and seized Mia after a struggle with Bilida. Bilida was then issued a summons for illegally possessing a raccoon but (according to Bilida) the officers promised her that Mia would not be killed. However, according to the state's rabies protocol, Mia had to be euthanized and tested for rabies. With no further notice to Bilida, Mia was then shot, tested, and found not to have any rabies infection.

Bilida filed her own complaint in the federal district court. She asserted federal claims under 42 U.S.C. § 1983 for violations of her constitutional rights of "privacy," due process, and protection against unreasonable search and seizure. As will be seen in later material, section 1983 claims have been used by citizens to attack actions by state agents. But in this case, assuming that the warrantless search was improper, the due process of the constitution requires the existence of a property interest before the right attaches. Does Bilida have a property interest in the raccoon? See **Bilida v. McCleod**, 211 F.3d 166 (5th Cir 2000).

Did Bilida have possession of the raccoon?

Does possession create a property interests? Does she have any legal options besides the federal 1983 action?

What do you think of the state law which required the killing of the raccoon?

A further point from the reported case:

"Whether the nature of Bilida's exposure to Mia required euthanizing the raccoon is not entirely clear from the language of the protocol; it refers inter alia to cases of possible exposure "via ... saliva ... and ... [a] pre-existing break in the skin...." There is no indication whether Bilida's feeding or handling of Mia resulted in such exposure."

The killing might have been discretionary for the agency and yet they chose, without any factual basis, to kill the raccoon. Why did this happen? Should it have happened? Also see **Fuller v. Vines**, 36 F.3d 65 (9th Cir. 1994); **Newsome v. Erwin**, 137 F. Supp.2d 934 (S.D. Ohio 2000).

Private Insurance Companies

In response to the large number of injuries caused by dogs, and the millions of dollars in settlement that insurance companies have had to pay out each year, some insurance companies are responding by refusing to issue policies if certain dogs are present or otherwise interfering with the free choice of a homeowner to have what animals they may want. Remember that most people have a mortgage on their private residence and mortgage companies require insurance on the home; having insurance is not normally optional for a home owner.

The Case Against Dog Breed Discrimination by Homeowners' Insurance Companies

by Larry Cunningham, 11 Conn. Ins. L.J. 1, 12–15 (2004). The 68-page article is available at *www.animallaw.info/articles/arus11conninslj1.htm.*

1. A Rise in Breed Discrimination

During 2003 and 2004, the media brought breed discrimination to light. The CBS Evening News with Dan Rather aired a story in June 2003 that featured a family that had difficulty obtaining insurance because they owned a Dalmatian. The report stated, "[a]nimal lovers have a term for what the insurance company did. They call it 'breed discrimination'—arbitrarily punishing all dogs of certain breeds because some are vicious." In the months that followed, several newspaper stories discussed the prevalence of breed discrimination and documented the effects this practice has had on families. These news reports replicate the experience I had in trying to get homeowners' insurance. Multiple insurers denied coverage because of the dogs I owned. I literally could not find a carrier in the Lubbock market willing to write a policy for me until I stumbled upon the Farm Bureau on the advice of one insurance broker who sympathized with my plight.

The practice of breed discrimination produces absurd results. Consider the case of Chris and Norm Craanen of San Antonio, Texas. They own a 12- year-old dog named Bukarus. He is a Rottweiler, a breed often targeted for discrimination by insurance companies. Yet, Bukarus does not pose much of a threat: he is deaf, partially blind, and has arthritis. Despite his bite-free history, his owners lost their homeowners' insurance.

Some of the most well-known insurers are engaging in breed discrimination. Some insurers have outright bans on specific breeds, while others take a more realistic and logical dog-by-dog approach. These decisions are predicated on insurers' assessment of relative risk. The "usual suspects" for breed discrimination are Pit Bulls, Rottweilers, German Shepherds, Doberman Pinschers, Chow Chows, Wolf hybrids, and Presa Canarios.

The Humane Society of the United States has documented an increase in the number of people being denied insurance because they own certain breeds of dog. As a result, the Society has started collecting data through the Internet, in the hopes of eventually convincing the insurance industry that there are alternatives to the current practice and that it must stop. To achieve their goal, the HSUS and the American Society for Prevention of Cruelty to Animals have created a joint grassroots campaign designed to educate the insurance industry.

2. The Insurance Industry's Defense of Breed Discrimination

Homeowners' insurance protects a policyholder in the event of financial loss. Most policies include two provisions: property damage and liability. Property damage provisions protect the policyholder in the event of fire, lightning, wind, water or hail damage, theft, and vandalism. Liability provisions protect the policyholder in the event that a claim is made against a homeowner for negligence. Liability coverage typically pays for bodily injury, medical payments, and property damage that is sustained because of the negligence of the property owner. Absent breed discrimination, most homeowners' insurance policies would cover injuries due to dog bites on the premises between the amounts of $100,000 and $300,000. In 1995, the average policyholder paid $418 in homeowners' insurance premiums. By 2004, the average premium climbed to $608.

"Insurance is a business." Insurers must make profits in order to continue in existence. Companies survive by minimizing risk, which reduces the likelihood of claims. Some companies have decided that certain breeds of dog are simply "too much of a risk" to insure. An industry representative claims that the issue of dog bites "is a major concern for insurers."

The industry has also pointed to the large amount of money that has been paid out in recent years for dog bite claims. The Insurance Information Institute ("III"), a trade group of the insurance industry, stated that in 2002, $345.5 million was paid out in dog bite liability claims, up from $250 million in 1995. The group argues that dog bite lawsuits are on the rise and juries are awarding larger claims. They claim, therefore, the need to curtail their risk.

Questions & Notes

1. Do you think this will save the insurance company money? Is this fair to homeowners?

2. Would you support a law that prohibited breed discrimination by home insurance companies? What about a company that refuses to write a liability policy if: (a) a dog is found by a local court to be a dangerous dog, or (b) if one claim for a dog bite has been filed under a previous policy?

3. The point of insurance is to spread the risk of negative events. What should be our public policy about insurance companies seeking to avoid the risk of payouts? Is it fair that the own-

ers of low risk dogs pay higher premiums to cover the cost of higher risk dogs?

Section 5

Obligations of Ownership

Civil Responsibility for Harm by an Animal

When an individual is injured or his or her property is harmed by an animal, the owner/keeper of the animal faces a number of potential consequences. At a minimum there is the likelihood of civil liability and monetary damages for the harm done. There is also the possibility of civil fines or criminal liability for the actions of animals owned or kept. Finally, the animal itself, particularly if it is a dog, is subject to possible confiscation and death. Traditionally, the principles of tort law have played a paramount role in determining the extent of an owner's monetary liability for injury by animals, but more and more frequently state and local statutory law can also be the basis for civil recovery. For both of these bases, some key phrases, such as "dangerous or vicious propensity" are constantly used and will be explored in some detail.

The fact patterns that arise in this area pose difficulties for the development of clear and fair social policy. For example, animals represent economic, recreational, and ecological interests for humans. Yet they also represent risk of harm, loss of property, and financial loss. This conflict of benefit and burden is particularly acute with the category of animals known as pets, or companion animals. As a nation, we love our pets and believe that great value can be obtained from having pets or access to animals.

> Near this spot are deposited the remains of one who possessed beauty without vanity, strength without insolence, courage without ferocity, and all the virtues of Man, without the vices. This praise, which would be unmeaning flattery if inscribed over human ashes, is but a just tribute to the memory of Boatswain, a dog. Lord Byron, *Inscription to the monument of a Newfoundland dog,* 1808.

However, these same loving pets can represent risk of significant and swift injury to humans and their property, particularly children. In 2007 33 humans were killed by dogs and in 2009 it was 30. (In 2002, 51 people were killed by lightning.) Sometimes significant injury can occur without any contact between the animal and the person. In one 1996 case, a jury awarded $190,000 for injuries when a person fell off a bike on a public sidewalk because a small white dog ran toward him. There was no contact between the dog and the human.

Tort law has traditionally sought to balance the "usefulness" of an animal with the risk it represents to the public. Low-risk animals such as sheep and cats impose no special duty of care on owners or possessors, unless they have specific knowledge that their specific animal possesses unusual risk to others. It is presumed that an individual coming face to face with these animals will not face risk of harm beyond the general knowledge and capabilities of the public. Additionally, the types of harm threatened by cats and cows are not normally life-threatening. Some animals, such as lions, are presumed by the law to represent high risk to others, and therefore, mere possession of one of these species will give rise to the highest duty of care for the owner/possessor, even strict liability. Some animals, particularly those of economic value, such as bulls, stallions, and rams, are not viewed by the law "as being abnormally dangerous animals, but rather as animals routinely kept for stud purposes, so that the particular danger involved in their dangerous tendencies has become a normal incident of civilized life." Obviously not every person in today's society would have equal personal knowledge of the dangers represented by these animals, but the owners of the animal receive the legal benefit of having their animals not being presumed dangerous.

> **News Bits**
>
> There are 4.5 million dog bites reported each year, resulting in $400 million in legal claims.
>
> In 2006, 31,000 people had reconstructive surgery from dog bites.

The following materials are only an introduction to the subject matter of owner responsibility.

CASE BY CASE

Sligar v. Odell
233 P.3d 914, 2010 WL 2674037 (Wash. App. Div. 1)

Here, Kara and David Odell's property was separated from Mary Sligar's property by a six-foot-high chain link fence at the time their dog bit Sligar's finger. Sligar's finger was protruding through the chain link fence enclosing the dog at the time of her unfortunate injury. Because Sligar fails to show the existence of any genuine issue of material fact for either her statutory strict liability claim or her common law negligence claim, we affirm summary judgment in favor of the Odells.

The material facts are largely undisputed. Sligar and the Odells are next-door neighbors. Their respective residences have a six-foot-high chain link fence between them. At the time of this incident, the Odells owned two dogs, Chico, a chocolate Labrador retriever, and Molly, a golden retriever. Sligar owned three miniature schnauzers, one of which was named Pearl. The dogs could see each other through the chain link fence and often barked at each other.

On the date of her injury, Sligar tripped and fell while she was trying to move Pearl away from the fence. According to Sligar's deposition testimony: "I was trying to catch Pearl, and I stumbled and lost my balance and fell onto the fence. My hand went on the fence, my finger went through the fence, and Chico bit it."

Sligar sued the Odells for damages for the dog bite. Her complaint alleged strict liability under RCW 16.08.040 and common law negligence. Following discovery, the Odells moved for summary judgment. The trial court granted their motion and denied Sligar's motion for reconsideration.

DOG BITE LIABILITY

Sligar first argues that the trial court erred by granting summary judgment to the Odells on her strict liability claim under RCW 16.08.040. That statute states:

> The owner of any dog which shall bite any person while such person is in or on a public place or lawfully in or on a private place including the property of the owner of such dog, shall be liable for such damages as may be suffered by the person bitten, regardless of the former viciousness of such dog or the owner's knowledge of such viciousness.

RCW 16.08.050 defines when entrance on private property is lawful for purposes of the above statute:

> A person is lawfully upon the private property of such owner within the meaning of RCW 16.08.040 when such person is upon the property of the owner with the express or implied consent of the owner: PROVIDED, That said consent shall not be presumed when the property of the owner is fenced or reasonably posted.

This " 'court's fundamental objective in construing a statute is to ascertain and carry out the legislature's intent.' "

Based on excerpts from the deposition testimony of Sligar, the Odells argued that her testimony demonstrated that she was not lawfully on their property at the time of the dog bite because they had not given her their express consent to be there. They also argued that their consent to her entry onto their property should not be presumed under RCW 16.08.050 because the property was fenced.

I response, Sligar argued that she had the Odells' implied consent to have her finger on their side of the chain link fence. She also claimed that they failed to prove she was a trespasser when she fell and her finger accidentally protruded through the fence. Neither of these arguments shows the existence of a genuine issue of material fact for trial.

The terms "implied consent" and "presumed" are not defined by the dog bite statute. " 'When a statutory term is undefined, the words of a statute are given their ordinary meaning, and the court may look to a dictionary for such meaning.' " Black's Law Dictionary defines "implied consent" as "[c]onsent inferred from one's conduct rather than from one's direct expression." Case law is consistent with this view that implied consent may be communicated based on "conduct, omission, or by means of local custom." A "presumption," on the other hand, is defined as "[a] legal inference or assumption that a fact exists, based on the known or proven existence of some other fact or group of facts."

At best, Sligar's arguments in response to the Odells' summary judgment motion attempt to show that she had their implied consent to be on their property at the time of her injury. She first claims that she had previously reached through the fence to pet Molly. She next claims she had attached chicken wire to her side of the fence which required placing her fingers through the fence to twist wire ties around the chain links. Lastly, she claims to have previously leaned on the fence while talking to the Odells. These assertions fail to show the existence of any genuine issue of material fact.

The proviso of RCW 16.08.050 plainly states that the consent of the owner "shall not be presumed when the property of the owner is fenced or reasonably posted." Here, a six foot fence separated the Odells' property from Sligar's property, containing Chico on the Odells' side of the fence. Thus, the statute mandates that there shall not be any presumption-no legal inference-of the Odells' consent to Sligar being on their property at the time of her injury. In short, she fails to show she was lawfully on their property at the time of her injury. Under such circumstances, there is no strict liability under the statute.

COMMON LAW CLAIM

Sligar next argues that the trial court improperly dismissed her common law negligence claim. She is wrong.

The common law recognizes two separate causes of action for injuries by animals. "First, if a dog owner knows the dog has vicious or dangerous propensities, the owner is strictly liable for any injuries the dog causes. Second, if a dog owner does not know of any vicious or dangerous propensities, the owner is liable only if negligent in failing to prevent the harm."

Common Law Negligence

To establish negligence, Sligar must prove (1) the existence of a duty, (2) breach of that duty, (3) injury, and (4) proximate cause between the breach and the injury. If the plaintiff fails to present evidence to prove each essential element of the negligence claim, then summary judgment for the defendant is proper.

In a dog bite case, "a negligence cause of action arises when there is ineffective control of an animal in a situation where it would reasonably be expected that injury could occur, and injury does proximately result from the negligence." "The amount of care required is commensurate with the character of the animal: 'The amount of control required is that which would be exercised by a reasonable person based upon the total situation at the time, including the past behavior of the animal and the injuries that could have been reasonably foreseen.'"

Sligar contends that the Odells were negligent in failing to protect her from harm because they failed to erect a solid fence on the property boundary until after the bite occurred and they failed to tie up or otherwise restrain Chico in their yard. Both theories suffer from the same problem: failure, under the circumstances of this case, to show any breach of a duty by the Odells.

As our supreme court has stated, "it is not per se unreasonable to keep a dog in a fenced backyard if the animal has not exhibited dangerous tendencies." Here, Sligar did not produce any evidence to demonstrate that the Odells either knew or should have known that their dog had any dangerous propensities. And the dog was in a fenced backyard when it bit Sligar's finger, which protruded through that fence.

Absent a showing that the Odells knew of the alleged dangerous propensities of their dog, Sligar fails to show any genuine issue of material fact regarding a breach of any duty they owed to her. Accordingly, she fails to show any common law negligence for the dog bite.

We affirm the summary judgment order and order denying reconsideration

Questions and Notes

1. Was this outcome fair? Would the outcome be any different if the fingers of the plaintiff's hand had been bitten off?

2. What kind of evidence might the plaintiff have presented for showing that the defendants had prior knowledge of a dog's dangerous propensity?

3. What might have been a negligence act that would have triggered liability?

4. Under the Ohio statute, what would happen if a UPS delivery person was bitten while bringing a package to the front door?

Criminal Responsibility for Actions of an Animal

State v. Ruisi, 9 Neb. App. 435, 616 N.W.2d 19 (2000). A large dog seriously attacked the defendants girl friend while she sat alone in a room with the dog. He was found guilty of criminal possession of a dangerous dog because of the event, even though there was no evidence before the event of the dangerous propensities of the dog. The court upheld the strict liability conviction and the sentence of six months in jail.

    Michigan v. Trotter, 530 NW.2d 516, 1995 Mich. App. LEXIS 82. Conviction for involuntary manslaughter was based on the fact that defendant's two bull terriers killed a two-year-old boy when the boy was left with the terriers. Some six months earlier the defendant had seen the dog bite another person. The Court upheld the conviction (three years probation) stating: "involuntary manslaughter occurs when death results from negligence that is gross, wanton or wilful, or criminal, indicating a culpable indifference to the safety of others." Michigan criminal statute: MCLA 287.323(1), provides: "The owner of an animal that meets the definition of a dangerous animal in [MCLA 287.321(a); MSA 12.545(21)(a)] that causes the death of a person is guilty of involuntary manslaughter, punishable under [MCLA 750.321]."

    Trisuzzi v. Tabatchnik, 666 A.2d 543, 1995 NJ Super LEXIS 514. In its opinion the court noted that the defendant dog owner had previously been found guilty of harboring a vicious dog.

    The California Penal Code § 399 creates a felony charge if a mischievous animal kills a human (1872 Act), while § 399.5 creates a misdemeanor if a dog, trained to fight, attacks or kills a human. Discussed in **Sea Horse Ranch, Inc. v. the Superior Court of San Mateo County,** 24 Cal. App. 4th 446, 1994 Cal. App. LEXIS 402:

> Petitioners Sea Horse Ranch, Inc. (the Ranch), and its president, Arbis "Al" Shipley, are charged by information with one count of involuntary manslaughter (Pen. Code, § 192, subd. (b)); the Ranch is also charged with one count of willfully suffering a mischievous animal to roam at large with the result that it kills a human being (Pen. Code, § 399). The charges arise from an incident in which a horse escaped from the Ranch onto an adjacent state highway and collided with a car, killing the passenger.

> Section 399 provides that "[i]f the owner of a mischievous animal, knowing its propensities, willfully suffers it to go at large, or keeps it without ordinary care, and such animal, while so at large, or while not kept with ordinary care, kills any human being who has taken all the precautions which the circumstances permitted, or which a reasonable person

would ordinarily take in the same situation, is guilty of a felony." As noted above, only the Ranch is charged with violation of this statue because it, and not petitioner Shipley, is the owner of the escaped horse. Petitioners argue that the statute requires the animal possess mischievous propensities per se, and that horses by their very nature are not mischievous. The People respond that the question is whether the animal is mischievous if allowed to run free.

The court held that the fact that an animal is allowed to roam does not make it mischievous. Therefore it dropped the criminal charge under this section, but allows the State to proceed with the charge of involuntary manslaughter against the President of the corporation, as there was sufficient evidence of actual knowledge by the person.

[In Colorado it is a felony if the dog is a dangerous dog and kills a human or twice inflicts serious injury on a human. C.R.S. 18-9-204.5(3); same in Georgia, O.C.G.A. § 4-8-28 (1997); same in Florida, Fla. Statutes § 767.13.]

CASE BY CASE

People v. Berry
1 Cal. App. 4th 778 (1991)

This case involves the killing of a small child by Willy, a pit bull owned by defendant Michael Patrick Berry. Defendant appeals from a judgment entered after a jury found him guilty of involuntary manslaughter, keeping a mischievous animal, keeping a fighting dog, and cultivating marijuana. (Pen. Code, § 192, subd. (b), 399, and 597.5, subd. (a)(1) and Health & Saf. Code, § 11358.)

In seeking to protect people from fatal attacks by "mischievous" animals, section 399 implies that a "mischievous" animal is one that may be dangerous to others if allowed to run free or is kept in a negligent manner. Knowledge of an animal's "mischievous propensities" therefore puts an owner on notice of such danger or risk of harm, and his or her liability under the statute arises from the failure to act reasonably with knowledge of this risk. Consequently, we hold that "mischievous propensities" as used in the statute means those propensities that may naturally pose a risk of harm or injury to others.

Section 6

New Issues Edging into the Property Arena

A New Aspect: Genetic Ownership

While the concept of owning individual animals must be as ancient as any legal system, new contexts of ownership pose new conceptual challenges. How about ownership of the genetic information necessary to make an animal as a patent? While back in the 1970s the U.S. patent office's position was that it was inappropriate to have a patent on a natural living being, the Supreme Court, in the case **Diamond v. Chakrabarty**, 447 U.S. 303 (1980), held that a living creature could be the subject of a patent. In 1994 Harvard received a patent for their special mouse — it had been genetically engineered for specific research. Some members of Congress have been uncomfortable with this approach and have sought to adopt new legislation. See Senator Mark O. Hatfield, *From Microbe to Man*, 1 Animal Law 5 (1995).

For an update on how the patent office is dealing with these issues, with a heavy dose of science, see Warren D. Woessner, *The Evolution of Patents on Life — Transgenic Animals, Animal Clones and Stem Cells*, 83 Journal of the Patent and Trademark Office Society 830 (2001). For discussion of the broader property concepts see Kojo Yelpaala, *Symposium: Biotechnology and the Law: Owning the Secrets of Life: Biotechnology and Property Rights Revisited*, 23 McGeorge Law Review 111 (2000).

This topic will undoubtedly be of increasing concern — particularly as human genes become intermingled with nonhuman animals, and genes from other plants and animals are intermingled. Particularly troublesome is this economic incentive to "create" new animals so that patents can be obtained. The quality of life for such creatures has to be suspect, and no government seems to control when this should or should not be allowed. See Dana Visser, *Who's Going to Stop Me from Patenting My Six-legged Chicken: An Analysis of the Moral Utility Doctrine in the United States*, 46 Wayne Law Review 2067 (2000).

As further evidence of the complexities of this topic in 2009 Sen. Sam Brownback, R-Kansas, has introduced the Human-Animal Hybrid Prohibition Act of 2009 (S. 1435), legislation that would "amend title 18, United States Code, to prohibit human-animal hybrids."

Does this require a new definition of what an animal is? Or does it, perhaps, require us to create a new category of animal? Is genetic engineering any different from the selective breeding of chickens or cattle over the centuries of domestication?

Should Animals be Property At All?

A number of writers find that the property status of animals and the resulting attitude and treatment that is promoted by the idea that animals are property is unacceptable. They seek to remove animals from the property status all together.

Animal Rights Theory and Utilitarianism

by Gary L. Francione, 3 Animal Law 75 (1987)

IV. Animal Rights and Personhood

Our treatment of nonhuman animals reflects a distinction that we make between humans, whom we regard as persons, and nonhumans, whom we regard as things. Although we may regard some animals as having certain "interests," we regard all of those interests to be tradable and dependent on our judgment that the sacrifice of the interests will benefit us. This trade is generally permissible even when the animal interest involved is significant and the human interest is admittedly trivial, as is the case of the use of animals for "entertainment" purposes such as pigeon shoots, rodeos, or circuses. Animals are not persons in either moral theory or under the law; they are property in that they exist solely as means to human ends. They have no interests that cannot be sacrificed, even when the "benefit" to be gained by humans is mere amusement at the cost of great pain or death to the animal. That is precisely what it means to be property.

***

If, however, we recognize that animals are not "things" (that their basic right to physical security cannot be sacrificed merely because we think the consequences justify the sacrifice), then we can no longer justify the institutionalized exploitation of animals for food, experiments, clothing, or entertainment. These forms of institutionalized exploitation necessarily assume that animals are things whose interests are contingent on human desires. Once we recognize that animals are not "things," we can no longer justify the use of animals in experiments any more than we could justify the use of humans. We have at least de jure ruled out the institutional use of coerced humans in biomedical experiments. And, although many people will tolerate the payment of low wages to workers, few would similarly tolerate human slavery.

Questions & Notes

1. Much of the emotional power behind the rejection of the property status of nonhuman animals is the history of having allowed humans to be property, slavery, and the unacceptable denegation of humans that the status allowed the owners to impose upon them. The solution to human property issue was the elimination of the status. The freed humans had the capacity for self direction and equal legal status with the prior owners. Is the loss of "property status" possible for nonhuman animals in today's or tomorrow's world? See *http://www.abolitionistapproach.com/*.

2. Another author focused upon the diffiuclty of animals being considered as faceless, nameless masses. For an insightful discussion of the consequence of seeing animals as individuals, see Joseph Vining, *The Mystery of the Individual in Modern Law*, 52 Vill. L. Rev. 1 (2007).

◇◇◇

Rather than abolition of property status, what about seeking modification of property concepts? First, self-ownership for wild animals:

Equitable Self-Ownership for Animals

by David Favre, 50 Duke L.J. 473 (2000)

B. Self-Ownership

As property laws are a human construct and not an inherent characteristic of physical objects, there is always conceptual space for innovation. One of the premises for our new property paradigm is that living objects have "self-ownership." That is, unless a human has affirmatively asserted lawful dominion and control so as to obtain title to a living object, then a living entity will be considered to have self-ownership. As will be shown, this is but a modest recasting of existing concepts, but one with significant consequences.

Our existing legal system does not now assert ownership in all physical things. Meteorites in the sky have no human-designated title, and particular molecules of water and air in their natural state have no human title constraining and defining them. Nor do newborn squirrels in the wilderness, or human babies in Lansing, Michigan, have human-based title claims against them. As will be seen, however, not all of these objects qualify for the concept of self-ownership, as the object in question must first be a "being."

In whichever category non-owned objects might be placed, our legal system does have a number of rules that allow humans to obtain ownership. Usually, as a prerequisite to title being acknowledged in a human, some assertion of possession and control over an object must be made by the person seeking title. This is logical, as the concept of title deals with the use and control of objects: until an object is within the possession and control of some human, the law will be without effect, and there will be no reason to assert title over an object.

As a wild animal, the squirrel of Yellowstone is not yet human-controlled; she retains self-direction, self-control and self-ownership. It is a misperception of existing property law to say that title is in the state when wildlife exists in its natural environment. If no human or human substitute has possession and control over a wild animal, there cannot be an assertion of title. The courts have long made it clear that using the word "title" as it relates to wildlife and state ownership issues is not title in the property sense. Rather, the word is being used as a surrogate for a different concept. The assertion of the common law is not that the state has title to the wild squirrel, but that it has the right to decide the conditions under which humans can obtain title to the squirrel. Under these rules, if Tom shows up in Yellowstone National Park and traps or shoots the squirrel, then the property rules of the state of Wyoming will decide if she becomes the owner of the squirrel, if she obtains "title" to the squirrel. Until the point of capture, the squirrel has self-ownership. Assuming that the property rules of the state allow Susan to assert title with the capture of the animal, then self-ownership is lost or transformed into human ownership. The fragility of the title asserted by humans over wildlife is reinforced by the existence of the property rule that that if the squirrel escapes back into its natural habitat, then Tom will lose her title. It evaporates with the disappearing squirrel. Thus, the existing property rules relating to wild animals do not hinder assertions of self-ownership.

Also, under existing concepts, it is fair to state that the newborn human is self-owned. Certainly in the negative sense, no one else is the owner of human Susan. The extent to which state legislatures have sought to regulate the sale of human body parts is additional support for the conceptual existence of human self-ownership. Susan's parents, while not having ownership, nevertheless have obligations toward Susan, and while she is a minor they certainly have physical possession and considerable control over Susan and what she experiences. But within the common law states today, these obligations do not rise to the level of having title in Susan, that is, the ability to use, kill, or transfer ownership to another. So our human child, like the squirrel, is not a being owned by a human and, therefore, must be considered to have self-ownership. A rock poses a different kind of problem. It has no "self" to which the concept of self-ownership can attach. It is not alive. Also, assuming that a rock, like all ageless rocks, is sitting on a tract of land, then property law dictates that the owner of the land has ownership of all the rocks located on, below, and above the land itself. The rock is part of the land ownership. Within the United States, all land is owned by someone—if not a private party, then by a government. Rocks in the Antarctic and on the moon, where no human asserts ownership of the underlying land, may be free from human ownership claims, but, as rocks have no self-interests, even in these locations it is not useful to say that they have self-ownership.

◇◇

Keeping and modifying the property status.

Equitable Self-Ownership for Animals

by David Favre, 50 Duke L. J. 473 (2000)

D. Human Retention of Legal Title and Duty of Care

While some authors have urged the elimination of the concept of title/property as it applies to animals, it is neither advisable nor feasible at this time. A key issue that the existing property law addresses is who is responsible for the care of this animal. Under our present system, full responsibility comes with ownership. Most animals within the domestic control of humans are not capable of self-care, regardless of their age, and if released or abandoned by their human owner would find themselves in an environment hostile to their existence. Therefore, at present, it is important that legal ownership continues to exist so that responsibility for the care of the self-owned animal can be squarely placed on a specific human.

Also for the foreseeable future, animals, even self-owned animals, could have economic value, and the only practical way to keep track of and transfer this value is through property ownership. Consider, for example, a racehorse. While the horse, Midnight, has her own intrinsic value as a living being, and this value is acknowledged by owner Jed who transfers her into a self-owned animal status, the horse will still have value in the external world of commerce. The new existence of equitable self-ownership does not preclude the realization of commercial value upon sale of an animal. However, the commercial value may well be negatively impacted, as the use of an animal must take into account the interests of the animal.

Another variation on the issue of value is what should happen at the death of the animal. If an animal dies, then self-ownership is destroyed, and the owner of the legal title has full title in the physical body of the self-owned after death. In effect, there is a reversion of title back to the legal title holder. It is meaningless to talk of duty to the animal after it is dead; it is then no different than a rock.

Finally, the continued use of legal title will exist so long as different jurisdictions have different laws about the status of animals. If an owner takes an animal from a jurisdiction that does recognize equitable self-ownership into one that does not, then the laws of the jurisdiction where the animal is located will govern the relationship. Since legal title would always be present, there will continue to be certainty as to ownership and responsibility for an animal, regardless of where he or she travels.

◇◇◇

Second, equitable self-ownership for domestic animals.

Equitable Self-Ownership for Animals

by David Favre, 50 Duke L.J. 473 (2000)

Having acknowledged that it is well within the legal mainstream to create and transfer equitable interests in personal property, an expansion of a second, related concept must be considered. Who is capable of holding a legal or equitable title? While historically only humans could hold title, is it not conceptually possible for other living entities be a holder of title, at least to the limited extent of holding their own equitable title? If self-ownership is an acceptable concept, is it not appropriate to say that title is being held by "self"? If the legal and equitable owner of an animal can change the title status completely by intentional acts, is there a policy reason to object to the returning of part of the title to an animal? Could not an owner of an animal return or transfer the equitable interests of the animal to the animal? Such a transfer would be but a partial return of title, a hybrid form of self-ownership.

[These issues will be considered in more detail in Chapter 11, Animal Rights.]

◇◇◇

Changing the Property Status in Other Countries

Have other countries developed a different legal status for animals?

New Zealand

A 1999 Act adopted in New Zealand gives acknowledgment of the interests of primates. Their Animal Welfare Act of 1999 provides that before any "research, testing, or teaching" involving a nonhuman hominid can be undertaken, a government official must give approval. This can be done only with a showing that the activity "is in the interest of the individual" or the species and "the benefits [of the activity] are not outweighed by the likely harm to the non-human hominid" (§ 85). Note that someone other than the owner of the property is having a voice in the treatment and use of the property. Why is this necessary? See generally Paula Brosnahan, *New Zealand's Animal Welfare Act: What Is Its Value Regarding Non-Human Hominids*, 6 Animal Law 185 (2000).

Germany

In 2002 the country of Germany amended its national constitution by adding the word "and the animals." This brought animals within the clear vision of constitutional concern but it did not give animals separate rights.

"... Und Die Tiere"

by Kate M. Nattrass, *Constitutional Protection for Germany's Animals*, 10 Animal Law 283 (2004)

The three words, "und die Tiere," did not give any rights to animals in Germany. Rights are reserved for humans, and human well-being remains at the center of the Grundgesetz. The Directive of the State (Staatszielbestimmung Tierschutz) declares protection of animals a value and goal of the state, and mandates the state to exercise this value in all its official capacities. By committing itself to protecting animals, the state holds itself to a much higher standard for fulfilling its obligations to animals.

> *Available at www.animallaw.info/journals/jo_pdf/vol10_p283.pdf. This article gives the full story of the adoption of the amendment and what it means in the German legal context.*

Brazil

Article VIII of Brazilian Constitution:

> Article 225. All have the right to an ecologically balanced environment. which is an asset of common use and essential to a healthy quality of life, and both the Government and the community shall have the duty to defend and preserve it for present and future generations.
>
> Paragraph 1 – In order to ensure the effectiveness of this right, it is incumbent upon the Government to:
>
> VII. protect the fauna and the flora, with prohibition, in the manner prescribed by law, of all practices which represent a risk to their ecological function, cause the extinction of species or subject animals to cruelty.

Note: The apparent effect of this provision is to put an obligation on the government. It does not give a private cause of action. Would you think it a good idea to put such a provision in our Constitution? Does this change the property status of animals?

A Focusing Question

Is it degrading for nonhuman animals to be considered human property?

India

Article 51-A of the Indian Constitution states:

> It shall be the duty of every citizen of India – (g) to protect and improve the natural environment, including forest, lakes, rivers and wild life, and to have compassion for living creatures.

Imagine a provision in the U.S. Constitution compelling compassion. Is such a thing possible? Such language, again, does not create legal rights for animals. Note that it is a duty imposed on individual humans, not the state. For a fuller discussion of how this phrase is used in the legal context, see Raj Panjwani, *Compassion and the Indian Judiciary*, International Animal Law Conference 147 (2004).

Switzerland

This country has developed its own legal balance between acknowledging a different status for animals while still having them within traditional legal rules:

Civil Code Article 641a

> 1. Animals are not chattels.
>
> 2. In so far as no special rules exist for animals, then the regulations that apply to chattels also apply to animals.

United States

As animals are property, and the U.S. Constitution does not delegate from the states to the federal government control over the issues of property, it is unlikely that animals will appear in the federal constitution. It is possible to contemplate the amending of state constitutions for the benefit of animals.

A few final questions for stretching the property concept:

1. What might the animal-human relationship be in 50 years?

2. What might be the legal status of animals in 50 years?

3. Will animals still be property?

CHAPTER 3

Veterinarian Malpractice

Section 1

Introduction

Animals are harmed by any number of different categories of people and in a wide assortment of fact patterns. Veterinarians receive a chapter of their own for a number of reasons. First, as a profession they are subject to a different set of legal standards from those standards considered in general tort law: professional malpractice. Second, veterinarians inherently deal with the health and well-being of the animals in a large number of fact patterns—indeed, it was estimated that in 2001 there were 200,000,000 visits to veterinarians. Third, the accusation of malpractice is often the issue that brings a member of the public to the office of a lawyer.

Malpractice is a standard of legal liability which applies only to professionals. Veterinarians are now accepted as being a professional group subject to this standard of care. "Who is a veterinarian?" is a question easily answered, because a state license is required. What if a farmer down the road, with 30 years of experience in raising hogs or horses, gives advice that turns out to be wrong? Because he is not a veterinarian, the farmer cannot be held to a standard of malpractice. However, anyone, including the farmer next door, is subject to the constraints of tort law concepts such as negligence. A key difference between ordinary negligence and malpractice is that the jury decides whether ordinary negligence has occurred. But, if it is an issue of malpractice, then only another veterinarian can state whether an act was malpractice. When there is a conflict between experts, then it is the role of the jury to decide which side's expert is more believable.

CASE BY CASE

Price v. Brown
545 Pa. 216, 680 A. 2d 1149 (1996)

ZAPPALA, JUSTICE.

The issue presented in this appeal is whether a complaint based upon an alleged breach of a bailment agreement states a cause of action for injury or death suffered by an animal that has been entrusted to a veterinarian for surgical and professional treatment. We hold that allegations of breach of a bailment agreement are insufficient to state a cause of action against a veterinarian who has performed surgery on an animal when the animal suffers an injury as a result or does not survive the surgery.

On May 4, 1993, Tracy Price filed a complaint against Nancy O. Brown, a veterinarian, alleging that she had delivered her English Bulldog to Dr. Brown for surgical treatment to correct a prolapsed urethra. Dr. Brown performed the surgery on August 30, 1991. The next evening,

Price visited the dog at the veterinary hospital. She inquired into the dog's condition after observing that the dog was panting strenuously and appeared groggy. She requested that the dog be monitored on a 24-hour basis and was assured that this would be done by an unidentified agent of Dr. Brown's. Price alleged that the dog was left unattended after midnight that evening. During the morning of September 1, 1991, the dog died.

In her complaint, Price asserted liability based only upon a theory of bailment. Price alleged that the dog had been entrusted to Dr. Brown in reliance upon the promise and representation that she would perform the necessary surgery and return the dog to her in the same general good health as before. Price alleged that Dr. Brown had breached the agreement by failing to monitor the dog's condition and by failing to return the dog in good health. Price alleged that the fair market value of the dog was $1,200.00 and demanded judgment in that amount.

> "A bailment is a delivery of personalty for the accomplishment of some purpose upon a contract, express or implied, that after the purpose has been fulfilled, it shall be redelivered to the person who delivered it, otherwise dealt with according to his directions or kept until he reclaims it." Smalich v. Westfall, 440 Pa. 409, 413, 269 A.2d 476, 480 (1970) (citation omitted).

Therefore, a cause of action for breach of a bailment agreement arises if the bailor can establish that personalty has been delivered to the bailee, a demand for return of the bailed goods has been made, and the bailee has failed to return the personalty.

When the bailor produces evidence to satisfy those elements, the bailee has the duty of going forward with evidence accounting for the loss and if the bailee fails to do so, he is responsible for the loss. It is assumed under those circumstances that the bailee has failed to exercise the duty of care required by the agreement. Schell v. Miller North Broad Storage Company, 142 Pa. Super. 293, 16 A.2d 680 (1940). On the other hand, should the bailee go forward with evidence showing that the personalty was lost and the manner in which it was lost, and the evidence does not disclose a lack of due care on his part, then the burden of proof again shifts to the bailor who must prove negligence on the part of the bailee. Id.

As to a cause of action based on the negligence of a veterinarian in the performance of his/her professional duties or services, we note at the

News Bits

In 2010 it is estimated that U.S. pet owners will expend:
- Food - $18.28 billion
- Vet Care - $12.8 billion
- Supplies/OTC Medicine - $11 billion
- Live Animal Purchases - $2.2 billion
- Grooming & Boarding - $3.45 billion

outset that malpractice claims have traditionally arisen in the context of services provided by the legal and medical professions. Similar to the practice of law or medicine, the vocation of veterinary medicine involves specialized education, knowledge, and skills. We conclude, therefore, that professional negligence concepts also extend to veterinary medicine.

The practice of veterinary medicine is extensively regulated in Pennsylvania under the Veterinary Medicine Practice Act, 63 P.S. § 485.1 et seq. "Veterinary medicine" is defined as the "branch of medicine which deals with the diagnosis, prognosis, treatment, administration, prescription, operation or manipulation or application of any apparatus or appliance for any disease, pain, deformity, defect, injury, wound or physical condition of any animal or for the prevention of or the testing for the presence of any disease." 63 P.S. § 485.3(9).

The Act established a State Board of Veterinary Medicine within the Department of State whose duties include, inter alia, the adoption of rules and regulations governing the practice of veterinary medicine, approval of qualifications of applicants for a license to practice, and regulation of licensed veterinarians. 63 P.S. §§ 485.4, 485.5. A person who intends to practice veterinary medicine in Pennsylvania must obtain a license and maintain registration. The board may license to practice veterinary medicine any applicant who pays the requisite fee and submits satisfactory evidence that he or she: (1) is at least eighteen years old; (2) has graduated from an approved school or college of veterinary medicine; (3) has passed a license examination required by the board; and (4) has not been convicted of a felonious act prohibited by The Controlled Substance, Drug, Device and Cosmetic Act. 63 P.S. § 485.9. To state a cause of action based upon the negligent acts or omissions of a veterinarian in the performance of professional duties or services, the plaintiff must plead (1) the employment of the veterinarian or other basis for the duty; (2) the veterinarian's failure to exercise the appropriate standard of care; and (3) that the veterinarian's departure from that standard was the proximate cause of the animal's injury or death. A plaintiff must specifically allege that the veterinarian was negligent in the performance of his professional services. In contrast, a claim based upon a breach of bailment agreement does not require an allegation of negligence to be made. Under a bailment theory, the plaintiff does not bear the initial burden of producing evidence of the negligent acts or omissions of the veterinarian; however, the plaintiff does bear that burden when professional negligence is asserted.

In this case, Price's complaint asserted a cause of action for her dog's death based solely upon breach of a bailment agreement. Price asserts that preliminary objections to the complaint should not have been sustained by the trial court because all of the traditional elements of a bailment were pled in the complaint, i.e., delivery of the dog to Dr. Brown [FN3]; that a demand was made for the dog's return; and that Dr. Brown failed to return the dog in the same general good health and did not provide any explanation therefor. Although allegations to that effect were stated in the complaint, Price also alleged that she delivered the dog to Dr. Brown for surgical treatment to correct a prolapsed urethra, that the surgery was performed, that Dr. Brown failed to monitor the dog's condition overnight, and that the animal died within two days after surgery.

> FN3. Under the Dog Law, 3 P.S. § 450-101 et seq., dogs are declared to be personal property and subjects of theft. 3 P.S. § 459- 601(a).

The trial court sustained the preliminary objections to the complaint, determining that liability could not be imposed upon a veterinarian for breach of a bailment agreement when an animal is delivered for the particular purpose of surgical procedure. The court recognized that a dog is personal property, but stated that "Allegations which might give rise to a bailment are, without more, insufficient to state a cause of action against a veterinarian for death or damage to an animal entrusted to his or her care for veterinary treatment." (Trial court slip opinion at 3.) The court concluded that in order to recover damages for such loss, the plaintiff must plead and prove that the veterinarian was negligent.

We agree with the trial court that the purpose for which an animal is entrusted to the care of a veterinarian is a material fact that must be considered in determining whether a plaintiff's complaint states a cause of action as a matter of law, and that Price's complaint failed to state a cause of action for professional negligence. The allegations relating to the professional services rendered by Dr. Brown cannot be deliberately excised from the complaint as if the veterinarian's services were no different than those offered by a kennel operator or dog groomer. There are significant differences between surgical services provided by a veterinarian and grooming or caretaking services.

Accordingly, the order of the Superior Court is reversed and the trial court's order is reinstated. [Two judges dissented, believing that bailment was an adequate and preferred remedy]

Questions & Notes

1. Which is the better approach from a public policy perspective? Who should bear the burden of proof? Does society want it to be easier or more difficult to file a lawsuit against veterinarians? What should the veterinarian prefer?

2. Why are veterinarians regulated by the state?

3. So what happens at trial? Assuming you can qualify someone as an expert, what is the critical question that has to be asked?

4. What about the tort element of causation? Did not having someone watch/check the animal result in the animal's death?

   Note that under the majority opinion, if professional services are involved then the animal owner must use the malpractice cause of action and is precluded from using bailments. But in other circumstances, a veterinarian can have bailment obligations when dealing with healthy animals. See David Favre, The Keeping of Animals, JA-VMA 1735 (Dec. 1 2006).

CASE BY CASE

The determination of what constitutes veterinarian care is also important to others that deal with animals. What can they do themselves or for others without a veterinarian?

Cady v. Tenn. Board of Vet. Medical Examiners
2009 WL 2707398 (Tenn. Ct. App.)

This is an appeal from two separate but related contested case hearings before the Tennessee Board of Veterinary Medical Examiners. The first case pertains to a Notice of Charges filed by the Tennessee Department of Health against Bonnie Cady, a breeder and trainer of horses, alleging that she had engaged in the unlicensed practice of veterinary medicine as defined by Tenn. Comp. R. & Regs. 1730-1-.02. Following a hearing before the Tennessee Board of Veterinary Medical Examiners, the Board found Ms. Cady had engaged in the unlicensed practice of veterinary medicine and assessed $17,000 in civil penalties against her. The second case was initiated by Ms. Cady who sought a Declaratory Order that the Rule she was alleged to have violated, Tenn. Comp. R. & Regs. 1730-1-.02, was void because the definition of the "scope of the practice of veterinary medicine" in the Rule adopted by the Board was impermissibly broader than and inconsistent with the statutory definition set forth in sections 63-12-103(9), (17) of the Tennessee Veterinary Practice Act.

On July 15, 2004, the Office of the General Counsel of the Department of Health ("Department") served Ms. Cady with a Notice of Charges alleging that she had engaged in conduct constituting the unlicensed practice of veterinary medicine as defined by Tenn. Comp. R. & Regs. 1730-1-.02, a Rule adopted by the Board of Veterinary Medical Examiners, for which the Department would seek civil penalties pursuant to Tenn.Code Ann. § 63-12-119. Specifically, the Department alleged that the following services provided by Ms. Cady were in violation of Rule 1730-1-.02: artificially inseminating mares, flushing mares, performing ultrasound examinations on mares to ascertain if they were pregnant, infusing horses with antibiotics, injecting Prostin and other drugs to get horses to come into season, and injecting HCG to get mares to ovulate.

Based upon these facts the Board concluded, as a matter of law, that Ms. Cady had engaged in the unlicensed practice of veterinary medicine for which an assessment of $17,000 in civil penalties was authorized.

Two statutory definitions within the Act are pertinent to our inquiry. One is the definition of "the practice of veterinary medicine," the other is the definition of "veterinary medicine." Tenn.Code Ann. § 63-12-103(9), (17). By statutory definition, "the practice of veterinary medicine" means to:

> 5 (A) Diagnose, prescribe or administer any drug, medicine, biologic, appliance, application or treatment of whatever nature for the cure, prevention or relief of any wound, fracture, bodily injury or disease of animals;
>
> (B) Perform any surgical operation, including cosmetic surgery, upon any animal;
>
> (C) Perform any manual procedure for the diagnosis or treatment for sterility or infertility of animals;
>
> (D) Represent oneself as engaged in the practice of veterinary medicine in any of its branches;
>
> (E) Offer, undertake or hold oneself out to be able to diagnose, treat, operate or prescribe for any animal disease, pain, injury, deformity or physical condition;
>
> (F) Use any words,....
>
> (G) Collect blood or other samples for the purpose of diagnosing disease or other conditions... and
>
> (H) Remove an embryo from a food animal or companion animal for the purpose of transplanting such embryo into another female animal or for the purpose of cryopreserving such embryo.

Tenn.Code Ann. § 63-12-103(9)(A)-(H) (2006).

Based upon the Board's interpretation of the Act in effect prior to the 2006 amendment to Tenn. Code Ann. § 63-12-133(c), which excluded artificial insemination from the practice of veterinary medicine, the Board adopted Tenn. Comp. R. & Regs. 1730-1-.02 which states:

> (1) The scope of practice of veterinary medicine means to diagnose, treat, correct, change, relieve, or prevent animal disease, deformity, defect, injury or other physical or mental conditions; including the prescription or administration of any drug, medicine, biologic, apparatus, application, anesthetic, or other therapeutic or diagnostic substance or technique, and the use of any manual or mechanical procedure for artificial insemination, for testing for pregnancy, or for correcting sterility or infertility or to render advice or recommendation with regard to any of the above.

Tenn. Comp. R. & Regs. 1730-1.-02.

WHETHER RULE 1730-1-.02 EXCEEDS THE STATUTORY PROVI-
SIONS

The Board was authorized to promulgate rules to aid it in carrying out
the purpose and intent of the Act. It was not, however, authorized to
expand the definition The statute does not state that "the use of any
manual or mechanical procedure for artificial insemination" and "for
testing for pregnancy" is within the scope of veterinary medicine. The
Rule, however, defines the practice of veterinary medicine to include
these activities. Neither of these activities are included within the statutory definition of the practice of veterinary medicine; thus, the Rule
expanded the statutory definition. We also note that neither of these
activities fall within the umbrella set forth in Tenn. Code Ann. § 63-12-
103(9)(A) regarding activities "for the cure, prevention or relief of any
wound, fracture, bodily injury or disease." (Emphasis added).

We find it significant that the Legislature included within the statutory definition of the practice of veterinary medicine "any manual procedure for the diagnosis or treatment for sterility or infertility of animals,"
Tenn. Code Ann. § 63-12-103(9)(C), and the Legislature included within
the statutory definition the act of removing "an embryo from a food animal or companion animal for the purpose of transplanting such embryo
into another female animal or for the purpose of cryopreserving such
embryo," see Tenn.Code Ann. § 63-12-103(9)(H); yet, the Legislature did
not include "artificial insemination" or "testing for pregnancy" within
the statutory definition of the practice of veterinary medicine.

The Board, however, contends these activities are properly included
due to Tenn.Code Ann. § 63-12-103(17)'s inclusion of "obstetrics" as a
branch or specialty of veterinary medicine. We, however, find this contention unpersuasive. The Legislature chose to identify specific activities
to be within the practice of veterinary medicine. The fact that the Legislature acknowledged the various branches of veterinary medicine, including obstetrics, does not authorize the Board to expand the definition
of the practice by including any activity that relates to obstetrics. To the
contrary, the Legislature identified specific activities in regards to animal reproduction that require licensure, specifically matters pertaining
to sterility, infertility, and transplanting embryos, as each of these activities were identified as constituting the practice of veterinary medicine.
Pursuant to the canon of statutory construction, expressio unius est ex-
clusio alterius, we must assume the Legislature by including the specific
terms, sterility, infertility, and transplanting embryos, but not artificial
insemination, which is one of the most frequently employed activities
in the field of equine obstetrics, intended to omit artificial insemination
from the definition of the practice of veterinary medicine. Based upon
the foregoing, we have determined that the Board's inclusion of artificial
insemination in its Rule constitutes an impermissible expansion of the

Legislature's definition of the practice of veterinary medicine and the Board's authority.[And therefore the fine against her must be set aside.]

Problem 3A

What if Mr. Jones, with 15 years of experience raising dogs, volunteers to administer vaccines (other than a rabies vaccine) to a dog with the consent of the dog's owner? The vaccines, which are available over-the-counter and not prescribed by a veterinarian, are administered for the purpose of preventing disease in the dog receiving the vaccine, as well as to protect other dogs boarded at Mr. Jones' kennel facility. Mr. Jones is not a licensed veterinarian. What if a veterinarian could testify that Mr. Jones possessed the skills and knowledge of a veterinarian for the purposes of giving shots to four-legged mammals? Would your answer be any different if he was giving shots to his own dogs? What are the social policy considerations that must be balanced?

Section 2

Scope of Liability

Veterinarians, by the nature of their occupation, deal with animals on a daily basis and in a variety of contexts. The core of their activities relate to the providing of professional services, which are usually performed to the satisfaction of both the animal and his or her owner. But, invariably some of the interactions do not have the desired outcome. As the following list suggests, the veterinarians who have been defendants in lawsuits may find themselves confronted with a wide variety of legal claims against them:

Malpractice. This is discussed in full later. Malpractice requires the testimony of an expert witness.

Res ipsa loquitur. This is an important alternative cause of action against a veterinarian, as an expert witness is not needed. Some mistakes are so obvious that the average person (the jury) can make an informed judgment without an expert witness.

Administrative action for malpractice. A person may file an action against a veterinarian with the state administrative licensing board that oversees veterinarians.

Negligence. As in discussion later, if the actions in question are not within the realm of malpractice, then there may be legal liability based on common negligence. For example, if a veterinarian was overseeing the loading of a horse into a trailer and did not properly secure the horse, the standard of care is that of negligence.

Gross negligence. This is the more egregious form of a claim of negligence. If an animal came in for a treatment for fleas, and the veterinarian removed a leg, that would be gross negligence. A claim of gross negligence may support different kinds of damage awards, such as punitive damages or emotional distress for the owner.

> **News Bits**
>
> In 2005 it was estimated that there were 80,000 veterinarians in the United States. For the same time the number of lawyers in the U.S. was estimated at 700,000.

Intentional and negligent infliction of emotional distress (on the owner). This may arise when the actions (against an animal) are intentional and likely to produce a strong reaction in the owner.

Duties of bailee. When a veterinarian acts as a bailee of an animal, for example when they board pets, then legal liability may arise either out of the negligent care of the animal or failure to redeliver the animal to the owner. (See the section in Chapter 2, "Bailments," for full discussion of this issue.)

Violation of a contract obligation. This may be a useful approach if there is a written contract. However, oral agreements may also constitute a contract. The normal conversation with a veterinarian before rendering services would not constitute an oral contract. A contract claim cannot be based on general statements of reassurance, "I'm sure Fluffy will be better after the operation." Rather, it must be a specific promise to do something or obtain a specific result. In a contracts action, the promise in the contract becomes the standard for conduct, not the general standard of veterinarian care appropriate to the community. There may be a difference in the statute of limitations for filing a contract action—which gives the plaintiff more time from the event in question to file a legal claim—rather than the filing of a tort or malpractice action.

Deceptive trade practices. However, professional services are often specifically excluded in the statutes that create the cause of action.

Taking. This may occur when the actions of an agent of the State result in the death of an animal. Only one case has been found to support such a cause of action. It first requires that the veterinarian be an employee of the State; second, that because of some state policy the injury to the animal occurred.

Case Study 3A

Defendant Kern, an employee of defendant Clinic, was the veterinarian on duty at the time. He asked Ms. Branks to bring the cat into the treatment room. He began the procedure with the plaintiff in the room, his veterinary assistant holding the cat. For medical and financial reasons, no anesthesia was used. The cat seemed in great pain. A few minutes into the procedure the cat wriggled loose and snapped at the assistant who was holding him. Plaintiff, who was standing at the cat's head and stroking his chest and paws in an attempt to soothe him, was aware that the cat had attempted to bite the assistant. The assistant adjusted his grip on the cat and the veterinarian resumed his work. A few minutes later, the cat again managed to free his head, this time biting the plaintiff, who was holding the cat's front paws. Plaintiff's injury did not seem particularly severe at the time; the receptionist bandaged the plaintiff's hand and Dr. Kern successfully opened the cat's blocked urethra. Plaintiff later went to an emergency room and discovered that she had severed a tendon in her hand. Plaintiff incurred medical expenses for treatment to her hand and lost wages as a result of her injury.

Is there a cause of action against the Clinic? See **Branks v. Kern**, 348 S.E.2d 815 (1986).

Case Study 3B

This case arises from the death of a Boer goat named Pancho. The Carters alleged that they were in the business of owning, breeding, and selling goats; that they placed Pancho with the Edwards "at their breeding facility for the purpose of standing him at stud, collecting, storing and selling his semen"; that an employee of the Edwards' spoke with and explained to Carter's wife that "Pancho's horns [were] growing into his head, and we need to do something about it"; that Carter consented to what he considered a "tip[ping]" of Pancho's horns; that Pancho was anesthetized at the Dublin Veterinary Clinic and dehorned; that approximately 15 to 20 minutes after the dehorning procedure was completed, Pancho died; that Vet Clinic sent tissue samples from Pancho to the Texas Veterinary Medical Diagnostic Laboratory and the tests showed that Pancho died of acute pulmonary congestion and edema; and that Vet appellees then burned Pancho's body without their consent.

Is there a cause of action against the Clinic?
See **Hight v. Dublin Veterinary Clinic**, 22 S.W.3d 614 (Tex. App. 2000).

Section 3

Malpractice Generally

For a plaintiff (animal owner) to recover damages for injury to an animal, in an action based on malpractice, all the following elements must be proven by the plaintiff:

1. The defendant was under a duty of care toward the animal in question. The veterinarian had accepted the responsibility to treat the animal.

2. The actions or nonactions of the veterinarian did not conform to the professional standard of conduct.

3. The failure to conform to the professional standard was the proximate cause of the injury or harm at issue.

4. The injury or harm resulted in damages to the plaintiff (not just the animal in question).

Veterinarians are under no legal duty to treat an ill or injured animal. The decision whether or not to provide a service is an individual decision. A decision to not provide treatment is not malpractice. One case suggests, however, that professional ethics may require some level of attention in emergency situations, but this does not give rise to a legal cause of action. Once the decision to treat an animal is made, the veterinarian has a duty to continue to treat or at least inform the owner of his or her decision to stop treatment of the animal in question.

Section 4

Determining the Standard of Treatment

A veterinary surgeon impliedly engages and is bound to use, in the performance of his duties in his employment, such reasonable skill, diligence and attention as may be ordinarily expected of persons in that profession. ... He did not undertake to perform a cure. **Barney v. Pinkham**, 45 N.W. 694 (Neb. 1890).

The recent cases dealing with injury to animals by veterinarians based on malpractice draw on the parallel problems and concepts developed in the judging of the conduct of other professions (doctors, lawyers, accountants, etc.). If a jurisdiction has few or no cases dealing with veterinary malpractice, the case opinions arising out of more extensive litigation-based doctor/human malpractice is an appropriate alternative source of legal principles.

While jurisdictions may have some variation in words or phrases, a general statement of the legal standard for veterinary practice is: "the exercise of the care and diligence as is ordinarily exercised by skilled veterinarians." Another Court stated the standard as "the standard of care required of and practiced by the average reasonably prudent, competent veterinarian in the community." The standard does not make the veterinarian an insurer of the recovery of an animal. The existence of an injury or a death after treatment does not give rise to a presumption of malpractice. In one case a court used the following: "nor does the legal standard set the threshold for liability at a particularly high level. The average or normal practitioner, not the best or most highly skilled, sets the standard." The plaintiff has the burden of proving that the defendant did not satisfy the legal standard. Because a layperson is unqualified to testify as to the proper exercise of judgment and skill, the testimony must be given by an expert, normally another veterinarian. One case noted that not only must the witness qualify generally as an expert on animal care, but for the particular issues before the court as well. In another case the plaintiff was unable to meet his burden of proof because no experts testified on his behalf.

> See Joseph H. King, Jr., *The Standard of Care for Veterinarians in Medical Malpractice Claims*, 58 Tenn. L. Rev. 1 (1990).

An important limitation on the application of the legal standard for veterinary practice is that of geographical setting. Some jurisdictions seek to limit the scope of the standard to comparisons on a local level. Three geographic variations have appeared in veterinary cases: Utah and Louisiana qualify their standard with the phrase "in the community." Iowa has rejected the "in the community" qualification, stating that location is but one factor for the jury to consider. North Carolina and Tennessee have taken a middle ground with the phrase "similarly situated": "It envisions a standard of professional competence and care customary in the field of practice among practitioners in similar communities which, in turn, suggests a consideration of such factors as the nature of the treatment involved; the degree of specialization, if any, required; the character of the community concerned; and the comparability of medical facilities available." It is reasonable to expect that whatever rule a jurisdiction adopted for medical malpractice would also apply to veterinarian malpractice. In the case of individuals who hold themselves out as an expert in a particular area, such as horses, then the standard of care will be statewide, if not national. The appropriate standard may be set by state statute.

CASE BY CASE

Ruden v. Hansen

206 N.W. 2d 713 (Iowa 1973)

JUDGE MOORE.

Defendant, Dr. L. R. Hansen, appeals from judgment on jury verdict for plaintiff in his action alleging malpractice by negligent vaccination of pregnant gilts. Plaintiff cross-appeals asserting the trial court erred in determination of the measure of damages. We reverse on both appeals.

In the fall of 1966 Plymouth County farmer, Melvin Bainbridge, decided to have a farm sale, including the sale of 67 pregnant gilts and 20 pregnant sows. In November or December 1966 he asked Plymouth County veterinarian, Dr. L. R. Hansen, to do whatever was necessary to get his animals ready for sale and transportation. He told Dr. Hansen the gilts had been bred and were due to farrow by March 7, 1967. Dr. Hansen was aware transportation regulations required certain vaccinations. In December he tested the gilts for brucellosis and vaccinated them for lepto and erysipelas. He decided to wait until January to vaccinate for hog cholera so the gilts would be further along in pregnancy. He vaccinated Bainbridge's gilts and sows with a modified live cholera vaccine on January 12, 1967. He thought this was the best way to qualify them for sale. Although the label on the cholera vaccine bottle stated the vaccine should not be used on pregnant sows, he had used it successfully on pregnant animals. Dr. Hansen testified such use was the best method and within good veterinary medical practice in the community.

Plaintiff, Eldon Ruden, bought the 67 gilts at Bainbridge's farm at public auction on January 12, 1967. He knew from a newspaper ad the gilts had been vaccinated and were due to farrow about March 7. He was not aware of when the gilts had been vaccinated. Within two days after purchase plaintiff trucked the gilts to his farm near Le Mars. They appeared to be in good condition.

The gilts started farrowing about a week after March 7. Several had only one, two or three live pigs. The normal litter is from eight to ten. Some had ten or eleven mummies—little dead pigs. Others were born alive but could not walk. Some were deformed. A number of the gilts just had after-birth. Many pigs had to be killed. Eighty lived to weaning time.

As a result of his loss plaintiff brought action against Bainbridge in division one of his petition for breach of warranty and in division two a tort action against Dr. Hansen, alleging negligence and malpractice. On trial the jury returned a verdict for Bainbridge and a $2000 verdict for plaintiff against Dr. Hansen.

As a veterinarian defendant was duty bound to bring to his service the learning, skill and care which characterizes the profession generally.

In other words, the care and diligence required was that as a careful and trustworthy veterinarian would be expected to exercise.

We have omitted reference to the veterinarian's duty "in the neighborhood or vicinity" as used in Morrison v. Altig, supra, first because all testimony in the case at bar refers to duty by veterinarians practicing in Plymouth County and secondly because we no longer approve that limitation. The standard of care practiced in the particular community or like communities may be one of the elements to be considered but it is not conclusive. We are convinced the correct standard of the veterinarian's care should be held to that exercised generally under similar circumstances. Such is the rule as applied to hospitals in the care of patients.

We return to the evidence as shown by the record. About March 15 plaintiff visited the office of Dr. John R. Conley, Le Mars, Plymouth County veterinarian and related his experience. He was given medicine to treat his sows. Dr. Conley's associate went to plaintiff's farm two days later. Dr. Conley was given a report but did not see plaintiff's animals until April 13. He drew blood for testing to eliminate two possible causes of plaintiff's problem. He was not qualified to run the brucellosis and leptospirosis test. Therefore he sent blood samples to the Diagnostic Laboratory at Iowa State University at Ames.

Dr. Conley's qualifications as a member of the profession are not questioned. His testimony includes:

"All right now, Doctor, based upon your experience as a veterinarian, with a reasonable degree of certainty, do you have a reason for the cause of the difficulty in the farrowing of these gilts and these gilts' litters?"

Over defendant's objection the witness answered:

"Yes. My opinion was as previously stated that the fetal deaths, of stillborn pigs, malformation in the pigs, and the high death rate in the pigs that were born alive, were the result of use of modified live vaccine, hog cholera vaccine, in the first part of their pregnancy."

He also testified he felt any violation of the contraindication enclosed with the vaccine or biological product is not proper and that use of modified live vaccine is not proper on bred animals. He further opined "the only proper procedure is serum."

Although Dr. Conley was not asked directly the standard of care to be exercised generally in vaccination of pregnant gilts we believe his testimony was sufficient to establish a jury question on that element of plaintiff's case.

Defendant also contends he was entitled to a directed verdict on the grounds plaintiff failed to prove proximate cause. The testimony of Dr. Conley set out above sufficiently establishes a jury question on the causal connection of defendant's alleged negligence and plaintiff's loss. Dr. Conley's testimony on cross-examination, that there are other possible causes of such problems as experienced by plaintiff, was not enough to negate as a matter of law his testimony that plaintiff's problems were the result of defendant's use of modified live vaccine.

Generally questions of negligence, contributory negligence and proximate cause are for the jury; it is only in exceptional cases that they may be decided as matters of law. Rule 344(f)10, Rules of Civil Procedure. The record before us does not establish such an exceptional case. The trial court did not err in overruling defendant's motions for directed verdict and for judgment notwithstanding the verdict.

II. Defendant's second assigned error is the trial court erred in allowing the witness William Mills to state his opinion as to the cause of his problem with the 20 pregnant sows which he had bought at the Bainbridge auction sale on January 12, 1967. Defendant had vaccinated the sows that day in the same manner as the gilts. At farrowing Mills had a similar experience with his pigs as that of plaintiff.

After stating his experience with his sows Mills testified he operated a 240 acre farm on which he fed 500 to 600 head of hogs per year. He was then asked: "Do you know, of your own knowledge — and answer yes or no — what the problem was?" He answered, "Yes" and then was asked, "What was that problem?"

Defense counsel objected to the question "as calling for an opinion and conclusion of the witness, without proper foundation having been laid as to the qualifications of this witness to speak as to what the problem was." The objection was overruled and Mills answered, "I felt that this was not the procedure to be followed. The procedure was to vaccinate with a modified live virus into a pregnant animal."

It is not enough that a witness be generally qualified in a certain area; he must also be qualified to answer the particular question propounded.

Mills' qualifications, if any, were indeed general. He said nothing concerning the length of time he had been feeding hogs, nor of any prior experience with the problem he experienced with his 20 sows. The showing of any knowledge of the proper method of vaccinating gilts or sows was entirely lacking. The inadequacy of Mills' qualifications is so manifest that no extended discussion is necessary.

The trial court committed reversible error in permitting Mills to express the opinion above set out.

IV. Defendant's fourth assigned error is that Dr. Conley over defendant's objection that the factual background was insufficient, was allowed to express an opinion of the cause of plaintiff's loss. We do not agree. Although Dr. Conley did not see plaintiff's animals until April 13, he had a full history of the animals, including the breeding and vaccination dates. Dr. Hansen's deposition was part of the record and its contents, including several admissions, were within Dr. Conley's knowledge. His associate's reports were within his knowledge. We note this evidence was not challenged as being hearsay. Dr. Conley had taken blood samples and made some tests. As we point out in Ganrud v. Smith, supra, and Fischer, Inc. v. Standard Brands, Inc., supra, the trial court is vested with discretion on the question of admissibility or exclusion of expert testimony. See also Hedges v. Conder, Iowa, 166 N.W.2d 844, 857, 858. We find no abuse of the trial court's discretion.

V. Finally defendant asserts the trial court erred in allowing Dr. Conley to testify to "the best method" to be used in vaccinating pregnant gilts for hog cholera. He argues this was an improper statement of the degree of care required to be exercised by Dr. Hansen. Dr. Conley's testimony was in response to defendant's testimony that use of modified live virus was the best method for vaccination of plaintiff's animals. We find no merit in defendant's last assigned error.

On defendant-appellant's appeal we find reversible error requiring remand of this case for a new trial.

[The discussion of the issue of damages is omitted.]

This case is reversed on each appeal and remanded for a new trial.

Questions & Notes

1. In this case, the attorney for the animal owner used a number of methods for introducing evidence of malpractice. Which were successful and why?

2. What is the public policy reason for requiring experts? What real-world burden does this place on the animal owner and the attorney preparing the case?

3. Note that, in the case, the court briefly mentions that it will not adopt an "in the community" standard for judging the presence of malpractice. Is a statewide standard preferable? What about nationwide?

Case Study 3C

In November 2005 Arlene Sherman purchased a six-week-old apricot colored toy poodle for $550. Sherman named the dog Ruby. At approximately 5:00 p.m. on May 26, 2006, Sherman brought Ruby to the Broadway Veterinary Hospital (BVH) to stay overnight in order to obtain a urine sample to determine if Ruby still had a urinary tract infection. Sherman signed a "Financial Responsibility Agreement and Authorization for Professional Services," authorizing BVH to perform diagnostic procedures and agreeing to assume all financial responsibility. According to Sherman, the receptionist told her that the urine sample would be collected from a plastic sheet placed beneath the dog's cage.

After reviewing the dog's chart, Jennifer Kissinger, D.M.V. decided to use cystocentesis to obtain a urine sample that evening. Cystocentesis is " 'a procedure in which a needle is placed into the urinary bladder through the abdominal wall of an animal and a sample of urine is removed.'" According to Kissinger " '[c]ystocentesis is essential for a urine culture (the procedure for which Ruby had been brought in for).' " BVH admits that no one told Sherman that a cystocentesis would be performed. When Kissinger inserted the needle into Ruby, she drew blood instead of urine. Kissinger said she immediately removed the needle, applied pressure, and placed Ruby back in her cage. About a minute later, Ruby collapsed. Despite efforts to resuscitate the dog, Ruby died.

Following Ruby's death, BVH performed a number of tests in an attempt to determine the cause of death. In June 2006, Kissinger sent Sherman a letter stating that the DNA test results did not indicate Ruby had a clotting disorder and that the cause of death was unknown. "The lack of blood clots in the abdomen at the time of her necropsy, as well as her propensity to have bruising and hematomas with blood draws are all suspicious for a coagulation defect.... We will never actually know if Ruby truly had a rare platelet coagulation defect or not, at this point. I am quite suspicious she did, since the necropsy showed that the cystocentesis procedure did not lacerate any of the major abdominal blood vessels."

Was there malpractice (consider the four elements)?

How will plaintiff meet the burden of proof?

See Sherman v. Kissinger, 195 P. 3d 539 (Ct. of Ap. Wash. 2008).

There are two policy considerations that support a general standard for practice of nationwide, or at least statewide scope, making the location of the events only one factor to be considered when deciding the presence or absence of malpractice. First, as a practical matter, it is often difficult for the plaintiff to get local veterinarians to testify against other members of the profession whom they may personally know. Yet, if a "within the community" standard is adopted, then only local veterinarians would qualify as expert witnesses. To make it practical for plaintiffs to prove their cases, use of experts outside the community should be allowed. Second, a standard without geographic limitations is in the public interest, for it would promote higher levels of competence within the profession, and, therefore, better care and treatment for animals. The "in the community" limitation aids primarily the small-town or rural practitioner, who historically has less access to new ideas and information than the urban practitioners. While there might have been reasons to tolerate this differing standard in the past, it is no longer justifiable to expect any less from a small-town veterinarian than from an urban veterinarian. With increased emphasis by all professions in continuing (post-degree) education, and with recent developments in communication and data-transfer facilities, everyone who seeks the aid of a professional ought to expect a more or less uniform standard within the entire state. One factor that would qualify such an expectation, however, is access to advanced equipment that may be available only in limited areas within a state (such as the teaching centers).

Case Study 3D

I took my dog to be spayed on 10/19/04. The surgery was performed and I brought her home on 10/21/04. The doctor used staples and the incision seemed to be fine until Saturday morning. I noticed that 3 of the staples were out on one side. I called the vet's office and told his technician that the staples were coming out and she asked if they were oozing or leaking. I said no, and she said that if they weren't there was no problem, that this was normal and nothing to worry about. Additionally, I was told to bring her in on 10/30/04 to remove the remaining staples.

I kept an eye on the incision for the rest of the day and it didn't appear that it was any worse. I went to bed around 1:00 a.m. Sunday morning and my dog was in the bedroom with me. She woke me up to go out around 5:10 and I let her back in about 5:15. She was walking fine and appeared to have no problems as she came back inside. However, within about 30 to 45 seconds of returning into the house she let out a howl of pain. I turned on the light and her intestines were outside of her body. We wrapped her in a wet towel and rushed her to a local after hours emergency clinic where they performed surgery and she again appears to be doing fine.

The reason I'm asking your advice is that the doctor states that he is not responsible for her after she leaves his office. He did not request that I bring her in after I notified him of the emergency clinic visit and insists that the only way the stitches could have come out was if she chewed them out. I spent the entire 3 days after the surgery with her and never saw her pay more than cursory attention to the staples. I feel that the doctor was negligent in allowing his technician to advise a customer with a concern like mine that everything was normal (and the doctor told me he would have told me the same thing if I had spoken to him). In my opinion my dog was under his care until the staples were taken out.

> This vet does not acknowledge that any of this situation may have been caused by himself or his office. The cost for the emergency surgery was 3 times the cost of the initial spaying. Thankfully that option was available to us and we didn't lose her.
>
> I need to know if from a legal standpoint you feel that we may have a case against this doctor.
>
> Thank you
>
> Questions: Was the above malpractice? Is there anything else that you need to know? How do you decide whether or not to take the case? What will the damages be?

Section 5

Proximate Cause

As with all tort actions, the veterinarian's malpractice must be shown to be the proximate cause of the injury. In the cases discussed in the prior section, the action of the individual clearly resulted in the harm to the animal.

CASE BY CASE

Southall v. Gabel

33 Ohio Misc. 194, 293 N.E. 2d 891 (1972)

WEST, JUDGE.

This action was brought by plaintiff as owner of a 3 year old thoroughbred race horse, named Pribal, against defendant, a veterinarian, charging defendant so mishandled the horse that it sustained physical injuries and emotional trauma; that the emotional stability of the horse worsened until finally it was exterminated. Plaintiff asks a total of $6,663 including $1,663 expense for care and medical attention for Pribal.

Plaintiff on September 11, 1967, brought Pribal to the O.S.U. Veterinary Clinic with apparent lameness. Radiographs and examination revealed: (1) chip fracture off antero-lateral aspect of distal left radius, (2) multiple areas of exostosis in left knee, (3) periostitis (splints) both right and left medial splint bones, front legs. The colt was sent home September 13, 1967, for stall rest for three weeks to a month because of heat in the knee and cortisone having been injected in the last three weeks.

Pribal was returned to the clinic October 1, 1967, and a bone chip was removed from the lateral radiocarpal joint of the left leg. According to clinic records he was ready to go home October 16, 1967, but instead of going home, on October 17, 1967, after dark Pribal was loaded by mistake by students at the clinic in defendant's two-horse, padded, rubber-floored van with another horse destined for the Ohio Thoroughbred Center at Sunbury, Ohio. Pribal was not tranquilized nor were standing bandages or shipping boots put on his legs. The horse loaded, traveled and unloaded well on this occasion. Horses are often tranquilized and have leg protection for transportation but not always. Before 1960 horses were never tranquilized.

The defendant left the horse at Sunbury after discovering the error and when plaintiff came to see Pribal at the clinic the next day and found the horse gone, defendant promised he personally would deliver the horse to the stable in Hilliard where plaintiff wanted it.

The evening of October 19, 1967, at about 11:00 p.m., defendant, with no trouble, loaded Pribal into his van, secured the horse and gave him hay. The horse was not tranquilized, no stall sheet, no bandages and no boots were used. The horse was not shod, his shoes having been removed for surgery. After traveling about a mile, defendant stopped because he could feel the horse moving about in the van. Defendant observed the horse was jumping up and down and moving from side to side and wouldn't calm down, so defendant gave Pribal an intravenous injection of a tranquilizer. The conduct of the horse was characterized as a "van fit."

Defendant returned Pribal to Sunbury, unloaded him, walked him, treated an abraded area on the hip, noted minor skin damage elsewhere and that Pribal was handling the operated leg well. Defendant notified plaintiff and she personally went to the stable at Sunbury at 2:30 a.m. October 20, 1967, and saw the horse was soaking wet, one hip was badly abraded, the ankles were swollen, the bandage had slipped from the operated knee down to the ankle and the incision was seeping.

Upon the insistence of plaintiff, Pribal was returned to the O.S.U. Veterinary Clinic by a company specializing in transportation of horses. Although plaintiff insisted the horse's legs be wrapped this time, they weren't. Pribal was kept at the clinic until December 13, 1967. Then it took six students to load the horse into the van and, according to plaintiff, Pribal was no longer kind, gentle and loving. Instead of wanting to nuzzle he wanted to bite.

No charge was ever made to plaintiff for the surgery or the clinical care of her horse. A horse cannot race for four to six months after surgery on its knee.

Pribal began racing again about April 1968, and ran nine times that year, but was never in the money. The horse was gelded in the fall of 1968 in an attempt to improve its disposition, but this did not help and he continued to be the most temperamental horse the trainer ever saw. The trainer didn't know if it was the starting gate, the van fit or what caused the horse to be that way. He had never been around a horse that became a killer other than Pribal. They ran Pribal seven times in 1969, but he was never up close and plaintiff had him destroyed August 24, 1969.

In this case, plaintiff has complained the defendant failed to use the care required when transporting plaintiff's horse October 17 and October 19, 1967; "(1) In moving the colt in a van so soon after surgery, and (2) In not preparing the colt's legs for transit with the use of proper standing and shipping bandages."

The evidence establishes there was nothing unusual or out of the ordinary in moving Pribal October 17, 1967, as the horse was ready to go home and the results of the surgery were in no way affected. Since the horse loaded, traveled and unloaded well two days before without a tranquilizer or leg protection, defendant's action in loading and starting to transport it October 19, 1967, was not unreasonable or imprudent.

Proximate cause is the active and efficient cause that sets in motion a train of events which brings about the result without intervention of any force started and working actively from a new or different and independent source.

What caused Pribal to become mean and a "killer" is speculative.

> **Think About It**
>
> What would/will be the economic consequences to veterinarians if malpractice claims about pets result in awards of $100,000 or more? Will this increase or decrease the level of care?

When admitted to the O.S.U. Veterinary Clinic September 11, 1967, it was noted: "This horse is highly spirited" and "Attitude: Alert—very hyper" and "Genital System: Suspect peri phimosis—always has penis extended over period of time—both testes descended." When admitted to the clinic for surgery October 1, 1967, it was noted: "Horse has been raced on cortisone injection into the knee and butazolidin treatment for lameness." On October 4, 1967, the chart shows: "Operated for carpal chip. Recovery was a bad trip (freak out)." The defendant explained this was the student veterinarian's way of indicating the horse had a violent recovery from anesthesia. A notation on the chart October 9, 1967, reads: "This horse masturbates—may be the reason for his loss of condition."

When Pribal was returned to the O.S.U. Veterinary Clinic October 20, 1967, after having had the "van fit" the previous night, the admission record showed: "Horse traveled roughly in a trailer—hip abrasion and swollen hind legs with multiple superficial abrasions." On October 28, 1967, the chart is noted: "Animal is ready to go home—looks better than ever did. All lesions healed—legs are down." The evidence was that plaintiff refused to take Pribal home then and another notation on the chart December 10, 1967, reads in part: "this is * * * the worst tempered animal I have ever come in contact with * * *."

A horse is personal property, yet where the alleged damage to such property is injury resulting in physical or mental disability, causal connection between the injury and the disability must be established in much the same way as required where the injury is to a person. As Justice Leach so well states in Darnell v. Eastman (1970), 23 Ohio St. 2d 13, 261 N.E.2d 114: "Except as to questions of cause and effect which are so apparent as to be matters of common knowledge, the issue of causal connection between an injury and a specific subsequent physical disability involves a scientific inquiry and must be established by the opinion of medical witnesses competent to express such opinion."

In this case, the defendant was the only veterinary medical witness. The O.S.U. Veterinary Clinic records are in evidence. Dr. Gabel did not and the clinical records do not indicate any causal relationship between the handling of Pribal by the defendant and the subsequent personality change resulting in Pribal becoming a "killer horse." The closest thing to expert testimony was that of plaintiff's trainer who did not know if it was the van fit, the starting gate or what made the horse so mean.

Questions & Notes

1. Why did the plaintiff file this suit?

2. What do you think of the use and treatment of the horse by the owner?

3. Which way would you rule in this case?

4. Would an action based on bailments have been any stronger?

Case Study 3D

Prior to and during the incident giving rise to this litigation, the plaintiff held a Connecticut veterinary license. On November 28, 1992, a car struck Allison O'Connell's dog. O'Connell subsequently took the dog to the plaintiff's veterinary hospital for emergency treatment. After the plaintiff diagnosed and treated the dog's injuries, he informed O'Connell—and his treatment notes indicate—that he diagnosed a fracture to the dog's radius and that part of the proximal surface of her olecranon bone was missing. The plaintiff also told O'Connell that he repaired the tendons in the dog's leg with surgical steel wire. The plaintiff testified, and his treatment notes indicate, that he used number one and number two gauge nylon to repair lacerated tendons in the dog's leg. On the basis of its own expertise, the board found that number one or number two gauge nylon is inappropriate for the treatment of injured tendons in a dog's leg.

On December 7, 1992, O'Connell took the dog to Jeffrey LaCroix, a veterinarian, for further treatment. LaCroix removed the splint and sutures that the plaintiff had applied to the dog's leg. LaCroix palpated and took X-rays of the dog's leg, as well as examined X-rays that the plaintiff had taken of the dog's leg. LaCroix concluded, and the board agreed, that the X-rays revealed no fractures. His palpation of the dog's leg revealed that no repair had been performed to any tendons because he found a fully mobile leg joint with no evidence of scar tissue on the leg. The board also found, on the basis of its expertise, that if the plaintiff had repaired the tendons with nylon, LaCroix should easily have been able to detect the nylon when he examined the dog. LaCroix also found that the dog was weight-bearing when he examined her on December 7, 1992. He testified, and the board found, that the dog would not be weight-bearing if she had sustained a tendon repair two weeks earlier. According to LaCroix's testimony, the dog would not have been weight-bearing for at least four weeks had she sustained a lacerated tendon in her leg.

After her visit to LaCroix's office with the dog, O'Connell contacted the department. The department held a compliance conference on August 10, 1993, and, on November 19, 1993, the department submitted charges against the plaintiff to the board. The statement of charges alleged that the plaintiff did not conform to the acceptable standard of care for veterinarians because the plaintiff (1) misdiagnosed the dog's condition, (2) misrepresented the dog's condition to her owners and (3) misrepresented to the owners the treatment that he provided to the dog.

Is there a cause of action against the Clinic?
See **Wasfi v. Department of Public Health**, 761 A. 2d 257 (Conn. App. 2000).

Section 6

Revocation of License to Practice

CASE BY CASE

Eastep v. Veterinary Medical Examining Board

22 Or. App. 457, 539 P. 2d 1144 (1975)

FORT, JUDGE.

Petitioner is a practicing veterinarian in Oregon. He was charged with violation of ORS 686.130(3), which he denied. Following notice and hearing before an examiner, the latter entered findings of fact and conclusions of law holding that petitioner's actions "constituted unprofessional conduct by his misrepresentation of services rendered" in violation of the statute. Upon review the Board concluded those findings were correct, denied his application for renewal of his license to practice, and permanently revoked his right to practice veterinary medicine in this state. He appeals, asserting essentially that the order was not supported by reliable and substantial evidence, that the proper evidentiary standard which should have been applied was that of clear and convincing evidence, and that both the hearing officer and the Board erred in refusing to strike the testimony of the licensed pathologist who performed the autopsy on the animal in question.

The facts found were summarized by the Board as follows:

1. That on October 3, 1974, Nancy Hunt was the owner of a nine months old Gordon Setter dog which she brought to the Animal Clinic of Dr. Eastep, a licensed veterinarian, for treatment.

2. That the said dog remained at the said Eastep Animal Clinic during the period October 3 through October 9, 1974, and was given treatment by Eastep including surgery.

3. That during said period Eastep represented to Hunt that the animal had a floating kidney, that he reattached the floating kidney; that the animal had an enlarged kidney which should be removed; that the animal had a hiatus hernia which was repaired, and that a portion of the liver of the animal was removed.

4. That Hunt paid Eastep the sum of $494.00 for his services.

5. That on or about the 9th day of October 1974, the dog was taken by the owner to another veterinarian, Dr. Ralph J. Plamondon, and stayed until October 14, 1974.

That the animal was given further treatment but that no further surgery was performed.

6. The animal was returned to Dr. Plamondon on October 16 and died on October 22, 1974. The immediate cause of death was a collapse of the left lung and pericardial effusion.

7. That at the request of the owner, Dr. Plamondon ordered an autopsy to be performed by Dr. Gene Bogaty, a licensed pathologist. That the dog was delivered to Dr. Bogaty for such autopsy on or about October 22, 1974.

8. That on said date an autopsy was performed on the said Gordon Setter dog by Dr. Bogaty, a qualified pathologist, who made a gross examination of the anatomy of the dog.

9. That as a result of said autopsy no sutures or adhesions were discernible.

10. That Dr. Eastep testified that he initially had made an exploratory operation and thereafter a second incision and operation upon the said dog during which he removed a two inch piece of bone from the intestines; that he repaired a hiatus hernia which included the moving of the liver and spleen and reattached to kidney, all of which required at least 16-18 sutures in the anatomy of the dog.

11. That the expert medical and veterinarian witnesses were in accord that sutures and adhesions for such type of operation should be readily apparent from an autopsy taken within ten days or two weeks following the alleged operations described in paragraph 10.

12. That Dr. Eastep, by reason of the foregoing, did not perform the alleged services of surgery involving the repair of a hiatus hernia or the reattachment of a kidney or removal of an object in the intestine or the moving or removal of a portion of the liver."

Examination of the record shows that there was "reliable, probative and substantial evidence" offered to support each of the foregoing findings of fact. It is clear that our review of an administrative agency finding on a question of fact is confined to that question. ORS 183.480(7)(d). It is not for us to weigh the evidence when, as here, there is conflicting evidence. Balduyck v. Morgan, 9 Or. App. 363, 497 P. 2d 377 (1972).

We conclude that there was ample evidence to support the findings of the Board, whether the standard adopted be that of "clear and convincing evidence," as petitioner urges, or that of "reliable, probative and substantial evidence" (ORS 183.480(7)(d)), as urged by respondent.

Affirmed.

Questions & Notes

1. What would the animal owner have to produce in court as evidence to recover in an action for malpractice?

◇◇

Besides legal liability, veterinarians have obligations to their professional organization and to the state, through its licensing board, for maintaining certain levels of professional conduct. If, because of lack of monetary damages or other legal problems, an animal owner is unable to obtain satisfaction through the courts for a grievance against a veterinarian, or in addition to any civil lawsuit, he or she can pursue the issue with the state licensing board or file a grievance with a professional organization of which the veterinarian is a member.

Most statutes that provide for the professional licensing of veterinarians also provide for the revocation or nonrenewal of the license for stated reasons. The statutes fall into two general categories. The first type lists the standard for revocation specifically in the statute:

- fraudulent deception or incompetence in the practice of veterinary medicine (Calif.);

- incompetence, gross negligence or other malpractice in the practice of veterinary medicine (Idaho and Miss.).

Other states give the licensing board the authority to pass regulations governing the practice of veterinary medicine. A license can be revoked for violation of these standards of professional conduct (Texas and Va.).

In one New Jersey case the standard for action against the veterinarian by the Board was "grossly neglectful actions or gross malpractice." This standard would not be broken by simple malpractice. The action would have to be much more serious, on the level of gross negligence, before administrative action could be justified. In an Oregon case a veterinarian had claimed that he had performed surgery on a dog. After the dog's death an autopsy revealed none had been done. The court felt the Board was justified in permanently revoking the defendant's right to practice. Finally, in a New Mexico case, a veterinarian's license was suspended for six months due to the following complaints:

- failure to communicate with owners of animals.

- failure to inform animal owners of actual conditions of animals.

- failure to inform owners of deaths of animals under his care.

- failure to administer timely treatment.

- improper record controls on animals.

- failure to maintain clean and sanitary conditions.

- lack of proper control over animals.

- misrepresentation to the public that one of the members of his staff was a doctor of veterinary medicine.

While the filing of complaints with state and professional organizations will give no damages or relief to the animal owner (or the animal), it does act as a check on the general level of practice of a particular veterinarian, and may be the only realistic option which an aggrieved individual may possess.

What is the appropriate level of punishment for misdeeds? Consider the following:

> On July 13, 2004, Patti Smith presented her eight-year-old Briard dog named "Bri" to appellant, a veterinarian specializing in orthopedic surgery, for treatment of recurrent lameness in the left hind leg. Appellant made the diagnosis of hip dysplasia with degenerative joint disease. On August 5, 2004, appellant performed a total hip replacement surgery. It is undisputed that appellant failed to take postoperative radiographs ("x-rays") on the date of the surgery. Within four days of the surgery, Ms. Smith telephoned appellant and expressed concerns about Bri's condition. On August 10, 2004, appellant conducted a follow-up examination, during which appellant again failed to take x-rays. Appellant conducted additional follow-up examinations on September 3, and October 12, 2004. During these examinations, appellant did take x-rays, which demonstrated that cement from the surgery had leaked into the pelvic area, thereby causing resultant nerve damage.

> Plaintiff filed a complaint with veterinary state licensing Board, alleging malpractice. The Board appointed a hearing examiner to take the evidence of the case. The hearing examiner recommended that appellant's veterinary license be suspended for 30 days. The board unanimously adopted the findings of fact and conclusions of law of the hearing examiner. However, the board modified the recommended sanction and instead imposed a $500 fine. Upheld on appeal by veterinarian. Harrison, D.V.M. v. Ohio Veterinary Medical Licensing Board, 2009 WL 1700141 (Ohio App. 10 Dist.).

What do you think? What are the different consequences for 30 days suspension of licence vs. $500?

For additional discussion see: **Coy v. Ohio Veterinary Med. Licensing Bd. Ohio**, 2005 Ohio App. LEXIS 756, 2005 WL 433518 and **Gilman v. Nevada State Board of Veterinary Medical Examiners**, 120 Nev. 263, 89 P. 3d 1000 (2004).

CHAPTER 4

Damages for Harm to Pets

Section 1

Overview

This topic shall discuss a critical right of an animal owner to recover damages for harm to her animal. It is through the measure of damages that the legal system assesses the value of an owner's property. The measure of damages is also important because it sets a practical frame of reference as to what kinds or degrees of harm to animals will justify seeking access to the courts. The reality of our legal system is such that, unless there is a minimal amount of damages recoverable, most attorneys will be unwilling to file a lawsuit; and, therefore, that property (animal) remains unprotected and unacknowledged by the law.

Note that the rights of the owner are the focus of this discussion—not the legal rights of the animal. While the animals categorized as property have many and varied interests, at present they cannot recover money damages at law for injuries to themselves.

Section 2

Legal Rights of Animal Ownership

The rights of animal owners may be summarized with the following list:

1. the right to convey;
2. the right to consume;
3. the right to use as collateral;
4. the right to obtain the natural dividends of the animal; and
5. the right to exclude others.

The right to convey ownership encompasses the ability to sell the animal, to give the animal away, and to devise the animal to others by will or provide for them with a trust. As these rights are discussed in detail in Chapter 2, further explanation at this point is unnecessary.

The right to consume or destroy property has been a long-standing part of animal ownership. As a major source of food, animals are killed by individual and corporate owners on a regular basis. The primary limitations on such activities are the cruelty laws of the states and the slaughter acts of the states and the federal government. The owner's property interest in the animal continues after its death. The change in the animal's status from living to nonliving does not deprive the owner of the title to or right of possession to the property. To the extent that animals represent a financial asset, they may be used as collateral for loans or other business transactions. The natural dividends of animals are as multitudinous as the animals themselves. Milk, eggs, wool, etc. all belong to the owner of the producing animal unless they have been specifically contracted away. Perhaps more important is the fact that the offspring (increase) of animals belongs to the owner of the mother.

The most critical legal right within our concept of private property is the ability to exclude others. This is a multifaceted right that includes the right to use force to protect one's property from outside threats. The legal system also provides the owner with methods of regaining possession of the animal (replevin) or financial reimbursement for the loss when someone has improperly interfered with the owner's possession (conversion). In addition, society, through the criminal law system, seeks to protect ownership rights by punishing those that interfere with the lawful possession of animals.

Section 3

Injury to Animals by Another — Torts

The number of ways that an animal can be injured by other animals or humans are too numerous to recite. The following list should act as a reference to the types of cases that deal with animals:

> **Think About It**
>
> Since the turn of the century, the veterinarian profession has been providing increasingly comprehensive and expensive care for animals: kidney transplants for cats ($6,000–$11,000), heart surgery for dogs ($6,000–$12,000) and chemotherapy for cancers.
>
> (Steve Dale, *Friend for Life*, USA Weekend June 13–15, 2003 at p. 6.)

1. Trespass — defendant's terrier trespassed and impregnated plaintiff's cow or injured neighbor's dog.

2. Negligence & gross negligence:
   - Defendant sprayed animals with a poisonous chemical.
   - Defendant left gaps in fences around pasture, escaped horse was killed.
   - Defendant delivered contaminated chicken feed.
   - Defendant improperly left a pipe trench uncovered, which injured a horse.
   - Defendant negligently mislabeled a chemical.
   - Defendant left gate open, dog was killed by a passing car.
   - Defendant animal hospital was found negligent in the use of heating pads on dogs (allowing recovery for emotional distress).
   - Defendant negligent in transportation of pet and pet dies

of heat stress. Facts support action for negligent infliction of emotional distress.

- Defendant negligent in care and control of dog resulting in impregnation of plaintiff's dog—for a second time.

3. Inherently dangerous product—chemicals.

4. Products liability—arsenic in horse feed.

5. Malicious destruction of body of dog, malicious killing of an animal (may support an action for intentional infliction of emotional distress or punitive damages).

6. Violation of a state statute.

7. Illegal state action under 42 U.S.C. 1983.

Regardless of the cause of action, after finding that a defendant is liable for the injury to an animal, the next critical step is the measure of damages.

Section 4

Overview of Damages for Injury to Animals

Assuming that an animal has been wrongfully injured or killed, a very important issue arises as to the appropriate method of calculating the monetary damages for compensation for the injury done. In a commercial context, when the market value for goods, such as timber, is readily ascertainable, the calculation is straightforward. With commercial animals such as pigs, the standard categories of compensation are used as the animal has no additional value to the owner. With pets, the answers are not so clear, as the court may consider a pet animal to be more than just property.

> This court now overrules prior precedent and holds that a pet is not just a thing but occupies a special place somewhere in between a person and a piece of personal property. **Corso v. Crawford Dog and Cat Hospital**, 415 N.Y.S. 2d 182 (1979).

Beginning in the 1990s there has been considerable variability in the attitude of courts toward pets; whereas several courts have found harm to a pet to justify more than market value, a number of other courts have flatly rejected any attempt to create new categories for injury to pet animals. A 1994 Minnesota case specifically declined to find that pet dogs had intrinsic value on which an award of damages could be based—a dog was just another form of property. Additionally, a 1996 case adopted the traditional view by declining to award any damages other than medical costs. In this case, a pet poodle had his left front leg and shoulder blade torn off by a kennel owner's dog. Obviously the dog experienced great pain, but he did survive and continued to be the three-legged family pet. The court stated:

> We reject the Nichols' argument that the intrinsic value of a dog should be considered in awarding damages for injury to the dog. The Nichols still enjoy the companionship of their pet and there is no evidence of the dog's special purpose. **Nichols v. Sukaro Kennels**, 555 N.W. 2d 689 (1996).

The issues of pet loss are also bound up in larger disputes over the appropriateness of allowing humans to recover for mental pain and suffering in a wide variety of circumstances. Additionally, the reality is that often the harm causes the most emotional trauma not to the "owner" of the animal but to another member of the family.

Animals pose a unique problem for the underlying theory of damage awards. The primary purpose of a damage calculation is to compensate for the harm, the injury, and the pain and suffering arising out of the wrongful acts of another. Yet, when an animal is harmed, injured or has suffered pain and anguish, the legal system has difficulty in addressing it directly. There is no case in the United States in which the pain and suffering of the animal was the measure of a financial award. This is because animals have not yet been recognized as legal "persons" for this purpose. Only legally recognized "persons" can receive financial reimbursement for legal wrongs inflicted on them.

So long as it is only the human's pocketbook that is harmed, the legal system has developed reasonable rules to handle most situations, and there is little disagreement among the jurisdictions. If it is a human's mental well-being or emotional bond with an animal that is injured, then the recovery is

---

A Focusing Question

Is it possible for an animal to recover for harm inflicted on the animal by the owner of the animal? Should it be?

---

much less certain and there is great disparity among the jurisdictions as to theory and result.

Section 5

The Traditional Calculation — Fair Market Value

In all personal property injuries, the measure of damages is the amount that will return the owner to his financial status prior to the injury. With animals, the primary focus is on fair market value and associated consequential damages (considered in the next section).

Where the animal has a market value, the market value at the time of the loss, or the difference in market value before and after injury, will generally be the measure applied. Any special value, particular qualities, or capabilities are generally considered as factors making up market value. For example, when an owner has received the market value of an animal, he will have been compensated for any use he might have made of the animal for breeding purposes. The high production rate of a slaughtered cow is to be considered as a particular quality along with breed, age, condition, and other factors in computing the animal's market value.

CASE BY CASE

Dillon v. O'Connor
412 P. 2d 126, 68 Wash. 2d 184 (1966)

This is "The Case of the Costly Canine." "Bimbo," an acknowledged "tree hound," [n2] but without pedigree or registration papers, lost a bout with defendant's automobile. For "Bimbo's" untimely demise, his owner, plaintiff, brought suit against defendant alleging that "Bimbo" was killed as a result of defendant's negligent operation of his automobile. Plaintiff alleged:

> That "Bimbo" had a reasonable market value of $2,000 as a trained four-year old animal experienced in hunting and of a bloodline known throughout the area and for its capacity in this regard.

> n2 Webster's Third New International Dictionary, Unabridged (1961), defines "tree dog" as "a dog (as a coonhound) used for treeing game."

Defendant appeals from a $1,650 money judgment entered against him after a jury verdict. l.

Defendant's first of three assignments of error is directed to instruction No. 18, requested by plaintiff and given by the court:

> In the event you decide to render a verdict in favor of the plaintiff, in determining the value of the dog which was destroyed, you may consider its original purchase price, if any, its age, and the condition of its health. You may also con-

sider the plaintiff's investment in said dog from the point of view of time devoted to its training, maintenance by way of food, and may also consider its pedigree, if any, its grade, if any, and its fair market value. The value of such an animal is determined by its market value which includes the foregoing factors amongst others.

The rationale of plaintiff's action, as illustrated by the allegations of the complaint quoted supra, is for recovery of the "reasonable market value" of "Bimbo." A careful reading of instruction No. 18 convinces us that it was intended originally by plaintiff and by the court to be a "market value" instruction. [n3] Absent the testimony, we must assume that the evidence justified giving a "market value" instruction, for no claim is made by appropriate assignment of error supported by the record that a "market value" instruction should not have been given.

> n3 On appeal, to mix a metaphor, plaintiff apparently "has switched dogs in the middle of the stream." He contends in his appellate brief that "the evidence did not support the giving of instructions on market value," although plaintiff requested the instruction given.

We believe, however, that instruction No. 18 is misleading, an erroneous statement of the law, and ambiguous.

The first two sentences of the instruction are misleading, for they authorize the jury to place a value, if any, upon the factors set forth and "its fair market value." Thus the instruction authorizes an amount over and above the "fair market value." While the factors mentioned (except "maintenance by way of food"), under proper instructions, may be elements to be considered as having a bearing upon a determination of the "fair market value," it is error to instruct the jury that they have a value in addition to the "fair market value." The last sentence of the instruction is not sufficient to correct the error. Further, the instruction is ambiguous by virtue of its "amongst others" phrase at the end of the last sentence. This makes it possible for the jury to speculate and add the value of unknown factors as an additional amount to an award otherwise determined. A proper instruction would also state the date on which the value is to be determined.

In Donaldson v. Greenwood, 40 Wn.2d 238, 242 P.2d 1038 (1952), the court said:

> "Fair market value" means neither a panic price, auction value, speculative value, nor a value fixed by depressed or inflated prices. We have defined it as the amount of money which a purchaser willing, but not obliged, to buy the property would pay an owner willing, but not obligated, to sell it, taking into consideration all uses to which the property is adapted and might in reason be applied. Ozette R. Co. v. Grays Harbor County, 16 Wn. (2d) 459, 133 P. (2d) 983.

The judgment is reversed and the case is remanded for a new trial which, since no error has been assigned to the ascertainment of defendant's liability, shall be limited to a determination of the amount of plaintiff's damage.

Defendant (appellant) shall recover his costs on this appeal.

It is so ordered.

Questions & Notes

1. If you were on the jury, how would you decide the fair market value of the dog? Is it what an average dog buyer would pay, or is it the amount that a highest bidder at a national dog auction would pay? How does the attorney prove value?

2. How would you draft the instructions for the jury? If you were seeking to broaden the possible award of damages for a dog, what would you add to the jury instructions?

3. See **Alaimo v. Racetrack at Evangeline Downs, Inc.**, 893 So. 2d 190 (La. Ct. App. 3rd Cir. 2005). A horse breeder and owner brought suit against a racetrack for lost revenue due to the death of a thoroughbred racehorse. The racehorse collided with a negligently maintained gate at the racetrack and was subsequently euthanized. The breeder sought damages for future winnings the racehorse may have won and based the amount on the horse's racing history. The trial court awarded plaintiffs $38,000, but did not specify what the award was for. The Court of Appeals affirmed the trial court holding the award was not unreasonable based on the horse's racing history. Also see **Leblanc v. Underwriters at Lloyd's**, 402 So. 2d 292 (1981).

<><><><><><><><><><><><><><><><><><><><><><><><><><><><>

The primary concern of a plaintiff is in knowing just what elements will be comprised in a market value determination. In essence, anything that affects commercial value may be considered. Various courts have agreed that the following elements are appropriate to consider:

1. the pedigree of the animal;
2. the purchase price of the animal and the sale price of its littermates;
3. the special abilities or training of the animal, also prizes and awards;
4. the age and the general health of an animal;
5. the fact that the animal was pregnant.

What should happen if the market value is practically zero? A 2001 Alaska case suggested a modest alternative.

In the more recent case of Landers v. Municipality of Anchorage, we recognized that the value to the owner, rather than the fair market value, is the proper measure of damages "where the destroyed or lost property has no real market value or where the value of the property to the owner is greater than the market value." We applied this measure to *Landers's* lost photographs and videotapes, concluding that damages under this standard would include the cost of purchasing and developing the film and purchasing blank videotapes. In *Landers*, we also reaffirmed that damages for a chattel's subjective emotional or sentimental value to the owner were generally unavailable, concluding that such considerations were limited to the context of intentional infliction of emotional distress claims.

We agree with those courts that recognize that the actual value of the pet to the owner, rather than the fair market value, is sometimes the proper measure of the pet's value. In determining the actual value to the owner, it is reasonable to take into account the services provided by the dog. Where, as here, there may not be any fair market value for an adult dog, the "value to the owner may be based on such things as the cost of replacement, original cost, and cost to reproduce." Thus, an owner may seek reasonable replacement costs—including such items as the cost of purchasing a puppy of the same breed, the cost of immunization, the cost of neutering the pet, and the cost of comparable training. Or an owner may seek to recover the original cost of the dog, including the purchase price and, again, such investments as immunization, neutering, and training. Moreover, as some courts have recognized, it may be appropriate to consider the breeding potential of the animal, and whether the dog was purchased for the purpose of breeding with other purebreds and selling the puppies.

See **Mitchell v. Heinrichs**, 27 P. 3d 309 (Alaska 2001).

Section 6

Consequential Damages

When one party injures another's property, that party is liable not only for the loss of value of the property itself, but is also liable for the normal and foreseeable consequential damages that arise from the injury. These consequential damages are divided into two different categories: additional expenses and loss of income or loss of use. To claim an expense, the animal owner would have to show that the expenditure of funds would not have happened, but for the injury, and is directly related to the injury. Expenses such as veterinary bills are often incurred in an effort to save an animal (mitigate damages). As long as these are reasonable the court will normally award them. Some of the expenses awarded by courts include:

1. the cost of treatment and labor for sick cattle;

2. the increased feed expense;

3. the veterinarian's fee; and

4. the cost of searching for lost cattle.

While the death of a pet may cause the owner the most harm, injury to animals is the most common of events. Harm during pet grooming (a bailment, see Chapter 2) seems to occur with some regularity. In such circumstances the availability of consequential damages is critical to recovery by the plaintiff.

CASE BY CASE

Burgess v. Shampooch Pet Industries, Inc.

131 P. 3d 1248 (2006 Kan. App.)

JUDGE BUSER, P.J.

Factual and Procedural Background

On April 10, 2004, Burgess took Murphy to Shampooch in Kansas City, Kansas, for pet grooming services. Two days prior, on April 8, 2004, a veterinarian had examined Murphy and determined the dog was in good health. Moreover, Murphy appeared healthy when Burgess left her at Shampooch. Burgess returned later, retrieved the newly groomed Murphy and paid the $30 bill.

Upon leaving Shampooch, Burgess noticed Murphy was acting strangely and was limping. Burgess immediately returned to the business and a representative of Shampooch denied any responsibility for Murphy's injury. The following day, Burgess sought treatment for Murphy at Veterinary Specialty and Emergency Center in Overland Park, Kansas. On April 13, 2004, 3 days after her ill-fated grooming, Murphy underwent surgery to repair a dislocated hip. Veterinary treatment also included x-rays, blood work-up, anesthesia, intravenous fluids, sutures, and pain medications. As a result, Burgess incurred veterinary bills totaling $1,308.89. According to the district court, Burgess testified at trial that Murphy "was back to her usual self within a short time after her treatment."

Burgess filed a Chapter 61 petition for damages in Wyandotte County District Court alleging negligence by Shampooch caused Murphy's dislocated hip. Following a trial to the court, judgment was entered for Burgess and against Shampooch in the amount of $1,308.89 plus court costs. Shampooch filed a timely appeal.

The Measure of Damages Recoverable for Murphy's Injury

Shampooch contends the damages awarded should be limited to Murphy's market value. This contention is predicated on the general rule that when repairs can restore personal property to its previous condition, the measure of damages is the fair and reasonable cost of repairs not to exceed the value of the property before damage. See PIK Civ.3d 171.10. Shampooch asks this court to reverse the award of damages and remand the case to redetermine damages based on Murphy's market value. In the context of this request, it should be noted that at oral argument counsel for the parties stated that Murphy was originally purchased for $175. Shampooch further requests this court to conclude, as a matter of law, that there is a rebuttable presumption that a pet has a market value.

In response, Burgess tacitly acknowledges that Murphy may have value but observes:

> "[W]hat is the value of a wet face licking received first thing in the morning? To a 'cat person' it is probably nothing but to a dog owner who has raised her friend from a puppy it is like the Master Card ad—priceless. What is the value of years of companionship, of training, of shared love? To put a value on a family pet all of this must be considered."

Burgess argues in support of the district court's damage award, however, because by

> "allowing her the veterinary bills, the trial court put Burgess back into the position she was in prior to entering Shampooch Pet Grooming. She had a pet who could walk without pain, again. She did not have to find another pet, housebreak it, treat and care for it, feed it, walk it, love it and travel the many thousands of steps involved in a 13 year journey."

Several jurisdictions have found that where recovery is sought for a dog's injury, however, the owner is entitled to recover the reasonable veterinary expenses incurred in treating those injuries. See Kaiser v. United States, 761 F. Supp. 150 (D.D.C. 1991) ($1786.50 in veterinary fees awarded pursuant to the Federal Tort Claims Act for injury to dog shot by United States Capitol Police officer).

In evaluating the propriety of the district court's award of the cost of veterinary bills as damages in this case, we are mindful of the practical, common-sense approach traditionally employed by Kansas courts in determining the appropriate measure of damages:

> "While Kansas decisions give the courts a great deal of latitude in arriving at the proper measure of damages depend-

ing on the facts present, it appears that all of the various approaches at computing damages have the same ultimate goal: to make the damaged party whole.... '[T]he sundry rules for measuring damages are subordinate to the ultimate aim of making good the injury done or loss suffered and hence "[t]he answer rests in good sense rather than in a mechanical application of a single formula. [Citations omitted.]" ' " Thatcher, 14 Kan. App. 2d at 617, 797 P. 2d 162.

Consistent with this long-standing common-sense jurisprudence, we find the district court did not err in its award of damages to Burgess. We hold that when an injured pet dog with no discernable market value is restored to its previous health, the measure of damages may include, but is not limited to, the reasonable and customary cost of necessary veterinary care and treatment.

In the instant case, unlike other types of personal property, there are no true marketplaces that routinely deal in the buying and selling of previously owned pet dogs. Moreover, Murphy's real value to Burgess as a household pet is noneconomic and, as a result, is difficult if not impossible to appraise in the purely economic terms of market value. Or, as one court observed, "it is impossible to reduce to monetary terms the bond between man and dog, a relationship which has been more eloquently memorialized in literature and depicted on the motion picture screen." Zager v. Dimilia, 138 Misc. 2d 448, 524 N.Y.S. 2d 968 (1988).

Moreover, the award of the amount Burgess spent on veterinary bills is in accord with the very purpose of the law of damages — to make Burgess whole and return her to the position she was in prior to Shampooch's tortuous conduct. It can hardly be said that a lesser award — for example, Murphy's original purchase price of $175 depreciated over 13 years — would " 'make good the injury done' " 14 Kan. App.2d at 618, 797 P. 2d 162, or fairly and adequately compensate Burgess for her out-of-pocket expenses.

Affirmed.

Questions & Notes

1. How do you think the plaintiff proved the negligence?

2. If you represent the business, would you offer the cost of veterinary care at the beginning? If you represent the dog owner, would you accept an offer to cover the cost of veterinary care at the beginning of the lawsuit?

3. What if the cost were $6,000? How would you define reasonable cost? How much financial risk should be on the defendant? The state of Maryland has adopted a statute that specifically allows cost of veterinary care for harm to pets, but places a ceiling of $5,000 on the cost. See **Md. Cts. & Jud. Pro.** § 11-110. Is this reasonable?

Case Study 4A

In November 1995 the Grants go to the local pound and pick up George, a laid-back German Shepard. For five years George and the Grants live together in bliss. In November 2001 a neighbor who is mad at the Grants' son Bobby, who had run a car into neighbor's barn, finds George on his land and hits him with a board with such force that it shatters a hip of George. The Grants immediately take George to their normal veterinarian, who tries to treat George by setting the bone. However, after two days and an X-ray, it is clear that her effort wasn't working and she referred the Grants to a specialist on shattered bones. After two operations and one permanent pin being implanted, George recovered, keeping his leg, but having a permanent limp. Grants sue Neighbor for the following:

    1. Initial veterinary cost – $520
    2. Second veterinary cost – $1,200
    3. Physical therapy cost – $400
    4. Increased cost of special diet – $80
    5. Value of having to live with a permanent limp – $1,000

Make the best policy arguments for the plaintiff's claims. How do you think a court would rule under today's rules. How would you rule and why?

Section 7

Intrinsic Value

For pets, having no market value, one category of damages has been suggested as an alternative to market value, a pet animal's intrinsic value. The term "intrinsic" suggest a focus on the animal as an individual. However, as damages in reality have to relate to the value of the animal to the human owner/ keeper the use of this word is unclear.

> Intrinsic value does not include "sentimental value." Sherman, 146 Wash.App. at 871-872, 195 P.3d 539. As we held in Sherman, in determining intrinsic value the finder of fact must consider objective evidence of the dog's utility and services and not the value the owner attributes to the dog's companionship or other sentimental value.
>
> **Brinton v. Codoni**, 2009 WL 297006 (Wash. App. Div. 1, 2009).

Whether this will develop into a separate category of damages for injury to animals only future cases will decide. In 2004 a California jury awarded a dog owner $39,000 in damages, including $30,000 as the dog's intrinsic or special value after a dog died of liver failure while in the care of the defendants. Market value was $10. "This jury did not give an emotional distress award. This jury did not give a loss of companionship award. This jury did not give a punitive damage award. What it did was give a special value award." R. Scott Nolen, *www.avma. org/onlnews/javma/apr04/040415e.asp* (2004). The judgment was paid in full and an appeal was dismissed so there is no appeals court language affirming the position of the jury.

Section 8

Intentional Acts & Punitive Damages

It is important to distinguish between a cause of action and the damages recoverable if a cause of action exists. This is a particular issue in this topic. A "cause of action" is a statutory or common law tort recognized by a court to support the filing of a lawsuit. Sometimes courts do not do a good job of keeping these concepts apart, and it causes difficulty when trying to understand the state of the law. In this area one possible cause of action is the "intentional infliction of pain and suffering on a pet" (or perhaps "malicious injury" of a pet). The possible damages arising from such a tort could include market value, emotional distress of owner, and punitive damages. Some confusion arises because the elements necessary to show the cause of action are also some of the same considerations used in deciding whether to grant punitive damages.

First the cause of action: Historically, a cause of action has always existed for negligent destruction of property—that is, an animal. However, almost no court is comfortable with "negligent infliction of pain and suffering on a pet" as a new cause of action, a new tort.

> Accordingly, for clarification purposes, we now hold that dogs are personal property and damages for sentimental value, mental suffering, and emotional distress are not recoverable for the negligently inflicted death of a dog. **Carbasho v. Musulin**, 618 S.E. 2d 368 (W. Va. 2005).

In such cases, negligent destruction of personal property is still available to support a lawsuit, but the damages are limited to traditional analysis of value of property discussed earlier.

However, several courts have recognized the "intentional infliction" as a cause of action. In 2006 a court of the State of Washington acknowledged a cause of action for malicious injury of a pet. **Womack v. Von Rardon**, 135 P. 3d 542 (Wash. 2006) (boy set cat on fire). Having found the existence of such a cause of action, the court went on to say that such an action would support damages of emotional distress by the owner.

The case in the next section, **Rabideau v. City of Racine**, considers two causes of action, one based on intentional actions and the other on negligent actions. In both cases the cause of action is not focused on the destruction of personal property, but on the emotional harm caused to the owner. Their requirements for intentional actions are stricter than that of some other state courts like Washington. In part this is because they are looking at a broader traditional tort action: the "intentional infliction of emotional distress," which has as focus the actor's knowledge of the impact of the action on bystander/owner. The Washington court allowed a new tort where the focus is on whether the harm to the animal was intentional/grievous. Only time will tell as to whether other jurisdictions agree with the new path allowed by the Washington court.

Attorneys, realizing that intentional infliction of emotional distress does often allow a plaintiff to reach the jury, often try to stretch negligent actions into intentional actions even if the facts do not seem to justify the claim. See **Harasymiv v. Veterinary Surgical Associates**, 2003 WL 22183946 (Cal. App. 1 Dist), and **Anzalone v. Kragness**, 356 Ill. App. 3d 365 (2005).

Under many different causes of action—torts—one of the damages allowed is punitive damages. Punitive damages are not meant to compensate an owner for injury to his or her property, but to punish the person causing the injury for his or her unacceptable conduct. Negligence alone will not support a claim for punitive damages. The actions of the individual must show a malicious, willful, or reckless disregard for the rights of the animal and its owner. For example, in one case, a city employee hurled a trash can at a miniature dachshund while collecting the trash. The injuries killed the dog. The court allowed punitive damages based on the nature of the conduct. It is not necessary that the individual causing the harm know the owner, only that he be aware that the animal is, in all likelihood, owned by someone. **La Porte v. Assoc. Independents, Ins.**, 163 So. 2d 267 (Fla. 1964). For example, one jury awarded $7,500 in punitive damages for killing his neighbor's dogs with antifreeze-soaked meat. [Lisa Sink, *Man Ordered to Pay $7,500 for Poisoning Neighbors' Dogs*, Milwaukee J. Sentinel, Oct. 13, 2000, at 15B.]

Case Study 4B

On May 29, 1997, Susan Tuccio Heinrichs noticed two dogs running loose on her property. Heinrichs recognized one of the dogs, a MacKenzie River husky, as a dog that had been on her property repeatedly, without permission, over the previous two months. According to Heinrichs, she had unsuccessfully attempted to find the owner in the past and did not know at that time that Jennifer Mitchell owned the husky.

Heinrichs saw the dogs running near her livestock pen, which contained chickens and goats. One of the goats had just given birth to two kids and it was still bloody from the birth. Heinrichs perceived that the dogs were excited by the smell of the blood and were threatening her livestock.

Heinrichs grabbed her shotgun, left her house, and walked toward the dogs, which were about twenty-five to thirty feet away. After she walked a few feet, the dogs turned their attention to Heinrichs. Maintaining that she felt threatened for her own personal safety, Heinrichs shot Mitchell's dog. Immediately after the shooting, Heinrichs walked back into the house. Ten to fifteen minutes later, Mitchell discovered her dead pet. She confronted Heinrichs and then removed her dog from Heinrichs's property. Mitchell files suit seeking punitive damages. Defendant files an action for summary judgment on the issue of punitive damages. How do you rule?

See **Mitchell v. Heinrichs**, 27 P. 3d 309 (Alaska 2001).

The doctrine of punitive damages provides, in effect, a civil alternative to criminal actions, in that the court will seek to discourage or punish unacceptable conduct by allowing the equivalent of civil fines, particularly when the traditional measure of damages is not sufficiently large to discourage such conduct in the future.

One Florida case stated that a plaintiff's pleadings supported a claim for punitive damages when the defendants cremated a dog that had died while in their care, even though they had been requested to hold the dog for an autopsy. **Levien v. Knowles**, 197 So. 2d 329 (Fla. 1967). Another court upheld an award of $500 in punitive damages when government employees captured a cat and then killed it on the same day, in contravention of a state statute. **Wilson v. City of Eagar**, 297 N.W. 2d 146 (Minn. 1980).

In determining the appropriate amount for a punitive damage award, the jury should consider:

1. the degree of malice involved;
2. the nature of the interest invaded;
3. the amount needed to deter such conduct;
4. the cost of bringing the suit; and
5. the wealth of the defendant.

Each jurisdiction may have its own requirements that must be satisfied. Claims for punitive damages arising out of an injury to an animal do not differ significantly from any other claim for damages. Therefore, the general rules of each state should apply directly to animal cases.

Section 9

Mental Anguish or Suffering of the Owner

The previous discussion of damages has focused on the economic injury to the animal's owner. This, however, may not represent the full extent of the loss incurred by the owner or caregiver. When dealing with pets in particular, emotional ties may have developed between the owner and the animal of a nature not unlike the ties between a parent and a child. As an animal becomes important in the daily life of an individual, the injury or death of the animal represents an increasingly significant threat to the mental well-being of the owner. A harm of this nature is categorized as either mental pain and suffering or, in a less extreme situation, loss of companionship (considered in the next section). Both of these bases of recovery deal with harm to the mental rather than physical well-being of a human.

To a large extent the recovery for the destruction or harm of pets under a theory of mental pain and suffering is subsumed within the broad policy and practical conflicts on the issue within each jurisdiction. The judicial system has shown a general reluctance to award damages for mental pain and suffering. This is particularly true when the distress is caused by the loss of a pet. Historically, two arguments have been suggested in justifying the courts' reluctance: "mental pain and suffering" were considered evanescent, intangible, peculiar, and entirely idiosyncratic; there were also questions as to the ability of the judicial system to quantify damages and to separate legitimate claims from the fraudulent or frivolous ones.

> **A Focusing Question**
>
> How much compensation should a parent receive for the negligent injury of a child (leg is broken in three places; run over by a car)? How much should a grandparent receive?

The 1970s and early 1980s saw a greater willingness to award damages for mental pain and suffering in some jurisdictions. In so doing the courts have sought to find the proper balance between two important considerations. There has been growing acceptance within the medical profession that mental distress is a real, predictable, and observable consequence of certain events. (This can occur with the disruption of emotional relationships with other beings.) This is particularly predictable if the injury or death of the being is observed. There has been a willingness in some courts to expand the legal concept of personal injury to include this new knowledge. In so doing the courts are seeking to fulfill the fundamental tort concept of full recovery for all unlawful injuries. On the other side of the issue, however, courts are reluctant to impose unlimited or unpredictable liability on a defendant. If the door is open for recovery in limited situations, based strictly on mental pain and anguish, where is the line to be drawn? What is the financial extent of the duty? How will it be measured? Is the defendant liable to all who see an event, such as the hitting of a cat by a car? Is he liable to those who hear the event or are told about it? What is a fair burden (risk) to impose upon a negligent actor (or an intentional actor)? How far will the judicial system expand the concept of foreseeable consequences? To date, the courts have drawn the line at various places. As a result there is a spectrum of holdings that make generalizations difficult and suggest that the development of this legal issue is not yet complete.

While some courts state the issue in terms of whether or not an award for mental distress will be allowed, in reality the question is whether or not a claim for mental distress constitutes a cause of action. The ultimate direction of this discussion is the creation of a new tort, the freedom from negligent infliction of mental distress.

CASE BY CASE

Rabideau v. City of Racine
627 N.W. 2d 795 (Wis. 2001)

At the outset, we note that we are uncomfortable with the law's cold characterization of a dog, such as Dakota, as mere "property." Labeling a dog "property" fails to describe the value human beings place upon the companionship that they enjoy with a dog. A companion dog is not a fungible item, equivalent to other items of personal property. A companion dog is not a living room sofa or dining room furniture. This term inadequately and inaccurately describes the relationship between a human and a dog.

The association of dogs and humans is longstanding. Dogs have been a part of human domestic life since 6,300 B.C. See Debra Squires-Lee, In Defense of Floyd: Appropriately Valuing Companion Animals in Tort, 70 N.Y.U. L. Rev. 1059, 1064 (1995). Archaeologists have uncovered a 12,000-year-old burial site in which a human being and a dog lay buried together. "The arm of the person was arranged on the dog's shoulder, as if to emphasize the bonds that existed between these two individuals during life." Id. (internal quotation marks and footnote omitted). Dogs are so much a part of the human experience that we need not cite to authority when we note that dogs work in law enforcement, assist the blind and disabled, perform traditional jobs such as herding animals and providing security, and, of course, dogs continue to provide humans with devoted friendship.

Rabideau and Officer Jacobi were neighbors. On March 31, 1999, Officer Jacobi had just returned home. Across the street, Rabideau was returning home as well. Dakota jumped out of Rabideau's truck. He crossed the street to the Jacobi house where Jed, the Jacobi's Chesapeake Bay retriever, was in the yard.

There is significant disagreement between the parties concerning what subsequently occurred. The City argued that Dakota came onto the Jacobi property and attacked Jed. Officer Jacobi, it is contended, shouted at Dakota to no effect. The City argues that Officer Jacobi, fearing for the safety of Jed, and for the safety of his wife and child who were nearby, fired a number of shots with his service revolver. Dakota moved toward the street and turned his head and was snarling. Officer Jacobi, believing the dog was about to charge, fired a third time and struck Dakota.

On the other hand, Rabideau contends that Dakota was sniffing Jed, not biting or acting aggressively. She asserts that she called Dakota and was crossing the street to retrieve him when shots rang out.

Although both parties agree that three shots were fired, Rabideau maintains that Dakota was stepping off the curb toward her when he was hit by Officer Jacobi's second shot. Rabideau asserts that while Dakota was struggling to crawl away, Officer Jacobi fired again and missed.

Two days after the shooting occurred, Rabideau was informed that Dakota died. Upon hearing this news, she collapsed and was given medical treatment.

A.

Rabideau argues that the tort of negligent infliction of emotional distress to a bystander should encompass the facts of this case. Our tort law recognizes a claim for damages where a bystander suffers great emotional distress after witnessing an accident or its gruesome aftermath involving death or serious injury to a close relative. See Bowen v. Lumbermens Mut. Cas. Co., 183 Wis. 2d 627, 517 N.W.2d 432 (1994). The elements of the claim are: "'(1) that the defendant's conduct [in the underlying accident] fell below the applicable standard of care, (2) that the plaintiff suffered an injury [severe emotional distress], and (3) that the defendant's conduct was a cause-in-fact of the plaintiff's injury.'" Wis JI—Civil 1510 Comment (quoting Bowen, 183 Wis. 2d at 632.) Rabideau's complaint sets forth these elements.

Nevertheless, even if a plaintiff sets forth the elements of a negligence claim, a court may determine that liability is precluded by public policy considerations. Gritzner v. Michael R., 2000 WI 68, ¶26, 235 Wis. 2d 781, 611 N.W.2d 906. Before a court makes such a determination, it is typically the better practice to submit the case to the jury. Id. If, however, the facts of the case are not complex and the attendant public policy issues are presented in full, then this court may determine before trial if liability is precluded by public policy. Id. Accordingly, we turn next to a consideration of the public policy concerns presented by this issue.

The *Bowen* analysis noted that two concerns have historically shaped the development of the tort of negligent infliction of emotional distress. These concerns are (1) establishing that the claim is genuine, and (2) ensuring that allowing recovery will not place an unfair burden on the tortfeasor. *Bowen*, 183 Wis. 2d at 655.

Where, as in the present case, the issue presented is negligent infliction of emotional distress on a bystander, *Bowen* identified three public policy factors to be applied in an effort to establish that the claim is genuine, the tortfeasor is not unfairly burdened, and that other attendant public policy considerations are not contravened. Id. at 655-58. First, the victim must have been killed or suffered a serious injury. Second, the plaintiff and victim must be related as spouses, parent-child, grandparent-grandchild or siblings. Third, "the plaintiff must have observed an extraordinary event, namely the incident and injury or the scene soon after the incident with the injured victim at the scene." Id. at 633.

We need not address each of these factors because it is plain that the victim in this case is not related to Rabideau as a spouse, parent, child, sibling, grandparent or grandchild. Accordingly, she cannot maintain a claim for negligent infliction of emotional distress.

Rabideau urges that we extend this category to include companion animals. In her words, "[a]nyone who has owned and loved a pet would agree that in terms of emotional trauma, watching the death of a pet is akin to losing a close relative." Further, she contends that we need not engage in an analysis of whether companion animals are "family," but should instead examine the rationale supporting the limitation to certain family members. Rabideau argues that the limitation of claims to family members is a means of assuring forseeability as well as a reasonable limitation of the liability of a negligent tortfeasor. According to Rabideau, the bond between companion animals and humans is one that is sufficiently substantial to ensure that these concerns are met.

We agree, as we must, that humans form important emotional connections that fall outside the class of spouse, parent, child, grandparent, grandchild or sibling. We recognized this in *Bowen*, and repeat here, that emotional distress may arise as a result of witnessing the death or injury of a victim who falls outside the categories established in tort law. However, the relationships between a victim and a spouse, parent, child, grandparent, grandchild or sibling are deeply embedded in the organization of our law and society. The emotional loss experienced by a bystander who witnessed the negligent death or injury of one of these categories of individuals is more readily addressed because it is less likely to be fraudulent and is a loss that can be fairly charged to the tortfeasor. The emotional harm occurring from witnessing the death or injury of an individual who falls into one of these relationships is serious, compelling, and warrants special recognition. Id. at 657.

We concluded in *Bowen* that for the present time these tort claims would be limited; we reach the same conclusion in this case. We note that this rule of nonrecovery applies with equal force to a plaintiff who witnesses as a bystander the negligent injury of a best friend who is human as it does to a plaintiff whose best friend is a dog.

Had Rabideau been a bystander to the negligent killing of her best human friend, our negligence analysis would be complete. However, as we have previously noted the law categorizes dogs as property. We turn, therefore, to consider whether Rabideau can maintain a claim for negligent infliction of emotional distress arising from property loss.

In Kleinke v. Farmers Cooperative Supply & Shipping, 202 Wis. 2d 138, 145, 549 N.W.2d 714 (1996), we concluded that under Wisconsin's formulation of tort law, "it is unlikely that a plaintiff could ever recover for the emotional distress caused by negligent damage to his or her property." This conclusion was founded upon public policy.

The public policy analysis in *Kleinke* drew upon the reasoning of *Bowen*. In *Bowen* this court listed six public policy factors addressed by courts when considering the authenticity and fairness of an emotional distress claim. These various public policy considerations set forth in *Bowen*, and cited in *Kleinke*, are:

1) Whether the injury is too remote from the negligence;

2) whether the injury is wholly out of proportion to the culpability of the negligent tortfeasor;

3) whether in retrospect it appears too extraordinary that the negligence should have brought about the harm;

4) whether allowance of recovery would place an unreasonable burden on the negligent tortfeasor;

5) whether allowance of recovery would be too likely to open the way to fraudulent claims; or

6) whether allowance of recovery would enter a field that has no sensible or just stopping point.

In this case we need only examine one of the *Bowen-Kleinke* factors to conclude that there is no basis for recovery here. This factor concerns whether allowance of recovery would enter a field that has no sensible or just stopping point. Rabideau suggests that limiting liability to the human companion of a companion animal who is killed may satisfy this concern. We find this proposed resolution unsatisfactory. First, it is difficult to define with precision the limit of the class of individuals who fit into the human companion category. Is the particular human companion every family member? the owner of record or primary caretaker? a roommate? Second, it would be difficult to cogently identify the class of companion animals because the human capacity to form an emotional bond extends to an enormous array of living creatures. Our vast ability to form these bonds adds to the richness of life. However, in this case the public policy concerns relating to identifying genuine claims of emotional distress, as well as charging tortfeasors with financial burdens that are fair, compel the conclusion that the definition suggested by Rabideau will not definitively meet public policy concerns.

Based upon all the above, we conclude that Rabideau cannot maintain a claim for the emotional distress caused by negligent damage to her property.

B.

Next, we consider Rabideau's claim of intentional infliction of emotional distress. Four elements must be established for a plaintiff to maintain such a claim. A plaintiff must demonstrate:

1) that the defendant's conduct was intentioned to cause emotional distress;

2) that the defendant's conduct was extreme and outrageous;

3) that the defendant's conduct was a cause-in-fact of the plaintiff's emotional distress; and

4) that the plaintiff suffered an extreme disabling emotional response to the defendant's conduct.

The first *Alsteen* element requires the plaintiff to demonstrate that the defendant acted with the intent to cause emotional harm. "One who by extreme and outrageous conduct intentionally causes severe emotional distress to another is subject to liability for such emotional distress and for bodily harm resulting from it." Id. at 358 (emphasis omitted). In this case, there is no material issue of fact in the record that suggests that Officer Jacobi acted for the purpose of causing Rabideau emotional harm.

Rabideau argues that she need only show that Officer Jacobi acted intentionally when he shot Dakota. She contends that by shooting Dakota while she was present, Officer Jacobi would have known that his act would cause her severe emotional distress. Rabideau argues that such knowledge is tantamount to intentionally causing severe emotional distress because "a person is presumed to intend 'the natural and probable consequences of his acts voluntarily and knowingly performed.'" Haessley v. Germantown Mut. Ins. Co., 213 Wis. 2d 108, 118, 569 N.W.2d 804 (Ct. App. 1997) (quoting State v. Gould, 56 Wis. 2d 808, 814, 202 N.W.2d 903 (1973)).

The presumption cited by Rabideau from *Haessley* is generally applied in criminal cases. See Hawpetoss v. State, 52 Wis. 2d 71, 80, 187 N.W.2d 823 (1971). Rabideau's application in this case of the general rule that an accused is presumed to intend the natural and probable consequences of his act obfuscates what is required by the first element of this cause of action. The plaintiff must establish that the purpose of the conduct was to cause emotional distress. There is no question that Officer Jacobi intended to fire his weapon at Dakota. However, there is no evidence to indicate he did so to cause emotional distress to Rabideau. Certainly that was a byproduct, but that is insufficient standing alone.

This is a limitation upon the cause of action for the intentional infliction of emotional distress. Anderson v. Continental Ins. Co., 85 Wis. 2d 675, 694-95, 271 N.W.2d 368 (1978). There must be something more than a showing that the defendant intentionally engaged in the conduct that gave rise to emotional distress in the plaintiff; the plaintiff must show that the conduct was engaged in for the purpose of causing emotional distress. While intent may be evidenced by inferences from words, conduct or the circumstances in which events occurred, in the present case there is no asserted fact as to this element. Accordingly, we are not persuaded by Rabideau's argument, and we affirm the court of appeals' grant of summary judgment.

II.

Although we affirm the court of appeals' decision as to Rabideau's claims for damages based upon emotional distress, we hold that the court erred in its conclusion that Rabideau's claim did not seek damages for lost property. A claim for damages for property loss as the result of Officer Jacobi's action is the most conventional claim Rabideau could have brought, and is without doubt the most widely recognized claim that arises when an animal is killed. See 1 Dan B. Dobbs, Law of Remedies § 5.15(3), at 898 (2d ed. 1993); Robin Cheryl Miller, Annotation, Damages for Killing or Injuring Dog, 61 A.L.R.5th 635 (1998). We therefore hold that Rabideau's complaint, liberally construed, also encompassed a demand for damages for property loss. We decline to further address the proper means to measure this property loss or whether other elements, such as veterinary expenses incurred in treating a companion animal's injuries, may be recovered.

Affirmed

Notes

1. For a discussion of the case see, Janice M. Pintar, *Negligent Infliction of Emotional Distress and the Fair Market Value Approach in Wisconsin: the Case for Extending Tort Protection to Companion Animals and Their Owners*, 2002 Wis. L. Rev. 735 (2002). In a 2009 case, the Vermont Supreme Court held no cause of action for Negligent Infliction of Emotional Distress when prescribed pills killed plaintiff's cats. Goodby v. Vetpharm, Inc., 974 A. 2d 1269 (Vt. 2009). Also see **Johnson v. Douglas**, 723 N.Y.S. 2d 627, 628 (N.Y. Sup. Ct. 2001) ('[S]ome pet owners have become so attached to their family pets that the animals are considered members of the family.... However, the law is clear that pet owners cannot recover for emotional distress based upon an alleged negligent or malicious destruction of a dog....'); Also see, **Krasnecky v. Meffen**, 777 N.E. 2d 1286, 56 Mass. App. Ct. 418 (2002), appeal denied, 782 N.E. 2d 516 (2003). Plaintiff had sheep that

were killed by defendant's dogs. Rather than market value, the plaintiff specifically sought damages under emotional distress. Appeals court held that form of damages was not available to the plaintiff.

> "In the circumstances, it was reasonably foreseeable that the plaintiffs would suffer emotional distress upon learning of the slaughter of the sheep and seeing their bodies. It would be illogical, however, to accord the plaintiffs greater rights than would be recognized in the case of a person who suffers emotional distress as a result of the tortuously caused death of a member of his immediate family. It has been explained in such a case that limiting liability on the basis of admittedly arbitrary factors such as presence or temporal proximity must be employed for policy reasons to prevent an unreasonable expansion of liability for the multitude of injuries that could fall within the bare principle of reasonable foreseeability."

But see a lower Conn. court, in an unpublished opinion, allows an action to proceed based upon the claim that a pet owner witnessed the beating of her dog, leading to its death. **Vaneck v. Drew**, 2009 WL 1333918.

2. For intentional infliction of emotional distress, see **Brown v. Muhlenbery Township**, 269 F. 3d 205 (3d Cir. 2001). Federal court finds that state would allow that cause of action against police officer who shot pet dog while owner was watching.

For updated material on the issue of damages to animals see the website of the Animal Legal and Historical Center and the topic on pet damages (*www.animallaw.info/topics/spuspetdamages.htm*). The website has a table of cases, with over 60 cases in full text.

Section 10

Loss of Companionship

The immediate shock of the harm to a pet results in one kind of mental pain and suffering. This is frequently succeeded by a long-term feeling of loss of the animal's companionship. To the extent that a particular pet is part of the family relationship, some attempt can be made to compensate for the loss. The most extreme situation may be when the pet is owned by an elderly person who lives without other humans. Frequently in such cases the pet has, in effect, become the family for that individual.

One Florida case allowed recovery for the "peculiar" value of a dog to its owner. A 1987 Illinois case, while disallowing loss of companionship as a separate cause of action, would have allowed it as part of the damage calculation and distinguished it from recovery for emotional distress that requires the owner to have been in the zone of danger when the events occurred. An earlier New York case not only allowed damages based on loss of companionship, but also on loss of protective value (but total damages awarded only came to $550). In 1988, Pennsylvania specifically disallowed this measure of damages, stating:

> The appellants also contend in Count II that they would be entitled to damages for loss of companionship due to their dog's death. This assertion is clearly without merit. Companionship is included in the concept of consortium, which is a right growing out of a marriage relationship giving to each spouse the right to the companionship, society and affection of each other in their life together. **Burns v. Pepsi-Cola Metropolitan Bottling Company**, 353 Pa. Super. 571, 510 A. 2d 810 (1986). Under no circumstances, under the law of Pennsylvania, may there be recovery for loss of companionship due to the death of an animal. **Daughen v. Fox**, 539 A. 2d 858 (1988).

Also see **Carbasho v. Musulin**, 217 West. Va. 359, 618 S.E. 2d 368 (2005). Dog owner brought action against a motorist whose car struck and fatally injured a dog. Court held that owner could not recover damages for the loss of companionship she suffered. The same holding was found in **Pickford v. Masion**, 98 P. 3d 1232 (Wash. 2004) (no cause of action for destruction of companionship relationship with a dog). The Court considered emotional distress different from loss of companionship. The court noted that "such an extension of duty and liability is more appropriately made by the legislature." Again, the same holding was reached in **Petco Animal Supplies, Inc. v. Schuster**, 2004 WL 903930 (Tex. App. 2004) (overturning a verdict of $47,000 which included $10,000 each for emotional anguish, loss of companionship, and punitive damages).

Another trial court has allowed this category of damages. On May 8, 2005, Seattle District Court Judge Barbar Linde ordered Wallace Gray to pay $45,480 to Paula Roemer for the fatal mauling of a cat by a dog. The award included $30,000 for the loss of the cat and $15,000 for emotional distress. It was not appealed, thus higher court confirmation will not be possible.

It is worth noting that there have been a number of juries and judges at the trial level that allow extensive claims of damages, such as loss of companionship, for plaintiffs with harmed or killed animals, but the appeals courts usually reverse when the case is considered on appeal. This suggests that there is a social need for new measures of damages but that the conceptual development of the theory of the law is not yet at the same point.

Section 11

Noneconomic, Nonemotional Value

In the case of the death or serious injury of pets, perhaps the better focus for a new theory of damages is on the value that the animal represented to the owner before the harm occurred rather than the suffering after the event. Not sentimental value, but other values. For example, studies have shown that the presence of pets helps the physical well-being of the owner by lowering blood pressure and boosting immunity. (See Josh Fischman, *The Pet Prescription*, U.S. News & World Report, Dec. 12, 2005 at 72.) Lower human health care costs may be shown to relate to pet ownership. Likewise, the presence of pets relates to general quality of life. See generally Sonia S. Waisman & Barbara R. Newell, *Recovery of "Non-economic" Damages for Wrongful Killing or Injury of Companion Animals: A Judicial and Legislative Trend*, 7 Animal L. 45 (2001):

The Significance of the Bond Has Been Further Documented in Recent Health Studies

Studies indicate that beyond loss of companionship and pure emotional distress, certain plaintiffs may be able to demonstrate entitlement to damages for bodily injury as well when an animal companion is wrongfully killed or injured. By the mid-1980s, there was considerable evidence indicating animal companions had the capacity to reduce the frequency of serious disease and to prolong life. One study of veterans, for example, identified a positive correlation between morale and living with a companion animal, and further supported previous findings that close contact with companion animals is associated with superior health status.

In the late 1980s and early 1990s, a study was conducted to examine prospectively the independent effects of companion animals, social support, disease severity, and other psychosocial factors on one-year survival after acute myocardial infarction. The researchers concluded the study provided "strong evidence" that companion animals, and dogs in particular, promote "cardiovascular health independent of social support and the physiological severity of the illness." The report noted previous findings that companion animals decrease their human companions' anxiety and sympathetic nervous system arousal in response to stressors. The report also noted that Medicaid recipients with animal companions visited their physicians less frequently than those without animals.

A similar study in the early 1990s compared risk factors for cardiovascular disease in people who shared their lives with animal companions and those who did not. The study demonstrated that those with animal companions had significantly lower systolic blood pressure and plasma triglycerides than those without animals. The researchers suggested further investigation of the positive correlation between companion animals and the prevention of cardiovascular disease.

Further evidence of that positive correlation was presented in a recent study of stockbrokers already taking medication for hypertension, wherein researchers found those who adopted an animal companion reduced by half the increase in blood pressure that accompanied stress. Moreover when participants were undergoing stressful verbal and mathematics tests, researchers found that companion animals calmed the participants the most, while the spouse caused the most stress.

In other studies, scientists have demonstrated that petting an animal releases the same endorphins as those which contribute to the so-called "runner's high" experienced by joggers; and that dogs are "powerful social catalysts" who make it easier for people to connect with other people and be healthier as a result.

Section 12

Statutory Provisions for Damages

Given the general unwillingness of the courts to expand the common law concepts of damages for the pain and suffering of an owner, upon the death of pet, it was inevitable that some state legislatures have taken up the issue. Since 2000 several states have adopted new laws to address these issues.

In 2000 Tennessee became the first state to enact legislation that allows companion animal owners to recover for emotional injuries when their pets are wrongfully killed. Tenn. Code Ann. § 44-17-403. The measure allows pet owners (dogs & cats only) to recover up to $5,000 in noneconomic damages "[i]f a person's pet is killed or sustains injuries which result in death caused by the unlawful and intentional, or negligent, act of another or the animal of another, ..." In addition, the statute defines noneconomic damages in terms of loss of "expected society, companionship, and love and affection of the companion animal."

Illinois has what may be the most comprehensive consideration of the topic to date. A few of the highlights of the law include:

- applies only to intentional acts against pets;
- specifically allows veterinary cost, attorney fees and cost of prosecution;
- provides for damages relating to emotional distress of the owner (no maximum is provided);
- provides for punitive or exemplary damages of not less than $500 or more $25,000.

510 ILCS 70/16.3 – Civil Actions

§ 16.3. Civil actions. Any person who has a right of ownership in an animal that is subjected to an act of aggravated cruelty under Section 3.02 or torture under Section 3.03 in violation of this Act or in an animal that is injured or killed as a result of actions taken by a person who acts in bad faith under subsection (b) of Section 3.06 or under Section 12 of this Act may bring a civil action to recover the damages sustained by that owner. Damages may include, but are not limited to, the monetary value of the animal, veterinary expenses incurred on behalf of the animal, any other expenses incurred by the owner in rectifying the effects of the cruelty, pain, and suffering of the animal, and emotional distress suffered by the owner. In addition to damages that may be proven, the owner is also entitled to punitive or exemplary damages of not less than $500 but not more than $25,000 for each act of abuse or neglect to which the animal was subjected. In addition, the court must award reasonable attorney's fees and costs actually incurred by the owner in the prosecution of any action under this Section.

Connecticut has also passed a statute dealing with the same topic and it tracks Illinois except that it does not provide for emotional distress damages, but does allow exemplary damages. C.G.S.A. § 22-351a.

Questions & Notes

1. Do you think that the Illinois statute strikes the correct balance of the interests of the various parties? Does it go too far? Suggest a modification of the law.

2. Tennessee covers negligence acts, but Illinois and Connecticut do not. Which do you prefer? Why?

3. Is veterinary malpractice covered by this statute? Should it be? How would you bring it in?

4. Part of the debate about awarding damages when the issue arises in the context of a pet veterinary malpractice claim is whether increasing damages awarded to plaintiffs would result in increased cost to veterinarians, in turn increasing cost to pet owners.

   "If soft or non-economic compensatory damages were allowed, costs of vets would zoom, and many animals would not get the care they need or would be put to sleep when not absolutely necessary," Schwartz said." Victor Schwartz was lobbyist for Animal Health Institute. From Judy Sarasohn, Tort Watch for Animal Lovers Washington Post, *December 29, 2005; A21, www.washingtonpost.com/wp-dyn/content/article/2005/12/28/AR2005122801383_pf.html.*

   For a full discussion that suggests no significant increase in the cost of veterinary care if damages awarded should increase, see Christopher Green, *The Future of Veterinary Malpractice Liability in the Case of Companion Animals,* 10 Animal L. 163 (2004) available at *www.animallaw.info/journals/jo_pdf/vol10_p163.pdf.* For a detailed consideration of the issue that rejects the call for noneconomic damages by the lobbyist who is also a leading scholar in the field of torts see Victor E. Schwartz and Emily J. Laird, *Non-Economic Damages in Pet Litigation: The Serious Need to Preserve a Rational Rule,* 33 Pepp. L. Rev. 227–73 (2006).

   > **Think About It**
   >
   > How long will it be before the pain and suffering of the pet will be recoverable?

5. What do you think? From a public policy point of view are increasing damages available to plaintiff pet owners a good or bad idea?

Problem

Consider drafting a statute for your state. What are the key terms that have to be defined? What level of damages would you allow? Should you distinguish negligent acts from intentional acts?

CHAPTER 5

State Regulation of Ownership

This chapter's focus is on the scope of power that the government, at the state and local level, can assert over domestic animals and their human owners, and in turn, the limits on the exercise of that government power.

Section 1

Police Power Generally

Individuals have the right to own, possess, use, and transfer title of personal property, and therefore animals. In the absence of a law to the contrary, a person may possess any animal that they might desire. However, with increasing frequency, society, through its laws, is seeking to control many aspects of animal ownership. Some common areas of concern include: the movement of animals between states; the registration and licensing of animals (particularly dogs); the keeping of exotic pets; the control of contagious and infectious diseases in animal populations; and the destruction of animals, particularly dogs, that pose a risk to humans or other animals. At the local level of government, many of the animal issues arise in the context of the zoning laws. These laws often attempt to control the number, type, and conditions of animals possessed by local citizens. Because the legal issues are basically the same for each category, the following discussion will consider police power generally, with examples from all types of animal issues in each section. The law is now the mechanism that balances the competing interest between those who wish the benefits of animal ownership against those who do not wish to deal with the risks of domestic animals.

"Police power" is a term of art within the legal world that refers to the power of the 50 states — historically derived from the sovereign power of the King of England — to pass legislation that is binding upon the members of that society. Any time a new law is passed by a legislature, or a regulation is promulgated by an agency under a law, it is an exercise of the police power. While at times this power may seem limitless, such is not the case. In our system it is the judiciary's role to determine whether or not a particular law or regulation is a proper exercise of police power. If the exercise of police power is found to be improper, then, in effect, the courts have declared the law void and unenforceable. It is difficult to find recent examples in which a court has found an exercise of police power over animals improper. Nevertheless, there are real limitations that exist and restrict the scope of the legislature's powers.

Generally, when testing the appropriateness of a law the court will first decide if the law is under the umbrella of the police power. Does the law represent an exercise of authority to further a state's legitimate interest in the public health, safety, and welfare of its people?

Exercise of Police Power by State and Local Government

Interference with Property Allowed

Public Health		Public Safety	Public Welfare
- Nuisance - Transmittable Disease		- Fire Control - Exotic Animal Control	- Zoning - Wildlife Protection
Quarantine of an animal	Taking & killing animal to test for disease	Prohibition of the possession of dangerous dogs	How much land to possess a horse? No possession of endangered species.

Assuming that the law deals with an appropriate topic (risk of dog bites to the public), then the second question is whether the restrictions of the law are rationally related to that lawful interest (a law that sought to reduce the dog bite problem by shooting on sight all dogs over 40 pounds found off a leash in public places would fail this rational relationship test). Third, assuming that the topic is appropriate and the provisions are rationally related, the court will set aside a law as inappropriate only if it violates some constitutional right of a citizen (this can be a state constitution, but is usually the federal constitution).

The criminal laws prohibiting cruelty against animals and requiring care of animals are exercises of the police power, are subject to police power and constitutional limitation. This will be considered in the next two chapters.

Section 2

Limitations on Police Power: Constitutional Rights

Even assuming there is a proper exercise of police power, an action may nevertheless be stricken down if it violates an individual's constitutional rights. An exercise of police power is improper, and therefore void, if it interfered with any of the constitutionally protected rights of an individual or with existing federal law (statute or constitutional authority). The three individual rights most often asserted as a limitation on the state exercise of police power in the animal area are: lack of due process accorded the individual (Fifth and Fourteenth Amendments), lack of equal protection under the law (Fourteenth Amendment), and improper taking of private property (Fifth Amendment). (The rights of free speech and free exercise of religion often impose limitations on police power in other areas of government, but seldom are used with animal issues.)

One potential conflict exists over whether a state should attempt to restrict the use of animals as part of sacrificial rites in rituals performed by religious groups. If the courts feel that a legitimate religious organization is involved, and the general cruelty laws are not being violated, then it would be difficult for the state to justify control unless further issues of public health, safety, or welfare are involved. **Church of the Lukumi Babalu Aye v. City of Hialeah**, 508 U.S. 520 (1993).

.

CASE BY CASE

Toledo v. Tellings

871 N.E. 2d 1152 (Oh. Sup. Ct. 2007)

Moyer, C.J.

Appellant, the city of Toledo, appeals from the judgment of the Court of Appeals of Lucas County that held R.C. 955.11 and 955.22 and Toledo Municipal Code 505.14 unconstitutional. For the following reasons, we reverse the judgment of the court of appeals.

Appellee, Paul Tellings, a resident of the city of Toledo, owned three dogs identified as pit bulls. Tellings was charged by the city for violating Toledo Municipal Code 505.14(a) and R.C. 955.22. The Toledo Municipal Code limits ownership of vicious dogs, as defined in R.C. 955.11, or dogs commonly known as pit bulls or pit bull mixed breeds, to one in each household, and the Ohio Revised Code requires an owner of a pit bull to obtain liability insurance for damages, injuries, or death that might be caused by the dog.

Tellings challenged the constitutionality of Toledo Municipal Code 505.14(a) and R.C. 955.22 and 955.11(A)(4)(a)(iii), which includes pit bull in the definition of "vicious dog." The trial court conducted a hearing on appellee's motion, and several witnesses testified for both parties regarding the traits and characteristics of pit bulls. The court found that as a breed, pit bulls are not more dangerous than other breeds but that the evidence supported the city's claim that pit bulls present dangers in an urban setting.

The trial court found that property rights are subject to a government's police powers. The court stated: "The fact that such legislation may have an adverse effect on a segment of the dog population not presenting a danger to the public does not make the legislation overbroad. Legislation will only be considered overbroad if it is applicable to conduct protecting a fundamental constitutional right * * * and this does not include the category of ownership of dogs." The court found that Tellings's evidence did not prove beyond a reasonable doubt that Toledo Municipal Code 505.14 was unconstitutional [FN1]

FN1. The trial court found only Toledo Municipal Code 505.14 unconstitutional, which was the law specifically challenged in the caption of Tellings's motion to dismiss, though he did argue the constitutionality of Toledo Municipal Code 505.14 and R.C. 955.11 and 955.22 in the action. When reviewing the decision of the trial court, the court of appeals reviewed the constitutionality of all three laws.

In a split decision, the court of appeals reversed the trial court, holding that R.C. 955.11 and 955.22 and Toledo Municipal Code 505.14 were unconstitutional.

First, the court of appeals held that R.C. 955.11 and 955.22 and Toledo Municipal Code 505.14 were unconstitutional because the three laws violated procedural due process. In Cowan, we held that "R.C. 955.22 violates the constitutional right to procedural due process insofar as it failed to provide dog owners a meaningful opportunity to be heard on the issue of whether a dog is 'vicious' or 'dangerous' as defined in R.C. 955.11(A)(1)(a) and (A)(4)(a)." Id. at syllabus. In this case, the court of appeals held that because Tellings did not "have an opportunity under [R.C. 955.22] to offer evidence that his pit bulls were not vicious in order to refute the charges,"Tellings, 2006-Ohio-975, 2006 WL 513946, at ¶ 48, the laws were unconstitutional.

The court of appeals also held that the laws violated Tellings's rights to equal protection and substantive due process because, once the trial court had determined that the American Pit Bull terrier was not inherently dangerous, the laws were not rationally related to a legitimate state interest. The court of appeals stated that the evidence presented at the trial court had disproved the presumption that pit bulls are inherently dangerous.

Finally, the court of appeals held that the three laws were unconstitutional because they were void for vagueness. The court of appeals stated that it was "troubled by the lack of an exact statutory definition of 'pit bull' " and the "highly subjective nature of the identification process." Tellings, 2006-Ohio-975, 2006 WL 513946, at ¶ 73.

R.C. 955.11 states:

"(A) As used in this section:

(4)(a) 'Vicious dog' means a dog that, without provocation and subject to division (A)(4)(b) of this section, meets any of the following:

(i) Has killed or caused serious injury to any person;

(ii) Has caused injury, other than killing or serious injury, to any person, or has killed another dog.

(iii) Belongs to a breed that is commonly known as a pit bull dog. The ownership, keeping, or harboring of such a breed of dog shall be prima-facie evidence of the ownership, keeping, or harboring of a vicious dog."

R.C. 955.22(A) states:

> As used in this section, 'dangerous dog' and 'vicious dog' have the same meanings as in section 955.11 of the Revised Code.

Toledo Municipal Code 505.14(a) states:

> (a) No person or organization or corporation shall own, keep, harbor or provide sustenance for more than one vicious dog, as defined by Ohio R.C. 955.11, or a dog commonly known as a Pit Bull or Pit Bull mixed breed dog, regardless of age, in the City of Toledo, with the exception of puppies commonly known as Pit Bull or Pit Bull mixed breed for which the owner has filed an ownership acknowledgement form in person with the Dog Warden of Lucas County, prior to reaching seven (7) days of age. The ownership of these puppies must be transferred according to Ohio R.C. 955.11 before they are three (3) months of age. Additionally, this section requires that all vicious dogs, as described in the Ohio Revised Code, or dogs commonly known as Pit Bull or Pit Bull mixed breed dogs are required, when off the owners' premises, to be securely confined as described in Ohio R.C. 955.22 and muzzled."

Our resolution of the issue presented turns on whether the statutes and the ordinance in question are valid exercises of police power by the state and the city. If R.C. 955.11 and 955.22 and Toledo Municipal Code 505.14 are rationally related to a legitimate interest of the state and the city in the public's health, safety, morals, or general welfare, they are constitutional.

We begin with the well-established legal principle that " '[t]he legislature is the primary judge of the needs of public welfare, and this court will not nullify the decision of the legislature except in the case of a clear violation of a state or federal constitutional provision.

The Ohio Constitution provides for the exercise of state and local police power in derogation of the right to hold private property. Section 19, Article I of the Ohio Constitution states: "Private property shall ever be held inviolate, but subservient to the public welfare." "As a result of this subordination, police power regulations are upheld although they may interfere with the enjoyment of liberty or the acquisition, possession and production of private property." State v. Anderson.

"Among the regulations which have been upheld as legitimate exercises of police power are those regulations addressing the ownership and control of dogs." Anderson, 57 Ohio St.3d at 170, 566 N.E.2d 1224. Despite the special relationships that exist between many people and their dogs, dogs are personal property, and the state or the city has the right to control those that are a threat to the safety of the community: "Although dogs are private property to a qualified extent, they are subject to the state police power, and 'might be destroyed or otherwise dealt with, as in the judgment of the legislature is necessary for the protection of its citizens.' * * * [L]egislatures have broad police power to regulate all dogs so as to protect the public against the nuisance posed by a vicious dog." Id., citing Sentell v. New Orleans Carrollton RR. Co. (1897), 166 U.S. 698, 17 S. Ct. 693, 41 L. Ed. 1169.

The state and the city have a legitimate interest in protecting citizens against unsafe conditions caused by pit bulls. We note that substantial reputable evidence was presented at the trial court by both parties: the parties produced 18 witnesses, dozens of exhibits were admitted into evidence, and more than 1,000 pages of testimony were taken. The trial court found that there is little evidence that pit bulls are a dangerous breed when trained and adapted in a social situation and that there is no evidence that pit bulls bite more frequently than other breeds of dogs. However, the trial court correctly noted that its finding that pit bulls are not inherently dangerous does not necessarily lead to the conclusion that the laws at issue are unconstitutional. Rather, the evidence was evaluated to determine whether pit bulls were associated with problem circumstances.

The trial court cited the substantial evidence supporting its conclusion that pit bulls, compared to other breeds, cause a disproportionate amount of danger to people. The chief dog warden of Lucas County testified that (1) when pit bulls attack, they are more likely to inflict severe damage to their victim than other breeds of dogs, (2) pit bulls have killed more Ohioans than any other breed of dog, (3) Toledo police officers fire their weapons in the line of duty at pit bulls more often than they fire weapons at people and all other breeds of dogs combined, and (4) pit bulls are frequently shot during drug raids because pit bulls are encountered more frequently in drug raids than any other dog breed. The trial court also found that pit bulls are "found largely in urban settings where there are crowded living conditions and a large number of children present," which increases the risk of injury caused by pit bulls.

The evidence presented in the trial court supports the conclusion that pit bulls pose a serious danger to the safety of citizens. The state and the city have a legitimate interest in protecting citizens from the danger posed by this breed of domestic dogs.

The statutes and the city ordinance are rationally related to serve the legitimate interests of protecting Ohio and Toledo citizens. R.C. 955.11(A) (4)(a)(iii) states that "vicious dog" includes a dog that "[b]elongs to a breed that is commonly known as a pit bull dog" and that owning, keeping, or harboring a pit bull is prima facie evidence of owning, keeping, or harboring a vicious dog. In view of the unique problems posed by pit bulls in this state, the General Assembly requires owners of pit bulls, like owners of vicious dogs, to meet certain statutory requirements. In R.C. 955.22(E), all persons having vicious dogs are required to obtain liability insurance, and under R.C. 955.22(F), vicious dogs cannot be surgically silenced. These requirements are rationally related to the state's interest in protecting its citizens from pit bulls and in assuring those who are injured by a pit bull that they will be compensated for their injuries.

Toledo Municipal Code 505.14 limits ownership to one pit bull per person, organization, or corporation, and requires that pit bulls be muzzled when not on the owner's premises. The limitation and requirement are rationally related to the city's interest in protecting its citizens from harm caused by pit bulls. In addition to the evidence cited above, the chief dog warden testified that an encounter with two aggressive dogs is much worse than an encounter with one aggressive dog because dogs in a pack are more likely to have increased aggressive behavior and act on predatory instincts.

The court of appeals found R.C. 955.11 and 955.22 and Toledo Municipal Code 505.14 unconstitutional with respect to procedural due process, substantive due process, and equal protection, and under the void-for-vagueness doctrine. We disagree.

First, the court of appeals declared that the laws violated procedural due process pursuant to State v. Cowan. In Cowan, the dogs were determined to be vicious under the first two subsections of R.C. 955.11(A)(4)(a) because they had caused injury to a person. Thus, the case concerned the dog warden's unilateral classification of the dogs as vicious. However, in this case, the "vicious dogs" at issue are those classified as pit bulls under the third subsection of R.C. 955.11(A)(4)(a). Unlike the situation in Cowan, the General Assembly has classified pit bulls generally as vicious; there is no concern about unilateral administrative decision-making on a case-by-case basis. The clear statutory language alerts all owners of pit bulls that failure to abide by the laws related to vicious dogs and pit bulls is a crime. Therefore, the laws do not violate the rights of pit bull owners to procedural due process.

Second, R.C. 955.11 and 955.22 and Toledo Municipal Code 505.14 are not unconstitutional for violating substantive due process or equal protection rights. Laws limiting rights, other than fundamental rights, are constitutional with respect to substantive due process and equal protection if the laws are rationally related to a legitimate goal of government. As we discussed previously when evaluating whether the statutes and ordinance in question are valid exercises of state and city police power, R.C. 955.11 and 955.22 and Toledo Municipal Code 505.14 are rationally related to a legitimate government interest.

Finally, the court of appeals erred in holding that R.C. 955.11 and 955.22 and Toledo Municipal Code 505.14 are void for vagueness. This court has previously held that the term "pit bull" is not unconstitutionally void for vagueness. In State v. Anderson, we stated: "In sum, we believe that the physical and behavioral traits of pit bulls together with the commonly available knowledge of dog breeds typically acquired by potential dog owners or otherwise possessed by veterinarians or breeders are sufficient to inform a dog owner as to whether he owns a dog commonly known as a pit bull dog." 57 Ohio St. 3d 168, 173, 566 N.E. 2d 1224.

In conclusion, the state and the city of Toledo possess the constitutional authority to exercise police powers that are rationally related to a legitimate interest in public health, safety, morals, or general welfare. Here, evidence proves that pit bulls cause more damage than other dogs when they attack, cause more fatalities in Ohio than other dogs, and cause Toledo police officers to fire their weapons more often than people or other breeds of dogs cause them to fire their weapons. We hold that the state of Ohio and the city of Toledo have a legitimate interest in protecting citizens from the dangers associated with pit bulls, and that R.C. 955.11(A)(4)(a)(iii) and 955.22 and Toledo Municipal Code 505.14 are rationally related to that interest and are constitutional.

Questions & Notes

1. Do you think the laws in question are unfair? Note that the law does not ban the ownership of pit bulls. Since the trial court and Supreme Court both accepted the evidence that pit bulls are not inherently dangerous, how can it be that the ordinances are upheld? Consider the argument of the appeals court:

    > The ownership and control of dogs in a crowded, urban setting is a legitimate concern which relates to all dogs. Once the finding is made that a specific breed does not inherently represent a greater danger than any other breed, a law that regulates that breed on the basis of mere ownership is arbitrary, unreasonable, and discriminatory. Even presuming a legitimate concern that pit bulls are used in dog fighting or by other criminals, evidence was presented that the breed-specific laws have had virtually no effect in abating or preventing dog fighting or other crimes. Therefore, since the trial court found that pit bulls as a breed are not inherently dangerous, we conclude that R.C. 955.11(A)(4)(a)(iii) is unconstitutional, since it has no real and substantial relationship to a legitimate state interest.

    2006 WL 513946.

2. The court rather preemptively dealt with the issue of identification of a pit bull. Do you agree with their position? Who is the final decider about which dog is or is not a pit bull? Does that require the application of due process?

3. Does the legislature have to set out the nature of the rational relationship at the time of the adoption of a law?

4. Note how the requirement of due process during administrative hearings, e.g., whether a dog is dangerous, is eliminated if the creation of the category is done by the legislature.

5. On the issue of banning breeds all together, see Safia Gray Hussain, *Attacking the Dog-Bite Epidemic: Why Breed-Specific*

Legislation Won't Solve the Dangerous-Dog Dilemma, 74 Fordham L. Rev. 2847 (April 2006). Also see B. G. Boucher, **Pit Bulls: Villains or Victims** (2011).

6. Rather than a total ban, a different approach is being tried in California. In 2006 a law took effect that allowed local governments to regulate the breeding, spaying, and neutering of specific dog breeds. In 2007 San Francisco adopted an ordinance that requires the neutering or spaying of all pit bulls in the city.

Problem 5A

Akron City Council amended an existing ordinance by inserting "cat" into the definition of animal for the following ordinance:

    1. Defintions: The term "animal" shall include dogs, goats, horses, and bulls.

    2. No animal shall be allowed off the land of the owner or keeper of the animal unless under the direct physical control of an adult human.

    3. Any animal found not under the control of a human may be taken by a government agent. If the animal is not claimed within three days, it shall be destroyed.

    What are the consequences of the ordinance to cat owners? What if, at the time of the adoption of the ordinance, one of the council members stated, "This will eliminate all those feral cats, the curse of my neighborhood." Is this ordinance a proper exercise of police power?

    See **Akron ex rel. Christman-Resch v. Akron**, 825 N.E. 2d 189 (Ohio 2005).

Case Study 5A

The Sanchez family home is situated on a 0.24-acre lot and is located within one of the city's subdivisions. The Sanchezes owned a Vietnamese pot-bellied pig, Eugenia, which they kept as a domestic pet. Eugenia spent much, but not all, of her time on the family's 0.24-acre lot. After adjoining property owners complained, the city cited and fined the Sanchezes for violating its municipal crime ordinance regulating the ownership of pigs:

(A) It shall be unlawful to keep hogs or pigs within the city.

(B) A purebred Vietnamese pot-bellied pig is considered a household pet, and is allowed, provided that the lot is at least one acre in size, no hobby breeding, and only one pig shall be allowed per lot. All adjoining property owners shall sign a statement that they have no objection to the pig. Lilburn City Code, § 11-3-3.

The Sanchezes sought a declaratory judgment that the ordinance was unconstitutional, claiming that it was not rationally related to an articulable legislative purpose.

It was established before the trial court by expert veterinary testimony that the smell emanating from pot-bellied pig waste is much stronger than that associated with dogs and cats.

What's more, evidence showed that pot-bellied pigs generate manure in quantities four times greater than dogs, and that, because they require greater care than other domestic pets, pot-bellied pig owners are more likely to neglect their responsibilities than are other pet owners. The impact of these organic statistics on the 0.24-acre lot where the Sanchez family kept their porcine pet, Eugenia, and on the surrounding property owners was evidenced by the testimony of the Sanchezes' neighbor, Hogan. Hogan testified that his house stands 15 to 20 feet from the Sanchez home, and that the smell associated with Eugenia, and her by-product, was reminiscent of a pig sty, and unbearable to the point of nauseating him. Hogan also testified that the smell of pig manure sometimes permeated the interior of his home.

Is the ordinance within the police power of the government to adopt? What is the plaintiff's burden of proof? Does this ordinance put too much power in the hands of one neighbor with whom the animal owner may being having other disputes, or "bad blood?" Is one acre reasonable?

See **City of Lilburn v. Sanchez**, 491 S.E.2d 353 (Ga. 1997).

CASE BY CASE

In the following case, a local government has sought to exercise its police power and restrict the possession of animals it deems unsafe for the public. The plaintiffs assert a number of their constitutional rights.

Peoples Program for Endangered Species v. Sexton

476 S.E. 2d 477 (S.C. 1996)

FINNEY, C.J.: Appellants commenced this action seeking declaratory judgment and injunctive relief. We affirm.

Appellants Jim and Nancy Saviano are principals of Peoples Program for Endangered Species (a non-profit corporation) and own three wolves who live in their home. Respondent Thomas Sexton is the Town of Mount Pleasant Chief of Police. Appellants instituted this action challenging the constitutionality of Mount Pleasant's Town Ordinance No. 93050. This ordinance prohibits the possession of any "vicious or dangerous domesticated animal or any other animal ... of wild, vicious or dangerous propensities." The ordinance specifically makes it unlawful to possess wolves within the Town. Exceptions are provided for private non-profit organizations established for educational purposes if: 1) the location conforms to the provisions of the Town's zoning code; 2) animals are kept in clean and sanitary conditions; 3) animals are maintained in quarters to prevent their escape; and 4) no person lives or resides within 200 feet of the animals' quarters. Appellants claim they can meet the first three conditions of the exception. Following a hearing, the circuit court denied appellants' claim for declaratory and injunctive relief. Appellants raise several issues on appeal.

Violation of Due Process

Appellants contend their due process rights were violated because the ordinance was passed after they had purchased the house and without notice that the ordinance was under consideration. The circuit court held the ordinance does not violate their due process rights because it pertains to the regulation of animals and an ordinance regulating the keeping of animals within municipal limits is a valid exercise of the police power delegated to a municipality if the ordinance is not unreasonable or arbitrary. 4 Am.Jur.2d Animals § 21 (1995). See *Sentell v. New Orleans and Carrollton R.R. Co.*, 166 U.S. 698, 17 S. Ct. 693, 41 L. Ed. 1169 (1897).

Appellants further claim the ordinance deprives them of the use of their house by banning wild animals. However, the ordinance governs the control of certain animals within the town and not the use of the house. The court properly ruled the ordinance regulating the keeping of animals within the town limits is a valid exercise of the police power. See

Darlington v. Ward, 48 S.C. 570, 26 S.E. 906 (1897). We find no violation of appellants' due process rights.

Preemption by Federal and State Law

Appellants assert the ordinance is preempted by the Federal Endangered Species Act, (FESA) 16 U.S.C. §§ 1531 et seq. and the S. C. Nongame and Endangered Species Conservation Act, S.C. Code Ann. §§ 50-15-10 et seq. (1992). To determine whether the ordinance has been preempted by Federal or State law, we must determine whether there is a conflict between the ordinance and the statutes and whether the ordinance creates any obstacle to the fulfillment of Federal or State objectives. *Gibbons v. Ogden,* 22 U.S. 1, 6 L. Ed. 23 (1824).

The circuit court found no conflict nor obstacles created by the ordinance that would pose any threat to wolves as an endangered species. The stated purpose of FESA is to preserve the habitat of endangered species and provide a program for their conservation. The stated purpose of the local ordinance is to regulate the care and control of animals within the town limits to protect the safety, health and general welfare of the community. Under the FESA a permit can be obtained to possess endangered animals. The ordinance does not run contrary to the permitting of animals, but regulates the conditions under which certain animals can be kept in the town. Furthermore, the FESA provides that any state law respecting taking of endangered species may be more restrictive than federal exemptions or permits. 16 U.S.C.A. § 1535(f) (1985).

Equal Protection Violation

Appellants contend the ordinance violates their equal protection rights because the 200 foot clearance zone has no rational basis and the classification of wolves as within the prohibition has no rational relation to public safety. We disagree.

The requirements of equal protection are met if:

1. the classification bears a reasonable relationship to the legislative purpose sought to be effected;

2. the members of the class are treated alike under similar circumstances; and

3. the classification rests on a reasonable basis.

Robinson v. Richland County Council, 293 S.C. 27, 358 S.E.2d 392 (1987).

The circuit court found there was a rational basis for the distance requirement in that virtually all residential subdivisions have houses closer than 200 feet. It was the intent of Town Council to limit the possession of wild animals by permitted entities to those areas outside of residential subdivisions. Accordingly, it is not arbitrary for a town to desire to keep wild animals at a distance of at least 200 feet from residents.

The classification of wolves as wild animals is not arbitrary. Appellants testified that a wolf is generally classified scientifically and by animal experts as a wild animal. Wolves are included on the federal endangered species list. Wolves are classified as being predatory animals in the State Endangered Species Act, S.C. Code Ann. § 50-11-1150. Consequently, wolves are appropriately classified as wild animals and the ordinance does not violate appellants' equal protection rights.

Appellants have not met their burden of proving beyond a reasonable doubt the ordinance is unconstitutional. The trial court properly denied declaratory and injunctive relief.

AFFIRMED.

CASE BY CASE

In this case, a locality asserts the right to kill dogs that have harmed others. Note that this is not really an attempt to prevent the harm but to punish for the bad acts. The dog owner asserts his constitutional rights. These cases are very difficult for the lawyer because the events move very fast and the attitude of the judge is critical to outcome. The holding of the dog during the hearing stage and during appeal raises substantial issues about the welfare of the dog.

Phillips v. San Luis Obispo County

183 Cal. App. 3d 372 (1986)

This is a death penalty case. We reverse. Missy, a female black Labrador, shall live, and "go out in the midday sun."

Facts

The Phillips own "Missy." In 1981 and twice again in 1982, the San Luis Obispo County Department of Animal Regulation (the department) received reports that Missy bit a child. These incidents occurred while Missy lived with Mary Phillips in Morro Bay. After the third report, the department directed Mrs. Phillips to confine Missy to an enclosed kennel run.

In May 1985 Mrs. Phillips entered the hospital for surgery and surrendered Missy to the care of her son and daughter-in-law in Atascadero. On May 20 Missy bit a child entering the Phillips' residence to play. The child's mother, a registered nurse, observed a single puncture wound on the child's buttocks. The department seized Missy three days later and on the following day ordered Missy destroyed.

The Phillips demanded a hearing concerning the destruction order. The director of the department believed that the Atascadero City and San Luis Obispo County ordinances [n1] did not permit a dog owner to appeal a destruction order. As an epilogue to this tale of two cities, Steve Carnes, a county environmental health officer, conducted a "courtesy" hearing at the request of a county supervisor to determine Missy's fate.

[n1] The San Luis Obispo Department of Animal Regulation provided animal control services to the City of Atascadero. Atascadero City Code section 4-1.212 and San Luis Obispo County Code section 9.08.130 were identical and provided in part: "If any dog within the City is known to have bitten any person or persons on at least two separate occasions, the Chief Animal Control Officer shall notify the owner or person having control of such dog to so keep or surrender the dog in such manner as the Chief Animal Control Officer shall direct. If it is determined by the Chief Animal Control Officer that the dog cannot be properly controlled in order to ensure public safety, then the Chief Animal Control Officer shall destroy the dog in a humane manner.

The department sought to prove the first three biting incidents by testimony that the records reflected reports of three bites. The victim and her mother testified as to the fourth bite. The Phillips acknowledged paying medical bills for the first and third bites. The hearing officer concluded that Missy had bitten four children and that she should be destroyed.

The Phillips filed a petition for a writ of mandamus requesting that the court vacate the destruction order and declare the ordinances unconstitutional because they fail to provide notice and a hearing before permitting a destruction order. The trial judge agreed that the ordinances did not expressly provide for notice and a hearing. He found, however, that the requirement of a hearing could be implied from the language of the ordinances and that the hearing afforded the Phillips satisfied due process and produced sufficient evidence to support Missy's condemnation.

On appeal the Phillips contend (1) the ordinances are constitutionally infirm because they fail to provide for notice and a hearing prior to destruction of a dog; (2) the ordinances do not impliedly permit a noticed hearing; (3) the gratuitous hearing afforded them does not satisfy due process of law; (4) in the absence of an ordinance requiring a noticed hearing, Civil Code section 3342.5 governs the destruction of a biting dog; and (5) they are entitled to attorneys' fees. (Code Civ. Proc., §1021.5.)

Discussion

I.

The Phillips contend the dog destruction ordinances deny them due process of law because the ordinances do not provide for a hearing prior to the

---

Think About It

In 2010 it was reported that the nonfish pet population of the United States was 229 million:

- Cats - 93 million
- Dogs - 77 million
- Birds - 15 million
- Equine - 13 million
- Small Animals - 16 million
- Reptiles - 14 million
- Fish - 182 million

American Pet Products Manufacturers Assoc.

seizure or the destruction of a dog. We agree that due process requires that a dog owner have an opportunity to be heard prior to the destruction of his dog unless there is need for prompt government action.

Procedural due process imposes constraints on governmental decisions depriving individuals of liberty or property interests.

Decisions construing the federal and state due process guarantees generally require that an individual receive notice and some form of hearing before he is deprived of his property or liberty. Nevertheless, important governmental interests may justify postponement of notice and hearing until after the initial taking has occurred. Whether special circumstances warrant summary seizure depend upon the nature of the governmental interest, the need for "very prompt action," and the duty of the seizing official under the standards of a narrowly drawn statute.

It is obvious that summary seizure of dogs must be permitted when of immediate danger to the public, as for example when the dog is vicious or rabid. In that situation, the governmental interest in protecting the personal and property rights of others is paramount to the property right of the dog owner. However, the constitutionality of the ordinance or statute justifying seizure rests upon its provision for a prompt post-seizure hearing. Ordinance 4-1.212 does not provide for a hearing either before or after the taking of a biting or vicious dog.

II.

The Phillips contend that the requirement of a hearing cannot be implied from the ordinance permitting the destruction of uncontrollable biting or vicious dogs. (Fn. 1, ante.) The trial judge found that the ordinance required the department to make two determinations: first, that a dog has either bitten two persons or is vicious and dangerous; and second, that the dog "cannot be properly controlled." The judge concluded that the second finding implied notice and hearing. (Simpson v. City of Los Angeles, supra, 40 Cal. 2d at pp. 281-282.) We disagree with this analysis.

IV.

We conclude that the ordinances here are unconstitutional for failure to provide for notice and a hearing either before or after the seizure of an uncontrollable biting or vicious dog [and that a gratuitous hearing does not cure a deficient law]. The judgment is reversed and remanded to the trial court for a determination whether the Phillips are entitled to attorneys' fees under Code of Civil Procedure section 1021.5, the private attorney general statute. The county is, of course, free to proceed against the Phillips and Missy under any other existing ordinance or statute that provides for notice and hearing prior to destruction of a dog. But, the ordinance in question here ends, "not with a bang but a whimper." [n3]

[n3] See The Hollow Men (1925), with apologies to T. S. Eliot.

The Phillips are entitled to the immediate return of Missy.

The judgment is reversed. Petitioners are entitled to costs on appeal.

Questions & Notes

1. What would be the point of a hearing? See Dangerous Dog statutes discussed later for how this requirement is being realized today in many jurisdictions. Is the topic within the police power of the state? Does this law protect the public, the dog owner, or the dog?

2. Does the dog have the right to assert the need for a hearing even if the owner does not?

3. Another example of a statute that provides for a death sentence for biting dogs is Arizona R. S. § 11-1014. Biting animals:

    > G. The county enforcement agent shall destroy a vicious animal by order of a justice of the peace or a city magistrate. A justice of the peace or city magistrate may issue an order to destroy a vicious animal after notice to the owner, if any, and the person who was bitten, and a hearing. The justice of the peace or city magistrate may impose additional procedures and processes to protect all parties in the interest of justice and any decision by the justice of the peace or magistrate may be appealed to the superior court.

    Do you think that the standard to be used for determining whether the death sentence should be given is adequately articulated? Where the standard is very unclear or unstated, then it can be argued that the statute is open to arbitrary application and therefore in violation of an individual's due process rights. In many death penalty cases for dogs, it seems this argument is available.

4. In the circumstance of infectious diseases, time is considered of paramount importance; as a result, the courts often allow the government to kill animals without a due process hearing. See **Nunley v. Texas Animal Heath Comm.**, 471 S.W. 2d 144 (Tex. 1971).

Problem 5B

Consider the Akron City Council Cat Ordinance again in light of the constitutional rights of the animal owners. Would the federal constitution act as a limitation on this ordinance? Has the constitutionally required due process and equal protection been provided in the ordinance?

Section 3

Dangerous Dogs

While the Ohio case at the beginning of this chapter was about a dangerous dog law, the focus of the case was on the naming of a breed as per se dangerous. We now turn to a more detailed consideration of the general provisions of such laws. One of the historical legislative provisions about dogs sought to do two things: reinforce the requirement of a dog license, and protect the public from risk of harm. In these statutes, having a dog running at large (off the owner's land and not under the control of a human) was itself a basis for the death sentence. Due process would be provided only if the dog had a tag. These statutes are old, written before present-day concerns over due process for the owners of dogs. Consider:

> Arkansas St. § 14-54-1102 (a) Municipal corporations shall have the power to prevent the running at large of dogs, and injuries and annoyances therefrom, and to authorize the destruction of them, when at large contrary to any prohibition to that effect.
>
> (b)(1)(A) Municipalities may impound and destroy any dog running at large within the municipality.
>
> (B)(i) Prior to destroying the dog, the municipality shall give the dog's owner at least five (5) days' notice of the date of the proposed destruction of the dog.
>
> (ii) The notice shall be by certified letter, return receipt requested. Dog owners may claim their dogs at the municipal pound by reimbursing the municipality for the cost of the notice plus other costs and requirements which may be established by ordinance of the municipal governing body prior to the date set for destruction of the dogs.
>
> (2) This subsection shall apply only in instances where the dog carries its owner's address.

Note that no standards are suggested for deciding whether or not the dog should be killed; and if the dog is untagged, it can be killed immediately. This lack of concern for the interests of the owners was in a context when it was not clear that dogs were even property (pre-1930s). If you lost a dog that was not tagged, you had no interests to protect. It is not clear how these statutes, some of which are still on the books, would stand up against the constitutional rights of dog owners today.

Beginning in the 1970s, legislatures, showing more respect for dogs and owners' rights, were not so quick to destroy dogs, but they did seek to create a process for dealing with those dogs that represented a threat to the public. Merely being "at large" will not trigger these statutes.

For the issue of dog bites, state legislatures realized that the existence of tort laws, which only allow recovery after the harm is done, is not sufficiently preventive. Neither is the power of the state to confiscate and destroy dogs after the fact an adequate deterrent to prevent the harm from occurring in the first place. The other factor that comes into play is that those dogs that are at risk of causing harm can sometimes be identified in advance of harm actually occurring. Thus,

> **News Bits**
>
> In 2001, a 13-year-old boy was bitten by two pit bulls, leaving one-inch scars on his back, arms, and face. A jury awarded him $500,000 in damages. In 2003 his attorney was beginning a campaign to draft a law to ban pit bulls from the state. Without effect.
>
> Detroit News, Aug. 25, 2003. *www.detnews.com/2003/ metro/0308/25/b01-253007.htm.*

a number of states have adopted Dangerous Dog laws. (Michigan's law uses the broader term "dangerous animal," and California's scope is "dog or other animal.") The purpose of these laws is to identify those dogs that pose a risk to the public and to put extra responsibility on the owners of the dogs or to empower local officials to collect, impound, and kill dogs that represent the most serious risk of injury to humans. These statutes are generally in addition to the dog bite statutes that provide a civil remedy for injuries incurred and the general power to pick up stray dogs [N.J.4.19-15.16]. These statutes seek to prevent the harm by controlling the problem, or removing the dog, before injury to humans occurs.

The controlling of a dog with a dangerous or vicious propensity is within the police power of the various states. The key limitation on the state's exercise of its police power in this area is the requirement of procedural due process. The removal of a dog from its owner is the taking of personal property, and the removal of property by a government agent is not normally allowed unless the requirements of due process are satisfied. If, under these laws, a dog is taken from its owner and killed in order to protect the public from risk of injury, then the law is in the nature of nuisance prevention or protection of public health regulation, and payment by the state for the loss of property is not normally required. When private property is taken for public benefit without compensation, then the requirement of due process is particularly important.

A number of states have adopted a dangerous dog law since 1975: Lousiana (2001), Maryland (2002), Georgia (2006), Texas (1997), New York (1997), Florida (1990), Virginia (1993) (authorization for local ordinance only), California (1989), Michigan (1988), Minnesota (1988), Maryland (1988), Georgia (1981), and Washington, D.C. (1979). These dog laws are clearly discernible from the older dog laws in several aspects. First, rather than using the old and inappropriate term "vicious dog," the statutes use the term "dangerous" and "potentially dangerous dog" (but California did keep the old term "vicious"). Most laws provide a process whereby a dog is identified as dangerous to the public, and possession by the owner is thereafter conditional. After a dog has been identified as a potentially dangerous dog, then criminal (sometimes felony-level) sanctions will attach to the owner's conduct that does not comply with the strict control provisions of the law. Finally, if the dog causes harm after having been identified as a risk, then the state has clear authority to kill the dog, and significant penalties for the owner may attach.

For example, Fla. Stat. § 767.11 (1997) says that "Dangerous dog" means any dog that, according to the records of the appropriate authority:

(a) Has aggressively bitten, attacked, or endangered or has inflicted severe injury on a human being on public or private property;

(b) Has more than once severely injured or killed a domestic animal while off the owner's property;

(c) Has been used primarily or in part for the purpose of dog fighting or is a dog trained for dog fighting; or

(d) Has, when unprovoked, chased or approached a person upon the streets, sidewalks, or any public grounds in a menacing fashion or apparent attitude of attack, provided that such actions are attested to in a sworn statement by one or more persons and dutifully investigated by the appropriate authority.

There are a number of words that are worrisome. "Aggressively bitten": aggressive has to refer to the attitude and action of the dog, not the seriousness of the injury. A dog could be very aggressive and yet inflict only a modest scratch. Equally troublesome is the phrase "endangered ... a human being." This is difficult to understand. The three other categories require the dog to have physical contact with the human; "endanger" suggests otherwise, but just what that is is not clear. The definitions in the last of (a) and then (b) and (c) are straightforward enough and typical of many statutes. However, (d) is very troublesome (from a policy perspective) because of its subjectivity: "approached a person upon a public street in a menacing fashion." If this phrase triggers the application of the law simply because of the subjective belief of a person walking down the street, then it is an unsupportable standard. If the law requires the testimony of an expert in dog behavior, then it may be a useful standard (remember, the purpose of the law is to identify those dogs that, in fact, represent a risk of harm to the public). Individuals not familiar with dog behavior may entirely misread what a dog is doing. It is not fair to put a dog's well-being at risk because of the response of an individual who is ignorant of dog culture.

The better and fairer definition is one that triggers the statute by the evidence of some specific act. Consider the Georgia Code:

(A) Inflicts a severe injury on a human being without provocation on public or private property at any time after March 31, 1989; or

(B) Aggressively bites, attacks, or endangers the safety of humans without provocation after the dog has been classified as a potentially dangerous dog and after the owner has been notified of such classification. O.C.G.A. § 4-8-21 (1997).

Note that this definition builds upon a dog having done something after being initially identified as a risky dog (Minnesota, California, and Maryland also have this two-step approach). The definition in the Washington, D.C., code uses a less event-oriented standard:

(3) The term "dangerous animal" means an animal that because of specific training or demonstrated behavior threatens the health or safety of the public. D.C. Code § 6-1001 (1997).

In the practice of dog law at the local level, events can flow fast and dog owners often find themselves in legal quagmires even before talking to lawyers. Also, because dogs are not usually the highest priority of local government, procedure/due process is often less than robust, and therefore the attorney for the dog owner often has a procedural battle to fight and can win dismissal of cases based on failure of procedure.

As you read the following case, consider the definition of a vicious dog. Who makes the determination, and under what legal standard the determination is made.

Case by Case

Mansour v. King County
128 P.3d 1241 (Wash. App. 2006)

Judge Agid, J. delivered the opinion of the court.

¶ 1 King County Animal Control issued an order requiring Peter Mansour to remove his dog from King County or give her up to be euthanized. The King County Board of Appeals upheld that order, and the superior court granted summary judgment for the County affirming the Board. Mansour appeals, arguing the Board hearing violated his due process rights.

Facts

¶ 3 Peter Mansour lives in Kirkland with his dogs, Maxine and Kobe. On September 25, 2002, King County Animal Control issued Mansour a Warning Notice stating that it had received a complaint about his dogs being loose in the neighborhood in violation of King County Code

(KCC) 11.04.230. It instructed him to abate the violation by confining the dogs to his property at all times unless on a leash and to control excessive barking. The notice included boilerplate language in bold print that said: "All cases involving a bite or attack may result in the issuance of a Notice and Order of Confinement or Removal and a civil penalty." In response to the warning, Mansour increased the height of his backyard fence.

¶ 4 On May 27, 2003, Mansour went to work and left his dogs at home with his housekeeper, Shelly Miller. Miller testified that she let the dogs out into the backyard despite Mansour's instructions to keep them inside. A short time later Kobe ran back inside whining and looking out the window. Miller assumed Maxine had gotten out, and when she went out the front door she heard Maxine barking. She saw Maxine trotting towards the neighbors, Robert and Dioni O'Brien's, driveway. Maxine picked up the O'Brien's cat, Lacie, in her mouth, at which point Miller yelled, "Max, no," and Maxine put the cat down. Miller put Maxine in the house and then checked on Lacie, who was severely injured. Miller notified Mansour, who immediately left work and took Lacie to Juanita Veterinary Hospital.

¶ 5 On May 28, the O'Briens moved Lacie to Cascade Veterinary Specialists where Dr. Thomas Fry diagnosed her with a broken jaw, fractured and dislocated pelvis, and severe spinal cord damage. On May 30, Lacie was euthanized because of her extensive injuries. After the euthanization, Dr. Fry performed a more thorough examination and discovered that Lacie also had numerous puncture marks consistent with animal bites on opposite sides of her body. He later testified that although the kind of fractures Lacie had often resulted from vehicular trauma, the punctures could not have resulted from an auto accident. Dr. Fry said the punctures were in an area consistent with the fractures, and animal bites could have caused the fractures on their own. The lack of abrasions and contusions indicated she had not been hit by a car.

¶ 6 Animal Control issued Mansour a Warning Notice that it had received a complaint that Maxine had exhibited "vicious propensities," and was a "[v]icious animal running" at large. The notice contained the same boilerplate "bite or attack" language as the September 25, 2002 notice. On July 10, 2003, Animal Control issued a Notice and Order of Removal (Removal Order) to Mansour informing him that Maxine was in "violation of King County Code 11.04.290(b), in that [she] has bitten, attacked or endangered the safety of a human being or domesticated animal. ..." It charged that Maxine was also in violation of RCW 16.08.090 "in that she has bitten, attacked or otherwise threatened the safety of a human being or domestic animal either on public or private property without provocation." Animal Control notified Mansour that "[a]nimals declared in violation of RCW 16.08.090 and/or King County Code 11.04.230 may be kept in King County only upon compliance with the requirements set by King County pursuant to King County Code

11.04.290." Because of the "severity of the incident and grave injuries to 'Lacie' and in order to protect the public safety[,]" Animal Control ordered Mansour to remove Maxine from King County within 48 hours and have her microchipped. Failure to comply would result in Maxine's being disposed of as an unredeemable animal. Animal Control also fined Mansour $100.

Discussion

¶ 8 Mansour asks us to determine what process a municipality must provide a dog owner before it significantly impacts his property interest in his dog.

I. Procedural Due Process

¶ 9 Mansour argues that the Board hearing did not meet minimum procedural due process requirements because the Board imposed an inadequate burden of proof on Animal Control and prevented him from subpoenaing records and witnesses. The County argues that Mansour had a contested hearing that followed Board rules. We determine de novo whether the hearing violated Mansour's due process rights.

A. Standard of Proof Before the Board

¶ 11 Mansour argues that the Board did not even use a "mere preponderance" standard of proof, but rather simply acted in an appellate capacity to determine whether Animal Control's order was arbitrary and capricious. He asserts that the intermediate "clear preponderance" standard is required here, where there is a risk of erroneous deprivation of an invaluable family-type relationship tantamount to that at stake in a parental termination proceeding. The County argues that the Board correctly determined that Animal Control did not act arbitrarily and capriciously when it issued the Removal Order. It further contends that substantial evidence supported the Board's findings of fact no matter what standard of proof it used.

¶ 13 Neither the King County Code nor the Board rules require a particular standard of proof in a removal proceeding. Nor does the record indicate what standard the Board applied here. The superior court ruled that Animal Control had to prove by "substantial evidence that it did not act arbitrarily or capriciously when it issued the Notice and Order. ..." But this is not an evidentiary standard. Rather, it is the standard by which the superior court and this court review the Board's decision. It is not the proper standard for the Board to use in its role as the ultimate fact finder.

¶ 14 As Mansour points out, his first opportunity to offer evidence and be heard was before the Board of Appeals. Before significantly impacting Mansour's interest in Maxine by forcing him to move out of King County to maintain their relationship and avoid her euthanization, due process requires that Animal Control prove more than that it simply did not act arbitrarily and capriciously. We recognize that the bond between pet and owner often runs deep and that many people consider pets part of the family. Other Washington counties require that when an owner appeals an Animal Control order, the agency must prove by a preponderance of the evidence that the dog is dangerous. A purely monetary dispute between private parties would warrant greater protection than King County advocates for removal hearings. The superior court erred in ruling that due process requires only that Animal Control prove to the Board that the Removal Order was not arbitrary and capricious.

¶ 16 A determination of removal does not sever the relationship between dog and owner; as long as Mansour moves out of King County, his relationship with Maxine can continue uninterrupted. While this is certainly a burden on Mansour, it leaves it up to him to determine whether the relationship can continue. Even a dependency proceeding, where a parent may lose custody of a child, requires proof only by a preponderance of the evidence. The government's decision to remove a child, even if temporary, cannot warrant less protection than the government's order to remove a dog, no matter how beloved, to another county. And although we have recognized the emotional importance of pets to their families, legally they remain in many jurisdictions, including Washington, property.

¶ 17 On this record, we cannot presume that the Board applied at least a preponderance of the evidence standard of proof. The lack of a clearly ascertainable adequate standard of proof violated Mansour's procedural due process rights.

B. Subpoena Powers

¶ 18 Mansour argues that procedural due process also required that he be able to subpoena witnesses and records. He contends that in order to effectively cross-examine Dr. Fry and rebut the evidence against him, he needed to subpoena Lacie's veterinary records and Steve Wegener and Catherine Usher. [The court holds that the plaintiff does have a right to subpoena evidence.]

II. Notice

¶ 23 Mansour further argues that he received insufficient notice because the Removal Order identified the wrong authority for removal. He contends the Removal Order is a charging document, and because he challenged the document's defects before the hearing and they were never cured, the Removal Order should be dismissed. [The court holds that notice of the charges were not adequate]

Attorney Fees

¶ 28 Mansour requests attorney fees on appeal under RAP 18.1 on the equitable basis that his argument protects constitutional principles affecting thousands of dog owners in King County. Washington courts follow the American rule in not awarding attorney fees as costs unless authorized by contract, statute, or recognized equitable exception. [The court did not grant attorney fees.]

Questions & Notes

1. How can the state law be changed to meet the court's requirements of due process? What happens if the legislature makes no change?

2. What is the difference between being the fact finder with a burden of proof and a reviewing court under the arbitrary and capricious standard?

3. What standards of proof might have been adopted? Do you agree with the court as to the standard adopted? If you were the government attorney, how would you meet this burden? If the Board had said it was adopting a preponderance of the evidence burden of proof, would the facts have supported a finding of vicious dog?

4. The attorney for the plaintiff, Adam Karp, reported the following about the case on remand:

   > The case was dismissed, the county paid costs of nearly $1300, and the designation of Maxine as potentially dangerous, dangerous, vicious, or potentially vicious was vacated. My client did have to provide proof of insurance, abide by the leash laws, and extend the height of one side of his fence to 6'.

5. Once the procedure is correct, there is usually great discretion in the trial court in ordering the death of a dog. This usually makes the taking of an appeal a fruitless enterprise. But sometimes the appeals court does reverse death sentences on the merits. For such a case—where the appeals court simply reweighed the facts presented—see, **State v. Lesoing-Dittoe**, 693 N.W.2d 261 (Neb. 2005).

Section 4

Local Government — Nuisance and Zoning

The exercise of governmental power at the local level may also affect the ownership and possession of animals. Through the state constitution, or by specific delegation from the state legislature, a local level of government has the power to pass ordinances to protect the health, safety, and welfare of its citizens—again the exercise of police power. In Virginia, a number of the animal issues, such as dangerous dogs discussed earlier, are allowed as local law, but the state legislature sets the key provisions of the local ordinances. Sometimes the states can act to specifically limit the authority of local government. For example, there is a Michigan state law that says "a city, village or ... shall not enact an ordinance which prohibits the orderly keeping of racing pigeons." Assuming that a local government does possess the necessary authority to deal with animal issues, attempts to control animal possession normally fall within either of three categories: nuisance regulations, public health, or zoning.

Case by Case

Commonwealth v. Ebaugh

783 A. 2d 846 (2002 Pa. Cmwlth.)

Opinion by President Judge Doyle.

Marvin Eugene Ebaugh appeals from an order of the Court of Common Pleas of York County, finding him guilty of seven violations of the Conewago Township nuisance ordinance for failure to control barking dogs.

Conewago Township enacted a nuisance ordinance in 1984 that provides, in pertinent part:

> *Section 1. Definitions and Interpretation:* The following words as used in this Ordinance, shall have the meanings hereby respectively ascribed thereto:
>
> A. *Nuisance:* any use of property or conduct, or activity or condition of property ... that shall cause or result in annoyance or discomfort beyond the boundaries of such property which disturbs a reasonable person of normal sensitivities. ... the word 'nuisance' shall include ... the following: ... (iii) Owning, possessing, controlling, or harboring any animal or fowl which barks, bays, cries, squawks, or makes other such noise continuously and/or intermittently for an extended period which annoys or disturbs a reasonable person of normal sensitivities.

(Ordinance 175, adopted December 17, 1984, Supplemental Reproduced Record (SRR) at 6b.) The ordinance provides for fines of not less than $10 nor more than $300, and, where a violator defaults in the payment of a fine or costs, imprisonment for not more than thirty days. (Section 4 of Ordinance 175.)

At all times relevant to the charges against Ebaugh, he owned a large number of dogs of various breeds, which he maintained at his residence in Conewago Township. Ebaugh himself testified that he has had upwards of 13 dogs during the period in question. All of the dogs are kept outside and to the rear of Ebaugh's home.

Joseph Marchione owns the property adjacent to Ebaugh's, and was disturbed by the barking of Ebaugh's dogs. Marchione complained to Ebaugh about the barking dogs; however, the problem was not corrected and Marchione began to alert the police. As a result of Marchione's complaints, the police issued seven "non traffic citations" to Ebaugh for violation of the nuisance ordinance, based on barking that occurred on the following dates and times: (1) June 22, 1999 (11:30 to 11:45 p.m.); (2) June 24, 1999 (4:30 a.m.); (3) November 6, 1999 (7:30 a.m.); (4) November 7, 1999 (11:45 p.m.); (5) December 12, 1999 (4:29 a.m.); (6) December 29, 1999 (11:30 p.m.); and (7) January 5, 2000 (11:30 p.m.). The trial court explained events surrounding the above complaints as followed:

> In each case, Mr. Marchione has described similar circumstances, that the barking noises continued rather uninterrupted for a period approximating ten minutes. After expiration of that time period, he in each instance called 911 and requested a police officer to be dispatched. He says that a period of approximating twenty to thirty minutes would typically pass until the police arrived, and in that period of time, the dogs would continue to bark intermittently, which he has described as twenty to thirty seconds, and then abate for a number of minutes and then start again, and then upon the Police arrival, they would either witness or not some barking, go to the Defendant's house, and the barking would generally cease. He ... typically heard more than one dog barking, upwards of two or three on any given occasion.

(Common Pleas Court order, May 24, 2000, at 3-4.)

Ebaugh challenged the seven citations before a District Justice, and he was found guilty of every violation. He appealed the convictions to the Common Pleas Court, which consolidated the matters for hearing. The Common Pleas Court found Ebaugh guilty of all seven violations of the nuisance ordinance and imposed a fine for each violation ranging from $10 to $150.

On appeal, Ebaugh contends that the Common Pleas Court erred in (1) concluding that he waived his right to challenge the constitutionality of the nuisance ordinance, (2) concluding that the ordinance was constitutional, and (3) finding him guilty of creating a public nuisance in violation of the ordinance.

... Hence, following *Waltz*, we must conclude that Ebaugh did not waive his constitutional issue by failing to raise it before the district justice.

However, even though the issue was not waived, it is nonetheless without merit. Ebaugh asserts that the nuisance ordinance is unconstitutionally vague because it refers to the offensive conduct as disturbing a person of "reasonable sensitivities," and thus does not contain a standard for defining the prohibited conduct.

We begin our analysis by stating the basic legal principle that Ordinances are presumed to be constitutional, and a heavy burden is placed on the one seeking to challenge the constitutionality of an ordinance. Commonwealth v. Fisher, 350 A.2d 428 (Pa. Cmwlth.1976), *cert. denied,* 429 U.S. 1026 (1976). An ordinance is unconstitutionally vague only when it fails to give a person of ordinary intelligence a reasonable opportunity to know what conduct is prohibited by the law. Widmyer v. Commonwealth, 458 A.2d 1048 (Pa. Cmwlth.1983).

In this case, we believe that the phrase "annoy or disturb a reasonable person of normal sensitivities" in the Township's ordinance is an objective standard that looks to the impact of noise upon a reasonable person under the particular circumstances of the incident. In our view, a person of ordinary intelligence would understand what conduct violates this provision and, accordingly, the ordinance is constitutional. *See* City of Philadelphia v. Cohen, 479 A.2d 32 (Pa. Cmwlth. 1984) (ordinance that defined noise as causing adverse psychological or physiological effects in persons was not unconstitutionally vague). *See also* Commonwealth v. Solon, 13 D. & C.3d 85 (1979) (ordinance that penalizes an owner of an animal that makes a noise that disturbs a reasonable person of normal sensitivities is not unconstitutionally vague); and Commonwealth v. Cromartie, 65 D. & C.2d 541 (1973) (disturbing the peace ordinance proscribing "any noise or disturbance ... whereby the public peace and tranquility is disturbed" implies that a noise must be sufficient to disturb a reasonable person and, for that reason, is not unconstitutionally vague).

Last, Ebaugh asserts that this case merely involves a private nuisance, not a public nuisance, and that his neighbor's remedy was to file an injunction petition to abate the nuisance. We disagree. A public nuisance is an unreasonable interference with a right common to the general public; circumstances that constitute a public nuisance are, among other things, conduct that is proscribed by statute or ordinance, or conduct that interferes with public peace. Muehlieb v. City of Philadelphia, 574 A.2d 1208 (Pa. Cmwlth. 1990). Here, owning, possessing or controlling a noisy animal is classified as a nuisance by the Township's ordinance, and excessive barking obviously interferes with the public peace. Therefore, the conduct here involves a public nuisance, and Ebaugh was properly sanctioned by the Common Pleas Court.

The judgment of the Common Pleas Court is affirmed.

Questions & Notes

1. Do you agree: Is the ordinance clear as to what is prohibited? Was the dog owner at risk of an overly unfriendly neighbor?

Section 5

Actions of State Agents

One of the most emotionally difficult issues for a dog owner to deal with is when police, or other agents of the state, shoot a pet dog, usually under claims of self-defense, without any warning, without any of the due process required in most of the dangerous dog laws. Consider the following:

CASE BY CASE

Brown v. Muhlenberg Township

269 F. 3d 205 (3d Cir. 2001)

STAPLETON, CIRCUIT JUDGE:

This is a civil rights action arising out of the shooting of a pet dog. The plaintiffs/appellants are Kim and David Brown, the owners of the pet. Police Officer Robert Eberly is alleged to be the primary constitutional tortfeasor. Officer Eberly's employer, Muhlenberg Township, its Board of Supervisors, and two of its Chiefs of Police are also alleged to be responsible for Officer Eberly's constitutional torts on various theories. Additionally, the Browns assert a state law claim. The District Court granted summary judgment to the defendants on all claims.

We first address the facts and law concerning whether a constitutional violation occurred. We then examine whether the defendants other than Officer Eberly share responsibility for any constitutional violations that may have occurred. Finally, we focus on the state law claim. Because this case comes to us on appeal from the District Court's grant of summary judgment to the defendants, we view the facts in the light most favorable to the Browns, drawing every reasonable inference in their favor. See *Beers-Capitol v. Whetzel*, 256 F.3d 120, 130 n. 6 (3d Cir. 2001).

I. Facts

The Browns lived in a residential section of Reading, Pennsylvania. On the morning of April 28, 1998, they were in the process of moving. Kim was upstairs packing, while David was loading the car. Immi, their three year old Rottweiler pet, had been placed in the Browns' fenced yard. Although the Browns had not secured a dog license for her, Immi wore a bright pink, one inch wide collar with many tags: her rabies tag, her microchip tag, a guardian angel tag, an identification tag with the Browns' address and telephone number, and the Browns' prior Rottweiler's lifetime license. Unbeknownst to the Browns, the latch on the back gate of their fence had failed, and Immi had wandered into the adjacent parking lot beyond the fence.

A stranger parked in the lot observed Immi as she wandered about in it. After three or four minutes of sniffing and casually walking near the fence, Immi approached the sidewalk along the street on which the Browns lived. As she reached the curb, Officer Eberly was passing in his patrol car. Seeing Immi, he pulled over, parked across the street, and approached her. He clapped his hands and called to her. Immi barked several times and then withdrew, circling around a vehicle in the parking lot that was approximately twenty feet from the curb. Having crossed the street and entered the parking lot, Officer Eberly walked to a position ten to twelve feet from Immi. Immi was stationary and not growling or barking. According to the stranger observing from his car, Immi "did not display any aggressive behavior towards [Officer Eberly] and never tried to attack him."

At this point, Kim Brown looked out of an open, screened window of her house. She saw Officer Eberly not more than fifty feet away. He and Immi were facing one another. Officer Eberly reached for his gun. Kim screamed as loudly as she could, "That's my dog, don't shoot!" Her husband heard her and came running from the back of the house. Officer Eberly hesitated a few seconds and then pointed his gun at Immi. Kim tried to break through the window's screen and screamed, "No!"

Officer Eberly then fired five shots at Immi. Immi fell to the ground immediately after the first shot, and Officer Eberly continued firing as she tried to crawl away. One bullet entered Immi's right mid-neck region; three or four bullets entered Immi's hind end.

Immi had lived with the Browns pre-school aged children for most of her three years and had not previously been violent or aggressive towards anyone.

Based on these facts and the reasonable inferences that can be drawn from them, we are thus faced with a situation in which a municipal law enforcement officer intentionally and repeatedly shot a pet without any provocation and with knowledge that it belonged to the family who lived in the adjacent house and was available to take custody.

II. Officer Eberly

A. Unreasonable Seizure

The Browns claim that Officer Eberly violated their constitutionally secured right to be free from unreasonable governmental seizures of their property. The Fourth Amendment to the United States Constitution, made applicable to the states by the Fourteenth Amendment, provides that "[t]he right of the people to be secure in their persons, houses, papers, and effects, against unreasonable searches and seizures, shall not be violated. ..." The people's "effects" include their personal property. A Fourth Amendment "seizure" of personal property occurs when "there is some meaningful interference with an individual's possessory interests in that property." *United States v. Jacobsen*, 466 U.S. 109, 113, 104 S. Ct. 1652, 80 L. Ed. 2d 85 (1984). Destroying property meaningfully interferes with an individual's possessory interest in that property. "[T]he destruction of property by state officials poses as much of a threat, if not more, to people's right to be 'secure ... in their effects' as does the physical taking of them." *Fuller v. Vines*, 36 F.3d 65, 68 (9th Cir. 1994).

The Browns had a possessory interest in their pet. In Pennsylvania, by statute, "All dogs are ... declared to be personal property and subjects of theft." 3 Pa. Stat. Ann. § 459-601(a). [FN1] It necessarily follows that Immi was property protected by the Fourth Amendment and that Officer Eberly's destruction of her constituted a Fourth Amendment seizure. Accordingly, we join two of our sister courts of appeals in holding that the killing of a person's dog by a law enforcement officer constitutes a seizure under the Fourth Amendment. *Fuller*, 36 F.3d at 68; *Lesher v. Reed*, 12 F.3d 148, 150-51 (8th Cir. 1994).

> FN1. Officer Eberly argues that an unlicensed dog under Pennsylvania law is as a matter of law an abandoned dog. We find no authority for this proposition and, accepting the evidence tendered by the Browns, are unpersuaded that Immi should be regarded as having been abandoned.

To be constitutionally permissible, then, Officer Eberly's seizure must have been "reasonable." "In the ordinary case, the [Supreme] Court has viewed a seizure of personal property as *per se* unreasonable within the meaning of the Fourth Amendment unless it is accomplished pursuant to a judicial warrant issued upon probable cause and particularly describing the items to be seized." *Place*, 462 U.S. at 701, 103 S. Ct. 2637. Where the governmental interest justifying a seizure is sufficiently compelling and the nature and extent of the intrusion occasioned by the seizure is not disproportionate to that interest, the seizure may be reasonable even though effected without a warrant. Thus, when the state claims a right to make a warrantless seizure, we "must balance the nature and quality of the intrusion on the individual's Fourth Amendment interests against the importance of the governmental interests alleged to justify the intrusion." *Id.* at 703, 103 S. Ct. 2637. Even when the state's interest is sufficiently compelling to justify a warrantless seizure that is minimally intrusive, the seizure will be unreasonable if it is disproportionately intrusive. While the state's interest in drug interdiction, for example, is sufficient to render reasonable a brief but warrantless detention of suspicious luggage for a canine "sniff," such detention for ninety minutes constitutes an unreasonable seizure under the Fourth Amendment. *Id.*

Where a pet is found at large, the state undoubtedly has an interest in restraining it so that it will pose no danger to the person or property of others. The dog catcher thus does not violate the Fourth Amendment when he or she takes a stray into custody. Moreover, the state's interest in protecting life and property may be implicated when there is reason to believe the pet poses an imminent danger. [FN2] In the latter case, the state's interest may even justify the extreme intrusion occasioned by the destruction of the pet in the owner's presence. This does not mean, however, that the state may, consistent with the Fourth Amendment, destroy a pet when it poses no immediate danger and the owner is looking on, obviously desirous of retaining custody. Striking the balance required by Place, we hold that Officer Eberly's destruction of Immi could be found to be an unreasonable seizure within the meaning of the Fourth Amendment.

> FN2. The state's interest in the protection of life and property undoubtedly occasioned enactment of 3 P.S. § 459-302(a) which states in relevant part:
>
> It shall be the duty of every police officer, State dog warden, employee of the department or animal control officer to seize and detain any dog which is found running at large, either upon the public streets or highways of the Commonwealth, or upon the property of a person other than the owner of such dog, and unaccompanied by the owner. Every police officer, State dog warden, employee of the department or animal control officer may humanely kill any dog which is found running at large and is deemed after due consideration by the police officer, State dog warden, employee of the department or animal control officer to constitute a threat to the public health and welfare.

While Officer Eberly relies on this statute, it would be clearly inapposite should the trier of fact credit the evidence that has been tendered by the Browns.

This brings us to Officer Eberly's qualified immunity defense. Qualified immunity absolves Officer Eberly from liability and, indeed, from the burdens of defending this suit, if he can show that a reasonable officer with the information he possessed at the time could have believed that his conduct was lawful in light of the law that was clearly established on April 28, 1998.

[The court held that a reasonable officer would not have shot the dog. The Dissent disagreed—"it is clear to me that Officer Eberly, when he shot and killed the Brown's Rottweiler which was unleashed, uncontrolled, barking and presenting an aggressive appearance, could not have reasonably understood that his act was unlawful. (It also was the fact that the officer during the past two years had shot four dogs, without any consequence to his status.) As such, he is entitled to qualified immunity and the District Court's judgment should be affirmed." Additionally the court held that the Plaintiffs' claim that the city was liable for actions of police officer was without merit.]

Questions & Notes

1. Do dogs, not under the control of a human, have a presumption of dangerousness? What should be the context that a police officer uses when confronted by a large dog not under anyone's control? Is this an issue of changing standards? What would have been the outcome 50 years ago? What has changed?

   Should the individual policeman bear the entire burden of the wrong, or should the government also be liable?

   See **Brandon v. Village of Maywood**, 157 F. Supp. 2d 917 (N.D. Ill. 2001) (immunity upheld since an officers' split-second decision emanated from their desire to avoid being injured by a dog with an unknown propensity for violence) and **U.S. v. Gregory**, 933 F. 2d 1016 (9th Cir. 1991) (shooting, though regrettable, was done excusably by an officer who reacted quickly to a perceived attack by an animal reasonably believed to be an attack dog).

   Also see **Hebert v. Broussard**, 886 So. 2d 666(LA 2004) (court held police officer had statutory immunity because the dog was vicious or dangerous). But also know that the organization Hells Angels reached a settlement with Santa Clara County for $990,000 because of police raids on several of their houses where, while obtaining evidence, they shot a number of dogs. Prior to settlement, a judge had ruled that the actions of the police were unreasonable.

2. What do you think the plaintiff will get as damages?

3. For the most recent information on this topic see the Police Shooting Pets topic of the Animal Legal and Historical Center (*www.animallaw.info*).

4. In a particularly difficult case, local officials raided a residence that contained hundreds of cats and dogs (a hoarder, see Chapter 7). By the next morning, without any hearing, all but a few of the cats had been killed at the local shelter. There had not even been individual examination of each animal. In a Section 1983 action, the court denied recovery saying that the state did not have control over such random and arbitrary actions. **Bogart v. Chapell**, 396 F. 3d 548 (4th Cir. 2005).

CHAPTER 6

Anti-Cruelty Laws — History and Intentional Acts

For over a century, animals within the dominion and control of humans have received some level of protection at the state level in the form of criminal anti-cruelty laws. This legal right of animals to be free from cruel practices by humans is both important and ignored. The implementation of the moral precept—that animals should not suffer pain (unnecessary pain) at the hands of humans—says much about the character and nature of our culture. While the law clearly applies to the pet owner, millions of other animals—in exempted institutional areas such as agriculture, sport hunting, and scientific research—receive little, if any, protection. These anti-cruelty laws represent the first acknowledgment by our society that animals are not as other property, but have interests of their own that the legal system ought to acknowledge and accommodate to the extent possible.

An examination of the history of anti-cruelty laws and their present-day implementation is one of the best windows available into the complex and contradictory thinking of Americans toward animals. The failure of the anti-cruelty laws to address critical issues and groups of animals has been a prime motivation for the animal rights movement in the United States.

In most countries, the laws relating to the use of animals resides at the national level. In the United States, the criminal anti-cruelty laws reside primarily at the state level of government because of the property status of animals. The present state laws are shaped primarily by their historical development in the 1800s, and that is where the tale shall begin.

Section 1

Historical Perspective

Much of the following text is from a law review article, David Favre and Vivien Tsang, "The Development of Anti-Cruelty Laws During the 1800's," 1993 Detroit Coll. of Law Review 1 (1993). As you read, consider the list of animals protected and the acts covered by the changing law.

The nineteenth century saw a significant transformation of society's attitude toward animals, which was reflected in the legal system. The legal system began the century viewing animals as items of personal property not much different than a shovel or plow. During the first half of the century, lawmakers began to recognize that an animal's potential for pain and suffering was real and deserving of protection against its unnecessary infliction.

The last half of the nineteenth century saw the adoption of anti-cruelty laws that became the solid foundation upon which today's laws still stand. As will be discussed, during the 1860s and 1870s, Henry Bergh of

New York City was a primary force in the adoption, distribution, and enforcement of these laws in the United States. Underlying the changes of the law were parallel changes of social attitude toward animals.

Early American Legislation

Statutory language expressly adopted by a legislative process usually reflects the broader societal attitudes that the legislature represents. The evolution of the statutory language concerning animals during the nineteenth century paralleled the evolution of society's attitude toward animals. Nowhere in the legislative examples set out next do we have any contemporaneous records about the debate in the legislature: We do not know the submitter of the legislation, the nature of the debate, or who supported the measures as adopted. This analysis is limited to the actual language adopted. Indeed, there is a dearth of both legal and nonlegal writing dealing with animal issues during that century. Indirect evidence of their concerns is the best available.

An example of a statute that reflects the strict property concept of animals, which existed at the beginning of the nineteenth century, is found in Vermont legislative law. Section 1 makes it illegal to steal a horse, but not a cow or dog. Section 2 states in part:

> Every person who shall wilfully and maliciously kill, wound, maim or disfigure any horse, or horses, or horse kind, cattle, sheep, or swine, of another person, or shall wilfully or maliciously administer poison to any such animal ... shall be punished by imprisonment [of] ... not more than five years, or fined not exceeding five hundred dollars. ... **1846 Vt. Laws 34**.

There was no provision prohibiting the cruel treatment of the animals, the word not being found in the statute. The list of animals protected was limited to commercially valuable animals, not pets or wild animals. The purpose of this law was to protect commercially valuable property from the interference of others, not to protect animals from pain and suffering.

A crime was committed only if the harmed animal was owned by someone else, thus the language "of another." Therefore, if a person maimed his own animal it would not be a crime. Nor was it a crime to harm a wild or ownerless domestic animal. Actions had to constitute willful and malicious conduct before they were deemed illegal. Finally, because the penalty was for up to five years of jail time, a violation of this law was a felony. The legislature sought to control humans harming valuable property of another, not to stop the unnecessary infliction of pain upon animals. (At this time family wealth might be held as commercial animals.)

The next step in the legal evolution is represented by the earliest statute yet uncovered, that established in Maine in 1821. This tentative law provides:

> 7. *Be it Further enacted*, That if any person shall cruelly beat any horse or cattle, and be thereof convicted, ... he shall be punished by fine not less than two dollars nor more than five dollars, or by imprisonment in the common gaol for a term not exceeding thirty days, according to the aggravation of the offence. **Me. Laws Ch IV, Sec. 7 (1821).**

In this case, the operative phrase is "cruelly beat." This is an extremely narrow range of conduct to control. Assuming the common sense definition of the term "cruelly," is that only a cruel beating is illegal, not killing, cutting, maiming, or one of a hundred other actions. Like the previously discussed statute, it applies only to commercially valuable animals: horses and cattle.

This law represented a new, tentative step forward because, in this case, no distinction was made as to who owns the animal. It was illegal to cruelly beat your own horses or cattle, as well as those of another. Because common law criminal law concepts did not limit what a person did with their own property, this law suggested a new societal interest; concern for the animal itself.

Finally, note the level of punishment: a two- to five-dollar fine and/or up to thirty days in jail. One of the best ways to gauge the seriousness with which the legislature views an issue is to examine the level of punishment provided. Unlike the felonious horse maiming statute set out earlier, the penalties provided here suggest the bare threshold of criminality.

The above anti-cruelty law was passed the year *before* the first such law passed in England. However, there is no record that this law was followed by the creation of any public organization to help enforce the law or compel change in public conduct, as was the case in England at this time or in New York in the 1860s. It marks the initiation of concern, but not the birth of a social movement.

More representative of the first wave of anti-cruelty laws in the United States was the New York law of 1829:

> 26. Every person who [part one] shall maliciously kill, maim or wound any horse, ox or other cattle, or any sheep, belonging to another, or [part two] shall maliciously and cruelly beat or torture any such animals, whether belonging to himself or another, shall upon conviction, be adjudged guilty of a misdemeanor. **N.Y. Rev. Stat. Tit. 6, Sec. 26 (1829).**

The criminal prohibitions consist of two distinct parts. The first part is qualified with the phrase "belonging to another" while the second is qualified "belonging to himself or another." The purpose of the first part is to provide protection for private property, while the second deals with cruelty to the animal regardless of ownership. The two parts prohibit very different actions. One result of the different language is that it was not illegal to maliciously kill or maim your own animal. The legislature most likely presumed that financial self-interest would protect against this possibility. However, if you killed your own horse by beating it to death, the beating, but not the killing, would be illegal.

Both parts of this legislation attempt to stop the affirmative acts of individuals. Under neither of the parts of the legislation would it be illegal to kill a horse by starvation. Requiring a person to care for an animal, imposing an affirmative act, has always been considered more burdensome than prohibiting an action. The affirmative duty of care would be added later as the concern for the well-being of animals became stronger.

The most serious limitation of this legislation is the limited list of protected animals. It was not yet illegal to torture a dog or a bear. The limited list set forth in both parts was most likely utilized because this was the list with which the legislature was familiar. The legislature had not yet made the conceptual bridge that, if it is wrong to cruelly torture a cow, it should also be wrong to torture a cat or dog. The critical new factor was not the value of the animal to the owner, but the ability of the animal to suffer.

Initially, the societal concern about cruelty to animals contained mixed motives. While some did not believe moral duties were owed to animals, they did accept that cruelty to animals was potentially harmful to the human actor, as it might lead to cruel acts against humans. Thus, the concern was for the moral state of the human actor, rather than the suffering of the nonhuman animal.

One case under the Minnesota law shows the continued confusion about the purpose of the these cruelty laws. A defendant was indicted for the shooting of a dog under the criminal statue providing that "[e]very person who shall wilfully and maliciously kill, maim or disfigure any horses, cattle or other beasts of another person." The court decided that the indictment would fail as a dog could not be considered a beast.

> [I]t seems to me, that all [animals] such as have, in law, no value, were not intended to be included in that general term. ... The term beasts may well be intended to include asses, mules, sheep and swine, and perhaps, some other domesticated animals, but it would be going quite too far to hold that dogs were intended. **United States v. Gideon, 1 Minn. 292, 296 (1856).**

This is reflective of the continued confusion about the intended purpose of the law: to protect valuable personal property or to restrict the pain and suffering inflicted upon animals.

The Bergh Era Begins

The life of Henry Bergh is set out elsewhere and will not be repeated here. His impact on the legal world began in 1866. After his return from a trip to Europe, where he observed both the cruelty inflicted upon animals and the efforts of the Royal Society for the Protection of Animals on behalf of animals, he became focused on the animal cruelty issue.

Because of his social and political connections, it was not difficult for him to approach the New York legislature in Albany.

Although not a lawyer, Henry Bergh was able to direct the drafting of substantially different legislation. He also understood that the mere passage of legislation was insufficient—without dedicated enforcement, the laws will never actually reach out and touch the lives of the animals about which he was concerned. Therefore, besides the drafting and passage of new criminal laws, he sought the charter of an organization which, like the Royal Society of London, would be dedicated to the implementation of the law. He asked the New York Legislature for a state-wide charter for the American Society for the Prevention of Cruelty to Animals ("A.S.P.C.A."), whose purpose, as set forth in its constitution, was "[t]o provide effective means for the prevention of cruelty to animals throughout the United States, to enforce all laws which are now or may hereafter be enacted for the protection of animals and to secure, by lawful means, the arrest and conviction of all persons violating such laws." This was granted on April 10, 1866. Henry Bergh was unanimously elected as the A.S.P.C.A.'s first president, a position he continued to hold until his death in 1888.

New Legislation

With the adoption of the A.S.P.C.A. charter and the passage of a modest law in 1866, Henry Bergh went to work and was immediately active in enforcing the law. However, he clearly wanted more because, within months, drafts for a new law were created. By the first anniversary of the A.S.P.C.A., a new, restructured, and greatly expanded law was passed by the New York Legislature. The following paragraphs set out a summary of the key points of the law. Section 1 provided for the law to apply to "any living creature." This marvelously sweeping statement finally eliminated the limitation that protection was only for animals of commercial value. All provisions of this section applied regardless of the issue of ownership of the animal. The list of illegal acts was greatly expanded to include: overdriving, overloading; torturing, tormenting; depriving of necessary sustenance; unnecessarily or cruelly beating; and needlessly mutilating or killing. Yet, note that none of the acts were qualified by the term "maliciously." The focus changed from the mind set of the individual to objective evidence of what happened to the animal.

To address the ongoing problems of animals being forced to fight each other, often to their death, for the owners' and spectators' delight, section 2 of the New York Act made animal fighting illegal for the first time. While specifically identifying bull, bear, dog, and cock fighting, it applied to any living creature. The ownership and keeping of fighting animals as well as the management of the fights themselves was illegal.

For the first time the law imposed a duty to provide "sufficient quality of good and wholesome food and water" upon anyone who kept (impounded) an animal. Just as important from a practical enforcement perspective, the new law allowed any persons, even the A.S.P.C.A., to enter private premises and care for the animal's needs. This was a very practical provision which allowed immediate help to the animals regardless of the criminal action that might or might not be brought later against the owner or keeper.

Another first for this legislation was its concern about the transportation of animals. Section 5 made it illegal to transport "any creature in a cruel or inhuman manner." Again with an eye to helping the animal, the law allowed the taking away by officials, such as A.S.P.C.A. officers, of any animal being transported cruelly so that they might be given the proper care.

Section 6 is a curious provision requiring the registration of dogs, but no other animal, used by businesses for the pulling of loads. The registration number was to be placed on the vehicle being pulled by the dog. Perhaps this was to make identification of owners easier, but little explanation of this section is found in the sources of the time.

As a follow up to the second section of the 1866 Act, section 7 of the 1867 Act made illegal the abandonment of any "maimed, sick, infirm or disabled creature." Under the previous law it was not at all clear what could be done with an abandoned animal. Under this law, a magistrate or the captain of the police could authorize the destruction of such a creature. It is very likely that the vision of abandon horses on the side streets of New York City created much of the public political support for the new law.

Focusing on the issue of enforcement, Mr. Bergh must have realized that the normal police forces could not be counted upon to seriously and vigorously enforce this new law. Therefore, section 8 specifically provided that agents of the A.S.P.C.A. could be given the power to arrest violators of the adopted law. This delegation of state criminal authority to a private organization was, and is, truly extraordinary. This, more than any other aspect of the 1867 Act, reflected the political power and trust that Bergh must have had within the city of New York and in the state capital. Another unusual provision was the requirement that all collected fines would be given to the A.S.P.C.A.; the pragmatic Bergh again at work.

With the threat of actual enforcement of meaningful anti-cruelty statutes came the first lobbying for an exemption from the law. Section 10 of the Act provided an exemption for "properly conducted scientific experiments or investigations," at a medical college or the University of the State of New York. Thus, one of the more heated debates of today must have been carried out over 120 years ago in the New York Legislature.

With the 1867 Act, an ethical concern for the plight of animals was transformed for the first time into comprehensive legislation. The focus of social concern was on the animals themselves. Although it is not known who drafted the specific words used, the language was visionary in scope while addressing a number of specific, pragmatic points.

Questions & Notes

1. Create a set of criteria by which to judge the scope and effectiveness of a criminal anti-cruelty law.

2. List five specific acts toward animals that you think should be controlled or banned by the criminal law. Would these acts have been covered by the language of the New York law? If your list includes the duty to provide care for animals, that topic will be more fully addressed in the next chapter, while this chapter focuses on prohibitions against certain acts.

3. By additional statutory language and common practice, a large number of exceptions and exemptions to the anti-cruelty law have developed since this first law. Some of these will be considered later in this chapter, but agricultural animals specifically shall be discussed in Chapter 9.

This early case, while providing some historical context, grapples with the legal issue which is still squarely before us today: which actions by humans are "needless" or in today's language, "unnecessary"?

CASE BY CASE

Grise v. State

37 Ark. 456 (1881)

EAKIN, J. The appellant was indicted, under an Act, approved March 11th, 1879. "For the prevention of cruelty to animals." The first section, inter alia, makes it a misdemeanor to "needlessly mutilate or kill" * * * "any living creature." The indictment simply charges that appellant did, unlawfully and needlessly, kill a hog, of the value of five dollars, being a living creature. No allegations of value, or of ownership, were essential.

The proof, on the part of the State, tended to show that appellant had killed a pig, belonging to a neighbor, by a blow on the head with a stick, producing sudden death. The pig was in a field belonging to appellant, in which corn and wheat were growing. It had, before that time, been in the habit of trespassing there with others, and the defendant had repeatedly applied to the owner, a lady, to pen her hogs, or keep them out of his field. This, for a while, she did. But they were again turned out, and the one in question being found again in appellant's field, he killed it on the spot—with no more circumstances of cruelty than would attend the taking of life at one blow.

Upon the trial, defendant asked six instructions, which were refused throughout. In lieu thereof, the court gave two of its own motion—all against objection. The defendant was found guilty, and sentenced to a fine of two dollars. He moved for a new trial upon the grounds of error, in refusing the instructions asked; in giving those by the court of its own motion; and because the verdict was against law and evidence. The motion was refused, and he appealed.

This court is called for the first time to construe a new statute, belonging to a class which must ever be more or less vague in their meaning, and extremely difficult of administration. They are the outgrowth of modern sentiment, and are of comparatively recent origin. They attempt to transcend what had been though, at common law, the practical limits of municipal government. They spring, originally, from tentative efforts of the New England colonists to enforce imperfect but well recognized moral obligations; a thing much more practical in small isolated communities than in populous governments. They first had in view only to compel benevolence and mercy to those useful animals, which being domesticated, and wasting their lives in man's service, were supposed to be entitled to his kind and humane consideration. Such statutes appealed strongly to the instincts of humanity. They were adopted in many of the States, and recently in England; and the impulse which favored them has endeavored to enlarge their beneficence, until, in our law they are made to embrace "all living creatures." It is obvious that laws of this class, pressed to this extreme limit, must be handled by the courts with great care, and we feel it due the Legislature to do so, to prevent their becoming dead letters. They must be rationally construed with reference to their true spirit and intention. It must be kept in mind that they are not directed at all to the usual objects of municipal law, as laid down by Blackstone. For example: They are not made for the protection of the absolute or relative rights of persons, or the rights of men to the acquisition and enjoyment of property, or the peace of society. They seem to recognize and attempt to protect some abstract rights in all that animate creation, made subject to man by the creation, from the largest and noblest to the smallest and most insignificant. The rights of persons and the security of property and the public peace, are all protected by other laws, with appropriate sanctions. The objects of the two classes should not be confounded. It will lead to hopeless confusion. The peculiar legislation we are now called to discuss must be considered wholly irrespective of property, or of the public peace, or of the inconveniences of nuisances. The misdemeanors attempted to be defined may be as well perpetrated upon a man's own property as another's, or upon creatures, the property of no one, and so far as one act is concerned, it is all the same whether the acts be done amongst refined men and women, whose sensibilities would be shocked, or in the solitude of closed rooms or secluded forests.

It is in this view that such acts are to be construed, to give them, if possible, some beneficent effect, without running into such absurdities as would, in the end, make them mere dead letters. A literal construction of them would have that effect. Society, for instance, could not long tolerate a system of laws, which might drag to the criminal bar, every lady who might impale a butterfly, or every man who might drown a litter of kittens, to answer these, and show that the act was needful. Such laws must be rationally considered, with reference to their objects, not as the means of preventing aggressions upon property, otherwise unlawful; nor so as to involve absurd consequences, which the Legislature cannot be supposed to have intended. So construed, this class of laws may be found useful in elevating humanity, by enlargement of its sympathy with all God's creatures, and thus society may be improved. Although results in other States and in England, have not, as we judge from the paucity of decisions, been such as to excite sanguine hopes, yet to a limited extent the objects of the laws may be practically obtained. It is the duty of the courts to co-operate to that end, so far as the rules of construction may warrant.

There are civil laws for the recovery of damages for trespass, and criminal laws for the punishment of malicious mischief, and trespass and injury to property. In a suit or indictment, under these, there are appropriate defenses, not applicable to an indictment for cruelty or for needless killing. They should, one or the other of them, have been resorted to by the individual, or the State, if the object had been to recover damages for the loss of the pig, or to protect society from violent aggressions on property. The law under which this indictment was framed has no such object, and cannot be made a substitute for the others. The issue was, did the defendant needlessly kill the pig. The burden of proof was upon the State to show not only the killing, but that it was done under such circumstances as, unexplained, would authorize the jury to believe that it was needless in the sense of the Statute. The controversy does not turn at all upon the lawfulness or unlawfulness of the act, except in so far as the Statute itself might make it unlawful as needless.

From the view we have taken of the nature and scope of this class of acts, it is obvious that the term "needless" cannot be reasonably construed as characterizing an act which might by care be avoided. It simply means an act done without any useful motive, in a spirit of wanton cruelty, or for the mere pleasure of destruction. Other portions of the act are directed to prevent undue torture, or suffering, which do not come here in question. However unlawful the act may be, and whatever penalties might be incurred under the Statutes, the defendant should not, under this indictment, have been convicted, if he had some useful object in the killing, such as the protection of his wheat and corn.

The provisions of different Statutes must be regarded; and acts really criminal, must be punished under appropriate indictments. Malicious mischief and needless killing are distinct.

The defendant, in effect, asked the court to instruct:

> First. That the burden was on the State to show not only the killing but that it was needless, and that "needless" meant a killing in mere idle wantonness, without being in any sense whatever beneficial or useful to defendant.

Second. That it was for the jury to determine whether or not it was "needless," and that they might consider the facts, that the pig was found in the field where there was corn and wheat, that it had frequently been there before, and all other facts and circumstances in evidence.

Third. That the jury must find before conviction that there was no necessity or cause whatever for the defendant to kill the animal.

Fourth. That considering the circumstances, if the jury found that the animal was trespassing upon the defendant's crops and destroying them, and that he had up to the time of the killing used all reasonable means to prevent it, and that the act of killing did prevent it, they would be warranted in finding that it was not needless.

Fifth. That the word "needlessly," used in the Statute, relates to a wanton and cruel act, and not to one which is the result of necessity, or reasonable cause.

Sixth. That unless the defendant was guilty of wanton and needless acts of cruelty to the animal, resulting in unjustifiable physical pain, they should acquit.

We think that the spirit of all the foregoing instructions, except the last, was in harmony with the true intent and meaning of the Act—as nearly so as moral acts can be characterized by the formulas of language—at all times a difficult task. They are very nearly in accord with the views we take of the Statute. The last was erroneous. A needless killing could not be justified by an easy death. Cruelty was no part of the charge, although it is made criminal under the other sections.

The instructions given by the Court, of its own motion, were as follows:

First. That the proof of killing a pig would support the allegation of the killing of a hog.

This is unquestionably correct.

Second. "If the jury believe from the evidence that defendant, in this county," etc ... "needlessly killed the animal mentioned in the indictment, they should convict, notwithstanding it may have been trespassing within defendant's enclosure at the time it was killed. "Needlessly" means without necessity, or unnecessarily, as where one kills a domesticated animal of another, either in mere wantonness or to satisfy a depraved disposition, or for sport or pastime, or to gratify one's anger, or for any other unlawful purpose."

But for the last clause of this instruction, it would not be, in the abstract, subject to criticism, but it is, we think, erroneous in holding all killing needless, in the sense of the Statute, done for an unlawful purpose. For unlawful trespasses, other remedies are provided. There are other Statutes for their prohibition. All acts of killing are not "needless," in the meaning of the Statute, which are unlawful. A man, for instance, might kill his neighbor's sheep for food, which would be unlawful, and either a trespass or felony, according to the circumstances; but such killing could not, with any show of reason, come within the intention of the Act in question. The lawfullness, or unlawfulness, of the act, has really no bearing upon its character, as charged.

Had the last clause been omitted, in this instruction, it would not, however, have been sufficiently instructive, in all points, to have caused the refusal to give the defendant's first five instructions, in substance, as asked. He was entitled to have them particularly impressed upon the jury, in a matter which, being new, they might misapprehend.

For error in overruling the motion for a new trial, reverse the judgment, and remand the cause for further proceedings, consistent with law, and this opinion.

Questions & Notes

1. Of what outcomes was the court fearful? Do you agree with the court in this case?

2. Who decides if an act is "needless"? What is the "tip point" where an act becomes illegal? How is it decided? Is there a moral basis for such judgment?

3. The judge suggested that a person should not be held to account for "every lady who might impale a butterfly, or every man who might drown a litter of kittens." What do you think of that statement? Would a judge say that today? Would a legislature distinguish between these two activities? Why?

4. In this case, is "needless killing" a different moral issue from "needless pain and suffering"? Was there suffering in this case? Does this suggest that beyond pain and suffering the life of the pig has recognizable interests and moral weight?

Section 2

Intentional Acts

Who Is Liable? Which Humans?

The question of whether the human actor is covered by the statute is fairly straightforward under statutes that prohibit the commission of certain acts (omission of acts is a little more complex). Generally, if the individual did the act or procured another to do the act, then he or she is within the purview of the statute. The mere fact that a person is an

employer, a principal, or a family relation of someone guilty of an illegal act does not make that person liable. On the other hand, it is not
a defense to an act that a person was simply carrying out corporate
policy. In one case, an employee of a dog-grooming establishment negligently burned a dog. The court found that the corporate owner/direc-
tor was not in violation of the criminal act without proof of knowledge
or intent. **People v. Miller**, 221 N.Y.S.2d 430 (1961). Civil liability for
acts of agents, on the other hand, is another issue. A business can be
financially liable for the acts of employees when they are acting within
the scope of their employment.

Which Animals Are Protected?

Most older statutes defined "animals" in the broadest sense, using
awkward terms such as "all," "dumb," or "brute creatures." Today,
as many states move toward making the statutory violations felonies
rather than misdemeanors, the legislatures are being more specific
about the definition. But, there remains great diversity in the language
used by legislatures.

- Cal. Pen. Code § 599b: "[E]very dumb creature" (added to
  code in 1905)

- Va. Code Ann. § 3.2-6500: "[A]ny nonhuman vertebrate
  species except fish" (substantial revisions of cruelty laws
  in 1990s)

- Mich. Comp. Laws § 750.50(1)(b): "Vertebrates other than
  a human being" (1994 Amendment)

- Miss. Code Ann. § 97-41-1: "Any living creature" (1930
  code—based on New York's 1867 law)

- Minn. Stat. § 343.20(2): "[E]very living creature except
  members of the human race" (added pre-1900)

- N. H. Code § 644:8: "[A]nimal means a domestic animal, a
  household pet or a wild animal in captivity."

Questions & Notes

1. Why the different terms? Do you think they really meant "every living creature" — oysters, flies, jellyfish, etc.? What do you
   think of limiting the definition to vertebrates? Why did Virginia exclude fish but Michigan did not? The word "dumb"
   was often used in the 1880s to refer to animals, and it should be
   considered reflective not of an issue of intelligence, but of their
   inability to speak for themselves. The publication of the Massachusetts Society for the Protection of Animals during the late
   1800s was "Our Dumb Animals."

2. Texas, like New Hampshire, limits its definition of animals to "domesticated living creatures and wild creatures previously captured" (Texas Penal Code § 42.09(c)(1)). Why it should be cruel to injure a dog or cat but not to injure a raccoon or hawk is not suggested. Why would Texas have this different view of the anti-cruelty laws? What does it suggest about their cultural context?

3. Courts may modify the definition of the statutory terms. Historically, several courts found that gamecocks (birds trained to fight) are not within the general definition of "animal," a finding owing more to culture than to scientific reasoning. See the section later on animal fighting.

Case Study 6A

One old case considered the problem of a fox that had been captured and caged for a few days, and then the cage was opened up and the fox released:

The evidence tended to prove that the defendant let a fox loose from his custody in the presence of several dogs; that the fox ran into a thick wood and disappeared; that about five minutes afterwards the dogs were let loose, and pursued the fox, and caught it and tore it in pieces. The jury might have found that the fox was let loose by the defendant to be hunted by the dogs, and that the dogs were procured by him, and were let loose by his direction, in order that they should hunt the fox. The evidence is sufficient to prove these facts. The question is whether these facts constitute or prove the offense described in the statute.

The statute in question reads:

Pub.St. c. 207, § 53, provides that "every owner, possessor, or person having the charge or custody of an animal, who cruelly drives or works it when unfit for labor, or cruelly abandons it, or carries it, or causes it to be carried, in or upon a vehicle, or otherwise, in an unnecessarily cruel or inhuman manner, or knowingly and willfully authorizes or permits it to be subjected to unnecessary torture, suffering, or cruelty of any kind, shall be punished."

There is no question that hunting by dog was an exception to this statutory language. Did the capture of the fox change his status so as to be an "animal" under the act, and therefore that the act of release constituted an illegal act of suffering and torture? See **Commonwealth v. Turner,** 145 Mass. 296, 14 NE 130 (1887).

What Is Cruel?

The term "cruelty" represents something of an enigma. Just what is cruel? Should the focus be on a determination of the physical or physiological impact of an act on the animal, or is the motivation of the human more important? Is the infliction of any pain cruelty? What if the pain is inflicted for the animal's well-being, for economic

> **A Focusing Question**
>
> Is it death that is cruel or pain that is cruel?

reasons, or for human recreational benefit? It is clear that the term "cruelty," like the term "interstate commerce," has no set definition, but a meaning that evolves over time as the attitudes, morals, and perspectives of society change.

The vast number of diverse situations that one statute must cover is also a problem. Principles and concepts must be applied to the hunter, the cowboy on the open range, the teenager in the subdivision, the scientist in the laboratory, and the elderly couple in their apartment with their pet. Additionally, while the United States is one country, there are many regional cultures with different attitudes toward animals. Humans brand cattle, boil live lobsters, make lions jump through fire, discipline dogs by hitting them, practice surgery on pigs, and inject rats with new chemicals. Thousands of activities, like killing baby seals, are done for the benefit or comfort of humans. Other things are done to animals out of caprice or malice. Additionally, animals often suffer through human neglect and negligence.

In the end criminal cruelty is an act that a jury finds is beyond the boundary of socially/culturally acceptable conduct. The vagueness of the criminal language seen in many statutes reflects this need to balance and test the present standards of conduct by a jury; that which was not cruel 100 years ago may well be cruel today, and that which is acceptable today may be a criminal act tomorrow.

CASE BY CASE

Horton v. State

124 Ala. 80, 27 So. 468 (Feb. 8, 1900)

Arthur Horton was convicted of cruelly killing a dog, and he appeals. Reversed.

McMillian & Thetford, for appellant. Chas G. Brown, Atty. Gen., for the State.

DOWDELL, J. The defendant was prosecuted and convicted in the county court of Shelby county, under section 5093 of the Code of 1896, for cruelly killing a dog. The evidence, without conflict, showed that the defendant shot the dog with a rifle, producing almost instantaneous death of the animal. The question now presented is, does such a killing come within the meaning and purview of the statute? The statute reads:

> "Any person, who overrides, overdrives, overloads, drives when overloaded, tortures, torments, deprives of necessary sustenance, cruelly beats, mutilatees, or cruelly kills, or causes or procures to be overridden, overdriven, overloaded, driven when overloaded, tortured, tormented, deprived of necessary sustenance, cruelly beaten, mutilated, or cruelly killed, any domestic animal," etc.

The manifest purpose of the statute is the prevention of cruelty to domestic animals, and it is immaterial whether the cruelty is inflicted by the owner of the animal or by another. The word "cruelly," as employed in the statute, must have some significance, and when taken in connection with such other words as "tortures," "torments," "mutilates," or "cruelly beats," found therein, as well as with the manifest purpose of the statute, evidently means something more than to kill — the manner of the killing, such as tormenting or torturing to death, or prolonging the agony, suffering, and pain of the animal in terminating its life. It not being the purpose of the statute to punish the accused for any offense against the owner of the property, but its enactment being for the prevention of cruelty to the animal itself, it might follow that if the mere act of killing the animal, without more, be cruelty, within the meaning of the statute, then he who kills his pig or ox for the market would fall within the letter of the law, and, no exception being made in the statute as to the purpose of the killing, we must eat no more meat. We are of the opinion that under the undisputed evidence in the case the killing did not come within the character or description denounced by the statute, and the general charge should have been given for the defendant, as requested. Com. V. Lewis, 140 Pa. St. 261, 21 Atl. 396, 11 L.R.A. 522; Bish. St. Crimes, 1110, 1119, and notes citing authorities. The above view which we have expressed renders it unnecessary to notice the other rulings by the court on the giving and refusal of charges. The judgment of the court is reversed, and the cause remanded.

Questions & Notes

1. The New Hampshire and Mississippi laws do not now cover the act of killing an animal, but the other states do with a variety of language.

   - Cal. § 579(a): "[E]very person who maliciously and intentionally maims, mutilates, tortures, or wounds a living animal, or maliciously and intentionally **kills** an animal."

   - Va. § 3.2-6570(A): "Any person who (i) overrides, overdrives, overloads, tortures, ill-treats, abandons, willfully inflicts inhumane injury or pain not connected with bona fide scientific or medical experimentation, or cruelly or unnecessarily beats, maims, mutilates, or **kills** any animal."

- Mich. § 50b(2):"a person shall not do any of the following without just cause: (a) Knowingly **kill**, torture, mutilate, maim, or disfigure an animal."

- Minn. § 343.20 (3): " "Torture" or "cruelty" means every act, omission, or neglect which causes or permits unnecessary or unjustifiable pain, suffering, or **death**."

- Wash. §16.52.205: "Animal cruelty in the first degree … (c) **kills** an animal by a means causing undue suffering."

Make a chart of the qualifying words and see if you can define them in a criminal law context.

Is the killing of a cow for fast food hamburgers "necessary"?

Problem 6A

You are the prosecutor for a criminal case in which the defendant, who was without any financial resources, had a dog with cancer who had a month to live unless over a $1,000 worth of treatment could be provided. He killed the dog with one swing of a baseball bat. He is charged with a felony for the unjustified/unnecessary killing of an animal. The judge ask you to prepare an instruction for the jury on the issue of what constitutes an "unjustified/unnecessary killing." It cannot be more than one paragraph. Please draft such an instruction.

Torture, Torment, or Injury

"Torture, torment, unjustifiably injure." This is but one of many examples of overlapping, uncertain terms found in statutory anti-cruelty laws. In most dictionaries there is almost no difference between "torture" and "torment." (For these and all future unfootnoted definitions the author has sought the aid of *Balentine's Legal Dictionary* and *Webster's Third International Dictionary*.) In common parlance, "torture" perhaps refers more to physical pain and suffering, while "torment" refers to emotional or psychological stress. Some torture also constitutes injury (damage or harm to the body). Some injuries would be torturous, others would not. The language of the statute, then, suggests three different categories: pain of the body, distress of the mind, and injury of a physical nature. While the statute only qualifies the term "injury," the connotation of "torture" or "torment" also suggests unjustified action. When would torture of an animal ever be justified? Therefore, one way to restate this phrase would be: "the unjustified (i.e., without legally

recognized defense) infliction of injury, pain or mental distress." Examples of violations of this portion of the statute would include:

(a) An animal is chained and unable to escape. Mr. X approaches the animal, waves a torch in front of the animal's face, causing great distress (torment) to the animal, as reflected by her noises and body language.

(b) In the same situation, if X then put the torch to the fur of the animal (torture, infliction of pain), the statute would be violated a second time.

(c) If, for some reason, an animal is unconscious and while unconscious has her leg broken in one swift motion, there could be injury but not torture or torment.

Would any of the following constitute "torture, torment, or injury"?

(a) If a horse were shot in the head bringing almost instant death.

(b) If one were to shoot a horse in the leg and two hours later the horse is killed by injection by a veterinarian because it would never be able to walk.

(c) If a horse was given feed containing a poison that results in five hours of heavy breathing and bloat that compressed the lungs before death occurs.

Case Study 6B

Florida law states:

A person who intentionally commits an act to any animal which results in the cruel death, or excessive or repeated infliction of unnecessary pain or suffering, or causes the same to be done, is guilty of a felony of the third degree, punishable as provided in § 775.082 or by a fine of not more than $10,000, or both.

The evidence in this case consists of two parts:

The first in the form of two phone calls Aaroe made to the police station. In the first call he stated:

"Yeah I shot him. The son of a bitch got up underneath my trailer and both my dogs are raising all kinds of hell, got me up in the middle of the god damn night."

In the second call Aaroe stated:

"Well, that cat is still moving and if you want to get it before it is dead you had better come because I'm going to go out there and put another round into it."

The second part of the evidence was that Aaroe told the two investigating deputies who came to his home that he had shot the cat with his nine millimeter pistol, and one of the deputies found two shell casings of that caliber at the scene. A veterinarian who treated the cat, which had miraculously survived the shooting, testified that its right eye had been shot out of the socket, its skull had been fractured by the shot, and the cat was in shock and in pain. The veterinarian further testified that there were no injuries to the cat that could have been caused by a dog bite. Aaroe claimed at trial that he shot the cat to put it out of its misery after it had been mauled by his dogs.

Is this a violation of the law? Why?

See **Aaroe v. State**, 788 So. 2d 340 (Fla. 2001)

CASE BY CASE

One of the qualifying words often found in anti-cruelty laws is "malicious". This term requires a consideration not of the effect of the act on an animal but upon the motivations of the actor.

State v. Avery
44 N.H. 393 (1862)

This was an indictment, which alleged substantially that the respondent at, &c., on, &c., did willfully, maliciously and cruelly beat and wound one horse, of the value of $100, then and there being in his possession and keeping, &c. The defendant moved to quash the indictment, but the court overruled the motion, and the respondent excepted.

The testimony tended to show that in the afternoon of the 20th of July, 1861, the defendant was driving his own horse in a gigwagon, in and about Campton village, for a considerable space of time, and while so driving he continued, although with intervals of a few minutes, to whip his horse severely. The respondent's counsel objected that it appeared by the testimony that the whipping had ceased, and that no evidence of any whipping afterward should be received; but the court admitted the evidence, subject to exception, as tending to show one continued beating.

The jury found the defendant guilty, and he moved that the verdict be set aside and a new trial granted, by reason of said exceptions.

BELLOWS, J. The motion to quash the indictment was properly refused. By the Revised Statutes (ch. 215, sec. 10; Comp. Stat. 229, sec. 11), it is enacted that,

> [I]f any person shall willfully and maliciously kill, maim, wound, poison or disfigure any horse, cattle, sheep or swine of another, with intent to injure their owner, or any other person, he shall be punished by confinement to hard labor not less than one year nor more than three years, or by fine not exceeding $1000, and imprisonment in the common jail not exceeding one year.

One of the main questions is, whether evidence was admitted of more than one beating. It would seem that the evidence went to prove that the respondent beat his horse quite a long time, although with intervals of a few minutes, and the judge who tried the cause was of the opinion that the evidence tended to show a continued beating, or that the jury might so find; and upon a careful examination of the testimony we are disposed to concur with him. No objection, then, being made to the instructions on that point, it furnishes no reason for disturbing the verdict.

> **Think About It**
>
> The legal system gives maximum protection to preventing loss of life of humans. For nonhuman animals, however, the law's primary concern is with the unnecessary infliction of pain, not loss of life.

The admission of the testimony of Bachelder that the horse always drove well, unless harassed with the whip, is nothing more than evidence that he was kind and manageable, and is not, we think, a matter of opinion but of fact. Whether testimony as to his ordinary character was admissible or not, is not made a question by the case; but the objection is, that it was but matter of opinion. See Mills v. Quimby, 31 N.H. 489; Spear v. Richardson, 34 N.H. 430.

So in relation to the question to Mrs. Foss, whether she saw any thing vicious or obstinate in the horse; and the court might very properly decline to make any distinction in this respect founded on the difference of sex in the witnesses.

So also as to the question relative to the apparent effect of the blows upon the horse, which may well be regarded as calling for a statement of facts whether they caused the horse to start, or whether they left marks of such blows; and the form of this question is not material.

The instructions prayed for were substantially given, except upon the point that the jury must find that the acts complained of were done out of a spirit of wanton cruelty; instead of which the court instructed the jury that malice was not limited to ill-will to an animal, or its owner, or to wanton cruelty; but the act will be malicious if it results from any bad or evil motive; as from cruelty of disposition, from violent passion, a design to give pain to others. Of these instructions we think the defendant had no cause to complain. If the beating was wrongful, because cruel and severe, and was done intentionally, and without just cause or excuse, the law would regard it as malicious; and if, therefore, it was done from any of the motives enumerated by the judge, malice would be implied.

The law in question was designed to restrain the exercise of cruelty to animals, and is founded on a high moral principle, which denounces the wanton and unnecessary infliction of pain, even on animals created for the use of man, as contrary alike to the principles of Christianity and the spirit of the age. At the same time, there is no purpose to interfere with the infliction of such chastisement as may be necessary for the training or discipline by which such animals are made useful. The distinction is between that chastisement which is really administered for purposes of training and discipline, and the beating and needless infliction of pain, which is dictated by a cruel disposition; by violent passions, a spirit of revenge, or reckless indifference to the sufferings of others. If resorted to in good faith and for a proper purpose, it will not be necessarily malicious because it may be deemed to be excessive; but the undue severity should be carefully weighed by the jury in determining whether it was not in fact dictated by a malevolent spirit, and not by any justifiable motive. It is not, however, like the case of a parent or master, who has the right to inflict only moderate and reasonable chastisement, and is liable to punishment if he exceed it; but, under the law now in question, there is no liability for such excess unless it be found to be malicious. At the same time it must be considered that the chastisement which at first may be inflicted with a lawful motive, may, in its progress, engender such brutal and malignant passions as in the end to change entirely its character, and render the beating malicious within the meaning of the act; and this should operate as a salutary admonition to keep guard over the passions, lest the beating which, although always, or at least generally, of questionable utility, may degenerate into an unmanly and malicious crime.

We are satisfied, then, that there was no error in declining to charge the jury that they must find that the act was done out of a spirit of wanton cruelty; for the malice upon the principals we have stated, can not be so limited.

There must, therefore, be judgment on the verdict.

CASE BY CASE

Elisea v. State
777 N.E. 2d 46 (Ind. 2002)

Facts and Procedural History

The facts most favorable to the verdict reveal that on May 8, 2001, Shawn and William Stratton had twelve pit bull puppies. The Strattons learned that Elisea performed ear croppings on dogs and hired him to crop the ears on two of the puppies at their home. Elisea purchased three of the puppies from the Strattons during his visit to perform the ear croppings. During the procedure, Elisea had an assistant bind the dogs' legs and mouths with tape. Once immobilized, Elisea marked a line along each ear with an eyeliner pencil and, after numbing the ears with ice, but without any anesthetic, cut the dogs' ears with a pair of office scissors. Vaseline and Bactine were placed on each cut, and Elisea told Shawn to keep the puppies outside in the cold because their ears would heal more quickly.

In response to an anonymous phone call about neglected puppies, Johnson County Animal Control went to the Stratton home on May 10, 2001 to investigate. Assistant Warden Michelle Gilbert saw that the two puppies had "no ears at all" and "were covered in blood." The ears were not wrapped or sutured and appeared to be swollen and infected. Additionally, Gilbert noticed that the puppies were feverish and sluggish. Gilbert requested permission to take the puppies to a veterinarian, but Shawn refused. Following the visit from Animal Control, the Strattons took the puppies to a veterinarian, who prescribed an antibiotic pill and ointment for the badly infected ears. The veterinarian opined that the procedure performed by Elisea was quite inappropriate.

On May 11, 2001, Animal Control officers executed a search warrant at the Stratton home and took the puppies into their care. The State subsequently charged Elisea with one count each of cruelty to an animal and practicing veterinary medicine without a license. After being found guilty of the crimes, the trial court sentenced Elisea to a one-year executed jail sentence. He now appeals.

Discussion and Decision

In this case, to convict Elisea of cruelty to an animal, the State was required to prove that Elisea knowingly or intentionally tortured, beat, or mutilated a vertebrate animal resulting in serious injury or death to the animal. IC 35-46-3-12(a). Subsection (b)(2) provides that it is a defense if the defendant "engaged in a reasonable and recognized act of training, handling, or disciplining the vertebrate animal." Elisea maintains that the evidence is insufficient to support the conviction for cruelty to an animal because the State failed to present sufficient evidence to rebut and overcome his defense that he engaged in a reasonable and recognized act of handling the puppies. We disagree.

The legislature has not defined torturing, beating, or mutilating an animal. Therefore, we must give the statutory language its plain, ordinary, and usual meaning. Because there is no evidence that Elisea beat the puppies, we examine the plain and ordinary meaning of the terms "torture" and "mutilate." The dictionary meaning of the word "torture" is "to cause intense suffering [or] subject to severe pain." *Webster's Third New International Dictionary Unabridged* 2414 (1967). "Mutilate" means "to cut off or permanently destroy ... an essential part of a body" and "to cut up or alter radically so as to make imperfect." *Id.* at 1493.

Here, there is no question that cutting off the ears of the puppies was severely painful. Veterinarian Edward O'Connor testified that cutting the ears of the puppies without anesthesia would have "hurt like heck for a short period of time [and] there is going to be some long term pain associated with it." He later explained that there would be both acute pain and chronic pain associated with cutting the puppies' ears without anesthesia:

[F]irst of all the initial pain is acute pain. ... They are going to scream or cry. They are going to wiggle. The first response is escape. ... It hurts. It hurts a lot for a short period of time. That is acute pain. So, in the very beginning there could be some screaming or some whining and wiggling and trying to get away.

Following this, the veterinarian testified that chronic pain would develop and would last "quite awhile for several days." The puppies would be rubbing and pawing at their ears and rolling around because of the pain. Additionally, Dr. O'Connor opined that there would be a physiological response, which would entail an accelerated heart rate, higher blood pressure, and the release of certain compounds in the puppies' systems.

Finally, despite Elisea's argument to the contrary, the evidence presented by the State was sufficient to overcome his defense that he engaged in a reasonable and recognized act of handling the puppies. Dr. O'Connor testified that the procedure employed by Elisea was "[m]ost inappropriate." He explained that the puppies should have been anesthetized to alleviate most of the pain and that the cuttings should have been sutured to avoid scarring, promote healing, and prevent infection. Given the foregoing evidence, the trial court could have reasonably inferred that Elisea committed the crime of cruelty to an animal. We find no error. [The court also upheld his conviction for practicing veterinary medicine without a license.]

Questions & Notes

1. Why did the dog owners want to cut the ears of the puppies? Does it make a difference if it was for the whim of the owner or for breed standards adopted by the American Kennel Association? This is a fact pattern that fairly clearly sets out the "interests" of the human owner versus the interests of the animal. How would you balance these interests? How does the criminal law balance those interests? Would it have made any difference if the owners did these acts to their own dogs?

2. The prior two cases allow a consideration of the motivation of the actors in criminal law. In the two cases, what was the motivation? What motivation did the law require in order for there to be a violation of criminal law?

3. Should the legislature specifically make illegal the cropping of dog ears? Consider the New York statute:

   § 365. *Clipping or cutting the ears of dogs*

   > Whoever clips or cuts off or causes or procures another to clip or cut off the whole or any part of an ear of any dog unless an anaesthetic shall have been given to the dog and the operation performed by a licensed veterinarian, is guilty of a misdemeanor, punishable by imprisonment for not more than one year, or a fine of not more than one thousand dollars, or by both.

CASE BY CASE

A number of states now seek to segregate out a special set of intentional actions under the heading of "aggravated cruelty." Usually this is for purposes of assigning a higher level of punishment, usually making such actions a felony. Consider the following case:

State v. Witham

876 A. 2d 40 (Me. 2005)

JUDGE LEVY delivered the opinion of the court.

I. Background

In February 2004, Witham lived part-time with his girlfriend in Augusta. On February 26, Witham, who claimed to be allergic to cats, got into an argument with his girlfriend over whether the girlfriend's cat, which was pregnant, would reside with them in her apartment. Later that evening, the girlfriend approached Witham as he was sitting in his truck. He had the cat in a cat carrier on the seat next to him. The two started arguing again, with Witham complaining to the girlfriend that she was choosing the cat over him.

As the argument continued, Witham said, "last chance, [it's] either me or your cat." He then held the cat carrier out the window, screaming, "last chance, ... I'm leaving," and "choose, choose." Witham then dropped the cat carrier. He began to drive away, and in maneuvering around another car he ran over the cat carrier and killed the cat. A neighbor testified that he heard Witham howling and laughing as he drove away.

In May 2004, Witham was charged with, among other things, aggravated cruelty to animals, 17 M.R.S.A. § 1031(1-B)(B). A jury trial was held in November 2004. The jury found Witham guilty, and the court entered a judgment of conviction. [FN2] Witham filed this appeal.

> FN2. Witham was sentenced to a term of five years, with all but four suspended, and four years of probation.

II. Discussion

Witham contends that the aggravated cruelty to animals statute is unconstitutionally void for vagueness. [FN3] The statute provides:

> A person is guilty of aggravated cruelty to animals if that person, in a manner manifesting a depraved indifference to animal life or suffering, intentionally, knowingly or recklessly:
>
> A. Causes extreme physical pain to an animal,
>
> B. Causes the death of an animal; or
>
> C. Physically tortures an animal.
>
> 17 M.R.S.A. § 1031(1-B) (Supp. 2003).

Witham asserts that the phrase "manifesting a depraved indifference to animal life or suffering" provides no intelligible standard to guide individual conduct. He points out that the statute does not define "depraved indifference to animal life or suffering," and contends that the lack of guidance leaves courts, law enforcement officials, and the public guessing at the statute's meaning.

"The Due Process Clause of the Fifth Amendment to the United States Constitution [and Article I, section 6-A of the Maine Constitution] require[ ] that criminal defendants be given 'fair notice of the standard of conduct to which they can be held accountable.' " State v. Weeks, 2000 ME 171, ¶ 7, 761 A.2d 44, 46 A statute is unconstitutionally vague "when it fails to 'define the criminal offense with sufficient definiteness that ordinary people can understand what conduct is prohibited and in a manner that does not encourage arbitrary and discriminatory enforcement.' " Weeks, 2000 ME 171.

People of common intelligence can understand that in the context of cruelty to animals, the term "depraved indifference" is an objective standard similar to that applied in the context of murder. Witham was not left to guess whether his conduct was in violation of the statute. See

Weeks, 2000 ME 171, ¶ 7, 761 A.2d at 46. He needed only to ask himself whether a reasonable person would find his conduct to be morally debased, posing a high degree of risk, and manifesting a total lack of concern for the cat's death or suffering.

Here, the trial court cogently instructed the jury that:

> [T]he State has to prove to convict the defendant of aggravated cruelty that he acted in a manner manifesting a depraved indifference to animal life. That means that regardless of what the creates a very high degree of risk [to] animal life or suffering. [T]he death producing [ ] conduct must be conduct which when objectively viewed demonstrates an almost total lack of concern or feeling for the value of animal life.

There is nothing vague or uncertain about assessing Witham's conduct by these standards. His actions created a very high degree of risk of causing the cat to suffer and its subsequent death. It is also conduct that, when viewed objectively, could be found by a reasonable jury to demonstrate an almost total lack of concern or feeling for the value of animal life. Accordingly, 17 M.R.S.A. § 1031(1-B) is not void for vagueness.

Questions & Notes

1. Is the focus of this crime that the animal suffered more than in other fact patterns? What justifies the enhanced status of this crime?

2. What is depraved indifference? Is he guilty?

3. What to you think about the appropriateness of the jail sentence?

Case Study 6C

Assume a man comes home drunk and shortly thereafter it is discovered that one of his dogs has been stabled to death and the other assaulted and later dies of his injuries. After conviction and a two-year sentence, the defendant appeals the conviction, claiming that the state had to prove he had the specific intention to violate the law. The state said that they only had to prove a general intention. The statute reads:

Every person who maliciously and intentionally maims, mutilates, tortures, or wounds a living animal or maliciously and intentionally kills an animal is guilty of a violation of section 597 [Calif.]

The appeals court holds that only general intent is required—that is, that he did indeed strike, or stab, the dogs in question. As a rule, the term "intentionally" requires only that the agent acted intentionally in engaging in the proscribed conduct, and not that the agent knew that the conduct was proscribed.

The Court said that to make it a specific intent crime, the law would have to be drafted differently:

If the Legislature intended section 597, subdivision (a) to describe a specific intent crime, it would have used language describing an act and an additional purpose for which the act was done. For instance, the statute could have read, "Every person who maliciously and intentionally strikes a living animal, with the intent to maim, mutilate, etc." Or, the statute could have read, "Every person who maliciously and intentionally maims, mutilates, tortures or wounds a living animal, for the purpose of inflicting pain and suffering. ..." Drafted in either manner, the statute would have described a specific intent crime.

Consider the difficulty the state would have in proving beyond a reasonable doubt the subjective intention of a person, rather the objective acts of a person. For an extensive discussion of this issue, which represents the clear majority rule for anti-cruelty statutes, see **People v. Alvarado**, 125 Cal. App. 4th 1179 (2005).

Section 3

Constitutional Issues

CASE BY CASE

The new age of technology has provided some individuals with opportunity and motivation to engage in a type of intentional cruelty that might make a court reiterate that one public policy reason for the anti-cruelty laws was to protect humans from immoral acts that might corrupt them or other humans. In this case some unique constitutional defenses are raised by the defendant to justify his acts.

People v. Voelker
172 Misc. 2d 564, 658 N.Y.S. 2d 180 (1997)

Defendant was arrested on October 2, 1996 and charged with three counts of Overdriving, Torturing and Injuring Animals pursuant to § 353 of the Agriculture and Markets Law ("AML"). These charges stem from a videotaped incident wherein defendant is alleged to have cut off the heads of three live conscious iguanas without justification. Defendant was arraigned in Criminal Court on November 19, 1996. A superseding complaint was filed on November 22, 1996.

Defendant moves to dismiss the accusatory instrument pursuant to CPL § 170.30(1)(a) and § 170.35(1)(a) upon the ground that it is facially insufficient in that it fails to adequately allege every element of the offense charged pursuant to CPL § 100.15 and § 100.40. Defendant also maintains that dismissal is required because the statute is being unconstitutionally applied.

The complaint in this case alleges, in pertinent part, that on or about and between February 6, 1996 and August 2, 1996 at 85 Havemeyer Street, apartment 1L in Brooklyn, the defendant allegedly cut off the heads of three live, conscious iguanas without justification. The complaint alleges further that Assistant District Attorney Todd Davis (hereinafter "deponent") is in possession of and has viewed a videotape showing the defendant committing the acts alleged. Additionally, the complaint alleges that deponent was informed:

> by Michael Pescatore that informant is the owner of the building at the above location, that he has viewed the videotape mentioned above, that the room pictured in said videotape is inside the above location, and that informant leased the apartment that includes said room at the above location to Eric Voelker from February 6, 1996 to the present;

[and]

by Frank Fitzgerald that informant recorded said videotape on August 9, 1996, from a television broadcast by Manhattan Neighborhood Network of the show entitled "Sick and Wrong," and that informant saw the same incident broadcast on an earlier edition of the show, "Sick and Wrong," aired on August 2, 1996.

Defendant maintains that an essential element of AML § 353 is an "unjustifiable act" toward an animal, and that the allegation that defendant cut off the heads of three live iguanas, "without justification," is conclusory and insufficient. Defendant contends that killing the animals in this case was justified and necessary and that any pain or suffering was temporary, unavoidable and without criminal intent.

The People maintain that the term "without justification" means just what it says, that defendant cut off the heads of three animals without apparent justification. Thus, the allegations in the accusatory instrument provide reasonable cause to believe that the defendant committed the offense charged and establish, if true, every element of the offense charged.

The People maintain further that defendant's alleged "justification defense" does not support the motion to dismiss and that the issue of justification is a question of fact to be determined at trial. Additionally, the People argue that defendant's acts were unjustified in that defendant violated the state's anti-cruelty statute by cutting off the heads of three conscious iguanas and that the mere fact that defendant thereafter allegedly cooked and consumed these animals does not justify defendant's actions.

Discussion

In this case, the Information consists of the complaint, taken together with the supporting depositions of Frank Fitzgerald and Michael Pescatore. Those depositions merely attest to the fact that each informant has read the accusatory instrument filed and that the facts stated in the complaint are true based upon personal knowledge. Thus, this Court is limited to reviewing the factual allegations as stated in the complaint.

AML § 353 provides that:

> A person who overdrives, overloads, tortures or cruelly beats or unjustifiably injures, maims, mutilates or kills any animal, whether wild or tame, and whether belonging to himself or to another, … or causes, procures or permits any animal to be overdriven, overloaded, tortured, cruelly beaten, or unjustifiably injured, maimed, mutilated or killed, … or in any way furthers any act of cruelty to any animal, or any act tending to produce such cruelty, is guilty of a misdemeanor. …

An "Animal" is defined as "every living creature except a human being," AML § 350(1), and "torture" is defined as "every act, omission, or neglect, whereby unjustifiable physical pain, suffering or death is caused or permitted" AML § 350(2).

In People ex rel. Freel v. Downs, 136 N.Y.S. 440 (1911), defendant, captain of a ship, was convicted of causing, procuring and permitting turtles to be transported in a manner that caused unnecessary and unjustifiable pain and suffering. The turtles had their fins pierced and were tied together through the holes with a string. The court explained that "[t]he question as to whether the pain caused to such creatures, often classed as dull nervous organisms, is 'justifiable' or not, cannot be easily answered." Id. at 445. Moreover, the court held that the question of what constitutes cruelty is an issue of fact to be decided upon all the evidence in a prosecution for cruelty to animals. Id. at 446.

Defendant cites the *Downs* decision for the proposition that where the acts against the animal are "temporary, unavoidable, and without criminal intent ... than [sic] it is not torture as that term is here employed." See, Defendant's Affirmation at § 5 citing, *Downs*, supra, at 444. Defendant's reliance on *Downs* is misplaced in that he misquotes the *Downs* decision. In *Downs*, supra, at 444, the court held that:

> [t]he torture that would justify a criminal prosecution must be some mode of inflicting bodily pain that is unjustifiable and unnecessary; but if the pain and suffering is temporary, unavoidable without criminal intent, and necessary to preserve the safety of the property involved and to overcome any danger or injury to such property, then it is not torture as that term is employed in legal parlance.

Thus, it is clear that the justification for killing or torturing the animals must be of the type necessary to preserve the safety of property or to overcome danger or injury, People v. Downs, supra; see also, People v. Bunt, 118 Misc.2d 904, 462 N.Y.S.2d 142 (1983), or the type of legal justification specifically authorized by statute. See PL § 35.05. Moreover, whether an act of cruelty and infliction of pain was justified or unjustified is a question to be determined by the trier of facts based upon the moral standards of the community. People v. Bunt, supra.

In this case, to establish a prima facie case of Overdriving, Torturing and Injuring Animals, the Information must contain non-hearsay factual allegations which establish that defendant did torture or unjustifiably injure, maim, mutilate or kill three live iguanas.

This Court holds that the acts of cutting off the heads of three conscious iguanas are acts which certainly injure, maim, mutilate and kill. This Court holds further that the term "without justification" is not a legal conclusion but a factual allegation that means what it says, i.e., with no apparent justification; to demand that the People address an infinite number of justification defenses would place an undue burden on the People requiring them to supply trial quality evidence in the body of an accusatory instrument. Whether or not the People can prove that defendant "unjustifiably" committed these acts is a matter best left to the trier of fact.

Accordingly, defendant's motion to dismiss for facial insufficiency is denied.

The Constitutional Issue

Defendant also moves for dismissal upon the ground that AML § 353 is being unconstitutionally applied in that the motivation for the prosecution of defendant is that he chose to televise an act that is normally relegated to the back room of a restaurant, and that such content-based restrictions on speech are unconstitutional.

There is no question that government action that stifles speech on account of its message, or that requires the utterance of a particular message favored by the government, contravenes an individual's rights under the First Amendment. Turner Broadcasting v. F.C.C., 512 U.S. 622, 114 S. Ct. 2445, 129 L. Ed.2d 497 (1994). However, it is well established that a content-neutral restriction on speech will be upheld if:

> it furthers an important or substantial governmental interest; if the governmental interest is unrelated to the suppression of free expression; and if the incidental restriction on alleged First Amendment freedoms is no greater than is essential to the furtherance of that interest.

Turner Broadcasting v. F.C.C., supra at 662, 114 S. Ct. at 2469, quoting, United States v. O'Brien, 391 U.S. 367, 377, 88 S. Ct. 1673, 1678, 20 L. Ed. 2d 672 (1968).

Contrary to defendant's contention, this Court holds that the animal cruelty statute at issue is not a content-based restriction on speech. Rather, it is a restriction against torturing, injuring, maiming, mutilating or killing animals. The statute is not directed at any form of communication. Furthermore, the People correctly point out that although the statute might prohibit the torturing of an animal as a form of expression, such a statute would not be unconstitutional where it serves a legitimate governmental interest, Barnes v. Glen Theatre, Inc., 501 U.S. 560, 567, 111 S. Ct. 2456, 2460, 115 L. Ed. 2d 504 (1991), and that the U.S. Supreme Court has indicated that a neutral anti-cruelty statute which is limited to the government's legitimate interest in the prevention of cruelty to animals may be upheld despite its effect on religious observance. Church of the Lukumi Babalu Aye, Inc., and Ernesto Pichardo v. City of Hialeah, 508 U.S. 520, 538, 113 S. Ct. 2217, 2229, 124 L. Ed. 2d 472 (1993).

Moreover, defendant is not being prosecuted because he televised the decapitation of the iguanas. The televising of the decapitations merely provided law enforcement officials with a way to observe a defendant engage in criminal activity. A defendant cannot shelter himself from prosecution by the mere televising of a criminal act. Taking defendant's argument to its logical conclusion, a defendant could televise any criminal act and seek to shield himself from prosecution on First Amendment grounds. Such an argument defies common sense and cannot be sustained.

The Court holds that AML § 353 is not being unconstitutionally applied in this case. Accordingly, defendant's motion to dismiss is denied on this ground.

If you were on the jury would you find the defendant guilty? In the next case study the presence of pain and suffering is much clearer.

Case Study 6D

A case of charged torture against animals arose in the late 1990s when the Internet became available as a means of distribution of film, bypassing normal retail outlets. Consider the case of **People v. Thomason**, 84 Cal. App. 4th 1064 (2000), which describes the following as the facts:

On information from a Ventura County District Attorney investigator who had learned, through a chat room and subsequent conversation with defendant, that he had produced a "crush video" [FN2] depicting rats, mice and baby mice ("pinkies") being crushed and killed by a female under heel of her shoe, Officer William Le Baron and other officers conducted a search of defendant's apartment for any evidence of his production and distribution of videos. Officer Le Baron found 30 or 40 videos in defendant's closet, then asked defendant for the crush video he had filmed with codefendant Diane Aileen Chaffin. Defendant told the officer the videotape was with the others and labeled "Diane." Officer Le Baron found two "Diane" videotapes which, defendant stated, had been filmed at the home of Chaffin's parents. Other items seized were defendant's computer containing chat room conversations relating to crush videos, clips taken from crush videos and still images.

> FN2 "Crush videos" are fetish videos in which small animals are taunted, tortured, then crushed to death under the feet of provocatively dressed women.

The videotape in evidence is 60 minutes long and shows Chaffin crushing numerous mice, baby mice and rats under the heel of her shoe and under her bare feet. Part of the videotape depicts a mouse being held down and Chaffin crushing the animal to death; the mice and rats were "stepped on to the point where intestines and innards are torn apart and taken out of them. It is then smashed into the ground until the mouse or rat or pinkie appears to be dead and it stops moving.

The defendants were found guilty of violating the following section:

"Except as provided in subdivision (c) of this section or Section 599c, every person who maliciously and intentionally maims, mutilates, tortures, or wounds a living animal, or maliciously and intentionally kills an animal, is guilty of an offense punishable by imprisonment in the state prison ..."

The defendants claimed that killing mice were exempted under the statute as either a wild animal or a health code concern. Additionally they claimed the statute was void for vagueness. How would you rule on appeal?

While the prior case and case study dealt with the death of animals recorded on video, the act of harm itself and not the distribution of the video was the legal focus. But, it quickly became apparent that crush videos in particular would be very hard to stop if only the act against the animal could be prosecuted. It is always done in private by parties seeking secrecy. A prosecutor viewing a tape will not be able to know when or where the tape was made, and thus prosecution is almost impossible. The best way to deal with this issue was to make the distribution of the videos on the internet a crime, just as it is a crime to distribute child pornography. In record time Congress adopted a new criminal law.

The original version of the statute read:

18 USC § 48. Depiction of animal cruelty

(a) CREATION, SALE, OR POSSESSION.-Whoever knowingly creates, sells, or possesses a depiction of animal cruelty with the intention of placing that depiction in interstate or foreign commerce for commercial gain, shall be fined under this title or imprisoned not more than 5 years, or both.

(b) EXCEPTION.-Subsection (a) does not apply to any depiction that has serious religious, political, scientific, educational, journalistic, historical, or artistic value.

(c) DEFINITIONS.-In this section-

(1) the term 'depiction of animal cruelty' means any visual or auditory depiction, including any photograph, motion-picture film, video recording, electronic image, or sound recording of conduct in which a living animal is intentionally maimed, mutilated, tortured, wounded, or killed, if such conduct is illegal under Federal law or the law of the State in which the creation, sale, or possession takes place, regardless of whether the maiming, mutilation, torture, wounding, or killing took place in the State; and

(2) the term 'State' means each of the several States, the District of Columbia, the Commonwealth of Puerto Rico, the Virgin Islands, Guam, American Samoa, the Commonwealth of the Northern Mariana Islands, and any other commonwealth, territory, or possession of the United States.

After this became law, the crush videos did fairly well disappear from the internet. However, it was the prosecution of a defendant with a long history of distribution of dog fighting videos that found its way to the U.S. Supreme Court.

CASE BY CASE

United States v. Stevens

130 S. Ct. 1577 (2010)

Two primary issues were addressed by the Court:

(1) Should the video materials described under this law be exempt from 1st Amendment protection as child pornography is exempt?

The eight judge majority stated, in part:

The First Amendment provides that "Congress shall make no law ... abridging the freedom of speech." "[A]s a general matter, the First Amendment means that government has no power to restrict expression because of its message, its ideas, its subject matter, or its content." Ashcroft v. American Civil Liberties Union, 535 U.S. 564, 573, 122 S. Ct. 1700, 152 L. Ed.2d 771 (2002). Section 48 explicitly regulates expression based on content: The statute restricts "visual [and] auditory depiction[s]," such as photographs, videos, or sound recordings, depending on whether they depict conduct in which a living animal is intentionally harmed. As such, § 48 is " 'presumptively invalid,' and the Government bears the burden to rebut that presumption."

When we have identified categories of speech as fully outside the protection of the First Amendment, it has not been on the basis of a simple cost-benefit analysis. In *Ferber*, for example, we classified child pornography as such a category, 458 U.S., at 763, 102 S. Ct. 3348. We noted that the State of New York had a compelling interest in protecting children from abuse, and that the value of using children in these works (as opposed to simulated conduct or adult actors) was de minimis. Id., at 756-757, 762, 102 S. Ct. 3348. But our decision did not rest on this "balance of competing interests" alone. Id. We made clear that *Ferber* presented a special case: The market for child pornography was "intrinsically related" to the underlying abuse, and was therefore "an integral part of the production of such materials, an activity illegal throughout the Nation." Id. As we noted, " '[i]t rarely has been suggested that the constitutional freedom for speech and press extends its immunity to speech or writing used as an integral part of conduct in violation of a valid criminal statute.' "

Judge Alito in his sole minority opinion stated:

It must be acknowledged that § 48 differs from a child pornography law in an important respect: preventing the abuse of children is certainly much more important than preventing the torture of the animals used in crush videos. It was largely for this reason that the Court of Appeals concluded that *Ferber* did not support the constitutionality of § 48. 533 F.3d, at 228 ("Preventing cruelty to animals, although an exceedingly worthy goal, simply does not implicate interests of the same magnitude as protecting children from physical and psychological harm"). But while protecting children is unquestionably more important than protecting animals, the Government also has a compelling interest in preventing the torture depicted in crush videos.

The animals used in crush videos are living creatures that experience excruciating pain. Our society has long banned such cruelty, which is illegal throughout the country. In *Ferber*, the Court noted that "virtually all of the States and the United States have passed legislation proscribing the production of or otherwise combating 'child pornography,' " and the Court declined to "second-guess [that] legislative judgment." Here, likewise, the Court of Appeals erred in second-guessing the legislative judgment about the importance of preventing cruelty to animals.

Section 48's ban on trafficking in crush videos also helps to enforce the criminal laws and to ensure that criminals do not profit from their crimes. See 145 Cong. Rec. 25897 (Oct. 19, 1999) (Rep.Gallegly) ("The state has an interest in enforcing its existing laws. Right now, the laws are not only being violated, but people are making huge profits from promoting the violations"); id., at 10685 (May 24, 1999) (Rep.Gallegly) (explaining that he introduced the House version of the bill because "criminals should not profit from [their] illegal acts"). We have already judged that taking the profit out of crime is a compelling interest.

In short, *Ferber* is the case that sheds the most light on the constitutionality of Congress' effort to halt the production of crush videos. Applying the principles set forth in *Ferber*, I would hold that crush videos are not protected by the First Amendment.

(2) Assuming the videos are protected speech then the question is the constitutionality of a statute that does limit speech activities. The court uses an "overbreadth" analysis to find the statute as written is overbroad and therefore must be set aside. A statute is guilty of overbreadth when it exceeds the police power of the state, asserting itself into fact patterns where the interests of the state does not justify the intrusion on to the rights of private individuals.

Majority of the Court:
Section 48 creates a criminal prohibition of alarming breadth. The statute's definition of a "depiction of animal cruelty" does not even require that the depicted conduct be cruel. While the words "maimed, mutilated, [and] tortured" convey cruelty, "wounded" and "killed" do not. Those words have little ambiguity and should be read according to their ordinary meaning. Section 48 does require that the depicted conduct be "illegal," but many federal and state laws concerning the proper treatment of animals are not designed to guard against animal cruelty. For example, endangered species protections restrict even the humane wounding or killing of animals. The statute draws no distinction based on the reason the conduct is made illegal.

Moreover, § 48 applies to any depiction of conduct that is illegal in the State in which the depiction is created, sold, or possessed, "regardless of whether the ... wounding ... or killing took place" there, § 48(c)(1). Depictions of entirely lawful conduct may run afoul of the ban if those depictions later find their way into States where the same conduct is unlawful. This greatly expands § 48's scope, because views about animal cruelty and regulations having no connection to cruelty vary widely from place to place. Hunting is unlawful in the District of Columbia, for example, but there is an enormous national market for hunting-related depictions, greatly exceeding the demand for crush videos or animal fighting depictions. Because the statute allows each jurisdiction to export its laws to the rest of the country, § 48(a) applies to any magazine or video depicting lawful hunting that is sold in the Nation's Capital. Those seeking to comply with the law face a bewildering maze of regulations from at least 56 separate jurisdictions.

Limiting § 48's reach to crush videos and depictions of animal fighting or other extreme cruelty, as the Government suggests, requires an unrealistically broad reading of the statute's exceptions clause. The statute only exempts material with "serious" value, and "serious" must be taken seriously. The excepted speech must also fall within one of § 48(b)'s enumerated categories. Much speech does not. For example, most hunting depictions are not obviously instructional in nature. The exceptions clause simply has no adequate reading that results in the statute's banning only the depictions the Government would like to ban.

We therefore need not and do not decide whether a statute limited to crush videos or other depictions of extreme animal cruelty would be constitutional. We hold only that § 48 is not so limited but is instead substantially overbroad, and therefore invalid under the First Amendment.

Dissenting opinion of Judge Alito:

The overbreadth doctrine "strike[s] a balance between competing social costs." *Williams*, 553 U.S., at 292, 128 S. Ct. 1830. Specifically, the doctrine seeks to balance the "harmful effects" of "invalidating a law that in some of its applications is perfectly constitutional" against the possibility that "the threat of enforcement of an overbroad law [will] dete[r] people from engaging in constitutionally protected speech." Ibid. "In order to maintain an appropriate balance, we have vigorously enforced the requirement that a statute's overbreadth be substantial, not only in an absolute sense, but also relative to the statute's plainly legitimate sweep." Ibid.

In determining whether a statute's overbreadth is substantial, we consider a statute's application to real-world conduct, not fanciful hypotheticals. Accordingly, we have repeatedly emphasized that an overbreadth claimant bears the burden of demonstrating, "from the text of [the law] and from actual fact," that substantial overbreadth exists. Similarly, "there must be a realistic danger that the statute itself will significantly compromise recognized First Amendment protections of parties not before the Court for it to be facially challenged on overbreadth grounds." Members of City Council of Los Angeles v. Taxpayers for Vincent, 466 U.S. 789, 801, 104 S. Ct. 2118, 80 L. Ed. 2d 772 (1984) (emphasis added).

III

In holding that § 48 violates the overbreadth rule, the Court declines to decide whether, as the Government maintains, § 48 is constitutional as applied to two broad categories of depictions that exist in the real world: crush videos and depictions of deadly animal fights. Instead, the Court tacitly assumes for the sake of argument that § 48 is valid as applied to these depictions, but the Court concludes that § 48 reaches too much protected speech to survive. The Court relies primarily on depictions of hunters killing or wounding game and depictions of animals being slaughtered for food. I address the Court's examples below.

A

I turn first to depictions of hunting. As the Court notes, photographs and videos of hunters shooting game are common. But hunting is legal in all 50 States, and § 48 applies only to a depiction of conduct that is illegal in the jurisdiction in which the depiction is created, sold, or possessed. §§ 48(a), (c). Therefore, in all 50 States, the creation, sale, or possession for sale of the vast majority of hunting depictions indisputably falls outside § 48's reach.

Straining to find overbreadth, the Court suggests that § 48 prohibits the sale or possession in the District of Columbia of any depiction of hunting because the District-undoubtedly because of its urban character-does not permit hunting within its boundaries. The Court also suggests that, because some States prohibit a particular type of hunting (e.g., hunting with a crossbow or "canned" hunting) or the hunting of a particular animal (e.g., the "sharp-tailed grouse"), § 48 makes it illegal for persons in such States to sell or possess for sale a depiction of hunting that was perfectly legal in the State in which the hunting took place.

The Court's interpretation is seriously flawed. "When a federal court is dealing with a federal statute challenged as overbroad, it should, of course, construe the statute to avoid constitutional problems, if the statute is subject to such a limiting construction." Ferber, 458 U.S., at 769, n. 24, 102 S. Ct. 3348. See also Williams, supra, at 307, 128 S. Ct. 1830 (STEVENS, J., concurring) ("[T]o the extent the statutory text alone is unclear, our duty to avoid constitutional objections makes it especially appropriate to look beyond the text in order to ascertain the intent of its drafters").

Applying this canon, I would hold that § 48 does not apply to depictions of hunting. First, because § 48 targets depictions of "animal cruelty," I would interpret that term to apply only to depictions involving acts of animal cruelty as defined by applicable state or federal law, not to depictions of acts that happen to be illegal for reasons having nothing to do with the prevention of animal cruelty. See ante, at ---- - ---- (interpreting "[t]he text of § 48(c)" to ban a depiction of "the humane slaughter of a stolen cow"). Virtually all state laws prohibiting animal cruelty either expressly define the term "animal" to exclude wildlife or else specifically exempt lawful hunting activities, so the statutory prohibition set forth in § 48(a) may reasonably be interpreted not to reach most if not all hunting depictions.

Within a few weeks of the release of this opinion in 2010, a new House Bill was drafted, indeed several were drafted. Not withstanding a gridlocked Congress and Congressional elections in the fall of that year, a bill was passes and signed by the President. The key part of the new law:

Public Law No: 111-294 (2010)

Sec. 48. <<NOTE: 18 USC 48.>> Animal crush videos

``(a) Definition.--In this section the term `animal crush video' means any photograph, motion-picture film, video or digital recording, or electronic image that--

``(1) depicts actual conduct in which 1 or more living non- human mammals, birds, reptiles, or amphibians is intentionally crushed, burned, drowned, suffocated, impaled, or otherwise subjected to serious bodily injury (as defined in section 1365 and including conduct that, if committed against a person and in the special maritime and territorial jurisdiction of the United States, would violate section 2241 or 2242); and

``(2) is obscene.

``(b) Prohibitions.--

``(1) Creation of animal crush videos.--It shall be unlawful for any person to knowingly create an animal crush video, if--

``(A) the person intends or has reason to know that the animal crush video will be distributed in, or using a means or facility of, interstate or foreign commerce;

or

``(B) the animal crush video is distributed in, or using a means or facility of, interstate or foreign commerce.

``(2) Distribution of animal crush videos.--It shall be unlawful for any person to knowingly sell, market, advertise, exchange, or distribute an animal crush video in, or using a means or facility of, interstate or foreign commerce.

``(c) Extraterritorial Application.--Subsection (b) shall apply to the knowing sale, marketing, advertising, exchange, distribution, or creation of an animal crush video outside of the United States, if--

``(1) the person engaging in such conduct intends or has reason to know that the animal crush video will be transported into the United States or its territories or possessions; or

``(2) the animal crush video is transported into the United States or its territories or possessions.

``(d) Penalty.--Any person who violates subsection (b) shall be fined under this title, imprisoned for not more than 7 years, or both.

Questions & Notes

1. Why did Congress do such a poor job of drafting the first version of the law? Do you think the new language adequately addresses the concerns of the Supreme Court?

2. A key to allowing an exception to 1st Amendment protection is that the interests of the state must be "compelling." Do you think the state interest in the case of crush videos is compelling? How about dog fighting videos? How about chopping off the heads of iguanas? What makes an interest compelling?

3. Which of the overbreadth arguments do you think is strongest? Does the draft of a new version of the statute overcome the concerns of the majority opinion?

4. Besides the cruelty to animals in fighting videos and crush videos, is there social concern about the moral corruption of the humans? Can this be a basis for legal intervention? Why is the original law a five year felony in this federal legislation when most state cruelty law violations are misdemeanors or up to two year felonies? What is the constitutional basis giving Congress the right to pass this animal related law, since the various states have primary jurisdiction?

5. Cruelty statutes have, on several occasions, been attacked as unconstitutionally vague. The concept of due process requires that a criminal statute be reasonably definite as to the persons and conduct that are intended to come within the scope of the stat-

ute. The two tests appropriate for cruelty statues are: (1) does the statute fail to give a person of ordinary intelligence fair notice that his contemplated conduct is forbidden by the statute, and (2) does the statute, as drafted, encourage arbitrary and erratic arrest and convictions? There is a potential problem with cruelty statutes in that most terms used in these statutes are broad in scope and not defined within the statutes themselves. On the other hand, it would be impossible to list, by particular acts, everything that would be unlawful. The number of animals, as well as the number of potential human activities, makes any listing impractical. Rather, generic terms like "torture," "injury," and "cruelty" are used. With the exception of the gamecock cases discussed later, cruelty statutes are seldom attacked as vague. Most courts and defendants are apparently well satisfied that the statutes give sufficient notice. **People v. Rogers**, 183 Misc.2d 538, 703 N.Y.S.2d 891 (2000).

Section 4

Defenses & Exemptions

Although not stated in the statutes, it is presumed that the common concept of self-defense is available to justify what would otherwise be a criminal act against an animal. The clearest example is when the animal actually attacks the human. In two cases, an animal (one a cat, the other a dog) affixed their jaws upon the defendants. In both cases, the animal was killed in the process of being dislodged, with varying evidence as to the amount of force used. The courts overturned both convictions on the grounds that the killing was in self-defense. **McMinnis v. State**, 541 S.W.2d 431 (Tex. 1976); **State v. Spencer**, 29 A.2d 398 (N.J. 1942). When an individual is seeking to use the concept of self-defense, only that force that is appropriate to the degree of the threat or danger may be used. It would be unreasonable force to kill with a shotgun a duck that was nipping at an individual's leg. The degree of force was not examined closely by either of the courts, as indeed it is difficult to judge such activities after the heat of the confrontation has passed. It should be noted that once the threat is removed, subsequent actions against the animal would be considered revenge, which is not a defense to a cruelty action.

The concept of self-defense also extends to reasonable fear of immediate harm to self and others, although again only reasonable force is justified. A more complicated issue is protection of property when there is no fear of personal injury. The outcome may depend on statutory language, particularly when dealing with dogs. Given the remedy of damages through civil suits, it would take an unusual situation to justify cruelty in defense of property (unjustified force). Many of these issues are the same as those surrounding the killing or injuring of human trespassers by a property owner.

CASE BY CASE

State v. Wrobel

3 Conn. Cir. Ct. 57, 207 A. 2d 280 (1964)

KOSICKI, JUDGE.

The defendant was found guilty, after a trial to a jury, of cruelly beating or unjustifiably injuring an animal in violation of General Statutes, § 53- 247, which is printed in the footnote.

> CRUELTY TO ANIMALS. Any person who overdrives, drives when overloaded, overworks, tortures, deprives of necessary sustenance, mutilates or cruelly beats or kills or unjustifiably injuries any animal, or who, having impounded or confined any animal, ... shall be fined not more than two hundred and fifty dollars or imprisoned not more than one year or both.

The essential facts which are not in dispute, may be summarized as follows: The defendant, on May 2, 1963, the date of the alleged offense, was, and for twenty years had been, the dog warden of East Hartford. In response to complaints which he had received on that date concerning roaming dogs in the vicinity of 99 Great Hill Road, he went there prepared to investigate the complaints and to act in his official capacity. Upon arrival, he noticed two stray dogs, one of which he caught and placed in a cage in his truck without incident. The other, a black dog, remained in the vicinity. The defendant learned from Mrs. Parker, who resided at the address, that the black dog and other dogs had been around her house because a female dog she owned was in heat. The defendant fastened a noose on the black male dog and proceeded to lead it away. The dog slipped out of the noose but remained close by. A large number of children, returning to school from lunch, had gathered at the scene. The defendant tried to fasten the noose again but the dog, in eluding him, bit him on the right hand, and arm. The defendant then lifted the dog by its hind leg and carried it to the truck.

While he was reaching to open the door, the dog turned and locked its teeth onto the defendant's knee, causing him severe pain. To extricate himself, the defendant seized the dog by both hind legs and slammed it against the truck. The dog then locked its jaws onto the defendant's right foot. The defendant tried to shake the dog loose but was unsuccessful. The defendant then, still holding the dog by its legs, stepped on the dog's head with his left foot and pinned the dog to the ground. He then secured the dog and put it in the cage in the truck. Subsequently, the defendant's leg and knee started to swell and, that same day, he was treated at the Hartford Hospital emergency room for dog bites of the right hand and thigh. On the following day, the dog was examined by a veterinarian and was found to have a bruise over the left eye, a small wound over the left ear, a small wound on the left shoulder, small wounds in the mucous membranes of the mouth, and inflammation around the wounds.

At the close of the evidence, the defendant moved for a directed verdict and the motion was denied. There was conflicting evidence on the issues of cruelty and justification and, on the state of the evidence, it could not be said that the issues of fact were left to conjecture, surmise and speculation. Blados v. Blados, 151 Conn. 391, 395, 198 A.2d 213. The court's action in submitting the facts to the jury was proper. [The jury found the defendant guilty of criminal acts.]

The [Defendant also claimed that the] charge was inadequate in that it failed to define and relate to the evidence the words "cruelly" and "unjustifiably" as they appear in the statute. It was not enough, for the guidance of the jury, to define cruelty in its general sense or abstract connotation. See, e.g., Greenberg v. Branciere, 100 Conn. 596, 600, 124 A. 216. What is cruelty under one set of circumstances may not be cruelty in another. The issue of justification, we believe, was treated too abruptly. It was left to the jury to determine whether the defendant was justified in doing what he did. Further, explication, it appears, was needed, pointing to the extent and limits of the defendant's duty and authority as dog warden: that in performing his duty he may not only resort to force, beating, injuring or killing a roaming dog but may be required to do so; that the application of such force, although it may appear to be cruel to bystanders, who are under no responsibility to act, may be the practicable and reasonable means to accomplish the capture and impounding of the offending dog, and therefore not within the statutory meaning of cruelty. On the other hand, the defendant was not immune from prosecution if he acted in excess of his authority or in abuse of the discretion vested in him; and it was for the jury to determine whether the acts of the defendant were such as were reasonably necessary to accomplish the lawful purpose of confining the dog, or whether they amounted to a wanton, brutal, or vicious use of force; and whether the conduct of the defendant was such as flowed from vengeful, inhuman motives or was impelled by the urgency of duty and the need for self-protection. The defendant's motion to set aside the verdict should have been granted. Fleischer v. Kregelstein, 150 Conn. 158, 161, 187 A.2d 241.

Questions & Notes

1. Is "cruel" determined by looking at the impact of the action on the animal in question or on the motivation of the actor?

2. Please define what constitutes a cruel act against a law student or an animal.

◇◇

Abandonment

A special category of intentional acts under cruelty law is the prohibition against abandonment. The common law definition of the term in the property law context, as it relates to personal property such as animals, requires an intentional mindset of relinquishment of title by an act showing the giving up of dominion and control over the animal. Thus, in the criminal law context, abandonment may be considered an intentional act of cruelty. Obviously it is not the actual act of walking or driving away from an animal that is cruel. Rather, it is the predictable harm or suffering that will arise after the abandonment. Note that it is not the death of the animal that is sought to be controlled, but the high possibility of future pain and suffering. It should not be surprising that a criminal prohibition against abandonment was in the first New York law (§ 7), as abandoned horses on the city streets of New York was a prime motivator for the adoption of that first law.

Case Study 6E

Would You Prosecute?

On July 24, 1999, McDonald stopped his van on the side of the road in front of the Holly Street power plant near an entrance to the Town Lake Hike and Bike Trail. McDonald opened the back doors of the van, pulled out a black bag, and dropped it on the ground next to the van. A puppy came out of the bag and ran toward the trail. Two security guards from the power plant witnessed these events. One guard approached McDonald and told him to take the dog with him. McDonald refused, saying "[t]hat dog ain't even mine." McDonald presented evidence at trial showing that his son's friend had found the stray dog and placed it in the van without McDonald's knowledge. McDonald and his wife were on their way to the grocery store when his wife first heard a noise coming from the back of the van. McDonald stopped the van by the trail to investigate. He opened the rear doors and saw a black bag that was moving. McDonald testified that he became scared, grabbed the bag, and dropped it on the ground, which is when the puppy jumped out.

The security guards reported the incident to animal control, and an investigator interviewed McDonald at his house three days later. According to the investigator, McDonald first denied knowing of the incident, then acknowledged that a friend of his son's had brought the puppy over and because it was not his dog, McDonald had taken it away. When the investigator indicated that lack of ownership did not excuse abandoning a dog, McDonald changed his story again to indicate he only discovered the dog in his van when he was driving to the store with his wife and was so startled he let it loose at the trail. McDonald maintained at trial that he did not know about the puppy's presence in his van until after he left home. The investigator determined otherwise from the interview and all the facts, concluding that McDonald found the puppy and intended to drive it to a remote area to abandon it because it did not belong to him.

Your jurisdiction has the following law: "A person commits an offense if he intentionally or knowingly … abandons unreasonably an animal in his custody." How would you define abandonment? How would you define his relationship to the animal? Would you file criminal charges? What level of punishment is appropriate?

See **McDonald v. State**, 2001 WL 837905 (Tex. App.-Austin).

News Bits

In September 2005 Ms. Murry of Ohio decided to abandon 33 kittens in a nearby woods as she was "moving and having personal problems." She was found guilty of abandonment of an animal and sentenced by the court to spend a night in the woods without water, food, or light.

Exemptions to Cruel Acts

As the materials of the this chapter suggest, the determination of what constitutes an illegal act under the anti-cruelty laws of the various states relates more to the social or cultural acceptability of the human action rather than the impact of the action on an animal. This occurs because the legal system is always balancing the interests of humans with those of animals. In the prior materials it was the role of the court to decide in a particular fact pattern whether an individual act was acceptable, and therefore not a crime, or unacceptable and thus a crime. The law gives the court a modest context in which to make this judgment, using terms such as "cruel," "unnecessary" and "overburden." The laws adopted by the legislature allow for this weighing of interests by the a judge or a jury.

The legislatures, beginning with the 1867 New York law, also decided that in some areas of human activity the interests of the humans would always outweigh the interests of the animals and when they created statutory exceptions to the cruelty law. If an action falls within an expressed exception, regardless of the pain, suffering or death of the animal, the human interest wins and the courts are unable to judge an action as being in violation of the cruelty laws. Section 10 of the 1867 New York law created an exemption for properly conducted scientific experiments, thus allowing the intentional infliction of pain and suffering on animals for the advancement of scientific knowledge. When human acts are within the scope of a legislatively created exemption, no court can seek to balance the interests of the humans against the animals.

As an example of the law today, consider the existing Michigan law, MCLA §750.50, which provides:

> 8) This section does not prohibit the lawful killing or other use of an animal, including, but not limited to, the following:
>
> (a) Fishing.
>
> (b) Hunting, trapping, or wildlife control regulated pursuant to the natural resources and environmental protection act.
>
> (c) Horse racing.
>
> (d) The operation of a zoological park or aquarium.
>
> (e) Pest or rodent control.
>
> (f) Farming or a generally accepted animal husbandry or farming practice involving livestock.
>
> (h) Scientific research pursuant to 1969 PA 224.

Questions & Notes

1. What public policy (human interests) supports each of the above exemptions?

2. Can changes in technology support changing the exemptions? What about the fact that rodents can sometimes be kept out of buildings with the use of sound generators? Is the use of poison still an acceptable balance of human versus animal interests? Are there any other categories where advancing technology might require a rebalancing of the interests?

3. There are now individuals and organizations within the United States who wish to revisit these exemptions to the anti-cruelty laws and take away the blanket exemptions that now exist (see *www.farmsanctuary.org/*). For example, is it really necessary to impose cruel conditions on agricultural animals in order to raise food animals? If the answer is no, then why is there a blanket exemption for farming practices?

4. The case of **Taub v. State**, 296 Md. 439, 463 A.2d 819 (1983) is the only criminal action ever brought against a scientist for violation of a state anti-cruelty law for acts in a research laboratory. The trial-level conviction was not based on the scientific experiment itself, but on the lack of care provided a set of monkeys used for research while housed for the experiment. The arrest and conviction were based on the undercover investigation of a private individual, Alex Pacheco, the co-founder of the People for the Ethical Treatment of Animals. The state prosecutor of this case went on to become a member of the Board of Directors of the Animal Legal Defense Fund. As a result of the trial court conviction, the Institute for Behavioral Research had its quarter-of-a-million-dollar research project suspended by the National Institute of Health. On appeal, the court created an exception for the defendant, which was later supported by an amendment to the Maryland law, § 10-603, exempting such activity in the future.

One human activity that impacts millions of animals annually is the practice of sport hunting and fishing. Every state has extensive regulations about hunting. Which portion of the state code applies when humans harm deer?

Case Study 6F

Mr. Cleve was the owner of a 100-acre ranch on which he attempted to raise cattle. His land was often visited by deer that ate his crops and pastures. After unsuccessful attempts to control the presence of the deer by the state game agency, Cleve shot at least 13 deer, five in the abdomen, and snared two others. In one of the snares, a fawn was caught by the neck and died of strangulation, probably within about five minutes of being caught. In the other snare, a spike buck was caught by its antlers and died of either stress-related fatigue, starvation, or dehydration.

The State charged Cleve with three counts of negligent use of a deadly weapon, see NMSA 1978, § 30-7-4 (1993), seven counts of cruelty to animals, see NMSA 1978, § 30-18-1 (1963), and 15 counts of unlawful hunting, see NMSA 1978, § 17-2-7(A) (1979).

The issue facing the court was whether the existence of the game laws (unlawful hunting) preempted the area so as to make the application of the cruelty law provisions inappropriate in his case. What would you decide? See **State v. Cleve**, 127 N.M. 240, 980 P.2d 23 (1999).

Another exception to the anti-cruelty laws presents a different set of difficulties. Animals used in agriculture were historically a localized activity, for the most part; the animals were supervised by the owners of the animals—the "traditional" family farm. Today, while localized animal use certainly continues to exist, vast numbers of animals destined for the food stores of the world are part of large commercial corporations whose primary purpose is to create maximum profits for shareholders. The owners of the animals never have to look their property in the eye, or listen to them complain.

A key issue in this area is what constitutes "traditional agricultural practices" as most statutory exemptions use that phrase. It is unclear what the word "traditional" might mean—those practices used by the average producer or the high-volume producer, 100-year-old practices vs. farming practices that are only 20 years old? State prosecutors seem entirely disinterested in pursing what is or is not protected by such exemptions. Why might this be the case?

> **Think About It**
>
> Research reported in 2003 suggested that fish felt pain when their lips were injected with bee venom. This was in contradiction with other research that suggested that fish brains did not have the structure necessary to feel pain as mammals do.
>
> Alok Jha, *Scientist claims fish do feel pain*, The Guardian, April 30, 2003.

Case Study 6G

Would You Prosecute?

Owners of Wards Poultry Farm had 30,000 egg layers who were past egg laying and would normally have been sent to slaughter. Because of a Newcastle disease outbreak in California, the farm was quarantined and therefore unable to send the chickens to slaughter. They asked a vet how to dispose of the chickens and were informed that they could kill them by putting them through a wood shredder, while still alive. This they proceeded to do. A humane society urged them to stop the process, but they continued. [Carbon dioxide gas was used at other farms unable to ship.] The farmer's defense is that he was only doing what the veterinarian said he could do. Is this a violation of the anti-cruelty law if the law provides that "acceptable agricultural practices" are exempt from the anti-cruelty law?

See Elizabeth Fitzsimmons, *Live Hens Were Put in the Wood Chipper*, Union-Tribune, April 11, 2003.

Section 5

Animal Fighting

When humans force animals to fight each other, significant pain and suffering occurs for the sake of the pleasure of the human observers. (Why it is pleasurable for humans to observe the pain and death of an animal is a critical issue not within the realm of a law course.) Unfortunately, the destruction of animals for human pleasure has a long history. The ancient Roman Circus is an opulent, but not isolated, example of the injury and death of animals for human gratification:

> In 13 BC 600 African Beasts were slain; in 2 BC 260 lions were slaughtered in the Circus Maximus. ... Under Claudius, 300 bears and 300 Libyan beasts; and Nero's bodyguard brought down with javelins 400 bears and 300 lions.

J.M.C. Toynbee, Animals in Roman Life and Art, 21 (1973).

The practice of animal death for human entertainment continues today. The bull fights of Mexico and Spain remain as public events. (However, in 2010 the Catalonia section of Spain adopted a law outlawing bull fighting within their portion of the country, so change is in the wind even in Spain.) Dog and cock fighting remain as a more private activity in many countries.

The interest of humans in engaging in animal fighting has been judged by most legislatures in the U.S. to be an unacceptable justification for the pain, suffering, and death of the animals. In many states, the judgment of the legislature is so firm as to make such activities felony criminal violations. Into the beginning of the 21st century, in a few states, the cultural tradition of this activity still has sufficient political power to allow the continued existence of cockfighting. An activity in Detroit might get a jail term of four years, while the same acts in Arizona are perfectly legal. This is an unusually clear example of how the cultural context is not uniform across the United States. For examples of those promoting cockfighting see *www.sabong.net.ph/*.

CASE BY CASE

An informal dog fight.

T.J. v. State of Indiana
932 N.E. 2d 192 (2010)

On August 28, 2009, Leah Slate (Slate) was driving near the intersection of Dearborn Street and Nowland Avenue in Indianapolis, Indiana, when she noticed two boys, eleven-year-old T.J. and thirteen-year-old L.M., standing in the fenced in yard of Felipa Maleonado (Maleonado). Slate observed the boys hitting a large brown dog that resembled a pit bull with a stick. About this same time Maleonado heard commotion in her back yard, looked out the window, and saw T.J. and L.M. in her back yard, standing there, watching a dog attack her dog. She heard one of the boys saying, "[g]et 'em, get 'em." (Transcript p. 27).

Slate got out of the car and noticed that the large dog was attacking a small dog, and the boys were making "sss, sss" sounds. (Tr. p. 5). Slate asked the boys, "[h]ey, what are you guys doing," but they did not respond. (Tr. p. 6). About this time, Maleonado's husband came out of their house and the boys left the yard through a gate that had been previously closed, but was open when they left the yard. Slate helped Maleonado's husband get the larger dog to stop attacking the small dog. The small dog was mangled from the attack and died from its injuries.

While separating the dogs, Slate told the boys that she was going to call the police, to which one boy responded: "F you B." (Tr. p. 10). Slate watched the boys walk to the porch of a neighboring house. After she and Maleonado's husband got the larger dog off of Maleonado's dog, the larger dog left Maleonado's yard and followed the boys onto the front porch of the neighboring house. Slate and Maleonado's husband approached the house and could hear "the people on the porch snickering and laughing." (Tr. p. 11).

T.J. contends that the State did not present sufficient evidence to prove beyond a reasonable doubt that he committed the offense of promoting or staging an animal fight, I.C. § 35-46-3-9.

Indiana Code section 35-46-3-9, entitled "Promotion, use of animals or attendance with animal at animal fighting contest," provides: "A person who knowingly or intentionally: (1) promotes or stages an animal fighting contest; (2) uses an animal in a fighting contest; or (3) attends an animal fighting contest having an animal in the person's possession; commits a Class D felony." By using the word "or" the statute is written in the disjunctive, and if charged accordingly, a defendant may be convicted of a Class D felony if he commits either of the three activities. However, Count II of the delinquency petition filed by the State alleged only that T.J. had knowingly or intentionally promoted or staged an animal fighting contest. Therefore, our consideration of the sufficiency of the evidence is limited to the elements of subsection (1) of the statute.

Fuller v. State, 674 N.E.2d 576 (Ind. Ct. App. 1996) is the sole published appellate decision considering the sufficiency of the evidence to sustain a conviction under I.C. § 35-46-3-9. Unlike in *Fuller*, here witnesses saw the dog attack. The testimony provided by Slate and Maleonado support a reasonable inference that T.J. and L.M. were encouraging the larger dog to attack the smaller dog. Maleonado heard the boys saying "[g]et em, get em." (Tr. p. 27). Slate heard the boys making "sss, sss" sounds. (Transcript p. 5). Further, Slate testified that during the vicious attack:

> [The boys] were just watching. They were just watching this dog attack this little dog. I mean they didn't even ... They didn't even look like ... To me, if they were gonna ... If they were like trying to attempt to stop the dog, they would've been like, "Stop ... [."]

[We] conclude that this eye-witness testimony supports a reasonable inference that T.J. made possible and encouraged the dog fight and is sufficient evidence to prove beyond a reasonable doubt that T.J. promoted or staged an animal fighting contest.

CONCLUSION

Based on the foregoing, we conclude that the State presented sufficient evidence to support the juvenile court's finding that T.J. knowingly or intentionally promoted or staged an animal fighting contest.

Affirmed.

CASE BY CASE

The next case represents the other extreme, a formal, organized dog fight and an undercover police investigation.

People of the State of Michigan v. Norfleet

2010 WL 3564829 (Mich. App. - unpublished)

I. Basic Facts

Wayne County Sheriff's Department Undercover Officer Shontae Jennings testified that on July 13, 2008, she went to a house on 263 Nevada, in Detroit, Michigan, to investigate a possible dogfight. When she arrived, there were 6 to 8 people in the backyard. Officer Jennings went into a detached garage and observed a square "arena" and a "weighing station." After leaving the garage, Officer Jennings was shown a pitbull dog that was going to fight that night. Officer Jennings then waited in the backyard, observing as more people arrived, until they numbered about 50 or 60. Officer Jennings observed the other people "[s]moking marijuana, drinking, getting dogfight bets, [and] talking about previous dog fights." Officer Jennings testified that she saw Norfleet and Smith among the people in the backyard.

After several hours of waiting, Officer Jennings then watched as the dogfight preparations began. She explained that she saw another pitbull brought into the backyard. Each dog was then washed with a milk solution to rinse off any chemicals that might discourage the other dog from biting. After the washing, one of the dogs was placed inside the arena, and people continued making bets. Officer Jennings also explained that people paid a $30-$35 entrance fee as they entered the garage. She testified that she waited until everyone else was inside the garage before she went in; she believed that she was the last person to enter because she did not recall anyone coming in behind her.

Once inside the garage, Officer Jennings had trouble seeing the arena, so she was allowed to move to the front of the crowd to watch the fight. She identified Smith as the referee. Officer Jennings testified that she also saw Norfleet in the garage. According to Officer Jennings, Smith read the rules and then the fight began. Officer Jennings then text messaged Lieutenant Walter Epps (whom she had been updating by text message all along) that the fight had begun. Shortly thereafter, a response team raided the garage. When the raid team entered, they yelled, "This is a raid. Everybody, lie down[.]" However, most of the people ran.

Sergeant Tyrone Jackson testified that he was assigned to the raid unit on the night of the dogfight. He was responsible for coordinating the outside perimeter to prevent suspects from escaping. Sergeant Jackson explained that he had eight to ten officers located around the perimeter. According to Sergeant Jackson, when the raid team went into the backyard, he stayed out in front of the house, and, after he heard the raid team announce the raid, he saw people scattering everywhere from the back-yard; it was a chaotic scene. Sergeant Jackson was able to detain three people, including Norfleet. Sergeant Jackson testified that he caught Norfleet as he was running from a yard just west of the address in question.

Mark Ramos, a senior investigator for the Michigan Humane Society, was qualified as an expert in the area of dog fighting. He went to the scene of the dogfight on July 14, 2008, and took photographs. At trial, Ramos explained that the photographs depicted dog-fighting equipment, including the washing items and the arena. Ramos testified that he also removed one of the dogs from the location when he went to the scene. Ramos explained that the dog had "active wounds[,]" including injuries to "his top muzzle, his head, [and] the side of his mouth, ... his neck and lower part of the chest." Ramos testified that the dog's injuries were bite wounds. The dog also had an open would on his leg and "significant scarring." Ramos testified that the dog's injuries were consistent with dog fighting. Ramos testified that three days later he received a call from the sheriff's department, asking him to pick up the other dog from a veterinarian's clinic. There were no wounds on the second dog's face, but the dog had a gunshot wound. It was stipulated that a deputy shot this dog when it ran from the scene. The jury found Norfleet guilty of attending the dogfight. Norfleet now appeals.

During the charge to the jury, the trial court instructed them as follows: "The prosecution must prove beyond a reasonable doubt that Armond Norfleet was present at 263 Nevada in Detroit, Michigan where an exhibition for the fighting or baiting of an animal was occurring, knowing that said exhibition was taking place and/or about to take place." MCL 750.49(2)(f) states, "A person shall not knowingly ... [b]e present at a building, shed, room, yard, ground, or premises where preparations are being made for an exhibition described in subdivisions (a) to (d), or be present at the exhibition, knowing that an exhibition is taking place or about to take place." "[A]n exhibition described in subdivisions (a) to (d)," includes fighting or baiting an animal.

Analysis

Norfleet's argument is essentially that his conviction was against the great weight of the evidence because Officer Jennings' identification of him was not credible. Norfleet attempts to call Officer Jennings' testimony into question by pointing out that, during cross-examination, she admitted that she had misidentified a certain man as being a principal participant. Norfleet also points out that, in her investigation report, Officer Jennings described the referee as having a "light complexion," while Smith, who she identified as the referee, actually had a dark complexion. Norfleet further points out that a photo taken of the scene on the night of the incident showed that it was dark and that it was not possible to identify the persons in the photo. Norfleet also points to Officer Jennings' own testimony that the garage was packed with people, that she had never seen nor met Norfleet before the incident in question, that she never specifically identified Norfleet in her text messages or in her report, and that she did not actually see Norfleet walk into the garage nor did she recall seeing him pay an entrance fee.

Officer Jennings also testified that, while she was waiting in the backyard for the fight to start, she saw Norfleet among the people in the backyard. She explained that there was a floodlight attached to the back of the house and that the area was "[v]ery well lit." Officer Jennings also testified that there were "regular incandescent lights" in the garage and that it was "[v]ery well lit." She confirmed that she did not have any problems seeing anything inside the garage. Mark Ramos, the senior investigator for the Michigan Humane Society, similarly testified that the there was "bright light" in the garage, and he confirmed that he had "very good visibility inside the garage." Moreover, Smith also testified that the garage was "well lit."

Additionally, Sergeant Jackson testified that he caught Norfleet as he was running from a yard just west of the address in question.

Considering the evidence as a whole and leaving any credibility issues to the province of the jury, we conclude that the evidence does not preponderate so heavily against the verdict that it would be a miscarriage of justice to allow the verdict to stand. Rather, there was competent evidence on the record to support Norfleet's presence at the dogfight. Norfleet cannot demonstrate that any plain error affected his substantial rights, and we will not vacate his conviction on the basis of this issue.
Affirmed.

Questions & Notes

1. Why did the dog fights in the prior two cases occur? What constitutes a "dog fight" for purposes of the criminal statute? How is it proven in court? What social and economic conditions support these activities?

2. Do you think that being a spectator at a dog fight should be a crime? Consider the difficulty of meeting the burden of proof, beyond a reasonable doubt, with 50 people running away in different directions. Having undercover police present at the fight itself is often critical to enforcement. Note the use of technology in making the bust happen. How did she get into the fight location?

3. Dog fighting is also a federal crime (7 U.S.C. Sec 2156). The most famous case being that of Michael Vick. In the summer of 2007 the quarterback for the Atlanta Falcons, a professional football team, was indicted on federal charges of dogfighting. (The 18-page indictment is available at www.animallaw.info.) The information in the charges suggest multiple years of activities, including professional fighting contracts with $10,000-plus purses and the killing of a number of dogs who were not good fighters. His visibility brought the national spotlight to the issue and it was discussed on radio sports channels, public television, and many newspaper articles. In December 2007 Vick was sentenced to 23 months in federal prison. He was also found guilty under state dog fighting charges on dogfighting, but did not serve any additional jail time. In July of 2009 he was released from jail and shortly thereafter returned to being a professional quarterback.

Cockfighting

In several states cockfighting remained legal even after dog fighting was outlawed. Cockfighting did not go away without several legal disputes. Why do you think cockfighting might be perceived differently by legislatures and courts?

Edmondson v. Oklahoma, 91 P. 3d 605 (Okla. 2004). In this case the petitioners (the attorney general and others) sought declaratory relief from the court by way of upholding the constitutionality of the statute outlawing cockfighting, after various companies and individuals obtained a temporary injunction preventing the enforcement of the statute. The Supreme Court held the following:

(1) The court is entitled to invoke original jurisdiction;

(2) the statute did not amount to an uncompensated regulatory taking;

(3) the statute did not violate the state or federal constitutional Contract Clause;

(4) the statute did not violate the state constitutional provision regarding the right to life, liberty, and the pursuit of happiness;

(5) the statute did not infringe on the right to travel between states; and

(6) the statute was not unconstitutionally overbroad.

In 2006 some individuals found it hard to believe that prohibitions on cockfighting would be enforced. See **Savage v. Prator**, 921 So. 2d 51 (La. 2006) where two Louisiana "game clubs" filed an action for declaratory judgment and injunctive relief against parish commission and parish sheriff's office after being informed by the sheriff that an existing parish ordinance prohibiting cockfighting would be enforced. The clubs contended that the ordinance was violative of the police power reserved explicitly to the state (the state anti-cruelty provision is silent with regard to cockfighting). The First Judicial District Court, Parish of Caddo, granted the clubs' request for a preliminary injunction. The Supreme Court of La. reversed the injunction and remanded the matter, finding that the parish ordinance prohibiting cockfighting did not violate general law or infringe on state's police powers in violation of the constitution.

In March 2007, New Mexico Gov. Bill Richardson signed into law a ban on cockfighting. As part of the press release he said: "Today, New Mexico joins 48 other states in affirming that the deliberate killing of animals for entertainment and profit is no longer acceptable." In the summer of 2008 Louisiana became the last state to outlaw the practice of cockfighting. It is now illegal in all of the United States.

While support for lawful cockfighting has almost faded, the idea of animal fighting seems to just find other forms. Another variation in animal fighting is where a dog is turned loose in a confined area with a hog, and the dog attacks the hog. See *www.cbsnews.com/stories/2006/01/27/national/main1245804.shtml*. Would this be illegal under standard cruelty laws? Will special laws be needed?

Another entertainment use of animals is the bull fighting of Spain, Portugal, and Mexico. How should historical traditions be balanced against the pain, suffering, and perhaps death of animals?

CHAPTER 7

Anti-Cruelty Laws — Duty to Provide Care

Another set of criminal statutes dealing with animals requires that a minimum level of care be provided by humans to animals within their possession and control. These statutes deal with nonfeasance or omissions rather than prohibitions against the commission of certain acts. (See Chapter 6.) The public policy supporting the "duty to provide care" statutes is more directly concerned with the interests of the animal than the conduct of the human. Animals are living entities, and those within the dominion of humans are often/ usually unable to care for themselves. When humans have taken control of animals or purchased or propagated them for their own purposes, society has decided there is an obligation for the humans to care for them. Thus, this section focuses on the duty of assuring care of the animals, rather than on prevention of unacceptable human conduct.

This chapter does not include materials about the key federal law, the Animal Welfare Act and its regulations that have much to say about the care of some animals by some owners. This important federal law has a chapter of its own—Chapter 10. It is different from the state laws discussed in this chapter in that the federal law is regulatory in nature, using a permit and inspection system with a focus primarily on civil enforcement rather than criminal law enforcement. Additionally, the number of animals covered is much more limited than the state anti-cruelty laws.

Henry Bergh's New York Law of 1867 contains only two short phrases on the issue of duty of care. In section 1 of the Act is the phrase "deprive of necessary sustenance" and in section 3 of the act, when discussing impounded animals, it says "a sufficient quantity of good and wholesome food and water" should be supplied. Most of the reported cases of the late 1800s dealt with intentional acts of cruelty, not duty to provide care. Perhaps public sentiment was not yet in a position to support criminal charges for neglect of animals versus infliction of pain on animals.

Whatever definitional problems exist with intentional acts, the problems for "duty of care" provisions are twice as difficult. It is fairly clear when a horse is being beaten; it is less clear when a horse has not received adequate food. Over time the statutory provisions for many states have become increasingly detailed in setting out specific standards for helping define what duty of care means. However, it is important to keep in mind that the criminal law only acts after the animal has suffered. It is not preventative in structure.

Section 1

Which Animals, Which People?

There must be some legally recognized connection between the animal and the human before the law will impose a duty of care. The most common phrases describing responsible parties are "owner," "possessor," or "person having charge or custody," the latter being a factual determination of dominion and control over the animal. One case held an individual responsible for animals in one house even though she had moved her residence to another. This was because she still had exclusive control and right of possession for the house and the animals located in the house. (**Smith v. State**, 285 S.E. 2d 749 (Ga. 1981).)

A more difficult question arises when the owner does not have custody, and the individual with custody fails to provide the required care. Most courts are reluctant to impose liability on the owner for the failure to provide care, based on ownership alone. The Michigan court has held that ownership alone is not sufficient. There must be a showing of actual custody (**Trager v. Thor**, 516 N.W. 2d 69 (1994)). In an Oregon case, five dogs were found in an underfed and abused state, and their only tie to the defendant was the name on the animals' collars. The court found this insufficient to find the defendant guilty (**Hunt v. Hazen**, 197 Or. 637, 254 P. 2d 210 (1953)). A Connecticut case concerned a pet owner who left on vacation after leaving her animal with another. The bailee, possessor of the animal, did not adequately care for the animal and the owner was charged. The state court reversed the conviction, noting that the defendant did not have custody and was not negligent in making the arrangements for care of the animal (**Malone v. Steinberg,** 138 Conn. 718, 89 A. 2d 213 (1952)). The courts are focusing on those in a position to carry out the care of the animals, rather than merely on ownership.

In the case of **State v. Klammer**, 230 Minn. 272, 41 N.W. 2d 451 (1950) the owner had an on-site manager for some 28 horses, but the owner fired the manager and never returned to care for the horses. The fired manager tried to feed the horses for a few weeks but then just walked away. All 28 died of starvation. The owner was held liable for violation of the cruelty statute. Death makes it easy to find a violation of the law, but the condition of being underfed makes application of the law of duty of care more difficult.

Case by Case

State v. Jackson
2010 WL 3011287 (Wash. App. Div. 2)

FACTS

On March 4, 2008, Donna Ray, Ryan Jackson's neighbor, called animal services to report on the condition of Jackson's two dogs. Ray spotted one of the dogs, Nikki, a shepherd mix, foaming at the mouth, and the other, Ginger, a beagle mix, so thin that she was having a hard time standing. Both dogs appeared very distraught. Upon closer examination, Ray found the dog kennel covered in feces and the food and water bowls empty.

Officers Kenneth Maynard and Erika Quinn-Ellenbecker of animal services responded to the call and transported the dogs to a nearby veterinary clinic. Dr. Karen Hook diagnosed Nikki with gastric dilatation (bloating) and volvulus (a twisted bowel), the latter requiring emergency treatment. Given Nikki's poor prognosis, animal services elected to euthanize her. Ginger was given food and water and kept in the hospital overnight.

On April 1, 2008, animal services received two more of Jackson's animals: a slightly underweight cat and a more severely underweight gecko. Dr. Tiffany Rainier-Quitania examined the cat, finding him stressed, dehydrated, and slightly thin. Dr. Noreen Jeremiah examined the gecko, finding him severely malnourished.

The State charged Jackson with two counts of first degree animal cruelty and two counts of failure to provide humane care. A jury convicted Jackson on both counts of animal cruelty (relating to Nikki and Ginger) and one count of failure to provide humane care (relating to the gecko). Before sentencing, Jackson moved for a new trial, arguing juror misconduct. The trial court denied Jackson's motion.

ANALYSIS

I. Sufficiency of the Evidence

Jackson contends the State failed to prove animal cruelty and failure to provide humane care. He argues he presented ample evidence contradicting the State's allegations, including evidence that he fed and cared for all his pets and that Nikki's extreme thinness was likely a result of Cushing's disease. Jackson also argues the State failed to prove that the dogs experienced "substantial and unjustifiable [pain] extending over a period of time." Br. of Appellant at 21.

To convict on a charge of animal cruelty, the State must prove beyond a reasonable doubt that the defendant, with criminal negligence, starved, dehydrated, or suffocated an animal, causing substantial and unjustifiable physical pain that extended for a period of time sufficient to cause considerable suffering or death. RCW 16.52.205(2). To convict for failure to provide humane care, the State must prove that a defendant owned a pet and failed to provide necessary food, water, shelter, rest, sanitation, ventilation, space, and medical attention in a way that imperiled the animal's health. Thurston County Code (TCC) 9.10.050(f).

The State elicited extensive testimony concluding that the animals were starved. On a scale of one (emaciated) to nine (fat), Officer Quinn-Ellenbecker rated both dogs as a one. Dr. Hook, who examined and treated both dogs, testified that they were emaciated and skeletal. Dr. Paul Mabrey, Jackson's expert witness, opined that Nikki's physical condition was attributable to Cushing's disease and that blood tests showed no indication of starvation. But Dr. Hook, who performed the tests and autopsy, testified that while Cushing's could have caused Nikki's symptoms, she could not say conclusively that Nikki had the disease. Dr. Hook also testified that several of the symptoms that could have been a result of Cushing's disease could have also been a result of starvation. Here, the jury was entitled to weigh the evidence, reasonably concluding that the physical condition of the dogs was a result of starvation.

The State also presented evidence of Jackson's negligence. Officer Quinn-Ellenbecker testified there was no food or water in the kennel and that she found dust covering the empty food bowl and dried up algae in the water bowl. While Jackson offered evidence of receipts for dog food, Officer Quinn-Ellenbecker calculated that, based on the food bag and receipts found in Jackson's house, he had been feeding the dogs only a fraction of what they should have been receiving. Dr. Hook confirmed that after performing an autopsy on Nikki, without finding an obvious cause for her thinness, she suspected Nikki had not been regularly fed. She also testified that Nikki's life-threatening condition upon arrival at the clinic may have been caused by a meal ingested by an animal not used to eating. Finally, Ginger improved significantly under the care of animal services, gaining back weight and muscle tone, primarily through regular feedings. All this evidence-taken in the light most favorable to the State-supports the conclusion that Jackson negligently caused the dogs' emaciated condition.

Lastly, Officer Quinn-Ellenbecker testified that Nikki was in pain when she first arrived at the scene. Dr. Hook confirmed that Nikki felt pain, particularly from the bloating. She also testified both dogs would have experienced pain lying on their kennel's concrete floor in their emaciated conditions; that they would have been cold due to their thin coats and little fat; and that it would have been distressing for them to live in their kennel's unsanitary conditions. Moreover, it was reasonable for the jury to infer that Nikki and Ginger experienced pain from hunger. "Pain," as this court previously defined, is "a state of physical or mental lack of well-being or physical or mental uneasiness that ranges from mild discomfort or dull distress to acute often unbearable agony"; "hunger" is "the discomfort, weakness, or pain caused by lack of food." State v. Zawistowski, 119 Wn. App. 730, 734, 83 P. 3d 698 (2004) (quoting Webster's Third New Int'l Dictionary at 1621 (1969) and Webster's II New Coll. Dictionary at 539 (1999)). In Zawistowski, the defendant's horses suffered unnecessary and unjustifiable pain as a result of being severely underweight. Zawistowski, 119 Wn. App. at 736-37 (reasonable to infer that the horses felt pain from being hungry and hunger from being underweight and malnourished). Here, a jury could similarly infer, based on these governing definitions, that both dogs experienced some degree of pain as a result of being severely underweight. In sum, this evidence was sufficient to convict Jackson of both animal cruelty counts.

With respect to failure to provide humane care, the State presented evidence that the gecko was extremely thin, had poor bone density, was unable to move and properly shed its skin, and that its color was washed out. The veterinarian testified that the gecko was deficient in calcium and vitamin D3 from lack of exposure to a heat and light source. The veterinarian concluded "that this animal had been lacking in not just its basic requirements, very, very basic requirements that this animal would need, but it also had been severely neglected and therefore that had amounted to this severe state of malnutrition." Report of Proceedings (RP) (Sept. 24, 2008) at 403. After being taken into custody by animal services, the gecko returned to normal weight and color. Jackson's testimony to the contrary, that he provide adequate care by obtaining the necessary cage, lighting, humidifier, and food, does not render the State's evidence insufficient. That evidence, taken as true, supports the reasonable inference that Jackson failed to provide minimal care in a way that imperiled the gecko's health. The evidence was sufficient to convict Jackson for failure to provide humane care.

Affirmed.

Questions & Notes

1. Consider the difficulty of the state prosecutor in meeting its burden of proof; proving a failure to do something. Also, why did the state charge cruelty rather than failure to provide care for the dogs? Was there a failure to provide care? Does the gecko provide any additional difficulties over a dog or cat? Which standards were violated? How do you prove pain and suffering in cases such as this?

2. In one Texas case, the defendant objected to the sufficiency of the charging language when being charged with failure to provide "necessary food" for a horse, as it might be referring to either quantity or quality. But the court found the language sufficient saying, "The quantity and quality of food necessary to sustain a horse is a matter of common knowledge among persons familiar with the care of horses. It would be unreasonable to require the State to specify in the information a minimum quantity and quality of food that appellant failed to provide when the statute provides no specific standard." **Cross v. State**, 646 S.W. 2d 514 (Tex. App. 1982).

Section 2

Scope of the Duty of Care

Presuming the level or scope of care has been determined, and the provider of the care identified, the critical question then becomes, by what standard shall the case be judged? How much food, what kind of food? How much water, how often? What will satisfy the requirement of shelter—a miniature, air- and watertight house, a lean-to, or just a roof? Again, the number of possible animals, different environments, different ages, and different times of the year make precise measurements in the law impossible. The lack of particulars within the statutes has not bothered the courts, perhaps because only the most serious of cases have been prosecuted. In cases where the animal died of starvation, the standard had obviously been violated, and the proofs consisted primarily of showing that the defendant had custody of the animal and that starvation was the cause of death. Proof of amounts of food actually given an animal might be sufficient to show a violation of the section, but the best evidence is the condition of the animal itself. Veterinarians and others familiar with animals can determine when the food and water have been insufficient by the physical condition of the animal (looseness of skin, lack of fat, showing of ribs/bones, etc.). The only difficulty with this standard is that by the time the breach of the standard is obvious, the animal has endured substantial suffering.

CASE BY CASE

Jordan v. United States

269 A. 2d 848 (D.C. App.1970)

The principal witness for the Government was a physician who testified that on January 10, 1970 at 11:00 a. m. he saw a full-grown German shepherd dog tied by a 3-foot chain on an open concrete back porch of appellant's home. He further testified that from a distance of about 40 yards he "thought the dog was undernourished; and, in addition, I thought the dog was apathetic and depressed" and that in his opinion there was no "adequate shelter" for the dog. He returned to appellant's home at 2:00 p.m. and 3:00 p.m. that afternoon and observed the same conditions. The president of the Washington Humane Society, who arrived at appellant's home at 3:00 p.m., and a police officer, who arrived at appellant's home about 4:15 p.m., confirmed the physician's testimony regarding the dog being tied by a short chain on the open porch with no shelter. All witnesses testified that the weather was extremely cold that day. A certified copy of the United States Weather Bureau weather report for the day in question indicates that the temperature was 23 at 11:00 a.m., 28 at 2:00 p.m. and 3:00 p.m., and 27 at 4:00 p.m.

> **Think About It**
>
> In 2001 a 30-year-old woman from Allegan County, Michigan, was charged with a number of cruelty counts. Investigators found 162 dogs and cats in her home. Animal control officers had to euthanize about half the animals on the spot. She claims that she was just running a rescue operation and placing animals in other homes.
>
> Can a positive motivation to care for animals result in illegal acts?

Although the witnesses testified they observed no food or water on the porch the trial court in finding appellant guilty made reference only to the fact that on the several occasions the dog was on the porch "in unusually cold weather." Since the trial court did not make any finding with respect to the charges of inflicting unnecessary cruelty or failing to provide proper food or drink [FN1] we assume the trial court limited its finding of guilt to a failure by the appellant to provide proper shelter or protection from the weather. [FN2] Consequently we review the evidence to determine whether it would sustain a finding that appellant failed to provide the dog with proper shelter or protection from the weather.

> [FN1] Apparently the judge recognized that it was not necessary that a dog have access to food and water during every hour of the day. While the physician stated that he thought the dog was undernourished on his first visit at a view from 40 yards, he did not repeat this after the third visit when he had a much closer view of the dog. The dog was impounded but if it was examined upon being impounded there is nothing in the record to show what that examination disclosed.

> [FN2] Appellant could have been convicted of unnecessarily failing to provide the dog with proper food, drink, shelter, or protection from the weather without a finding that he inflicted unnecessary cruelty upon the dog. See Commonwealth v. Curry, 150 Mass. 509, 23 N.E. 212 (1890). See also Annotation at 82 A.L.R.2d 794 (1962).

Before it can be determined that an animal is not supplied with adequate shelter and protection from the weather, it must first be determined what shelter or protection is necessary for the animal. This court professes no expertise on the subject of the care and handling of dogs, and we assume the trial court likewise had none and there was no expert testimony on the subject. [FN3] It is a matter of common knowledge that some breeds of dogs can remain exposed to extremely cold weather for many hours without injurious effects. In the absence of testimony by someone experienced in the care of a dog of this type, not necessarily a veterinarian, that the shelter or protection from the weather supplied this dog on this occasion would to cause the dog to suffer, the evidence was insufficient to sustain the conviction.

> [FN3] Although it was stipulated at trial that the physician was a qualified physician we do not understand this stipulation to have the effect of qualifying the physician as an expert on the care and handling of dogs.

Reversed with instructions to enter a judgment of acquittal.

Questions & Notes

1. The judge ties the issues of adequate shelter to a standard of causing the dog to suffer. Do you agree with this approach? How do you establish in court that a dog has suffered? Who

could testify as to the state of suffering? Is this an objective standard or a subjective standard.

CASE BY CASE

State v. Dresbach

122 Ohio App. 3d 647, 702 N.E. 2d 513 (1997)

On September 4, 1996, an employee of the Cruelty Investigations Division of the Capital Area Humane Society responded to an anonymous report that an emaciated Rottweiler was seen chained to a doghouse in an alley behind the 800 block of Champion Avenue and Forest Street in Columbus. According to the investigator, the dog tied in the yard at 1039 Forest Street was very thin, its ribs and spine could be seen through the skin, and the area in which the dog was chained contained numerous piles of loose feces resembling "cow patties."

The investigator spoke to an individual who lived at the address. That individual told the investigator that the dog was owned by his roommate, defendant herein. The individual gave the investigator permission to take the dog to the humane society for medical treatment.

Later that day, defendant contacted the humane society to check on the condition of the dog. Defendant told the investigator that he had been taking care of the dog ever since the dog owners were arrested in a drug raid. According to the investigator, defendant told him that he owned the dog and that he had obtained a license for the dog. The investigator asked defendant if he would execute a "permission to treat" form allowing the humane society to examine and treat the dog. Defendant personally executed the document as the owner of the dog.

The dog was examined by a veterinarian, who concluded that the dog was suffering from a heavy internal parasite infestation, commonly known as hookworm. She estimated that the dog was approximately thirty to forty pounds underweight due to this condition. The veterinarian stated that once identified, such an infestation could be treated with a powder mixed in the dog's food. The veterinarian also observed lesions on the dog's ears from untreated fly bites. ...

Problem 7A

Using the facts from this case, is there a violation of any of the three following state laws dealing with duty of care? If you do find a violation, how much jail time is appropriate under the given facts?

Texas Penal Code Ann. § 42.09 (Vernon 2002)

(a) A person commits an offense if the person intentionally or knowingly:

(2) fails unreasonably to provide necessary food, care, or shelter for an animal in the person's custody;

(b)(5) "Necessary food, care, or shelter" includes food, care, or shelter provided to the extent required to maintain the animal in a state of good health.

Ohio Statutes § 959.13 Cruelty To Animals

(A) No person shall:

(1) Torture an animal, deprive one of necessary sustenance, unnecessarily or cruelly beat, needlessly mutilate or kill, or impound or confine an animal without supplying it during such confinement with a sufficient quantity of good whole-some food and water;

(3) Carry or convey an animal in a cruel or inhuman manner;

(4) Keep animals other than cattle, poultry or fowl, swine, sheep, or goats in an enclosure without wholesome exercise and change of air, nor or [sic] feed cows on food that produces impure or unwholesome milk.

Michigan Compiled Laws 750.50 General Prohibitions

(2) An owner, possessor, or person having the charge or custody of an animal shall not do any of the following

(a) Fail to provide an animal with adequate care.

(1) As used in this section and section 50b:

(a) "Adequate care" means the provision of sufficient food, water, shelter, sanitary conditions, exercise, and veterinary medical attention in order to maintain an animal in a state of good health.

(i) "Sanitary conditions" means space free from health hazards including excessive animal waste, overcrowding of animals, or other conditions that endanger the animal's health. This definition does not include a condition resulting from a customary and reasonable practice pursuant to farming or animal husbandry.

(j) "Shelter" means adequate protection from the elements and weather conditions suitable for the age, species, and

> **Think About It**
>
> Do you have a legal duty to keep your mother in a state of good health? A moral duty?

physical condition of the animal so as to maintain the animal in a state of good health. Shelter, for livestock, includes structures or natural features such as trees or topography. Shelter for a dog shall include 1 or more of the following: (omitted)

(k) "State of good health" means freedom from disease and illness, and in a condition of proper body weight and temperature for the age and species of the animal, unless the animal is undergoing appropriate treatment.

Note that the more detail that is provided in the statute the easier it is to show specific conduct is a violation. See **State v. Wools** 2001 WL 935466 (Tenn. Crim. App.).

Section 3

Special Case — Puppy Mills

A puppy mill is usually a small business, perhaps a family business, where the goal of selling puppies dominates, and the care for the breeding mothers, as well as, the puppies becomes secondary. There is a lack of socialization of the dogs; there is a risk of infection and genetic defects that will not become apparent for considerable time. While the cruelty laws clearly apply to these fact patterns, there is a dearth of cases. In part these puppy mills act more like the agricultural animals discussed in the next chapter. These businesses are hidden from public view. They involve many animals, making it hard for local officials to deal with. How would a police agency or local humane society deal with 100 terriers that need to be removed from one facility in one day? Most of these dogs are shipped to retail dealers so the purchasers never see the conditions under which the animals are raised. The process is supported by impulse purchasing followed by emotional attachment by the purchasers to the puppies who are in poor health. (For a discussion of the sales law aspect of the process, see Chapter 2.)

The reality is that the criminal law is a poor regulator of commercial conditions of animals. There needs to be a right of inspection without a search warrant. What constitutes an appropriate level of care needs to be set out in more detail than the criminal law provides. If criminal charges are brought then the dogs often are evidence that must be "kept" until after trial - six months or more. Who is able to do this? What does it do the dogs? Therefore more focused information about puppy mills are found in the world of administrative law, with requirement of federal, state, or local permits. The federal law does have a substantial roll in this area under the provisions of the Animal Welfare Act; see Chapter 10. The following case is an administrative appeal of a state level license for breeding dogs. It provides an opportunity to discuss the facts of the issue more than administrative law.

CASE BY CASE

Burkholder v. Department of Agriculture
989 A. 2d 73 (Pa. Cmwlth. 2010)

Aaron Burkholder, t/d/b/a Burkholder Farm Kennel (Burkholder) petitions for review of the May 15, 2009 adjudication and final order of the Secretary of the Department of Agriculture that affirmed the decision of the Department's Bureau of Dog Law Enforcement (Bureau) to refuse to approve Burkholder's 2009 kennel license application pursuant to Section 211(a) of the Dog Law (the Law).

On December 30, 2008, Burkholder sent the Bureau an application for a 2009 commercial kennel class license permitting fifty-one to one hundred dogs of any age during a calendar year. The Bureau received the application and a check for $200 on January 2, 2009. On February 5, 2009, the Bureau sent Burkholder a kennel license refusal order, noting that its personnel had inspected the kennel on nine occasions and found numerous serious violations of the Law and its regulations. Burkholder appealed the refusal order on February 12. The Bureau then sent him a notice of operating under suspension of kennel license and a letter scheduling an administrative hearing for March 24, 2009.

Prior to taking testimony at the hearing, the parties stipulated that Burkholder had entered pleas of guilty in the Court of Common Pleas of Berks County to four violations of Section 207(b) of the Law, 3 P.S. § 459-207(b), failure to maintain the kennel in a sanitary and humane condition in compliance with regulations. Those violations included failure to provide adequate shelters for dogs kept outdoors; failure to keep buildings and grounds of kennels clean and in good repair; failure to maintain indoor and outdoor housing facilities for dogs in a manner to protect them from injury and to contain the dogs; and failure to provide ample lighting by natural or artificial means in indoor housing facilities. 7 Pa.Code §§ 21.24(b), 21.29(c), 21.21(a) and 21.27. Thereafter, the Bureau presented the testimony of the three inspectors who had conducted the nine inspections between May 9 and September 8, 2008. The first inspector, Ms. Donmoyer, testified that she inspected the kennel in response to its inclusion in a feature by Oprah Winfrey dealing with puppy-mills and that she also visited the other Pennsylvania kennels that were featured. In summary, the inspectors testified that their inspections revealed numerous violations of the Law and its regulations.

Burkholder testified that even though he has had a kennel license since 2002, he has been breeding dogs since 1974. In general, he acknowledged that it was his responsibility to be in compliance with the regulations. He stated his belief that there were two things that he had to do following Ms. Donmoyer's initial inspection, but that he could not remember them.

On May 15, 2009, the Secretary affirmed the Bureau's decision to refuse to approve Burkholder's application. In so ruling, the Secretary noted that, pursuant to Section 211(a)(3) and (4) of the Law, 3 P.S. § 459-211(a)(3) and (4), he has the power to revoke or refuse to issue a kennel license for any one or more of the following reasons: "the person holding or applying for a license has failed to comply with this act [or] the person holding or applying for a license has failed to comply with any regulation promulgated under this act." In the present case, the Secretary set forth the following specific reasons in support of the refusal:

Over a number of months, the photographic evidence revealed metal strand flooring which was not coated with vinyl and not kept in good repair. Jagged metal edges posed a danger to the dogs. Further, the size of the mesh did not prevent dogs' feet from passing through the openings. It took the kennel many months to make the necessary corrections.

The photographs of this dirty, cobweb ridden, fly-infested and debris-strewn kennel are prima facie evidence of a violation of 7 Pa.Code § 21.29(c), which requires that "[t]he buildings and grounds of kennels shall be main-tained, kept clean and in good repair to protect the animal from injury and to facilitate practices required by [the regulations]. Kennels shall have an effective program that controls ingress by insects...." Secretary's Adjudication at 26.

[We] note that the General Assembly afforded the Secretary broad discretion in administrative licensing under Section 211, the provision upon which Burkholder's license renewal was denied. Section 211(a) provides that "the Secretary may revoke or refuse to issue a kennel license ... for any one or more of the following reasons[,]" including, inter alia, conviction of a violation of the Dog Law and failure to comply with any regulation promulgated under the Law. 3 P.S. § 459-211(a). In the present case, those reasons were undeniably established by Burkholder's pleas of guilty.

Accordingly, we affirm the Secretary's order affirming the Bureau's decision to refuse to approve Burkholder's 2009 kennel license application.

Questions & Notes

1. Were the conditions at the kennel a violation of the normal anti-cruelty laws? Note the focus on the physical conditions of the premises, not on the conditions of the dogs.

2. What happens to the animals while the defendants await trial? During the year or more of legal appeals? Does the arrest of an individual shift the property ownership of the animal? Should it? What happens if the defendants are found not guilty? A key practical issue in the enforcement process against puppy mills is the cost of holding 100 or more dogs for months. One option is to get the defendants to release their ownership. Another is to seek a court order requiring the forfeiture of the animals or

the posting of a bond to cover the cost of care while the criminal charge proceeds. See Mich. C.L. § 750.50(3)

3. Preventive laws would include local laws with limitations on the number of animals that can be kept in a home without a kennel license. States can impose conditions and inspections on sellers of pets. Also, the federal Animal Welfare Act may be triggered to deal with commercial sale of pets, but there are a considerable number of issues about the scope and effectiveness of this law (see Chapter 10). All of the preventive measures assume that someone has the financial and human resources to support an inspection of premises program.

4. What would you suggest to preclude the conditions of this case?

Section 4

Duty to Provide Veterinary Care

While the need to provide food and water for animals is obvious to everyone, and sufficiency of food and water relatively straightforward, the duty to support the general well-being of an animal, including the duty to take the animal to a veterinarian, is not yet clearly formalized in the collective judgment of our society.

CASE BY CASE

People v. Arroyo

777 N.Y.S. 2d 836 (2004)

Defendant is charged with Overdriving, Torturing and Injuring Animals and Failure to Provide Proper Sustenance (Agriculture and Markets Law § 353). Defendant has moved for dismissal of the information on the grounds that the statute is unconstitutionally vague.

Relevant Facts

The factual part of the information in this case states as follows:

Deponent [a special investigator of the ASPCA] states that, at the above time and place, the deponent observed a dog sitting behind a fence at the above-mentioned location and that said dog did have difficulty walking due to large tumor hanging from said dog's stomach and that said tumor was bleeding.

The deponent is further informed by the defendant's own statements that the defendant resides at the above-mentioned location and that the defendant is the owner of the dog and that the defendant owned the dog for approximately six years, he knew that she had a tumor and was in pain, he decided not to provide medical treatment for the dog because it was to [sic] expensive.

The deponent is informed by Doctor Bunni Tan of the ASPCA, that the informant did examine the above-mentioned dog, and that said dog did have a very large mammory [sic] gland tumor on the lower stomach area, and that the surface of said tumor had several ulcerations that leaked fluid causing a chronic medical condition, which was neglected to the point where her tumor was uncomfortable and painful for the dog, and that the tumor was approximately the size of a large grapfruit [sic] and that said tumor required a painful and extensive surgery and that said dogs [sic] condition is terminal.

Upon his return from vacation, at Ms. Lucas' request, defendant went to the A.S.P.C.A. offices to meet with her. The minutes of a hearing held before another judge of this court, pursuant to People v. Huntley, 15 N.Y. 2d 72, 255 N.Y.S. 2d 838, 204 N.E. 2d 179 (1965), reveal that during that meeting, defendant acknowledged to Ms. Lucas that he was the owner of the dog, that he knew the dog had a tumor, and that he had not provided medical care to the dog because of his limited finances. Defendant added that he was familiar with cancer because a relative had had cancer and painful chemotherapy and stated that he believed that the dog should live out her life without intervention. Ms. Lucas then arrested defendant.

The Parties' Contentions

In support of his motion, defendant argues that A.M.L. § 353 is vague because the terms "necessary sustenance" and "unjustifiable physical pain" (this latter one included in the definition of "torture" and "cruelty" of A.M.L. § 350) are not specific enough to provide notice that an owner must provide medical care to a terminally ill animal.

In opposition, the People argue that A.M.L. § 353 is not so vague as to violate Due Process standards and that the statute gave enough notice to defendant that he was required to get veterinary care for his dog. In particular, the People argue that "[t]he intent of the legislature and wording of the applicable statute" make it clear that the term sustenance means more than food and drink. The People also argue that the statute's failure to define the term "unjustifiable" does not make the statute vague because that term has "an extremely common" meaning in the vernacular.

The Statutes in Question

Section 353 of the Agriculture and Markets Law provides:

> A person who overdrives, overloads, tortures or cruelly beats ..., or deprives any animal of necessary sustenance, food or drink, or neglects or refuses to furnish it such sustenance or drink, or ..., or to be deprived of necessary food or drink, or who wilfully sets on foot, instigates, engages in, or in any way furthers any act of cruelty to any animal, or any act tending to produce such cruelty, is guilty of a mis-

demeanor, punishable by imprisonment for not more than one year, or by a fine of not more than one thousand dollars, or by both.

"Torture" or "Cruelty" is defined by section 350 of the Agriculture and Markets Law as "includ[ing] every act, omission, or neglect, whereby unjustifiable physical pain, suffering or death is caused or permitted."

Necessary Sustenance

The court in this case must then determine whether A.M.L. § 353 gives sufficient notice to a pet owner that not providing medical care to an ill animal is a crime. In particular, the court should determine whether the term "necessary sustenance" includes the provision of medical care to an animal, such that defendant should have been on notice that his decision not to provide veterinary care to his pet was a crime. Defendant does not argue that the phrase "necessary sustenance" as used in the statute is vague per se or on its face, but that it is vague as applied to the facts of this case. As stated above, the People argue that the wording of A.M.L. § 353 makes clear that the term "sustenance" refers to more than food or drink, and that it also includes medical care

When constructing a statute, the intention of the Legislature is first to be sought from a literal reading of the act itself. (McKinney's Cons.Laws of N.Y., Book 1, Statutes 92[b], at 182). The language of the statute in this case is anything but clear. The first time the statute mentions the term "sustenance," it refers to depriving an animal of "necessary sustenance, food or drink." Then, within the same sentence, the statute refers to neglecting or refusing to furnish the animal "that sustenance or drink." Finally, the statute states, again within the same sentence, that it is also a violation of the statute to permit any animal to be deprived "of necessary food or drink." From the grammatical construction employed the first time the phrase is used, i.e, the use of an appositive set off by commas, the court infers that the legislature intended to define sustenance as "food or drink." The use of the term "sustenance" in place of the word "food," as in "sustenance or drink," the second time the phrase is used within the same sentence, supports this inference. The third time the phrase is used, the statute omits the word sustenance and refers merely to "necessary food or drink," which further supports the notion that the legislature meant "food or drink" when it wrote "sustenance."

Unjustifiable Physical Pain

The court must also determine whether, when measured by common understanding and practice, as well as society's sense of morality, the language of the statute, and specifically, the term "unjustifiable," conveys sufficient notice to a person that his or her decision not to provide a pet with medical care is a crime. The answer to this question requires the court's analysis of common understanding, practice and moral standards and how these notions inform the meaning of the term "unjustifiable" in the context of laws protecting animals.

Thus, anti-cruelty statutes, including A.M.L. § 353, do not prohibit causing pain to animals but causing "unjustifiable" pain. People v. Downs, 26 N.Y. Crim. R. 327, 136 N.Y.S. 440, 445 (City Magistrates' Court, 1911); Hammer v. American Kennel Club, 304 A.D. 2d 74, 78, 758 N.Y.S.2d 276 (1st Dept. 2003). In the context of these statutes, an act is considered justifiable, "where its purpose or object is reasonable and adequate, and the pain and suffering caused is not disproportionate to the end sought to be attained." 4 Am Jur 2d, Animals, § 29, at 370. That is, not all pain and suffering is prohibited and some pain, even if substantial, is considered justifiable. For instance, branding is allowed, even though it causes pain, because it is found to be justified by the owner's need to enjoy his or her property. Hunting and fishing as sports are not prohibited by anti-cruelty statutes, even though they are arguably the ultimate form of cruelty, because these activities are found to be justified by the need of some people to engage in killing animals as a recreational activity. Similarly, the killing of animals for their pelts to adorn clothing and accessories is permitted.

The question of what is justifiable — or unjustifiable — in the context of anticruelty statutes protecting either children or animals has also been the subject of discussion in judicial opinions from several states. A review of these decisions reveals that courts across the nation are split on the issue of whether the term "unjustifiable" is a vague term, incapable of conveying a proscription. Appellate courts of at least two states have held that statutes containing the phrase "unjustifiable physical pain" are unconstitutionally vague as a result of the uncertainty of that phrase. See State v. Meinert, 225 Kan. 816, 594 P. 2d 232 (1979); State v. Ballard, 341 So.2d 957 (Ct. Crim. App. Alabama, 1976). The opposite result was reached in People v. Smith, 35 Cal. 3d 798, 201 Cal.Rptr. 311, 678 P. 2d 886 (1984); State v. Eich, 204 Minn. 134, 282 N.W. 810 (1938); and State v. Comeaux, 319 So. 2d 897 (La. 1975).

It is clear from the above discussion that what is "unjustifiable" in the context of anti-cruelty statutes is what is not reasonable, defensible, right, unavoidable or excusable. This court agrees with the reasoning in People v. Rogers, supra, and is not inclined to accept that merely adding the term "unjustifiable" to the word "pain" transforms conduct that is inherently innocent, like allowing an animal to die of natural causes without providing medical care, into a crime. As the Court of Appeals held more than a century ago, "purely statutory offenses cannot be established by implication, and [...] acts otherwise innocent and lawful do not become crimes, unless there is a clear and positive expression of the legislative intent to make them criminal. The citizen is entitled to an unequivocal warning before conduct on his part, which is not malum in se, can be made the occasion of a deprivation of his liberty or property." People v. Phyfe, 136 N.Y. 554, 32 N.E. 978 (1893).

Neither does the court believe that society's current practice or the moral standards of our community expand the meaning of the term "unjustifiable" to include a duty on owners to provide their animals with medical care. This is especially true in the case of a terminally ill pet. Reading into A.M.L. § 353 an affirmative duty to provide medical care in all cases, regardless of the expenses or the owner's ability to meet them, implies a standard of morality and decency that the court is not persuaded society has adopted. Judging by the current lack of national consensus regarding the provision of affordable health care for our less affluent citizens, to impose seemingly limitless mandates on owners to provide health care for their pets based on the vague language of this statute would be overreaching on the part of this court. The court concludes that, as used in § 350, the term "unjustifiable physical pain" is too vague to warn pet owners that not providing medical care for their pets is a crime.

Furthermore, the court is troubled by the imposition of a duty to provide care in light of a statute that, like § 353, is so general in its terms. Reading this duty into the statute will create a myriad of logistical problems. For instance, how is the standard of medical care that must be provided to be determined? (i.e., To what extent must treatment be provided to avoid prosecution? Is providing regular veterinary care sufficient? Or, in light of the sophisticated medical procedures that are now available for animals — chemotherapy, radiation therapy, organ transplants — will that level of treatment be required? Will mental health treatment be required?); and how would that standard be judged? (What kind of expense is it mandated to be incurred to avoid prosecution?) It will also create ethical issues that are difficult to discern in the absence of a legislative pronouncement (When is extending a pet's life permissible? When is putting an animal to death mandated? Up to what point do we respect the owners' choice to refuse invasive treatment for their pets and allow them to die at home in the company of their human and non-human companions, rather than in a strange and antiseptic environment?).

> **Think About It**
>
> Is it better that pets continue life with pain or that they be put to death and stop the pain? What about children?

Conclusion

The court finds that A.M.L § 353 is unconstitutionally vague as applied to the facts of this case. In particular, the court finds that § 353 does not give notice to a person of ordinary intelligence that he or she is obligated to provide veterinary care to a terminally ill animal. Therefore, defendant's motion to dismiss is granted.

Questions & Notes

1. Michigan has a specific provision requiring the providing of veterinarian care: "'Adequate care' means the provision of sufficient food, water, shelter, sanitary conditions, exercise, and veterinary medical attention in order to maintain an animal

in a state of good health." Mich. C.L.A. § 750.50 (1)(a). Do you think this language would have resulted in a conviction in the preceding case? Does the Michigan law answer the questions raised at the end of the opinion?

What about the owners who are in denial about the health conditions of their animals? They see a lump but do not believe it should be looked after, or decide to self-treat with herbs. Or what about the many owners who overfeed their animals, and end up with obese animals. Do the owners understand the health risk of being overweight? Given the number of overweight humans, having overweight pets is unlikely to trigger much action. But being overweight clearly will jeopardize the animal's health. Is this what the legislature had in mind? How overweight would an animal need to before for the filing of criminal charges would be appropriate?

> **News Bits**
>
> The city of Rome, Italy, adopted an ordinance that requires that goldfish must be kept in full-size aquariums and cannot be used as contest prizes. The ordinance also required dog owners to walk their dogs daily. *L.A. Times* Nov. 9, 2005 at A3.

2. If the defendant did not have sufficient money to pay for veterinary care of a tumor, the other lawful action that he could have taken was to have the animal killed by a veterinarian. Is death an acceptable alternative? Can the law force a pet owner to expend money not in the bank?

CASE BY CASE

Consider what can happen when a statute requiring veterinary care is in place.

Martinez v. State

48 S.W. 3d 273 (Tex. App. 2001)

JUSTICE TOM RICKHOFF delivered the opinion of the court.

This appeal requires us to review a sad case. We reach this legal result with some discomfort. As appellate judges we cannot apply our own philosophy of justice, but may only apply the law to the facts of a particular case. After doing so here, we must affirm.

Appellant Andrea Martinez, an eighty-three year old widow, is known in her neighborhood for taking in homeless animals. She was charged with cruelty to animals, and convicted by a jury. See Tex. Pen. Code Ann. § 42.09(a)(2) (Vernon Supp. 2000). The trial court assessed punishment at one year confinement and fined Martinez one thousand dollars. The trial court probated the sentence and the fine for two years on the condition that Martinez perform one hundred hours of community service at a local animal shelter. Martinez raises five appellate issues.

Sufficiency of the Evidence

In two issues, Martinez challenges the sufficiency of the evidence supporting her conviction. Specifically, Martinez argues that the evidence is legally and factually insufficient to prove she "intentionally or knowingly" withheld care for the animal she called "Lobo."

Martinez was charged with intentionally and knowingly "fail[ing] unreasonably to provide necessary food, care, or shelter for an animal in [her] custody." See Tex. Pen. Code Ann. § 42.09(a)(2) (Vernon Supp. 2000). To prove this allegation, the State presented the testimony of Rudy Davila, an animal cruelty investigator for the City of San Antonio. Davila explained that he was asked to investigate a complaint of animal cruelty involving a dog being kept at Martinez's home. Davila testified that upon arriving at Martinez's home, he observed several dogs in the back yard, one of which was separated from the others. Davila stated that most of the dogs appeared healthy, but the separated dog was lethargic, non-responsive, and suffering from a severe skin condition. Davila described the dog as having very little hair and open wounds. Davila explained that he could not determine the dog's skin color because its skin was completely crusted-over. Davila further testified that the dog appeared malnourished, explaining that the dog's back vertebrae were distinctly visible and the dog's abdominal wall had a severe tuck. Davila identified the infected dog in several photographs that were admitted into evidence.

Davila explained that he questioned Martinez about the dog's condition. According to Davila, Martinez told him a friend gave her the dog two years before after trying to cure the dog's skin condition with flea powder. When questioned about Martinez's demeanor, Davila indicated that Martinez did not appear upset or worried about the dog. Davila opined that the dog had not received reasonable care, noting the dog did not appear to have been treated for parasitic sarcoptic mange. Davila explained that he did not smell sulfur on the dog, a scent that would indicate the dog was being treated. Davila stated he decided to seize the dog due to the severity of the dog's condition. He explained how Martinez signed a consent form, marking it to indicate the dog was "not wanted." Davila stated that after he took the dog to the animal control facility, a veterinarian decided to euthanize the dog.

After viewing this evidence in the light most favorable to the verdict, we conclude that a rational jury could have found all elements of the State's allegation. The evidence demonstrates that an animal in Martinez's custody did not receive the medical treatment it needed to survive. The decision to euthanize the animal upon its arrival at the shelter shows the unreasonableness of failing to treat the animal. Although Martinez maintains that no evidence of intent or knowledge exists, a jury may infer a culpable mental state from the circumstances surrounding the offense of cruelty to animals. See Pine v. State, 889 S.W. 2d 625, 629 (Tex. App.--Houston [14th Dist.] 1994, pet. ref'd). Here, the evidence indicates obvious and severe illness, and a long-neglected need for treatment. Presented with such an obvious need for treatment, a jury could easily infer intent or knowledge. As a result, the evidence is legally sufficient to support the verdict. However, even viewed without the light of the prism of "in the light most favorable to the prosecution," the evidence is still sufficient.

Conclusion

The jury, faced with the evidence discussed above, had no choice but to find Martinez guilty. She should not have accepted the dog or kept it without treatment for so long. The facts, however, offer compelling mitigation. [FN1]

> FN1. In my view, anyone visiting this home should have realized Martinez, poor, isolated, and elderly, needed assistance. One would think the first question these authorities would ask after, "Where is the dog?" would be, "Do you have any children, grandchildren, friends, or relatives who can help you so this does not happen again?" After Davila investigated she surrendered the dog and was compliant. Perhaps she could have been educated without the rigors of a full courtroom experience—nothing more than a helpful follow-up visit for the benefit of the other, healthy dogs. Failure to provide necessary care is cruelty to animals and a criminal offense, even though the record in this case reveals neglect arising out of a lack of resources rather than outright cruelty. Whether a case like this one rises to the level of outrageousness suggested by intentional behavior is properly for others to decide. Cf. Tilbury v. State, 890 S.W. 2d 219, 220 (Tex. App.-Fort Worth 1994, no pet.) (upholding conviction of cruelty to animals committed by shooting and killing two dogs). Whether there is a need to deter others similarly situated from committing this violation is also beyond our judgment. Martinez lives on four-hundred dollars monthly Social Security benefits, has no transportation, her husband passed away two months prior to trial, and the record failed to reveal any helpful family members. She did what she could short of calling for the dog's removal. Performing community service at an animal shelter may be difficult in light of Martinez's prior hardship in traveling to the veterinarian. Perhaps another Good Samaritan will appear to assist her. We can only hope Martinez's love for animals will find an appropriate outlet in her community service, allowing this sad experience to become meaningful.

Questions & Notes

1. The prior two cases present an issue that society has not yet faced directly in the adoption of sweeping criminal law language: What should be done about individuals who seek to keep pets but do not have adequate knowledge or resources to do that which is in the best interests of the pet? Is this issue parallel to those without resources who raise children? Is criminal prosecution the best tool to deal with this sort of problem? Might it make a difference if one or two dogs are involved versus 100 dogs?

2. There is a growing gap between the cost of routine care for pets and that of special care for diseases, injuries, and cancers. Should pet owners be criminally responsible if they do not seek out the $5,000 operation or treatment now available for an injury to a pet? Suggest language for the criminal law statute that would acknowledge this issue.

3. Should the criminal law standard vary depending on the resources of the defendant, so that poor families would not be held to the same standard as rich families?

4. What about agricultural animals? Should the duty to provide veterinary care apply if the care costs more than the commercial value of the animal?

Section 5

Special Case — Hoarders

CASE BY CASE

State v. McDonald

110 P. 3d 149 (Ut. 2005)

JUDGE THORNE delivered the opinion of the court.

Sydney McDonald appeals her conviction of fifty-eight counts of cruelty to animals, each of them a class C misdemeanor. See Utah Code Ann. § 76-9-301 (2003). We affirm in part and reverse in part.

Background

McDonald was convicted of multiple counts of animal cruelty following the discovery of fifty-eight diseased cats, and one dead cat, in a trailer on a farm in Cache County. McDonald brought the trailer to the farm in January 2001, with the apparent purpose of creating a "sanctuary" for stray cats that she trapped in and around Salt Lake City. McDonald brought cats to the trailer on multiple occasions between January 2001 and the discovery of the cats by authorities in April 2001.

McDonald arranged for the landowner to feed and water the cats and provide litter, but instructed the landowner not to open any windows in the trailer or go near the cats. McDonald also told the landowner that she would provide veterinary care for the cats, but failed to do so. After the cats were discovered, they were all determined to be ill to one extent or another, with their illnesses caused by their close confinement with other cats and insufficient ventilation in the enclosed trailer. Following their discovery, many of the cats had to be euthanized due to illness or injury.

McDonald was charged with fifty-eight class B misdemeanor counts of cruelty to animals, and was convicted of fifty-eight counts of class C cruelty to animals, a lesser included offense

Following her convictions, the trial court sentenced McDonald to ninety days of jail time for each count, to be served consecutively. The consecutive sentences totaled approximately fourteen and one-half years, but the trial court suspended all but two days of the sentence. The trial court then placed McDonald on two years of formal probation and twelve and one-half years of informal probation. The probation included terms tailored to the animal cruelty offenses, including prohibiting McDonald from harboring or owning any animals.

Analysis

1. Evidentiary Rulings

McDonald appears to object to two lines of testimony that were presented by the State at trial. First, McDonald objects to the testimony of a Salt Lake County Animal Services officer regarding a previous incident in Salt Lake County where he found McDonald in possession of fifty-three cats. Second, McDonald objects to various statements that, she alleges, suggest that she had stolen or otherwise improperly obtained the cats in her possession. We can identify no error in the trial court's decision to admit this evidence.

As to the prior incident in Salt Lake County, the main thrust of the officer's testimony was that he had contacted McDonald in 2000 regarding fifty-three cats that were found in ill health at a kennel. The officer testified that he had told McDonald that keeping multiple cats in a confined area for too long a time could cause sickness or injury to the cats. During the officer's testimony, the trial court instructed the jury that the officer's testimony regarding the 2000 incident was "to be considered by you only for the purpose of proof of knowledge. That is[,] was she aware, was the defendant aware, that her conduct was reasonably certain to cause the result."

This testimony tends to establish McDonald's knowledge that her conduct was likely to result in sickness or injury to the cats that she was confining. Such knowledge goes directly towards proving McDonald's state of mind, a defining element of the crimes charged, and is clearly relevant. See Utah R. Evid. 401. Further, there is no character evidence problem under Rule 404(b) because the State's need to demonstrate McDonald's knowledge of a likelihood of injury constitutes a valid, noncharacter reason for offering this evidence; because the evidence is relevant; and because the evidence is not overly prejudicial. See Utah R. Evid. 404(b); State v. Nelson-Waggoner, 2000 UT 59,¶¶ 18-20, 6 P.3d 1120.

McDonald also complains that the prosecution improperly suggested to the jury that McDonald had stolen the cats that were found in her possession. McDonald does not cite to any such testimony in the record, other than testimony that the authorities were investigating reports of stolen cats when they discovered McDonald's trailer. This is not tantamount to alleging that McDonald stole the cats in question, and we find no merit in McDonald's argument in this regard.

Having examined McDonald's evidentiary arguments, we cannot say that McDonald has identified any instance where the trial court exceeded its discretion in admitting the challenged evidence.

2. Sufficiency of the Evidence

McDonald next argues that there was insufficient evidence to convict her of class C misdemeanor cruelty to the fifty-eight cats in the trailer. Utah Code section 76-9-301 provides that a person commits a class C misdemeanor when, acting recklessly or with criminal negligence, he:

(a) fails to provide necessary food, care, or shelter for an animal in his custody;

(b) abandons an animal in the person's custody;

(c) transports or confines an animal in a cruel manner;

(d) injures an animal;

(e) causes any animal, not including a dog, to fight with another animal of like kind for amusement or gain; or

(f) causes any animal, including a dog, to fight with a different kind of animal or creature for amusement or gain.

Utah Code Ann. § 76-9-301(1), (2) (2003). [FN2] A person acts "[w]ith criminal negligence or is criminally negligent with respect to circumstances surrounding his conduct or the result of his conduct when he ought to be aware of a substantial and unjustifiable risk that the circumstances exist or the result will occur." Id. § 76-2-103(4) (2003).

> FN2. The same acts, committed intentionally or knowingly, constitute class B misdemeanors. See Utah Code Ann. § 76-9-301(1), (2) (2003).

To successfully challenge her jury verdict on the grounds of insufficient evidence, McDonald must " 'marshal the evidence in support of the verdict and then demonstrate that the evidence is insufficient when viewed in the light most favorable to the verdict.' " State v. Pritchett,

2003 UT 24,¶ 25,. Assuming that McDonald properly marshaled the evidence against her, that evidence suggests that McDonald knew that it was unhealthy to house large numbers of cats together, but proceeded to do so without providing them with proper ventilation or veterinary care. This evidence is sufficient to support a jury finding that she failed to provide necessary care or shelter for the cats, and that she was aware of a substantial and unjustified risk that the care and shelter she provided for the cats did not meet their basic needs. Accordingly, she has failed to demonstrate that the jury verdict was based on insufficient evidence.

3. Sentencing Issues

Finally, McDonald alleges that the trial court erred in sentencing her to jail and probation for a period exceeding fourteen years when her offenses, albeit multiple, were only class C misdemeanors.

We agree with McDonald that the trial court erred when it sentenced her to over fourteen years of probation for her misdemeanor offenses.

Questions & Notes

1. Was she a collector? Why do you think the jury found her guilty of a Class C misdemeanor — "recklessly or with criminal negligence" — rather than a Class B — "intentionally or knowingly."

2. Do you think the punishment is appropriate for past acts? Do you think the punishment will deter future conduct? Of her? Of others?

CASE BY CASE

State v. Mauer
688 S.E. 2d 774 (N.C. App. 2010)

Defendant Barbara Yvonne Mauer appeals her conviction of misdemeanor cruelty to animals, arguing primarily that the trial court erred in denying her motion to dismiss the charge for insufficient evidence. Contrary to defendant's contention, the State presented substantial evidence of the offense, and, therefore, the trial court properly denied defendant's motion.

Facts

The State's evidence tended to establish the following facts at trial: At roughly 11:00 a.m. on 6 September 2007, Officer Melissa Hooks with the Cumberland County Animal Control Department responded to a complaint about the conditions in a home on Sandstone Lane in Cumberland County, North Carolina. When no one answered the door, Hooks looked around the outside of the home, noticing a "moderate" smell of rotting garbage and the smell of urine and feces. Hooks saw food and water bowls on the front step with bugs in them. In the yard, Hooks saw multiple pans of cat litter and litter bags, animal traps, animal carriers, roof tiles, hay, and overflowing garbage cans. She tried to enter the backyard through a gate but was unable to do so because the gate was blocked on the other side with debris. Hooks took pictures of the house and reported her investigation to her supervisor.

Animal Control obtained an inspection warrant, and the next day, Hooks, along with other Animal Control officers and Cumberland County Sheriff's deputies, returned to the residence, which they had learned was owned by defendant. Getting out of their vehicles to execute the warrant, they noticed that the smell of feces and urine became stronger as they approached the residence. When no one answered the front door, the deputies pushed open the door, although it was difficult to do so because it was blocked by feces, trash, and clothes on the inside. As the officers tried to enter the house, the smell was "overpowering," making their eyes water. The officers were unable to go inside and had to call the fire department to come and use positive pressure fans to ventilate the house. The fire department also provided Hook and other officers with breathing apparatus so that they could inspect the inside of the house.

When the animal control offers finally went inside, they saw at least 15 to 20 cats running around. The floor was covered with feces and urine and the officers could not walk around inside without stepping in it. Some of the feces were fresh, but some of it was old, with mold on it. In the front room of the house, eight to 10 cats were running around several metal cages covered with feces and fur. In the kitchen, the stove, sinks, and counter tops were covered with feces and urine. The furniture had feces on it and "leftover" food. The cats also had feces on them, and around the windows and doors were "streaks" from where, according to the animal control officers, the cats had been jumping trying to get out of the house.

Inside the house were several bags of cat food, but none of them were open. There were also litter boxes inside, most of them having been turned over. There were piles of clothes and trash on the floor in the rooms and halls and they were covered in cat hair, feces, and urine. In a back room of the house there was a feeder with fresh cat food in it. All the windows and doors in the house were shut and locked, with no access for the cats to go outside.

The officers were able to catch three of the cats before they had to leave the premises due to the expiration of the inspection warrant. Three days later, on 10 September 2007, animal control officers returned to the residence to search for more cats. The inspectors from the county health department were there and they had condemned the house. The animal control officers saw defendant walking in and out of the house, cleaning it out. They saw several feral cats running around outside the house, but when they went inside, they found no animals.

Around the same time as the investigation at Sandstone Lane, animal control was also called out to investigate a complaint about a dead animal on Elliot Farm Road in Cumberland County. Officers Jason Seifert and Alan Canady found a dead cat in an upstairs room of the house. Inside the house, Seifert and Canady found the floors covered in two-to-three inches of feces. There was one room, above the garage, with clean carpet and no cat feces in it. A bed was in the room, with covers messed up like someone had recently slept in it. In the front yard near the driveway, they found a piece of mail with defendant's name on it.

Defendant was charged with one count of cruelty to animals. Defendant was tried and convicted in district court and defendant appealed for a trial de novo in superior court. At the close of the State's evidence in superior court, and, after electing to not present any evidence in her defense, defendant moved to dismiss the charge for insufficient evidence. The trial court denied both motions. The jury found defendant guilty and the trial court ordered a 30 day suspended sentence and 12 months probation, with no animals on her property or in her possession during her pro-bation period. The court further ordered defendant to undergo a mental health evaluation and to pay $259.25 in restitution to animal control. Defendant gave notice of appeal in open court.

I

Defendant first argues on appeal that the trial court should have granted her motion to dismiss the charge of cruelty to animals for lack of sufficient evidence. On appeal, the trial court's denial of a motion to dismiss for insuf-ficient evidence is reviewed de novo.

To prove misdemeanor cruelty to animals, the State must present evidence that the defendant did "inten-tionally overdrive, overload, wound, injure, torment, kill, or deprive of necessary sustenance, or cause or procure to be overdriven, overloaded, wounded, injured, tormented, killed, or deprived of necessary sustenance, any animal[.]" N.C. Gen. Stat. § 14-360(a) (2007); State v. Coble, 163 N.C. App. 335, 338, 593 S.E. 2d 109, 111 (2004). Under the statute, the term "torment" denotes "any act, omission, or neglect causing or permitting unjustifiable pain, suffering, or death." N.C. Gen. Stat. § 14-360(c). The State's theory at trial was that defendant tormented cat C142 by confining and exposing the cat to unsanitary conditions inside defendant's house for a prolonged period. Defendant argues that the "evidence failed to establish that mere exposure to the living conditions constituted torment as defined by § 14-306(c)."

The evidence presented at trial, viewed in the light most favorable to the State, tends to establish that the odor of cat feces and ammonia emanating from defendant's house was strong enough that it could be smelled outside of the property. The smell was so "overwhelming" that the animal control officers were unable to enter the house without the fire department first ventilating the house and giving the officers the breathing apparatus used when going into burning buildings. While the fire department was ventilating defendant's house, neighborhood residents from two blocks away came outside to find out what the smell was.

When the officers were able to enter the residence, there was so much fecal matter and debris on the floor that the front door was difficult to open. The officers observed that all the doors and windows were closed and feces and urine covered "everything"-including all the floors, furniture, and counter tops. Some of the feces were fresh while some were old and had mold on them. The officers, as well as the cats, were unable to walk in the house without stepping in the feces and urine. The officers also observed that cats, covered in their own feces and urine, were leaving streak marks from jumping on the walls, windows, and doors trying to get out of the house. We conclude that this evidence is sufficient to support a conclusion by a reasonable jury that defendant "tormented" cat C142, causing it unjustifiable pain or suffering, under N.C. Gen. Stat. § 14-360(c). See People v. Reed, 121 Cal. App. 3d Supp. 26, 31, 176 Cal.Rptr. 98, 101 (Cal. App. Dep't Super. Ct. 1981) (finding sufficient evidence of failure to provide animals with proper care and attention where evidence indicated that when animal regulation officers executed a search warrant on defendant's property, 22 dogs had been found in the garage and almost every room of the house; that the doors and windows in the house were closed; that dog feces had nearly covered the floors; and the dogs had been without food or water). The trial court, therefore, did not err in submitting the cruelty to animals charge to the jury.

◇◇

Hoarding is a particular human activity triggered by psychological problems and a certain clouding of awareness and judgment.

Hoarding of inanimate objects has been linked to a variety of psychological disorders, and a significant percentage of animal hoarders are eventually institutionalized or placed under some type of protective care. The hoarding of inanimate objects is a relatively new area of study in the psyhological and psychiatric literature, and even less has been reported about the subcategory of animal hoarding. Experts are still unsure of the exact causes for hoarding, and because the behavior is seen in a range of disorders, it is likely that a variety of conditions can ultimately result in pathological hoarding.

Hoarding is characterized in DSM-IV (the bible of psychiatric disorders) as a symptom of obsessive-compulsive disorder (OCD) and obsessive-compulsive personality disorder (OCPD). There is very little literature about treatment, and what exists suggests that hoarders may be particularly resistant to both psychotherapy and commonly used medications.

www.tufts.edu/vet/cfa/hoarding/mental.htm.

◇◇◇

Often hoarders swear that they love their animals, and in a subjective sense, this is true. One definition would include the following:

- more than the typical number of companion animals;
- the inability to provide even minimal standards of nutrition, sanitation, shelter, and veterinary care, with this neglect often resulting in starvation, illness, and death;
- a denial of the inability to provide this minimum care and the impact of that failure on the animals, the household, and human occupants of the dwelling.

www.tufts.edu/vet/cfa/hoarding/abthoard.htm#A1

◇◇◇

There are really two different threads that need to be followed for these fact situations. The first is how to help the animals held by a hoarder who is not providing adequate levels of care. Second, what to do with the person? Clearly jail time is not helpful for the animals. Because a hoarder does not realize the risk she or he is imposing on the animals, punishment of hoarders will seldom be an example sufficient to change conduct of others in the community. A combined intervention of social services for the humans and a humane society for the animals would be ideal, but it is difficult to combine public and private organizational efforts. What would you suggest should be the goals of intervention if a hoarding situation comes to light?

A key shortcoming in the present law is the necessity of filing criminal charges in order to get access to the animals. Additionally, the animals often must be held as evidence. The ownership of rescued animals may be in limbo for months or a year or more as usually ownership can be taken away only if the person is found guilty of a crime.

Because of the complexities of such cases and the need to care for large numbers of animals, most local prosecutors are reluctant to bring criminal cases. One possible answer is to allow qualified citizen organizations to file civil law suits for violations of the cruelty laws and obtain control and title to the harmed animals. North Carolina seems to have a statute that allows a civil action that can be used to address these difficult fact patterns. See William Reppy, *Citizen Standing to Enforce Anti-Cruelty Laws by Obtaining Injunctions: The North Carolina Experience*, 11 Animal L. 39 (2005).

Cat Champion Corp. v. Jean Marie Primrose, 149 P. 3d 1276 (Or. Ct. App. 2006) (A woman had 11 cats, which were in a state of neglect and were taken away from her and put with a cat protection agency. Criminal charges were dropped against the woman when it was found she was mentally ill and incapable of taking care of herself or her cats. The court found that it could grant the cat protection agency ownership over the cats so they could be put up for adoption, even though the woman had not been criminally charged and had not forfeited her cats.)

It is not just dogs and cats that can be the focus of hoarder/collectors. In March 2007 a man in Apex, North Carolina, was arrested on animal cruelty charges for having 80 sheep in his suburban home. Unfortunately, 30 of the sheep were in such poor condition that they had to be euthanized. Why did it take so long for authorities to intervene?

◇◇

For additional consideration of the issue of animal hoarding, see Colin Berry, Gary Patronek, Randall Lockwood, *Long-term Outcomes in Animal Hording Cases*, 11 Animal Law 167 (2005), available at: *http://www.animallaw.info/journals/jo_pdf/vol11_p167.pdf*. The most extensive website dealing with the issue has been established by Tufts University, *www.tufts.edu/vet/cfa/hoarding/*; for an article discussing the individuals see: *http://www.psychiatrictimes.com/p000425.html*.

◇◇

Illinois is one of the first states to acknowledge this new category of animal issue by adding the phrase in the definition section of its cruelty law.

> Il.C.S. 70 § 2.10. Companion animal hoarder. "Companion animal hoarder" means a person who (i) possesses a large number of companion animals; (ii) fails to or is unable to provide what he or she is required to provide under Section 3 of this Act; (iii) keeps the companion animals in a severely overcrowded environment; and (iv) displays an inability to recognize or understand the nature of or has a reckless disregard for the conditions under which the companion animals are living and the deleterious impact they have on the companion animals' and owner's health and well-being.

Section three of the Illinois law, upon a conviction of a failure to provide care, provides:

> If the convicted person is a juvenile or a companion animal hoarder, the court **must** order the convicted person to undergo a psychological or psychiatric evaluation and to undergo treatment that the court determines to be appropriate after due consideration of the evaluation.

News Bits

In 2005 in Michigan a couple was found in violation of the criminal cruelty laws for keeping animal in illegal conditions. There were 95 dogs on the property and 33 were removed from the home, some had missing teeth, infected eyes and ears, and it was found that their leg bones would fracture easily. They were infected with fleas and underweight. They agreed to plead guilty in return for no jail time. The judge sentenced them for two years of probation, during that time there can be no ownership or keeping of animals. *Lansing State Journal*, Dec. 16, 2005 p. B1.

CHAPTER 8

Agricultural Animals

This is a different type of topic as the United States is presently in the midst of a public policy discussion about these animals. It is not an issue of old laws or federal regulations. The issue is what the law should be, not what the law is. The number and plight of agricultural animals represents an area in need of public attention. While most recently a few states have adopted new laws, there are few constraints on the use or living conditions of agricultural animals. Indeed, most of the material in this chapter focuses on what steps might be taken to help the welfare of agricultural animals when it seems difficult to get significant change in the law.

This chapter is not about individual employees who intentionally harm by striking, kicking, throwing or beating agricultural animals. It is about the industrial system now in place in the U.S. for most agricultural animals. One focus of this chapter is the concept of "suffering" and the degree to which it does or should direct the law. Additionally, the reader will be introduced to regulations and administrative law issues.

Section 1

Conditions Faced by Animals

There are many books, articles and websites that reveal and discuss the conditions faced by the agricultural animal. In this modest chapter all of the agricultural animals and the conditions they face cannot be touched on. The following materials will focus on pork production and egg production.

From Paddocks to Prisons: Pigs in New South Wales, Current Practices, Future Directions

Excerpt from a report prepared by Voiceless (*www.voiceless.org.au*) (December 2005)[The conditions and issue of this report apply to the US and only a little has changed since the release of the report.]

Australians have had a love affair with ham, pork and bacon for generations, with the great Aussie breakfast of bacon and eggs having become an integral part of our national diet. Yet the farming of pigs has changed more rapidly than arguably just about any industry in Australia over the past generation.

The figures speak for themselves. Between 1970-71 and 2002-03 the number of Australian pig producers fell by an astounding 94 percent. What other industry has suffered such a labor decline? Astonishingly rather than total output falling by a similar margin, production actually increased by 130 percent over the same period. The reason is that well-managed family-run farms are being run out of business, unable to compete with larger factory-style operations that increasingly are being run by foreign interests. The implications for the welfare of pigs have been sinister and largely invisible to the Australian consumer.

The sad reality for pigs now is that mothers no longer forage in the earth in the open air, but are confined for most of their lives to steel stalls so cramped they cannot turn round, with cold concrete floors on which to feed.

About Pigs

a) Every year we discover more about the cognitive abilities and emotional complexity of animals, including farm animals. They can feel pain and suffer physically and they also experience psychological well-being and distress.

b) Pigs are recognized to be at least as good at problem-solving as dogs. Scientists have discovered that pigs "have an understanding of what is going on in other pigs' minds and make their own decisions accordingly in order to get what they want." This type of thinking has often been assumed to be unique to apes and humans.

c) Pigs are extremely active and inquisitive. When free to roam, pigs spend much of their day smelling, nibbling, manipulating objects with their snouts and rooting ("nosing") about in the soil for tidbits. Their powerful but sensitive snout is a highly developed sense organ. Rooting, exploring and manipulating natural materials are essential elements of pig welfare.

d) Few species are more social than pigs; they form close bonds with each other and other species, including humans. They cooperate with, and defend, one another. Adults will protect a piglet, leaving their own litters if necessary to defend an endangered youngster. Pigs may be able to recognize and remember up to 20-30 individuals. Touch and bodily contact are especially important to pigs. They seek out and enjoy close contact, and will lie close together when resting.

e) Pigs are vocal and communicate constantly with one another. More than 20 of their vocalizations have been identified. They have an elaborate courtship ritual, including a song between males and females. Newborn piglets learn to run to their mother's voice, and the mother pig sings to her young while nursing. After nursing, a piglet will sometimes run to her mother's face to rub snouts and grunt.

f) When she is ready to give birth, a sow selects a clean, dry area apart from the group, sometimes walking 5-10km to search for a good nest site and to gather preferred bedding materials. She hollows out a depression in the ground and lines it with grass, straw or other materials. For several days after her piglets are born, she defends the nest against intruders. When her piglets are five to ten days old, she encourages them to leave the nest to socialize with other pigs.

g) Weaning occurs naturally at three months of age, but young pigs continue to live with their mothers in a close family group. Two or more sows and their piglets usually join together in an extended family, with particularly close friendships developing between sows. Young piglets play with great enthusiasm, play-fighting and moving or throwing objects into the air. Pigs appear to have a good sense of direction too, as they have found their way home over great distances. Adults can run at speeds of about 15 km an hour.

What They Get

Sow Stalls

- Sow stalls are so small that pregnant pigs are not able to turn around or take more than one step forward or back.
- Stalls cause stereotypes, repetitive purposeless behaviors, and a sign of suffering.
- Some studies have shown that over 90% of stall-housed sows exhibit stereotypic behaviour.
- Pigs can spend up to half their time in stereotypic behaviour.
- Stereotypies can result in physical damage or illness.
- Sows in stalls may well be "clinically depressed."
- Stalls rate the lowest of all sow housing systems in terms

of welfare.

- It is widely accepted that sow welfare is better in alternative systems.

Farrowing Crates and Premature/Abrupt Weaning

- Farrowing crates allow almost zero movement.

- Sows give birth on concrete and are unable to fulfill their need to make a nest.

- Slatted or solid floors in farrowing crates increase the incidence of foot lesions in piglets.

- The stress of abrupt weaning results in piglets having a high incidence of clinical disease and diarrhoea.

Mutilations

- Tail docking of piglets without pain relief causes considerable pain leading to trembling, leg shaking, sliding on their hindquarters, tail-jerking and vomiting.

- It is unclear how effective tail docking is in reducing tail biting.

- Provision of straw-based bedding (or some other natural material) in pens, providing adequate feeding space and managing stocking densities is known to reduce the incidence of tail biting.

- Teeth clipping of piglets is a serious welfare concern and makes no clear contribution to sow welfare.

Space Allowance

- Pig aggression generally increases as space allowance decreases.

- Crowded living conditions leads to chronic stress in growing pigs.

Biological Facts on the Domestic Chicken

by Veronica Hirsch, Animal Legal and Historical Center
(*www.animallaw.info*) (2003)

Archaeological evidence suggests that the bird commonly known as the chicken (Gallus domesticus) is a domesticated version of the Indian and Southeast Asian Red Jungle Fowl (Gallus gallus) which is still found in the wild today. It is thought that the bird was first tamed in China around 6000 B.C., with the birds moving into India by 2000 B.C. The chicken then spread from China to Russia and from there into Europe between 750 B.C. – 42 A.D. Some scholars believe

that the bird may have been domesticated first for its use in cockfighting, and only later used as a food source. The White Leghorn breed or crosses of this breed is the large white bird most commonly used in agriculture and for research, but there are over 400 different breeds of chickens.

Most of the almost nine billion chickens in the United States today are used for either egg production or meat, and most of these chickens are raised using intensive husbandry practices commonly known as "factory farming." Prior to WWII, most chickens were raised on small family farms, but today, technology, antibiotics, and mechanization lets factory farmers raise more birds in less space, and with lower costs. Intensive farming uses less land and protects the animals from the extremes of climate. It also allows farmers to diagnose and treat diseases and other problems quickly, and control the length and intensity of daylight to increase egg production and/or encourage faster growth. Laying hens live a season-free life of unending 16 hour days, while broiler chickens live in almost constant daylight, getting just one hour of darkness every 23 hours.

The per capita consumption of chicken has increased from 23.4 pounds per year in 1960 to over 70 pounds today. It is thought that chickens currently supply up to 25% of the world's meat supply, and in the United States, over 20 million chickens are slaughtered every 24 hours. Today 36 percent of all meat consumed in the United States is poultry, and chicken remains the least expensive meat. In 1990 the average price of poultry was 89.9 cents a pound, compared to $2.13 per pound for pork, and $2.81 for beef. The average price of a dozen large eggs in the year 2000 (67 cents) was less than the average price paid in 1984 (84 cents).

The life led by these factory farmed birds depends on whether they will be used for eggs or meat. Laying chickens are bred for intense egg production, and therefore any male chicks born from egg-laying hens are killed, often by piling them into garbage bags and suffocating them, or through carbon-dioxide induced asphyxiation, or by decapitation. Occasionally, they may be ground up alive as meal for other animals. There are no legal restrictions on the disposal of chicks.

> **Think About It**
>
> The advances in breeding made quite an impact: In 1900 a typical chick took 16 weeks to reach 2 lbs (0.9 kg), which was considered frying weight. Today a commercial broiler chicken lives only about six weeks and weighs about 4 lbs (1.8 kg) at slaughter.

Egg-laying chickens are often referred to as cage hens or battery hens because they live their life in a "battery cage." Typically, each battery cage is a 12-inch by 18-inch wire cage that may hold up to six birds. In a six-bird cage, each bird would have approximately 36 in^2 of room. The cages are stacked on top of each other in a layer house that may hold over 80,000 birds. The hens begin laying at 16-22 weeks old, and may produce up to 300 eggs by 70 weeks. The crowded conditions mean that the hens cannot engage in most of their normal behaviors. They cannot walk, fly, perch, preen, nest, peck, dust-bathe, or scratch for food. Hens may not even be able to stand up and their feet may actually grow into the wire floor of their cages.

In these conditions the hens' normal behavior of establishing a pecking order is thwarted and hens may peck at and injure each other or even become cannibalistic. To prevent the hens from injuring one another, the chicks are de-beaked immediately after hatching. De-beaking is a process where a very hot blade is used to trim off and cauterize up to 3 mm of the top beak and 2.5 mm of the lower beak. Re-trimming may be necessary as the bird grows.

Chickens used for meat (broilers) are not raised in battery cages, but are usually raised in deep litter on the floor of a large warehouse that is carpeted with as many as 40,000 birds.

A four-level traditional battery cage system from a producer in Maryland. Reprinted with permission from Compassion Over Killing.

Broilers are also de-beaked, and may have their toes removed to prevent injuries from fighting that may occur because of the cramped living conditions. The birds have been bred to achieve a market weight (about four pounds) in just six weeks. Thirty years ago, it took twelve weeks for the birds to reach market weight. Upon reaching market weight, the broilers are packed into crates and shipped to the slaughterhouse. There are no federal regulations regarding the transportation or slaughtering of chickens, although there are a small minority of states that have enacted some protections in this area regarding chickens.

Because broilers are bred to grow fast, they gain weight faster than their bones, heart and lungs can support. For comparison, at six weeks of age, the average female broiler chicken is 4 times bigger than the average laying hen. Broiler's leg and breast muscles are especially large, and this causes the broiler chicken a multiple of health problems, including crippling leg disorders, ascites (a disease of the lungs and heart) and sudden death syndrome (akin to a heart attack). The birds are very inactive (perhaps due to lameness) and show a reduced capacity for antibody production. These health problems increase as the bird ages, and the mortality rate for broilers is up to 5% over the production cycle, or seven times that of egg-laying birds.

The super fast growth of broiler chickens has created an additional problem in the breeding of broilers. A full-grown, sexually mature hen is needed to produce the eggs that will grow into broiler chickens, but the broiler hen's fast rate of growth may shorten her life span. In order to keep the broiler hens from growing too large, too fast, these hens are fed only 25% of what they would eat if allowed to eat at liberty. These birds weigh only a quarter of what they would weigh if they were being grown for slaughter, and studies have shown them to be chronically hungry, frustrated and stressed. This chronic underfeeding is necessary in order to "dwarf" the breeding stock and prevent obesity, lameness and heart failure, and keep the hens alive long enough to lay eggs.

◇◇

The Five Freedoms

Before considering a batch of differing agricultural animal welfare standards, there should be established a context in which to judge the standards. In the United Kingdom, the welfare of farm animals has been on the public agenda for a number of decades. After considerable discussion among a variety of groups, the idea of the five freedoms was developed. This concept is fairly widely accepted in Europe today, but has only slight visibility in the United States.

The British RSPCA (Royal Society for the Prevention of Cruelty to Animals) has taken a leadership position within the U.K. to implement the five freedoms as a consumer choice labeling program in the grocery stores of the nation. From their website comes the following explanation of the program.

Freedom Food is the RSPCA's farm assurance and food labelling scheme, set up by the RSPCA in 1994. The aim of the scheme is simple — to improve the lives of as many farm animals as possible. It works towards this by implementing the RSPCA species specific welfare standards on farms, hauliers and abattoirs across the country. These practical standards apply to both indoor and outdoor systems, as long as they meet the requirements.

RSPCA Welfare Standards

The RSPCA's strict but achievable set of farm animal welfare standards have been devised by the society's experienced animal welfare specialists in consultation with veterinary experts and the industry. They are updated as new research and information is gathered to develop better ways to rear animals. The standards are based on concept of the five freedoms as defined by the Farm Animal Welfare Council. Examples of the way in which the RSPCA standards work towards these 'ideals' within a practical farming context can be found below:

Freedom from fear and distress

By providing conditions and care that avoid unnecessary fear and distress. Everyone that plays a part in managing and handling livestock must understand basic animal behaviour and Freedom Food members are required to avoid mixing animals of different ages, sexes and social groups, which can be very stressful to the animals and may result in injury through fighting.

Freedom from hunger and thirst

By providing a satisfying, appropriate and safe diet as well as consistant access to adequate fresh water. Allowing generous feeding and drinking spaces helps minimise bullying and competition.

Freedom from discomfort

By providing an appropriate environment including shelter and a comfortable resting area. A clean dry bedded area for mammalian species, and plenty of space to move around must be provided.

Freedom from pain injury and disease

By prevention or rapid diagnosis and treatment using good veterinary care when required. The environment must be well maintained to provide good health.

Freedom to express normal behaviour

By providing enough space, appropriate environmental enrichment and company of the animals own kind.

How the scheme works

Before a farm, haulier or abattoir can join the scheme, a Freedom Food approved assessor must carry out a detailed audit on the farm. Once in the scheme, members are then subject to reassessments. In addition, the RSPCA's Farm Livestock Officers also carry out random spot checks on at least 30% of members annually to help ensure that the standards are adhered to.

But that isn't the end of the story. Consumers can be confident that before products can appear on the supermarket shelves bearing the Freedom Food trademark, traceability must be established through the supply chain. If the farmer is a chicken producer, for example, the hatchery from which they were sourced must be accredited. The haulier who delivered them to the farm and who will eventually take them on to the abattoir must have been successfully assessed, and the abattoir itself must also satisfy all the RSPCA welfare conditions.

The actual standards can be downloaded from the website under their Freedom Food Project (*www.rspca.org.uk*). Under RSPCA standards the use of battery cages for laying hens is prohibited. Remember that these are voluntary standards; those that ask for inspections and pass are allowed to display a marketing logo. In turn it is presumed that some segment of the buying public would purchase their products because of the logo. This requires the existence of an educated public. The RSPCA and others have spent considerable resources promoting the logo and the purpose behind it.

> **Think about it**
>
> Is "quality of life" a meaningful phrase for chickens and pig (or dogs and cats)?

Questions & Notes

1. Perhaps the most difficult part of the animal welfare debate is deciding on the appropriate context, or mix of factors, that will set the stage for deciding which standards are appropri-

ate. Ethics and morals can only really bring us to the threshold of acknowledging the presence of a duty toward the animals. The Five Freedoms is an animal-focused perspective. Will this be acceptable to the public? What about human health or economic profitability? How about the environmental impact of industrial agriculture?

2. Veal calves — Removed from their mothers at birth so the mothers can produce milk, they are usually then isolated and fed a milk substitute. Historically it has been believed that the best veal meat comes from calves that are confined in small containers, alone and unable to exercise, because those conditions produce the whitest and softest of the meats. Is this suffering? If not, why object? To what degree should human taste preference drive the living conditions of calves? Should geese be required to endure forced feeding so as to create abnormally large livers resulting in the celebrated food — foie gras?

3. Should chickens be kept in sealed buildings so that they can be protected from the risk of various outside diseases like aviary flu? It is not clear that this is the best answer. See, *www.guardian.co.uk/birdflu/story/0,,2006377,00.html* (Monday, Feb. 5, 2007), which gives the story of the slaughter of 159,000 turkeys that had lived in a confined building but caught H5N1 bird flu anyways.

4. How much impact should economic cost have on living conditions? What if the cost of free-range layer eggs doubles farmers cost or egg production? (Assuming that free-range is defined as housing that allows a bird the choice of going outside into the natural environment to search for food *and they do so.*)

◇◇◇

While this book focuses on the welfare of agricultural animals, it must be understood the conditions under which these animals are required to live have significantly broader effects on human health and the environment. The full scope of all these issues have been set out in the final report of a two year national study by the Pew Charitable Trust.

Pew Commission on Industrial Farm Animal Production, Final Report: *Putting Meat on The Table: Industrial Farm Animal Production in America* (2008).

Full Report, *http://www.ncifap.org/bin/e/j/PCIFAPFin.pdf*

Executive Summary *http://www.ncifap.org/bin/s/a/PCIFAPSmry.pdf.*

The industrial farm animal production system, as it exists today, too often concentrates economic power in the hands of the large companies that process and sell the animal products, instead of the individuals who raise the animals. In many cases, the "open market" for animal products has completely disappeared, giving the farmer only one buyer to sell to, and one price to be received.

In addition to raising animals in closer proximity, steps were taken to streamline the process of raising animals for food, including standardized feed for rapid weight gain and uniformity; genetic selection to accentuate traits, such as leanness, that create uniform meat products; and mechanization of feeding, watering, and other husbandry activities. This streamlined processing and standardization is typical of the evolution of industrial pursuits, and is intended to be more economical by lowering the amount of input required to achieve a marketable product, as well as to ensure a uniform product. This process in food animal production has resulted in farms that are easier to run, with fewer and often less-highly-skilled employees, and a greater output of uniform animal products. However, there are unintended consequences of this type of animal production.

This transformation, and the associated social, economic, environmental, and public health problems engendered by it, have gone virtually unnoticed by many American citizens. Not long ago, the bulk of the fruit, grain, vegetables, meat, and dairy products consumed by the American people were produced on small family farms. These farms once defined both the physical and the social character of the US countryside. However, the steady urbanization of the US population has resulted in an American populace that is increasingly disassociated from the production system that supplies its food. Despite the dramatic decline in family farms over the past 50 years, many Americans, until very recently, continued to think that their food still came from these small farms.

While increasing the speed of production, the intensive confinement production system creates a number of problems. These include contributing to the increase in the pool of antibiotic-resistant bacteria because of the overuse of antibiotics; air quality problems; the contamination of rivers, streams, and coastal waters with concentrated animal waste; animal welfare problems, mainly as a result of the extremely close quarters in which the animals are housed; and significant shifts in the social structure and economy of many farming regions throughout the country. It was on these areas that the Commission focused its attention.

At p.2-3 Ex. Summary.

The Commission recommends the phase-out, within ten years, of all intensive confinement systems that restrict natural movement and normal behaviors, including swine gestation crates, restrictive swine farrowing crates, cages used to house multiple egg-laying chickens, commonly referred to as battery cages, and the tethering or individual housing of calves for the production of white veal. In addition, the Commission recommends the end to force-feeding of fowl to produce foie gras, tail docking of dairy cattle, and forced molting of laying hens by feed removal. Due to the capital investment in these intensive confinement systems by many contract producers, particularly in swine production, the Commission recommends targeted assistance be made available to contract producers to facilitate the conversion from intensive confinement systems, either through accelerated depreciation or some other mechanism.

At p. 22. Ex Summary.

Questions & Notes

1. Global corporations prefer high-capital investments and cheap labor. Family farm-based agriculture can work with low capital investment and highly educated and diverse individuals. Which is better for society? Is there a value in re-establishing the family farm — to the humans, in addition to the welfare of the animals? How much weight should be given to the high negatives to the environment that arise out of waste pollution from concentrated animal sites?

2. To make the whole thing even more complex, consider that all adoption of laws will occur in a political context. Animal welfare outcomes are subject to all the cross currents of hundreds of individuals' different political agendas. Do you think a Democrat or a Republican is more likely to sponsor a bill for agricultural animal welfare in the United States?

3. For fuller discussion of many of these issues, see, Michigan Law Review, Volume 106, First Impressions: An Online Symposium on Agricultural Animals and Animal Law, (April 2008) *http:// www.michiganlawreview.org/assets/fi/106/animals.pdf.*

Section 2

Agricultural Animal Welfare Standards

The ethical premise for this topic is that the general public does not reject the concept of eating animal products and flesh but that they require basic humane considerations for such animals. The child's storybook picture of family farms and happy animals no longer exists for the vast majority of farm animals. Yet, nothing has replaced those images in the minds of the average consumer, who do not give a thought as to where their food comes from.

An Innocent Inquiry into a Very Difficult Topic

[Farm Animal Protection Ad #45] Scene Set-Up: the camera is looking down one of the long aisles in a large food store. A mother and child are standing in front of the meat counter and the mother takes up a package. Camera zooms up close enough to have half body shots of the two and pick up their voices:

> **Daughter** (about 5 years old, nicely dressed, look of intelligence): Mommy, what is that?
>
> **Mother:** It's a package of chicken for dinner tomorrow.
>
> **Daughter** (Slight pause while thinking): But chickens have pretty feathers, and walk around on two feet, crowing out the welcome song.
>
> **Mother:** Well, yes but this one was killed so we could have the meat to eat.
>
> **Daughter:** Did it hurt to be killed? What happened to the feathers?
>
> **Mother:** I hope it did not hurt the chicken, and I don't know what happened to the feathers.
>
> **Daughter:** Where did the chicken live? How old was it when it was killed? (pause) How did they kill it?
>
> **Mother:** Ok, enough of the questions. Let's go find the eggs ...
>
> **Daughter:** Are the chickens that lay the eggs the same ones we eat? Where do they live?
>
> **Mother:** I have no idea, now stop all the questions; I have to find the donuts.

Dissolve this scene and phase in the picture of the five chickens in a small cage. Voiceover with male voice, "Do you know where your chicken comes from? Do you know how they lived and died? Shouldn't you?"

Questions & Notes

Several key questions remain unresolved in the area of agricultural animals:

1. Agricultural animals are not pets; they share a different community with humans. While people may well decide to expend money on behalf of a pet well beyond its economic value, this will not normally be the case for agricultural animals who must exist almost entirely in the context of economic value. Therefore it is important to distinguish between ideal conditions for farm animals and minimum acceptable conditions for an economic activity.

    What minimum standards should be imposed for the raising, transporting, and slaughtering of agricultural animals? Who should make this decision?

2. Assuming standards are agreed upon, who should enforce the standards? Consider the list of possibilities for both the source of standards and their enforcement:

    • State or federal prosecutors – criminal law

    • State or federal agency inspectors – civil fines

    • Informed consumers – labeling laws

    • Private organizations – both as inspectors and by civil lawsuits

3. The issues are much more complex than simply being free from pain. Is it acceptable to deprive animals from access to sunlight, dirt, bugs, and grass? How do we measure or value providing or denying a cow access to a green pasture for grazing? Do we know enough about animal pain and suffering to establish bans on or conditions for the raising of laying hens and pigs? Can the mental well-being of sheep be discussed intelligently by humans? [As you might imagine the elite sheep often have discussions about the possibility of human intelligence but have been without firm conclusion as of yet.]

4. Review the materials in the first part of this chapter and outline what steps you would suggest. Do you think these steps would be politically acceptable?

    Now consider how close the present law is to your suggestions.

◇◇

Think About It

Can their be life without suffering?

State Criminal Anti-Cruelty Laws

When introduced to commercial animals and issues of welfare, most students assume that some law must exist to provide a minimum level of protection for chickens. This is not the case. Most state anti-cruelty laws have a specific exemption for agricultural practices. For example, the Michigan law has the following provision at the end of the anti-cruelty law:

> MCLA §750.50 **(8)** This section does not prohibit the lawful killing or other use of an animal, including, but not limited to, the following:
>
> (a) Fishing.
>
> (b) Hunting, trapping, or wildlife control regulated pursuant to the natural resources and environmental protection act.
>
> (c) Horse racing.
>
> (d) The operation of a zoological park or aquarium.
>
> (e) Pest or rodent control.
>
> (f) **Farming or a generally accepted animal husbandry or farming practice involving livestock.**

The above language would extend to hogs, cattle, and other animals, as well as chickens. A key issue in this area is what constitutes "traditional agricultural practices," as most statutory exemptions use that phrase. It is unclear what the word "traditional" might mean—those practices used by the average producer or the high-volume producer; 100-year-old practices versus farming practices that are only 20 years old? State prosecutors seem entirely disinterested in pursuing what is or is not protected by such exemptions.

In 1996 the State of New Jersey took the progressive step of directing the state agricultural agency to adopt humane standards for the raising of agricultural animals. However, the regulations adopted were nearly identical to many of the existing industrial practices. See the case in Section 3 for more details. As of 2010 several states have adopted farm animal specific legislation but no modifications of general cruelty laws for this topic.

Questions & Notes

1. There are no cases in the law books questioning any of the current industrial practices used on animals. Why might this be the case? Criminal law prosecutions for farm animal issues usually arise only when animals have been starved to death. Apparently everyone can agree that starvation is not a "generally accepted

farming practice." See **State v. Klammer**, 41 N.W. 2d 451 (1950) (28 horses died of starvation); **People v. Johnson**, 305 N.W. 2d 560 (Mich. 1981) (four horses had been starved); **McClendon v. Story County Sheriff's Office**, 403 F. 3d 510 (8th Cir. 2005)(farm with 35 horses was not providing adequate food and care).

2. Remembering the "duty of care" materials from Chapter 7, does the keeping of a laying hen in a little wire cage violate the general prohibitions of the state anti-cruelty laws?

◇◇◇

The Federal Animal Welfare Act

The outcome for the agricultural animals is no better at the federal level in the United States. The Animal Welfare Act specifically says that agricultural animals are exempt from its provisions.

> 7 U.S.C. Sec. 2132(g) The term "animal" means any live or dead dog, cat, monkey (nonhuman primate mammal), guinea pig, hamster, rabbit, or such other warm-blooded animal, ... **but such term excludes** ... (3) horses not used for research purposes and other **farm animals**, such as, but not limited to livestock or **poultry**, used or intended for use as food or fiber, or livestock or poultry used or intended for use for improving animal nutrition, breeding, management, or production efficiency. ...

Additionally, the federal Humane Methods of Livestock Slaughter Act, 7 USC §§ 1901-1907, that deals with the slaughter of commercial food animals, again by definition, does not cover chickens, even though it does cover beef and pigs.

Because there were no laws in place when the chicken industries built up over the past 40 years, there are now millions of dollars invested in equipment and facilities. Any change to better the life of the chicken will be and has been met by sharp opposition by the commercial operations, saying that any change would be too expensive.

Seller-Based Standards

Sellers of animal products might have a number of different motives for the use of self-adopted standards:

- To forestall government regulation
- To assure the public about the product
- To provide a consistent product by all producers
- To assure an acceptable profit
- As a response to actions by animal activist

As you consider the following materials, try to make a judgment about why certain actions have occurred.

1. National Chicken Council

Within the United States, one of the industrial organizations that seeks to protect and promote those that raise chickens for meat is the National Chicken Council.

> The National Chicken Council (NCC), based in Washington, D.C., is the national, non-profit trade association representing the U.S. chicken industry. NCC is a full-service trade association that promotes and protects the interests of the chicken industry and is the industry's voice before Congress and federal agencies. NCC member companies include chicken producer/processors, poultry distributors, and allied industry firms. The producer/processors account for approximately 95 percent of the chickens produced in the United States.

From their website, *www.nationalchickencouncil.com*.

One response of the NCC to the issue of animal welfare concerns was the development of a set of standards and an inspection and certification process. The entire statement of 2010 standards can be found at www.nationalchickencouncil.com. These standards apply to the conditions for meat chickens who are not normally kept in cages, but instead allowed to roam on a building floor for their short lives.

The NCC has not adopted standards for caged egg-laying chickens. The industrial group more closely related to egg-laying chickens is the U.S. Poultry and Egg Association, a member of the NCC.

United Egg Producers Animal Husbandry Guidelines for U.S. Egg Laying Flocks (2010 edition)

RECOMMENDATIONS

While most of these guidelines are currently being used or can be implemented rather quickly, the recommendations dealing with cage configuration and size are intended for new construction....

1. Cage configuration and equipment maintenance should be such that manure from birds in upper cage levels does not drop directly on birds in lower level cages.

2. All hens should be able to stand comfortably upright in their cage. The slope of the cage floor should not exceed 8 degrees.

3. Space allowance should be in the range of 67 to 86 square inches of usable space per bird to optimize hen welfare.

4. Feeder space should be sufficient to allow all birds to eat at the same time.

The document also provides guidelines for "cage free" flocks. For the issue of space: "A minimum of 1.5 sq. ft. per hen must be allocated to allow normal behavior. In a house with perching/roosting area over a droppings pit/belt, the minimum space can be 1.2 sq. ft. for Brown Egg Layers and 1.0 sq. ft. for White Leghorns."

◇◇

Science-Based Organization Standards

The American Veterinary Medical Association is a science-based organization that might be expected to have a focus on the needs of animals. As an organization, they have drafted a number of policy statements to deal with a variety of animal issues, including commercial animals. See *www.avma.org/animal_welfare/position.asp*. Under AVMA policy, as of January 2007 the following is stated:

Housing Layer Chickens in Cages

Cages should be designed and maintained so as to avoid injury to birds. Construction of cages, feeders, and waterers should take into account scientifically documented advantages for bird comfort and health, and facilitate the safe removal of birds. Cage configuration should be such that manure from birds in upper level cages does not drop directly on birds in lower level cages. All hens should be able to stand comfortably upright in their cages. Feeder space should be sufficient to permit all birds to eat at the same time.

In 2010 there was a major revision of the Layer Position with the following language:

Laying hen housing systems must provide feed, water, light, air quality, space and sanitation that promote good health and welfare for the hens. Housing systems should provide for expression of important natural behaviors, protect the hens from disease, injury and predation, and promote food safety. Participation in a nationally recognized, third-party audited welfare program is strongly advised.

Support for the cage system is removed and acknowledgement of "natural behaviors" is given some focus. But is it clear what is and what is not within this statement? List three natural behaviors.

Buyer-Based Standards

Buyers come in two basic categories: retail individual consumers and large-volume purchasers. If an individual goes into a store to buy chicken meat or eggs, looking at the packages in front of them, how can they know the conditions, or even location of where the meat or eggs came from? Without detailed product labeling the consumer cannot make a choice. Therefore the consumer needs more information and some degree of assurance that the information on the package is truthful; thus the debate over logos. In the U.K. the Freedom  Foods line has the backing of the RSPCA, a long respected, highly visible organization that brings credibility to the presence of a logo on foods in the U.K.

In the United States a number of humane organizations have created a single program using a "Certified Humane" logo. (See *www.certifiedhumane.org/index.html*.)

The guidelines for layer hens do not allow for any cages, but may be in buildings under the following standards:

D. Space Allowance

E15: Sufficient freedom of movement

a. All hens must have sufficient freedom of movement to be able, without difficulty, to stand normally, turn around, and stretch their wings.

b. They must also have sufficient space to be able to perch or sit quietly without repeated disturbance.

E16: Stocking density

a. A minimum of 1.5 sq ft. per hen must be allocated to allow normal behavior. [This is 216 sq. inches per bird as compared to the 67-86 inches provided under the historical industry standard for when in a cage.]

http://www.certifiedhumane.org/uploads/pdf/Standards/English/Std09.Layers.1AD. pdf

Section 3

Initial Efforts for Legal Change

Over the past decade, two primary paths have been attempted in order to enhance the welfare of farm animals: legal prohibitions and legal regulations. The following case represents the regulatory approach, and following that case is a consideration of legislatively adopted prohibitions.

CASE BY CASE

This is a very long case – twenty six pages of small font. It was a national case, with big names and amicus briefs, and the Court treated it as such. It is a thoughtful opinion with which many in the animal movement disagree about the outcome, but the case is very instructive about how agencies handle difficult farm issues and how to expect courts to review agency actions, specifically the adoption of regulations. It also shows the burden is on the legislature to carefully state the goals of farm animal regulations, particularly addressing the balance between animal welfare concerns and a profitable animal enterprise. Finally, consider how important the role of science is in this outcome of the case. The battle for better animal welfare standards cannot be successful in the regulatory environment until there is better science about animal suffering under existing and alternative methods of agricultural production. Significant editing was required to fit this case into this chapter, reading the entire case is useful if time permits.

New Jersey Society for the Prevention of Cruelty to Animals v. New Jersey Department of Agriculture

196 N.J. 366, 955 A. 2d 886 (2008)

JUSTICE HOENS delivered the (unanimous) opinion of the Court.

In 1996, with little discernable fanfare, the Legislature enacted a new section of the existing statute regulating animal cruelty. Although that statute, since at least 1898, had essentially left animal welfare and the protection of animals to the New Jersey Society for the Prevention of Cruelty to Animals ("NJSPCA") and its related county organizations, the Legislature decreed that the Department of Agriculture ("the Department") would be vested with certain authority relating to the care and welfare of domestic livestock, commonly referred to as farm animals.

In doing so, the Legislature directed the Department to create and promulgate regulations that would set standards governing the raising, keeping, and marketing of domestic livestock, but it specified that the guiding principle to be utilized in establishing those standards was to be whether the treatment of these animals was "humane."

This matter presents us with a broad challenge to the regulations promulgated by the Department pursuant to this legislative directive. More particularly, we are called upon to consider whether the Department, in promulgating the regulations relating to the care of domestic livestock: (1) failed in general to comply with the mandate of the Legislature that it create standards that are "humane," either objectively or as tested against the definition that the Department itself adopted; (2) created an impermissibly broad and vague category of permitted practices by referring to "routine husbandry practices" as generally acceptable; (3) failed to create an adequate regulatory scheme by utilizing undefined or ill-defined terms that cannot serve as objectively enforceable standards; and (4) embraced a variety of specific practices that are either objectively inhumane or supported by inadequate scientific evidence as to their usefulness, or that fail to meet any accepted definition of the term humane.

In part, the issues before this Court require us to evaluate the very methodology utilized by the Department in its creation of the challenged regulations; in part, the issues before us raise questions and debates arising from deeply held notions concerning the welfare of animals generally. Nonetheless, the dispute before this Court has nothing to do with anyone's love for animals, or with the way in which any of us treats our pets; rather, it requires a balancing of the interests of people and organizations who would zealously safeguard the well-being of all animals, including those born and bred for eventual slaughter, with the equally significant interests of those who make their living in animal husbandry and who contribute, through their effort, to our food supply.

In the end, our focus is not upon, nor would it be appropriate for us to address, whether we deem any of the specifically challenged practices to be, objectively, humane. To engage in that debate would suggest that we have some better understanding of the complex scientific and technical issues than we possibly could have, or that we are in some sense better able to evaluate the extensive record compiled by the Department than is that body itself. To engage in that discussion would also suggest that in a realm in which the Legislature has expressed its intention that an administrative agency bring its expertise to bear upon the issues, this Court is better equipped to do so. More to the point, it would suggest that we, rather than the Legislature or the Department, know which farming and livestock practices are objectively humane and which are not.

To accept such a challenge would be to overstep our role in our constitutional system, for it would be little more than our effort to substitute our view for that of the bodies authorized to act. It is, simply put, an invitation that we decline to accept. Rather, we confine our analysis, as we must, to a consideration about whether the agency in question did or did not carry out the function assigned to it by the Legislature, as tested in accordance with our ordinary standard of review of final agency actions and with due deference to the considerable expertise of that agency.

I.

The statute that created the underpinnings for the challenged regulations was first introduced for consideration by the Legislature on March 3, 1994. Designated as Senate Bill 713, it proposed the creation of an entirely new statutory section, and was entitled "AN ACT concerning domestic livestock and animal cruelty and welfare laws, amending R.S. 4:22-16,

As enacted, the bill had two sections, the first of which was codified as N.J.S.A. 4:22-16.1. That section provides, in relevant part, as follows:

a. The State Board of Agriculture and the Department of Agriculture, in consultation with the New Jersey Agricultural Experiment Station and within six months of the date of enactment of this act, shall develop and adopt, pursuant to the "Administrative Procedure Act," P.L. 1968, c. 410 (C. 52:14B-1 et seq.): (1) standards for the humane raising, keeping, care, treatment, marketing, and sale of domestic livestock; and (2) rules and regulations governing the enforcement of those standards.

b. Notwithstanding any provision in this title to the contrary:

(1) there shall exist a presumption that the raising, keeping, care, treatment, marketing, and sale of domestic li-vestock in accordance with the standards developed and adopted therefor pursuant to subsection a. of this section shall not constitute a violation of any provision of this title involving alleged cruelty to, or inhumane care or treatment of, domestic livestock ....

[N.J.S.A. 4:22-16.1.]

A.

Notwithstanding the six month time frame within which the Department was directed to act, regulations designed to implement this statutory mandate were not drafted and published as proposed regulations for public comment until 2003. See 35 N.J.R. 1873-88 (May 5, 2003). In response to the proposed regulations, the Department received over 6,500 written comments, and heard testimony from numerous witnesses who appeared at a public hearing on the proposals. See 36 N.J.R. 2586(a) (June 7, 2004). After considering the comments and the testimony, the Department amended certain of the proposed regulations and formally adopted the regulations, to be codified at N.J.A.C. 2:8-1.1 to -8.7, on June 7, 2004. See 36 N.J.R. 2637-715 (June 7, 2004). In doing so, the Department stated that it intended to "establish the minimum level of care that can be considered to be humane." 36 N.J.R. 2637 (June 7, 2004). Moreover, the Department noted that the regulations were developed after extensive "consultations with the New Jersey Agricultural Experiment Station, as well as with other academicians, the New Jersey Society for the Prevention of Cruelty to Animals, veterinarians, Department staff, extension agents, producers, and allied industries." Ibid. As explained by the Department:

> [t]he rules were also developed with consideration of the Department's overarching mission as reflected in Governor James McGreevey's statement to Charles M. Kuperus, Secretary of Agriculture: "My charge to Charlie is clear-preserve our farms, fight for our farmers, and ensure that our agricultural industry is profitable and strong, innovative and poised for a bright future."

[Ibid.]

As the Department understood its legislative mandate, and as it expressed that understanding as part of its adoption of these regulations in 2004, "[t]he rule proposal was designed to meet the complementary objectives of developing standards to protect animals from inhumane treatment and ... fostering industry sustainability and growth."

B.

Petitioners are a variety of entities, including the NJSPCA, and individuals which describe themselves collectively as "a wide coalition of animal protection organizations, consumers, farmers, and concerned citizens." Petitioners, many of whom had participated in the notice and comment process that led to the adoption of the regulations, raised this challenge to the final agency action adopting the regulations through an appeal in the Appellate Division, see R. 2:2-3(a)(2).

As part of the appeal, petitioners asserted that the regulations violated the directive of the Legislature as set forth in the statute itself. More particularly, petitioners contended that in adopting the statute, the Legislature expressed an intention to elevate the treatment of farm animals so as to permit only those practices, procedures, and techniques that meet the definition of "humane." As such, petitioners argued that the regulations fell short of that mandate in several particulars. First, petitioners argued that several subsections of the regulations include a broadly-worded exemption for any practice that meets the definition of a "routine husbandry practice" and that the definition as adopted is both impermissibly vague and not grounded on any evidence in the record. Second, petitioners asserted that some of the subsections included vague or undefined terms and failed to create enforceable standards. Third, petitioners asserted that the regulations authorized a variety of specific practices that do not meet the Department's definition of "humane" and are not in fact humane.

III.

We begin with a recitation of the well-established principles that inform our review of the final decisions of administrative agencies like the Department. Because the challenge brought by petitioners proceeds on multiple levels, we set forth the standards that apply to each.

First, the general parameters of our review are not controversial. Appellate courts ordinarily accord deference to final agency actions, reversing those actions if they are "arbitrary, capricious or unreasonable or [if the action] is not supported by substantial credible evidence in the record as a whole." Henry v. Rahway State Prison, 81 N.J. 571, 579-80, 410 A.2d 686 (1980). Similarly, an appellate court generally will not reverse an agency action, including its action in promulgating regulations, unless: (1) the regulations at issue "violate[ ] the enabling act's express or implied legislative policies;" or (2) "there is [not] substantial evidence in the record to support the findings on which the agency based its action;" or (3) "in applying the legislative policies to the facts the agency clearly erred by reaching a conclusion that could not reasonably have been made upon a showing of the relevant factors." In re Rulemaking, N.J.A.C. 10:82-1.2 & 10:85-4.1, 117 N.J. 311, 325, 566 A.2d 1154 (1989).

Moreover, in our review of an agency's interpretation of statutes within its scope of authority and its adoption of rules implementing its enabling statutes, we afford the agency great deference.

IV.

C.

In its lengthy consideration of the questions about animal cruelty in the context of domestic livestock, the Department compiled an extensive record. That record includes a wide variety of materials, representing input from numerous organizations (e.g., Animal Welfare Institution, National Pork Board, United Egg Producers), individuals and interest groups from New Jersey and nationally (e.g., Temple Grandin, Bernard Rollin, People for the Ethical Treatment of Animals, Farm Sanctuary, Professional Rodeo Cowboys Association), as well as materials from other states (e.g., Pennsylvania, New York, Maine, Texas, West Virginia, Montana, New Mexico), and even from other countries (e.g., England, Australia, New Zealand).

The record before this Court is not only extensive, but it is broad in its scope. On its face, the record demonstrates that the Department took seriously its charge to consider all aspects of the questions about the welfare of domestic livestock. In doing so, the Department did not simply consider the views and the input of farmers, agriculture professionals and their trade organizations, but it also received and took into account the views of animal rights activists and animal welfare organizations.

At the same time, the Department received input into its decisions from a wide variety of professionals, scholars, veterinarians, and other experts in all phases of animal welfare, animal health, and farming practices. The record includes a large number of scientific studies and scholarly publications reflecting both existing practices and trends, in this country and abroad, and representing current thinking about humane practices in the fields of animal husbandry, veterinary sciences, and agriculture. In addition, during the rulemaking process, the Department received and responded to thousands of comments, including many objections to its proposed regulations, in its effort to adopt regulations that more accurately carried out the legislative goal of ensuring that farm animals are treated humanely.

V.

Petitioners first assert that the regulations, in their entirety, fail to carry out the fundamental goal of the Legislature to have the Department create regulations that embody standards that are humane. They assert that the regulations neither comply with the meaning of humane as it is contemplated by the statute, nor do they even accord with the definition of humane that the agency itself adopted.

Plainly, the Department recognized that part of its charge was to adopt regulations that would ensure that the treatment of farm animals was humane, as opposed to merely reciting those practices that were accepted, routine, common, or prevalent. Just as plainly, the Department understood that the effectuation of its legislative mandate required that it adopt a definition of humane, because this is the critical term in the statute. As a result, the Department included in its regulations, both as originally proposed and as finally adopted, the following definition: " 'Humane' means marked by compassion, sympathy, and consideration for the welfare of animals." N.J.A.C. 2:8-1.2(a).

In addition, although not part of the definition of "humane," the Department also proposed and adopted definitions of two related terms. As such, it defined both "Animal welfare" and "Well-being." The former, which is included in the list of defined terms, "means a state or condition of physical and psychological harmony between the animal and its surroundings characterized by an absence of deprivation, aversive stimulation, over stimulation or any other imposed condition that adversely affects health and productivity of the animal." Ibid. The latter, found in the same part of the regulations, is defined as follows: " 'Well-being' means good health and welfare." Ibid.

We do not read in this statute or in these definitions any standard that requires that the regulations be invalidated in their entirety.

The extensive record and careful response of the Department to the overwhelming number of comments does not permit us to so conclude.

Even though there may be particular practices that the regulations specifically embrace and that might fall short of this lofty language, we cannot say that this is true as to each and every aspect of the regulations, or as to all of the practices that they permit.

VI.

Petitioners next challenge the inclusion in the regulations of language creating a safe harbor for any act or technique that meets the definition of "routine husbandry practices." N.J.A.C. 2:8-1.2. This exception, included in one of the subsections of each subchapter, see, e.g., N.J.A.C. 2:8- 2.6(f) (cattle); N.J.A.C. 2:8-4.7(e) (poultry); N.J.A.C. 2:8-7.6(d) (swine), essentially authorizes the use of any and all techniques that meet this definition because it identifies this class of practices as not being prohibited.

The phrase "routine husbandry practices" is among the terms that the Department included in its section on definitions as follows:

> "Routine husbandry practices" means those techniques commonly taught by veterinary schools, land grant colleges, and agricultural extension agents for the benefit of animals, the livestock industry, animal handlers and the public health and which are employed to raise, keep, care, treat, market and transport livestock, including, but not limited to, techniques involved with physical restraint; animal handling; animal identification; animal training; manure management; restricted feeding; restricted watering; restricted exercising; animal housing techniques; reproductive techniques; implantation; vaccination; and use of fencing materials, as long as all other State and Federal laws governing these practices are followed.

[N.J.A.C. 2:8-1.2.]

Petitioners assert that the definition of "routine husbandry practices" is so broad and all-encompassing that it amounts to an improper delegation of the agency's authority, contrary to its legislative mandate. Moreover, they argue that the record reveals that the Department, in adopting this definition and this standard for what constitutes "humane," failed to even review or evaluate the practices that it would permit. In particular, they assert that the definition includes a wide variety of institutions, each of which has become the arbiter of which practices are humane, but that the Department did not undertake any analysis of these institutions. In part, they point out that the record includes no evaluation of any of the texts used or the curricula that they follow, and no investigation of their course catalogs or instructional personnel. In short, petitioners argue that there is nothing in the record that would suggest that any of these institutions teaches practices that would meet the Department's own definition of "humane."

Amicus Rollin concurs, arguing that merely because a practice is routinely employed or taught, even if taught at a veterinary school, does not mean that it is humane. Rather, he argues that many practices taught at these institutions are motivated by concerns about the economics of agriculture, focusing on productivity alone, and ignoring any concerns about the welfare of the animals involved. As such, he argues that these practices, even if commonly taught, simply cannot be equated with practices or techniques that are also humane.

Our analysis of petitioners' objections to the several subsections of the regulations that create a safe harbor by reliance on "routine husbandry practices" compels us to conclude that these objections have merit. By adopting a definition of exceptional breadth, by failing to create an adequate record in support of this decision, and by implicitly permitting techniques that cannot meet the statutory mandate to base its regulations on a determination about what is humane, the Department has adopted regulations that are arbitrary and capricious. We therefore strike as invalid the definition of "routine husbandry practices," see N.J.A.C. 2:8-1.2, and that part of each of the subsections of the regulations referring thereto, see N.J.A.C. 2:8-2.6(f), -3.6(f), -4.7(e), -5.7(e)(2), -6.6(d), -7.6(d).

VII.

Petitioners also challenged individually a number of practices that are specifically permitted by the regulations, as-serting that they are demonstrably inhumane and that the Department's authorization thereof is unsupported by sound science. In particular, petitioners point to several procedures utilized by some farming operations that are physically painful and, they contend, are emotionally distressing to the animals. At the same time, they argue, these same practices cannot be justified because they are often of little or no value. In response, the Department counters that there is ample scientific evidence in the record that supports the continued use of each of these procedures. Moreover, the Department asserts that because the regulations include limits on the manner and circumstances in which any of these disputed practices is permitted, the practical result is that each of them is only performed in a humane manner.

A.

The first specific practice that petitioners attack relates only to dairy cattle. This practice, known as "tail docking," see N.J.A.C. 2:8-2.6(f), is a procedure that involves "the amputation of the lower portion of a dairy cow's tail." Lawrence J. Hutchinson, Tail Docking for Cattle (1997). Petitioners contend that tail docking cannot meet the Department's definition of humane, and they point to evidence of a consensus among scientists that tail docking is without any "apparent animal health, welfare, or human health justification." See C.L. Stull et al., Evaluation of the scientific justification for tail docking in dairy cattle, 220 J. Veterinary Med. Assoc. 1298, 1302 (May 1, 2002).

They further assert that tail docking causes acute pain and interferes with the ability of the affected animals to perform natural behaviors, including flicking their tails to chase away flies in the summer. See S.D. Eicher & J.W. Dalley, Indicators of Acute Pain and Fly Avoidance Behaviors in Holstein Calves Following Tail-docking, 85 J. Dairy Sci. 2850 (2002). Moreover, petitioners note that both the American (AVMA) and Canadian (CVMA) Veterinary Medical Associations oppose tail docking of dairy cattle, and they point to the AVMA's position paper that states: "[c]urrent scientific literature indicates that routine tail docking provides no benefit to the animal, and that tail docking can lead to distress during fly seasons." See AVMA, Animal Welfare Position Statements: Tail Docking of Cattle (2005), see also CVMA, Animal Welfare Position Statements: Tail Docking of Dairy Cattle (2003). Petitioners argue that a practice from which the animal derives no benefit, and that will cause it to suffer distress, cannot be humane.

The Department contends that, despite the AVMA's position paper, its decision to permit tail docking to continue to be performed complied with its statutory mandate to create humane standards. The agency points out that it responded to comments objecting to the practice, and that it reasoned that the practice should be permitted because it may lead to better milk quality and udder health, and it may also reduce the spread of diseases. 36 N.J.R. 2652 (June 7, 2004).

In the absence of evidence in the record to support the practice or to confine it to circumstances in which it has a benefit and is performed in a manner that meets an objective definition of humane, this aspect of the regulation cannot stand.

B.

For purposes of our analysis, we have identified several of the challenged practices that we find it appropriate to consider together. This group comprises three specific practices that are similar in terms of petitioners' focus and our evaluation of the record: (1) castration of swine, N.J.A.C. 2:8-7.6(d), horses, N.J.A.C. 2:8-3.6(f), and calves, N.J.A.C. 2:8-2.6(f); (2) de-beaking of chickens and turkeys, N.J.A.C. 2:8-4.7(e); and (3) toe-trimming of turkeys, N.J.A.C. 2:8-4.7(f). Each is a procedure that petitioners assert is, by and large, unnecessary, because each seeks to prevent behaviors, or the effects thereof, in which animals would likely not engage were they not raised in close quarters. In addition, petitioners challenge these practices because each is performed without anesthetics, thus causing the animals significant, if not severe, pain.

[A critical policy premise is in the following sentence. — Ed.] As to each of these practices, the Department implicitly recognizes that there are sound animal husbandry and management reasons for raising livestock in relatively close quarters that it elects not to prohibit. In light of that largely philosophical viewpoint, the Department asserts that its review of the scientific and professional literature supports its conclusion that the specific practices provide benefits to the health and safety of livestock. Moreover, the Department points out that its regulations address the question of pain and do so by adding the limitation on use of each of these procedures, requiring that they be performed by "knowledgeable persons" who are required to "minimize pain." In this manner, the agency asserts that it has ensured that each procedure will be performed in a manner that is in fact humane.

That debate about whether domestic livestock should be kept in close quarters or left relatively unconfined, however, is not addressed in the statute. Nothing in the statute suggests that the Legislature intended to embrace the latter and reject the former; the record instead reflects that the agency was charged with finding an appropriate balance between the interests of animal welfare advocates and the need to foster and encourage agriculture in this state. Notwithstanding the ardent views of some of the individuals who have voiced opinions throughout the regulatory process, we do not view our role as including the right or the obligation to weigh in on that debate; we consider instead that it remains within the scope of the agency's expertise to strike a balance between the competing positions of the parties, guided only by the standards of review to which we have adverted.

The record reflects that there is evidence that demonstrates these practices confer a benefit on the animals in light of their living conditions. For example, castration is generally employed to reduce aggression between male animals, including horses and cattle, when they are kept together in a herd. [The court quotes from article on both sides of the issue.]

Our review of the record certainly supports the conclusion that the agency's determination, in general, that these procedures should be permitted is neither arbitrary nor capricious. We are, as part of this analysis, mindful of the significant limitations imposed relating to the age of the particular livestock on which some of these procedures may be performed, which we see as evidence of the agency's care in the decision-making process. Notwithstanding the foregoing, however, the limitation that the agency asserts is the lynchpin of ensuring that these procedures are per-formed in a humane manner cannot pass muster. The regulations do not define the terms "sanitary manner," "knowledgeable individual," or "minimize pain," nor is there any objective criteria against which to determine whether any particular individual performing the procedure measures up to these standards. As a result, the regulations that the Department suggests will ensure that the procedures will be accomplished in a humane manner provide no standard against which to test that they are in fact so performed. Although one farm may conclude that a knowledgeable individual, for example, means someone with either veterinary training or some similar level of expertise, another might conclude that merely having performed the procedure in the past, humanely or not, or merely having observed it being performed by others, humanely or not, meets the standard set forth in the regulations.

Similarly, without any standard as to what the regulation means in terms of minimizing pain, there is no standard at all. One could, of course, conclude that each of these practices causes pain for a period of time, but that the benefits outweigh that adverse consequence. At the same time, one might conclude that, in light of the mandate of the Legislature that all of these practices be performed only consistent with being humane, they can only be performed if sufficient pain medication or anesthesia is utilized. Alternatively, one might conclude that a particular practice is only humane if it is performed on an animal of a particular age or if a particular instrument is utilized. As it is, the Department adopted none of these standards.

C.

Petitioners next attack the regulations relating to the use of crates and tethering for swine (sow gestation techniques) and for veal calves (cattle intended to be raised as "Special-Fed veal"), each of which they assert fails to meet the statutory standard of humane. In short, petitioners contend that these techniques do not permit the animals to move freely and to turn around and that they therefore cause significant distress in the animals not consistent with humane treatment. They rely on a number of publications relating to the use of crates for swine gestation that so conclude. See, e.g., European Union, Report of the Scientific Veterinary Committee, The Welfare of Intensively Kept Pigs, ¶ 5.2.2, EU Doc XXIV/ B3/ScVC/0005/1997, (Sept. 30, 1997) ("The Welfare of Intensively Kept Pigs"); J.L. Barnett, et al., A review of the welfare issues for sows and piglets in relation to housing, 52 Austl. J. Agric. Res. 1-28 (2001); J.N. Marchant et al., The effects of housing on heart rate of gestating sows during specific behaviours, 55 Applied Animal Behav. Sci. 67, 75 (1997) (concluding that use of sow gestation crates likely causes cardiovascular disease). Petitioners further point out that this practice is banned in Florida, see Fla. Const. Art. X, § 21 (2005), and is currently being phased out and scheduled to be banned in member states of the European Union by 2013, see European Union Council Directive 2000/88/EC of 23 October 2001. [The parallel analysis for veal crates is omitted.]

In response, the Department also points to an impressive array of scientific studies that, it asserts, support the regulations that permit the use of crating and tethering techniques, particularly as they relate to sows. See, e.g., The Welfare of Intensively Kept Pigs, supra; J.J. McGlone et al., Review: Compilation of the Scientific Literature Comparing Housing Systems for Gestating Sows and Gilts Using Measures of Physiology, Behavior, Performance, and Health, 20 Prof. Animal Sci. 105-06 (2004) (concluding that "gestation stalls (non-tethered) or well managed pens generally (but not in all cases) produced similar states of welfare for pregnant gilts or sows in terms of physiology, behavior, performance and health"); J.L. Barnett et al., A Review of the Welfare Issues for Sows and Piglets in Relation to Housing, 52 Austl. J. Agric. Res. 1 (2001).

Far from simply adopting techniques already in place or embracing practices that serve only the economic ends of the agricultural community as petitioners suggest, these regulations reflect that the Department took seriously its mandate to identify humane practices, but did so in recognition of the need to balance those concerns with the interests of the farmers whose livelihood depends on such techniques and whose existence would be threatened were they to be banned. More to the point, because those aspects of the regulations are supported by sufficient credible evidence in the record, and because they are neither arbitrary nor capricious, we find no basis on which to interfere with them.

D.

[Finally, petitioners argue that the regulations permit the transport of sick and downed animals to slaughter, a practice that is not humane. Discussion is omitted; the Court allows the regulations to stand as written.]

The judgment of the Appellate Division is affirmed in part and reversed in part and the matter is remanded to the Department for further proceedings consistent with this opinion.

Questions & Notes

1. Do the regulations carry out the mandate of the law? What is the purpose of the law?

2. Given the concept of "administrative discretion", do you think the analysis of the court is supportable? How protective might the agency have been before the court would overturn the regulation?

3. What is the role of science is setting regulatory standards? Can science determine what living conditions are humane?

4. What would the legislature need to say to have more protective regulations adopted?

State Ballot Issues

As an alternative to the passage of new law by adoption of a legislature where the key committees often seem to be controlled by those with an industrial agriculture perspective, organizations sought the ballot initiative with its direct access to the voters. In 2005 a ballot initiative in the State of Florida was passed at the general election. Some of the provisions of the initiative include:

> This ballot proposal addresses the inhumane treatment of animals, specifically, pregnant pigs. To prevent cruelty to animals and as recommended by The Humane Society of the United States, no person shall confine a pig during pregnancy in a cage, crate or other enclosure, or tether a pregnant pig on a farm so that the pig is prevented from turning around freely, except for veterinary purposes and during the prebirthing period; provides definitions, penalties, and an effective date. Note: this measure passed in the November 2002 election with 54% of the vote.

This first successful effort only dealt with pigs in a state that had almost no industrial presence. The next major event was in California. In 2008 a California initiative measure added to the Health & Safety Code a law entitled, "The Prevention of Farm Animal Cruelty Act." Specifically, the proposed law requires that calves raised for veal, egg-laying hens, and pregnant pigs be confined only in ways that allow these animals to lie down, stand up, fully extend their limbs and turn around freely. The law provides misdemeanor penalties, including a fine not to exceed $1,000 and/or imprisonment in jail for up to 180 days, and would go into effect on January 1, 2015. It was approved in November 2008 by a margin of 63% to 37%.

In both of these cases the Humane Society of the United States played a major role, particularly in the financing of the multi-million dollar media battle. After these wins, HSUS was seeking out other states to change the animal agricultural laws. In 2009, in Michigan, the state farm organizations sought to preempt a battle with HSUS by the introduction of very industrial friendly legislation by the chair of the Agriculture Committee in the Michigan House. But the industrial farm interests did not have the political power to force though the legislation and ended up negotiating directly with HSUS for a substitute bill which was built upon the language of the California ballot measure.

In all of these state actions, many local individuals and organizations were important in the realization of changing the law, but HSUS was always the partner more important than the others. In 2010 in different political circumstances, HSUS negotiated with organizations in Ohio and reached a compromise on legal changes for animal law which went beyond the farm animal focus of other prior efforts to deal with such issues as cock fighting and puppy mills.

The HSUS approach was not like that done in New Jersey, which sought a set of regulations to be defined by a state agency. Rather, the approach is that of a prohibition of what cannot be done. While there are dozens of issues with agricultural animals the initial housing is a critical one and that is the focus of HSUS. The goal of these laws is to outlaw specific types of housing without stating exactly what would be acceptable. In that way HSUS is not in the position of promoting any particular conditions for farm animals. They are simply against certain existing conditions.

The following chart sets out some of the specifics

◇◇

Issue	Calif. Prop. 2 - 2008	Mich. Law - 2009
egg-laying hen - CA & MI - defined as domesticated chicken, turkey, duck, goose, or guinea fowl kept for the purpose of egg production	a person shall not confine any covered animal, on a farm, for all or the majority of any day, in a manner that prevents such animal from: (a) Lying down, standing up, and fully extending his or her limbs; and (b) Turning around freely.[futher defined as fully spreading both wings without touching the side of an enclosure or other egg-laying hens.] Effective date: January 1, 2015	shall not confine in a manner that prevents such animal from doing any of the following: (a) lying down, standing up, or fully extending its limbs.(b) turning around freely. "Fully extending its limbs" means fully extending all limbs without touching the side of an enclosure. In the case of egg-laying hens, fully extending its limbs means fully spreading both wings without touching the side of an enclosure or other egg laying hens and having access to at least 1.0 square feet of usable floor space per hen. Effective Date – 2020

Calf raised for veal	a person shall not confine any covered animal, on a farm, for all or the majority of any day, in a manner that prevents such animal from: (a) Lying down, standing up, and fully extending his or her limbs; and (b) Turning around freely. "Fully extending his or her limbs" means fully extending all limbs without touching the side of an enclosure Effective date: January 1, 2015	shall not confine in a manner that prevents such animal from doing any of the following: (a) lying down, standing up, or fully extending its limbs.(b) turning around freely. "Turning around freely" means turning in a complete circle without any impediment, including a tether, and without touching the side of an enclosure or another animal. Effective Date – 2011
Pig during pregnancy [but does not cover the other times of pig confinement.]	a person shall not confine any covered animal, on a farm, for all or the majority of any day, in a manner that prevents such animal from: (a) Lying down, standing up, and fully extending his or her limbs; and (b) Turning around freely. "Fully extending his or her limbs" means fully extending all limbs without touching the side of an enclosure Effective date: January 1, 2015	shall not confine in a manner that prevents such animal from doing any of the following: (a) lying down, standing up, or fully extending its limbs.(b) turning around freely. "Turning around freely" means turning in a complete circle without any impediment, including a tether, and without touching the side of an enclosure or another animal. Effective Date – 2020
Horses, turkeys, meat chickens	No provisions	No provisions

Is a violation criminal?	ENFORCEMENT. Any person who violates any of the provisions of this chapter is guilty of a misdemeanor, and upon conviction thereof shall be punished by a fine not to exceed one thousand dollars ($1,000) or by imprisonment in the county jail for a period not to exceed 180 days or by both such fine and imprisonment.	Not criminal offence
Is a violation civil? Who enforces? Fine? Injunction?	No provisions, no injunctions available	No fines, only Attorney General may file an action for injunction.

Questions & Notes

1. What do you think of the general approach of these efforts? To what degree does the nature of the public battle for passage help shape the actual provisions proposed. Why is it that cages are unacceptable? Is this a pain issue or a suffering issue? Will the new laws eliminate suffering? Can we say any better at the end of this chapter that we understand what constitutes suffering? When is it unacceptable as a matter of public policy?

2. Does the language actually adopted outlaw the cages these animals are kept in? Why was the battery cage not simply outlawed? If you are an attorney for an egg producer, what legal advice would you give to your client to assure compliance with the law?

3. What are the pros and cons of the two very different approaches to enforcement?

4. Would it have been better to leave the details to a state agency?

5. If you could have drafted sections for two more issues, what would they have been?

Section 4

International Law & the WTO

The organization that is perhaps the most abstract and furthest removed from the barnyard may ultimately have the most impact on the commercial conditions of chickens and other agricultural animals. Like all parts of agriculture, animal production is increasingly part of a global trade network. The set of rules that govern international trade is under the World Trade Organization (WTO). A detailed consideration of this issue is not possible in this short space. The purpose of the treaty is to foster free trade. Restrictions on trade such as quotes or tariffs are reduced or prohibited. Only in limited circumstances may trade be limited as it arrives from another country. A key concern for animal welfare issues is what happens in a global market if one country adopts protective welfare standards that make local production more expensive than foreign production.

Consider what would happen if the United Kingdom passed a law that said all eggs sold or consumed in the U.K. must be from free-range, noncaged chickens. This is what is known in the world of trade as a restriction on the method of production. It is not making a distinction based on the nature or content of the product—the egg—but rather on how the product was made. The treaty specifically prohibits such national limitations on imports. Thus, at first analysis, the U.K. could only control the conditions of layer chickens in their own country. If this is done and the cost of eggs rises locally, then foreign eggs, not limited in the methods of production, will come into the marketplace and reduce the sale of the eggs from the protected chickens.

The WTO treaty has, within its provisions, only a few exceptions of which individual countries can take advantage. The key language to one of the exceptions allows a country to adopt controls over methods of production in another country if:

> "(a) necessary to protect public morals; (b) necessary to protect human, animal or plant life or health; ... (g) relating to the conservation of exhaustible natural resources if such measures are made effective in conjunction with restrictions on domestic production or consumption."

Article 21

Thus, to block the importation of beef from countries with mad cow disease or an outbreak of hoof and mouth disease is acceptable under the treaty. But, the blocking of the importation of eggs laid in battery cages is more difficult to justify. While it would seem to be fairly easy to make the argument that animal health includes animal welfare, the proposition has not yet been fully established or accepted. (The issue of protecting environmental values is also not clear under WTO standards.) This uncertainty makes the adoption of welfare protection legislation more difficult at the national level because producers will fight the provisions under a fear of being put at an economic disadvantage in a global marketplace.

For a full discussion of this legal quagmire, see Peter Stevenson, *The World Trade Organization Rules: A Legal Analysis of Their Adverse Impact on Animal Welfare* (2003) available at Animal Legal and Historical website, *www.animallaw.info/articles/arukstevensonwto2003.htm.*

The issues of animal heath, as in disease-control issues, are clearly allowed under the provisions of the WTO. For many decades the primary source of these international health standards has been the OIE (World Organisation for Animal Health). It is a science-based organization first formed in 1924, now with 167 country members. Part of its role is stated as:

> Within its mandate under the WTO SPS Agreement, to safeguard world trade by publishing health standards for international trade in animals and animal products. The OIE develops normative documents relating to rules that Member Countries can use to protect themselves from the introduction of diseases and pathogens, without setting up unjustified sanitary barriers [prohibited by provisions of WTO].

From *www.oie.int/eng/oie/en_oie.htm.*

One of the stated objectives of the organization is:

> To provide a better guarantee of the safety of food of animal origin and to promote animal welfare through a science-based approach.

www.oie.int/eng/OIE/en_objectifs.htm.

Beginning in 2001, the organization agreed to begin a discussion on animal welfare issues with the goal of the adoption of international standards. (See *www.oie.int/eng/bien_etre/en_introduction.htm.*) Any standards adopted by the organization do not become operative law by themselves; instead they become recommendations to the world at large. It is presumed that any national law that adopts their proposed animal welfare standards will be in compliance with the provisions of the WTO and thus create lawful limitations on the welfare conditions of animals in agriculture outside the border of the adopting country.

Therefore, the battle has been engaged at the global level. The conditions of battery chickens are not first on their list, so it is not known when this one issue might be addressed. A process has started that may ultimately overcome the political difficulties faced by those seeking change in the U.S. legal system. The standards may come from outside the United States but be of such stature that they cannot be ignored.

CHAPTER 9

Access to Courts —
Standing and Legal Injury

Section 1

Introduction

The prior chapters have focused upon substantive laws dealing with animals. This chapter will address a key procedural issue: who can obtain access to the courts in order to help animals.

Courts are uncomfortable with allowing anyone to sue anyone about anything any time they might wish. The preliminary step in any court action is to decide if the plaintiff is an appropriate person for the filing of a lawsuit. Therefore, there are a series of tests — or hurdles — that must be passed over before the courthouse door will be opened, allowing access to the minds and pens of the judges therein. Of course, there isn't any physical barrier to filing a lawsuit; the sorting and denial will occur only after the suit has been filed and a plaintiff has asserted access to that court against a particular defendant over a specific topic. The courts will then first decide whether to allow the access and may issue an opinion at an initial stage that ignores the claims of the plaintiff and simply tells them that their access is denied, "please go away." Such a decision by a court may be appealed to a higher court, perhaps going as high as the United States Supreme Court just on the issue of whether to allow the plaintiff access to a court. All of this denial of access is usually discussed under the heading of "standing to sue." (Whether an individual has picked the right court is an issue of "jurisdiction," but that issue will not be addressed in this set of materials. This discussion assumes that the lawyer will be able to find the correct court in which to file the papers.)

Standing has an entire chapter of this book because it is a legal concept with which anyone filing a lawsuit about animal issues must consider. If the animal in question is the property of a plaintiff, then the principles of standing do not pose a difficulty. If a plaintiff seeks the court to address issues about animals not owned by the plaintiff, then many issues arise. An introduction follows.

The rules about standing are the result of decades of legal development by the U.S. Supreme Court in the context of our Constitution. As of now, any plaintiff in a federal lawsuit must show the following elements in order to satisfy the requirement of standing (this does not mean that the plaintiff will win, only that the court will address the merits of the claim):

As required by the U.S. Constitution:

1. That the plaintiff has suffered an injury-in-fact that is both concrete and particularized.

2. That there is a causal connection between the injury and the actions of the defendant.

3. Even assuming that a legally recognized harm exists, is it likely that the injury will be redressed by a favorable decision of the court.

As required by the Courts (prudential requirement):

> Where Congress has created the source of the violations—
> the law at issue—then the plaintiff must show that they, the
> human plaintiffs, are within the zone of interests that Con-
> gress sought to protect with the adoption of the law.

See **The Cetacean Community v. Bush,** 386 F. 3d 1169 (9th Cir. 2004).

Federal Article III analysis dominates the discussion about standing,
but state claims should not be dominated by this analysis. Distinguish
suits against federal government under congressional legislation (issues of private enforcement of public laws and allocation of authority
between the three branches of government) from civil common law action between private parties or government granted standing at the state
level.

The application of the rules of standing in a number of judicial opinions may cause confusion because often a number of different questions (sub-issues) are being discussed under this one concept. Some of
the most important, from the perspective of animal litigation, include:

1. Does the plaintiff possess legal personhood?
2. Has the plaintiff suggested a legally recognized harm?
3. Assuming a legally recognized harm does exist, does this
   plaintiff have the right to bring the cause of action?

The key to understanding the scope of the term "injury-in-fact" in
the federal context is to understand that there is an unstated qualifier
after the term: "which is a harm recognized as being within the family
of rights and interests protected by the legal system and is one that the
plaintiff is allowed to pursue." Consider the following:

> **Example A** Roger, an eight-year-old alley cat, is shot with
> three arrows by Sam, an 18-year-old human male, out hav-
> ing some "fun." The physical injury is one acknowledged
> by the legal system, but the cat is not allowed to be a plain-
> tiff over this injury. Instead, a prosecuting attorney of the
> government may file criminal law charges against Sam for
> the legally recognized harm (the cruel and unjustified inflic-
> tion of pain and suffering).

It is settled law at the moment that while the State may sue, Roger the
cat is without the status of a legal person (personhood) and therefore
without status to pursue Sam's legally wrong actions, even though it
was Roger's personal interests that were harmed.

However, humans and their private organizations, in some circumstances, can file lawsuits over harm to animals. One category of human

that can clearly sue about legal harm to an animal is the owner of an animal. As an owner of an animal, it is not the pain of the animal that is the harm; rather, it is the harm to the human property interests that is at issue. If the owner has suffered damages that arose because of harm to an animal, then there has been an injury-in-fact to the plaintiff that is both a recognized harm and one for which the owner is allowed to sue. If Roger the cat in Example A is owned by Sally, then Sally will have standing to sue Sam for the damage caused to Sally's property interest. (See Chapter 4 for a discussion of what categories of damages will be allowed by courts.) However, in no jurisdiction at the moment may Sally be considered to have standing to sue for the pain and suffering of the cat. Again, only a state prosecutor has that standing.

What about someone who is not the cat's owner but who has personal harm because of the events?

> **Example B** Assume that the act of Roger's injury is viewed by a neighbor, George. George is horrified by what he has seen, and his viewing of the events gives him nightmares for weeks. There are two possible injuries-in-fact, but neither one will work in this case. Again, the pain and suffering of the cat is redressable only by the state prosecutor, so George has no standing to file a lawsuit for the injury to the cat. Additionally, while George has his own injury or has suffered for having viewed the event, in no state do these facts create a legally recognized harm, or a cause of action. Therefore George has no standing on which to base a lawsuit.

The more remote case is when someone did not view the events but is concerned about what has happened to an animal. As one Supreme Court justice has written, "A plaintiff must allege some particularized injury that sets him apart from the man on the street." (**U.S. v. Richardson,** 418 U.S. 166, 194 (1974).

> **Example C** News of the shooting gets in the local newspaper, and the Garden Club of Rosebud discusses the event at a meeting and passes a resolution condemning the action and directing that Sam be sued so that suitable punishment will be realized for the evil deed. However, this organization is even further removed from the events than neighbor George. As the garden club has no property interest in the cat, no financial stake in the events, and has suffered no injury to itself, neither the club nor its members have any injury-in-fact relative to the events surrounding Roger's harm. Therefore, they have no standing to file a lawsuit.

If a lawsuit is filed, the judge will dismiss the suit for lack of standing by the plaintiffs. (See **Animal Lovers Volunteer Ass'n Inc. v. Weinberger,** 765 F. 2d 937 (1985), in which the court said, "A mere assertion of organizational interest in a problem, unaccompanied by allegations of actual injury to members of the organization, is not enough to establish standing." The plaintiffs had objected to the shooting of feral goats who were harming the natural environment on a government island.)

> **Example D** If Sally, owner of Roger the cat, is a member of the Garden Club of Rosebud and the club files a suit on behalf of its members, the court will nevertheless dismiss the suit for lack of standing.

An organization may file a suit only in the following circumstances:

1. There is harm to the organization itself.

2. There is harm to some of the members of the organization, and;

> a. the members could sue on their own,
>
> b. the interests they seek to protect are germane to the purpose of the organization,
>
> c. the claims and relief requested do not require the participation of the individual members.

Even with Sally as a member of the club, element 2(b) is not satisfied; and, therefore, the club is without standing to redress the legal harm.

Humans and the organizations that they form have many diverse interests in animals. The Audubon Society and Sierra Club have long-existing interests in wildlife in its natural habitat. The American Society for the Prevention of Cruelty to Animals (ASPCA) has been interested in domestic animal issues since its formation in 1867. As we will see, these interests, as well as a budget of millions of dollars and hundreds of thousands of members, does not provide standing for access to the courts automatically. The organizations must satisfy the tests of "standing" on a case-by-case basis.

Section 2

Human Interests Standing

As the above suggest, the dominant and practical concern in most animal cases is how to find the human interests which allows a case to be filed. But, the last two sections of this chapter suggests there can be circumstances were the focus is indeed on the interests of the animal as a basis for filing a lawsuit. These two sections are intertwined with broader issue of animal jurisprudence, the topic of the next chapter. This discussion will help provide a context for that discussion.

The best way to understand where we are today on the issue of standing for humans when dealing with animals is through an examination of the historical development of the concept. The key concern is which injuries or harms are those that will justify access to the courts, thus giving plaintiffs standing. Historically, physical injury or economic loss have always satisfied the test. But these injuries are not helpful if the focus of concern is harm to the environment or specific animals. The conceptual path for animal welfare issues started almost 40 years ago. The first case presented next was a landmark in its time. While holding against the Sierra Club for lack of standing, the Supreme Court articulated a new definition of injury-in-fact. This definition became a key to the courthouse, allowing the powerful environmental movement into the courts of the United States during the 1970s and 1980s. It contains the conceptual basis on which all future cases dealing with animals are built.

CASE BY CASE

Sierra Club v. Morton

405 U.S. 727, 92 S. Ct. 1361 (1972)

MR. JUSTICE STEWART

The Mineral King Valley is an area of great natural beauty nestled in the Sierra Nevada Mountains in Tulare County, California, adjacent to Sequoia National Park. It has been part of the Sequoia National Forest since 1926, and is designated as a national game refuge by a special Act of Congress. Though once the site of extensive mining activity, Mineral King is now used almost exclusively for recreational purposes. Its relative inaccessibility and lack of development have limited the number of visitors each year, and at the same time have preserved the valley's quality as a quasi-wilderness area largely uncluttered by the products of civilization.

The United States Forest Service, which is entrusted with the maintenance and administration of national forests, began in the late 1940's to give consideration to Mineral King as a potential site for recreational development. Prodded by a rapidly increasing demand for skiing facilities, the Forest Service published a prospectus in 1965, inviting bids from private developers for the construction and operation of a ski resort that would also serve as a summer recreation area. The proposal of Walt Disney Enterprises, Inc., was chosen from those of six bidders, and Disney received a three-year permit to conduct surveys and explorations in the valley in connection with its preparation of a complete master plan for the resort.

The final Disney plan, approved by the Forest Service in January 1969, outlines a $35 million complex of motels, restaurants, swimming pools, parking lots, and other structures designed to accommodate 14,000 visitors daily. This complex is to be constructed on 80 acres of the valley floor under a 30-year use permit from the Forest Service. Other facilities, including ski lifts, ski trails, a cog-assisted railway, and utility installations, are to be constructed on the mountain slopes and in other parts of the valley under a revocable special-use permit.

Representatives of the Sierra Club, who favor maintaining Mineral King largely in its present state, followed the progress of recreational planning for the valley with close attention and increasing dismay. They unsuccessfully sought a public hearing on the proposed development in 1965, and in subsequent correspondence with officials of the Forest Service and the Department of the Interior, they expressed the Club's objections to Disney's plan as a whole and to particular features included in it. In June 1969 the Club filed the present suit in the United States District Court for the Northern District of California, seeking a declaratory judgment that various aspects of the proposed development contravene federal laws and regulations governing the preservation of national parks, forests, and game refuges, and also seeking preliminary and permanent injunctions restraining the federal officials involved from granting their approval or issuing permits in connection with the Mineral King project. The petitioner Sierra Club sued as a membership corporation with "a special interest in the conservation and the sound maintenance of the national parks, game refuges and forests of the country," and invoked the judicial-review provisions of the Administrative Procedure Act, 5 U.S.C. § 701 et seq.

II.

The first question presented is whether the Sierra Club has alleged facts that entitle it to obtain judicial review of the challenged action. Whether a party has a sufficient stake in an otherwise justiciable controversy to obtain judicial resolution of that controversy is what has traditionally been referred to as the question of standing to sue. Where the party does not rely on any specific statute authorizing invocation of the judicial process, the question of standing depends upon whether the party has alleged such a "personal stake in the outcome of the controversy," Baker v. Carr, 369 U.S. 186, 204, 82 S. Ct. 691, 703, 7 L. Ed. 2d 663, as to ensure that "the dispute sought to be adjudicated will be presented in an adversary context and in a form historically viewed as capable of judicial resolution." Flast v. Cohen, 392 U.S. 83, 101, 88 S. Ct. 1942, 1953, 20 L. Ed. 2d 947.

The Sierra Club relies upon section 10 of the Administrative Procedure Act (APA), 5 U.S.C. § 702, which provides:

"A person suffering legal wrong because of agency action, or adversely affected or aggrieved by agency action within the meaning of a relevant statute, is entitled to judicial review thereof."

Early decisions under this statute interpreted the language as adopting the various formulations of "legal interest" and "legal wrong" then prevailing as constitutional requirements of standing. But, in Association of Data Processing Service Organizations, Inc. v. Camp, 397 U.S. 150, 90 S. Ct. 827, 25 L. Ed. 2d 184, and Barlow v. Collins, 397 U.S. 159, 90 S. Ct. 832, 25 L. Ed. 2d 192, decided the same day, we held more broadly that persons had standing to obtain judicial review of federal agency action under § 10 of the APA where they had alleged that the challenged action had caused them "injury in fact," and where the alleged injury was to an interest "arguably within the zone of interests to be protected or regulated" by the statutes that the agencies were claimed to have violated.

III.

The injury alleged by the Sierra Club will be incurred entirely by reason of the change in the uses to which Mineral King will be put, and the attendant change in the aesthetics and ecology of the area. Thus, in referring to the road to be built through Sequoia National Park, the complaint alleged that the development "would destroy or otherwise adversely affect the scenery, natural and historic objects and wildlife of the park and would impair the enjoyment of the park for future generations." We do not question that this type of harm may amount to an "injury in fact" sufficient to lay the basis for standing under § 10 of the APA. Aesthetic and environmental well-being, like economic well-being, are important ingredients of the quality of life in our society, and the fact that particular environmental interests are shared by the many rather than the few does not make them less deserving of legal protection through the judicial process. But the "injury in fact" test requires more than an injury to a cognizable interest. It requires that the party seeking review be himself among the injured.

The impact of the proposed changes in the environment of Mineral King will not fall indiscriminately upon every citizen. The alleged injury will be felt directly only by those who use Mineral King and Sequoia National Park, and for whom the aesthetic and recreational values of the area will be lessened by the highway and ski resort. The Sierra Club failed to allege that it or its members would be affected in any of their activities or pastimes by the Disney development. Nowhere in the pleadings or affidavits did the Club state that its members use Mineral King for any purpose, much less that they use it in any way that would be significantly affected by the proposed actions of the respondents.

The Club apparently regarded allegations of individualized injury as superfluous, on the theory that this was a '"public" action involving questions as to the use of natural resources, and that the Club's longstanding concern with and expertise in such matters were sufficient to give it standing as a "representative of the public." This theory reflects a misunderstanding of our cases involving so-called "public actions" in the area of administrative law.

Some courts have indicated a willingness to take this latter step by conferring standing upon organizations that have demonstrated "an organizational interest in the problem" of environmental or consumer protection. Environmental Defense Fund, Inc. v. Hardin, 138 U.S. App. D.C. 391, 395, 428 F. 2d 1093, 1097. It is clear that an organization whose members are injured may represent those members in a proceeding for judicial review. See, e.g., NAACP v. Button, 371 U.S. 415, 428, 83 S. Ct. 328, 335, 9 L. Ed. 2d 405. But a mere "interest in a problem," no matter how longstanding the interest and no matter how qualified the organization is in evaluating the problem, is not sufficient by itself to render the organization "adversely affected" or "aggrieved" within the meaning of the APA. The Sierra Club is a large and long-established organization, with a historic commitment to the cause of protecting our Nation's natural heritage from man's depredations. But if a "special interest" in this subject were enough to entitle the Sierra Club to commence this litigation, there would appear to be no objective basis upon which to disallow a suit by any other bona fide "special interest" organization however small or short-lived. And if any group with a bona fide "special interest" could initiate such litigation, it is difficult to perceive why any individual citizen with the same bona fide special interest would not also be entitled to do so.

As we conclude that the Court of Appeals was correct in its holding that the Sierra Club lacked standing to maintain this action, we do not reach any other questions presented in the petition, and we intimate no view on the merits of the complaint. The judgment is

Affirmed.

Mr. Justice DOUGLAS, dissenting.

I share the views of my Brother BLACKMUN and would reverse the judgment below.

The critical question of "standing" would be simplified and also put neatly in focus if we fashioned a federal rule that allowed environmental issues to be litigated before federal agencies or federal courts in the name of the inanimate object about to be despoiled, defaced, or invaded by roads and bulldozers and where injury is the subject of public outrage. Contemporary public concern for protecting nature's ecological equilibrium should lead to the conferral of standing upon environmental objects to sue for their own preservation. See Stone, *Should Trees Have Standing?--Toward Legal Rights for Natural Objects*, 45 S. Cal. L. Rev. 450 (1972). This suit would therefore be more properly labeled as Mineral King v. Morton.

So it should be as respects valleys, alpine meadows, rivers, lakes, estuaries, beaches, ridges, proves of trees, swampland, or even air that feels the destructive pressures of modern technology and modern life. The river, for example, is the living symbol of all the life it sustains or nourishes — fish, aquatic insects, water ouzels, otter, fisher, deer, elk, bear, and all other animals, including man, who are dependent on it or who enjoy it for its sight, its sound, or its life. The river as plaintiff speaks for the ecological unit of life that is part of it. Those people who have a meaningful relation to that body of water — whether it be a fisherman, a canoeist, a zoologist, or a logger — must be able to speak for the values which the river represents and which are threatened with destruction.

Mineral King is doubtless like other wonders of the Sierra Nevada such as Tuolumne Meadows and the John Muir Trail. Those who hike it, fish it, hunt it, camp in it, frequent it, or visit it merely to sit in solitude and wonderment are legitimate spokesmen for it, whether they may be few or many. Those who have that intimate relation with the inanimate object about to be injured, polluted, or otherwise despoiled are its legitimate spokesmen.

Questions & Notes

1. Why did the Sierra Club not discuss their individual members' use of the area?

2. The key sentence of the opinion is "We do not question that this type of harm may amount to an 'injury in fact' sufficient to lay the basis for standing under § 10 of the APA." Explain in detail what you think this means. Is this based on an intellectual or emotional response to potential and real harm to the environment? How would you plead and prove the facts necessary to support standing in an environmental case. What role might wildlife play in such a case?

3. While the Sierra Club lost in its attempt to create organizational standing based on a long-existing institutional concern, they were quick to pick up the language of the court and file suits under the court-articulated standard. With members everywhere, all they needed was someone who used the area in question. This became the door through which many environmental organizations developed a strong litigation muscle for pushing the government down the road of environmental awareness and protection.

4. What about the line of thought in the dissent by Justice Douglas? Is this a path forward for animals?

5. The Administrative Procedure Act, joined with the requirement of an environmental impact statement, under the National Environmental Policy Act joined with this definition of injury-in-fact was and continues to be a powerful club over U.S. agencies on behalf of a large number of wildlife issues. See **Robertson v. Methow Valley Citizens Council**, 490 U.S. 332 (1989) (Court considered the scope of an environmental impact statement for a ski development on national forest land);

Progressive Animal Welfare Society v. Dept. of the Navy,
725 F. Supp. 475 (W.D. Wash. 1989) (Court held that the Navy
had to stop deployment of dolphins at a sub base until an environmental impact statement was drafted. This is one of the
few cases that considered the well-being of individual animals
as part of the natural environment and under the umbrella of
NEPA.)

༺༛༺༛༺༛༺

Harm to Individual Domestic Animals

While standing was fully available for environmental groups by the
mid-1970's, there was no path available for animal welfare groups. The
following case is an example of the inability of groups to gain access to
the court because of the lack of an appropriate human interest.

While a decision by a judge on the issue of standing is not supposed
to reflect any opinion on the possible outcome of the merits of the case,
every judge knows that if a plaintiff is found to not have standing, then
in effect the plaintiff loses the case without the judge having to address
the merits of the case. There is always the unspoken public policy issue
of whether it is a good or bad idea to allow private parties to "turn over"
certain stones—such as the use of animals in research institutions.

*While the term standing is used in the following case, this judge is primar-
ily concerned about allowing this cause of action on behalf of animals held in
scientific labs.*

CASE BY CASE

IPPL v. Institute for Behavioral Research, Inc.
799 F.2d 934 (4th Cir. 1986)

WILKINSON, CIRCUIT JUDGE.

In this case we must decide whether a group of private individuals may
challenge a medical researcher's compliance with federal standards for
the care of laboratory animals. Because we find that the plaintiffs lack
standing to bring such a lawsuit, we affirm the judgment of the district
court in its dismissal of this action.

To imply a cause of action in these plaintiffs might entail serious consequences. It might open the use of animals in biomedical research to the
hazards and vicissitudes of courtroom litigation. It may draw judges into
the supervision and regulation of laboratory research. It might unleash
a spate of private lawsuits that would impede advances made by medi-

cal science in the alleviation of human suffering. To risk consequences of this magnitude in the absence of clear direction from the Congress would be ill-advised. In fact, we are persuaded that Congress intended that the independence of medical research be respected and that administrative enforcement govern the Animal Welfare Act.

I.

The principal complainant in this case, Alex Pacheco, first met the principal defendant, Dr. Edward Taub, in May 1981. Pacheco, an undergraduate student in the program of Environmental Studies at George Washington University in Washington, D.C., had worked frequently for the protection of animals, participating in projects of the Fund for Animals, the Friends of Animals, the Ohio Capital Area Humane Society, and the Alaska Department of Fish and Wildlife. He had founded the Ohio Animal Rights Committee and, in Washington, D.C., had founded People for the Ethical Treatment of Animals, Inc. (PETA), on which he continued to serve as director. Taub, the chief of the Behavioral Biology Center of the Institute of Behavioral Research (IBR), was studying the capacity of monkeys to learn to use a limb after nerves had been severed. Funded by the National Institutes of Health (NIH), the project amplified Taub's earlier research in this area and attempted to discover benefits for the rehabilitation of human patients suffering from a serious neurological injury such as a stroke. Pacheco offered to work as a volunteer for Taub on the neurological study at an IBR facility in Silver Spring, Maryland. Taub gave Pacheco the keys to the premises and permission to enter at any time, and Pacheco came regularly to the laboratory during the summer of 1981. He concluded from his observations that IBR did not provide the monkeys with sufficient food or water, a sanitary environment, or adequate veterinary care. On several nights during the week of August 27, 1981, Pacheco brought other researchers to IBR to confirm his impressions. Collecting affidavits from these visits with his own statement and photographs of the laboratory, Pacheco asked Sgt. Richard W. Swain, Jr. of the Montgomery County Police Department to investigate IBR for violations of Article 27, § 59 of the Maryland Code, which defines the criminal misdemeanor of cruelty to animals and authorizes a maximum imprisonment of ninety days and a maximum fine of $1,000 for each offense.

Swain obtained a search warrant from the Circuit Court for Montgomery County and on September 11 seized from IBR the seventeen monkeys in the experiment. Nine days later, the Assistant State's Attorney for Montgomery County filed criminal charges against Taub in the county District Court, alleging seventeen violations of the animal cruelty statute. [Dr. Taub had previously been the subject of a charge of criminal violation of anti-cruelty laws of Maryland. In Chapter 6, see Taub v. State, 296 Md. 439, 463 A. 2d 819 (1983) at p. 322.]

On October 9 the Circuit Court for Montgomery County, without opposition from IBR, instructed Sgt. Swain and Dr. James Stunkard, a veterinarian, to supervise the transfer of the monkeys to an NIH facility in Poolesville, Maryland that Swain and Stunkard had chosen as the best place for temporary care and custody. The order was to remain in effect "until further Order of this Court or the termination of the pending criminal prosecution against Dr. Taub, whichever occurs first."

Dr. Taub stood trial in November 1981 in the District Court for Montgomery County, which on December 2 entered orders of conviction on six of the seventeen counts and acquittal on the other eleven counts. Fearing that the court order on custody of the monkeys would partially expire with the acquittals, PETA acted quickly to prevent the return of any animals to IBR. Along with the International Primate Protection League, the Animal Law Enforcement Association, and several named individuals, PETA filed a bill of complaint on December 3 in the Circuit Court for Montgomery County. The complaint, in which the plaintiffs purported to speak for "their own and class interests and as next friends of seventeen (17) non-human primates," alleged that a civil inquiry would show IBR violations of the Maryland animal cruelty laws which the criminal trial had not established and further alleged that IBR had violated the federal Animal Welfare Act, 7 U.S.C. §§ 2131 *et seq.* Naming IBR, NIH, Swain, and Stunkard as defendants, the plaintiffs asked the equity court to verify these claims, to designate the plaintiffs as new guardians of the monkeys, and to enjoin all parties from permitting IBR to regain possession.

On December 17, NIH requested removal of the case to the U.S. District Court for the District of Maryland. The plaintiffs did not oppose removal; as the complaint had noted, the claims arising under the Animal Welfare Act supported federal jurisdiction.

II.

In order to sue in federal court, plaintiffs must show that they "personally [have] suffered some actual or threatened injury as a result of the putatively illegal conduct of the defendant," Plaintiffs argue that they would suffer both financial and non-financial injuries if IBR regained control of the monkeys. Close examination of the allegations, however, shows that the claims do not provide standing for the plaintiffs.

Plaintiffs assert that this case implicates their financial interests in two different ways. First, they argue that their tax payments entitle them to ensure that the law is respected by NIH, a federal agency, and by IBR, a recipient of federal funds. The Supreme Court rejected this reasoning in United States v. Richardson, 418 U.S. 166, 174-75, 94 S. Ct. 2940, 2945, 41 L. Ed. 2d 678 (1974), holding that payment of taxes does not purchase authority to enforce regulatory restrictions. Second, plaintiffs argue that they contributed to the maintenance of the monkeys after Sgt. Swain seized the animals and before NIH took possession. But as the transfer receipt shows, this expenditure represented a voluntary offer to help the Maryland authorities. The plaintiffs did not acquire any interest in the monkeys, who remained the property of IBR and in the legal custody of

Sgt. Swain. Like attorneys' fees or other litigation costs, the maintenance payments were part of the response to the contested conduct, not part of the conduct itself, and therefore do not establish "a personal stake in the outcome of the controversy."

The plaintiffs also assert that this case implicates their non-financial interests in two ways. On the more general level, the plaintiffs sought standing by describing themselves as individuals and members having a personal interest in the preservation and encouragement of civilized and humane treatment of animals, whose own aesthetic, conservational, and environmental interests are specifically and particularly offended and affected by the matters hereinafter described, and which interests, along with their educational interests, will be detrimentally impacted upon if the relief sought is not granted.

This statement of interest resembles the pleading that the Supreme Court found to be inadequate in Sierra Club v. Morton, 405 U.S. 727, 735 n. 8, 92 S. Ct. 1361, 1366 n. 8, 31 L. Ed. 2d 636 (1972). The Court held that "a mere interest in a problem; no matter how longstanding the interest and no matter how qualified the organization is in evaluating the problem, is not sufficient by itself" to create standing. Id. at 739. That conclusion applies precisely to these plaintiffs' asserted commitment to the humane treatment of animals. The commitment of an organization may enhance its legislative access; it does not, by itself, provide entry to a federal court.

Plaintiffs try to distinguish *Sierra Club v. Morton* by presenting a second, more specific, form of non-financial injury: the disruption of their personal relationship with these monkeys by the return of the animals to IBR. This theory seeks to compare plaintiffs with the parties who suffer injury from the disturbance of national parks or forests because they use those areas. But that analogy fails because these plaintiffs have been with the monkeys primarily because of this litigation. Whereas the parties described in *Sierra Club v. Morton* could use the park if the defendants complied with the law, these plaintiffs could not see the monkeys in the IBR laboratory if the defendants satisfied all requirements of care.

III.

Not only do plaintiffs fail to allege cognizable injuries; they fail also to prove that the implicated federal statute authorizes their right to seek relief. The two shortcomings provide related, though alternative, bases for dismissal of this action.

The Animal Welfare Act, 7 U.S.C. §§ 2131 *et seq.,* is the federal statute on which plaintiffs rely in defining their allegations of mistreatment. The Act seeks to insure that "animals intended for use in research facilities... are provided humane care and treatment." 7 U.S.C. § 2131(1). There is no indication, however, that Congress intended this goal to come at the expense of progress in medical research. To the contrary, both the language of the statute and the means chosen by Congress to enforce it preserve the hope that responsible primate research holds for the treatment and cure of humankind's most terrible afflictions. The statutory design is, in turn, inconsistent with the private right of action that plaintiffs assert.

The administrative enforcement that Congress envisioned for this statute is readily apparent. The Act directs the Secretary of Agriculture to "promulgate standards to govern the humane handling, care, treatment, and transportation of animals," but cautions that "nothing in this chapter shall be construed as authorizing the Secretary to promulgate rules, regulations, or orders with regard to design, outlines, guidelines, or performance of actual research or experimentation by a research facility as determined by such research facility."

The *amicus curiae* brief of sixty-eight scientific and medical organizations reviews the history underlying these priorities. Research with primates helped to lead, for example, to the development of the polio vaccine, and other animal research has contributed to the discovery of insulin, the invention of transplantation techniques, and the improvement of cancer therapies. *Amici* predict that animal research will play some part in the prevention and treatment of such illnesses as multiple sclerosis, AIDS, and Alzheimer's disease. Recent amendments to the Animal Welfare Act have accordingly reaffirmed the Congressional finding that "the use of animals is instrumental in certain research and education or for advancing knowledge of cures and treatments for diseases and injuries which afflict both humans and animals." H. Conf. Rep. No. 99-447, 99th Cong., 1st Sess., *reprinted in* 1985 U.S. Code Cong. & Ad. News 1676, 2518.

The Act, as our description suggests, does not imply any provision for lawsuits by private individuals as a complement to the authority of the Secretary of Agriculture. The plaintiffs therefore can draw no support from cases involving other statutes that do create standing for private individuals to challenge a particular treatment of animals. "The question whether a statute creates a cause of action, either expressly or by implication, is basically a matter of statutory construction." Transamerica Mortgage Advisors, Inc. v. Lewis, 444 U.S. 11, 15, 100 S. Ct. 242, 245, 62 L. Ed. 2d 146 (1979). Here, we are convinced that Congress intended the administrative remedy to be the exclusive remedy. To accord plaintiffs standing to sue by virtue of a private cause of action would not conform to the aims of Congress in the Animal Welfare Act.

Affirmed.

Questions & Notes

1. Is this suit about the absence of an injury-in-fact to any animal or to any human? What is the harm to the animals, and does the harm violate any law? Did anyone have a right to file a law suit over the injury or harm? Do you agree with the court that the best public policy would be to disallow this sort of suit?

2. Would the court have had a different attitude if Congress had adopted a citizen suit provision for the AWA?

3. IPPL, the named plaintiff, is the International Primate Protection League, formed in 1973 to help primates around the world. It is still a very active organization. Plaintiffs consisted of three corporations and seven individuals.

4. Another, more recent example of the barrier of standing for animal organizations dealt with the issue of foie gras in New York. Plaintiffs sought declaratory judgment against the Department of Agriculture and Markets, seeking a declaration that foie gras was adulterated food product pursuant to Agriculture and Markets Law. **Humane Soc. of U.S., Inc. v. Brennan**, 63 A.D.3d 1419, 881 N.Y.S.2d 533 (N.Y.A.D. 3 Dept., 2009). The Court found that they did "not suffer an injury within the zone of interests protected by State Administrative Procedure Act § 204. Nor are we persuaded that petitioners established either statutory or common-law taxpayer standing." State courts do have some differences in standards to apply for standing tests.

Breakthrough Standing for AWA Issues

[Disclosure: The author, Prof. David Favre, was on the Board of Directors for the Animal Legal Defense Fund during the period of this series of cases.]

Preview

There is a basic public policy issue that is present when a government agency is the defendant in a lawsuit: Should the government agency — APHIS in this case—be subjected to the pressures/checks of private litigation, as is the Department of Interior on environmental issues? One way of disallowing external public pressure on an agency is by allowing or disallowing private parties standing to sue the agency. Remember that the Fourth Circuit in **IPPL v. Institute for Behavioral Research**, supra, decided that Congress did not want research facilities subject to "the hazards and vicissitudes of courtroom litigation." In ALDF's loss in the DC Circuit Court in 1997, the dissenting opinion of the three-judge panel raised the issue most clearly, and this may have been one of the key policy reasons that a full *en banc* rehearing of the case was ultimately allowed.

> Judge Wald, This case hardly requires us to recognize the independent standing of animals; Mr. Jurnove's allegations fall well within the requirements of our existing precedent. But it is striking, particularly in a world in which animals cannot sue on their own behalf, how far the majority opinion goes toward making governmental action that regulates the lives of animals, and determines the experience of people who view them in exhibitions, unchallengeable. *See* Oral Argument (statement of government counsel) (voicing

his inability to identify one party who would have standing to challenge the USDA regulations implementing the AWA provisions on animal exhibitions). Because such a result offends the compassionate purposes of the statute, and our precedents do not require it, I respectfully dissent.

Animal Legal Defense Fund, Inc. v. Glickman, 130 F.3d 464, at 476, 327 U.S. App. D.C. 235, at 247 (D.C. Cir. Dec. 09, 1997).

Think About It

The Animal Legal Defense Fund spent almost a decade in litigation before reaching the opinion set out next. The following case was the second case the organization had filed on this issue. The first one was filed in 1991 and met its final demise at the Court of Appeals in 1995 with a decision that standing did not exist for any of the named plaintiffs. In 1996 the second case (with a new set of plaintiffs) was filed. It did not reach final conclusion until 2000, when the merits of the case were finally decided. The following is a quick summary of the path of the second case:

Animal Legal Defense Fund, Inc. v. Glickman, 943 F. Supp. 44 (D.D.C. Oct 30, 1996) (NO. CIV. A.96-00408(CRR)) (Court allowed standing and held for the plaintiffs on the merits of the case.)

Judgment Vacated by

Animal Legal Defense Fund, Inc. v. Glickman, 130 F. 3d 464, 327 U.S. App. D.C. 235 (D.C. Cir. Dec. 09, 1997) (NO. 97-5074, 97-5031, 97-5009) (None of the plaintiffs had standing to sue, suit was to be dismissed without reaching the merits of the case.)

Rehearing in Banc Granted, Judgment Vacated by

Animal Legal Defense Fund, Inc. v. National Ass'n for Biomedial Research, 136 F. 3d 829, 329 U.S. App. D.C. 89, 28 Envtl. L. Rep. 20,395 (D.C. Cir. Mar 10, 1998) (NO. 97-5009, 97-5031, 97-5074)

AND On Rehearing in Banc

Animal Legal Defense Fund, Inc. v. Glickman, 154 F. 3d 426, 332 U.S. App. D.C. 104, 29 Envtl. L. Rep. 20,202 (D.C. Cir. Sep. 01, 1998) (NO. 97-5009) (case set out below.)

Certiorari to U.S. Supreme Court Denied by National Ass'n for **Biomedical Research v. Animal Legal Defense Fund, Inc.**, 526 U.S. 1064, 119 S. Ct. 1454, 143 L. Ed. 2d 541, 67 USLW 3438, 67 USLW 3470, 67 USLW 3633, 67 USLW 3641 (U.S. Apr. 19, 1999) (NO. 98-1059)

CASE BY CASE

Animal Legal Defense Fund v. Glickman

154 F. 3d 426, 332 U.S. App. D.C. 104 (1998)

(the en banc opinion)

WALD, CIRCUIT JUDGE [this judge wrote the dissent in the prior three-judge opinion]:

The 1985 amendments to the Animal Welfare Act ("AWA") direct the Secretary of Agriculture to "promulgate standards to govern the humane handling, care, treatment, and transportation of animals by dealers, research facilities, and exhibitors." Pub. L. No. 99-198, § 1752, 99 Stat. 1354, 1645 (1985) (codified at 7 U.S.C. § 2143(a) (1994)). They further provide that such standards "shall include minimum requirements" for, *inter alia*, "a physical environment adequate to promote the psychological well-being of primates." *Id.* Pursuant to this authority, the United States Department of Agriculture ("USDA") issued regulations for primate dealers, exhibitors, and research facilities that included a small number of mandatory requirements and also required the regulated parties to "develop, document, and follow an appropriate plan for environment enhancement adequate to promote the psychological well-being of non-human primates. The plan must be in accordance with the currently accepted professional standards as cited in appropriate professional journals or reference guides, and as directed by the attending veterinarian." 9 C.F.R. § 3.81 (1997). Although these plans must be made available to the USDA, the regulated parties are not obligated to make them available to members of the public. *See id.*

The individual plaintiffs, Roseann Circelli, Mary Eagan, and Marc Jurnove, challenge these regulations on the ground that they violate the USDA's statutory mandate under the AWA and permit dealers, exhibitors, and research facilities to keep primates under inhumane conditions. The individual plaintiffs allege that they suffered aesthetic injury during their regular visits to animal exhibitions when they observed primates living under such conditions. A divided panel of this court held that all of the plaintiffs lacked constitutional standing to pursue their claims. *See* Animal Legal Defense Fund, Inc. v. Glickman, 130 F.3d 464, 466 (D.C.Cir.1997). This court subsequently vacated that judgment and granted rehearing *in banc*.

We hold that Mr. Jurnove, one of the individual plaintiffs, has standing to sue. Accordingly, we need not pass on the standing of the other individual plaintiffs.

I. Background

A. Marc Jurnove's Affidavit

Mr. Jurnove's affidavit is an uncontested statement of the injuries that he has suffered to his aesthetic interest in observing animals living under humane conditions. *See* Animal Legal Defense Fund, Inc. v. Glickman, 943 F. Supp. 44, 49 (D. D.C. 1996) (granting summary judgment to plaintiffs on all legal claims except one that plaintiffs have not appealed; defendants did not allege any genuine disputes of material fact, but instead moved only to dismiss for lack of standing).

For his entire adult life, Mr. Jurnove has "been employed and/or worked as a volunteer for various human and animal relief and rescue organizations." Jurnove Affidavit § 3. "By virtue of [his] training in wildlife rehabilitation and [his] experience in investigating complaints about the treatment of wildlife, [he is] very familiar with the needs of and proper treatment of wildlife." *Id.* § 6. "Because of [his] familiarity with and love of exotic animals, as well as for recreational and educational purposes and because [he] appreciate[s] these animals' beauty, [he] enjoy[s] seeing them in various zoos and other parks near [his] home." *Id.* § 7.

Between May 1995 and June 1996, when he filed his affidavit, Mr. Jurnove visited the Long Island Game Farm Park and Zoo ("Game Farm") at least nine times. Throughout this period, and since as far back as 1992, the USDA has not questioned the adequacy of this facility's plan for the psychological well-being of primates.

Mr. Jurnove's first visit to the Game Farm, in May 1995, lasted approximately six hours. *See id.* While there, Mr. Jurnove saw many animals living under inhumane conditions. For instance, the Game Farm housed one primate, a Japanese Snow Macaque, in a cage "that was a distance from and not in view of the other primate cages." *Id.* § 14. "The only cage enrichment device this animal had was an unused swing." *Id.* Similarly, Mr. Jurnove "saw a large male chimpanzee named Barney in a holding area by himself. He could not see or hear any other primate." *Id.* § 8. Mr. Jurnove "kn[e]w that chimpanzees are very social animals and it upset [him] very much to see [Barney] in isolation from other primates." *Id.* The Game Farm also placed adult bears next to squirrel monkeys, although Jurnove saw evidence that the arrangement made the monkeys frightened and extremely agitated. *See id.* § 11.

The day after this visit, Mr. Jurnove began to contact government agencies, including the USDA, in order to secure help for these animals. Based on Mr. Jurnove's complaint, the USDA inspected the Game Farm on May 3, 1995. According to Mr. Jurnove's uncontested affidavit, however, the agency's resulting inspection report "states that [the USDA inspectors] found the facility in compliance with all the standards." *Id.* § 18. Mr. Jurnove returned to the Game Farm on eight more occasions to observe these officially legal conditions.

On July 17, 18, and 19, 1995, he found "virtually the same conditions" that allegedly caused him aesthetic injury during his first visit to the Game Farm in May. *Id.* § 20. For instance, Barney, the chimpanzee, and Samantha, the Japanese Snow Macaque, were still alone in their cages. *See id.* This time, Mr. Jurnove documented these conditions with photographs and sent them to the USDA. *See id.* §§ 19-20. Nevertheless, the responding USDA inspectors found only a few violations at the Game

Farm; they reported "nothing" about many of the conditions that concerned Mr. Jurnove and that he had told the agency about, such as "the fact that numerous primates were being housed alone" and the lack of adequate stimulation in their cages. *Id.* § 21.

Mr. Jurnove devoted two trips in August and one in September to "videotaping the conditions that the inspection missed," and on each trip he found that the inhumane conditions persisted. *Id.* §§ 22-28. At the end of September, the USDA sent three inspectors to the Game Farm in response to Mr. Jurnove's continued complaints and reportage; they found violations, however, only with regard to the facility's fencing. *See id.* § 29.

Mr. Jurnove returned to the Game Farm once more on October 1, 1995. Indeed, he only stopped his frequent visits when he became ill and required major surgery. *See id.* § 30. After his health returned, Mr. Jurnove visited the Game Farm in April 1996, hoping to see improvements in the conditions that he had repeatedly brought to the USDA's attention. He was disappointed again; "the animals [were] in literally the same conditions as [he] had seen them over the summer of 1995." *Id.* § 33. Mr. Jurnove's resulting complaints prompted the USDA to inspect the Game Farm in late May 1996. For the fourth time, the agency found the facility largely in compliance, with a few exceptions not relevant to the plaintiffs' main challenge in this case. *See id.* § 42. In June 1996, Mr. Jurnove filed the affidavit that is the basis of his claim here. He concluded this affidavit by stating his intent to "return to the Farm in the next several weeks" and to "continue visiting the Farm to see the animals there." *Id.* § 43.

B. The Plaintiffs' Complaint

The plaintiffs' complaint elaborates a two-part legal theory based on the factual allegations in the individual plaintiffs' affidavits. First, the plaintiffs allege that the AWA requires the USDA to adopt specific, minimum standards to protect primates' psychological well-being, and the agency has failed to do so. *See, e.g.,* First Amended Complaint § 97 ("In issuing final Part 3 regulations, USDA violated its statutory obligation [under 7 U.S.C. § 2143(a)(2)(B)] to set standards 'for a physical environment adequate to promote the psychological well-being of primates,' and instead delegated this responsibility to regulated entities by requiring that regulated entities devise 'plans' for this purpose.").

Second, the plaintiffs contend that the conditions that caused Mr. Jurnove aesthetic injury complied with current USDA regulations, but that lawful regulations would have prohibited those conditions and protected Mr. Jurnove from the injuries that he describes in his affidavit. *See id.* § 53 ("Marc Jurnove has been and continues to be injured by USDA's failure to issue and implement standards for a physical environment adequate to promote the psychological well-being of primates because this harms the nonhuman primates he sees at the Long Island Game Farm and Zoo which in turn caused and causes him extreme aesthetic harm and emotional and physical distress."); *id.* ("[B]ecause USDA regulations permit the nonhuman primates in zoos, such as the Long Island Game Farm and Zoological Park to be housed in isolation, Marc Jurnove was exposed to and will be exposed in the future to behaviors exhibited by these animals which indicate the psychological debilitation caused by social deprivation. Observing these behaviors caused and will cause Marc Jurnove personal distress and aesthetic and emotional injury."); *id.* § 58 ("Marc Jurnove experienced and continues to experience physical and mental distress when he realizes that he, by himself, is powerless to help the animals he witnesses suffering when such suffering derives from or is traceable to the improper implementation and enforcement of the Animal Welfare Act by USDA.").

II. Analysis

"The question of standing involves both constitutional limitations on federal-court jurisdiction and prudential limitations on its exercise." Bennett v. Spear, 520 U.S. 154, 117 S. Ct. 1154, 1161, 137 L. Ed. 2d 281 (1997) (citation and quotation marks omitted). To meet the "case or controversy" requirement of Article III, a plaintiff must demonstrate: (1) that she has suffered "injury in fact;" (2) that the injury is "fairly traceable" to the defendant's actions; and (3) that a favorable judicial ruling will "likely" redress the plaintiff's injury. Id.; *see also* Lujan v. Defenders of Wildlife, 504 U.S. 555, 560-61, 112 S. Ct. 2130, 119 L. Ed. 2d 351 (1992). In addition, the Supreme Court has recognized prudential requirements for standing, including "that a plaintiff's grievance must arguably fall within the zone of interests protected or regulated by the statutory provision or constitutional guarantee invoked in the suit." Bennett, 117 S. Ct. at 1161.

We find that Mr. Jurnove's allegations fall well within these requirements.

A. Injury in Fact

Mr. Jurnove's allegations solidly establish injury in fact. As his affidavit indicates, Mr. Jurnove "enjoy[s] seeing [animals] in various zoos and other parks near [his] home" "[b]ecause of [his] familiarity with and love of exotic animals, as well as for recreational and educational purposes and because [he] appreciate[s] these animals' beauty." Jurnove Affidavit § 7. He decided to tour the primate cages at the Game Farm "in furtherance of [his] appreciation for exotic animals and [his] desire to observe and enjoy them." *Id.* During this tour and the ones that followed, Mr. Jurnove suffered direct, concrete, and particularized injury to this aesthetic interest in observing animals living under humane conditions. At this particular zoo, which he has regularly visited and plans to keep visiting, he saw particular animals enduring inhumane treatment. He developed an interest, moreover, in seeing these particular animals living under humane treatment. As he explained, "[w]hat I observed [at the Game Farm] was an assault on my senses and greatly impaired my ability to observe and enjoy *these captive animals.*" *Id.* § 17 (emphasis added). "I want to observe, study, and enjoy these animals in humane conditions." *Id.* § 43.

Simply put, Mr. Jurnove has alleged far more than an abstract, and uncognizable, interest in seeing the law enforced. To the contrary, Mr. Jurnove has made clear that he has an aesthetic interest in seeing exotic animals living in a nurturing habitat, and that he has attempted to exercise this interest by repeatedly visiting a particular animal exhibition to observe particular animals there. This interest was allegedly injured, however, when Mr. Jurnove witnessed the actual living conditions of the primates described and named in his affidavit. It is, of course, quite possible that many other people might visit the same zoo, observe the same animals there, and suffer similar injuries upon seeing these animals living under inhumane conditions. But the fact that many may share an aesthetic interest does not make it less cognizable, less "distinct and palpable."

The Supreme Court has repeatedly made clear that injury to an aesthetic interest in the observation of animals is sufficient to satisfy the demands of Article III standing. *Defenders of Wildlife* states explicitly that "the desire to use *or observe* an animal species, *even for purely esthetic purposes,* is undeniably a cognizable interest for purpose of standing." 504 U.S. at 562-63, 112 S. Ct. 2130 (emphasis added).

[T]he Animal Welfare Act, with which we deal here, is explicitly concerned with the quality of animal life, rather than the number of animals in existence. It seeks "to promote the psychological *well-being* of primates." Pub. L. No. 99-198, § 1752, 99 Stat. 1354, 1645 (1985) (codified at 7 U.S.C. § 2143(a) (1994)) (emphasis added). Quite naturally, suits alleging violations of this statute will focus on the conditions under which animals live. Along these lines, this court has already noted in Animal Welfare Institute, which recognized injury in fact based on an aesthetic interest in seeing animals living under humane conditions, that "[w]here an act is expressly motivated by considerations of humaneness toward animals, who are uniquely incapable of defending their own interests in court, it strikes us as eminently logical to allow groups specifically concerned with animal welfare to invoke the aid of the courts in enforcing the statute." 561 F.2d at 1007. Moreover, and perhaps more importantly, it does not make sense, as a matter of logic, to suppose that people suffer aesthetic injury from government action that threatens to wipe out an animal species altogether, and not from government action that leaves some animals in a persistent state of suffering. To the contrary, the latter seems capable of causing more serious aesthetic injury than the former.

B. Causation

Plaintiffs allege that the AWA, 7 U.S.C. § 2143, requires the USDA to adopt explicit minimum standards to govern the humane treatment of primates, and that the agency did not do so. *See* First Amended Complaint §§ 97, 106, 107. They further contend that the conditions that caused Mr. Jurnove injury complied with current USDA regulations, but that lawful regulations would have prohibited those conditions and protected Mr. Jurnove from the injuries that his affidavit describes. *See id.* §§ 53, 58. We find that these allegations satisfy the causation prong of Article III standing.

The USDA's own actions in this case further support the plaintiffs' allegation that the agency's current regulations allow the conditions that allegedly caused Mr. Jurnove injury. [T]he USDA has not questioned the legality of the Game Farm's plan since 1992. Since May 1995, when Mr. Jurnove began visiting the Game Farm and complaining to the agency, the USDA inspectors have examined, and largely approved, the actual conditions at the facility at least four times.

C. Redressibility

We also find that Mr. Jurnove has satisfied the redressibility element of constitutional standing. [Court stated that changing the regulations would most likely result in better living conditions at the zoo Mr. Jurnove visited.]

D. Prudential Standing/Zone of Interests

Mr. Jurnove also falls within the zone of interests protected under the AWA's provisions on animal exhibitions. As the Supreme Court has recently reaffirmed, the zone of interests test is generous and relatively undemanding. Instead, the test, a gloss on APA § 10(a), 5 U.S.C. § 702 (1994), asks only "whether the interest sought to be protected by the complainant is *arguably* within the zone of interests to be protected by the statute," National Credit Union Admin., 118 S. Ct. at 935

In this case, logic, legislative history, and the structure of the AWA, all indicate that Mr. Jurnove's injury satisfies the zone of interests test. The very purpose of animal exhibitions is, necessarily, to entertain and educate people; exhibitions make no sense unless one takes the interests of their human visitors into account. The legislative history of both the 1985 amendments to the Animal Welfare Act and the 1970 act that first included animal exhibitions within the AWA confirms that Congress acted with the public's interests in mind.

In introducing the 1985 amendments, Senator Robert Dole explained "that we need to ensure *the public* that adequate safeguards are in place to prevent unnecessary abuses to animals, and that everything possible is being done to decrease the pain of animals during experimentation and testing." 131 Cong. Rec. 29,155 (1985) (statement of Sen. Dole) (emphasis added). The Congressmen who went on the House floor to introduce the act that first extended the AWA to cover animal exhibitions recognized that their bill "ha[d] been a focal point of concern among animal lovers throughout the Nation for some time" and spoke of the "great pleasure" that animals bring to the people who see them. 116 Cong. Rec. 40,159 (1970) (statement of Rep. Mizell).

III. Conclusion

Mr. Jurnove has standing to sue. He satisfies the injury, causation, and redressibility elements of constitutional standing, and also falls within the zone of interests for the Animal Welfare Act. We accordingly have no need to consider the standing of the other individual plaintiffs. We leave a determination of the merits of the plaintiffs' claim to a future panel of this court.

So ordered.

[There is a strong dissent by four judges who find no standing. The dissenting opinion states: "Granted, 'the desire to use or observe an animal species, even for purely esthetic purposes, is undeniably a cognizable interest for purpose of standing.' *Defenders of Wildlife*, 504 U.S. at 562-63, 112 S.Ct. 2130. However, as we have observed before, the Supreme Court cases addressing aesthetic injury resulting from the observation of animals are limited to cases in which governmental action threatened to reduce the number of animals available for observation and study."]

Questions & Notes

1. For the decision on the merits once ALDF got past the barrier of standing, see **Animal Legal Defense Fund, Inc. v. Glickman,** 204 F. 3d 229, 340 U.S. App. D.C. 191 (D.C. Cir. Feb. 01, 2000)(The Court upheld the regulation.)

2. Again, what was the injury-in-fact in this case? How is the test as formulated for this case alike or different from the test set out in **Sierra Club v. Morton**? While the standing allowed in this case opens a crack in the courtroom door for issues under the AWA, it is not yet clear what advantage will be made of this opportunity. Based on this opinion, another set of plaintiffs were allowed standing in **Alternatives Research & Development Foundation v. Glickman**, 101 F. Supp. 2d 7 (D.D.C. 2000), where the plaintiffs challenged the limited definition of "animal" in the federal regulations.

3. How is the factual context of this case different from the prior IPPL case?

4. For a fuller discussion of the animal-related standing issues see 29 Wm. & Mary Envt'l L. & Policy Rev. 681 (2005). Also see Robert J. Pushaw, Jr., *Limiting Article III Standing to "Accidental" Plaintiffs: Lessons from Environmental and Animal Law Cases*, 45 Ga. L. Rev. 1 (2010)(Author argues against the extension of the standing doctrine obtained in the above case).

The next major case that made use of this development of standing concepts was within the context of the federal Endangered Species Act and harm to captive elephants held by Ringling Brothers Circus. On a motion to dismiss, the issue of standing went up to the D.C. Court of Appeals where the Court held that assuming the facts were proven at trial, the plaintiff did have standing. See **American Society for Prevention of Cruelty to Animals v. Ringling Bros. and Barnum & Bailey Circus***, 317 F. 3d 334 (C.A. D.C. 2003).*

Some five years later a trial was held. The following is the district court memorandum opinion after a five week trial and years of pretrial discovery. It is quite long, as the Judge is clearly going to great lengths to show support for his decision to dismiss the case. Unlike the prior ALDF case, it appears that this plaintiff did not have the required "injury-in-fact." There was no appeal of this decision by plaintiffs. Just a few sample paragraphs are presented.

CASE BY CASE

American Soc'y for Prevention of Cruelty to Animals v. Feld Entertainment, Inc.

677 F. Supp. 2d 55 (D.D.C. 2009)

JUDGE EMMET G. SULLIVAN, District Judge delivered the opinion of the court.

MEMORANDUM OPINION

Plaintiff Tom Rider was formerly employed by Defendant Feld Entertainment, Inc. ("FEI"), where he worked with several of defendant's Asian elephants in defendant's Ringling Bros. and Barnum & Bailey ("Ringling Bros.") traveling circus. Plaintiff Animal Protection Institute ("API") is a non-profit organization which conducts advocacy and public policy campaigns focused on animals in entertainment. Plaintiffs brought this action against FEI, alleging that FEI's use of bullhooks and prolonged periods of chaining with respect to its circus elephants violates the Endangered Species Act ("ESA"), 16 U.S.C. § 1531, et seq. The Court presided over a non-jury trial from February 4, 2009 to March 18, 2009, during which time the Court heard testimony from approximately thirty fact and expert witnesses and reviewed and admitted hundreds of documents into the evidentiary record.

B. Plaintiffs' Claims
Rider and API contend that FEI "takes" the Asian elephants in its possession in violation of Section 9 of the ESA by "harming," "harassing," and "wounding" the elephants. Specifically, plaintiffs allege that

defendant's employees "take" the elephants by routinely hitting them with bullhooks to train, handle, "correct," and "discipline" the animals, and by chaining them on hard surfaces for many hours each day, and for even longer durations while the elephants are transported on train cars from one location to the next. Plaintiffs maintain that the use of the bull-hook "wounds," "harms," and "harasses" the elephants in violation of the ESA's "take" prohibition because it causes physical, psychological, and behavioral injuries to the elephants, and also significantly impairs and disrupts the elephants' essential and normal behavioral patterns, including their ability to move freely without being hit, their ability to explore their surroundings, and their ability to socialize with other elephants. Plaintiffs also contend that defendant's practice of chaining the elephants "harms," "harasses," and "wounds" the elephants in many ways, such as by contributing to serious foot, leg, joint, and other injuries and diseases, as well as significantly impairing and disrupting their essential and normal behavior patterns, including their need to walk, their need to turn around and to explore their surroundings, and their need to socialize with other elephants.

B. Article III Standing

The Court of Appeals found that, assuming the allegations in the complaint were true, Rider had established a sufficient "injury-in-fact" to satisfy the first element of the standing requirement because "Rider alleged a strong personal attachment to the elephants[,]" and "stated a desire to visit the elephants, making his injury present or imminent[.]" Id. at 337-38. The court found that the second element of Article III standing, causation, was easily demonstrated because "[i]t is unquestioned that Ringling Bros.'s alleged actions-inhumane treatment of the elephants-are the source of the aesthetic injuries that Rider alleges." Id. at 338.

As for the third element, redressability, the Court of Appeals referenced the two forms of relief that Rider was seeking at that time: (i) an injunction halting Ringling Bros.' mistreatment of the elephants in violation of the ESA; and (ii) an order directing the defendant to forfeit possession of the elephants. The Court of Appeals then concluded that "[i]f Rider wins the case, we must assume-because the case is at the pleading stage-that his injury will be resolved." Id. The court explained:

III. ANALYSIS
A. Rider Does Not Have Article III Standing
1. Findings of Fact

1. Mr. Rider claims that he has a strong personal and emotional attachment to the elephants that he worked with while employed by FEI from June 3, 1997 through November 25, 1999. Mr. Rider also claims that what he contends is FEI's mistreatment of these animals causes him aesthetic and emotional injuries. Based upon the following Findings of Fact ("FOF"), the Court does not find Mr. Rider's testimony to be credible.

The Court finds that Mr. Rider failed to prove either a strong and personal attachment to the seven elephants at issue or that FEI's treatment of those elephants caused and continues to cause Mr. Rider to suffer aesthetic or emotional injury. Mr. Rider was repeatedly impeached, and indeed was "pulverized" on cross-examination. The Court finds that Mr. Rider is essentially a paid plaintiff and fact witness who is not credible, and therefore affords no weight to his testimony regarding the matters discussed herein, i.e., the allegations related to his standing to sue.

48. From the time he returned to the United States on March 20, 2000 through December 31, 2008, Mr. Rider has been paid at least $190,000.00 by PAWS, ASPCA, AWI, FFA/HSUS and API (directly or through MGC or WAP) and by WAP itself. The organizational plaintiffs and Mr. Rider claim that this money is to reimburse Mr. Rider for the expenses he has incurred in conducting a media and educational outreach program about the treatment of FEI's elephants. The Court does not find this testimony to be persuasive. Plaintiffs certainly established during the trial that Mr. Rider engages in media and educational outreach activity regarding FEI's Asian elephants, including speaking out about what he allegedly witnessed regarding elephant mistreatment, and publicizing his involvement in this litigation. The Court does not doubt that the plaintiff organizations willingly support those efforts. Nevertheless, based on the totality of the evidence, the Court concludes that while the organizational plaintiffs may see Mr. Rider's media and outreach activities as a benefit, that is not the primary purpose for the payments to Mr. Rider. Rather, the primary purpose is to keep Mr. Rider involved with the litigation, because he is the only plaintiff who alleges a personal and emotional attachment to the elephants and an aesthetic injury based on the alleged mistreatment he claims to have witnessed while working for FEI.

53. The Court finds that the primary purpose of the funding provided by the organizational plaintiffs by and/or through MGC and WAP was to secure Mr. Rider's initial and continuing participation as a plaintiff in this litigation. This is not a case in which the financial support began years-or even months-after Mr. Rider's advocacy efforts, which might suggest that the organizations were simply providing financial support so that Mr. Rider could continue advocating for an issue or cause to which he had long since demonstrated a commitment. To the contrary, the financial support in this case began before the advocacy efforts and suggests that absent the financial incentive, Mr. Rider may not have begun or continued his advocacy efforts or his participation as a plaintiff in this case.

55. Mr. Rider was not forthright about the payments that he had received from the organizational plaintiffs and their (and his) counsel. In his June 9, 2004 response to FEI's Interrogatory No. 24, which asked whether Mr. Rider had received any compensation from any animal advocate or animal advocacy organization for services rendered, Mr. Rider stated-under oath-that "I have not received any such compensation." This statement was false.

61. In pleadings and other filings in this Court and in the Court of Appeals during the period from July 2000 through 2002, Mr. Rider represented that he would like again to visit or observe the Blue Unit elephants with whom he had worked and formed a personal attachment, but was refraining from doing so in order to avoid subjecting himself to further aesthetic injury. The evidence demonstrates, however, that contrary to his claims, from March 2000 through June 2004, Mr. Rider had seen or observed these elephants on numerous occasions-approximately ten (10) or fifteen (15) times per year since 1999.

2. Conclusions of Law

4. Mr. Rider's testimony at trial about his personal and emotional attachment to these elephants is not credible in light of his own undisputed actions at the time he worked for FEI and thereafter, which were undertaken long before this lawsuit was filed and before there was a motive to falsify. Mr. Rider never complained to management about the treatment of the elephants while at FEI and made no effort to complain about that treatment after he left, to either the USDA or anyone else, even though he had ample opportunity to do so. Moreover, while he claims that he quit his job at FEI due to elephant abuse, he immediately took another job tending elephants for Mr. Raffo, one of the very persons whom Mr. Rider claimed had abused the FEI elephants as well as the three elephants from England as to which Mr. Rider also claims a personal and emotional attachment. His credibility with regard to his personal and emotional attachment to the elephants is further undercut by Mr. Rider's own use of the bullhook while employed by Mr. Raffo.

6. While Mr. Rider claimed in pleadings and filings in this Court and the D.C. Circuit that he was refraining from visiting his "girls" in order to spare himself further aesthetic injury and that he would frequently visit his "girls" if they were no longer with FEI, those claims were false. Shortly after he began taking money from the organizational plaintiffs and/or their counsel (and his), Mr. Rider began following FEI's circus units and observing the elephants, including elephants on the Blue Unit. Therefore, contrary to his representations to the Court, Mr. Rider was not refraining from seeing his "girls." Moreover, after Mr. Rider began working for animal activists, three (3) of his "girls" were donated to a sanctuary or zoo by FEI. Mr. Rider made no attempt to visit any of them until after he was deposed in October 2006 and this issue was pointed out to him; even then he still failed to visit two (2) of these elephants (Minnie and Rebecca) who were placed in a sanctuary (PAWS). Mr. Rider used to work for PAWS, and there is no evidence that he was precluded from visiting Minnie while she was still alive or that he is precluded from visiting Rebecca now.

Questions & Notes

1. Compare and contrast the plaintiff in the ALDF case with the plaintiff in this case. What is a list of good qualities for a test case plaintiff?

2. Is it legally ethical for an organization's attorney to "find" a plaintiff? To pay a plaintiff?

Section 3

Standing for Individual Animals

The following case is an example of the response of a court when an attempt is made to put forward the injured animal the plaintiff of the case.

CASE BY CASE

C.E.A.S.E. v. The New England Aquarium
836 F. Supp. 45 (D.C. Mass. 1993)

WOLF, DISTRICT JUDGE.

This case is brought by Kama, a dolphin, Citizens to End Animal Suffering and Exploitation ("CEASE"), the Animal Legal Defense Fund, Inc. ("ALDF"), and the Progressive Animal Welfare Society, Inc. ("PAWS"), to protest the transfer of Kama from the New England Aquarium to the Department of the Navy.

I. Facts

Plaintiffs' factual contentions primarily concern the transfer of Kama from the Aquarium to the Navy. Except as noted, the following relevant facts are undisputed.

Kama was born in captivity at Sea World in San Diego in 1981. Kama was transferred to the Aquarium in 1986 for breeding purposes and/or for public display. Kama, however, did not fit into the social climate at the Aquarium. As a result, he was not regularly on public display, nor featured in the Aquarium dolphin shows. In 1987, the Aquarium wrote to Commerce requesting authorization to transfer Kama and another dolphin to the Naval Oceans Systems Center. The Navy also wrote to Commerce, requesting authority to purchase and transport the two dolphins, noting, "These two dolphins will be housed in floating bay pens as specified in Marine Mammal Permit Number # 195. Commerce authorized both requests, and sent the Navy a Letter of Agreement (# AN108), to be signed by the Navy, which set forth the obligations of the Navy to ensure the safety and well-being of the dolphins."

In late 1987, Kama was transferred from the Aquarium to the Navy pursuant to this Letter of Agreement. Kama is now located in Hawaii, where he is being studied for his sonar capabilities. The Navy has invested over $700,000 and over 3,500 man hours training Kama. *Id.* at § 4. The Navy contends that Kama is able to associate with wild dolphins on a daily basis, and could swim away if he so desired.

A. Kama Lacks Standing

There is little case law addressing whether an animal who has allegedly been injured has standing to bring a suit. Plaintiffs assert that Kama has standing, relying on Palila v. Hawaii Dept. of Land and Natural Resources, 852 F.2d 1106, 1107 (9th Cir.1988). In Palila, the court stated in its introduction:

As an endangered species under the Endangered Species Act,...the bird (Loxioides bailleui), a member of the Hawaiian honey-creeper family, also has legal status and wings its way into federal court as a plaintiff in its own right...represented by attorneys for the Sierra Club, the Audubon Society, and other environmental parties.

However, in *Palila*, the defendants did not challenge the propriety of having an animal as a named plaintiff. Similarly, animal species have remained named plaintiffs in other cases in which the defendants did not contest the issue. *See* Mt. Graham Red Squirrel v. Yeutter, 930 F. 2d 703 (9th Cir. 1991); Northern Spotted Owl v. Lujan, 758 F. Supp. 621 (W.D. Wash. 1991); Northern Spotted Owl v. Hodel, 716 F. Supp. 479 (W.D. Wash. 1988).

However, in the only reported case in which the naming of an animal as a party was challenged, the court found that the animal did not have standing to bring suit. In *Hawaiian Crow ('Alala) v. Lujan*, No. 91-00191-DAE (D. Haw. Sept. 13, 1991), the court ruled that the 'Alala, an endangered species of birds, did not have standing to maintain a suit challenging the implementation of a program under the Endangered Species Act ("ESA"). The court, while recognizing the authority cited above, denied the 'Alala standing on the bases that: (1) the ESA provided for citizen suits brought by "persons;" (2) the other named parties — various Audubon Societies — could obtain the relief sought; and (3) F. R. Civ. P. 17(c) which provides for suits on behalf of infants or incompetent persons does not apply to animals. *Id.* at 4-6.

The same considerations apply in this case. The MMPA [Marine Mammal Protection Act] does not authorize suits brought by animals. Rather, the MMPA provides for judicial review of the grant or denial of permits for permit applicants or "any party opposed to such permit" pursuant to 5 U.S.C. § 701 *et seq. See* 16 U.S.C. § 1374(d)(6). Section 702 of Title 5 provides that, "A *person* suffering legal wrong because of agency action, or adversely affected or aggrieved by agency action within the meaning of a relevant statute, is entitled to judicial review thereof." 5 U.S.C. § 702 (Emphasis added). Thus, as with regard to the ESA in 'Alala, the MMPA expressly authorizes suits brought by persons, not animals. This court will not impute to Congress or the President the intention to provide standing to a marine mammal without a clear statement in the statute. If Congress and the President intended to take the extraordinary step of authorizing animals as well as people and legal entities to sue, they could, and should, have said so plainly. Furthermore, as in 'Alala, citizen groups, if they satisfy the standing requirements, could seek to obtain the relief the amended complaint requests for Kama.

This conclusion is reinforced by consideration of F. R. Civ. P. 17(b), which falls within the section of the Rules entitled "Parties," and discusses the "capacity of an individual ... to sue or be sued." It provides that such capacity "shall be determined by the law of the individual's domicile." While this provision generally addresses the capacity of corporations, partnerships, and other business entities to litigate, there is no indication that it does not apply to other non-human entities or forms of life. While neither Massachusetts nor Hawaii law addresses the precise question of animal standing, cases in each state indicate that animals are treated as the property of their owners, rather than entities with their own legal rights. *See e.g.,* Massachusetts Society for Prevention of Cruelty to Animals v. Commissioner of Public Health, 339 Mass. 216, 158 N.E. 2d 487 (1959); State of Hawaii v. Pokini, 45 Haw. 295, 367 P. 2d 499 (1961).

Accordingly, the MMPA and the operation of F. R. Civ. P. 17(b) indicate that Kama the dolphin lacks standing to maintain this action as a matter of law. Defendants have moved, therefore, for the removal of Kama's name from the caption of this case. This motion must be allowed.

[The case was dismissed for lack of either human or dolphin standing. The plaintiff's attorney for this case was Steven Wise, subsequently the author of **Rattling the Cage** and first professor of an Animal Law course at Harvard Law School in 1999.]

Questions & Notes

1. Why did the Navy want Kama? What was the injury-in-fact for Kama? For the plaintiffs?

2. Why not allow animals to sue? Do you see any problems if the Court had said that a dolphin could have standing?

3. In **The Cetacean Community v. Bush**, 386 F.3d 1169 (9th Cir. 2004) the court specifically held that the language from the Palila case was nonbinding dicta:

> After due consideration, we agree with the district court that *Palila IV's* statements are nonbinding dicta. A statement is dictum when it is " 'made during the course of delivering a

judicial opinion, but ... is unnecessary to the decision in the case and [is] therefore not precedential.' "

****

An alterative to naming an animal as plaintiff is to allow human plaintiffs to make claims based upon injuries to animals. As set out in Chapter 6, there is long history of making harm to animals illegal through anti-cruelty criminal laws. But being criminal law means that normally only the state may be the plaintiff. However, there is no conceptual barrier to allowing private parties to bring a civil action to assert this right to be free from unnecessary pain and suffering on behalf of animals. In this context humans are the plaintiffs, but the harm they bring before the court is the violation of the legal rights of animals.

There is a North Carolina Statute which provides a clear example of this variation of standing.

> It shall be the purpose of this Article to provide a civil remedy for the protection and humane treatment of animals in addition to any criminal remedies that are available. A real party in interest as plaintiff shall be held to include any person even though the person does not have a possessory or ownership right in an animal; a real party in interest as defendant shall include any person who owns or has possession of an animal.

N.C. Gen. Stat. Ann. § 19A-2 (West 2007).

This statute provides standing for a private party to file an action. Upon the showing that an animal is being subjected to "cruelty" or "cruel treatment" a plaintiff is allowed to obtain relief, which is limited to injunctive remedies (like the citizen suits of federal environmental law). Under the injunctive relief power of the courts, ownership of the harmed animal may be severed without compensation. (§ 19A-4.)

The full scope of this law was tested in a contested hoarding case brought by the Animal Legal Defense Fund in North Carolina. ALDF filed suit to remove more than 300 dogs from the defendants' home because of the adverse conditions in which the animals were living. The court ordered all the animals removed from the Woodleys' home and title was transferred to ALDF, which found homes for almost all the animals. ALDF's trial court win was upheld in this appeals case.

CASE BY CASE

Animal Legal Defense Fund v. Woodley

640 S.E. 2d 777, 2007 WL 475329 (N.C. App. 2007)

JUDGE ELMORE,

Barbara and Robert Woodley (defendants) appeal from an injunction forfeiting all rights in the animals possessed by defendants and the removal of the animals from defendants' control, and an order granting temporary custody of the animals to the Animal Legal Defense Fund (plaintiff), both of which were entered 12 April 2005 by Judge Albert A. Corbett, Jr. After careful review of the record, we find defendants' contentions on appeal to be without merit; we therefore affirm the trial court's order and injunction.

On 23 December 2004, plaintiff filed a complaint against defendants seeking preliminary and permanent injunctions under North Carolina's Civil Remedy for Protection of Animals statute (Section 19A). N.C. Gen. Stat. § 19A-1 et seq. (2005). Plaintiff alleged that defendants had abused and neglected a large number of dogs (as well as some birds) in their possession. Defendants answered the complaint on 7 January 2005. On 13 January 2005, after the lower court reviewed the evidence, held two hearings, and visited defendants' property, Judge Resson O. Faircloth entered a preliminary injunction prohibiting defendants from any further violation of the statute, requiring defendants to properly maintain those parts of their property in which the animals were kept, and granting plaintiff access to defendants' property for the purpose of giving care to the animals.

Defendants first contend that the trial court lacked subject matter jurisdiction to hear the matter because plaintiff's complaint was not verified as required by N.C. Gen. Stat. § 19A-3. However, as plaintiff points out in its brief, § 19A-3 applies only to preliminary injunctions. Defendants' first assignment of error is without merit.

Defendants also argue that N.C. Gen. Stat. § 19A-1 is unconstitutional in that it purports to grant standing to persons who have suffered no injury. To support their contention, defendants rely on Article IV, Section 13 of the North Carolina Constitution, which states, "There shall be in this State but one form of action for the enforcement or protection of private rights or the redress of private wrongs, which shall be denominated a civil action...." N.C. Const. art. IV, § 13. This reliance, however, is misplaced. While defendants contend that "this provision places a constitutional limit on standing in civil actions to those individuals who have suffered some individualized and concrete harm," they rely almost entirely on federal authority. However, as defendants themselves note, "North Carolina courts are not constrained by the 'case or controversy' requirement of Article 3 of the United States Constitution." See Neuse River Found., Inc. v. Smithfield Foods, Inc., 155 N.C. App. 110, 114, 574 S.E. 2d 48, 52 (2002), disc. review denied, 356 N.C. 675, 577 S.E. 2d 628 (2003). Moreover, defendants, in maintaining that our Constitution restricts our legislature's ability to give standing by statute, simply misinterpret the language of the Constitution. In actuality, "[t]his section abolished the distinction between actions at law and suits in equity, leaving such rights and remedies to be enforced in the one court, which theretofore had administered simply legal rights." Reynolds v. Reynolds, 208 N.C. 578, 624, 182 S.E. 341, 369 (1935).

Because we hold that Article IV, Section 13 of the North Carolina Constitution merely "abolished the distinction between actions at law and suits in equity," *Reynolds*, 208 N.C. at 624, 182 S.E. at 369, rather than placing limitations on the legislature's ability to create actions by statute, defendants' contention is without merit.

Accordingly, we will not review defendants' unargued assignments of error. Having found no meritorious assignments of error, the judgment of the trial court is

Affirmed.

Questions & Notes

1. While this statute would appear to be the answer to many problems about animal standing, it is not used very often. Indeed, there is no evidence of any flood of litigation on behalf of animals. No other state has adopted this law.

2. If you were to take this statute to your state legislature for adoption, what do you think might be the compelling arguments for its adoption? Against adoption?

3. Because of the number of animals that were involved in this case, the cost to ALDF was in the six figure range. Not a responsibility lightly undertaken.

Allowing Animal Interest Before the Courts

There are a diversity of legal context where the interests of animals have been before a court, even if the plaintiff is not the animal. Presently in the United States, a primary area where an animal interest may be brought before the courts is under the "Uniform Trust Act ". (See discussion in Chapter 2.) This law provides a legal right to protect the financial interest of animals. Obviously a human would have to bring the issue to the attention of the court, but it would be the animals interests, not the human's, which would be before the court. The enforceability of the trust is made very clear with the following language:

> 408 (b) A trust authorized by this section may be enforced by a person appointed in the terms of the trust or, if no person is so appointed, by a person appointed by the court. A person having an interest in the welfare of the animal may

request the court to appoint a person to enforce the trust or to remove a person appointed.

For example consider the following order entered in 2002 on behalf of a chimpanzee:

In re The Florida Chimpanzee Care Trust
[Circuit Court, Palm Beach Florida, Probate Division, File No CP-02-1333-IY]

> This matter having come before this Court on the Petition of Carole Noon and David G. Armstrong, trustees of the Florida Chimpanzee Care Trust dated October 9, 2001 ("Trust"), for an order to appoint a guardian ad litem for the beneficiaries of the Trust; the Court having reviewed the Petition, the Memorandum of law in support of the Petition, and upon the advice of counsel;
>
> IT IS HEREBY ORDERED:
>
> 1.   Carol M. Standley, Esq. is hereby appointed as guardian ad litem to represent the interests of the beneficiaries of the Trust in all future matters involving the Trust; and
>
> 2.   Carol M. Stanley's reasonable fees for serving as guardian ad litem for the Trust Beneficiaries shall be paid from the assets of the Trust.
>
> DATED: April 1, 2002
>
> Signed by Circuit Court Judge

****

Beyond the area of trusts, the need for a court to take into account the living nature of dogs has arisen in several contexts. In 2007 a probate court in Tennessee appointed an attorney as a guardian ad litem for a dog in a contested estate where it was not clear who should obtain possession of the dog. The order stated that:

> "The Guardian Ad Litem owes a duty to this Honorable Court to impartially investigate to determine the facts and report the facts to the Court. The Guardian Ad Litem is not an advocate for the dog, but has the duty to determine what is best for the dog's welfare."
>
> In Re: Estate of Ronald Callan, Jr. No. D-2252. Probate Court of Shelby County, Tennessee. March 20, 2007.

The judge is slightly uncomfortable with the dog being treated this way, specifically saying the attorney is not an advocate, but at the same time requiring him to determine the best outcome for the dog's welfare, clearly making him an advocate. Note that property status is not a factor.

A unique, and highly visible, case arose with the prosecution of the professional football player, Michael Vick for a violation of the federal dog fighting laws. (See discussion on dog fighting at end of Chapter 6.) A very visible issue after his arrest was the issue of what to do with his dogs, the pit bulls that were found on the property and part of the dog fighting venture. The court appointed a guardian attorney at law and asked for advice concerning the disposition of the dogs.

United States v. Approximately 53 Pit Bull Dogs

U.S. Dist. Court of Eastern Virginia, Civil Action No.: 3:07CV397 Second Ord. as to Disposition and Appointing Guardian/Special Master 2 (Oct. 16, 2007)

> "COMES NOW the United States, by counsel, and herewith moves the court to enter an order 1) appointing a guardian/special master to recommend to the Court final dispositions as to each forfeited dog, 2) permit the guardian/special master to arrange for interim housing of the forfeited dogs, and 3) provide for the spaying and neutering of the forfeited dogs."
>
> 1. Rebecca J. Huss is hereby appointed as guardian/special master to consider appropriate options for a final disposition of the remaining 48 pitbull dogs previously forfeited to the United States.
>
> 2. Professor Huss shall have the following powers and duties to fulfill her obligations:
>
> (a) Consider available disposition and placement options as she deems appropriate for the final disposition of the remaining dogs;
>
> (b) Engage and employ any individuals or entities the guardian/special master deems necessary to assist in her duties ("Retained Personnel");
>
> (c) Take such action as necessary and appropriate to provide for the interim care prior to final permanent disposition of the dogs.
>
> 3. In evaluating the permanent disposition options, Professor Huss shall consider the following factors, among others:
>
> (a) The need to protect the public and other animals from any dogs which may be aggressive; and

(b) The quality of life for any dog which may need to be housed in a restrictive environment for the long term.

[Rebecca Huss is a professor of law at Valparaiso Law School and has a long history of writing and working in the animal law area.]

Note that Professor Huss had a mixed charge. She had to decide about the best interests of the individual animals but in the context of protection of the public. Her interests were not relevant; their property status was not relevant. While the dogs were not plaintiffs, the court (and federal prosecutors) accepted that the dogs were not simply personal property, but had independent interests and asked Professor Huss to ascertain what course of action would be best for the dogs and the public. It is also important to acknowledge that this was being done for dogs that were part of a dog fighting enterprise; and, in most prior circumstances the dogs would have been killed by the government or humane society as unadoptable For a discussion of the events by the Professor Huss, see Rebecca J. Huss, *Lessons Learned: Acting as Guardian/ Special Master in the Bad Newz Kennels Case*, 15 Animal Law 69 (2008). For many of the documents that were part of this case, see, *http://www. animallaw.info/pleadings/pbusfdvick.htm.*

As the above suggests, at least some individuals presently within the legal system accept that animals have interests deserving of consideration by the courts, whether or not they are full "legal persons". Perhaps is it helpful to think of animals as partial legal persons. It would help this process if the legislatures could more specifically set out the circumstances when animal interests may come directly before the courts in a civil law context, rather than criminal law context.

Appendix A

Many in the animal welfare movement have believed that it would be helpful for federal standing issues if there was a citizen suit provision like that found in the environmental laws. Below the provision from the Endangered Species Act is set out. Do you see a way that this could be adopted to animal welfare laws such as the Animal Welfare Act?

Portions of the Endangered Species Act

16 USC 1540(g) Citizen Suits

(1) Except as provided in paragraph (2) of this subsection any person may commence a civil suit on his own behalf —

(A) to enjoin any person, including the United States and any other governmental instrumentality or agency (to the extent permitted by the eleventh amendment to the Constitution), who is alleged to be in violation of any provision of this Act or regulation issued under the authority thereof; or

(B) to compel the Secretary to apply, pursuant to section 6(g)(2)(B)(ii) of this Act [16 USCS § 1535(g)(2)(B)(ii)], the prohibitions set forth in or authorized pursuant to section 4(d) or section 9(a)(1)(B) of this Act [16 USCS §§ 1533(d), 1538(a)(1)(B)] with respect to the taking of any resident endangered species or threatened species within any State; or

(C) against the Secretary where there is alleged a failure of the Secretary to perform any act or duty under section 4 [16 USCS § 1533] which is not discretionary with the Secretary.

The district courts shall have jurisdiction, without regard to the amount in controversy or the citizenship of the parties, to enforce any such provision or regulation, or to order the Secretary to perform such act or duty, as the case may be. In any civil suit commenced under subparagraph (B) the district court shall compel the Secretary to apply the prohibition sought if the court finds that the allegation that an emergency exists is supported by substantial evidence.

[notice: provisions omitted]

(3) (A) Any suit under this subsection may be brought in the judicial district in which the violation occurs.

(B) In any such suit under this subsection in which the United States is not a party, the Attorney General, at the request of the Secretary, may intervene on behalf of the United States as a matter of right.

(4) The court, in issuing any final order in any suit brought pursuant to paragraph (1) of this subsection, may award costs of litigation (including reasonable attorney and expert witness fees) to any party, whenever the court determines such award is appropriate.

(5) The injunctive relief provided by this subsection shall not restrict any right which any person (or class of persons) may have under any statute or common law to seek enforcement of any standard or limitation or to seek any other relief (including relief against the Secretary or a State agency).

CHAPTER **10**

The Animal Welfare Act

Section 1

Introduction

The Animal Welfare Act (AWA, 7 USC § 2131, available at *www.animallaw.info/statutes/stusawa.htm*) is a federal law of limited purpose and scope. It is not a broad anti-cruelty law. It does not deal with all species of animals, as most state anti-cruelty laws do. Instead, the law focuses on several very specific animal-related activities which have a national level of recognition.

Concern about the use of animals for science has a long history. (See Descarte's & Voltaire's discussion in Chapter 1.) The issue of how the activity might be regulated from the national level first arose in Great Britain. The National Anti-Vivisection Society was formed in Britain in 1875 and the first law concerning the use of animals in science passed in 1876. In the United States, the first detailed national discussion occurred 1896-1900, culminating in a U.S. Senate Hearing on Vivisection. (February 21, 1900 Hearing on SB 34 — For the Further Prevention of Cruelty to Animals in the District of Columbia. Published by Government Printing Office 1900.) However, no law was adopted at that time.

During the early 1960s the issue was again on the national agenda. There was considerable discussion in Congress concerning the issue of the use of animals in science, research, and testing. At the same time, a related topic became a front-page issue. There was significant public and media outcry over a story about how pet dogs and cats were being stolen and ultimately sold to research facilities. (See *Concentration Camps for Dogs*, Life, Vol. 60, No. 5, Feb. 4, 1966, at pages 23–29.) These two topics formed a critical mass in the national political arena promoting the adoption of the AWA in 1966.

This initial law created a licensing system for animal dealers and laboratories that use dogs, cats, hamsters, guinea pigs, rabbits, or non-human primates. Subsequent amendments expanded the list of animals and the degree of federal regulation in the laboratory setting. Pet protection and provisions against the use of interstate shipment of animals used in illegal animal fighting ventures have also been added to the AWA. The scope continues to expand but is nevertheless limited. (For the full story of the history, see Christine Stevens, *Laboratory Animal Welfare*, in the 4th Edition of **Animals and Their Legal Rights** (1990, Animal Welfare Institute)).

There is a wide assortment of issues with which the AWA is concerned, including:

- The thief of pet dogs and cats being sold to research and testing facilities
- Mammals in zoos & exhibitions
- Animal fighting (dogs and cocks primarily)

- The breeding and wholesale distribution of some mammals
- Auctions of animals/mammals
- Animals in research labs (universities and private industry)
- The transportation of listed animals by other than common carriers

Among the topics that are not covered by the federal law are:

- Slaughter of animals (but see federal Humane Slaughter Act)
- Animals in agriculture production
- Retail pet stores
- Injuries by animals or inflicted upon animals
- Animals other than mammals

The Animal Welfare Act seeks to address many of these issues by establishing a regulatory scheme of licenses and inspections and establishing minimum conditions of care for animals when they are within the custody of these licensed individuals or registered institutions. As Congress had neither the time nor the expertise to decide the specific care provisions for a wide assortment of animals, the task of developing the particular provisions for the care of animals was delegated to the U.S. Department of Agriculture and its Animal and Plant Health Inspection Service (APHIS). This agency has adopted an extensive set of regulations that set out species-specific care provisions. See 9 Code of Federal Regulations §1 (9 CFR §1, available at *www.animallaw.info/administrative/ adusawaregtofc.htm*). As an example, if a cat is kept in a cage in an institution registered under the AWA, then the keeper of the cat must satisfy the following:

> Regulation Sec. 3.3 Sheltered housing facilities.
>
> (a) Heating, cooling, and temperature. The sheltered part of sheltered housing facilities for dogs and cats must be sufficiently heated and cooled when necessary to protect the dogs and cats from temperature or humidity extremes and to provide for their health and well-being. The ambient temperature in the sheltered part of the facility must not fall below 50 deg. F (10 deg. C) for dogs and cats not acclimated to lower temperatures....

Although the AWA has criminal provisions for violations of the Act, these are seldom used. Instead, the agency uses a civil enforcement process of inspections, corrections, administrative hearings, fines, and license withdrawal as its primary tools of enforcement. In 1999 there were 313 investigations carried out by APHIS. The enforcement process resulted in 143 warnings and 79 settlements; as well, 28 cases went to administrative law judge hearings. In total, $667,000 in penalties were assessed that year in civil fines. In 2007 there were 613 cases, 433 warnings 68 ALJ decisions, and $414,050 in civil penalties (note that in 2008 the amount was over $1 million).

Historical Development of the AWA

As stated in Senate Report No. 1280 (this and other historical legal materials are available at *www.animallaw.info/topic_subcat/lhusawa.htm*) there were three main purposes for the proposed law in 1966:

1. To protect the owners of pet dogs and cats from the theft of their pets;

2. To prevent the use or sale of stolen dogs or cats for purposes of research or experimentation; and

3. To establish humane standards for the treatment of dogs, cats, and certain other animals by animal dealers and research facilities.

In order to accomplish these goals, the law directed the U.S. Secretary of Agriculture to set up a regulatory program to license all dealers in dogs and cats, to register all animal research facilities, and to provide humane care provisions, enforceable through inspections. To help eliminate the black market in pets, research facilities were required to purchase dogs and cats only from licensed dealers. To help track down stolen pets, a system of record keeping was required for all animal dealers and animal research facilities. To assure the humane treatment of animals, the Secretary of Agriculture was authorized to establish an inspection program and adopt the necessary regulations. One of the more curious aspects of the 1966 Act was the limited list of animals that came under it: dogs, cats, primates, guinea pigs, hamsters, and rabbits.

By 1970 it was apparent that changes in the law would be required if the goal of humane treatment of animals was to be realized. There were four areas of significant change to the AWA in the 1970 amendments.

1. The definition of "animal" was expanded to include warm-blooded animals generally (with certain exceptions).

2. More human entities were brought under the regulatory provisions of the Act: animal exhibitors (i.e., circuses, zoos, and roadside shows), and wholesale pet dealers (including breeders who sell to others under the Act).

3. The lab door of research facilities was opened more, requiring that certain humane standards be maintained at all times, and that animals be given the appropriate use of pain-killing drugs, if that did not interfere with the research.

4. The Secretary's enforcement powers were strengthened and protection for government inspectors was provided from individuals who interfered with enforcement actions under the Act.

When the 1970 amendments brought exhibitors under the requirements of the AWA, they (like dealers) had to have licenses to operate and became subject to inspections and compliance with the Act's humane standards, as promulgated through USDA regulations enforced by APHIS. Most of the discussion in Congress in 1970 focused on seeking a balance between the rights of scientists to use animals in their research and the interests of the animals to receive humane care.

By 1976, other animal protection issues had come to the forefront of public and congressional discussion. Those provisions dealing with research facilities and dealers were pretty much left alone by the 1976 amendments, which instead dealt with several new topics:

1. Transportation carriers and intermediate handlers of animals were brought under the provisions of the Act.

2. A number of specific transportation problems were addressed by Congress.

3. A new provision was added that made it a crime to knowingly sponsor, participate in, transport, or use the mails to promote fights between live birds, live dogs, or other mammals.

4. The penalty provisions were rewritten allowing the broad use of civil fines.

Some of the specific transportation provisions Congress added dealt with the C.O.D. shipment of animals and the shipment of underaged animals. They required that veterinary certificates must accompany animals during the transportation process. There were also some adjustments to the definition of exactly what constitutes an animal dealer.

The set of amendments that Congress adopted in December 1985 focused almost entirely on the issue of animal research. Throughout the early 1980s, animal welfare and rights advocates, and the general public, had been persistently attempting to get new legislation passed to protect research animals. As of 1985, all of those efforts, ideas, and compromises had been compressed into a Senate bill (S. 1233) sponsored by Senator Robert Dole (R-KS). A companion bill had also been submitted to the House of Representatives by Rep. George Brown (D-CA). During congressional work on appropriations bills on the floor of the Senate just prior to adjournment for the 1985 Christmas holiday, Senator Dole succeeded in getting his bill passed by tacking it, as an amendment, onto the Food Security Act of 1985. Because of this procedure there are no House or Senate committee reports that discuss this amendment. (In 1983 and 1984 Congressional hearings were held on this issue.) Its provisions comprise only eight sections of Public Law 99-198, a very long law dealing with all aspects of the federal farm subsidy program.

1. The minimum level of care is stated with more specificity.

2. Animal research facilities are required to create Institutional Animal Committees, which include the presence of a public member from outside the facility.

3. Trade secrets of research facilities are protected by a new section of the AWA.

4. The law clarifies the responsibility of federal animal research facilities.

One long fought-for provision is the requirement that dogs held by research facilities be exercised. Another requires research facilities to provide "a physical environment adequate to promote the psychological well-being of primates." This represents the first time that Congress has extended the concern and scope of the law beyond certain obvious physical requirements like food and water. It is a recognition by our lawmakers that primates have legally recognizable interests in a mental life of quality.

The 1990 amendment added a new section 28 that provided more specific details as to the protection of pets.

In 2002 the Farm Bill again addressed AWA issues. Although a number of changes were offered up, very few were adopted. The final version of the bill as adopted in the Senate House Conference killed the provisions that would have stiffened penalties for bird and dogfighting. Early versions of the bill mandated the humane euthanasia of "downers" (animals who are too sick or injured to walk into a slaughterhouse), but these proposed changes were later eliminated. Congress also discarded provisions that would have curtailed abuses in U.S. puppy mills and protected bears from farms that extract bile from their gall bladders for sale overseas. Two items were adopted:

1. The Farm Bill included an amendment by Sen. Jesse Helms (R–NC) that denied Animal Welfare Act protection to birds, rats, and mice, the subjects of a majority of all research experiments in the United States. The USDA had just agreed to expand the definition of "research animal" to include rats, mice, and birds. So this amendment eliminated that possibility as they are now specifically excluded from the law.

2. The second amendment further restricts the interstate shipment of animals that might be used in animal fighting ventures.

Questions & Notes

1. Is it not curious how Congress chooses to deal with these animal issues as amendments to the periodic farm bill, a very complex and detailed bill that allocates billions of dollars to U.S. agriculture? Also, note that the agency responsible for the well-being of animals under the AWA is the Department of Agriculture. And yet, farm animals are specifically exempted from the operation of the AWA. The result is an orphaned responsibility for an agency primarily concerned about transmittable animal diseases and marketing for U.S. producers of agricultural products and animals.

2. Why might this be the case? When the agency seeks to reward administrators, how high will be the enforcement of the AWA in the evaluation of agency goals?

3. Where would you locate an agency home for the AWA?

4. There is nothing in the U.S. Constitution to suggest that the U.S. Congress is authorized to deal with animal issues. The federal government is limited in its power and may exercise only those powers allocated to it by the sovereign states through the U.S. Constitution. By legal tradition, the control of animals is a state power. (See Chapter 5, "State Regulation of Ownership.") In the Constitution, however, Congress is clearly given authority over laws relating to interstate commerce. Further, not only is Congress allowed to control the conditions of interstate commerce but, under analysis by the U.S. Supreme Court, the Constitution allows Congress to also deal with concerns before and after the object of commerce is actually shipped. Thus, the term "affect such commerce" appears in the opening paragraph of Section 1 of the AWA quoted earlier.

Section 2

Class A & B Dealers

The Source of the Dogs and Cats—Illegal, Stolen Animals

The concern about pet dogs and cats being used in research was one of the prime catalyzes for adoption of the law. As noted in the 1966 Senate Report No. 1280:

> The demand for research animals has risen to such proportions that a system of unregulated dealers is now supplying

hundreds of thousands of dogs, cats, and other animals to research facilities each year.... Stolen pets are quickly transported across State lines, changing hands rapidly ... [and] State laws ... proved inadequate both in the apprehending and conviction of the thieves who operate in this interstate operation. See Senate Report No. 89-1281, at 4-6 (1966), reprinted in 1966 U.S.C.C.A.N. 2635, 2636.

To gain control of this problem the AWA first deals with the source of the demand for the stolen animals. Section 7 of the AWA, prohibits any registered institution from obtaining dogs or cats from other than government licensed sources:

It shall be unlawful for any research facility to purchase any dog or cat from any person except an operator of an auction sale subject to section 12 of this Act or a person holding a valid license as a dealer or exhibitor issued by the Secretary pursuant to this Act unless such person is exempted from obtaining such license under section 3 of this Act.

As the cost of animals is a very small part of the budget of a research institution, and as there are very negative public relations that can occur from the use of stolen pets, institutions have almost no incentive to deal in stolen animals. Additionally, there are extensive record-keeping requirements for research facilities (see Reg. Sec. 2.35 (b)) to make the tracking of possible stolen animals easier. Therefore, the real risk of pet theft is further back in the chain of commerce in animals. Consider the chain of commerce, or flow chart, for dogs and cats (somewhat simplified). [See the "Chain of Commerce for Dogs and Cats" chart on page 359.]

The critical step for the elimination of stolen pets is to make sure that licensed dealers find it difficult to use these animals as a source; to increase the risk of the dealer being part of the criminal chain if they use stolen dogs and cats. For the moment, use the simplified definition that licensed dealers (Class B license) are those that buy and resell animals, while private breeders (Class A license) purchase animals only to add to their breeding stock and sell the animals they breed on their premises. Therefore, it is the Class B dealers that must be focused on.

The AWA has two primary approaches in dealing with the issue of pet theft. First, an identification/information record trail is required that is supposed to follow the animal through the chain (see Reg. Sec. 2.50). Second, there is a required holding period when a dog or cat enters the chain of transfer. Both start with the Class B dealer. Now that the system has been in place for 30 years, it is unlikely that a licensed dealer would steal animals to be later sold—the risk/reward ratio does not make it worth the dealer's while to engage in criminal conduct. Rather, the real risk is that someone who does steal animals will sell them to a licensed dealer. Realizing this, the regulations for source identification imposed upon the dealers try to discourage this activity by being very specific about proof of ownership.

Reg. Sec. 2.75 Records: Dealers and exhibitors.

(a)(1) Each dealer, other than operators of auction sales and brokers to whom animals are consigned, and each exhibitor shall make, keep, and maintain records or forms which fully and correctly disclose the following information concerning each dog or cat purchased or otherwise acquired....

(i) The name and address of the person from whom a dog or cat was purchased or otherwise acquired whether or not the person is required to be licensed or registered under the Act;

(ii) The USDA license or registration number of the person if he or she is licensed or registered under the Act;

(iii) The vehicle license number and state, and the driver's license number and state of the person, if he or she is not licensed or registered under the Act;

(vii) A description of each dog or cat which shall include:

(A) The species and breed or type;

(B) The sex;

(C) The date of birth or approximate age; and

(D) The color and any distinctive markings;

The second requirement to discourage the use of stolen animals is a holding period requirement. Section 5 of the AWA:

No dealer or exhibitor shall sell or otherwise dispose of any dog or cat within a period of five business days after the acquisition of such animal or within such other period as may be specified by the Secretary: Provided, that operators of auction sales subject to section 2142 of this title shall not be required to comply with the provisions of this section.

This holding period at least makes it possible for the tracing of a stolen pet before it moves so far away from the point of origin that the animal is not recoverable. For a case dealing with the five-day rule see, **In re E. Lee Cox and Becky Cox, D/b/a Pixy Pals Kennel**, 49 Agric. Dec. 115, 1990 WL 320949 (U.S.D.A.).

The Source of the Dogs and Cats—Legal, Random Source

The issue of stolen random source dogs (and cats) being used by laboratories was what helped bring the AWA into political reality. While today there is considerably less theft of dogs than in the 1960s, the issue is still present for lawful sources and it can be a hot and emotional local political topic. The issue arises when local shelters or government pounds decide to sell prior pet animals rather than euthanize them. The prior owners who may have turned over a pet are normally not aware of this possible outcome for their animal. Some owners have said that they would rather have their animal killed than have it placed in the hands of researchers. Neither federal nor state law prohibits the transfer of previous pet animals to laboratories, it only regulates it.

The political question is whether animals from a local humane society or government-run animal pound should be available for use in science and testing. Some states prohibit the practice, others allow it while a few require the transfer by local shelters.

Just how many animals are transferred? The national report gives total animals used in research as reported by institutions as set out the table below. But, the research institutions do not have to say the source of the animals. The three primary sources are: directly from pounds and shelters, from Class B dealers, or from breeding facilities such as Charles River who raises animals specifically for sale to research facilities. The Humane Society of the U.S. a few years ago reported that there were only 10 class B dealers in the United States that use random source dogs.

The Use of Dogs and Cats

Animals in Research*:

	1990	2004	2007
Dogs	109,992	64,932	72,037
Cats	33,700	23,640	22,689
Primates	47,177	54,998	69,990
Rabbits	399,264	261,573	236,511

* Rats and mice are not reported; estimates for them run into the millions per year.

CHAIN OF COMMERCE FOR DOGS AND CATS

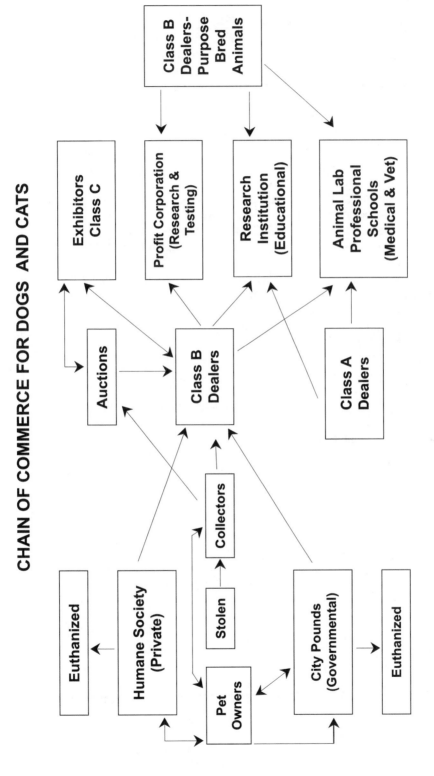

Suppliers → Users ← Suppliers

Problem 10A

Sue and David came into the office of Attorney Jones on May 10 with the following story:

On May 7 they returned home from work between their normal times of 5:30 p.m. and 6:00 p.m. Their golden retriever was not in either the garage or the backyard. The gate had been opened, but only a human could open it. Sue and David searched the neighborhood that evening and the next day, posted notices of a lost dog and told local children about a $100 reward for the dog's return. On the evening of the 8th, a person who lived on the next block stopped by and told them that on the previous day when he had been out jogging, he noticed a van in their driveway and someone carrying a large dog—which might have been a golden retriever—out of the backyard and toward the van. The truck had the name of "something" Kennels on the side—he wasn't sure. He did say it was an early-model blue-panel van with windows in the back but not on the sides.

Sue and David had read an article earlier about the local university beginning a study using retrievers, and they are afraid that someone has stolen their dog and that he will be sold to the University.

If they are right, is there a chance that they can find their dog? How would you go about this?

What are the possible chains of transfer that would result in the dog ending up at the University? Could a dealer sell an animal to another dealer out of state? How does AWA govern this chain?

If the stolen dog was to be used by out-of-state breeders, does the AWA help?

In deciding what to do, you should check out Reg. Sec. 2.128, Inspection for Missing Animals.

Case Study 10A

Baird is licensed under the AWA as a Class B animal dealer and operates the Martin Creek Kennel. Baird buys dogs and cats and, after conditioning, sells them to research institutions. Baird has purchased cats and dogs from 1,156 different individuals.

Baird acquired an old kennel in 1988 and started the business. He invested between $150,000 and $200,000 to upgrade the facility. The facility is inspected approximately four times a year by APHIS inspectors. There is no record of violations prior to those upon which this proceeding is instituted.

In 1993 APHIS set up an investigation task force charged with examining the records of buyers in order to check the persons from whom the dealers were buying dogs. The task force consisted of nine investigators, each of whom was given names of individuals Baird had purchased dogs from.

Of the 1,156 individuals that Baird had purchased dogs from, 23 of those individuals could not be located by the task force investigators. Two other individuals had died, with one dying before Baird had purportedly purchased dogs from him. Eighteen of the individuals traced by the investigators gave statements indicating that they had sold random source dogs, 11 of which signed affidavits that they had sold random source dogs to Baird. Another person located was a "fugitive from justice" and was selling dogs under another name. Two individuals denied selling dogs to Baird. Another individual stated that he admitted to Baird that he had three different driver's licenses. One individual stated that he used the names of relatives when he sold dogs, and that some of the dogs were raised, others were "just dumped," and others had been traded for at dog swaps. This individual also testified that he was told by an investigator that if he obtained a license he would not be penalized for his actions. No investigator reported evidence that any of the dogs had been stolen.

Following the reports of the investigators, Baird changed his procedures for purchasing dogs. He prepared a form that each dog owner is required to complete, requires the seller display his or her driver's license, and requires the seller to sign a statement that they understand that the animals may be sold for research or educational purposes and that they had bred and raised the animals themselves.

Baird's facility was inspected on July 12, 1994. This inspection resulted in the following violations of the AWA: The inspector found a rusty gate, chewed and rotted wood, and poor water drainage.

At the administrative hearing, Baird testified that he corrected these violations by painting the metal, replacing the wood, and filling the mudhole with concrete.

What violations of the AWA have occurred? If you were the Administrative Judge what sanctions would you impose?

See **In re C.C. Baird, d/b/a Martin Creek Kennel**, 57 Agric. Dec. 127 (1998).

Once the animals, whatever the source, arrive at a research facility another, larger, set of issues arise. The AWA clearly has a voice in the welfare of the animals, but that track will not be pursued in this chapter. Besides the brief mention at the end of this chapter, the author has an entire chapter on animals used in science which is available as a .pdf file.

The AWA does not deal with the purchase of pet animals, it does not provide any remedies to dismayed buyers; nor does it deal with animal welfare in the retail store environment, or promises made by sellers. It does deal with those who breed for sale and those who are whole sellers of animals for the consumer market. It is a tool to deal with puppy mills, the conditions under which animals are held and raised. [The issue of exhibitors will be in the next section.]

As the following material gets deeper and deeper into the agency process, keep in mind the Congressional mandate:

> 7 USC §2143 (a)(1) The Secretary shall promulgate standards to govern the humane handling, care, treatment, and transportation of animals by dealers, research facilities, and exhibitors.(2) The standards described in paragraph (1) shall include minimum requirements--
>
> (A) for handling, housing, feeding, watering, sanitation, ventilation, shelter from extremes of weather and temperatures, adequate veterinary care, and separation by species where the Secretary finds necessary for humane handling, care, or treatment of animals; and.

The only substantive mandate to the agency is that regulations must be "humane". But with no other context, what does that mean? (This is the same difficulty as in the New Jersey law mandating humane standards for agricultural animals, Chapter 8). There are no cases that pursue the issue of what constitutes a humane regulation.

Class A & B Dealers

Before reading some of the administrative cases set out here, some background on how the administrative process works will provide a useful context for the cases.

The AWA is a regulatory scheme. Its internal definitions set out who has responsibilities under this Act. The general thrust of the law is to define those categories of people who must be licensed in order to engage in particular activities. The law will then seek to prohibit unqualified individuals from obtaining a license. Additionally, there is an inspection program in place to assure that those who have a license meet the standards of animal care set out in the USDA regulations. Failure to provide care can result in criminal charges, civil fines, and revocation of licenses, making the individual unable to continue to engage in the activity in question. Under this law, individuals within each functional classification have to make themselves known to the USDA by obtaining a license or by registering.

Section 4 of the AWA creates the license requirement with the following language:

> No dealer or exhibitor shall sell or offer to sell or transport or offer for transportation, in commerce, to any research facility or for exhibition or for use as a pet any animal, or buy, sell, offer to buy or sell, transport or offer for transportation, in commerce, to or from another dealer or exhibitor under this chapter any animals, unless and until such dealer or exhibitor shall have obtained a license form the Secretary and such license shall not have been suspended or revoked.

Note that research facilities, the destinations for many animals, are not licensed. Instead, they must register under Section 6 of the AWA. The apparent focus on transportation is because the justification for federal law in this area is that the interstate shipment of animals is part of the problem.

The law defines more sharply the key terms of dealers and exhibitors,

> AWA Sec. 2(f)
>
> The term "dealer" means any person who, in commerce, for compensation or profit, delivers for transportation, or transports, except as a carrier, buys, or sells, or negotiates the purchase or sale of, (1) any dog or other animal whether alive or dead for research, teaching, exhibition, or use as a pet, or (2) any dog for hunting, security, or breeding purposes, except that this term does not include—
>
> (i) a retail pet store except such store which sells any animals to a research facility, an exhibitor, or a dealer; or
>
> (ii) any person who does not sell, or negotiate the purchase or sale of any wild animal, dog, or cat, and who derives no more than $500 gross income from the sale of other animals during any calendar year;

(but see AWA Reg. Sec. 2.1 which has a long list of categories of activities that are not dealers.)

◇◇◇

Administration of the Animal Welfare Act (2000)

by Katherine Zopf

Pursuant to the Animal Welfare Act ("AWA"), the Secretary of the United States Department of Agriculture is charged with the promulgation of regulations necessary for the carrying out of the AWA.

Within this Department, the Animal and Plant Health Inspection Service ("APHIS") conducts investigations of facilities subjected to the regulations promulgated by the Secretary under the AWA. There are two distinct types of investigations conducted by APHIS:

1. The first type of investigation occurs solely as a result of the fact that inspection of both facilities and records is provided for under the regulations. These routine inspections can take place at any time, and APHIS is not required to give advance notice to the owners of a facility that an inspection is scheduled to take place.

2. The second type of inspection occurs as the result of a complaint filed with the USDA or APHIS regarding suspected violations of the regulations promulgated under the AWA (see In re: Marilyn Shepherd, 57 Agric. Dec. 242 (1998). Any time a complaint is filed, APHIS is required to conduct an inspection, at least of the facility.

In the event that violations are found to exist, either with regard to the condition of the facility or of the records required to be maintained by the licensees, inspectors often will allow time for the licensees to correct the violations (i.e., provide a "correct-by" date) at which time a follow-up inspection will automatically be conducted.

When the Agency believes that there is a violation deserving of some level of sanctions, then civil complaints against individuals who violate the law or the regulations are filed within the USDA. The USDA is represented by its own general counsel in subsequent administrative proceedings. Although defendants may be represented by their own counsel during these administrative proceedings, representation by counsel in an administrative disciplinarian proceeding is not guaranteed by the Constitution.

The Administrative law Judge ("ALJ") presides at the presentation of evidence in a formal administrative proceeding. ALJs are appointed by the USDA; however, they are assigned cases by rotation in order to ensure their independence from the prosecutors of the cases. The ALJ must provide a record showing a ruling on each finding and conclusion that is presented at the proceeding. Remedies available to the agency are suspension or revocation of a license as well as civil fines. Criminal charges are available, but seldom used.

If the findings, conclusions, and proposed order of the ALJ are sufficient, the USDA may adopt them without a change.

In the event that the proposed order of the ALJ is challenged, the Judicial Officer ("JO") handles all appeals. The JO can reverse a decision of the ALJ whenever a preponderance of the evidence suggests that the decision of the ALJ was incorrect. However, JOs are generally deferential to the decisions of the ALJ, and thus very often will adopt the initial decision of the ALJ.

The Administrative Procedure Act allows for an individual to seek redress of an adverse agency action in court. However, as a general principle, all administrative processes must be exhausted before an individual may seek judicial review of the deci-

> **News Bits**
>
> In June 2003 it was reported that Michigan State University purchased 39 dogs and cats from Class B dealers, 42 from Class A dealers, and 155 directly from animal shelters during a prior one-year period. *The State News*, June 12, 2003 at p. 1.

sion of the USDA. The decision of the JO would be final agency action for purposes of the APA. Additionally, although courts review the final decisions of the USDA, they are often deferential to the expertise of the agency, and very often will affirm the final decision of the agency.

Avoidance of licensing does not always work.

CASE BY CASE

In re David M. Zimmerman
57 Agric. Dec. 1038 (1998)

Zimmerman operated as a dealer under the AWA from a facility which housed 200 to 300 dogs. Following the voluntary termination of his license, Zimmerman sold 33 dogs for resale for use as pets. Each sale constituted a separate violation of the AWA.

USDA investigators testified that they had obtained records from three different pet stores and a licensed dealer that showed Zimmerman was the source for dogs.

Zimmerman attempted to rebut this evidence with testimony from Mr. Kreider, a pet store owner that relied on Zimmerman as a source of dogs while Zimmerman was licensed under the AWA. Mr. Kreider testified that Zimmerman stopped selling him dogs, that Kreider then bought dogs from Zimmerman's children, and that the appearance of

Zimmerman's name in records of purchases was just a mistake. Kreider changed his story upon cross-examination, which made his testimony less reliable.

Zimmerman also called his son to testify that he had sold the dogs to the pet stores. When asked on cross-examination for the records to prove this, the son could not produce any records. Thus, his evidence was not considered to be reliable.

Zimmerman also testified as a separate defense that he had been told that an individual could sell 24 dogs without being subject to the AWA. The individual who allegedly made these statements testified to the contrary, stating that pursuant to the regulations promulgated pursuant to the AWA, only a person with 3 or less breeding females can sell offspring of those females to the wholesale pet trade without being licensed. The number 24 is used as a guideline because 3 reproducing females, producing an average of 8 puppies per year would produce 24 puppies. Additionally, Zimmerman was told when he voluntarily terminated his license that he was unable to engage in regulated activities without being licensed. Finally, because Zimmerman has always had more than 3 breeding females and sold more than 24 dogs, he was not acting within the parameters of the exception

Zimmerman's violations were deemed to be serious because the failure to obtain a license inhibits the ability of APHIS to enforce the AWA. Zimmerman was assessed a $20,000 civil penalty and was permanently disqualified from obtaining a license under the AWA. Because Zimmerman did not have a license that could be revoked, the appropriate sanction to be imposed against an individual whose license would be revoked is the disqualification from becoming licensed.

Questions & Notes

1. Why would someone voluntarily terminate their license?

2. What is the threshold for dog sales that requires a "class B" AWA license? The definition from the language of the law quoted earlier is vague. The detailed definition is in the regulations. The structure of the regulations is more in the negative (that is, there is a list of activities that are not within the definition).

◇◇

The legal trigger is 7 U.S.C. Sec. 2134:

> **No dealer** or exhibitor **shall sell or offer to sell** or transport or offer for transportation, in commerce, to any research facility or for exhibition or **for use as a pet any animal** ... **unless and until such dealer or exhibitor shall have obtained a license.**

Well, then the critical issue is: who is a dealer? From a hassle and expense prespective it will be best to avoid the status of dealer. AWA Reg. Sec. 2.1 provides a number of excluding categories, including:

(i) *Retail pet stores* which sell nondangerous, pet-type animals, such as dogs, cats, birds, rabbits, hamsters, guinea pigs, gophers, domestic ferrets, chinchilla, rats, and mice, for pets, at retail only: Provided, That, Anyone wholesaling any animals, selling any animals for research or exhibition, or selling any wild, exotic, or nonpet animals retail, must have a license;

(ii) Any person who sells or negotiates the sale or purchase of any animal except wild or exotic animals, dogs, or cats, and who derives *no more than $500 gross income* from the sale of such animals to a research facility, an exhibitor, a dealer, or a pet store during any calendar year and is not otherwise required to obtain a license;

(iii) Any person who maintains a total of *three (3) or fewer breeding female dogs and/or cats* and who sells only the offspring of these dogs or cats, which were born and raised on his or her premises, for pets or exhibition, and is not otherwise required to obtain a license;

(iv) Any person who sells *fewer than 25 dogs and/or cats per year* which were born and raised on his or her premises, for research, teaching, or testing purposes or to any research facility and is not otherwise required to obtain a license. The sale of any dog or cat not born and raised on the premises for research purposes requires a license;

Questions & Notes

1. Are all of the above exemptions justified under the language of the law itself? (Review sec. 2F of the AWA.) It is normal that regulations have more details than the law on which it is based. However, the agency can neither contradict the law or "make up" new requirements. For example, if the regulations had required retail pet stores to obtain a class C license, a court would strike the regulation as being in contradiction with subpart (i) of Section 2F. More difficult to deal with are regulations that do not contradict specific language of the law but that fill in a gray area. For example, the regulation above allows individuals selling less than 25 dogs or cats per year to research facilities to do so without a license. But is this what Congress intended? The only exemption of this nature speaks to a person having sales of less than $500 per year. Has the agency amended the law? Would a court uphold this agency-authorized exemption?

2. Mrs. Abbott has five female poodles. In 1999 these five had a total of 15 puppies, all of whom she placed with friends and neighbors. In 2000 there were 30 puppies, five of which went to friends and 25 of which went to Neighbor Pet Store. In 2001 there were 40 puppies. Can she sell these puppies without obtaining an AWA license?

3. What if Mrs. Abbott wants to sell ten puppies to Big University for a diet study the University is beginning. However, the University has a policy that they only buy from licensed dealers. Can she get a license even if she is not required to have a license?

∞∞∞

The number of licenses:

	2001	2007
Class A	3,573	4,182
Class B	1,166	1,021

Questions & Notes

1. Mr. Bojangles comes into your office asking you about his dog breeding operation. He breeds and sells beagles to Small State University, which is 50 miles away in the same state. He sells about 30 dogs a year ($50 per dog). He also picks up dogs at the local pounds and sells about 30 of those dogs a year ($40 per dog) to the same University. He has heard that he might need a federal license to do this selling, but cannot believe this, as all his activity is local.

   Does the AWA apply to this individual?

   What license might he need? How much will it cost him?

2. In 1999 it was reported by the APHIS that 70,541 dogs were used in research and 25,238 cats. From where do you think all of these animals came? Check the Internet.

   On July 14, 2006, Class B Dealer C.C. Baird and his wife Patsy were sentenced for violations of AWA for supplying random source dogs to institutions without appropriate documentation. This was the first felony conviction obtained for violations of AWA by a Class B dealer. The sentence included several years of supervised probation, six months of home detention, and a $7,500 fine. The no jail time sentence was a result of a deal with the prosecutor for full cooperation with the government. The defendants had previously surrendered 700 acres of land valued at $1.1million and forfeited $200,000 cash. The defendants were the focus of an HBO special "Dealing Dogs," which shows undercover footage of their dog collection and housing operation.

Once it is determined that an individual must have a licence, then the purpose of the AWA comes to the front: are the animals held by these licence holders being kept in humane conditions, as might be defined under the regulations of the USDA?

Regulatory Permits and Inspections

Before you read the following cases it is important to be aware that a regulation can usually be categorized into one of two types: performance or outcome regulations and those that impose engineering or number standards. Consider the following language alternatives for a regulation on the well-being of a dog held in a Class B dealer's kennel.

A. "All dogs shall be in fit and good condition unless under the care of a veterinarian."

B. "All dogs shall be fed and watered daily."

C. "All dogs over 50 pounds shall receive at least two pounds of food a day and have access to a one quart water bowl filled with clean water for at least eight hours a day."

If the goal of the law is to promote the well-being of the dog in the kennel, which language is most likely to accomplish the desired result? The first alternative language states the goal, but does not suggest how to judge whether the goal is satisfied. This is outcome, performance language. It suggests the endpoint desired without saying how to get there. Each owner of a dog kennel could adopt a different program to realize the performance outcome desired.

The language of alternative C reflects an agency decision: that the agency knows what actions should be undertaken to achieve the goal of a well-conditioned dog and therefore they will impose the actions required of the dealer with the presumption that if the engineering, number-based standard is met, the goal of dog well-being will be achieved.

Another context in which to judge the language is effectiveness of enforcement—in the courtroom and by agency inspectors. Inspectors arrive at a facility with a form to fill out that requires the inspector to identify violations of the laws and regulations. He or she will have two hours to inspect a facility with 100 dogs. While inspectors may receive some species-specific training, they may or may not know much about the species present at any one facility. If the regulation is the A alternative, when would the inspector put on the report that there is a violation? What about alternative B or C? Remember that whatever is written on the report may become part of a civil enforcement action and will have to be defended at a later point in time against the blistering cross examination of the licensee's attorney.

From an inspector's perspective, the most defensible violations to write up are when an observed condition violates a specific number, size, or quantity. Either the dog received two pounds of food or the dog did not. It is simple and defendable. The obvious problem is that a violation of the number/engineering standard may or may not relate to the initial concern of the law—is the dog in a good condition? The number standard could be satisfied and yet a particular dog might not be in good condition, or in the alternative, the standard might not be met and yet the dog would be in good condition. There is the risk of both false positives and false negatives. A key issue when looking at the regulations of APHIS under the AWA is what is the risk that the regulations as written and enforced will not accomplish the policy purpose of the law itself. Additionally, there is a practical resource allocation issue—what do you want the inspectors to accomplish with the limited time and resources that they have available to them?

CASE BY CASE

In re Marilyn Shepherd

57 Ag. Dec. 242 (1998) (summary by Katherine Zopf)

Marilyn Shepherd owned and operated a kennel which housed approximately 200 adult breeding dogs and a varying number of puppies. She also owns six dogs as personal pets that are free to roam the area of the kennel. In March 1994 a complaint was received by APHIS that Shepherd was not providing food and water to the dogs. On March 2, 1994, there was an APHIS "complaint-driven" inspection of every pen, dog, and run. The inspector found a few violations which were typical of the operation she was running. All violations were corrected. On a follow-up inspection on April 1, 1994 conducted by a different inspector, the only violation found was that ID tags had not been put on the dogs. This problem had not been corrected by August 30, 1994, and Shepherd was given until September 16, 1994 to correct the violation. Reports from inspections on September 19, 1994, March 27, 1995, May 19, 1995, June 5, 1995, and December 18, 1995 all revealed the typical violations including damage to doghouses from the dogs chewing on them, too many bones in the dogs' pens, and violations regarding the perimeter fence. However, on February 15, 1996 the inspector reported numerous violations, stating that the kennel was in the worst condition he had ever seen it. Despite the poor condition of the kennel, the inspector noted that all of the dogs appeared to be healthy and Shepherd was given until March 15, 1996, to correct the violations. All of the violations were corrected by the inspection on April 17, 1996, except that 3 doghouses needed repair and 2 new violations were found. The inspector was accompanied by Mark Westrich, whose function is to investigate and document the "habitual" AWA violators. His confidential report resulted in the filing of charges against Shepherd for willful violations of the AWA by failing to identify animals and by failing to provide adequate care and housing for the animals.

[After a decision by the Administrative Law Judge, an appeal is taken to the Judicial Officer which in turn resulted the following findings of facts and conclusions of law.]

1. The Judicial Officer (JO) held that an electronic fence used as a primary enclosure is not a violation of 9 C.F.R. § 3.6(a)(1) unless it appears that the fence is unsound or in bad repair. (Reversal of the ALJ).

2. Because windbreaks and rainbreaks are required for outdoor housing facilities pursuant to 9 C.F.R. § 3.4(b)(3), violations existed with regard to polystyrene calf huts used as outdoor facilities that did not have such wind or rainbreaks on them. (Upheld the ALJ ruling).

3. No due process is denied as a result of Shepherd being denied access to the confidential report because discovery is not available in administrative proceedings.

4. Shepherd did not provide adequate veterinary care to an emaciated dog. The fact that it is normal practice to first worm an emaciated dog, which Shepherd did, the fact that Shepherd tried to treat the dog herself does not alleviate her from the obligation to provide adequate vet care (it turned out that the dog was emaciated because of a liver disease, and the dog was put down).

5. Although disease resulting from the remodeling of Shepherd's kennel was only temporary, the failure to remove debris constituted a violation of 9 C.F.R. § 3.1(f).

6. Shepherd is required to be in compliance with the AWA at all times, and should not be afforded one free violation (this pertains to a violation because the lid was off the trash can, and Shepherd argued that the first instance should not constitute a violation).

7. Due process was satisfied because the complaint was adequate notice of the issues in controversy.

8. Shepherd was not being discriminated against by the APHIS inspector. The AWA does not have to be enforced everywhere in order for it to be enforced somewhere.

9. The fact that one individual complained to APHIS, thus requiring the complaint-driven inspections, is not relevant to whether Shepherd in fact violated the AWA.

Because Shepherd corrected the deficiencies and treated her animals in a humane manner, and considering the gravity of the violations (they were all minor in scope), sanctions were a $2,000.00 civil penalty and a 7-day suspension of Shepherd's AWA license.

CASE BY CASE

In re Judie Hansen
57 Agric. Dec. 1072 (1998)

Hansen does business as the Wild Wind Petting Zoo, and has exhibited animals in North Dakota, South Dakota, and Minnesota. She was licensed as a Class C animal exhibitor from 1992 to 1996. In 1996 she changed her license from Class C to Class A dealer.

The complaint against Hansen asserts that she violated the AWA by failing to identify her dogs. Hansen testified that the tags were temporarily removed from the dogs for the purpose of grooming and were removed at night. Although the AWA is applicable both during the day and at night, and there is no exception for grooming, there is an exception for dogs that are not yet weaned. The inspector's report noted that the unidentified dogs were puppies, but there was no note regarding whether they were weaned. Thus, it was found that the USDA did not meet its burden of proving that Hansen failed to identify her dogs.

Third, the complaint alleges that Hansen failed to keep the facilities in good repair so as to keep the dogs from being injured. The inspector noted that there was wire fencing with sharp points that needed to be trimmed. Hansen stated that although the wire did have sharp points, the wire was pushed into the ground and covered with gravel in order to prevent injury to the dogs. It was determined that wire with sharp points must be repaired because they could potentially harm the dogs. Therefore, even though the sharp points were pushed into the ground and covered with gravel, it still constituted a violation of the AWA.

Fourth, the complaint alleges that Hansen did not keep the kennel area free of clutter. The inspector's report notes that there was scrap metal, wood, and other discarded matter around the outside runs. Hansen testified that there was clutter, but that it was around the shop area. The JO determined that there was sufficient evidence to support a violation from the failure to keep the facility free from clutter.

Fifth, the complaint alleges that Hansen failed to keep supplies stored in a manner that they would be safe from spoiling, vermin infestation, and contamination. The inspector's report notes that feed must be kept in containers with lids on them, and that bleach and other toxic substances needed to be kept in the shop area in cabinets with doors. Hansen testified that the bleach had been diluted and that she had, on one occasion, forgotten to keep the feed in proper containers. The JO determined that this constituted a violation of the AWA.

Sixth, the complaint alleges that Hansen violated the AWA by her failure to provide for the frequent collection, removal, and disposal of animal waste and bedding. The inspector's report noted that the soiled newspapers laying in front of the enclosures needed to be placed in a leak-proof container with a tightly-closed lid. Hansen testified that she was in the process of collecting the soiled paper but had put them down in order to answer the phone. She stated that the papers had been placed there for no longer than 5 minutes. With regard to the open pails, Hansen testified that an employee was in the process of cleaning the cages and had stopped working in order to accompany the inspector through the facility. The JO determined that the placing of the newspapers on the ground was not a violation of the AWA because that occurred as a part of cleaning the facility. However, the open pail constituted a violation because the AWA requires pails to be closed at all times.

Seventh, the complaint alleges that Hansen failed to ensure that the walls and floors of the indoor enclosures were impervious to moisture.

Ninth, the complaint alleges that Hansen failed to provide an elevation in an enclosure for kittens that was large enough to hold all of the kittens in the enclosure. Hansen testified that she had taken the kittens from a friend in order to find homes for them and had just placed them in a traveling pen. Additionally, she stated that she was unaware of the requirement for elevations in enclosures. The JO determined that this constituted a violation of the AWA. Regardless of whether an individual knows of the requirements, they are expected to follow them.

Tenth, the complaint alleges that Hansen failed to keep the food receptacles clean and sanitized.

Twelfth, the complaint alleged that Hansen failed to keep the premises clean and free from weeds.

Thirteenth, the complaint alleged that Hansen failed to maintain an effective pest control program.

[There are six more points discussed by the court on the same level of detailed concern about "conditions" but nothing about actual animals being in poor health.

The administrative officials recommended an $8,000.00 civil penalty and a 30-day suspension of Hansen's license. The ALJ recommended a $3,000.00 civil penalty and a 30-day suspension of Hansen's license. The JO modified the recommended sanction, imposing a $4,300.00 civil penalty and a 30-day suspension of Hansen's license.]

Questions & Notes

1. Does the outcome in these two cases provide support for the realization of the policy that Congress adopted with the Animal Welfare Act? Do you detect any arrogance from the agency and its inspectors? What outcomes are being promoted? In the two cases, did the inspector do a good job? Should they get a raise, or be promoted based on the number of violations that

they report? What level of intrusion by the federal government is appropriate for the goal of assuring the well-being of dogs in Class B facilities?

2. For the year 2004 the agency carried out 11,883 inspections at 8,300 facilities with less than 100 inspectors.

◇◇

Section 3

Class "C" Exhibitors

Who are these licensed exhibitors? The obvious ones are the public zoo's, but there are other types as well.

CASE BY CASE

U.S. Dept. of Agriculture
In re Karl Mitchell, and Big Cat Encounters
AWA Docket No. 09-0084 (Aug. 2010)

This is an administrative disciplinary proceeding initiated by a complaint filed by the Administrator of the Animal and Plant Health Inspection Service ("APHIS"), an agency of the United States Department of Agriculture ("USDA"), that alleges Respondents violated the Animal Welfare Act, as amended (7 U.S.C. §§ 2131- 2159; "the Act"), and the Regulations and Standards issued under the Act (9 C.F.R. §§ 1.1-3.142; "Regulations and Standards").

Findings of Fact

1. Respondent Big Cat Encounters is a Nevada, non-profit corporation. Its registered agent is Legal Forms Depot/Lance Kreigh, 1161 South Loop Road A-4, Pahrump, Nevada 89048. Its business address is Post Office Box 1085, Pahrump, Nevada 89048.

2. Respondent Karl Mitchell is an individual whose mailing address is Post Office 1085, Pahrump, Nevada 89041. Respondent Karl Mitchell has always been an officer of Respondent Big Cat Encounters.

3. Respondents jointly operate a moderate-size business that owns exotic animals. The business purports to be a non-profit animal rescue shelter and, for that reason, Respondents contend their operations are exempt from the licensing, handling and inspection requirements of the Act and the Regulations and Standards.

5. On April 17, 2004, February 1, 2008, February 2, 2008 and August 22, 2009, Respondents exhibited one or more tigers to the public for compensation by requiring "donations" from persons who were either photographed with the tigers, or were allowed to pet, touch or otherwise be in close proximity to the tigers that were not separated from the public by barriers. In 2009, Respondent Karl Mitchell was engaged as the trainer of a tiger that he brought to the set of the Paris Hilton reality show where, in June of 2009, it was filmed while being petted by various cast members. These exhibitions took place without sufficient distance and/ or barriers between the tigers and the general viewing public so as to assure the safety of the animals and the public.

6. On May 4, 2004 and March 6, 2008, Respondents denied APHIS inspectors access to inspect the facilities, records and animals at a zoo operated by Respondents at which live animals were kept for public exhibition.

Discussion

A. The Violations

After his APHIS license was revoked [in 2001], Respondent Karl Mitchell continued to operate as an exhibitor. He has done so both as an individual and through Big Cat Encounters, the non-profit corporation he formed in an effort to exempt his activities from governmental regulation. But his activities are not exempt. Just as before, he is a trainer of lions, tigers and other exotic animals that he and the corporation he formed exhibit to the public for compensation.

The meaning of "Exhibitor" is specifically defined in the Act:

> The term "exhibitor" means any person (public or private) exhibiting any animals, which were purchased in commerce or the intended distribution of which affects commerce, or will affect commerce, to the public for compensation, as determined by the Secretary, and such term includes carnivals, circuses, and zoos exhibiting such animals for profit or not;...

7 U.S.C. § 2132 (h)

The Regulations and Standards reiterate this definition:

> Exhibitor means any person (public or private) exhibiting any animals, which were purchased in commerce or the intended distribution of which affects commerce, or will affect commerce, to the public for compensation, as determined by the Secretary. This term includes carnivals, circuses, animal acts, zoos, and educational exhibits, exhibiting such animals whether operated for profit or not....

9 C.F.R. § 1.1

The Regulations and Standards clarify that a lion or tiger is an "exotic animal" that is within the ambit of the Regulations and Standards:

> Exotic animal means any animal not identified in the definition of "animal" provided in this part that is native to a foreign country or of foreign origin or character, is not native to the United States, or was introduced from abroad. This term specifically includes animals such as, but not limited to, lions, tigers, leopards....

9 C.F.R. § 1.1

The term "Zoo" is also defined in the Regulations and Standards:

> Zoo means any park, building, cage, enclosure, or other structure or premise in which a live animal or animals are kept for public exhibition or viewing, regardless of compensation.

9 C.F.R. § 1.1

Exhibitors require valid, current licenses issued by the Secretary of Agriculture (7 U.S.C. §§ 2133, 2134; 9 C.F.R. § 2.1). They are also required to comply with the Regulations and Standards for the handing of animals that have been promulgated by the Secretary of Agriculture (7 U.S.C. §§ 2142, 2143, 2151; 9 C.F.R. § 2.100).Exhibitors must also allow inspection by APHIS inspectors to assure that the provisions of the Act and the Regulations and Standards are being followed (7 U.S.C. §§ 2142, 2143, 2143 (a)(1) and (2), 2146 (a)).

Respondents did not have a license on each of five occasions (April 17, 2004, February 1, 2008, February 2, 2008, a day in June, 2009, and on August 22, 2009) when they exhibited one or more tigers to the public for compensation.

In addition, on each of those occasions, they did not comply with the regulation that applies to the handling of animals when exhibited to the public. Specifically:

> During public exhibition, any animal must be handled so there is minimal risk of harm to the animal and to the public, with sufficient barriers between the animal and the general viewing public so as to assure the safety of the animals and the public.

9 C.F.R. § 2.131 (c)(1)

The care to be taken when handling lions, tigers and other "exotic animals" or "big cats" at public exhibitions has been the subject of a number of decisions issued on behalf of the Secretary of Agriculture. Under those decisions, Respondents did not observe the procedures that the cited regulation requires for the handling of tigers when it exhibited tigers to the public for compensation on April 17, 2004, February 1, 2008,

February 2, 2008, a day in June, 2009, and on August 22, 2009. Witnesses testified and photographs were received in evidence that show, on each of those occasions, although Karl Mitchell held the exhibited tiger and it was tethered, it was not separated by distance and/or a barrier from members of the public. In fact, various persons were permitted to pet or otherwise come in close contact with the exhibited tiger; and, in response to Respondents' invitations, some people had their photographs taken, for a fee, touching or next to the exhibited tiger.

The facts of In re: The International Siberian Tiger Foundation, et al., 2002 WL 234001 (2002), illustrate the dangers of allowing members of the public to come in close proximity to tigers without the presence of physical barriers, even when tigers are declawed, chained, and ostensibly controlled by not one, but by two trainers. Person after person was bitten, with one person requiring 50 stitches. These facts were reviewed against the objectives of the Act and the pertinent regulation (9 C.F.R. § 2.131), and the decision concluded:

> The purpose of the Animal Welfare Act, as it relates to exhibited animals, is to insure that they are provided humane care and treatment (7 U.S.C. § 2131).The Secretary of Agriculture is specifically authorized to promulgate regulations to govern the humane handling of animals by (7 U.S.C. §§ 2143(a), 2151). The Regulations deal almost exclusively with the care and treatment of animals. However, section 2.131 (b)(1) also provides that exhibited animals must be handled in a manner that assures not only their safety but also the safety of the public.

Animals that attack or harm members of the public are at risk of being harmed. The record establishes that effective methods of extricating people from the grip of an animal can cause the animal harm and can cause the animal's death…Even after an animal attacks a person, the animal is at risk of being harmed for revenge or for public safety reasons…. (In the latter respect, a) tiger that attacked a small girl was confiscated by the health department and decapitated to test it for rabies. Thus section 2.131(b)(1) of the Regulations (9 C.F.R. § 2.131 (b)(1)), which requires that, during public exhibition, animals be handled so there is minimal risk of harm to the public, with sufficient distance or barriers between the animals and the general viewing public so as to assure the safety of the public, is directly related to the humane care and treatment of animals and within the authority granted to the Secretary of Agriculture.

Respondents further violated the Act and the Regulations and Standards on the two occasions when they refused to allow APHIS inspectors to inspect their facilities, records and animals at Mr. Mitchell's ranch in Pahrump, Nevada. The brochures circulated by Respondents to the public encouraged them to tour Mr. Mitchell's ranch and have their picture taken with a Bengal tiger for a fee of $150, or for $250, if in addition to the tour and photograph, they chose to attend a lecture. (CX-6). This activity meets the definition of "zoo" set forth in 9 C.F.R. §1.1, supra (In Re:Petersen, 53 Agric. Dec. 80, 84-85 (1994).Therefore, when the APHIS inspectors came to the ranch, Respondents were required to provide them access to the facilities, records and animals, and Respondents violated the Act and the Regulations and Standards when they did not.

B. Cease and Desist Order and Civil Penalties

Respondents are jointly responsible for violating the Act and the Regulations and Standards on each occasion when they were found to have exhibited exotic animals without a license, and when, on each of those occasions, the animals were handled in violation of the requirement of 9 C.F.R. § 2.131 (c)(1) for sufficient distance and barriers between exhibited animals and the general viewing public so as to assure the safety of the animals and the public. Respondents also jointly violated the Act and the Regulations and Standards on the two occasions when they denied APHIS inspectors access to inspect the facilities, records and animals they maintained at Mr. Mitchell's ranch.

In an effort to deter future violations, a cease and desist order is being entered for a third time against Mr. Mitchell that shall also be applicable, for the first time, to Respondent Big Cat Encounters.

Under 7 U.S.C. § 2149(b), those who violate any provision of the Act or the Regulations and Standards may be assessed a civil penalty for each violation. The maximum civil penalty that may be assessed for each violation was modified under the Federal Civil Penalties Inflation Adjustment Act of 1990, as amended (28 U.S.C. § 2461 note) and various implementing regulations issued by the Secretary. Though the Act originally specified a $2,500 maximum, between April 14, 2004 and June 17, 2008 the maximum for each violation was $3,750. In addition, 7 U.S.C. § 2149(b), was itself amended and, effective June 18, 2008, the maximum civil penalty for each violation has been increased to $10,000.

In addition to these violations by both Respondents, Respondent Karl Mitchell violated the two cease and desist orders previously issued against him.

Respondent's violation, continuing to operate without a license, with full knowledge of the licensing requirements, strikes at the heart of the regulatory program. Accordingly, the maximum civil penalty should be imposed for each occasion that Respondents are known to have exhibited animals for compensation while unlicensed. Civil penalties are therefore being assessed against Respondents jointly and severally for their violations of the Act and the Regulations and Standards in the total amount of $50,625.

Lastly, Respondent Karl Mitchell knowingly failed to obey cease and desist orders made by the Secretary of Agriculture under the Act on each of the 12 occasions when he violated the Act and the Regulations and Standards. Under these circumstances the maximum civil penalties should apply. They have been calculated at $1,500 per offense for a total of $18,000, and that amount is being separately assessed against Mr. Mitchell, individually.

Victor W. Palmer, Administrative Law Judge

Questions and Notes

1. What is the source of such exotic animals? Can anyone buy them? (Make sure you are very careful to distinguish possession, sale, transport, buy, offer for sale etc.) Spend five minutes on the internet looking for sources.

2. Why is this responsibility given to the Department of Agriculture? Does it direct them to adopt regulations for public safety?

3. What do you think of the strength of the argument that as a non-profit rescue center they should not be subject to the AWA requirements?

4. In February of 2011 as this chapter was being written the defendant organization's website was fully active with no sign of closing down. Visit *http://bigcatencounters.org/* and consider the nature of the operation. From the website the operation is described as:

   Currently, the ranch has 5 rare tigers both white and tabby hetrozigous species, a liger and ten rescued stray dogs. Visitors can pet the tigers and romp with the baby tigers, who are as playful as kittens. The Ranch also offers a "Swim with the Tiger" program and a unique "Big Cat Educational Program".

5. Is this a non-profit business that should be licensed by the federal government, or should the government accept that individuals can do their own risk assessment as to what to do, or not do, and not have the government interfere by requiring licences?

Pubic Safety

A major concern in the prior case was safety for the public. What is the legal basis for this focus? The AWA has no provision or sentence which directs the agency to protect the public. The only possible hook is the phrase "humane conditions" being stretched to include risk to the animal if the public is too close. The regulation 9 C.F.R. § 2.131 states:

> (c)(1) During public exhibition, any animal must be handled so there is minimal risk of harm to the animal and to the public, with sufficient distance and/or barriers between the animal and the general viewing public so as to assure the safety of animals and the public.

But what does this mean: glass walls, or a six foot high chain length fences twenty feet away from the cage? How is an inspector to check if the inspection box "in compliance" or "not in compliance"? Remember the inspectors have to deal with all dealers, exhibitors and research facilities; they are not zoo architects. With this much uncertainty the problem of arbitrary, or vindictive enforcement arises.

This is a problem recently pointed out by the Inspector General of the Dept. of Agriculture in the report *Controls over APHIS Licensing of Animal Exhibitors*, Audit Report 33601-10-Ch June 2010:

> Finally, due to factors including a lack of periodic onsite supervision, we noted several instances in which APHIS Animal Care inspectors either failed to identify safety-related deficiencies during inspections, or failed to document the conditions and require corrective actions. As a result, we found a lack of consistency in the safety determinations made by APHIS Animal Care inspectors from one facility to another, and in some cases between different Animal Care inspectors at a single facility. In addition, at two facilities we visited, we identified potentially dangerous situations which, at other similar facilities, had allowed dangerous animals to escape their enclosures. Without clear and consistent standards to follow and a process that ensures that potentially dangerous conditions are identified and remedied, APHIS cannot adequately ensure the safety of the animals, or of the public who visits the various zoos, circuses, and other exhibitors who operate under an APHIS license. (At p. 16.)

What might be done?

CASE BY CASE

U.S. Dept of Agriculture
In re Great Cats of Indiana, Inc.
AWA Docket No. 07-0183 (2010)

DECISION AND ORDER

This proceeding was instituted under the Animal Welfare Act, as amended (7 U.S.C. § 2131 et seq.)(the "Act"), by a complaint filed by the Administrator, Animal and Plant Health Inspection Service, United States Department of Agriculture, and subsequently amended, alleging that the respondents willfully violated the regulations and standards issued pursuant to the Act (9 C.F.R § 1.1 et seq.).

The hearing of this matter was scheduled to commence on January 4, 2010, by notice filed April 29, 2009, following a teleconference held by me on that date. Respondents were represented by respondent Robert B. Craig. On December 15, 2009, I filed a Hearing Room Designation stating that the hearing would be held in Lafayette, Indiana. On January 4, 2010, I presided over an oral hearing in this matter in Lafayette, Indiana. Respondents failed to appear at the hearing without good cause.

FINDINGS OF FACT

1. Respondent Great Cats of Indiana, Inc. ("GCI"), is an Indiana corporation (number 2001112600247, incorporated November 21, 2001) whose address is 10471 East Highway 24, Idaville, Indiana 47950. At all times mentioned herein, respondent GCI operated as an exhibitor as that term is defined in the Act. Respondent GCI has never held an Animal Welfare Act license.

2. Respondent Laurob, LLC ("Laurob") is an Indiana limited liability company. Respondent Laurob operated as an exhibitor as that term is defined in the Act, and since February 24, 2004, has held Animal Welfare Act license 32-C-0186, issued to "LAUROB,LLC, DBA: GREAT CATS OF INDIANA." In its initial license application submitted in July 2003, Laurob identified itself as a limited liability company doing business as "Great Cats of Indiana." Its 2005 through 2008 license renewal forms represent that it is a corporation. In its application, Laurob identified the nature of its business as both a "zoo" and a "broker."

5. Respondents Craig and Proper were the principals of Cougar Valley Farms, Inc., an Indiana corporation that validly held Animal Welfare Act license 32-B-0136, from its incorporation until its dissolution by the Indiana Secretary of State on December 8, 2001. Although a defunct corporation is not a "person," as defined in the Act and the Regulations, and therefore cannot legitimately hold a license, for almost two years, between December 8, 2001, through September 19, 2003, respondents Craig and Proper continued to operate as dealers under the name "Cougar Valley Farms, Inc.," and to use (and renew) the license that APHIS had issued to Cougar Valley Farms, Inc., as their own for their own purposes.

6. Respondents operate a moderately-large business, and have regularly had custody and control of approximately 30 to 50 animals, including canids, felids and bears. The gravity of the violations in this case is great. They include repeated instances in which respondents exhibited animals without adhering to the handling Regulations, failed to provide minimally-adequate veterinary care to animals that were suffering, and failed to provide minimally-adequate housing and husbandry to animals. Respondents have not shown good faith. They have continually failed to comply with the Regulations and Standards, after having been repeatedly advised of deficiencies, and on August 30, 2004, APHIS issued a notice of warning to Respondent Laurob. Respondents Craig and Proper operated for two years ostensibly using a dealer's license issued

to a defunct corporation (Cougar Valley Farms, Inc.). On November 1, 2006, respondent Craig misrepresented to inspectors that on October 25-26, 2006, he sought veterinary care from two veterinarians for a jaguar in distress, when both veterinarians confirmed to APHIS that respondent Craig had never so communicated with them.

8. On January 16, 2008, respondents GCI, Laurob, Craig and Proper failed to allow APHIS officials to enter their place of business, during normal business hours, to conduct an inspection of respondents' facility, animals and records.

9. On September 19, 2003, respondents Craig and Proper failed to employ an attending veterinarian under formal arrangements, as required, and specifically, failed to employ either a fulltime attending veterinarian, or a part-time veterinarian under formal arrangements that include a written program of veterinary care and regularly-scheduled visits to the premises.

11. On September 15 and September 26, 2005, respondents GCI, Laurob, Craig and Proper failed to establish and maintain a program of adequate veterinary care that included the availability of appropriate equipment and services and the use of appropriate methods to treat injuries, and failed to provide adequate veterinary medical treatment to

(i) two emaciated juvenile tigers with brittle coats,

(ii) a cougar (Buddy Boy) with unhealed wounds on his right front paw that occurred months before, and

(iii) wolves in poor condition with bloody diarrhea.

12. On November 30, 2005, respondents GCI, Laurob, Craig and Proper failed to establish and maintain a program of adequate veterinary care that included the availability of appropriate equipment and services and the use of appropriate methods to treat injuries, and failed to provide adequate veterinary medical treatment to

(i) three bears with loose stools,

(ii) three juvenile tigers,

(iii) wolves, and

(iv) a cougar (Buddy Boy) with unhealed wounds on his right front paw from an amputation that occurred months before, or to following the bandaging and surgical debridement prescription.

13. On November 30, 2005, and February 28, July 12 and November 1, 2006, respondents

GCI, Laurob, Craig and Proper failed to establish and maintain a program of adequate veterinary care that included the availability of appropriate equipment and services, and housed juvenile tigers in enclosures that were too small for them, and would not accommodate their rapid growth.

15. On February 28, 2006, respondents GCI, Laurob, Craig and Proper failed to establish and maintain a program of adequate veterinary care that included the availability of appropriate equipment and services and the use of appropriate methods to treat injuries, and failed to provide adequate veterinary medical treatment to:

(i) animals recommended for worming with fenbendazole,

(ii) animals needing testing for heartworm (dirofilaria immitis) and hookworm (ancylostoma),

(iii) a lion (Mufasa) with a dental abscess,

(iv) a cougar (Buddy Boy) with unhealed wounds on his right front paw from an amputation that occurred months before, and

(v) animals in need of fecal exams for the treatment of parasites.

16. On July 12, 2006, respondents GCI, Laurob, Craig and Proper failed to establish and maintain a program of adequate veterinary care that included the availability of appropriate equipment and services and the use of appropriate methods to treat injuries, and failed to provide adequate veterinary medical treatment to

(i) a lion (Mufasa) with a dental abscess,

(ii) thin cougars,

(iii) a cougar (Buddy Boy) whose wounds were treated not by a veterinarian but by respondent Craig, and

(iv) animals in need of fecal exams for the treatment of parasites.

17. – 25. [The omitted sections contain equal facts of the same nature as above for different dates.]

26. On June 14, 2004, APHIS inspectors determined that on June 14, 2003, respondents GCI, Laurob, Craig and Proper failed to handle animals during public exhibition so there was minimal risk of harm to the animals and to the public, with sufficient distance and/or barriers between the animals and the general viewing public so as to assure the safety of animals and the public, and specifically, respondents exhibited a bear (Trouble) without sufficient distance and/or barriers to prevent the public from approaching and having direct contact with the bear, and a customer on a tour of the facility put her hand into the bear's cage, whereupon the bear bit off part of the customer's left index finger.

27. – [This paragraph contains 28 individual charges of failure to provide care, for example: inadequate housing, failure to provide for the removal and disposal of food and animal waste in animal enclosures, and excessive maggots on the ground of the pathway outside the lion and tiger enclosures.]

CONCLUSIONS OF LAW

2. On January 16, 2008, respondents GCI, Laurob, Craig and Proper failed to allow APHIS officials to enter their place of business, during normal business hours, to conduct an inspection of respondents' facility, animals and records, in willful violation of section 2.126 of the Regulations. 9 C.F.R. § 2.126(a)(1).

3. On September 19, 2003 [and a long list of dates], respondents Craig and Proper failed to employ an attending veterinarian under formal arrangements, as required, and specifically, failed to employ either a full-time attending veterinarian, or a part-time veterinarian under formal arrangements that include a written program of veterinary care and reg-

ularly-scheduled visits to the premises, in willful violation of the Regulations. 9 C.F.R. § 2.40(a)(1).

ORDER

1. Respondents, their agents and employees, successors and assigns, directly or through any corporate or other device, shall cease and desist from violating the Act and the regulations and standards issued there under.

2. Animal Welfare Act license 32-C-0186 and Animal Welfare Act license 32-B-0136 are hereby revoked. The provisions of this order shall become effective immediately. Copies of this decision shall be served upon the parties.

Done at Lafayette, Indiana this __4__ day of January, 2010

Jill S., Administrative Law Judge US Dept. of Agriculture

Questions & Notes

1. Why was this allowed to go on for years?

2. Do you think these conditions violated state anti-cruelty laws?

3. Note that no civil fines were awarded. Is this sufficient penalty for the acts committed?

4. Why is this responsibility under the Department of Agriculture? What do they know about lions and tigers and bears?

5. What do you think of the arrogance of the defendants to not even show up for the hearing? Perhaps they don't care and intend to ignore the agency, as they have for years without any consequence. The defendant's web site is active as of the publication of this book, see, *http://greatcatsofindiana.org*. It is noted on their web site that they no longer can have visitors, but they are not closing. If they do not have a federal licence, what new issues arise? Are the cats and other animals better off now that the owners licence has been revoked?

6. Often people who are collectors do not really have the resources to keep and feed large animals such as bears, tigers, or chimpanzees but have a deep desire to keep the animals. To make it happen they may seek to use/exhibit the animals or to breed the animals to raise money to help pay for the cost of keeping such animals. But, they never quite get enough resources to provide the facilities that will be seen at accredited zoos. What do you think is the quality of life for these "exhibited" animals?

Chimpanzee Dealer Fined $1,000

IPPL News, Vol. 28 No. 2 (Aug 2001) p. 26 (International Primate Protection League)

David Sabo, a chimpanzee breeder/exhibitor doing business as the "New York Primate Center," Amenia, New York, USA, recently agreed to pay a fine of $1,000 to the United States Department of Agriculture (USDA) for keeping chimpanzees and other primates in sub-standard conditions.

The fine was to be $4,000, but USDA allowed Sabo to keep $3,000, which he is supposed to spend on improvements to his facilities.

IPPL first heard of David Sabo when, on 19 December 1985, the Associated Press wire service told the story of how an exploding kerosene heater set fire to a shed used for animal housing, causing the deaths of five chimpanzees by smoke inhalation, with other chimps dying later and some animals requiring reconstructive surgery (reported in the April 1985 issue of IPPL News).

In the "Consent Decision and Order" signed by Sabo on 25 April 2001, he agreed to cease and desist from,

> *failing to provide sufficient space for animals in primary enclosures,*
>
> *failing to maintain programs of disease control and prevention and adequate veterinary care,*
>
> *failing to store supplies of food and bedding so as to adequately protect them against contamination,*
>
> *failure to keep the premises clean and in good repair and free of accumulations of trash, junk, waste and discarded matter,*
>
> *failure to establish and maintain an effective program for the control of pests,*
>
> *failing to utilize a sufficient number of trained employees,*
>
> *failing to maintain records of the acquisition, disposition, description, and identification of animals, as required.*

◇◇

Possessors of Exotic Animals

Under the AWA, the federal government seeks to intervene into private activities with exotic animals (mammals) only if they become exhibitors or commercial breeders of the animals. The law does not deal with private pets, regardless of the animal involved. Possession and ownership are issues for the state and local government. A number of states have passed statutes which seek to limit the ownership of animal. For example, Illinois has adopted a law prohibiting the keeping of dangerous animals such as big cats and bears:

> § 1. Dangerous animals and primates; prohibitions.
>
> (a) No person shall have a right of property in, keep, harbor, care for, act as custodian of or maintain in his possession any dangerous animal or primate except at a properly maintained zoological park, **federally licensed exhibit**, circus, college or university, scientific or educational institution, research laboratory, veterinary hospital, hound running area, or animal refuge in an escape-proof enclosure.

Notice the state's deference to the federal government's exhibitor licence. This creates a large incentive for people with small private collections. So an individual with a exotic or dangerous mammal simply applies for an exhibitors permits saying that the animals will be shown to the public. Once the permit is obtained, they may or may not ever show it to the public. They can get renewals of the permit without ever showing that they are in fact exhibitors. This was made very clear in the 2010 Inspector Generals report:

> A second licensee stated that she no longer advertised her cougar exhibit, and that no records were kept of instances where she had exhibited her cougars. She stated that her "boyfriend sometimes brings people to the facility to show them the animals," and that this was how she met APHIS' requirements to be a USDA licensed exhibitor. Based on her statements, we concluded that her activities were those of a pet owner, not an exhibitor.

> A third licensee provided scraps of paper—without specific dates—that listed the names of several people who had visited her property over the past 2 years (2007-2008). She explained that all but one of these visitors were either co-workers, friends, relatives, or neighbors. She added that she considered her bobcat and other animals as her pets, and that she treated them in that manner. As a result, we considered her evidence of exhibition to be very questionable.

> The other two licensees were unable to provide proof of exhibition, with one licensee stating that he obtained his bears so his son could have a pet.

U.S. Department of Agriculture, Office of Inspector General, Controls Over APHIS Licensing of Animal Exhibitors, Audit Report 33601-10-Ch June 2010, p. 15.

Just who should be allowed to keep dangerous animals and under what conditions?

Section 4

Enforcement

USDA Office of Inspector General

"Audit Report: APHIS Animal Care Program

Inspection and Enforcement Activities"

Report No. 33002-3-SF, September 2005

Available at *www.usda.gov/oig/webdocs/33002-03-SF.pdf*

[From Executive Summary]

We found that most AC [animal care] employees are highly committed to enforcing the AWA through their inspections and are making significant efforts to educate research facilities and others on the humane handling of regulated animals. However, we identified several ways in which AC should improve its inspection and enforcement practices to ensure that animals receive humane care and treatment and that public safety is not compromised.

> • *Due to a lack of clear National guidance, AC's Eastern Region is not aggressively pursuing enforcement actions against violators of the AWA.*

We found that regional management significantly reduced its referrals of suspected violators to IES from an average of 209 cases in fiscal years (FYs) 2002-2003 to 82 cases in FY 2004. During this same period, regional management declined to take action against 126 of 475 violators that had been referred to IES. In contrast, the Western Region declined action against 18 of 439 violators.

We found cases where the Eastern Region declined to take enforcement action against violators who compromised public safety or animal health. For example, one AC inspector requested an investigation of a licensee whose primate had severely bitten a 4-year-old boy on the head and face. The wounds required over 100 stitches. Although this licensee had a history of past violations, IES has no record of a referral from AC. In another case, the Eastern Region did not take enforcement action when an unlicensed exhibitor's monkey bit two pre-school children on separate occasions. The exhibitor failed to provide a sufficient public barrier and failed to handle the animal to ensure minimal risk to the public.

As a result, the two regions are inconsistent in their treatment of violators; the percentage of repeat violators (those with 3 or more consecutive years with violations) is twice as high in the Eastern Region than in the Western Region. Eastern Region inspectors believe the lack of enforcement action undermines their credibility and authority to enforce the AWA.

- *Discounted stipulated fines assessed against violators of the AWA are usually minimal.*

Under current APHIS policy, AC offers a 75-percent discount on stipulated fines as an incentive for violators to settle out of court to avoid attorney and court costs. In addition to giving the discount, we found that APHIS offered other concessions to violators, lowering the actual amount paid to a fraction of the original assessment. An IES official told us that as a result, violators consider the monetary stipulation as a normal cost of conducting business rather than a deterrent for violating the law.

- *Some VMOs did not verify the number of animals used in medical research or adequately review the facilities' protocols and other records.*

We found that 13 of 16 research facilities we visited misreported the number of animals used in research. In reviewing the protocols, some Veterinary Medical Officers (VMOs) did not ensure that the facilities provided them with a complete universe of protocols from which to select their sample. These VMOs told us that the selection process was based on "good faith" and that they relied on the facilities to provide them with accurate records. In addition, a VMO did not review readily available disposition records that disclosed unexpected animal deaths at a research facility.

- *AC's Licensing and Registration Information System (LARIS) does not effectively track violations and prioritize inspection activities.*

The LARIS database records AC inspections and archives violation histories for all breeders, exhibitors, research facilities, and others. We determined that the system generates unreliable and inaccurate information, limiting its usefulness to AC inspectors and supervisors.

- *FMD and IES did not follow the law and internal control procedures in their processing and collection of penalties.*

APHIS Financial Management Division (FMD) did not transfer 81 of 121 delinquent AC receivables totaling $398,354 to the U.S. Department of Treasury for collection as required by the Debt Collection Improvement Act of 1996 (see exhibit A). In addition, IES did not comply with APHIS internal cash controls to secure the collection of fines.

Questions & Notes

1. Historically it has been the attitude of the agency to "work with" facilities rather than go for strict, immediate enforcement of the regulations and laws. What are the pros and cons of such an approach?

2. Another aspect of the national enforcement program is the number of inspectors available to do the job. How many do you think would be necessary to cover the country? One way that Congress can kill the effectiveness of a regulatory program is to reduce funding or even not increase funding over a decade or so. During the last half of the 1990s the budget was flat at just over $9 million for the Animal Welfare Program. By 2007 the budget was $17 million. But even so, there are only 90+ inspectors for the entire U.S. who carried out 16,487 inspections in 2007. What level of funding would be required if enforcement was made a national priority?

3. In consideration of all the above, how should the animal care regulations be written and enforced?

◇◇

Section 5

Animals Used by Science

Another primary focus of the AWA is to regulate the use of some of the millions of animals used in scientific research. This is a very complex issue with considerable detailed regulations and a requirement that the nature of science be considered in order to understand why animals are used. This is a topic by itself and is otherwise available for class use. The following just sets out how the law defines the issue at the highest level.

Section 13 of the AWA contains the humane care requirements. The first subsection applies generally to dealers, exhibitors, and research facilities. The next subsection, (a)(3) is specifically focused on animals in research (the structure of the law requires the USDA to adopt regulation for):

(3) In addition to the requirements under paragraph (2), the standards described in paragraph (1) shall, with respect to animals in research facilities, include requirements —

(A) for animal care, treatment, and practices in experimental procedures to ensure that animal pain and distress are minimized, including adequate veterinary care with the appropriate use of anesthetic, analgesic, tranquilizing drugs, or euthanasia;

(B) that the principal investigator considers alternatives to any procedure likely to produce pain to or distress in an experimental animal;

Note the key phrase "in experimental procedures." This language from the 1985 amendments represents the first time that Congress directly stated its intent to govern by regulation certain actions that might occur during a scientific experiment. Congress has chosen to concern itself first with the housing of animals before and after experiments, and second, to a limited degree, during experiments. But, leaving the decision of what issues should be researched to the scientific community.

Considering the public policy of all these issues also requires some consideration of what is pain; a difficult topic in and of itself. The reader should consider this an advanced topic in animal law.

CHAPTER 11

Animal Rights — The Jurisprudence

Section 1

Philosophy and Religion — Moral Perspectives

Where does the discussion start? No human is urging the adoption of legal rights for automobiles, but a number of humans are urging the adoption of legal rights for animals. How are animals and automobiles the same? How are they different?

The overarching issue is this: within our society, what should be the nature of our relationship with the nonhuman animals? What are the possibilities? On the list of possible answers will, without doubt, be the suggestion that humans should "use animals for X." Therefore, a threshold question to ponder is whether it is morally correct to use animals for human benefit under any circumstance. Or, to approach it from the other direction, are there any uses of animals that ought to be prohibited? Separate the reality of what humans presently do with animals—the "is"—from the moral question of what we "ought" to be able to do with animals. Once the question of the nature of the relationship is decided on a personal basis, then the even more difficult question must be faced of what should be done with the law. The transition from discussion in the realm of philosophy and religion into that of law will not be an easy one.

> ### A Focusing Question
>
> Must animals be of moral concern before they can be of legal concern? What might make them a moral concern?

Law is built upon the moral beliefs of the members of a society. Before we can talk about the legal position of animals, there must first be a consideration of the moral status of animals. The following materials are offered to provide a context for that discussion.

Religion

1. The Bible, Genesis 1:20-31

And God said, "Let the water teem with living creatures, and let birds fly above the earth across the expanse of the sky." So God created the great creatures of the sea and every living and moving thing with which the water teems, according to their kinds, and every winged bird according to its kind. And God saw that it was good. And God blessed them and said, "Be fruitful and increase in number and fill the waters in the seas, and let the birds increase on the earth." And there was evening and there was morning—the fifth day.

And God said, "Let the land produce living creatures according to their kinds: livestock, creatures that move along the ground, and wild animals, each according to its kind." And it was so. God made the wild animals according to their kinds, the livestock according to their kinds, and all the creatures that move along the ground according to their kinds. And God saw that it was good.

Then God said, "Let us make man in our image, in our likeness, and let them rule over the fish of the sea and the birds of the air, over the livestock, over all the earth, and over all the creatures that move along the ground."

So God created man in his own image, in the image of God he created him; male and female he created them.

God blessed them and said to them, "Be fruitful and increase in number; fill the earth and subdue it. Rule over the fish of the sea and the birds of the air and over every living creature that moves on the ground."

Then God said, "I give you every seed-bearing plant on the face of the whole earth and every tree that has fruit with seed in it. They will be yours for food. And to all the beasts of the earth and all the birds of the air and all the creatures that move on the ground—everything that has the breath of life in it—I give every green plant for food." And it was so.

And God saw all that he had made, and it was very good. And there was evening, and there was morning—the sixth day.

Questions & Notes

1. Although the above suggests a basis for the relationship between humans and animals, the Bible also suggests obligations toward the animals used by humans. How would you describe this duty? To what degree do you think that the laws of the United States reflect this view of animals?

2. Are you aware of any other religious views of animals? Consider:

    > Many of the religions that arose in the East have a strong respect for all living creatures. Hinduism is a way of life that holds a core belief in the unity of all creation. As with some of the Greek philosophers, one of the tenets of Hinduism is the belief in the transmigration of souls. Animals that are kept as pets are "to be cared for particularly well by Hindus."

    > Under Buddhist teachings, a larger unified life force contains all life forms, and all life forms are thereby interrelated. By doing harm to any part of this unified life force, persons not only harm themselves, but all life. Under Buddhism, animals, as well as humans, have the potential for attaining enlightenment.

    > The Koran (Qur'an) teaches the followers of Islam "that the bond between man and nature is inseparable." Animals, as well as natural resources, are always to be treated with reverence and respect, and animals have traditionally been treated with compassion. Notwithstanding the

Think About It — Who Has the Rights?

The development of civilizations and legal systems over the centuries suggests an expanding consideration of who should be rights holders, both in the realm of philosophy and in law. Consider the following board game:

Group of Beings	No Moral Concern	Moral Concern (Religious or Philosophical)	Legal Concern	Legal Rights
Humans Adult Males ○ Adult Females ○ Children ○ Foreigners ○	⇨ ⇨	⇨ ⇨	⇨ ⇨	○
Beings Dolphins ○ Chimpanzees ○ Dogs & Cats ○ Chickens ○ Snakes ○ Redwood Trees ○				
Nonbeings Computers ○ Cars ○ Family Pictures ○				

The winners of this game are those who make it to the far right side of the board. A key issue of the game is the degree to which winners will help or hinder other groups from reaching the far right. It is a game that has been playing out since at least the time of the ancient Greeks. Not all movement has been to the right; sometimes there are reversals. Where are the pieces for each group presently located? In this game the rules are not provided; each player must discover the rules that promote the movement of the groups across the board. This issue is a primary focus of this chapter. By the end of this topic you will have a deeper understanding of what rules might exist to move groups over, and you will want to consider where you think the groups ought to be in the future.

teachings regarding the benevolent treatment of animals, is it acceptable to kill animals for food so long as the slaughter is done as humanely as possible?

Rebecca J. Huss, *Valuing Man's and Woman's Best Friend: The Moral and Legal Status of Companion Animals*, 86 Marq. L. Rev. 47 (2002). Also see Tina S. Boradiansky, *Conflicting Values: The Religious Killing of Federally Protected Wildlife*, 30 Nat. Resouces Jour. 709 (1990). [Both are available at *www.animallaw.info*.]

◇◇

Philosophy

The reader may wish to review some of the material in the Introduction, particularly the exchange between Descartes and Voltaire in Chapter 1 and the heading "New Issues Edging into the Property Arena" in Chapter 2. The following from Jeremy Bentham represents one of the first articulations of a philosopher showing concern for animals and basis for that concern.

A Utilitarian View

by Jeremy Bentham, *The Principles of Morals and Legislation*, Chapter XVII Section 1 (1789)

IV. What other agents then are there, which, at the same time that they are under the influence of man's direction, are susceptible of happiness? There are of two sorts: (1) Other human beings who are styled persons. (2) Other animals, which, on account of their interests having been neglected by the insensibility of the ancient jurists, stand degraded into the class of *things*.

Under the Hindu and Mahometan religions, the interests of the rest of the animal creation seem to have met with some attention. Why have they not, universally, with as much as those of human creatures, allowance made for the difference in point of sensibility? Because the laws that are have been the work of mutual fear; a sentiment which the less rational animals have not had the same means as man has of turning to account. Why *ought* they not? No reason can be given. If the being eaten were all, there is very good reason why we should be suffered to eat such of them as we like to eat: we are the better for it, and they are never the worse. They have none of those long-protracted anticipations of future misery which we have. The death they suffer in our hands commonly is, and always may be, a speedier, and by that means a less painful one, than that which would await them in the inevitable course of nature. If the being killed were all, there is very good reason why we should be suffered to kill such as molest us: we should be the worse for their living, and they are never the worse for being dead. But is there any reason why we should be suffered to torment them? Not any that I can see. Are there any why we should *not* be suffered to torment them? Yes, several. The day has been, I grieve to say in many places it is not yet past, in which the greater part of the species, under the denomination of slaves, have been treated by the law exactly upon the same footing as, in England for example, the inferior races of animals are still. The day may come, when the rest of the animal creation may acquire those rights which never could have been withholden from them but by the hand of tyranny. The French have already discovered that the blackness of the skin is no reason why a human being should be abandoned without redress to the caprice of a tormentor. It *may come* one day to be recognized, that the number of the legs, the villosity of the skin, or the termination of the *os sacrum*, are reasons equally insufficient for abandoning a sensitive being to the same fate. What else is it that should trace the insuperable line? Is it the faculty of reason, or, perhaps, the faculty of discourse? But a full-grown horse or dog is beyond comparison a more rational, as well as a more conversable animal, than an infant of a day, or a week, or even a month, old. But suppose the case were otherwise, what would it avail? The question is not, Can they *reason*? nor, Can they *talk*? but, Can they *suffer*?

Questions & Notes

1. Do you agree that suffering is a basis for moral status? Define "suffer." Is this the same as the capacity to feel pain? Which animals have the capacity to suffer?

2. Does it make a difference if an individual's concern arises out of religious beliefs or philosophical reflection? How do you think the average person develops their animal perspective?

◇◇

The next two articles are a blend of philosophy and jurisprudence. The concept of "person" is important in both realms, as it denotes those who are deserving of consideration.

Dolphins and the Question of Personhood

by Denise L. Herzing and Thomas I White, *Ethics & Animals* 9/98 p. 64 (entire issue is dedicated to the topic of Nonhuman Personhood)

Although philosophers debate the appropriate criteria for personhood, there is a rough consensus that a person is a being with a particular kind of sophisticated consciousness or inner world. Persons are aware of the world of which they are a part, and *they are aware* of their experiences. In particular, persons are aware of the fact that they are aware, that is, they have some sort of self-awareness and reflective consciousness. And the presence of such a sophisticated consciousness is evident in the actions of such beings.

If we translate this general idea into a more specific list of criteria, we arrive at something like the following:

1. A person is alive.
2. A person is aware.
3. A person feels positive and negative sensations.
4. A person has emotions.
5. A person has a sense of self.
6. A person controls its own behavior.
7. A person recognizes other persons.
8. A person has a variety of sophisticated cognitive abilities.

Conclusion

What, then, can we conclude from this admittedly brief survey? How well do dolphins measure up against a fairly traditional set of criteria for personhood? It should be clear, as suggested at the outset of this paper, that dolphins actually do quite well — even without taking into account the distinctive features that emerge from the fact that they are aquatic mammals. They appear to be self-aware beings with personalities and emotions; they are the authors of their own actions; they have significant intellectual capabilities; and their behavior towards humans suggests that they recognize other beings who share their cognitive and affective abilities. In this respect dolphins measure up well against a fairly traditional set of criteria for personhood. But without a more unbiased and holistic view on intelligence, its emergence and criteria, we can never fairly assess another species' use of the brain and mind. Such discussion tends to be left only for human-like relatives, based on our knowledge of one direction in evolution, that of land-based and human intelligence. Nonetheless, even in light of this concern, it does seem that dolphins should be recognized as members of the community of equals.

Questions & Notes

1. Is the presence of self-awareness a better basis for moral consideration than the capacity to suffer? Does this suggest young humans are not moral persons?

2. Is there any fact pattern in which you would award moral concern for the well-being of a worm? Why or why not? Is it morally acceptable to intentionally kill a worm in order to catch a fish? Should the law deal with that concern?

3. One book released in 2002 suggested that mercy should be the basis for our relationship with animals.

Matthew Scully, *Dominion: The Power of Man, the Suffering of Animals, and the Call to Mercy:*

> We are called to treat them with kindness, not because they have rights or power or some claim to equality, but in a sense because they don't; because they all stand unequal and powerless before us. Animals are so easily overlooked, their interests so easily brushed aside. Whenever we humans enter the world, from our farms, to the local animal shelter to the African savanna, we enter as lords of the earth bearing strange powers of terror and mercy alike.

Another book, by Steven Wise, *Drawing the Line* (2002), suggests that a particular set of animals should receive the attention of the legal community — those possessing practical autonomy. And, "a being has practical autonomy and is entitled to personhood and basic liberty rights if she:

1. can desire;

2. can intentionally try to fulfill her desires; and

3. possesses a sense of self-sufficiency to allow her to understand, even dimly, that it is she who wants something and it is she who is trying to get it."

Do you think this is useful? How broad would the circle of inclusion be using Wise's focus of concern?

4. Does there have to be agreement about why animals should be considered by the legal system? See Thomas G. Kelch, *The Role of the Rational and the Emotive in a Theory of Animal Rights*, 27 B.C. Envtl. Aff. L. Rev. 1, 2-3 (1999) (concluding that there is no single principle on which to base animal rights and that compassion has been neglected as a basis for rights theory); Thomas G. Kelch, *Toward a Non-Property Status for Animals*, 6 N.Y.U. Envtl. L.J. 531, 582 (1998) (arguing that animal rights should be teleologically based, rather than based on special characteristics such as sensibility and identity over time, in order to protect a broader range of creatures).

A Focusing Question

Is it morally wrong for humans to bring into existence nonhuman animals solely for human benefit?

A Dialogue on Animal Rights

by Richard A. Posner and Peter Singer. Posted on *www.slate.com* in June 2001. (These are only the introductions to what was an exchange of six different letters.)

Dear Judge Posner:

I'm not a lawyer, let alone a judge, but I've noticed increasing interest in legal circles in the topic of the legal status of animals. This seems to have been triggered in part by the efforts of the Great Ape Project, by the publication of Steven Wise's *Rattling the Cage,* and by the fact several law schools, including Harvard, are now teaching courses on law and animals. You reviewed *Rattling the Cage* in the *Yale Law Journal,* and while you were critical of Wise's argument that the law should recognize chimpanzees and other great apes as legal persons, your tone was respectful, and you took his argument seriously. That has encouraged me to attempt to persuade you that—for I am an ethicist, not a lawyer—there is sound *ethical* case for changing the status of animals.

Before the rise of the modern animal movement there were societies for the prevention of cruelty to animals, but these organizations largely accepted that the welfare of nonhuman animals deserves protection only when human interests are not at stake. Human beings were seen as quite distinct from, and infinitely superior to, all forms of animal life. If our interests conflict with theirs, it is always their interests which have to give way. In contrast with this approach, the view that I want to defend puts human and nonhuman animals, *as such,* on the same moral footing. That is the sense in which I argued, in *Animal Liberation,* that "all animals are equal." But to avoid common misunderstandings, I need to be careful to spell out exactly what I mean by this. Obviously nonhuman animals cannot have equal rights to vote and nor should they be held criminally responsible for what they do. That is not the kind of equality I want to extend to nonhuman animals. The fundamental form of equality is *equality of interests,* and it is this that we should extend beyond the boundaries of our own species. Essentially this means that if an animal feels pain, the pain matters as much as it does when a human feels pain—if the pains hurt just as much. How bad pain and suffering are does not depend on the species of being that experiences it.

Dear Professor Singer:

I am impressed by your lucid and forceful argument for changing the ethical status of animals; and there is much in it with which I agree. I agree, for example, that human beings are not infinitely superior to or infinitely more valuable than other animals; indeed, I am prepared to drop "infinitely." I agree that we *are* animals and not ensouled demi-angels. I agree that gratuitous cruelty to and neglect of animals is wrong and that some costs should be incurred to reduce the suffering of animals raised for food or other human purposes or subjected to medical or other testing and experimentation.

But I do not agree that we have a duty to (the other) animals that arises from their being the equal members of a community composed of all those creatures in the universe that can feel pain, and that it is merely "prejudice" in a disreputable sense akin to racial prejudice or sexism that makes us "discriminate" in favor of our own species. You assume the existence of the universe-wide community of pain and demand reasons why the boundary of our concern should be drawn any more narrowly. I start from the bottom up, with the brute fact that we, like other animals, prefer our own — our own family, the "pack" that we happen to run with (being a social animal), and the larger modalities constructed on the model of the smaller ones, of which the largest for most of us is our nation. Americans have distinctly less feeling for the pains and pleasures of foreigners than of other Americans and even less for most of the nonhuman animals that we share the world with.

I do not feel obligated to defend this reaction; it is a moral intuition deeper than any reason that could be given for it and impervious to any reason that you or anyone could give against it. Membership in the human species is not a "morally irrelevant fact," as the race and sex of human beings has come to seem. If the moral irrelevance of humanity is what philosophy teaches, and so we have to choose between philosophy and the intuition that says that membership in the human species is morally relevant, then it is philosophy that will have to go.

What is needed to persuade us to alter our treatment of animals is not philosophy, let alone an atheistic philosophy (for one of the premises of your argument is that we have no souls) in a religious nation, but to learn to feel animals' pains as our pains and to learn that (if it is a fact, which I don't know) we can alleviate those pains without substantially reducing our standard of living and that of the rest of the world and without sacrificing medical and other scientific progress.

> **Think About It**
>
> Rather than focusing on the characteristics of individual beings, perhaps moral status should arise out of relationships, out of the relationships that exist between particular humans and particular animals.

Most of us, especially perhaps those of us who have lived with animals, have sufficient empathy for the suffering of animals to support the laws that forbid cruelty and neglect. We might go further if we knew more about animal feelings and about the existence of low-cost alternatives to pain-inflicting uses of animals. And so to expand and invigorate the laws that protect animals will require not philosophical arguments for reducing human beings to the level of the other animals but facts, facts that will stimulate a greater empathetic response to animal suffering and facts that will alleviate concern about the human costs of further measures to reduce animal suffering.

◇◇◇◇◇◇◇◇◇◇◇◇◇◇◇◇◇◇◇◇◇◇◇◇◇◇◇◇◇◇◇◇◇◇◇◇◇◇◇

Transition from Philosophy to Law

```
                              Is
       Philosophy          ⇦ ⇨            Law
       Personal Positions /   Ought     Group Position /
       Logically Consistent             Politically Acceptable
```

To what degree are emotion, economics, and culture part the development of a particular philosophy? The development of a particular law?

Social, religious, or philosophical attitudes create the context in which laws are adopted. But given the complex and conflicting view held by the citizens of the United States there is seldom an easy or complete transformation of attitudes into laws. Words such as "person" and "rights" are used both in philosophy and in law but the definitions and use of the words are different. Readers should be careful to understand the context in which they appear. In law if you are a "person" who has a "legal right" then consequences will flow from that status, but defining a person or a legal right is more difficult.

∞∞∞∞∞∞∞∞∞∞∞∞∞∞∞∞∞∞∞∞∞∞∞∞∞∞∞∞∞∞

Persons and Non-Persons

by Mary Midgley, from Peter Singer (ed.), *In Defense of Animals* 52–62 (1985)

Is a Dolphin a Person?

This question came up during the trial of the two people who, in May 1977, set free two bottle-nosed dolphins used for experimental purposes by the University of Hawaii's Institute of Marine Biology. It is an interesting question for a number of reasons, and I want to devote most of this chapter to interpreting it and tracing its connection with several others which may already be of concern to us. I shall not go into the details of the actual case but shall rely on the very clear and thoughtful account which Gavin Daws gives in his paper *"Animal Liberation" as Crime*, published in Ethics and Animals, edited by Harlan B. Miller and William H. Williams.

Kenneth Le Vasseur, the first of the two men to be tried, attempted through his counsel what is called a "choice of evils" defense. In principle the law allows this in cases where an act, otherwise objectionable, is necessary to avoid a greater evil. For this defense to succeed, the act has to be (as far as the defendant knows) the only way of avoiding an imminent, and more serious, harm or evil to himself or to "another." Le Vasseur, who had been involved in the care of the dolphins, believed that their captivity, with the conditions then prevailing in it, actually endangered their lives.

> [I]n his opening statement for the defense, [his counsel] spoke of the exceptional nature of dolphins as animals; bad and rapidly deteriorating physical conditions at the laboratory; a punishing regimen for the dolphins, involving overwork, reductions in their food rations, the total isolation they endured, deprived of the company of other dolphins, even of contact with humans in the tank, deprived of all toys which they had formerly enjoyed playing with — to the point where Puka, having refused to take part consistently in experimental sessions, developed self-destructive behaviors symptomatic of deep disturbance, and finally became lethargic — "comatose." Le Vasseur, seeing this, fearing that death would be the outcome, and knowing that there was no law that he could turn to, believed himself authorized, in the interests of the dolphins' well-being, to release them. The release was not a theft in that Le Vasseur did not intend to gain anything for himself. It was intended to highlight conditions in the laboratory.

But was a dolphin "another?" The judge thought not. He said that "another" would have to be another person, and he defined dolphins as property, not as persons, as a matter of law. A dolphin could not be "another person" under the penal code. The defense tried and failed to get the judge disqualified for prejudice. It then asked leave to go to Federal Court in order to claim that Thirteenth Amendment rights in respect of involuntary servitude might be extended to dolphins. This plea the judge rejected:

> Judge Doi said, "We get to dolphins, we get to orangutans, chimpanzees, dogs, cats. I don't know at what level you say intelligence is insufficient to have that animal or thing, or whatever you want to call it, a human being under the penal code. I'm saying that they're not under the penal code and that's my answer."

At this point — which determined the whole outcome of the trial — something seemed perfectly obvious to the judge about the meaning of the words "other" and "person." What was it? And how obvious is it to everybody else? In the answer just given, he raises the possibility that it might be a matter of intelligence, but he rejects it. That consideration, he says, is not needed. The question is quite a simple one; no tests are called for. The word "person" means a human being.

I think that this is a very natural view but not actually a true one, and the complications which we find when we look into the use of this very interesting word are instructive. In the first place, there are several well-established and venerable precedents for calling non-human beings "persons." One concerns the persons of the Trinity and, indeed, the personhood of God. Another is the case of "legal persons" — corporate bodies such as cities or colleges, which count as persons for various purposes, such as suing and being sued. As Blackstone says, these "corporations or bodies politic ... are formed and created by human laws for the purposes of society and government," unlike "natural persons," who can be created only by God. The law then can, if it chooses, create persons; it is not merely a passive recorder of their presence (as, indeed, Judge Doi implied in making his ruling a matter of law and not of fact). Thirdly, an instance that seems closer to the case of the dolphins, the word is used by zoologists to describe the individual members of a compound or colonial organism, such as a jellyfish or coral, each having (as the dictionary reasonably put it) a "more or less independent life." (It is also interesting that "personal identity" is commonly held to belong to continuity of consciousness rather than of bodily form in stories where the two diverge. Science fiction strongly supports this view, which was first mooted by John Locke in his Essay Concerning Human Understanding.)

There is nothing stretched or paradoxical about these uses, for the word does not in origin mean "human being" or anything like it at all. It means "a mask," and its basic general sense comes from the drama. The "masks" in a play are the characters who appear in it. Thus, to quote the Oxford Dictionary again, after "a mask," it means "a character of personage acted, one who plays or performs any part, a character, relation or capacity in which one acts, a being having legal rights, a judicial person." The last two meanings throw a clear light on the difference between this notion and that of being human. Not all human beings need be persons. The word *persona* in Latin does not apply to slaves, though it does apply to the state as a corporate person. Slaves have, so to speak, no speaking part in the drama; they do not figure in it; they are extras. There are some similar, and entertaining, examples about women. The following is taken from Susan Moller Okin's book *Women in Western Political Thought*:

> One case, brought before the U.S. Supreme Court in the 1890's, concerned Virginia's exclusion of a woman from the practice of the law, although the pertinent statute was worded in terms of "persons." The Court argued that it was indeed up to the State's Supreme Court "*to determine whether the word "person" as used (in the Statute) is confined to males,* and whether women are admitted to practice law in that Commonwealth." The issue of whether women must be understood as included by the word "persons" continued even into the twentieth century.... In a Massachusetts case in 1931 ... women were denied eligibility for jury service, although the statute stated that every "person qualified to vote" was so eligible. The Massachusetts Supreme Court asserted; "No intention to include women can be deduced from the omission of the word male." (Emphasis added)

What is going on here? We shall not understand it, I think, unless we grasp how deeply drama is interwoven with our thinking, how intimately its categories shape our ideas. People who talk like this have a clear notion of the drama which they think is going on around them. They know who is supposed to count in it and who is not. Attempts to introduce fresh characters irritate them. They are inclined to dismiss these attempts sharply as obviously absurd and paradoxical. The question of who is and who is not a person seems at this point a quite simple and clear-cut one. Bertie Wooster simply is not a character in Macbeth and that is the end of the matter. It is my main business here to point out that this attitude is too crude. The question is actually a very complex one, much more like "Who is important?" than "Who has got two legs?" If we asked "Who is important?" we would know that we needed to ask further questions, beginning with "Important for what?" Life does not contain just one purpose or one drama but many interwoven ones. Different characters matter in different ways. Beings figure in some dramas who are absent from others, and we all play different parts in different scripts. Even in ordinary human life it is fatal to ignore this. To insist on reducing all relationships to those prescribed by a single drama — for instance, the social contract — is disastrous. Intellectuals are prone to such errors and need to watch out for them. But when we come to harder cases, where the variation is greater — cases such as abortion, euthanasia or the treatment of other species — this sort of mistake is still more paralyzing. That is why these cases are so helpful in illuminating the more central ones.

Questions & Notes

1. Do any of the dramas of which you are a part contain animals in significant or supporting roles?

2. Consider the original question, "Is a dolphin a person?" What is the legal answer? What is the moral answer? Should a dolphin be considered a legal person? For a full discussion of the jurisprudence of the term person, unrelated to animal issues, see 4 R. Pound, Jurisprudence 210 (1959).

3. Do you agree that some people might be frightened by the prospect of animals gaining a status in the legal system other than that of personal property? Why do you believe this to be the case?

4. If you were on a jury, would you convict Kenneth Le Vasseur of theft of government property? Why or why not?

American Veterinarian Medical Association Animal Welfare Principles

(Approved by AVMA Executive Board November 2006)

The AVMA, as a medical authority for the health and welfare of animals, offers the following eight integrated principles for developing and evaluating animal welfare policies, resolutions, and actions.

- The responsible use of animals for human purposes, such as companionship, food, fiber, recreation, work, education, exhibition, and research conducted for the benefit of both humans and animals, is consistent with the Veterinarian's Oath.
- Decisions regarding animal care, use, and welfare shall be made by balancing scientific knowledge and professional judgment with consideration of ethical and societal values.
- Animals must be provided water, food, proper handling, health care, and an environment appropriate to their care and use, with thoughtful consideration for their species-typical biology and behavior.
- Animals should be cared for in ways that minimize fear, pain, stress, and suffering.
- Procedures related to animal housing, management, care, and use should be continuously evaluated, and when indicated, refined or replaced.
- Conservation and management of animal populations should be humane, socially responsible, and scientifically prudent.
- Animals shall be treated with respect and dignity throughout their lives and, when necessary, provided a humane death.

The veterinary profession shall continually strive to improve animal health and welfare through scientific research, education, collaboration, advocacy, and the development of legislation and regulations.

Favre's Proposed Ethical Principles for Domestic Animals

1. Living property shall not be held or put to unnecessary uses.

2. Living property shall not be subjected to unnecessary pain, injury, suffering, or death.

3. Those who own or posses living property must provide respectful care and living space.

Questions & Notes

1. The first principle accepts as a premise that some uses of animals by humans would be acceptable. What do you think? What would be the outcome if the operating principle is that no use of animals by humans is acceptable? The second principle pivots on the word "unnecessary". The dynamic of this term was discussed extensively in Chapter 6 – Intentional Cruelty. The word would have the same public policy context here. Can the word be removed from the principle? In the third principle both the words "care" and "living space" are modified by "respectful". What might the term mean in this context? Is this a it useful modifier?

2. What would you add to the list? How might the law implement these principles? Should all unethical conduct be brought within the legal system?

3. As an example of application of these principles, consider the big cats in two USDA cases in Chapter 9 — In re Karl Mitchell, and Big Cat Encounters and In re Great Cats of Indiana, Inc. Apply the above ethical principles on behalf of those cats. Should the situation be allowed? What should be done about it?

4. It must be acknowledged that these principles are existent in a world where human interests will be balanced against specific animal interests. Will the human interest always win? Why not? In a conflict between the two, there is no clear measurement which givens us an answer, and humans are the one's doing the weighing. Human logic and emotion both play a role.

A Focusing Question

Assuming that it is within your power to give legal rights to animals, what are three rights you would give them?

Section 2

Jurisprudence — What Is a Legal Right? An Interest?

The Concept of Rights and the Competence of Courts

by Iredell Jenkins, 18:1 The Amer. J. of Jurisprudence 1 (1973)

The basic issue, obviously, is that of the status of rights—of what a right is—for on this hinges the identification of rights. On this issue I think it is fair to say, without becoming superficial or simplistic, that there are two broad views which have disputed the field for centuries. One of these holds that rights have a real metaphysical and moral status. They are extra- and supra- legal. Rights derive directly from God or Nature—from the ultimate structure of things—and they belong to man as part of his intrinsic nature, as much as do his body, his mind, and his various powers. Law merely recognizes these rights and enforces respect for them. This is the classical view, as expressed in the doctrines of Natural Law and Natural Rights, and it was the dominant influence for centuries.

The other view holds that rights are strictly legal entities or notions. They owe their being and their nature exclusively to law—to the substantive and procedural apparatus of a legal system—whose creatures they are. Law literally creates rights: the legislative or judicial act accords certain privileges and protections to some persons, and imposes corresponding duties on other persons, and it is this act that brings the right into being and constitutes its content. This is the view made famous by Holmes and Gray, and associated with the schools of Legal Positivism, Formalism, and Analytical Jurisprudence.

These statements are admittedly so general as to seem almost a caricature of the subtle and labyrinthine arguments that have been spun out in support of the different theories of rights. But I think that these broad interpretations constitute the only real

> ### Think About It
>
> From page 20 of *America's First Freedom* (August 2002) (Journal of the NRA):
>
> > Freedom took a hit when: Harvard author and litigator Steven Wise published his new book, *Drawing the Line*, in which he offers evidence that animals qualify for basic legal rights. Will you be dragged to court by the family dog? Not likely. But trial lawyers may soon have powerful new arguments to launch assaults on medical researchers, labs, circuses, cosmetic companies... and hunters.

and fundamental alternatives. Regarded substantively, rights are either legal or metalegal. They are either conceived and created by law; or they exist as aspects of reality prior to their legal annunciation, and are merely recognized by law. However sophisticated and exotic legal theory may become, it must adopt one or the other of these substantive views.

Furthermore, and most importantly, the essential functional characteristic of rights is the same on both of these views. In either case, rights are basically means to ends. Their value is instrumental, not inherent. Men are "endowed" with rights—by God, Nature, or law—in order to serve certain purposes that lie beyond these rights themselves. The claims, privileges, liberties, and immunities that make up the body of rights are all of them particular means to the general end of human well-being. Their role is to assure to men the security and protection that they need if they are to develop to their full potential.

◇◇

Toward Legal Rights for Animals

by Stephen I. Burr, 4 Environmental Affairs 205 (1975)

The Nature of a Legal Right

In a society such as ours, where formal inter-human and human-governmental relationships are controlled by laws, the amount of protection one receives is a function of the legal rights one holds. Fundamentally, a legal right involves the assurance by society that when another person acts inconsistently with a right that you hold, an authoritative public body will give some amount of consideration to your protest. However, more than this authoritative review must be present before one can really be said to be protected by a legal right. Christopher Stone, Professor of Law at the University of Southern California, has argued that before one can be said to be a holder of legal rights, three other criteria must be satisfied:

> ... first, that the thing can institute legal actions *at its behest;* second, that in determining the granting of legal relief, the court must take *injury to it* into account; and, third, that relief must run to the *benefit of it* [his emphasis].

Stone then gives us an example of just what these criteria imply:

> To illustrate, even as between two societies that condone slavery there is a fundamental difference between S¹, in which a master can (if he chooses), go to court and collect reduced chattel value damages form someone who has beaten his slave, and S², in which the slave can institute proceedings *himself*, for his own recovery, damages being measured by, say *his* pain ad suffering. Notice that neither society is so structured as to leave wholly unprotected the slave's interests in not being beaten. But in S² as opposed to S¹, there

> are three operationally significant advantages that the slave
> has, and these make the slave in S^2, albeit a slave, a holder
> of rights [his emphasis].

The three operationally significant advantages are that slave S^2 can institute proceedings in his own behalf, and not have to depend on his master to defend him; that once in court, the court will look to his injuries, what he rather than his master has suffered; and that whatever relief is given will run to his benefit, not his owner's.

Real protection in our legal system, then, involves more than protection as mere property. It involves the right to be heard, the right to be treated as having a unique worth. Such protection has not been limited exclusively to humans. Corporations, ships and governmental entities all are granted legal identity. Obviously these non-human parties could not appear in court to seek remedy for injuries unless human spokesmen were allowed to argue in their behalf. Yet we have been willing to confer on them the status of rights-holders because we have made the judgment that they are sufficiently unique and valuable to deserve protection in and of themselves. Similarly, humans who are incompetent to assert their own rights are still granted full protection. Children and the mentally ill or retarded may argue for their own interests before our courts through guardians.

Questions & Notes

1. Consider the claim of author Steve Wise: chimpanzees should be accorded the legal rights to bodily integrity and personal freedom. Others should not be able to make them take pills, medical tests, or be put under the knife against their will. Additionally, chimpanzees should have the legal right to not have their personal freedom infringed upon by being placed in 5' x 5' x 7' metal bar cages. See Steven Wise, *Rattling the Cage* (2000).

◇◇◇◇◇◇◇◇◇◇◇◇◇◇◇◇◇◇◇◇◇◇◇◇◇◇◇◇◇◇◇◇◇◇◇◇◇◇

The Role of the Rational and the Emotive in a Theory of Animal Rights

by Thomas Kelch, 27 Bost. Col. Env't Aff. L. Rev. 1 (1999)

V. Analysis and Synthesis of Rights Theories

Western thought tends to attempt to reduce disparate concepts to a unified theory. We look for one explanation that resolves all of our questions about a subject. For example, the Holy Grail of physics is the search for a unified theory, resolving conflicts in quantum theory and general relativity theory. While such a structure may fit hard sciences, in human affairs one must question its efficacy.

Similarly, we look at the issue of rights as one that requires a *single* explanation. Hohfeld sees rights as correlative with duties. Wellman refines this by founding rights on a set of Hohfeldian elements, revolving around a single central core. Regan and others see rights as founded in interests. Other theories see rights variously as remedies, reasons, goals, or rhetoric. The common theme is that there is *an* explanation.

Is there *an* explanation of the foundations or sources of rights? Might rights have diverse sources? The notion that a single conceptual foundation adequately describes legal rights appears dubitable. It seems wrong as a matter of fact because it has been widely recognized in the law, at least since Hohfeld, that rights can be described in many ways. As a matter of theory it appears wrong because "importantly different notions of a right, each of them proper, might profitably coexist in the law."

Emotion and Moral Theory

Generally, emotions are thought to be unimportant to moral theory. It is a maxim of Western thought that one is to avoid contamination of moral theory with compassion, sympathy, or caring. This extension of a religion of science into moral theory may ultimately be credited to Kant. In Kant's moral theory, duty is the foundation of morality, and through the application of reason we discover our duties. Reason is distinguished from emotion. This distinction assumes that emotion is irrational.

While most philosophers hold the view that reason must conquer passions, David Hume reversed this idea and claimed that reason should be the slave of passion. Hume was of the view that the passions are the basis for all moral thought. His view was based on the idea that reason is inert; it is just the mechanism used for the discovery of truth or falsehood — it concerns the relation of ideas or the existence of facts. Passions, volitions, and actions are not susceptible to being true or false and, thus, cannot be the subject of reason. Morality is concerned with actions, and since actions have their basis in passions, passions are the foundation of morals.

To the extent that the interests of animals are considered in the composite view of rights that I have described, these interests will include animal pain, anxiety, and the like. To evaluate these matters is, at least in part, to have feelings of compassion. Thus, to the extent that interests are part of the reason that we grant rights to an entity, the only way that these interests may be properly gauged is through our own emotional experiences and evaluations.

On the issue of whether it is fitting to attribute rights to animals in order to protect them from ill treatment, we might ask whether we feel compassion for their suffering. We might ask whether we feel attachment to them, whether we feel a sense of kinship to them, whether we feel a sense of awe at their resilience, and whether these feelings give us a reason to grant them rights. These feelings, none of which put us across an impenetrable gulf from reason, can be seen as elements counting in the analysis of whether rights ought to be accorded to animals.

If we conclude that animals should be accorded rights, as I believe they should, what role might emotion play in determining what rights we grant to animals? Our primary emotional response to animals is to feel compassion for their suffering. As Jeremy Bentham stated, "the question is not, Can they reason? nor, Can they talk? but Can they suffer?" Our emotional response to animal suffering must be considered in determining whether a practice violates an animal right given that most, if not all of us feel compassion for animals in laboratories or factory farms, this response is a strong reason supporting the abolition of such practices as a matter of right.

> One suggested roadblock to the awarding of legal rights to animals is the existing property status of animals (review materials in Chapter 2). In the broader sense of the word "rights," the property status is not a limitation. To understand how legal rights and property status might coexist, it will be necessary to approach the topic from a different direction, that of an "interest" paradigm. We begin with the perspective of one of the best legal thinkers of the twentieth century, Roscoe Pound. Admittedly Dean Pound was not contemplating animals when he wrote this, and never expressed any thoughts that he might have had about animals. But science is now showing that much of that which is human interests also exist in the lives of other beings.

Interest

by Roscoe Pound, Vol 3, Jurisprudence, ch 14 (1959)

Interests [edited]

A legal system attains the ends of the legal order (1) by recognizing certain interests, individual, public, and social; (2) by defining the limits within which those interests shall be recognized and given effect through legal precepts developed and applied by the judicial (and today the administrative) process according to an authoritative technique; and (3) by endeavoring to secure the interests so recognized within the defined limits.

For the present purpose an interest may be defined as a demand or desire or expectation which human beings, either individually or in groups or associations or relations, seek to satisfy, of which, therefore, the adjustment of human relations and ordering of human behavior through the force of a politically organized society must take account [italics added]. It will be noticed that while this is put psychologically, it seeks to avoid controverted questions of group psychology. It does not speak of group demands or desires but of the strivings of men, in, or perhaps we should say through, groups and associations and relations to satisfy certain demands or desires. The legal order or the law, in the sense of the body of authoritative guides to or grounds of determination of controversies, do not create these interests.

There is so much truth in the old idea of a state of nature and theory of natural rights. Interests in this sense would exist if there were no legal order and no body of authoritative guides to conduct or decision. Claims of human beings to have things and do things have existed wherever a number of human beings have come into contact. There has never been a society in which there has been such a surplus of the means of satisfying these claims or of room for every one to do all that he sought and urged a claim to do, that there has not been competition to satisfy them. Conflicts or competition between interests arise because of the competition of individuals with each other, the competition of groups or associations or societies of men with each other, and the competition of individuals with such groups or associations or societies in the endeavor to satisfy human claims and wants and desires.

We begin, then, with the proposition that the law does not create these interests. It finds them pressing for recognition and security [italics added]. First, a legal system classifies them and recognizes a larger or smaller number. Second, it fixes the limits within which it endeavors to secure the interests so selected. These limits may be fixed in view of the possibilities of effectively securing them through the judicial or administrative processes. Third, a legal system works out means by which the interests may be secured when recognized and as delimited. It prescribes canons of values for determining what interests to recognize, for fixing the limits of securing recognized interests, and for judging of the weight to be accorded in any given case to the practical limitations on effective legal action.

Hence in determining the scope and subject matter of a legal system we have to consider five points. (1) We must take an inventory of the interests which press for recognition and must generalize and classify them. (2) We must select and determine the interests which the law should recognize and seek to secure. (3) We must fix limits of securing the interests so selected. (4) We must weigh the means by which the law may secure interests when recognized and delimited. We must take account of the limitations upon effective legal action which may preclude complete recognition or complete securing of interests which otherwise we should seek to secure. (5) In order to do these things we must work out principles of valuation of interests. Their chief importance is in determining what interests to recognize; in selection of interests to be recognized. But we must use them also in fixing the limits of securing recognized interests, in fixing upon the means of securing interests, and in judging of the weight to be attributed in any given case to the practical limitations upon effective legal action.

Interests, that is, the claims or demands or desires for which or about which the law has to make some provision if civilization is to be maintained and furthered and society is not to be disrupted or dissolved, are asserted by individual human beings [italics added]. But they are not for that reason all individual interests. We must not confuse interest as claim, as jurists use the term, with interest as advantage as economists use it. Thinking of the claims and demands which men assert and press upon the legal order, interests fall conveniently into three classes, individual interests, public interests, and social interests. Individual interests are claims or demands or desires involved in and looked at from the standpoint of the individual life immediately as such—asserted in title of the individual life. Public interests are the claims or demands or desires asserted by individuals involved in or looked at from the standpoint of political life—life in politically organized society. They are asserted in title of that organization. It is convenient to treat them as the claims of a politically organized society thought of as a legal entity. Social interests are claims or demands or desires, even some of the foregoing in other aspects, thought of in terms of social life and generalized as claims of the social group. They are the claims which are involved in the maintenance, the activity and the functioning of society; the wider demands or desires asserted in title of social life and looked at from the standpoint of social life in civilized society.

What, then, are the claims or demands which the individual makes or may make which jurist and lawmaker must consider and provide for?

Questions & Notes

1. The threshold question is: do animals have interests? What might be the interests of a dog, a kangaroo, or a snake? Might we know more about mammal interests than we do about the interests of birds or reptiles? How about chickens being raised for egg production. What are their interests?

2. A second question is how should the interests in question be sorted into legally important categories? Assuming that the normal male dog has an interest in mating with female dogs, and that this interest is fundamental to his nature, how can humans justify mandatory neutering laws?

3. Does the circle of animals with "interests" overlap with the circle of animals with the capacity to "suffer" and those with "self-awareness"? Is "interests" a useful category by which to award moral and/or legal status?

4. Setting aside the possible interests of animals to not be human property, is there any conceptual reason why the legal system should not acknowledge and protect the interests of animals? Do not the anti-cruelty laws presently acknowledge and protect, at least to a limited degree, the interests of animals to be free from unnecessary pain and suffering?

5. To admit that animals have interests does not suggest in the world of law what outcome will occur when animal interests conflict with human interests. Through the political process, compromise is reached between conflicting interests; in the

arena political power, not logic is king. Pushing the "ought" to the "is" may face great political barriers.

Section 3
Present Legal Status

If animal interests are going to be the lexicon by which animals can obtain status in the legal system, then the first step in the analysis has to be the determination that nonhuman animals have interests. Remember in the context of human interest, Pound "*defined [interests] as a demand or desire or expectation which human beings, either individually or in groups or associations or relations, seek to satisfy.*" For animals the term will have to be slightly changed as most cannot speak for themselves. Animals have demands and expectations and at least some desires. (The cat desires the bird in the tree; the dog desires his tummy to be rubbed.) But we humans, with both personal experience and scientific information, can have a more complex view. We know animals have interests in food and water, shelter from weather extremes, and freedom from pain and suffering. Some animals have complex minds to which boredom is a relevant factor; many raise their young and the mother-child bond is important. In total, animal interests are those biological and psychological needs which shape and support the well-being of a particular animal. Some species, such as chimpanzees, will have significant overlap with human interests; others, such as sea turtles may have overlap with human interests' only at the most basic biological level. A fair sense of our present community judgment about what interests animals have and which are significant interests that might concern the law can be gained by examining the state anti-cruelty laws. (Unfortunately the law does not yet promote and protect the right of dogs to have a daily tummy rub.)

A Focusing Question

Is it better that an animal should have not been born rather than experience pain and premature death? Is it better that a human should have not been born rather than experience pain and premature death?

Those who assert that animals have no rights within our present legal system are using a narrow definition of the term, usually based on the premise that it is not a legal right unless the animal is the plaintiff. This creates a yes/no black/white sort of world. But the reality of the legal world is one of many shades of gray. (See discussion in Chapter 9 on standing for animal interests.) It will be more useful for charting the present and future of animal legal rights to suggest three different kinds of legal rights:

Weak Legal Rights exist where animal interests are acknowledged within the legal system but only the State may assert or protect them.

Strong Legal Rights are interests acknowledged within the legal system that can be asserted by nongovernmental humans on behalf of animals.

Preferred Legal Rights are interests acknowledged within the legal system that can be asserted directly by the animal possessing the interest in question.

The state anti-cruelty law is the classic example of a weak legal right. If state law allowed private citizens or groups to file an action for the benefit of animals based on the anti-cruelty laws, then that would be a strong legal right. As an example consider the North Carolina statute allowing civil enforcement of its anti-cruelty laws. This is discussed in detail in a law review article, William Reppy Jr., *Citizen Standing to Enforce Anti-Cruelty Laws by Obtaining Injunctions: The North Carolina Experience*, 11 Animal Law 39 (2005).

◇◇◇

The following was presented as a speech at a Conference on Chimpanzees held at Harvard Law School on September 30, 2002 by the author. Consider which category of legal right might be involved with each category considered.

Present Legal Presence

I feel comfortable in asserting that chimpanzees, for some purposes, for some of their interests, are presently within our legal community. There are three primary legal arenas we can look to for evidence of this state of affairs: Criminal law, Civil law and Regulatory law.

The first beachhead for all animals on the shores of our legally relevant community of beings was in the area of criminal law. Beginning after the U.S. Civil War, the various states around the country adopted criminal laws to protect animals from unnecessary pain and suffering. The existence of these laws clearly acknowledges the existence of an animal's interests to be free from unnecessary pain and suffering. In the case of **Stephens v. State**, 3 So. 458 (Miss. 1888) the court found that, "This statute is for the benefit of animals, as creatures capable of feeling and suffering, and it was intended to protect them from cruelty, without reference to their being property, or to the damages which might thereby be occasioned to their owners." [Also see **Grise v. State**, 37 Ark. 456 (1881), where the court acknowledged this new concern when it noted, these new laws "are not made for the protection of the absolute or relative rights of persons, or the rights of men to the acquisition and enjoyment of property, or the peace of society. They seem to recognize and attempt to protect some abstract rights in all that animate creation, ... from the largest and noblest to the smallest and most insignificant."]

Today under state cruelty laws in every state it is illegal to inflict unnecessary pain upon a chimpanzee. Additionally anyone with the care and custody of a chimpanzee has a legal duty to provide care for the chimpanzee. There are a number of statutory exceptions to this criminal law, but this is not the time to take up that level of detail.

A second example of chimpanzees being acknowledged within the relevant legal community came with the adoption of the 1985 Amendments to the federal Animal Welfare Act. In this case, for the first time, the mental well being, rather than the physical well being was recognized and supported. The law requires that all holders of chimpanzees under the jurisdiction of the AWA, have "a physical environment adequate to promote the psychological well-being of chimpanzees." USDA has developed regulations to deal with this issue. A number of books, a few lawsuits and many conferences have been held over the past decade to develop more fully how this legal obligation should be carried out.

A more recent example, in the civil law arena, is equally interesting. Under the Uniform Trust Act of 2000, which has been adopted in several states, another long-standing legal barrier has been lowered for animals. Section 408 allows for the creation of trusts for the benefit of animals. Not just honorary trusts, which may or may not be enforceable, but trusts in which the animal is the beneficiary and for which the court can substitute trustees and for which third parties can be appointed as enforcers to assure that the trustees have carried out their obligations. Thus a chimpanzee becomes a legally relevant being, one who has assets which must be protected. And, this has occurred in that most conservative of legal areas — trust and estates. [Uniform Trust Code, Last Revised or Amended in 2001, Drafted by the National Conference of Commissioners on Uniform State Laws. Section 408. Trust for Care of Animal.]

A final, fourth example is the most recent and perhaps most interesting. Last year the Congress passed the Chimpanzee Retirement Act [42 USC 287a(3a)]. Underlying the passage of the Act was a recognition by Congress that chimpanzees used in research are morally relevant beings about whom we as a society have obligations. Among other provisions, was the acknowledgment of a fundamental interest of chimpanzees: continued life. For the law states that chimpanzees within the sanctuary system, shall not be "subjected to euthanasia except as in the best interest of the chimpanzee involved." This is a powerful statement about the presence of the interests of chimpanzees within our legal system.

Questions & Notes

1. Do you agree that animal interests are already within the legal system? Are the preceding examples just human interests in a different form? To say that a human interest is promoted by a

provision is not to deny that animal interests may also be present and promoted.

2. See Jonathan R. Lovvorn, *Animal Law in Action: The Law, Public Perception, and the Limits of Animal Rights Theory as a Basis for Legal Reform*, 12 Animal Law 133 (2006).

◇◇◇

Note: The Issue of Property Status

As Chapter 2 has made clear, animals are presently categorized and treated as property in our legal system. The philosophy of many in the animal rights movement is to reject this as morally unacceptable. This author and many others have asserted that as a matter of philosophy, animal are beings deserving of moral status, on that point there is wide agreement. But, a key question over which there is dispute asks whether it is possible to acknowledge this moral status within the legal system without the total elimination of the property status of animals. If it is accepted that legal rights are the acknowledgment within the law of individual interests that are deserving of protection, then it may not be necessary to eliminate the property status in order to create legal rights. If the working premise is that property cannot be the holder of legal rights, then there exists a significant barrier to the realization of animal rights.

It is possible to imagine the creation of a new category of property, Living Property, which consists of property that can possess defined legal rights of their own. Regardless of the arguments within the realm of philosophy of the unacceptability of animal property status made by the abolitionist, it is not clear to this author that a paramount interest of animals is to not be the property of humans. For what is the alternative for their continued existence within our community? (See the end of Chapter 2 for the argument about keeping animals as property.) It will be in the interest of animals for humans to acknowledge that unlike other personal property, an owner of an animal has a legal obligation to the animal, thus creating a relationship closer to the nature of a guardianship.

The following chart is a summary of present attitudes about animals. In this chart welfare rights refers to animal interests that can only be asserted by the state (weak rights), while legal rights refers to animal interests assertable by private individuals (strong rights) or the animals themselves (preferred rights).

Corporate Agriculture "Is"	Average American "Is"	Favre (law) "Ought"	Animal Abolitionist (philosophy) "Ought"
Property	Property	Living Property	Not Property
No Moral Status	Some Moral Status	Greater Moral Status	Equal Moral Status
No Legal Rights	Welfare Rights	Legal Rights	Legal Rights
Example: Battery Hens	Pets & Zoo Animals	Beneficiaries of Animal Trusts; Tort Recovery for Companion Animals	Wildlife

Today the law reflects, as is fully predictable, the corporate and average American view. The battle will be the direction of the future. Do you fit on this chart, or do you have a different column to add to the chart?

Now returning to the initial board game at the beginning of the chapter, how would you place the groups for the present?

Section 4

Future Possibilities

A Focusing Question

Will the creation and possession of legal rights by animals assure the elimination of animal suffering? Does the presence of legal rights eliminate human suffering?

CASE BY CASE

The future of animal law might arise through case law development. Consider the following from Brazil.

Correio da Bahia

9th Criminal Court

Habeas Corpus – 833085-3/2005

In favor of: Suica [case has been edited]

Hons. HERON JOSE DE SANTANA and LUCIANO ROCHA SANTANA, Prosecutors from the Environmental Department and other entities and individuals indicated in the petition (page 2), have requested a REPRESSIVE HABEAS CORPUS in favor of "Suica," a chimpanzee (scientific name Anthropopithecus troglodytes), who is caged at Parque

Zoobotanico Getulio Vargas (Salvador's zoo), located at Av. Ademar de Barros, in this capital, and the co-plaintiff authority in this case is Mr. Thelmo Gavazza, Director of Biodiversity of the Environmental and Hydrological Resource Department, SEMARH.

To support the request, the petitioners alleged that "Suica" is caged in a cage that has severe infiltration problems in its physical structure, which would hinder the animal's access to the direct transit area, which is larger, and also to the hall used to handle the animal; the cage's total area is 77.56 square meters and 4.0 meters high in the solarium, with a confinement area 2.75 meters high, thus preventing the chimpanzee to move around. With the purpose of showing the grounds of this writ, the petitioners allege, in short, that "in a free society, committed to ensuring freedom and equality, laws evolve according to people's thinking and behavior, and when public attitudes change, so does the law, and several authors believe that the Judiciary can be a powerful social change agent." They also state, in short, that as of 1993 a group of scientists began to openly defend the extension of human rights to large primates, giving rise to the Great Ape Project, which is supported by primatologists, ethologists and intellectuals, which is based on the premise that human beings and primates became different species about 5 to 6 million years ago, and some evolved into the current chimpanzees and bonobos, and another into 2-footed erect primates, wherefrom Homo Australopithecus, Homo aridipithecus and Homo paranthopus descend, in short, the intent is to equate primates to human beings for the purposes of granting habeas corpus. Lastly, the petitioners say that this instrument alone, can extend the definition of personality (or humanity) to hominids. They base it on the concept of environmental safety, and seek a grant of Habeas Corpus in favor of "Suica" the chimpanzee, determining its transfer to GAP's Great Ape Sanctuary in the city of Sorocaba, State of Sao Paulo, having already made available the transportation for this transfer.

One could, from the very topic of the petition, have enough grounds to dismiss it, from the very outset, arguing the legal impossibility of the request, or absolute inapplicability of the legal instrument sought by the petitioners, that is, a Habeas Corpus to transfer an animal from the environment in which it lives, to another. However, in order to incite debate of this issue, with persons and entities connected to Criminal Procedural Law, I decided to admit the argument. In fact this is an unprecedented case in Bahia's law. I have been on the bench for 24 years, always working in criminal courts, and this the first case I have been assigned where the subject of the Habeas Corpus is an animal, to wit, a chimpanzee. However, the theme is deserving of discussion as this is a highly complex issue, requiring an in-depth examination of "pros and cons", therefore, I did not grant the Habeas Corpus writ, preferring rather to obtain information from the co-plaintiff authority, in this case, Mr. Thelmo Gavazza, Director of Biodiversity of the Environmental Department, requesting he did so within 72 hours.

On the last day of the 72-hour deadline for submission of information, the illustrious co-plaintiff, SEMARH's Biodiversity Director, filed a petition in this Court (page 166), requesting the extension of the deadline, by another 72 hours. However, surprisingly, I became aware, through a second petition sent to this Criminal Court, signed by the SEMARH's Biodiversity Director (page 168) received today at this Court (on 09/27/2005), that "Suica" the chimpanzee, the subject of this Habeas Corpus, was deceased inside the Salvador Zoo. The petitioner indicated that this sad fact took place "in spite of all efforts made and all care provided to the chimpanzee."

The news took me by surprise, no doubt causing sadness, as I visited the Ondina Zoo, covertly, on the afternoon of 10/21/2005, last Saturday, and did not perceive any apparent abnormality concerning "Suica" the chimpanzee, although I would like the record to show that I am not an expert on the matter. I am sure that with the acceptance of the debate, I caught the attention of jurists from all over the country, bringing the matter to discussion. Criminal Procedural Law is not static, rather subject to constant changes, and new decisions have to adapt to new times. I believe that even with "Suica's" death the matter will continue to be discussed, especially in law school classes, as many colleagues, attorneys, students, and entities have voiced their opinions, wishing to make those prevail.

The topic will not die with this writ, it will certainly continue to remain controversial. Thus, can a primate be compared to a human being? Can an animal be released from its cage, by means of a Habeas Corpus? As for the final decision, I recall article 659 of the CPPB: "If a Judge or Court finds that violence or illegal coercion has ended, the request will be dismissed." Thus, with the death of the chimpanzee, subject hereof, the Habeas Corpus has lost its purpose, its reason of being, thus ending the action.

Therefore, I dismiss the case. Enter. Notify and file a certified copy with the Court of record. Salvador, September 28, 2005.

Edmundo Lucio da Cruz, Judge.

Translation Prepared by Carlos de Paula (the full case, in original Portuguese, is available at *www.animallaw.info/nonus/cases/cabrsuicapt2005.htm*).

Questions & Notes

1. Why the chimpanzee died is still not known to the public.

2. Do you think the plaintiff's attorneys had a good context in which to raise the argument? Do you think they would have won? Could this be done in the United States? Why do you think this occurred in Brazil before it happened in the United States?

3. In any brief in support of the plaintiff's motion the argument will have to be made on the issue of why the chimpanzee should be treated as a legal person. What would be the strongest argument to present to the judge? If the motion was granted, would it be proper to say the case created a legal right for animals? Would the granting of the motion remove the chimpanzee from the status of property? Should the chimpanzee be given full personal liberty, as would be the case of humans?

4. Can you suggest another test case scenario for pushing the legal system toward acknowledging the legal personhood of animals? Which species do you think would make the best case?

5. For a European perspective on animal rights see Fernando Arajuo, *The Recent Development of Portugese Law in the Field of Animal Rights,* 1 Jour. of Animal Law 61 (2005) available at *www.animallaw.info.*

Partial Juristic Persons

While there are those seeking immediate significant legal change, by making animals full juristic persons, perhaps there is a better next step. Not full legal brothers, but a status of partial juristic persons, individuals with a few specifically acknowledged legal rights. This may be a way station to full status or a permanent status always being adjusted; only time will tell. Some animals may have some rights, if not full rights. Both the individuals within and principles of the legal system need to adjust to the idea of animals as rights holders; to try out the concept in limited circumstances to see what happens without creating significant uncertainty for everyone. For example, the North Carolina statute discussed in the Chapter 10 – Standing, has been on the books for a number of years and as of yet there has not been legal, economic, or social consequence of any significance, while being helpful to some animals.

CASE BY CASE

Does there exist the possibility for a change in the legal status of animals within the United States? The federal Ninth Circuit Court of Appeals is ready to accept some change if Congress will act.

The Cetacean Community v. Bush
386 F. 3d 1169 (9th Cir. 2004)

The sole plaintiff in this case is the Cetacean Community ("Cetaceans"). The Cetacean Community is the name chosen by the Cetaceans' self-appointed attorney for all of the world's whales, porpoises, and dolphins.

The Cetaceans challenge the United States Navy's use of Surveillance Towed Array Sensor System Low Frequency Active Sonar ("SURTASS LFAS") during wartime or heightened threat conditions.

Animals have many legal rights, protected under both federal and state laws. In some instances, criminal statutes punish those who violate statutory duties that protect animals. *See, e.g.,* African Elephant Conservation Act, 16 U.S.C. §§ 4201-4245; Animal Welfare Act, 7 U.S.C. §§ 2131-2159; Horse Protection Act, 15 U.S.C. §§ 1821-1831; Wild Free-Roaming Horses and Burros Act, 16 U.S.C. §§ 1331-1340; *see also, e.g.,* N.Y. Agric. & Mkts. Law § 356 (obliging anyone who has impounded or confined an animal to provide good air, water, shelter, and food); Cal.Penal Code § 597a (imposing criminal penalties on anyone who transports an animal in a cruel or inhumane manner). In other instances, humans whose interests are affected by the existence or welfare of animals are granted standing to bring civil suits to enforce statutory duties that protect these animals. The ESA and the MMPA are good examples of such statutes.

It is obvious that an animal cannot function as a plaintiff in the same manner as a juridically competent human being. But we see no reason why Article III prevents Congress from authorizing a suit in the name of an animal, any more than it prevents suits brought in the name of artificial persons such as corporations, partnerships or trusts, and even ships, or of juridically incompetent persons such as infants, juveniles, and mental incompetents. *See, e.g., Sausalito,* 386 F.3d at 1202, 2004 WL 2348385 (city is a "person" that can bring suit under the APA); *Walker v. City of Lakewood,* 272 F.3d 1114, 1123 n. 1 (9th Cir. 2001) (non-profit corporation had standing to sue under FHA and FEHA); *The Gylfe v. The Trujillo,* 209 F. 2d 386 (2d Cir. 1954) (discussing counterclaim by ship as "injured party" in collision litigation); *Cruzan by Cruzan v. Director, Missouri Dept. of Health,* 497 U.S. 261, 266, 110 S.Ct. 2841, 111 L.Ed. 2d 224 (1990) (plaintiff Nancy Cruzan was in "persistent vegetative state"); *see also* Christopher D. Stone, *Should Trees Have Standing?-Toward Legal Rights for Natural Objects,* 45 S. Cal. L.Rev. 450, 452 & n.13 (1972) ("The world of the lawyer is peopled with inanimate rights holders: trusts, corporations, joint ventures, municipalities, Subchapter R partnerships, and nation-states, to mention just a few.").

If Article III does not prevent Congress from granting standing to an animal by statutorily authorizing a suit in its name, the question becomes whether Congress has passed a statute actually doing so. We therefore turn to whether Congress has granted standing to the Cetaceans under the ESA, the MMPA, NEPA, read either on their own, or through the gloss of Section 10(a) of the APA.

We agree with the district court in *Citizens to End Animal Suffering & Exploitation, Inc.,* that "[i]f Congress and the President intended to take the extraordinary step of authorizing animals as well as people and legal entities to sue, they could, and should, have said so plainly." 836 F. Supp. at 49. In the absence of any such statement in the ESA, the MMPA,

or NEPA, or the APA, we conclude that the Cetaceans do not have statutory standing to sue.
   AFFIRMED.

Questions & Notes

1. If Congress were to do as suggested by the 9th Circuit Court of Appeals, it would be a movement from weak species right to strong species rights. What do you think would be the nature of the debate in Congress if it considered letting suits be filed in the name of species? Do you think it would be important to have named specific animals as plaintiffs rather than just a species?

2. Consider how this would change the nature of the standing debate for actions under the Endangered Species Act or Marine Mammal Protection Act.

◇◇

What are the Possible Pathways for the Greater Legal Recognition of Protection of Animal Interests?

1. Adoption of legislation at the state level. As the government with the residue power of the sovereign, there is no real question that the states could expand the protection of animal interests by the adoption of legislation.

2. Change of law through the opinions of judges. Judges, particularly the common law judges of a state, have the capacity to modify the law as might be necessary in a fair and just society. See discussion later.

3. Change of law at the federal level is perhaps possible but has the difficulty faced in the **Dred Scott** opinion, 60 US 393 (1857), when a slave sought the support of the federal courts. Does the federal level of government have the constitutional authority to extend civil rights, any rights, to a new class of "persons," given that animals did not have any civil rights at the formation of the U.S. Constitution, nor have animals been the subject of any constitutional amendment since then?

4. The market force of consumers can produce outcomes that acknowledge the desirability of reduced pain and suffering of animals. For example, educated consumers can chose to purchase eggs only from producers who do not use battery cages. McDonald's and Wendy's may decide to purchase animal products only from slaughterhouses that comply with standards more beneficial to animals than the present law demands. The dolphin-free tuna campaign is a very successful example of consumer impact.

5. *Constitutional:* It may be that only by amendments to the state or federal constitutions will the legal system accept animals as legal "persons."

Incremental change will be part of the future. This incrementalism will result in the law treating different communities of animals differently. For example, for over a century a dog and cow have been in the same category of animal for purposes of the state anti-cruelty laws. Since the beginning of this century, as laws have become more complex and have moved from misdemeanor to felony status, there have been examples of creating a subdivision of animals. There has been a political and legislative focus on pets; as a result sometimes the new law has resulted in a higher level of protection for the interests of pets, companion animals, than for other animals. For example consider creation of a new felony in Illinois:

> § 70.3.02. Aggravated cruelty. No person may intentionally commit an act that causes a companion animal to suffer serious injury or death. Aggravated cruelty does not include euthanasia of a companion animal through recognized methods approved by the Department of Agriculture.

So, the same person committing the same act on a cow will be guilty of a misdemeanor, but if it is against a companion animal, then the act is a felony. Is the reason for this special treatment justified on an ethical basis? Might there be a political basis for this approach?

◇◇◇

One example of how animal interests might be protected on the civil side of the legal system is suggested by the following material, derived from a speech presented to the Harvard Conference on Chimpanzees 2002.

A New Tort—Substantial Interference with a Fundamental Interest

Property status is not a barrier to the recognition and protection of interests within the legal system. As the preceding example suggests, our legislature has the authority to expand the presence of animal interests within our legal system — and hopefully will continue to do so.

But more needs to be done: The presence of chimpanzee interests must be expanded, for they are nevertheless not receiving all the protection that they need. And while the legislative arena is always open, I want to suggest that there is also another route available — that of common law state courts. These traditional courts also have the capacity for the expansion of legal recognition of animal interests. In order to give form and substance to this avenue, I urge for the adoption of a new tort — *the intentional interference with the primary interests of a chimpanzee.*

This tort would allow for the resolving of conflicts between the competing interests of humans and chimpanzees by courts of law.

Under this cause of action the plaintiff must show the following elements:

1. Assert the existence of an interest.

2. Show that the interest is of fundamental importance to the plaintiff.

3. Assert that the being's interest has been interfered with or harmed by the actions or inactions of the defendant.

4. Show that the weight and nature of the interests of the chimpanzee plaintiff substantially outweighs the weight and nature of the interests of the defendant.

Before considering these elements in more detail, let me give you three examples so that you can have a context in which to understand what I want to accomplish. We will deal with a hypothetical chimpanzee — JoJo.

#1

JoJo lives in the Potsville zoo. He is one of a group of ten chimpanzees on a three-acre tract that was part of the $6 million project the zoo built three years ago. Zoo visitors can see the chimpanzees from five viewing positions. However, chimpanzees have the ability to retreat out of view if they wish. There is a trained caregiver on duty ten hours a day. The caregiver has the obligation to observe the chimpanzees for medical needs, to feed them with creative gathering challenges, to assure that their individual interactions do not cause harm, to control humans, and to generally assure their well-being. David Favre, attorney, files a law suit on behalf of client JoJo, claiming that regardless of the size of the cage, JoJo is still not able to move about in as large an area as he would in nature, and that the confinement interferes with his fundamental interest in personal freedom. The court would not rule for JoJo under these facts. While assuming that personal freedom may be a fundamental interest, the zoo has provided an environment which allows significant exercise in the interest of freedom of movement, and therefore the plaintiff will not be able to show a substantial interference with a fundamental interest.

#2

JoJo lives in the basement of the home of Big Jones in a commercial 5 x 5 x 7 cage. Big Jones collects exotic animals and shows off JoJo to all his beer-drinking friends by banging on the cage to get a reaction out of JoJo. After several months in residence, JoJo no longer reacts to cage rattling and has cut back on eating the table scraps that Big Jones feeds him. This comes to the attention of attorney David Favre who brings an action for JoJo under this tort seeking a guardianship for JoJo and an injunction requiring the transfer of JoJo to better facilities. The first two elements are easily satisfied. The fundamental interests of JoJo are clearly at risk; no socialization, no physical exercise, no enrichment of the environment, lack of appropriate food and clear psychological abuse. He is basically a live trophy for Big Jones. Therefore the court will move to the fourth element: do the interests of JoJo substantially outweigh the interests of Big Jones? The interests of the owner Big Jones are personal: he has a modest financial investment in the animal, and he feels important as the center of attention within his community of human friends with JoJo as an "attraction" in his house. It makes him feel special, providing part of his self-identity. The interests of Big Jones can be fulfilled in other ways and do not justify the interference with JoJo's fundamental interests. Jones' property interest in JoJo is not a defense. The court should be willing to enjoin the continued possession of JoJo by Big Jones. Because of the harm caused by Jones, the court could award damages or require the title transfer of JoJo to a third party without compensation.

#3

As a final example, consider JoJo, having lived for twenty years in an institutional lab at Big University, in a cage that meets the requirements of AWA in physical dimensions. However, he never sees the natural light of the sun, or the touch of any other chimpanzee, human or other, unless handlers have sought to do a procedure with him. There is nothing for him to do in the cage. He has been part of three different scientific protocols over the past fifteen years. If attorney David Favre brings an action for violation of the tort and seeks removal of JoJo from this environment, it should not be too difficult to show intentional interference with his fundamental interests as discussed earlier. The legal focus would quickly turn to element four and the court would have to determine whether JoJo's interests clearly outweigh the interests of the owner, Big University, in utilizing this animal in the name of science. This is not an abstract argument about the use of animals in science; it would be about this particular chimpanzee being used by this particular university. Whereas in the past researchers have only had to justify the use of chimpanzees to themselves, and did not have to give any weight to the interests of JoJo, under the proposed tort, Big University would have to make their case to the judge. Perhaps they can justify the interference, but I suspect not.

Now let us return to some of the concepts embedded in this new tort.

Duty

The premise of a tort is that a duty exists between the defendant and the plaintiff. I submit that the existence of this duty has already been acknowledged within our legal system. Remember that the criminal law adopted in every state imposes duties of no harm without justification and an affirmative duty of care. This proposed tort simply allows recognition of the duty within the civil side of the legal system.

There are those that might object to the acknowledgment of this new duty, as it does not impose a legal obligation on the chimpanzee. But we have many duties toward those without the capacity to have reciprocal legal duties; infants and insane persons being two quick examples.

Existence of an Interest

The threshold question requires the court to be convinced that scientific information, and not speculation, supports the claim of the existence of an interest. There should be a dual aspect to this inquiry. First, information about the species generally; secondly, information about the individual before the court. The last 30 years have produced considerable information about chimpanzees — enough that a court should be comfortable in being able to understand the nature of their interests. Obviously the test cannot be whether humans know everything about a species, as we do not yet even know everything about ourselves. Sufficiency of the knowledge should be judged in the context of the specific interests that is at issue before the court. Satisfying the court as to the base of information is the burden of the plaintiff.

Fundamental Nature of the Interests

Only interests of fundamental importance to the animal should be before the court, not the trivial, or obscure interests of the chimpanzee. This is about both the reality of limited judicial resources and the political support that will be necessary to sustain the new tort. For the most part these interests should also be the ones about which the most scientific information exists. This is not a bright line test and obviously will call upon the court to make a judgment call. The term "fundamental" should be considered in light of our knowledge about what is important to chimpanzees as a species and perhaps as individuals. Life is fundamental — freedom from pain, activity space, reproductive opportunity and social interactivity are all potentially fundamental. But again, both the individual and the species must also be considered. A touchstone for what is fundamental already exists in the legal system in the form of the legislation discussed earlier.

Actions of the Defendant

It is axiomatic that the plaintiff must show that the defendant is the source of actions causing the interference with the plaintiff's interest. This is fundamental to common law tort actions, and the usual concepts and theories would apply in this circumstance as well.

Substantially Outweighs

The phrase "substantially outweighs" is very important. If the balance of interests is close, then the human interests should prevail. As my proposed tort is a new approach and will require adjustment on the part of many people, this power should be exercised only when the case is clear. To do otherwise will result in the undermining of the public's confidence in the right of courts to address these novel issues.

While the burden is on the plaintiff, the nature of the claim would normally result in the defendant coming forward with information about the nature of the defendant's interests in pursuing the course of action of which the plaintiff complains. Presumably the plaintiff would be required to show initially a prima facie case of "substantially outweigh" and then the burden would shift to the defendant to show the plaintiff's interests do not outweigh their own.

The difficult issue the court will face is how to weigh disparate interests. Undoubtedly issues of morality, money, fairness, and social policy will become intermixed. This difficulty is precisely why it is important to engage the courts in the debate about the use of chimpanzees. At the moment this decision is usually made by the owner of the chimpanzee. There can often be a significant conflict of interests, as some owners give no weight to any interests of any chimpanzee in their charge.

Standing

It is not expected that any chimpanzee has the capacity to call a lawyer and ask to initiate a lawsuit, but this is not a bar to creating a tort. Courts on a regular basis adjudicate issues concerning beings who are incapacitated: children, mentally incompetent, the insane, the aged. It is beyond the scope of this speech to address who is the best to represent the interests of chimpanzees before courts. Our legal system has mechanisms, such as guardianships, next friends, legal representatives, and social workers to deal with this issue. This procedural issue is not a bar to the adoption of the substantive law, a tort law.

Remedy

Against nonowners of chimpanzees money damages will normally be sufficient. Against an owner, the remedies will also need to include equitable remedies such as injunctions, which may be necessary to stop certain actions and to improve conditions or remove a chimpanzee from unacceptable conditions. When money is awarded, then one of the trusts discussed earlier can be used as a way to hold the money for the benefit of the plaintiff chimpanzee.

Internationality

If the defendant is not a possessor/keeper/owner of the plaintiff, then the plaintiff would have to show a knowing interference. (A second cause of action could be the negligent interference with a fundamental interest, but that is a topic for another day.) However, if a defendant is a possessor/keeper/owner of a chimpanzee, then the law will conclusively presume the person has the knowledge of what are the fundamental interests of a chimpanzee. As a matter of public policy no human should have control or ownership of an animal as complex as a chimpanzee without such knowledge, and therefore it is appropriate to charge them with the knowledge whether or not they actually possess it.

[For a fuller consideration of the issue see David S. Favre, *Judicial Recognition of the Interests of Animals-A New Tort*, 2005 Mich. St. L. Rev. 333 (2005).]

Questions & Notes

1. If the Supreme Court of a state recognized that such a cause of action existed, then would it follow naturally that the animal in question would have standing to bring the claim before the court? How could it be decided who should bring the action on behalf of the animal; that is, how is the lawyer chosen?

2. Would you be willing to extend this analysis beyond chimpanzees? How far?

3. If this tort was recognized, would JoJo the chimpanzee have a legal right? Is he still property?

4. Do you think a court would ever be willing to adopt the suggested tort?

5. In what fact patterns do you think this tort might be asserted? What would you suggest as a test case?

6. Would it be a better course of action to take the proposed tort to a legislature?

◇◇

As suggested, a key component of the process of obtaining legal rights for animals is its incremental nature. As a result of this reality, it is predictable that some animals will have legal rights different from other species of animals. The pet dog and cat may well have medical treatment requirements different from commercial animals. Different legal rights will cluster around different sets of animals. The following chart suggests three such categories. Pets or companion animals will have the most political support being the closest to voting humans. Commercial animals will have legal rights more circumscribed by economic reality. Another set of self-aware beings such as parrots, dolphins, and chimpanzees may well receive a different set of legal rights. The chart suggests some possibilities for the future evolution of law.

	Government Action "Weak rights"	Guardian/ Owner Action "Strong rights"	Humans Filing Action v. Owner "Strong rights"	Animals Bringing Legal Action "Preferred rights"
Pets Community	• State anti-cruelty laws • Federal AWA	• Divorce proceedings • Protection from domestic violence	• Civil action for enforcement of anti-cruelty law	• Animals as beneficiary of pet trust • Tort recovery
Commercial Community	• Living regulations • Federal AWA expansion		• Civil action for enforcement of welfare standards	• Farm-focused lawsuits based on groups of animal not individuals
Conscious Beings Community	• Endangered Species Act • New international treaties		• Civil actions under ESA & NEPA • State action under treaty	• National law & international law on behalf of a species & individuals

What would you add to the chart?

Please now return to the board game at the beginning of this chapter and mark where the groups will be in ten years, in 50 years. Can you now state clearly the rules of the game?

CHAPTER 12

Animal Rights — The Social Movement

Section 1

The Breadth of the Animal Movement

Is there a social movement for the betterment of the conditions of animals? Within the United States and a number of countries around the world the answer is clearly yes. This book exists as evidence of the movement. The World Wide Web is clearly the place to get a taste of the vast array of organizations that touch on animal issues.

Consider the following sources:

- http://en.wikipedia.org/wiki/List_of_animal_welfare_groups
- http://en.wikipedia.org/wiki/List_of_animal_rights_groups
- http://www.worldanimal.net/ [Listing 17,000 organizations worldwidel.

Many individuals and organizations devote considerable human and financial resources for the betterment of animals. Some support and protect feral cat colonies, others build shelters for unwanted animals, others write books or march in protests. Millions of individuals have expressed some level of interest in local, state, or national issues.

The development of the movement is visible within the world of legal institutions.

◇◇

The Gathering Momentum for Animal Rights

by David Favre, 1 Brazilian Animal Rights Review 13 (2006)

While the roots of the present animal welfare social movement reaches back into the 1950's with the efforts of a number of individuals to pass a national animal protection, it was not until the publication of Professor Peter Singer's *Animal Liberation* (1977) and Professor Tom Regan's *A Case for Animal Rights* (1983) that the philosophical claim for animal rights got ignited and the movement achieved intellectual traction.

On Thanksgiving weekend in 1981, at Brooklyn Law School, the first national conference was held for lawyers to consider animal legal issues. The next year at a meeting in San Francisco, the first national organization of attorneys was formed to promote animal welfare/rights. The initial name was Attorneys for Animal Rights, but several years later the name was changed to the Animal Legal Defense Fund (ALDF). Also in the 1980's the activist organization PETA (People for the Ethical Treatment of Animals) and many others were formed. Thus began the legal and social movement to create awareness of animal suffering and to obtain change within the legal system. This growing movement had sufficient activity and interests in the general population that in the summer of 1990 there was a "March for the Animals" in Washington D.C. Upwards of 10,000 people showed up to march from the White House to the steps of the Capitol building, chanting slogans and giving speeches on behalf of animals.

I. Law Schools

All of this broader social activity in the 1980's and early 1990's had very little impact within the legal profession or the law schools of the country. As the animal issues obtained increasing public awareness college students, in the tradition of environmental movement thirty years earlier, began arriving at law schools to pursue the goal of legal change on behalf of animals. It was back in 1994 that I was asked to write an introduction to the first volume of the Animal Law Review. It should be noted that within the United States legal journals are published primarily by law schools through the efforts of law students, so change can occur by the efforts of students, long before the acceptance of the issue at high levels of authority within legal education. In this case the law review was produced by the law students at Lewis and Clark Law School, in Portland, Oregon, USA. The Law School itself would not pay the cost of printing the Journal, so the ALDF paid the cost of printing, to get animal legal issues formally before the thinking lawyers of the country.

At approximately the same time at the same school, an overlapping group of law students formed the first Student Animal Legal Defense Fund (SALDF). Since that time interest in the topic of Animal Law has exploded in the realm of the law schools across the nation. This past summer I wrote the introduction to a second, new journal dealing with animal legal issues, the Journal of Animal Law, a peer reviewed law review of the Michigan State University College of Law. Law students at the University of Pennsylvania have also announced their intentions to create a third animal focused law journal.

The existence of these journals is important as they allow the development of ideas and theories within the legal community, at a level of sophistication which could not be realized in the public press. While the first debate within a movement is of philosophy, this lays the conceptual foundation for the direction in which the law ought to proceed. The philosophical debate creates the desire and justification for social change, but does not suggest how to obtain the change within existing laws and institutions. The debate in the law journals occurs when the discussion becomes more focused upon how to change the law. Thus there is a critical role for law journals, where the debate about how to proceed can occur among the lawyers. This is modestly important for changes of the nature of animal welfare improvements, but is critical for that much more difficult concept of animal rights.

Besides the publication of scholarly articles, another important measure of progress is the teaching of the course within law schools. While a few courses on Animal Law were taught in the 1980's and early 1990's it was the teaching of the course at Harvard Law School that really was a landmark event. There are two aspects of this occurrence that are important to note. First, it was taught by Steven Wise, past president of ALDF and activist attorney, as an adjunct professor, not by one of the tenured professors. In 2005 it is still the case that only a few of the law school's animal law courses are taught by tenured faculty. Secondly, the occurrence of the class at Harvard gave legitimacy to the issue that had not previously existed. An article in the New York Times about the course and the movement resulted in a large cascade of press coverage about the movement generally and possible legal changes specifically.

Omitting the intervening details, consider the scope of the interests today, as measured by both the number of law schools who are offering the course and the number of law schools where students have self organized to promote animal issues. The best count is kept by the Animal Legal Defense Fund and is available from their website. In of the fall of 2005 the site listed 62 law schools as offering the courses, and 68 law schools had student organizations (SALDF) . (There are approximately 190 American Bar Association (ABA) approved law schools in the U.S.) [As of January 2011 the number of law school teaching animal law was 125 and the number of SALDFs at law schools was up to 150 within the United States and eight internationally. See *http://www.aldf.org/userdata_display.php?modin=51*]

Celebrity Profile: Bob Barker

A true hero for all animals
By Sue Shaw, SORT Staff Writer
Published 05-26-2006, *www.sort.org/print_article.php?article_id=236*

The Bob Barker Endowment Fund for the Study of Animal Rights Law exists at several different colleges. The first one was established in June of 2001 at the Harvard Law School. It received a $500,000 gift to establish the Endowment Fund by Pearson Television in honor of Bob Barker's 30 years as the host for Price Is Right. Bob Barker continued this Endowment by donating $1 million to the UCLA School of Law to create its own Bob Barker Endowment Fund for the Study of Animal Rights Law. He has also established this Endowment at Duke University, Stanford University and Columbia University, and Northwestern Law School.

It is easy to say that a social movement on behalf of animals exists, but just where does the movement want to go? How should it proceed to generate awareness, change laws, get animals out of horrible conditions? There is no real way to obtain agreement on any of these questions. Individuals and groups just try to do what they think is important, like a headless blob the movement flows into the future. There is debate with those not in the movement and debate within the movement.

Section 2

Players in the National Debate

Those Against Change

The following memo was forwarded to the author during the fall of 2002.

From: Bob Kane
To: Undisclosed Recipient List
Date: 9/26/02 11:34AM
Subject: What You Need to Know About Animal Rightists

Dear Animal Enthusiast,

Time is running out. Running out due to our own apathy and failure to become involved. The Animal Rights movement is gaining significant ground to deprive you of your age-old rights to interact with animals. That's right, everything from enjoying a dinner of your choice to enjoying the comfort and companionship of a pet. At stake is your right to take your children and grandchildren hunting and fishing, to let them see the newborn colt lying in the grass next to his mother, or for that matter just to enjoy a lazy Sunday afternoon at the zoo with them. Animal Rights organizations have organized and become well funded. They are now a significant force on the political landscape. And what have we done? Most of us are not even aware of what these people stand for.

Did you know that the Animal Rights movement regards the rights of animals above human rights?

While expounding on the rights of animals, Peter Singer, recognized as the father of the Animal Rights movement, stated that human societies should kill retarded infants and incapacitated elderly members of society and that mainstream Christianity is a "problem."

Did you know that the Animal Rights movement regards violence and terrorism as viable methods to bring about change to their way of thinking?

"Every social justice movement has embraced violence and every successful social justice movement has utilized violent tactics to achieve their goals. I don't think it is possible without that. I think we have to quit waiting until everyone is behind us before we embrace new tactics."
—Jerry Vlasak, Animal Defense League

Volkert van der Graaf is charged with murdering Dutch politician Pim Fortuyn. Van der Graaf is a vegan animal rights activist who as a teenager founded a branch of the Animal Liberation Front and had spent his adult life fighting animal agriculture in court.

PETA founder and president Ingrid Newkirk in a keynote address at AR2002 stated: "I stand before you this year a little baffled because I have been named by name by the State of Wisconsin as a good reason to pass their state's anti-terrorism legislation. Was it something I said? It turned out it actually was. Right here in America, formerly the land of free speech, I said that yes, I do hope that foot and mouth disease would come here."

PETA payouts to violent radicals include:

- $5,000 to Josh Harper, who was convicted of assaulting police and firing on a fishing vessel;
- $2,000 to Dave Wilson, convicted of firebombing a fur co-operative;
- $7,500 to Fran Trutt, convicted of attempted murder of a medical executive;
- $20,000 to Rodney Coronado, convicted of burning a research lab at Michigan State.

Were this Hamas or Al Qaeda, the federal government would have long ago taken action against these people as a terrorist group.

Did you know that the Animal Rights movement supports ideas far from the mainstream of American ideals? Peter Singer, father of the animal rights movement has gone as far as to provide a qualified defense of sex between humans and non-human animals.

Did you know that the Animal Rights movement considers all uses of domesticated animals to be wrong?

Rutgers law professor Gary Francione and Fund for Animals legal director Lee Hall have gone as far as to label the provision of guide dogs for the blind as an "abominable practice."

Biomedical research as a whole is facing a well-financed, multi-faceted and sophisticated offensive designed to stop all use of laboratory animals in basic, disease and injury research, pharmaceutical R&D and safety testing.

Rather than advocate for humane treatment of non-human animals, Francione and Hall argue for essentially a complete separation and end all contact between humans and animals (except, perhaps, where humans are simply unnoticed observers).

Gary Francione: "If, however, we did accord animals this one right, not to be treated as property, we would be committed to abolishing and not merely regulating animal exploitation because our uses of animals for food, experiments, product testing, entertainment, and clothing all assume that animals are nothing but property. If we accepted that animals have the right not to be treated as our property, we would stop--completely--bringing domestic animals into existence."

Did you know that the activities of Animal Rights groups are being stepped up on all fronts?

At the Animal Rights 2002 convention a common focus of the panels and workshops was on developing new coalitions and alliances, manipulating the political and legal systems to achieve activist objectives, and framing the campaign for animal rights within a broader social justice movement.

PETA spokesman Andrew Butler claimed that activists showed up at 300 March of Dimes Walk America fundraising events in the past year. He discussed PETA's tactic of visiting local chapters of charities such as the March of Dimes, the American Cancer Society and the American Heart Association, that can be pressured directly and, he believes, more effectively than the national headquarters of those charities. Butler also noted PETA's use of billboards, letters to newspapers and leafleting to raise local public and media awareness of PETA's ongoing campaign against health charities.

Claiming that "opponents" are better organized than the animal rights movement now and are in control of the political landscape in every state, activist Julie Lewin, National Institute for Animal Advocacy said, "We are squandering our potential by not being organized," and not having "an accountability system" in place for politicians. Lewin said that full-time lobbyists need to be placed in every state capital and statewide databases need to be established of legislative voting records and animal rights-interested voters by district. To support her point, Lewin offered this axiom: "A politically organized minority on an issue can drive public policy on that issue because every politician knows that a politically organized minority can swing elections."

Did you know that unless you begin, right now, to become involved in this fight you will surely lose the right to:

- Enjoy a steak dinner (Vegans don't eat meat, cheese, eggs or fish)

- Hunt & Fish

- Raise livestock on your farm or ranch

- Buy clothes made of any type of animal product

- Avail yourself of lifesaving medical discoveries that involved animal testing

- Reach over and pet your favorite cat or dog

- Obtain a guide dog if you are blind

- Live in safety knowing that you disagree with the Animal Rightist concept

The Sportsmen's and Animal Owners' Voting Alliance (SAOVA) is helping in this fight. We have formed political coalitions across the United States working toward the election of individuals who believe, as you and I do, that the humane enjoyment of animals is our right. SAOVA urges you to become involved, investigate the voting record of your local representatives and let them know your feelings on this matter. And if they ignore your concerns then VOTE THEM OUT OF OFFICE.

SAOVA is working to do just that. Our grass roots level organization has been active in questioning and evaluating the answers of those running for political office in all of the states. We have been successful in helping to defeat some of the country's biggest Animal Rightist supporters in this year's primaries and look forward to similar success on November 5, 2002. It's important that you inform yourself of candidates' positions and agendas. If you are interested in participating in this fight visit *http://saova.org* and review our endorsements and contribution suggestions. There you will find the results of our analysis of both incumbent candidates running for re-election to Washington, as well as new candidates for such office. It's crucial that you vote for and financially support those candidates willing to fight this spreading menace. Help us help the candidates who will fight for our age-old heritage.

Please share this message with your friends, neighbors and relatives. Thank you.

Bob Kane, Sportsmen's and Animal Owners' Voting Alliance

http://saova.org — Forwarding and cross posting permission granted. [As of 2011 this site is still active on these issues.]

Questions & Notes

1. Did Bob Kane convince you of the need for action? Did you visit the website?

2. Do you think his characterization of the Animal Rights movement is accurate and fair?

3. Why is this postured as a political battle? Do you agree with the author about the risk of change?

⬦⬦⬦⬦⬦⬦⬦⬦⬦⬦⬦⬦⬦⬦⬦⬦⬦⬦⬦⬦⬦⬦⬦⬦⬦⬦⬦⬦⬦⬦⬦⬦⬦⬦

Others who seek to counter the efforts of the animal rights movement include the following.

I. The Center for Consumer Freedom

The Center for Consumer Freedom describes itself as:

> Founded in 1996, the Center for Consumer Freedom is a non-profit organization devoted to promoting personal responsibility and protecting consumer choices. We believe that the consumer is King. And Queen.

> A growing cabal of activists has meddled in Americans' lives in recent years. They include self-anointed "food police," health campaigners, trial lawyers, personal-finance do-gooders, animal-rights misanthropes, and meddling bureaucrats.

> Their common denominator? They all claim to know "what's best for you." In reality, they're eroding our basic freedoms — the freedom to buy what we want, eat what we want, drink what we

want, and raise our children as we see fit. When they push ordinary Americans around, we're here to push back.

So what exactly is "consumer freedom"?

Consumer freedom is the right of adults and parents to choose how they live their lives, what they eat and drink, how they manage their finances, and how they enjoy themselves.

But you're opposed to "good" groups. Doesn't that make you the "bad guys"?

We speak up whenever activists propose curtailing consumer freedom. What makes us different from many organizations is that we aren't afraid to take on groups that have built "good" images through slick public relations campaigns. Just because they claim to be "ethical" or "responsible" or "in the public interest" doesn't mean they are. Just because they claim to be "scientific" doesn't mean it's true. Activists are maneuvering to tax your favorite foods, throw the book at popular restaurants with tobacco-style lawsuits, limit the options you have for managing your money, and even criminally harass people with whom they disagree. We make sure you know about it.

From www.consumerfreedom.com/about.cfm (last visited January 2011).

II. Americans for Medical Progress

Animal research is a vital component in scientists' search for treatments and cures. Americans for Medical Progress protects society's investment in research by nurturing public understanding of and support for the humane and necessary use of animals in medicine.

• AMP provides information to bolster public opinion of animal-based research through its website, various publications and posters.

• AMP highlights the stories of those who have benefited from research to illustrate the relevancy of animal-based research.

• AMP provides materials to inspire research advocacy.

From http://www.amprogress.org/programs.

AMP has a very distinguished Board of Directors: http://www.amprogress.org/amp_board (last visited Jan. 2011).

III. Anti-PETA

P.E.T.A. (People For the Ethical Treatment Of Animals) has been around a while making life miserable for most decent folks with their hyped up, false stories of how we need to treat animals as equals and grant them rights that only we, as humans, should enjoy.

These assumptions are false and most of the claims they use to further their cause are not founded in reality but in some vegan induced fog of silliness.

This site is not intended to blast P.E.T.A. (everyone is entitled to their own opinion) but rather to tell folks the real story and hopefully stop them from joining an organization or way of life that may be harmful to themselves or others.

From http://www.anti-peta.com/ (last visited Jan 2011).

◇◇

Those for Change

The Humane Society of the United States (HSUS) is perhaps the largest animal welfare organization in the United States. In its 2006 annual report HSUS reported 9,980,589 members and constituents, as well as 569 staff and consultants. A few years ago they created a litigation division for the filing of lawsuits to aid in animal issues. Visit their website at *www.hsus.org* to see the scope of their activities. They are not an umbrella group for animal shelters around the country, but a single large issues focused organization.

The following is a small sample of other organizations seeking change. The information provided has been taken from each organization's website. For each group consider the following:

1. What is the size of the organization?

2. What are the goals of the organization?

3. What do you think their approach is for realization of their goals?

4. What is their level of working with the legal system?

5. How effective have they been in obtaining their goals?

I. Greyhound Protection League

The work of the Greyhound Protection League is dedicated to the hundreds of thousands of gentle, trusting greyhounds killed in the prime of life during the 80 years of pari-mutuel dog racing in America. The primary purpose of this website is to bear witness to the tragic history of the racing greyhound so that the world will never again be lulled into silence, ignorance or indifference.

The unbridled expansion of dog racing during the 20th Century spawned a greyhound breeding frenzy that culminated in the death of tens of thousands of uncompetitive greyhounds every year. As expendable by-products of the racing system, the sacrifice of these young lives was considered acceptable in the interest of state-budget deficits, gambling profits and free market enterprise; but not to everyone . . .

Founded in 1991, the Greyhound Protection League was the first organization of its kind to break the silence and speak out nationally against the atrocities inflicted upon racing greyhounds. GPL is a national, non-profit, all volunteer organization committed to protecting racing greyhounds from exploitation, mistreatment and abuse. Our work is pursued both on the front lines and behind the scenes through the valiant efforts of dedicated volunteers across the country, each of whom is also involved in the hands-on greyhound rescue movement.

In addition to our educational and investigative work, GPL is dedicated to all aspects of greyhound welfare, including the use of our financial resources for special-needs adoptions and emergency hauling expenses for the relocation of at-risk greyhounds.

For nearly two decades GPL has been the primary source for well-researched information about the internal workings of the greyhound racing system. Our in-depth investigations and exposés revealing the seamy underbelly of dog racing have altered the perception that greyhound racing is a harmless spectator "sport" to the blunt reality that greyhound racing has been responsible for incalculable animal suffering and the routine killing of thousands of young, healthy greyhounds each year. The League's fact-based revelations about what goes on beyond the glitz and glamour of the grandstand has put immense pressure on the racing industry to reform and focus on the welfare of the greyhound racing dogs who are the very life-blood of industry profits.

Fate has brought us full circle. In 21st Century America, it is the racing industry itself that is facing a death sentence for failure to deliver a winning performance in the economic arena. Changes in societal values, competition from other forms of gaming, media exposés and pressure from the humane community have all taken their toll.

However, complacency is not in order; numerous tracks and breeding farms remain in operation. Reduced breeding numbers have not eased the burden on adoption groups and the shuttering of a track puts hundreds more greyhounds at risk. With accountability for dogs exiting a track remaining the single most elusive element in the racing system, the Greyhound Protection League will continue its vigilance and the pursuit of justice and a decent life for every greyhound.

From www.greyhounds.org/gpl/contents/entry.html (as of January 2011).

II. Animal Legal Defense Fund

Who We Are, What We Do

For more than three decades, the Animal Legal Defense Fund has been fighting to protect the lives and advance the interests of animals through the legal system. Founded in 1979 by attorneys active in shaping the emerging field of animal law, ALDF has blazed the trail for stronger enforcement of anti-cruelty laws and more humane treatment of animals in every corner of American life. Today, ALDF's groundbreaking efforts to push the U.S. legal system to end the suffering of abused animals are supported by hundreds of dedicated attorneys and more than 100,000 members. Every day, ALDF works to protect animals by:

• Filing groundbreaking lawsuits to stop animal abuse and expand the boundaries of animal law.

• Providing free legal assistance to prosecutors handling cruelty cases.

• Working to strengthen state anti-cruelty statutes.

• Encouraging the federal government to enforce existing animal protection laws.

• Nurturing the future of animal law through Student Animal Legal Defense Fund chapters and our Animal Law Program.

• Providing public education through seminars, workshops and other outreach efforts.

http://aldf.org/section.php?id=3 (as of January 2011).

◇◇

III. PETA

Our Mission Statement

People for the Ethical Treatment of Animals (PETA) is the largest animal rights organization in the world, with more than 2 million members and supporters.

PETA focuses its attention on the four areas in which the largest numbers of animals suffer the most intensely for the longest periods of time: on factory farms, in the clothing trade, in laboratories, and in the entertainment industry. We also work on a variety of other issues, including the cruel killing of beavers, birds, and other "pests" as well as cruelty to domesticated animals.

PETA works through public education, cruelty investigations, research, animal rescue, legislation, special events, celebrity involvement, and protest campaigns.

http://www.peta.org/about/default.aspx (last visited Jan. 2011).

A Sense of the Activities of PETA

"McDonald's: First in U.S. History to Stop Some Abuses of Chickens, Other Farmed Animals" — Fall 2000 (from *www.peta.org*, as of August 2003).

In June 1997, McDonald's was found by the British High Court to be "culpably responsible for cruelty to animals." PETA immediately called on McDonald's to make improvements, holding news conferences and demonstrations around the country. After a "Day of Action" in October generated dozens of protests around the country, McDonald's invited PETA into negotiations, which lasted for two years.

After McDonald's refused to do a single thing to improve life for even a single animal, on October 16, 1999, PETA launched a campaign against McDonald's. Our campaign lasted 11 months and included more than 400 demonstrations at McDonald's restaurants in more than 23 countries, as well as provocative advertisements and campaign materials, celebrity involvement, and more. On September 6, 2000, PETA declared a one-year moratorium on the McDonald's Campaign, as the company had agreed to make important, but basic animal welfare improvements.

The McDonald's improvements marked the first time in U.S. history that any large corporation had done anything at all for farmed animals. Furthermore, since the U.S. government refuses to cover birds under the Animal Welfare or Humane Slaughter acts, before McDonald's implemented its new standards, egg and chicken farmers could do anything to these animals with complete impunity.

Vital Statistics (for the year 2010)

- PETA's Web site *PETA.org* was visited by more than 50,000,000 users—putting it in the top 1 percentile of all sites on the World Wide Web—and won a prestigious Webby Award.

- PETA's Media Department booked more than 4,500 interviews.

- PETA's International Grassroots Campaign Department helped organize 900 demonstrations.

- PETA's Sexiest Vegetarian Next Door was a smashing success with more than 684,000 page visits.

- PETA's Research & Investigations Department responded to more than 17,000 calls regarding cruelty to animals.

From: http://features.peta.org/Annual-Review-2010/default.aspxl (as of July 2011).

Questions & Notes

1. Are you aware of any PETA campaigns? If so, describe one. Are they effective?

2. For another view of PETA activities see, *www.anti-peta.com* (as of January 2007) and *www.petakillsanimals.com/about.cfm*.

The following table will give the reader a sense of the size of some of the organizations and the resources available to the movement. The information is from federal tax forms 990, available at *www.guidestar.com* or the websites of the organizations. The information is usually from the tax year 2010.

Organization	2010 Annual Revenue	Net Assets
Humane Society of U.S.	$101,680,000	$200,000,000
PETA	$35,851,000	$17,212,000
ALDF	$3,781,000	$4,718,000
Friend of Animals	$6,190,000	$5,021,000

Even though nonprofit organizations are the major players in the movement, "nonprofit" does not mean everyone in the movement is poor. Consider some of the salaries reported to the IRS.

Person	Organization	Salary
Wayne Pacelle	President, HSUS	$234,375
Roger Kindler	General Counsel, HSUS	$181,000
Priscilla Feral	President, Friends of Animals	$101,865
Steve Well	Exec. Director ALDF	$93,713

IV. Animal Liberation Front

ALF Mission Statement / Credo

The Animal Liberation Front (ALF) carries out direct action against animal abuse in the form of rescuing animals and causing financial loss to animal exploiters, usually through the damage and destruction of property.

The ALF's short-term aim is to save as many animals as possible and directly disrupt the practice of animal abuse. Their long-term aim is to end all animal suffering by forcing animal abuse companies out of business.

It is a nonviolent campaign, activists taking all precautions not to harm any animal (human or otherwise).

Because ALF actions are against the law, activists work anonymously, either in small groups or individually, and do not have any centralized organization or coordination.

The Animal Liberation Front consists of small autonomous groups of people all over the world who carry out direct action according to the ALF guidelines. *Any group of people who are vegetarians or vegans and who carry out actions according to ALF guidelines have the right to regard themselves as part of the ALF.*

The ALF guidelines are:

1. TO liberate animals from places of abuse, i.e. laboratories, factory farms, fur farms, etc, and place them in good homes where they may live out their natural lives, free from suffering.

2. TO inflict economic damage to those who profit from the misery and exploitation of animals.

3. TO reveal the horror and atrocities committed against animals behind locked doors, by performing non-violent direct actions and liberations.

4. TO take all necessary precautions against harming any animal, human and non-human.

From www.animalliberationfront.com/ALFront/alf_credo.htm (as of January 2011).

Questions & Notes

1. Just where is the battle ground for animal rights: Congress, corporate board rooms, evening news?

2. Who defines the agenda and who sets the strategy for obtaining the goals? How is the movement alike and different from the civil rights movement from the 1920s to 1950s? Is it alike or dissimilar from the women's rights movement for the right to vote or for equal rights?

Section 3

Change by Public Protest

CASE BY CASE

Dubner v. City and County of San Francisco
266 F. 3d 959 (9th Cir. 2001)

D.W. NELSON, CIRCUIT JUDGE.

I. FACTUAL AND PROCEDURAL BACKGROUND

On October 7, 1996, the American College of Surgeons ("ACS") held a convention at the Moscone Convention Center in San Francisco. The Moscone Center is owned by the City of San Francisco. During the convention, ACS leased the entire facility and controlled who was allowed into the building. That morning approximately twenty members of the animal rights group, In Defense of Animals, gathered outside the entrance to protest medical experimentation on animals. Dubner, an attorney and amateur photographer, went to the demonstration intending to take photographs, perhaps meet a potential client, and serve as a "legal observer," but not as a participant.

> The Moscone Center consists of two buildings (Moscone North and Moscone South). The demonstrators focused their attention on the entrance to Moscone North where there is a half circle driveway for cars and buses to drop off and pick up conventioneers. Between this driveway and the street--inside the half circle—eated by the driveway—is a pedestrian island. During the course of the demonstration, protestors alternatively stood on this pedestrian island waving placards, distributing literature, and shouting at conventioneers, or stood in the driveway and in front of the entrance to the convention center thereby impeding the conventioneers from entering and exiting the building.

At approximately 12:30 p.m., Sgt. Ziegler received word that a demonstration was taking place and proceeded to the Moscone Center. Ziegler first spoke to Gayle Grimes, who she believed was the organizer of the protest, and explained that they could continue the demonstration so long as they did not block traffic or prevent conventioneers from entering and exiting the building. Soon thereafter, Grimes and the other protestors tried to enter Moscone North, but were stopped by convention center security guards who locked the doors. Ziegler witnessed the protestors' attempts to enter the building and called for back up. Approximately fifteen officers responded to her call, including Lieutenant

Ehrlich and Captain Dennis Martel. After several minutes of chanting slogans outside the convention center doors, the demonstrators returned to the pedestrian island.

The officers informed Niespodziewanski that the sidewalk and driveway were considered private property controlled by ACS and asked if he wanted the police to make arrests. Niespodziewanski said that the demonstration could continue, but that he wanted the demonstrators to stay on the pedestrian island. At that point, an officer showed Niespodziewanski a citizen's arrest form and told him that if he signed it, "those people" would be arrested. The form provided space where the name of the offender and the relevant offense could be written in, but these were blank when Niespodziewanski signed the form. [FN1] Several officers testified that it was common practice to have the complainant sign the form and then fill in the name of one of the arrestees later followed by "et al."

FN1. The citizen's arrest form reads as follows:

I made a CITIZEN'S ARREST on the person of _____ for the violations(s) of _____ on _____ committed in my presence at _____ and I did thereupon request the San Francisco Police Department to assume custody of the above subject. I understand that I will be contacted by the District Attorney of the City and County of San Francisco should I be required to sign a formal complaint charging the above named subject with the commission of the violation(s) hereon indicted.

After the citizen's arrest form was signed, Captain Martel directed Ehrlich to give a dispersal order using a bull-horn. Ehrlich gave the dispersal order two or three times standing in different locations outside the Moscone Center. Ehrlich testified that the dispersal order was not the "textbook" version because the language in that order applies to dispersal orders given in public streets. He recalled using words to the effect of "I ask you to leave the area in front of the doors and go to the pedestrian island. You can no longer remain on private property. Go to the public sidewalk. If you do not leave the area you will be arrested." The dispersal order did not specifically mention the protestors because Ehrlich's goal was to get "all non-credentialed people" out of the area.

At that point, some of the protestors moved to the pedestrian island and others remained on the driveway and sidewalk. Several convention attendees also remained near the entrance. Martel directed Ehrlich and Captain Tachini to start arresting people, and then pointed out a few individuals to arrest first "because they were more animated." Martel assumed it would be obvious to the officers who to arrest because they were dressed differently than the conventioneers or because they had signs and leaflets. Sixteen people were arrested, including Dubner.

Dubner was at the demonstration for approximately one hour. For most of that time she was positioned on the sidewalk near the entrance to Moscone North, taking photographs of the protestors, and speaking with both demonstrators and conventioneers. At one point, Dubner entered the doorway to the convention center to take photographs of the protestors through the glass doors and was mistakenly locked inside. After being let out of the building, Dubner moved 8- 10 feet to the east of the line of glass doors, and approximately 8-10 feet out from the building where she remained standing on the sidewalk that runs along the curved driveway. There is no evidence in the record that she was carrying any signs or leaflets.

According to her testimony prior to the arrest, Dubner was talking to one of the convention attendees and did not hear any dispersal order or anyone ask her to move to the pedestrian island. A male police officer came up to her and told her she would have to leave. She replied, "Excuse me?" and the officer repeated his statement. Dubner asked "Does this gentleman have to leave, too?," referring to the convention attendee. At that point, the officer said, "Arrest her," and two other officers handcuffed Dubner and took her into custody. Dubner is unable to identify either the first male officer who said, "Arrest her," or the two officers who handcuffed her. The only information available as to the identity of these officers is her arrest report which lists Ehrlich and Ziegler as the arresting officers. Dubner and the other fifteen people arrested were then transported to the county jail where they were booked and detained. [FN2]

> FN2. Dubner alleged in her complaint that her camera was forcibly removed while she was in the jail cell and that the guards seized her and brought her to the floor with one arm twisted behind her back in order to remove the camera.

Dubner filed suit in state court against Officers Ziegler and Ehrlich, Police Chief Lau, and the City and County of San Francisco asserting several state law claims, and a § 1983 claim for unlawful arrest. The case was removed to federal court where both parties agreed to a bench trial before Magistrate Judge Phyllis J. Hamilton.

At trial and in deposition testimony, Ziegler and Ehrlich did not remember whether they had arrested Dubner. Ziegler explained that her name was listed as the arresting officer for fourteen or fifteen of the sixteen people arrested because she was the first officer on the scene. She testified that she did not arrest all fourteen or fifteen people for whom she was listed as the arresting officer. At the close of plaintiff's evidence, the trial judge dismissed Dubner's punitive damages claim because there was "simply insufficient evidence to support an allegation as to punitive damages."

III. DISCUSSION

We agree with the trial judge that the citizen's arrest was invalid because the citizen who signed the form did not see Dubner, describe her alleged offense, or point her out to the police. We also agree that the inaccuracies in the arrest report seem calculated to hide the identity of the arresting officers. We agree with the magistrate judge that the arrest was invalid. We disagree, however, with the conclusion that Dubner failed to establish a prima facie case against the defendants.

A. Identity of the Arresting Officers

A claim for unlawful arrest is cognizable under § 1983 as a violation of the Fourth Amendment, provided the arrest was without probable cause or other justification.

Although the plaintiff bears the burden of proof on the issue of unlawful arrest, she can make a prima facie case simply by showing that the arrest was conducted without a valid warrant. At that point, the burden shifts to the defendant to provide some evidence that the arresting officers had probable cause for a warrantless arrest. The plaintiff still has the ultimate burden of proof, but the burden of production falls on the defendant.

Since Dubner was not arrested pursuant to a valid warrant or citizen's arrest form, defendants had the burden of producing some evidence that the arresting officers had probable cause. None of the officers testified to having seen Dubner during the demonstration, much less to having seen her break the law. Appellees' references to the collective knowledge of the officers are, therefore, misplaced. Based on the total lack of evidence as to who arrested Dubner or what they knew at the time, it follows that the defendants failed to satisfy their burden of production and that Dubner has made out a valid claim of unlawful arrest.

B. Probable Cause

Appellees contend that, even if Dubner's failure to identify the arresting officers does not bar her claim, we should affirm because there was probable cause to arrest her for violating California Penal Code § 602.1 and § 409.

The arrest report states that Dubner violated Cal. Penal Code § 602.1. Section 602.1 provides that:

> [a]ny person who intentionally interferes with any lawful business or occupation carried on by the owner or agent of a business establishment open to the public, by obstructing or intimidating those attempting to carry on business, or their customers, and who refuses to leave the premises of the business establishment after being requested to leave by the owner or the owner's agent, or by a peace officer acting at the request of the owner or the owner's agent, is guilty of a misdemeanor,....

Thus, a violation of § 602.1 has two elements: (1) intentional interference, and (2) refusal to leave. Dubner may have refused to leave the sidewalk in front of the Moscone Center. She denied hearing either dispersal order, but the district court found her testimony incredible. Based on our review of the record, we cannot say this finding was clearly erroneous. Nevertheless, there is no evidence that Dubner intentionally interfered with the business of the Convention Center. Instead, the record shows that Dubner was taking photographs of the protestors from a position 8-10 feet away from the doors and conversing with convention attendees and protestors.

We reject Appellees' argument that intent to interfere can be inferred from Dubner's refusal to leave. Dubner's undisputed testimony is that she was at the Moscone Center to observe the demonstration and take photographs of the protestors. There is no indication that her conversations with attendees were intended to or had the effect of intimidating them. In fact, her behavior was indistinguishable from that of any member of the press, a curious passerby, or a legal observer. As the district court pointed out, there was no evidence that Dubner was "engaged in any traditional 'protest' activities, such as chanting, carrying a sign, handing out literature, or blocking the building entrances." Therefore, we conclude that, even if whoever arrested Dubner was privy to all of the information available to the officers at the scene and Dubner's testimony, there was insufficient evidence to warrant a prudent person to believe she had violated section 602.1.

Because the record does not support probable cause to believe Dubner had violated either code section, we reverse and remand for the trial court to determine whether Ziegler and Ehrlich can reasonably be held liable for the unlawful arrest.

Questions & Notes

1. What was the reason for the protest? Do you think the person in this case broke the law? Why was she arrested? Why were the police so willing to arrest?

2. What should happen when the case is returned to the lower court? What is the scope of responsibility for a person in a demonstration, for the subject of the demonstration and for the police? (Against a research facility, a zoo, a fur dealer, or a circus?)

3. Consider if you were a judge and 40 people are brought before you on charges of unlicensed demonstrations and public disorder. The demonstration was in the front of a store selling lawful fur coats. Thirty of those arrested have no prior criminal record, three have the additional charge of resisting arrest (one officer was hit with an umbrella), and one is charged with setting a police car on fire. Further, half of these people are

from out of state, and you happen to know that there is room for only ten people in the local jail and that any overflow taken by the county jail will cost $100 per day.

How should you deal with this mess and why? What would you do if an attorney for the demonstrators says that they have everything on videotape and intend to release it to the press if any of them spends one hour in jail?

4. How would you advise someone who wants to join a public demonstration/protest and does not want to get arrested? How would you advise a person who does want to be arrested in order to show the strength of her beliefs?

In the next story, both types of people were present. During the late 1980s and early 1990s many people in the movement went to Pennsylvania to take part in the annual event described next. While reading this, recognize that in many states the use of birds for target practice is a specific violation of the criminal cruelty law.

◇◇

Pennsylvania's Killing Fields

by Leslie Pardue, 6 The Animals' Agenda 10 (Nov. 1986) (reprinted with permission)

Every Labor Day for the past 53 years, thousands of pigeons are trucked into the tiny rural community of Hegins, Pennsylvania, to be killed in one of the area's most popular events of the year: the annual Fred Coleman Memorial Shoot. It is the largest single-day live bird shoot in the world, drawing some 5,000 spectators and from 250 to 300 shooters from all over the country. The shoot is a fundraiser for the 40-acre park and sports complex where the event takes place. Each year, residents from the surrounding small towns and farming communities bring their families, lawn chairs and picnic baskets, and spread their blankets on the ground among the trees to settle in and watch approximately 8,000 pigeons get shot. This year, however, there was a new twist to the event. About 300 animal rights activists were on hand to confront the organizers, participants and spectators and to demand an end to the Coleman Shoot.

Efforts by the Wildlife Information Center of Allentown, Penn., to convince the shoot organizers to consider alternatives to the use of live birds failed, despite offers to help farm animal activists to assist the park in conducting a humane fundraiser. Trans-Species Unlimited (TSU), an animal rights group based in Williamsport, Penn., went ahead with plans for the protest only after their attempts to meet with park and town officials also failed. Other organizations participating in the protest included the National Alliance for Animal Legislation, Lehigh Valley Animal Rights Coalition, Mobilization for Animals (Pittsburgh), Pennsylvania Animal Protection Association, and the Pittsburgh Society for the Prevention of Cruelty to Animals. Activists from all over the Northeast, and as far away as Florida attended, making this protest one of the largest and most visible actions for animals not organized and financed by one of the big national animal protection organizations. "The campaign and protest show the strength and unity of the grassroots movement and the split between that movement and the animal welfare organizations," said George Cave, president of TSU. "This was the vanguard of the movement at work – the people who will put their own lives on the line to end animal suffering and death."

Many of the protesters spent the night before the shoot camped out on a nearby farm in cold and uncomfortable conditions, arriving at the park about dawn the next day to confront the shooters. Shooters and protesters alike were greeted by a swarm of photographers, newspaper reporters, and radio and television crews at the park's entrance. According to TSU, the event received more media attention than any other single event in the history of the animal rights movement. The protest was covered by NBC Nightly News, CBS National Morning News, NBC National Radio, Cable Network News, Associated Press and United Press International, as well as numerous local radio and television stations and newspapers. It made the front pages of the *Philadelphia Inquirer,* the *Pittsburgh Press,* and the *Harrisburg Patriot,* and the front sections of the *New York Times* and the *Boston Globe.* At least 50 media people were in Hegins on Labor Day.

The emotionally-charged atmosphere and the confrontational nature of the protest no doubt contributed to the extensiveness of the media coverage. As the morning dew lifted off the surrounding fields, a long line of demonstrators carrying placards proceeded down a hill to the entrance of the park where a sizable crowd of reporters, shooters, police and onlookers waited. Nothing like this had ever happened in Hegins before. The protesters, in blue T-shirts reading "Stop Live Bird Shoots," were greeted by a jeering crowd of shooters in red-and-white T-shirts imprinted with the slogan "Save the Hegins Labor Day Shoot – for the S.P.O.R.T. of it." S.P.O.R.T. is an acronym for "Shooters Protect Our Rights Together." Many fans of the shoot also wore camouflage clothing and other macho military apparel, sporting caps and shirt patches with slogans such as "Pigeon Killer" and "Clean Up The City – Eat a Pigeon." Doris Gitman, a local resident and one of the protesters, displayed before the clicking cameras a handful of sharp tire-piercing spikes she had found in her driveway that morning. Similar spikes punctured the tires of several squad cars at the state police station in nearby Reedsville. Apparently, the shooters regarded the police with almost as much disdain as they did the protesters.

There has probably never been an animal rights protest with heavier police presence — all in all, 50 Pennsylvania state troopers including half a dozen mounted officers and 10 local police were at the site. The officers escorted the protesters into the park, where two long columns of activists formed along a path leading to the shooting areas. The shooters, carrying their rifles, walked between the two lines as animal rights chants and slogans rose up from the ranks of the protesters.

Meanwhile, the park's three baseball diamonds were being transformed into killing fields for the pigeons. Several small metal boxes, called "flipper traps," were placed on each field 32 yards away from where the shooter was to stand. The doors to the boxes were operated with strings which ran to a small booth on the edge of the field near the shooter's platform. Each flipper trap contained a pigeon. At a signal from the shooter, one of the several boxes would be opened and a pigeon released. The single-shot event allowed only one shot at each bird; the double-shot event allowed two. The boxes were restocked with birds every few minutes; each shooter was to shoot until he missed a bird completely. The average number of birds killed by each shooter would average out to about 20 or 25. For every five birds killed, the shooter would move back a yard.

The protesters gathered nearby as the first shooter in the double-shot event made ready. "I hope he whacks the first one ... don't miss the first one," an anxious shooter in red-and-white T-shirt whispered to his companion. The signal was given, the flipper trap opened, and a pigeon stepped out and tentatively spread its wings as the first shot rang out. It missed, and a cheer went up from the animal rights activists. The shooter aimed again as the bird fluttered off the ground. "What do we want? ANIMAL RIGHTS! When do we want it? NOW!," shouted the demonstrators. But the second shot hit its target, and the bird fell to the ground in a burst of blood and feathers. It was to be the first of thousands of birds to die.

Throughout the morning, the booming of the guns was countered by the shouts of protest. As each bird was killed, a raucous roar of hooting and cheering went up from the shooters and fans; when an occasional bird managed to escape (either wounded or unharmed) to the branches of nearby trees, the protesters whooped with joy. Many birds were not killed after two shots, and flapped pathetically on the ground amongst other dead or dying birds. After each round of shooting, young boys— called "trapper boys"—ran out onto the fields to retrieve the downed birds. The boys carried the pigeons behind plywood partitions where they killed the ones still living and threw them along with those already dead into 50-gallon barrels. (The bodies were later transported to a rendering plant to be processed into fertilizer.) According to TSU, the injured birds are killed by the trapper boys in one of four ways: pulling off their heads, beating them on the ground, wringing their necks, or stomping them to death. The partitions, not used in previous years' shoots, kept these grisly scenes from the eyes of the protesters and spectators, and from the lenses and notebooks of the media.

At one point, an injured bird escaped the second shot to fly into the trees and perch on a limb directly above the crowd. A few minutes later, the bird fell and was seized by a young boy in a red-and-white shirt. "Pull its head off! Pull its head off!" yelled several men in the crowd, and the boy did just that, to the horror of the protesters nearby. When asked by a reporter how he felt about what he had done, the boy replied, "It was easy." A short time later, several protesters were tending an injured bird when the pigeon was suddenly snatched away by a shooter, who tore the bird's head off. Spectators roared with laughter. One of the protesters subsequently remarked, "The laughing, jeering spectators in the stands would not have been out of place around the guillotine in 18th-century France."

Many of the local people consider the event to be a positive experience for the many children in attendance. "I don't think it desensitizes them," said one woman. "These are third and fourth generations of shooters. Almost everybody in this valley shoots. They [the protesters] have their opinions, and we have ours." "Death is a part of life—children should learn about it," said another shoot supporter. A young boy said, "I don't really think it's right, but it's a way of life, a tradition ... to try to stop it is a little harsh, I think." Indeed, the weight of tradition seems to be the biggest obstacle animal rights advocates face in attempting to stop the shoot. "We thought we were doing a good thing for our community," said Bob Tobash, a local insurance salesman and the shoot's chairman for the past ten years. "Here we are trying to provide entertainment and boost the economy of our town. It's been a part of the town for as long as I can remember."

The local people seemed threatened by the protesters' presence. Many dismissed the activists as city-slickers who simply did not understand the rural way of life. Others asked if the protesters ate meat or wore leather and were surprised and perhaps disappointed that many did not. Shouted epithets of "commie," "druggie" and "faggot" directed at the protesters by disgruntled shoot supporters were perhaps ways of dismissing ideas about cruelty which hit uncomfortably close to home. Throughout the day, the park was buzzing with conversation; in addition to the many heated exchanges between the two sides, there were some relatively calm discussions about the ethics and issues involved.

However, as the day wore on and more of the shooters began drinking, they became increasingly belligerent towards the protesters and the prospect of violence seemed more likely. (Subsequent to the protest, two such outbursts were reported: one protester was thrown to the ground in an unprovoked attack; and another was surrounded by four men and threatened with a knife.) All morning, warnings had been broadcast at regular intervals over the park's public address system. "If there is a disturbance at the traps, please do not take matters into your own hands. There are personnel here to deal with any problems," the announcer said, apparently directing this message not to the protesters but to the shooters. The protesters decided to leave at noon to avoid any further violent incidents. Explained TSU's George Cave: "The protest itself combined militant, aggressive confrontation with a commitment to non-violence.... Repeated chanting and verbal harassment of the shooters resulted, we believe, in a higher incidence of misses by the shooters and more birds escaping with their lives. In short, we feel that we pushed the confrontation up to the possible limits of what would result in an eruption of violence on the part of the shooters and the crowd. By noon, the drinking in the park had elevated the level of tension to a peak where we felt that it would be very dangerous for people to continue the protest, and so we left the park under police escort at that point."

The Hegins shoot uses 8,000 birds at a cost of $3 per bird—a total outlay of about $24,000 in order to raise $10,000 a year. Most of the profit comes from food concessions, which could be used with equal success at some other type of fundraiser. Trans-Species has suggested the option of skeet-shooting, a marksmanship event using clay "pigeons" which are ejected from a machine in an unpredictable and erratic pattern. This would certainly make the event more challenging than shooting live birds, since many birds do not even become airborne or manage a few steps out of the boxes before getting shot.

Many shooters try to justify the Hegins event by arguing that the birds are captured in cities where they would otherwise "spread disease" before eventually falling prey to poison. One spectator, a woman from Philadelphia, said, "I'm delighted to see these `flying rats' destroyed. I think they suffer more on the streets of Philadelphia." However, while a few of the pigeons are trapped in farmers' barns or captured in cities, the vast majority are purpose-bred and purchased from breeders. In any case, humane options for the population control of city pigeons *do* exist. A sterilization agent, Ornitrol, has been used successfully in Cleveland, St. Louis and other cities. This substance causes no suffering to the birds and stabilizes the population within one to two years.

Live bird shoots are prohibited in all but a handful of states. Even by hunters' standards, the shoots can in no way be deemed "sporting events." At most, 5 to 10 per cent of the birds escape with their lives, and many of these are wounded. The contests are simply displays of marksmanship with live animals used as targets.

The ASPCA, along with the Hillside SPCA of Schuylkill County, tried unsuccessfully to stop the shoot through legal action before this year's event. The groups petitioned to obtain a court injunction against the shoot in Schuylkill County Court, Commonwealth Court and the Supreme Court of Pennsylvania. The lower court ruled, incredibly, that pigeons are not animals and that therefore the shoot does not constitute cruelty to animals under state statutes. The two higher courts upheld this opinion.

Animal rights activists are not giving up on pursuing legal avenues, however. The ASPCA intends to pursue a permanent court injunction against the shoot, while TSU is concentrating its efforts on having legislation passed at the state level to ban all live bird shoots. The publicity generated by the protest will help fuel the legislative effort. TSU is currently in the process of obtaining a commitment of sponsorship for the bill, and expects to have the bill introduced very soon. At least three major Pennsylvania newspapers have published editorials calling for an end to the Hegins shoot and similar events, and interest in the issue is at an all-time high. TSU says the protests will be held every year until the shoot is banned. Until then, Hegins deserves to be known as America's "Town Without Pity."

Why has the seemingly peaceful little community of Hegins allowed this brutality to occur unchallenged for over half a century? Part of the answer lies in the nature of the rural community itself—change does not come easy in an insulated small town. In large cities, where much mixing of ideas, cultures, backgrounds, and viewpoints occurs, a city-dweller finds that open-mindedness is a much more natural process; in fact, personal flexibility could be said to be necessary for survival in the urban environment. However, in many rural areas, a willingness to listen to "outside" ideas is both unnatural and unnecessary, and may in fact jeopardize one's relationships with others in the community. Hence it is much more difficult for an individual growing up in such an environment to break away from established rituals and traditions, especially when lacking any outside impetus or support to do so, and in the absence of, say, church or media involvement in the issues. Animal rights activists should remember this fact, and approach rural people on their own terms, without the urban arrogance which so easily mistakes lack of information for lack of intelligence. Cave remarks, "We are very opposed to urban chauvinism and classism towards these people." It is to TSU's credit that the majority of the protesters conducted themselves with respect for the local people, criticizing not rural life *per se*, but simply one of its more brutal manifestations.

The significance of the shooters' connection of the event to militarism should not be overlooked. In addition to the military garb worn by many shooters and spectators, a number of others proudly proclaimed their status as veterans of World War II, Korea and, most especially, Vietnam. "Who are these jerks to tell us what to do? We fought in Vietnam!" one shooter remarked in reference to the protesters. "I fought for this country," said another. "Why don't you go protest in front of the Soviet Embassy?" Apparently, to them the logic is obvious: after making such a sacrifice for their country, they should be allowed to do as they please without interference. The implication seems to be that veterans are entitled to more freedom of action, especially violent action, than other Americans. Many of these vets seemed reluctant to relinquish the "license to kill" they had been granted years ago, and were not utilizing it on the only available and socially acceptable targets: the pigeons. Did these men's experiences in war harden them to killing? When a human life becomes cheap, does an animal life becomes less than nothing? For many veterans, few things in ordinary life can quite compare to the feeling of constant excitement and danger they once experienced in war. These veterans feel a driving need to restore the exhilaration, the "adrenalin rush" back into their lives. Some do it by becoming police officers or firefighters; others take up aggressive or dangerous sports; still others become criminals; and some become hunters, dogfighters, rodeo contestants or pigeon-shooters.

Two of the protesters, Harry Proctor and Ed Perlis, were also veterans — Perlis served in the Navy and Proctor in the Marines in World War II. Both men were disturbed at the behavior of the veterans who participated in the shoot, and felt that their own experiences in war had taught them a very different lesson. Perlis, not a vegetarian, said of his fellow veterans, "I don't consider them fellow anything if they're killing. And there's going to be another generation of killers [the trapper boys] doing the same sick thing. They should shoot the pigeons with a camera instead of a gun." Proctor remarked, "War disgusts you to the idea of killing *anything*. The shoot is just a big ego trip for a bunch of beerbellies."

Questions & Notes

1. Some people thought they should be able to kill pigeons. What are the interests of these people that are furthered by this activity. Do the interests of the pigeons in continued life have any impact on this activity?

2. Why would someone participate in such an event? Is this a type of sport hunting? Is the life of a pigeon of any moral value? What is the moral value of the event to either the city or the participants that might outweigh the value of the life of a pigeon, or 8,000 of them?

3. Does the economic value of the activity (to pigeon sellers, beer sellers, etc.) outweigh the interest of the pigeons?

4. What do you think of children being such active participants in the events? The participants do not believe their actions are immoral. Is it appropriate for animal rights activists to try to impose their values on the participants? Where should this debate occur? What role does the legal system play in this debate?

5. How could a judge rule that a pigeon is not within the definition of "animal" for purposes of the anti-cruelty laws?

6. Do you think the confrontational approach of the animal rights activists is justifiable, appropriate, or useful?

7. Over the next few years, several attempts to outlaw pigeon target shooting were made in the Pennsylvania legislature. All failed to pass. What political interests would oppose a ban on pigeon shooting?

In 1991, the 58th Annual Pigeon Shoot was held. Approximately 10,000 spectators, 1,000 animal rights activists, and

8,000 pigeons were present. (These numbers were reported by U.S. News and World Report. The Animal's Agenda reported the numbers as 2,000 paying spectators, 263 gunners, 1,200 protesters and 5,000 pigeons.)

This time, some of the protestors were more aggressive in their tactics. A number were successful in releasing pigeons from their cages before they could be shot. Ten protesters registered incognito as shooters and, when their time arrived to shoot, they would grab pigeons, in one case a crate of 40, and attempt to release them before the police could stop them. Approximately 400 pigeons were either released by this method or escaped the shooters. By the end of the day, the state police had arrested 86 people for criminal trespass. Prearranged legal help obtained release on bail by nightfall for all of those who chose not to stay in jail. Four men and fourteen women spent up to 12 days in the Schuylkill jail. The shoot organizers claimed cash receipts of about $20,000. Upwards of $100,000 was spent by the state to provide adequate police protection, including the use of three helicopters for the day.

In 2000 the Shoot came to an end when the Supreme Court of the State held that the general anti-cruelty laws would apply to the event. In the end it was the lawyers, not the protestors, who stopped the hunt.

Section 4

Change by Break-In and Violence

Comments: Animal Liberation and the Law: Animals Board the Underground Railroad

by Laura G. Kniaz, 43 Buffalo L. Rev. 765 (1995)

Proponents of animal rights use various legal means to pursue their agenda. They attempt to protect animals via lawsuits, political protest, and economic campaigns. Their efforts often include aggressive, yet peaceful techniques, such as civil disobedience, boycotts, picketing, and demonstrations. By the early 1980s, however, the United States' animal rights movement developed a fringe element whose members identified themselves as animal liberators. In contrast to their self-naming, animal liberators have been labeled animal rights terrorists or extremists by the FBI and others not sympathetic to the activists' goals. These animal liberators are a small but vocal contingent of the current animal protection movement.

Frustrated by what they perceive to be an insufficient pace of change in ending animal oppression, and likening themselves to the conductors of the Underground Railroad used to free human slaves, liberators protect nonhumans by engaging in direct action against animal enterprises. This direct action includes criminal, clandestine tactics such as vandalism, property destruction, and animal theft. Unlike those who engage in routine civil disobedience, liberators act covertly and attempt to evade arrest. In the United States, approximately sixteen different groups have claimed responsibility for animal liberation actions. The most infamous and active of all these organizations is the Animal Liberation Front (ALF).

Whether ALF can be characterized as an organization, per se, or as an "umbrella" ideology or cause, is an issue still being debated. Regardless of how it may be characterized as a whole, it is widely believed that ALF is a loose configuration of small, autonomous "cells," with no centralized command structure. It is also believed that there are no formal membership requirements beyond the willingness to inflict damage upon an animal enterprise.

A Focusing Question

Is it morally wrong to inflict economic damages on those who engage in immoral acts against animals? Is it morally wrong to remove an animal from a cage and situation in which there is the infliction of pain and suffering on that specific animal? Is it illegal?

◇◇◇

Consider the following reflections of an ALF member seeking to learn from his activities.

ALF Mission Statement

To effectively allocate resources (time and money) to reduce animal suffering in the world.

Lessons through mistakes of an ALF member:

I spent two weeks of vacation time and $1000 protesting and getting support to save a whale trapped in a bay, ignoring the fact that a week spent at the animal shelter (where I volunteer) would likely have saved 10 lives (finding homes, additional cost savings to the shelter).

This is possibly more reprehensible than a person who eats beef believing that cows live a happy life before they die and that eating beef gives life to a cow who otherwise would have never existed.

I knew what I was doing. Knowledge should be more than power — it should be obligation.

Ironically, I sometimes find it frustrating that the public is not aware of the animal abuse that goes on behind closed doors. Yet, I sometimes spend time saving one animal at the expense of many due to my laser focus on events in front of me. Not all actions are equal. I am frequently faced with the choice of "Do I save animal A or animal B?" Here are some suggested things to consider when evaluating a potential AR activity (beware of "paralysis of analysis"):

1. Cost. Time, money, and emotional energy spent (my mistake: rescuing an animal that was near-death and spending large amounts of money on medical bills, then running out of money for an operation that would have saved an otherwise healthy animal).

2. Danger to other sentient beings. Take into account humans as well as rodents you can't see. Realize that "change" may upset a miniature ecosystem on which some beings may rely.

3. Improvement in the quality of life of the "to-be saved" animal (is there a good home or safe environment for it?).

4. Public opinion. (My mistake: rescuing an animal and then, in frustration, spray-painting an obscenity on the wall). The obscenity made the news (nowadays there is no news without pictures) and the slant of the news-story was anti-AR. Result: More folks will probably turn a deaf ear to AR issues.

5. Effect on the business losing the animal. (My mistake: liberating an animal from an experiment that was subsequently replaced with a "brand new" test subject. Although the liberation forced the company to buy a new security system, the company did not reduce the amount of testing. The only effect of causing economic damage was to stockholders — NOT a good reason).

From www.animalliberationfront/ALFront/mission_statement.htm (as of July 2003).

CASE BY CASE

U.S. v. Fullmer,

584 F. 3d 132 (3rd Cir. 2009)

FUENTES, CIRCUIT JUDGE:

Defendants Darius Fullmer, Andrew Stepanian, Kevin Kjonaas, Joshua Harper, Lauren Gazzola, Jacob Conroy, and Stop Huntingdon Animal Cruelty ("SHAC") collectively challenge their convictions for conspiracy to violate the Animal Enterprise Protection Act ("AEPA"), 18 U.S.C. § 43 (2002). Notably, our interpretation of this statute is an issue of first impression in this, or any, circuit court of appeal.

SHAC, Kjonaas, Gazzola, and Conroy also challenge their convictions for conspiracy to commit interstate stalking, as well as three substantive counts of stalking. Finally, SHAC, Kjonaas, Gazzola, Conroy, and Harper challenge their convictions for conspiracy to use a telecommunications device to abuse, threaten, and harass.

The overarching issues in this appeal are whether the AEPA violates the First Amendment, whether there was sufficient evidence to convict Defendants of the various charges against them, and challenges to the jury instructions. [All convictions are upheld.]

I.

We begin by setting forth the two principal statutes implicated by the lengthy facts of this case: The version of the AEPA in force at the time of the conduct at issue provided, in relevant part

Whoever-

(1) travels in interstate or foreign commerce, or uses or causes to be used the mail or any facility in interstate or foreign commerce for the purpose of causing physical disruption to the functioning of an animal enterprise; and

(2) intentionally damages or causes the loss of any property (including animals or records) used by the animal enterprise, or conspires to do so, shall be punished as provided for in subsection (b).

18 U.S.C. § 43(a)(1)-(2) (2002). The interstate stalking statute provides, in relevant part

Whoever travels in interstate or foreign commerce ... with the intent to kill, injure, harass, or place under surveillance with intent to kill, injure, harass, or intimidate another person, and in the course of, or as a result of, such travel places that person in reasonable fear of the death of, or serious bodily injury to, or causes substantial emotional distress to that person, a member of the immediate family ... of that person, or the spouse or intimate partner of that person ... shall be punished as provided in section 2261(b) of this title.

18 U.S.C. § 2261A(1) (2000).

A.

Huntingdon Life Sciences ("Huntingdon") is a research corporation that performs testing for companies seeking to bring their products to market. The testing that Huntingdon provides to its clients is mandated by the laws and regulations of the United States and Europe to ensure the safety and efficacy of pharmaceuticals, agricultural products, veterinary products, and medical implants. Huntingdon has three laboratories, two in the United Kingdom and one in New Jersey. All Huntingdon laboratories use animals as test subjects. Approximately eighty-five percent of the animals used by Huntingdon are rats and mice, and the remaining fifteen percent is composed of other species, including fish, dogs, monkeys, and guinea pigs.

In the late 1990s, an individual posing as a laboratory technician videotaped the conditions inside a Huntingdon laboratory in the United Kingdom. The footage, which depicted animal abuse, became public when it was used in a television program, igniting protests against Huntingdon by a number of animal rights organizations. At about the same time, Stop Huntingdon Animal Cruelty was formed in the United Kingdom ("SHAC-UK"). The organization's mission is to close Huntingdon laboratories.

Immediately after SHAC-UK formed in November 1999, the organization published a newsletter that listed the names and addresses of the Huntingdon directors in the United Kingdom. Following the publication of the newsletter, animals rights protestors subjected the Huntingdon directors to an ongoing campaign of harassment, including vandalizing their homes and cars.

In February 2001, the Chief Operating Officer and Managing Director of Huntingdon, Brian Cass, was physically assaulted by three masked individuals in front of his home in England. Cass suffered cracked ribs, several lacerations, and a four-inch gash on his head that required nine stitches. David Blinkinsopp, who had been identified in video footage of SHAC-UK protests in front of Huntingdon, was convicted of the assault. The remaining two assailants were never identified.

B.

SHAC's campaign was multi-faceted in its approach, targeting companies that were directly and indirectly involved with Huntingdon [who had moved to New Jersey to protect shareholder names], as well as the people who worked for those companies. Because of the length of the record, we recount only a representative sample of the incidents that are the subject of this case. In particular, we discuss the general content of SHAC's website and the protest activity coordinated through the SHAC website, including protests directed at specific individuals.

SHAC Website

SHAC's primary organizing tool is its website, through which members coordinate future protests. It also publishes information about protests that have previously taken place.

The website includes a page dedicated to the concept of "direct action," which all parties concede is a type of protest that includes the illegal activity in this case. With regard to its position on the use of direct action, SHAC stated the following on its website:

We operate within the boundaries of the law, but recognize and support those who choose to operate outside the confines of the legal system.

Big business has shown time and time again their lack of concern for ethics, instead focusing their attention on their profit. Often, simply targeting said business proves fruitless. However, as above ground activists have successfully targeted [Huntingdon]'s financial pillars of support, underground activists have too targeted [Huntingdon]'s pocketbooks. Unidentified individuals as well as underground cells of the Animal Liberation Front and the Earth Liberation Front have engaged in economic sabotage of [Huntingdon] and their associates.

They have also spent their time directly intervening and liberating the animals who are slated to die inside of [Huntingdon]. Animals have been liberated from breeders as well as the laboratories themselves.

SHAC does not organize any such actions or have any knowledge of who is doing them or when they will happen, but [SHAC] encourage[s] people to support direct action when it happens and those who may participate in it.

(J.A. at 775.)

The website often posted the organization's "accomplishments," which lauded both legal and illegal protest activity. The illegal activity included, among other things, a break-in at the Huntingdon lab in New Jersey, during which protestors broke windows and "liberated 14 beagles," in addition to overturning a worker's car; detonating a "stink bomb" in the Seattle office of a Huntingdon investor; destroying Bank of New York ATMs, windows, and other property; sinking a yacht owned by the Bank of New York's president; launching repeated "paint attacks" in the New York offices of a Huntingdon investor; and "rescuing" dogs and ferrets from a Huntingdon breeder farm.

The website also posted "anonymous" bulletins of successful, but illegal, protest activities. One such bulletin stated

Late last night, August 30th, we paid a visit to the home of Rodney Armstead, MD and took out two of his front windows ... gave him something to labor over this Labor Day weekend. Rodney serves as an officer and agent of service for "Medical Diagnostic Management, Inc.," a scummy little company [associated with Huntingdon]. Any ties with [Huntingdon] or its executives will yield only headaches and a mess to clean up.

(J.A. at 935.) The name and home address of Dr. Armstead followed. This bulletin was prefaced by SHAC's statement that it was "excited to see such an upswing in action against Huntingdon and their cohorts. From the unsolicited direct action to the phone calls, e-mails, faxes and protests. Keep up the good work!" Similar bulletins included photographs of extensive vandalism at the homes of people indirectly affiliated with Huntingdon, such as employees of Bank of New York. These bulletins almost always contained a disclaimer that "all illegal activity is done by anonymous activists who have no relation with SHAC." (J.A. at 1233.)

The SHAC website also posted a piece called the "Top 20 Terror Tactics" that was originally published by an organization that defends the use of animals in medical research and testing. With its standard disclaimer about SHAC not organizing illegal activity, SHAC re-published the list on its website. Some of the tactics included abusive graffiti, posters, and stickers on houses, cars, and in neighborhoods of targeted individuals; invading offices, damaging property, and stealing documents; chaining gates shut or blocking gates with old cars to trap staff on site; physical assaults against the targeted individuals, as well as their partners, including spraying cleaning fluid into their eyes; smashing windows in houses when the occupants are home; flooding houses with a hose attached to an outside tap inserted through a letterbox or window while the home is unoccupied; vandalizing personal vehicles by gluing locks, slashing tires, and pouring paint on the exterior; smashing personal vehicles with a sledgehammer while the targeted individual is inside; firebombing cars, sheds and garages; bomb threats to instigate evacuations; threatening telephone calls and letters, including threats to injure or kill the targeted individual, as well their children and partners; abusive telephone calls and letters; ordering goods and services in the targeted individual's name and address; and arranging for an undertaker to collect the target's body. Following the list, the SHAC website stated, "Now don't go getting any funny ideas!" (J.A. at 780.) [Court noted that the posting of this information is protected speech, unless part of a campaign to incite imminent and likely unlawful action.]

Through its website, SHAC also invited its supporters to engage in electronic civil disobedience against Huntingdon and various companies associated with Huntingdon. Electronic civil disobedience involves a coordinated campaign by a large number of individuals to inundate websites, e-mail servers, and the telephone service of a targeted company. Electronic civil disobedience also includes the use of "black faxes," repeatedly faxing a black piece of paper to the same fax machine to exhaust the toner or ink supply. SHAC sponsored monthly electronic civil disobedience campaigns on the first Monday of every month. SHAC reminded its supporters that electronic civil disobedience is illegal, so supporters should only participate if they "are like Martin Luther King and are ready to suffer the consequences ... or if [the supporters] want to live to fight another day, do the electronic civil disobedience from a public computer that cannot be traced...." (J.A. at 835.)

One specific example of SHAC's coordination of electronic civil disobedience was an e-mail from "shacuse@envirolink.org" that was disseminated on October 26, 2003. The subject line of the e-mail was "Electronic Civil Disobedience," and it advised SHAC supporters that on the following day, SHAC's website would provide a link to the SHAC-Moscow website where "electronic civil disobedience will be taking place."

The e-mail stated that "participation is mandatory," and that by taking part in the coordinated electronic civil disobedience, supporters would "help ... halt the ever important web medium for particular companies sponsoring Huntingdon." Participation would also "send[ ] a loud message that no silly injunctions or crooked politicians can derail the campaign to close Huntingdon." (J.A. at 2615.) [This will not be protected speech.]

At trial, the government presented evidence that the cyberattacks against Huntingdon caused the company's computer systems to crash on two separate occasions, resulting in $400,000 in lost business, $50,000 in staffing costs to repair the computer systems and bring them back online, and $15,000 in costs to replace computer equipment.

Protests Against Individuals

One of the strategies SHAC frequently employed was to target the employees of Huntingdon and affiliated companies, as well as their family members. To accomplish this goal, SHAC posted the names, home addresses, and home phone numbers of the individuals on the organization's website. SHAC also posted bulletins about what happened at the protests, including acts of vandalism committed by protestors.

[The court recounts the events of four individuals, only one is provided below.]

4. Robert Harper

Robert Harper is a property broker in Marsh's Boston office. In April 2002, his home address appeared on the SHAC website, and protests at his home began shortly thereafter. The protestors also engaged in other harassing activities, such as submitting an unauthorized mail-forwarding order to the United States Postal Service and posting advertisements for cars or concert tickets, listing Harper's home number. On Father's Day 2002, activists threw red paint on his front door. The following post subsequently appeared on the SHAC website:

Received anonymously:
Happy Father['js [D]ay Rob Harper. I hope you liked our gift[.]
In the wee hours of the mourning (sic) on June 15, Marsh Boston Employee, Rob Harper [home address redacted] received an early Father['js Day gift that he will never forget. A few gallons of red paint were thrown all over Harper's front steps and door. This left the front of his house caked in a huge pool of red paint.

Rob Harper is responsible for 500 animals dying within [Huntingdon] today and as long as Marsh has ties with [Huntingdon], Marsh will be a target. This also goes for any other company or business that has times [sic] with Huntingdon-
they will pay for it.
There will be no rest for these murders. [Huntingdon] will be closed.

This action is dedicated to the 500 animals that were murdered inside of [Huntingdon] today.

Love,

The Animal Liberation Front

(J.A. at 1225 (emphasis in original).)

Harper testified that after these protests began, his workday was "consumed" with checking the SHAC website. He testified that he became aware of other protests and other targets, including the physical assault of Brian Cass in the United Kingdom, as well as protestors destroying vehicles. He stated that this made him feel "vulnerable" and "concerned for his family," as well as angry and helpless because his life was so profoundly disrupted. (J.A. at 2979-80.)

On August 9, 2002, Harper was at work when a protest occurred at his home. His wife called him, crying and frantic. He arrived home to find his wife and two-year-old son upset. The protestors outside were screaming "puppy killer" and threatening to burn the house down. A video played at trial showed that Lauren Gazzola, a Defendant in this case, was present at this demonstration, shouting into a bullhorn,

Where were the police when a [Huntingdon] worker's car got flipped over in his driveway? Where were the police when a Marsh executive had all his windows smashed in and his house covered in red paint in Chicago? And where were the police when your house was covered in red paint a few weeks ago? They can't protect you. Your injunctions can't stop us. We'll always find a way around whatever they throw at us.

(G.E. 4006; J.A. at 2980 & 2985; Appellee's Br. at 65-66.) Harper testified that this was "one of the worst days of [his] life." (J.A. at 2980.) He feared that someone would "throw a molotov cocktail" into the house, or that someone would physically assault him or his family. (J.A. at 2981.) He contemplated moving and quitting his job, but the protests stopped when Marsh ended its business relationship with Huntingdon.

C.

The Individual Defendants

In addition to SHAC, this case involves the following individual Defendants who participated in protest activity on behalf of the organization. [Each defendant is discussed separately.]

1. Kevin Kjonaas

Kevin Kjonaas was the President of SHAC. Kjonaas lived at SHAC's Somerset, New Jersey, headquarters with two co-Defendants, Lauren Gazzola and Jacob Conroy.

Although SHAC often attributed illegal activity to other organizations or anonymous sources, the government presented evidence that Defendants coordinated, directed and personally participated in the illegal acts. Here, we recount a sample of specific instances that demonstrate Kjonaas's involvement, in chronological order.

In the fall of 2000, a website called www.stephenskills.com was published online. The website explained that Stephens, an investor with Huntingdon, had provided a financial "bailout" for the lab. Under a heading labeled "Consequences," the site stated,

We must show all other financial institutions via our actions against Stephens Incorporated that having any financial connections to Huntingdon will mean blocked up phone lines, flooded e-mail systemse [sic] and mailboxes, demonstrations outside and inside of offices, protests at the homes of the CEO's [sic] and company Directors....

At trial, a Stephens employee testified that these threats became a reality in the fall of 2000. In January 2001, the Stephens employee met with Kjonaas at Kjonaas's request. As a pre-condition, Stephens asked Kjonaas to remove www.stephenskills.com from the internet. A few days later, the website was down. During their meeting, the two sides "agreed to disagree" about Huntingdon. Shortly thereafter, Stephens was targeted by a massive direct action campaign that included a "virtual sit-in," a protest that involved hundreds of activists attempting to access Stephens's website simultaneously and repeatedly in an effort to shut it down. Approximately 1,300 people participated in this virtual sit-in, which resulted in major disruptions to Stephens's day-to-day business operations.

When two members of the Huntingdon Board of Directors resigned in January 2003, Kjonaas led the effort to obtain the identities of the new directors so that SHAC could disseminate their personal information in order to target them. The record contains dozens of pages of transcribed phone calls between Kjonaas and various individuals that demonstrate his intense effort to obtain this information.

In a February 2003 phone call, Kjonaas discusses how "awesome" it was that a company had severed ties with Huntingdon only ten days after the protests began. Kjonaas explained that the campaign against Marsh had been an example of what would have happened if the target did not end its relationship with Huntingdon. Kjonaas stated, "It's like how we beat Quilcap too." (J.A. at 2240.)

In August 2003, a bomb exploded at the California offices of Chiron, Inc., a pharmaceutical company that was a Huntingdon client. SHAC posted a bulletin on its website announcing the explosion, stating that a group called "The Revolutionary Cells" claimed responsibility. In the post, Kjonaas was quoted as saying, "[T]his action against Chiron marks a drastic escalation in severity. Although SHAC-USA may share the same passion for ending injustice and closing Huntingdon, we know nothing more about 'The Revolutionary Cells' and their intentions. If I were Huntingdon or Chiron, I would be very worried." (J.A. at 1550.) Less than twelve hours after the bomb detonated, telephone records show that Kjonaas called Daniel Andreas San Diego, the man later charged with the bombing.

III.

1. The threshold issue is whether the AEPA is unconstitutional either on its face, or as-applied to Defendants. This Court reviews challenges to the constitutionality of a statute under a de novo standard of review. United States v. Weatherly, 525 F. 3d 265, 273 (3d Cir. 2008).

A.

Constitutionality of the AEPA

1. Void for Vagueness

Defendants argue that the AEPA violates the Due Process Clause and the First Amendment because the statute does not clearly define prohibited conduct. Specifically, Defendants argue that the terms "economic damage" and "physical disruption" are not clearly defined. As a result, Defendants argue that the statute has a chilling effect on speech because protestors will refrain from all speech, even protected speech, due to the ambiguity of what the statute proscribes. In addition, Defendants argue that the vague nature of the statute allows prosecutors to determine what conduct is covered by the statute, inevitably permitting prosecutorial decisions based on content.

"A statute is void on vagueness grounds if it: (1) 'fails to provide people of ordinary intelligence a reasonable opportunity to understand what conduct it prohibits'; or (2) 'authorizes or even encourages arbitrary and discriminatory enforcement.' " United States v. Stevens, 533 F. 3d 218, 249 (3d Cir. 2008). The inquiry is undertaken on a case-by-case basis, and a reviewing court must determine whether the statute is vague as-applied to the affected party. San Filippo v. Bongiovanni, 961 F. 2d 1125, 1136 (3d Cir. 1992).

The AEPA proscribes the use of an instrument of interstate commerce with the "intent [to] damage [or] cause [ ] the loss of any property (including animals or records) used by the animal enterprise...." 18 U.S.C. § 43(a) (2002) (emphasis added). The definitions section of the AEPA states that " 'physical disruption' does not include any lawful disruption that results from lawful public, governmental, or animal enterprise employee reaction to the disclosure of information about an animal enterprise." 18 U.S.C. § 43(d)(2) (2002) (emphasis added). The AEPA also defines "economic damage" as "the replacement costs of lost or damaged property or records, the costs of repeating an interrupted or invalidated experiment, or the loss of profits...." 18 U.S.C. § 43(d)(3) (2002).

We do not agree with Defendants that the AEPA is void for vagueness. First, the term "physical disruption" has a well-understood, common definition. Defendants argue that the term "physical disruption" could be read to proscribe legal protest activity, such as a letter-writing campaign, because that could be interpreted as an intent to cause a physical disruption resulting in economic loss to the targeted enterprise. However, the statute provides an exception that exempts legal protest activity from proscribed conduct. In this case, Defendants engaged in various "direct action" campaigns, which even SHAC's website concedes constitute illegal activity. Therefore, Defendants cannot argue that the statute was vague. The record is rife with evidence that Defendants were on notice that their activities put them at risk for prosecution, including the extensive use of various encryption devices and programs used to erase incriminating data from their computer hard drives. Because Defendants' conduct was clearly within the heartland of the statute, speculation as to the hypothetical ways that the AEPA could be unconstitutionally vague would require us to "formulate a rule of constitutional law broader than is required by the precise facts" before us.

2. As-Applied

Defendants next argue that we should reverse their convictions for conspiracy to violate the AEPA because the statute is unconstitutional as-applied to them. Specifically, Defendants argue that their actions constituted political speech, and that the SHAC website neither incited violence nor constituted a true threat. Moreover, Defendants argue that their protected speech cannot be converted into unprotected speech by the independent action of others who engaged in illegal conduct.

We must first decide whether the content on the SHAC website, the cornerstone of the government's case, is protected by the First Amendment. If so, the AEPA's criminalization of the speech on and through the website is unconstitutional.

All parties agree that the postings on the website speak to an issue of political, moral, and ethical importance in today's society-the humane treatment of animals. Therefore, the issues here fit squarely within the rubric of the First Amendment because they contribute to the "marketplace of ideas," as well as educate and urge others to action. Moreover, the speech at issue is speech that many find offensive and uncomfortable, which is precisely the type of speech that requires First Amendment protection. However, provocative political speech can run afoul of the First Amendment.

In Brandenburg v. Ohio, 395 U.S. 444, (1969), the Supreme Court held that the First Amendment "do[es] not permit [the government] to forbid or proscribe advocacy of the use of force or of law violation except where such advocacy is directed to inciting or producing imminent lawless action and is likely to incite or produce such action." Id. at 447. The Court elaborated by stating, "the mere abstract teaching ... of the moral propriety or even moral necessity for a resort to force and violence, is not the same as preparing a group for violent action and steeling it to such action." Therefore, for the speech at issue in this case to fall outside the purview of the First Amendment, this Court must determine that the speech (1) invited imminent lawlessness and (2) that the imminent lawlessness was likely to occur.

Electronic civil disobedience is unlawful, as SHAC acknowledged on its website. When SHAC's website included links to the tools necessary to carry out virtual sit-ins, those posts were clearly intended to incite imminent, lawless conduct that was likely to occur. SHAC sometimes posted ongoing updates as virtual sit-ins progressed, noting that their efforts were having the desired effect because the Huntingdon servers were slowing down. As described above, an October 26, 2003, e-mail titled "Electronic Civil Disobedience," urged SHAC supporters to participate in electronic civil disobedience at a specified time. This message encouraged and compelled an imminent, unlawful act that was not only likely to occur, but provided the schedule by which the unlawful act was to occur. This type of communication is not protected speech under the Brandenburg standard.

With regard to the individual Defendants in this case, they attribute the illegal activity of the Huntingdon protestors to "anonymous activists" or unaffiliated organizations, and now argue that they cannot be held responsible for the illegal acts of others. However, there was ample evidence at trial to demonstrate that Kjonaas, Gazzola, Conroy, Stepanian, Harper and Fullmer coordinated and controlled SHAC's activities, both legal and illegal. Direct action, electronic civil disobedience, intimidation and harassment were part and parcel of SHAC's overall campaign, and these individual Defendants employed those tactics because they were effective. The record also supports a jury inference that these individual Defendants personally participated in illegal protests, in addition to orchestrating the illegal acts of others.

Further, other conduct constituted "true threats," which also removes Defendants' speech from the realm of First Amendment protection. In particular, Defendants used past incidents to instill fear in future targets. For example, SHAC displayed placards with photos of Brian Cass after his beating, with his injuries highlighted in red, at protests. Indeed, they attributed the quick exit of some targets, such as Deloitte and Touche, to the past experiences of employees at companies like Stephens and Marsh. In this regard, their actions meet the standard of a "true threat" as articulated in Watts, because viewed in context, the speeches, protests, and web postings, were all tools to further their effort. Moreover, given the success of the campaign in the past, including the destruction of private property and the telecommunication attacks on various companies, the implied threats were not conditional, and this speech rightly instilled fear in the listeners.

We therefore conclude that some of the speech on SHAC's website, viewed in context, is not protected by the First Amendment. Likewise, we find that any Defendant who created or disseminated that speech, or who personally participated in illegal activity, is likewise not protected by the First Amendment. We discuss the individual Defendants below.

b. Gazzola

One of the more incriminating pieces of evidence against Gazzola was her participation in the demonstration at the home of Robert Harper. The government showed a video at trial, in which Gazzola can be heard threatening to burn down Harper's house and warning him that the police cannot protect him. Under the Watts framework, this act, viewed in context with Gazzola's other conduct, constitutes a true threat and is sufficient to remove her protest activity from First Amendment protection.

We find it hard to see how threatening to burn down someone's house is "political hyperbole" such that it might be protected by the First Amendment in the first place. However, even assuming that it has some underlying political value, viewed in the totality of the circumstances, this constituted a "true threat." When this protest took place, Robert Harper and his family had been a target of the campaign for a few weeks. Robert Harper was keenly aware of what was happening, and what had happened, to others who had been targeted during the campaign to close Huntingdon, including the physical assault on Brian Cass. He lived in fear that something similar would happen to his family, and from the record, his fear of the protestors acting on their threats was reasonable. Gazzola could reasonably foresee that Harper would interpret her words as a serious expression of intent to harm Robert Harper and his family.

3. Conclusion

We hold that the AEPA is not void for vagueness and is not unconstitutional as-applied to all Defendants.

V.

The next issue on appeal is whether there was sufficient evidence to support the jury's guilty verdict. We conduct an "independent review" of the entire record because First Amendment principles are involved. [The court has no difficulty in finding sufficient evidence to support the jury verdict.]

FISHER, Circuit Judge, dissenting.

I write separately to express disagreement with my colleagues' conclusions regarding the sufficiency of the evidence to convict the Defendants on Count One, the conspiracy to violate the Animal Enterprise Protection Act (AEPA). Although I agree with most of the majority's analysis as to why the AEPA is constitutional on its face and as applied to the Defendants, I part company with my colleagues in assessing whether the Government in fact proved that the Defendants committed a conspiracy to violate the AEPA. This issue, though narrow, is nonetheless significant for this case. In light of the statutory prohibitions of the AEPA and the evidence that the Government presented at trial, I cannot conclude that there was sufficient evidence, as a matter of law, to convict the Defendants of conspiring to violate the AEPA. Therefore, I would reverse the convictions as to all Defendants on this count.

Questions & Notes

1. Were the activities described in the case above within the ALF guidelines set out earlier? Are these people part of the "animal rights movement"? Do their actions further the "movement"? Is the preceding terrorism?

2. Is a high moral purpose, the elimination of animal suffering, a defense to a criminal charge? Should it be? Why or why not? For discussion of this issue see: Review of book – Matthew Liebman, *I Fought the Law: A Review of Terrorists or Freedom Fighters: Reflections on the Liberation of Animals*, edited by Steven Best and Anthony J. Nocella II. 1 Journal of Animal Law 151 (2005); Lee Hall, *Animal Rights Advocacy in the Age of Terror* (2006).

The above case was decided under the prior version of the AEPT. Provided below is the language from the current version. As you read it consider whether it would easier or harder to prosecute the defendants under this new language.

PL 109-374 (S 3880), 120 STAT 2652, 18 USCA §43
November 27, 2006
Animal Enterprise Terrorism Act (edited)
"§ 43. Force, violence, and threats involving animal enterprises
"(a) OFFENSE.--Whoever travels in interstate or foreign commerce, or uses or causes to be used the mail or any facility of interstate or foreign commerce--
"(1) for the purpose of damaging or interfering with the operations of an animal enterprise; and
"(2) in connection with such purpose--

(A) intentionally damages or causes the loss of any real or personal property (including animals or records) used by an animal enterprise, or any real or personal property of a person or entity having a connection to, relationship with, or transactions with an animal enterprise;

(B) intentionally places a person in reasonable fear of the death of, or serious bodily injury to that person, a member of the immediate family (as defined in section 115) of that person, or a spouse or intimate partner of that person by a course of conduct involving threats, acts of vandalism, property damage, criminal trespass, harassment, or intimidation; or

(C) conspires or attempts to do so;

....

(d) DEFINITIONS.--As used in this section--
(1) the term 'animal enterprise' means—

(A) a commercial or academic enterprise that uses or sells animals or animal products for profit, food or fiber production, agriculture, education, research, or testing;

(B) a zoo, aquarium, animal shelter, pet store, breeder, furrier, circus, or rodeo, or other lawful competitive animal event; or

(C) any fair or similar event intended to advance agricultural arts and sciences;

(2) the term 'course of conduct' means a pattern of conduct composed of 2 or more acts, evidencing a continuity of purpose;

(3) the term 'economic damage' —

(A) means the replacement costs of lost or damaged property or records, the costs of repeating an interrupted or invalidated experiment, the loss of profits, or increased costs, including losses and increased costs resulting from threats, acts of vandalism, property damage, trespass, harassment, or intimidation taken against a person or entity on account of that person's or entity's connection to, relationship with, or transactions with the animal enterprise; but

(B) does not include any lawful economic disruption (including a lawful boycott) that results from lawful public, governmental, or business reaction to the disclosure of information about an animal enterprise;

(e) RULES OF CONSTRUCTION.--Nothing in this section shall be construed —

(1) to prohibit any expressive conduct (including peaceful picketing or other peaceful demonstration) protected from legal prohibition by the First Amendment to the Constitution;

(2) to create new remedies for interference with activities protected by the free speech or free exercise clauses of the First Amendment to the Constitution, regardless of the point of view expressed, or to limit any existing legal remedies for such interference; or

Questions & Notes

1. Of the millions of individuals that are part of the movement, how many are involved in these sorts of enterprises? Why has this sort of events received such high-profile attention from Congress? Who requested such a law? A report of the federal Department of Homeland Security was released on April 13, 2006, and entitled "Preventing Attacks by Animal Rights Extremists and Eco-Terrorists: Fundamentals of Corporate Security." Again why was it perceived as necessary for this agency to expend time and effort addressing this issue?

TABLE OF CASES

INDEX

477

Index 483